KU-178-904

WORKING HOLIDAYS 1995

THE COMPLETE GUIDE TO SEASONAL JOBS

CENTRAL BUREAU
FOR EDUCATIONAL VISITS & EXCHANGES
LONDON   EDINBURGH   BELFAST

Every effort has been made to ensure the accuracy of the information contained in **Working Holidays 1995**, but the Central Bureau for Educational Visits & Exchanges cannot accept responsibility for any errors which may exist, or for changes made after publication. The Central Bureau and officers accept no responsibility collectively or individually for the services offered by agencies or persons advertised or announced in the pages of this book or any misdescriptions, defaults or failures by any of them. Although publishing in good faith, the Central Bureau gives no express or implied warranty in relation to such matters. All rights reserved throughout the world. No part of this publication may be reproduced, stored in a retrieval system, or transmitted, in any form or by any means, electronic, mechanical or otherwise, without the prior permission in writing of the publishers.

43rd edition   © Central Bureau for Educational Visits & Exchanges

ISBN   1 898601 01 1

Published by the Central Bureau for Educational Visits & Exchanges, Seymour Mews, London W1H 9PE
℡ 0171-725 9402   ℻ 0171-935 5741
Director Tony Male
Head of Publications/Editor Thom Sewell
Contributing Editor Moira Jenkins
Editorial support Rebecca Sewell
Production support Louise Larkin

Distributed to the book trade by Kuperard (London) Ltd, No 9 Hampstead West, 224 Iverson Road, London NW6 2HL
℡ 0171-372 4722   ℻ 0171-372 4599

Cover illustration: David Jonason/Image Bank

Working Holidays 1995 was compiled, edited and produced for print by the Information, Print & Design Unit, Central Bureau, London

Printed and bound in Britain by Page Bros

USING THIS GUIDE

The opportunities in **Working Holidays 1995** are given alphabetically by country/area, and are arranged into various categories depending on the type of work on offer. If you are interested in working in a particular country turn to that section and check out the jobs detailed there. If you are intending to undertake a particular type of work, for example on an environmental or ecology project, but are open as to which country you want to work in, consult the **Conservation** sections under each country (see **Work Index** opposite). If you are undecided as to which area of work or country your skills and enthusiasm may be best employed in, consult the **Work Profiles** section which describes in more detail the different opportunities.

Under the **Info** heading at the beginning of each country section in the **Jobs Index** you will find a list of addresses including embassies, consulates, tourist offices and youth and student travel centres - all useful sources of help and advice as you plan your working holiday and travel around. As a rule, tourist offices and embassies cannot help you to find employment, but they may be able to provide useful details, for example of hotels that may employ temporary staff, or information about the country you plan to visit. This section also details entry and work permit regulations, possibilities for budget travel and accommodation, relevant publications and information centres. Further advice and information on health, insurance, discount cards, social security, unemployment benefit and advertising for a job is given under the **A-Z** section.

The available paid jobs and voluntary opportunities are listed under each company or recruiting organisation in the various categories. A description is given of the work available, any skills or qualifications required, general conditions, wages and application procedures. Within each entry the jobs on offer or type of work available is given in **bold** and the following symbols are also used to aid in selection:

☎	Telephone number
🖷	Fax number
⊕	Flags any age limits
☒	Highlights application deadlines

When writing to any organisation it is essential to mention **Working Holidays 1995** and enclose a stamped, self-addressed A4 envelope, or if in another country, an addressed A4 envelope and at least two IRCs (International Reply Coupons, available from post offices). Where no telephone number is given this is at the employer's request; the handling of telephone enquiries is more time consuming and expensive than for written enquiries. **Before applying**, read carefully all the information given. Pay particular attention to:

⊘ skills/qualifications/experience needed

⊘ the period of employment expected

⊘ age limits

⊘ nationality restrictions (see also **Nationality** page 12)

⊘ application deadlines

⊘ any other points, particularly details of insurance, and other costs you may have to bear such as travel

To apply for work, you must contact the employers/recruiting organisations **direct**, and not the Central Bureau. In the case of workcamp organisations in other countries, refer to the application details at the end of each entry and the information given under **Joining an international workcamp** on page 31.

Unless otherwise indicated, applications should be made in writing. Note that some employers will request that applicants complete their standard application forms; others will take applications direct, usually with at least an outline cv. **When applying** include the following:

✎ your name, address, date of birth, marital status, nationality, sex

✎ details of your education, qualifications, relevant experience, skills, languages spoken

✎ your period of availability for work

✎ a passport-size photo, particularly if you will be working with the public

✎ anything else recommended or asked for in their listing (such as a cv)

Your application may be acknowledged or you may be told straight away whether or not you have a job. Any membership or registration fee should usually be sent when you **return the application form.** Note that for au pair work although you may pay an initial registration fee, the placement fee should not be payable until you have been offered and accepted a position. In busy periods you may have to wait some time before your application is acknowledged, so remember to apply in good time.

Some types of jobs, for example seasonal farmwork, are more likely to be offered to those applying in person. However applicants should note carefully the entry regulations for countries where such work is on offer. Certain nationalities are not allowed to enter some countries either without proof of sufficient funds or a prearranged work offer.

When you are offered a job, check what is offered against your original expectations. You will also need to confirm that you have the necessary paperwork- valid passport, visa or work permit - to meet the requirements of the job. When offered a job you will need to accept as soon as is possible. Even if you have applied for a number of jobs and are awaiting offers, it is in your own interest to inform employers speedily of your acceptance or rejection of their job offer.

Many organisations provide facilities for, or will consider applications from those with a disability. Opportunities open to those with restricted ability are indicated by the following codes. In most cases applications for work will be considered on an individual basis, depending of the applicant's ability and mobility in relation to the job in question.

B   Blind/partially sighted
D   Deaf/hard of hearing
PH   Physically handicapped
W   Wheelchair access

Prices, costs and wages throughout this guide are given either in £ Sterling or in the currency of the host country. Prices were correct at the time of publication, although they may be liable to currency fluctuation. In particular, where wages and registration fees are concerned, the figures generally given apply to rates in 1994. The approximate exchange rates when this guide was compiled were as follows (all rates = £ Sterling):

Australia 2.04 AU$	Japan 151 ¥
Austria 16.25 AS	Malta 0.56 LM
Belgium 47.75 BF	Morocco 13.33 D
Canada 2.08 Can$	Netherlands 2.62 Fl
Czech Republic 46.50 Kcs	New Zealand 2.53 NZ$
Denmark 9.23 DKr	Norway 10.28 NKr
Finland 7.73 FIM	Portugal 238.50 Esc
France 7.92 FF	Slovak Republic 46.5 SK
Germany 2.33 DM	Spain 193.25 Pt
Greece 354.00 Dr	Sweden 11.76 SKr
Hungary 130.00 Ft	Switzerland 1.96 SF
Ireland 1.00 IR£	Turkey 47,078 TL
Israel 4.18 NIS	United States 1.52 $
Italy 2390 L	

A - Z

The main section, the **Jobs Index**, not only gives full details on the thousands of work opportunities, but also sources of information that can help in planning your working holiday, including advice on accommodation, travel and on getting to know the area and country in which you will be working. This **A-Z** of practical advice and information provides virtually everything else you need to know to make your working holiday a success.

ADVERTISING If you are looking for work it is worth finding out about national or local newspapers where seasonal jobs may be advertised, or where you could place an advertisement in the *Situations Wanted* column. Details of British representatives that can place advertisements in foreign newspapers can be found under **Job advertising** in the country sections. You could also consult a number of international media directories in reference libraries, for example *Benn's Media Directories* or the *Willings Press Guide*. Many countries and large cities have English-language newspapers; an advertisement in one could gain you a job within the English-speaking community. In many cases youth information centres or hostels will have noticeboards advertising casual work, especially in tourist areas or during the harvest season.

BAGGAGE What to include or exclude from your suitcase or rucksack can make or break any holiday. The basic list of what to take may already be drawn up for you by virtue of the job you are going to. If you have to take your own tent, sleeping bag, equipment and work clothes, then you may not have room for much else. Even if accommodation is provided, taking your own sleeping bag will allow you to be more flexible, especially if you are going to be travelling around afterwards. If you plan to do a fair amount of travelling, think carefully about how you

will carry your belongings; you may wish to invest in a good rucksack. If you've not travelled much, and are unsure how much to take with you, a good rule of thumb is to pack what you think you'll need, and then halve it! Some recruiting organisations will provide work clothes such as overalls or a uniform, which will allow you space to pack more of your own clothes. Try to get as much background information as you can on the area or country you are visiting, investigate the climate and weather patterns so that you will be taking the right sort of clothes, particularly if you will be involved in much outdoor work. Take clothes which are hard-wearing and easy to care for, and don't forget to leave space for presents and souvenirs.

CUSTOMS If you are going to work abroad you should be fully aware of the Customs regulations governing all the countries you will be visiting and what you may or may not bring back home. Full details of UK Customs regulations are given in the various *Customs Public Notices* obtainable from Customs & Excise local offices or from Customs at ports and airports in the UK. There are prohibitions and restrictions on the importation of certain goods including controlled drugs, firearms, indecent or obscene books, magazines, video tapes, animals and birds, articles derived from endangered species and certain counterfeit goods. Further information from local Customs enquiry offices or from HM Customs & Excise Advice Centre, Dorset House, Stamford Street, London SE1 9NG © 0171-202 4227.

DRUGS If you are taking prescribed drugs whilst travelling it is advisable to carry a doctor's letter giving details of the medical condition and the medication, avoiding the possibility of confusion. It will also be useful to find out the generic rather than the brand name of the medicine, so that if need arises further supplies can be obtained abroad. If you are prescribed any tablets or medicine when overseas it may not be legal to bring them back into your own country; if in doubt, declare the drugs at Customs when you return. Further details on health precautions and treatment can be found under the **Health** and **Jabs** headings. Don't make the mistake of assuming you will be let off if you are caught buying or possessing small amounts of controlled or illegal drugs abroad. Penalties for drug-related offences can be severe, even for so-called soft drugs, and may also involve lengthy detention before trial without any chance of bail. Keep an eye on your luggage whilst travelling, and don't let anyone tamper with it. Don't agree to carry anyone else's bags or drive someone's car over the border. In some countries possessing or selling alcoholic drinks may also be illegal. Some community service projects involve working with ex-drug abusers, and participants will be asked to refrain from the use of tobacco, alcohol and other drugs whilst working on these projects. Those who feel unable to cope with this should not apply; conversely, those with drug-related problems themselves should also think very carefully about participating.

EMBASSIES Addresses and telephone numbers of embassies/consulates are given under each country throughout this guide. It should be noted that they cannot help in finding work, cannot provide money (except in certain specific emergencies), telex or telephone facilities, interpreting or legal advice services, or pay bills, whether legal, medical, hotel, travel or any other debts, though in an emergency they may help with repatriation. British citizens should note that there are consular offices at British Embassies in foreign capitals and at Consulates in some provincial cities. Consuls maintain a list of English-speaking doctors and will advise or help in cases of serious difficulty or distress. As a last resort a consul can arrange for a direct return to the UK by the cheapest possible route, providing the person concerned agrees

to have her/his passport withdrawn and gives written confirmation that s/he will pay the travel expenses involved.

FOOD One of the joys of any holiday abroad is sampling the local food. This is no exception on a working holiday, though depending on the job being undertaken, such as working in a holiday centre, regular access to authentic local cuisine may be somewhat difficult. In many instances the working holiday will involve cooking for yourself. Given that you may be involved in heavy manual labour you should ensure that you are eating well, and consider resolving any conflict you may have if the best you have achieved in home cooking relies heavily on the freezer contents. On workcamps catering is often undertaken on a rota basis; before you inflict your culinary skills on yourself, let alone others, you may care to buy a basic but practical cookery guide.
The Coordinating Committee for International Voluntary Service, UNESCO, I rue Miollis, 75732 Paris Cedex 15, France publish *Cookbook for Workcamps* which contains a variety of nutritious recipes and tips on cooking cheaply for large numbers. Cost FF5 or 5 IRCs plus 20% to cover postage.

GUIDES Under the **Publications** heading for each country *Working Holidays 1995* details a number of down-to-earth guides to areas and countries in which you will find yourself working and travelling. A good traveller's guidebook and map can make all the difference between a missed opportunity and a memorable experience. Forward planning and advance reading can give you a flavour of the country and some idea of sights worth seeing. Your library should give you the opportunity to compare the available guides before buying your own copies. Tourist offices are a good initial source of free maps and guides. A good map can help you make the most of your free time; locally available maps, for example those issued free at petrol stations, can be invaluable.

HEALTH Changes in food and climate may cause minor illnesses and, especially when visiting the hotter countries of southern Europe, North Africa, Latin America and the Far East, it is wise to take extra care in your hygiene, eating and drinking habits. Native bacteria, to which local inhabitants are immune, may cause the visitor stomach upsets, so it is worth avoiding tap water and doing without ice in your drinks. In a hot climate never underestimate the strength of the sun, nor overestimate your own strength. Drink plenty of fluids, make sure there is enough salt in your diet, wear loose-fitting cotton clothes, even a hat, and guard against heat exhaustion, heat stroke and sunburn, especially if you are working outdoors. See the section on **Jabs**, below, for further information on health precautions. In the UK the Department of Health issues a booklet *T4 Health Advice for Travellers*, available from post offices, travel agents, libraries and doctors' surgeries, or by phoning 0800 555777. This includes details of compulsory and recommended vaccinations, other measures that can be taken to protect one's health, information on rabies, AIDS, malaria and other diseases. There is also advice on types of food and on water supplies which may be a source of infection. A person is only covered by the NHS while in the UK, and will usually have to pay the full costs of any treatment abroad. However, there are health care arrangements between all EEA countries (Austria, Belgium, Britain, Denmark, Finland, France, Germany, Greece, Iceland, Ireland, Italy, Luxembourg, the Netherlands, Norway, Portugal, Spain and Sweden). British citizens resident in the UK will receive free or reduced cost emergency treatment in other EEA countries on production of form *E111*. An application form for *E111* is included in the *Health Advice for Travellers* booklet, mentioned above, which explains who is covered by the arrangements, what treatment is free or at reduced cost, and gives the procedures which must be followed to get treatment in countries where form *E111* is not needed (usually Austria, Denmark, Finland, Gibraltar, Ireland and Portugal). Form *E111* must be taken abroad and, if emergency treatment is needed, the correct procedures must be followed. There are also reciprocal health care arrangements between Britain and Australia, Barbados, Bulgaria, Channel Islands, the Czech Republic, Hong Kong, Hungary, Isle of Man, Malta, New Zealand, Poland, Romania, Russia and the former Soviet Union (not Baltic States), the Slovak Republic, the former Yugoslavia and the British Dependent Territories of Anguilla, British Virgin Islands, Falkland Islands, Montserrat, St Helena, and Turks and Caicos Islands. However, private health insurance may still be needed in these countries; *Health Advice for Travellers* gives full details. Despite reciprocal health arrangements it is still **essential** to take out full medical insurance whenever travelling overseas. The health treatment available in other countries may not be as comprehensive as in the UK, and **none** of the arrangements listed above covers the cost of repatriation in the event of illness. See **Insurance**, below.

Travellers' Health - How to Stay Healthy Abroad by Dr Richard Dawood is considered the definitive guide to all aspects of health abroad, and offers comprehensive advice for those planning journeys anywhere in the world. Published by Oxford University Press, price £7.99, available from most good bookshops and specialist travel shops.

INSURANCE You **must** find out from the organisation you will be working for whether they provide insurance cover against risk of accident, illness and possible disability. Where possible, details will have been given in the *Working Holidays* entry, but it is still wise to check on this point. The insurance cover provided automatically by many employers is often solely against third party risks and accidents. It may not cover you when you are not at work, and is unlikely to extend to loss or damage to your personal belongings. You may therefore have to take out further insurance, especially if you plan to do any travelling when the work is finished. If you do not have a job arranged in advance, and are hoping to combine work with travel, it is wise to inform the insurance company of this. Some travel insurance policies will not cover accidents at work, but they may be prepared to insure you for this if they are informed in advance what work you will be undertaking, or if you are prepared to pay a higher premium.

The International Student Insurance Service (ISIS) policy provides, at competitive rates, a wide range of benefits covering death, disablement, medical and other personal expenses, loss of luggage, personal liability and cancellation, loss of deposits or curtailment. An advantage of this policy is that medical expenses can be settled on the spot in many countries by student organisations cooperating with ISIS. A 24-hour assistance service is provided to handle all medical emergencies. Details in the UK from 150 local Endsleigh Insurance centres; see *Yellow Pages* for details.

The Patrick Leigh Travel Insurance Agency, PO Box 984, Lewes, Sussex BN8 6RW ℭ Lewes (01273) 858536 provides insurance cover to pay for an economy round trip air ticket should a family member or person close to you fall very seriously ill in the UK. 24-hour emergency telephone service can arrange booking on next obtainable flight home.

JABS Even if you are not planning to do your working holiday abroad, you should make sure you have an anti-tetanus injection if you are going to be involved in any type of manual outdoor work such as construction work, gardening, an archaeological dig or a conservation project. If you will be

travelling abroad, a certificate of vaccination against certain diseases is an entry requirement for some countries, and it is wise to consult embassies on this point, since requirements are continually subject to review. As a general rule it is wise to make sure that your protection against typhoid, polio and tetanus is up-to-date if you are travelling outside Europe, North America or Australasia. Within the UK, printouts indicating the immunisations and malaria tablets appropriate for any specific journey are available from the Medical Advisory Service to Travellers Abroad (MASTA). Call ℭ 0891 224100 to leave a recorded message listing countries you will be visiting, the month of arrival in each and the living conditions (rural, towns, cities, business, tourist). The required information will be sent by return; calls are charged at 39p/48p a minute (cheap rate/all other times). MASTA printouts are also available without charge for those attending British Airways Travel Clinics for their immunisations; for details of the clinic nearest to you call ℭ 0171-831 5333.

Remember that protection against some diseases takes the form of a course of injections over several weeks, so allow plenty of time. Whilst abroad it is unwise to have your skin pierced by acupuncture, tattooing or ear piercing, for example, unless you can be sure that the equipment is sterile. A major cause of the spread of viruses, including AIDS, is the use of infected needles and equipment. In some countries blood for transfusions is not screened for the presence of the AIDS virus, but there may be arrangements for obtaining screened blood. The doctor treating you, or the nearest consulate or embassy may be able to offer advice. If you are concerned about the availability of sterile equipment whilst abroad, emergency medical travel kits are available through MASTA, see above, and other suppliers, and can be ordered through retail pharmacists. They contain a variety of sterilised and sealed items such as syringes and needles for use in emergencies. MASTA also has a range of health care items such as mosquito nets, insect repellent and water purifiers, available on mail order by calling ✆ 0171-631 4408.

KNOWLEDGE This edition of *Working Holidays* builds on over forty years of our knowledge in gathering together information on opportunities to experience life through a period of work in another environment. Every employer listed in this guide has been selected as offering a genuine working holiday; that is, you may be on holiday, but you will be expected to do a real job of work. Those employers who we feel cannot offer an authentic experience are not included; neither are those who can offer only one or two vacancies. However, we need your help in monitoring that the jobs on offer live up to their promises. We also very much welcome any other comments you may have about *Working Holidays 1994* and if you know of any organisations who should be included in future editions, do please let us know.

LANGUAGE Fluency in another language will increase the range of work opportunities open to you; it will also make your time in another country that much more enjoyable. Local education authority evening classes offer a range of courses to develop foreign language skills. The vocabulary and confidence gained will stand you in good stead when you find yourself abroad, even if, unless tuition is undertaken well in advance, you are unlikely to be totally fluent in the new language. *Study Holidays* £8.99, is a comprehensive guide to hundreds of organisations offering courses in 26 European languages, from I week to 12 months. Practical information on language resources and sources for grants is also given. Published by the Central Bureau for Educational Visits & Exchanges, Seymour Mews, London WIH 9PE ✆ 0171-725 9402. While you

are abroad, even the best phrase books will have limited use; if you are keen to develop your vocabulary a pocket dictionary will prove better value.

MONEY It's important to work out how much money you'll need. The exact amount will depend on a variety of factors, including the location, the country itself, the total length of time you will be away, how long you'll spend travelling rather than working, and the type of work you are undertaking. You will need some money to live on until your first pay day; this need only be pocket money if food and accommodation are being found for you. On the other hand, you may have to pay for your board, lodging and other needs, and you may be paid monthly, not weekly. If you're undertaking voluntary work in a remote location, with food and accommodation provided, pocket money may be enough to cover your needs, and you may even find difficulty in finding somewhere to spend that! A good guide as to how much to take is to make sure you've got enough to pay for at least two nights' accommodation and food, a long-distance telephone call, and return travel, if not already accounted for. If you do run out of funds it is possible to arrange for money to be transferred to a bank abroad, provided of course that you have the necessary funds available back home. Large amounts of money are best taken as travellers' cheques; when obtaining these from a bank or travel agency you'll generally need to give a few days notice, and produce your passport. Shop around beforehand to compare commission rates charged. Read carefully any instructions given, particularly with regard to signing cheques and keeping a note of the numbers. Some travellers' cheques can be replaced while you're still abroad; others will be honoured by the issuing bank on your return. If you have a current bank account you will probably be able to obtain a supply of Eurocheques and a cheque card. These can be cashed throughout Europe at banks where the Eurocheque sign is displayed, and in many cases are accepted by shops and restaurants. You'll also need to carry some foreign currency; you can get this at major travel agents and banks. Again, shop around for the best exchange and commission rates. Don't forget to take some of your own currency with you, for use on outward and return journeys.

NATIONALITY The information given in *Working Holidays 1995*, particularly with reference to entry and work regulation, applies to UK nationals and, as applicable, nationals of the other European Economic Area (EEA) countries. The EEA comprises all the European Union countries (Belgium, Denmark, France, Germany, Greece, Ireland, Italy, Luxembourg, the Netherlands, Portugal, Spain and the United Kingdom) plus five member countries of the European Free Trade Association (Austria, Finland, Iceland, Norway and Sweden). The EEA Agreement, which came into force on 1 January 1994 gives reciprocal rights of movement, residence and employment to all EEA nationals. This means that nationals of one EEA country may work in another EEA country without a work permit. Where possible, *Working Holidays 1995* also gives details of employment regulations for other nationalities, but if in doubt you should check out job availability, entry and work permit regulations with employers and with the appropriate embassy.

In general, voluntary work opportunities are open to all nationalities, with the official letter of invitation acting as an entry permit. However, some European voluntary organisations are wary of recruiting non-EEA nationals, as they have experience of sending letters of invitation to prospective volunteers who have simply used this as a means to enter the country and then do not turn up for work. Except for cases involving the EU/EEA, see above, or reciprocal

arrangements, for example Commonwealth countries and the UK, or under specific opportunities such as the Exchange Visitor Programme in the United States, a work permit will usually be required for all paid work, which depending on the country in question may be very difficult to obtain, and may be issued only for the job in question.

OPPORTUNITIES The thousands of opportunities to undertake paid and voluntary work, from as short as one weekend up to 52 weeks, are all detailed under the main **Jobs Index** section of this guide. Before this, the **Work Profiles** section details the categories of work on offer, and if you are in any doubt as to what type of work and in which country will be best suited to your needs, these work profiles will enable you to decide where your skills and enthusiasm may be best employed. They will also answer some of the basic questions like where and when does the grape harvest take place, what is involved in being an au pair, exactly what is a kibbutz, where can I literally dig up the past, and how can I practically contribute to the conservation of this planet?

PASSPORTS /VISAS If you intend to work abroad and are not in possession of a valid passport, application for one should be made at least three months in advance. In most countries you will need to hold a full passport in order to undertake work. If a passport is lost or stolen while abroad the local police should be notified immediately; if necessary your nearest embassy or consulate will issue a substitute. It is therefore wise to keep a separate note of your passport number.
Within western Europe and certain other specified countries, British citizens can travel on a British Visitor's Passport; however, those travelling for purposes of work should obtain a full passport. Application forms for BVPs, valid for 12 months, are obtainable from any main UK post office, Monday-Saturday; they

are not obtainable from passport offices other than the Passport Office, Belfast, and are only available to British citizens, British Dependent Territories citizens, and British Overseas citizens for holiday purposes of up to 3 months. Full UK passports, valid for 10 years, can be obtained from the regional offices below.

Passport Office, Clive House, 70-78 Petty France, London SW1H 9HD
℡ 0171-279 3434 (personal callers only).

Passport Office, 5th Floor, India Buildings, Water Street, Liverpool L2 0QZ ℡ 0151-237 3010

Passport Office, Olympia House, Upper Dock Street, Newport, Gwent NP9 1XA
℡ Newport (01633) 244500/244292

Passport Office, Aragon Court, Northminster Road, Peterborough, Cambridgeshire PE1 1QG
℡ Peterborough (01733) 895555

Passport Office, 3 Northgate, 96 Milton Street, Cowcaddens, Glasgow G4 0BT
℡ 0141-332 0271

Passport Office, Hampton House, 47-53 High Street, Belfast BT1 2QS
℡ Belfast (01232) 232371

The *Essential Information* booklet contains notes on illness or injury while abroad, insurance, vaccinations, NHS medical cards, consular assistance overseas, British Customs and other useful advice, and is available from all passport offices.

Nationals of other countries will need to consult their own passport-issuing authorities as to the issuing and validity of passports, and should read carefully details given under the **Info** and other headings for each country in this guide, so they are aware of the restrictions governing certain nationalities and their freedom to take some jobs, particularly where the work is paid. For entry to some countries a visa or visitor's pass is required, and in many a work and/or residence permit will be required. Requirements and regulations are noted in this guide under the **Entry regulations** headings for each country. Entry and work regulation requirements vary considerably, particularly outside the EU/EEA, and it is advisable to apply early to the relevant embassy or consulate as it may take some time to obtain the necessary documentation.

QUALIFICATIONS Although this guide has a large number of opportunities for those with no particular qualifications other than enthusiasm and a willingness to be fully involved with the job in hand, before applying for any job check that you fully meet any credentials required. These need not be formal requirements either: for example, it's no use opting for farmwork if you suffer badly from hayfever; it's no use settling for a volunteer post if you must cover all your expenses; and it's no use choosing a workcamp if you don't like working hard and mixing with an international group. On the formal side, the more you can offer as regards language skills, teaching or training certificates, formal education or previous experience, then the wider range of options you will have, and consequently the better chance of being selected. It is always worthwhile listing relevant qualifications and experience when applying for any job; the competition for many of these jobs is strong, and employers can afford to be very selective.

REDUCTIONS Youth and student cards offer a range of reductions on travel, accommodation, restaurants, shopping and entry to cultural sites, and if you are eligible it is worth getting one of the available cards.

The International Student Identity Card (ISIC) scheme is operated by the International Student Travel Confederation, a group of major official student travel bodies worldwide.

ISIC provides internationally accepted proof of student status and consequently ensures that students may enjoy many special facilities, including fare reductions, cheap accommodation, reduced rate or free entry to museums, art galleries and historic sites. Obtainable from official student travel offices, students' unions and by mail order, the card is available to all full-time students, along with a copy of the *ISIC Handbook*. The card costs £5 and is valid for up to 15 months (1 September-31 December of the following year). For further details call in at your local student travel office or contact ISTC, St Kongensgade 40H, 1264 Copenhagen K, Denmark ✆ (45) 33 11 21 55.

The Federation of International Youth Travel Organisations (FIYTO) aims to promote educational, cultural and social travel among young people. The FIYTO International Youth Card is a recognised card offering concessions including transport, accommodation, restaurants, excursions, cultural events and reduced rates or free entry to many museums, art galleries, theatres and cinemas. The card costs £6 and is valid for one year from date of issue. Available to all those aged 12-26, together with a booklet giving details of concessions. Available in the UK from Campus Travel offices; London office: 52 Grosvenor Gardens, London SW1W 0AG ✆ 0171-730 3402.

European Youth Cards are concessionary cards issued by a number of European youth agencies, entitling holders to a range of discounts and special offers on travel, cultural events and goods in high street shops in 18 European countries. Cards are renewable annually, and holders receive a directory of discounters and a regular magazine informing them of new discounts and activities available to card holders.

England and Wales: Under 26 Card available from Under 26, 52 Grosvenor Gardens, London SW1W 0AG ✆ 0171-823 5363. Cost £6.

Scotland: Young Scot Card available from youth information points, tourist boards, theatres and the Scottish Community Education Council, Rosebery House, 9 Haymarket Terrace, Edinburgh EH12 5EZ ✆ 0131-313 2488. Cost £6.

Northern Ireland: European Youth Card available from USIT, Fountain Centre, Belfast BT1 6ET ✆ Belfast (01232) 324073 and other USIT offices. Cost £6.

Ireland: European Youth Card available from USIT, Aston Quay, O'Connell Bridge, Dublin 2 ✆ (353 1) 677 8117, and other USIT offices. Cost IR£6.

SOCIAL SECURITY If a person undertakes paid employment abroad in a country having reciprocal social security arrangements, advice as to their position should be sought from their social security authority. The UK has reciprocal agreements with Australia, Bermuda, Canada, Croatia, Cyprus, Israel, Jamaica, Jersey and Guernsey, Malta, Mauritius, New Zealand, Philippines, Switzerland, Turkey, United States and the former Yugoslavia. Leaflets explaining these arrangements and how they affect UK nationals are available from the Contributions Agency, Overseas Contributions, see below.

Leaflet *SA29* gives details of the social security rights available to UK nationals working in the European Economic Area (EEA) and how to claim them. Separate booklets are available describing the social security schemes (including health services) in certain EEA countries. Leaflet *NI38 Social Security Abroad* is a guide to National Insurance contributions and social security benefits in non-EEA and non-reciprocal agreement countries. For copies of these leaflets and any further information contact the Contributions Agency, Overseas Contributions (EC/RA), Longbenton, Newcastle upon Tyne NE98 1YX ✆ 0191-213 5000. See also **Health**, above and **Unemployment benefit**, below.

TRAVEL A number of operators specialise in youth/student fares and in long-haul travel; details are given in each country section. In addition to these there are various travel outlets ranging through high street travel agencies, bucket shops and individual airline offices. There are many discount fares on offer, so it is a good idea to compare as many types of ticket as possible to see what constitutes the best deal.

For example, students may find that last-minute charter flight bookings are as cheap as student tickets, but not as flexible. Inter-Rail passes are good value for multiple destinations, but extra charges may be levied, for example on high speed trains. Bucket shops usually supply tickets direct from the airline or from consolidators (responsible for filling seats on scheduled flights). If you want to be sure that the shop you are dealing with is reliable, check that they are licensed by the International Air Transport Association (IATA), and see if they will accept payment by credit card, as this will give some form of protection against loss of payment. The Air Travel Advisory Bureau (© 0171-636 5000) should be able to refer you to a reputable agency, or an airline may be able to refer you to their own preferred agent or consolidator. High street travel agents might be more convenient, but may be limited in their range of destinations as they tend to offer specific holiday resorts and are subject to seasonal demands on tickets.

The availability of tickets to many destinations will also vary according to national and regional holidays, religious festivals, and specific tourist events. Another important area to consider is internal travel within your working holiday destination. Certain countries (for example CIS/Russia) can have extremely complicated systems for obtaining internal travel tickets, which make things difficult for independent travellers. Some countries also have restrictions on internal travel to certain places. On the other hand if you book with some national airlines at certain times of the year they may throw in a free or discounted return ticket to a selected destination on their domestic network, simply to fill internal flights. For some countries, including Australia, Canada and the United States, it is possible to buy a pass before you leave which will allow up to a month's unlimited travel on the internal air, coach or rail network.

If you're planning for long-term travel and going far afield, Round-The-World (RTW) air tickets are a popular, good value option. They are usually valid for a year and include at least three stopovers. Another option is an air ticket with an 'open-jaw' facility, which means that you can enter a country or continent by one airport and leave by another; very useful if you want to work your way across America, for example.

Wherever you travel by air, don't forget to re-confirm your flight booking at least 72 hours before departure. Phone the airline and make sure you're booked onto the flight, as there's nothing worse than checking in to find your seat has been given to someone else and the plane is full. If you're only staying a couple of weeks re-confirm your return flight at the airport as soon as you arrive. Specialist books and periodicals often contain up-to-the-minute tips and advice from travellers, covering anything from visa problems through to personal security.

UNEMPLOYMENT BENEFIT If you are an EEA citizen and unemployed and want to look for work in another EEA country you may be able to get unemployment benefit there for up to 3 months. Claimants must have registered at an unemployment benefit office or a careers office in their own country, normally for at least 4 weeks, and must be getting benefit when they leave. They must immediately register for work and also for benefit in all the countries they go to but may encounter problems if they cannot speak the languages of the countries they visit. Unemployed British citizens should ask at their nearest Employment Services Jobcentre for leaflet *UBL22*.

Those who qualify for benefit, and are staying temporarily at workcamps away from their home areas in Great Britain, Northern Ireland or the Isle of Man run by charities or local authorities and providing a service to the community, may receive unemployment benefit for one period of up to 14 days in a calendar year provided they continue to be available for work during this period. They will not be required to attend the unemployment office during the workcamp. On return, their claims will be considered to see whether they continued to satisfy the conditions for the payment of unemployment benefit. It is essential, however, that they give the office details of the workcamp in advance. Unemployed people may earn up to £2 per day when working for voluntary groups, charities or the community, without having to forfeit their unemployment benefit, providing that they also remain available for work. However, if a person earns more than £57 in any week, benefit is forfeited for that week. See also **Social security**, above.

VOLUNTARY SERVICE Short-term voluntary work opportunities are listed under various headings throughout this guide. *Volunteer Work* £8.99, is an authoritative guide to agencies recruiting volunteers for medium and long-term service. Information on each agency covers its background and objectives, countries of operation, projects, experience and personal qualities required of the volunteer, and details of orientation and debriefing. Practical information includes details on preparation and training, understanding development, advisory bodies, insurance, travel, social security and health requirements. Published by the Central

Bureau for Educational Visits & Exchanges, Seymour Mews, London W1H 9PE ✆ 0171-725 9402.

The International Directory of Voluntary Work £8.95 is a guide to short and long term volunteer opportunities in Britain and abroad. *The Directory of Work and Study in Developing Countries* £7.95 is a guide to employment, voluntary work and academic opportunities in the Third World for those who wish to experience life there not just as a tourist. Both available from Vacation Work, 9 Park End Street, Oxford OX1 1HJ ✆ Oxford (01865) 241978.

Community Service Volunteers, 237 Pentonville Road, London N1 9NJ ✆ 0171-278 6601 is the UK national volunteer agency which aims to involve young people as full time volunteers in the community and to encourage social change. Anyone aged 16-35 who can be away from home for 4-12 months can volunteer and work with people in need: physically disabled and elderly people; people with learning difficulties; homeless people; young offenders and children in care. Volunteers go where their help is most needed in the UK, and work alongside professionals for 4+ months, receiving accommodation, food, pocket money and some travel expenses. Also places overseas volunteers, ages 18-35 with good English and able to meet British visa requirements. Overseas volunteers pay a £475 placement fee and work on the same projects as UK volunteers, receiving pocket money, food, accommodation, and some travel costs within Britain.

WORKING FULL TIME This guide does not attempt to cover permanent employment abroad; those interested in finding such employment should apply through normal channels and advertisements. From time to time employment offices receive details of overseas vacancies, mainly in the EU. The majority of vacancies are for skilled persons aged 18+ with a good working knowledge of the language of the country chosen; applicants must be prepared to work abroad for 6 months or more. In Britain contact the Training Agency, Employment Service Division, through Jobcentres or employment offices, for further information.

The Directory of Jobs and Careers Abroad £9.95, is a guide to permanent career opportunities worldwide, and outlines methods of finding work. Includes information on jobs in computer services, oil, mining and engineering, medicine and nursing, journalism, banking and accountancy, transport and tourism, and also includes information on work permits, visas, taxes and social security. Published by Vacation Work, 9 Park End Street, Oxford OX1 1HJ ✆ Oxford (01865) 241978.

The factsheet *Working Abroad* gives broad guidelines relevant to working abroad, with useful information for UK nationals on how to apply for an overseas job and what they should ask before accepting it. Published by the Employment Service, Overseas Placing Unit, Steel City House, c/o Rockingham House, 123 West Street, Sheffield S1 4ER and available from Jobcentres and employment offices. Also publish a series of factsheets on working in EU countries.

XENOPHOBIA If you suffer from this condition, then a working holiday in another country, experiencing a different life and culture, and speaking another language, could prove to be just the cure. Even in your own country, taking part in an international workcamp could provide relief from some of the more extreme symptoms of xenophobia. However, if the condition has persisted for some time, then a working holiday, where international teamwork, shared experiences, opportunities to make and develop new friendships, and the challenges of new situations in far away environments are just some of the highlights, is probably not for you!

YEAR BETWEEN A number of options are open to those who choose to widen their experience by taking a year off between school and higher education, school and work, or higher education and a career. Like a working holiday, this time is a valuable opportunity to develop personal skills, become more self-reliant and achieve an understanding of your own strengths and weaknesses. The opportunities listed in *Working Holidays 1995* are mainly geared towards the short-term. Whilst these are bound to be of interest to those who would like to spend a year doing a variety of short projects, details of medium-term work opportunities, voluntary projects, work placements and adventure opportunities specifically aimed at those taking a year out can be found in *A Year Between*, £8.99, which offers authoritative advice and guidance, as well relating the experiences of those who have taken a year out. Published by the Central Bureau for Educational Visits & Exchanges, Seymour Mews, London W1H 9PE ✆ 0171-725 9402.

Z As in algebra, so in a working holiday, Z is the third unknown quantity. Having decided on a job and the country in which you want to work, the third variable is **you** yourself. No matter that this guide lists thousands of opportunities all over the world, and provides a wealth of advice and information, at the end of the day you will need to use your own initiative, determination and imagination in order to obtain the job you want. Those with faint hearts will never get that opportunity to work their way round the world, undertaking for example, courier work on the Côte d'Azur in France, working in the orchard groves of a moshavim in Israel, picking pears in the Murray Valley in Australia, teaching sports at an American summer camp, and doing conservation work in Iceland. On the other hand, those lacking in wanderlust will find a host of opportunities nearer home. To all, the best of luck.

WORK PROFILES

This section gives brief profiles on the types of work covered in this guide. If you're not sure what sort of work you want to do, or where your skills and enthusiasm will be best employed then these pages will help you find out. More detailed information will be found in the **Jobs Index**, but these profiles highlight the main opportunities available, with general details on age limits, requirements, entry regulations and periods of work.

ARCHAEOLOGY

Sitting in the bottom of a trench for hours on end, carefully brushing away decades of deposits is not everyone's idea of a holiday, but involvement in a project that may discover important finds of Palaeolithic, Bronze Age or Roman habitation has particular rewards. Learning from the archaeological past is to seek to understand the Earth's history and discover how humans, plants and animals have adapted to change over millions of years. We can learn a lot, for example, by finding out what caused dinosaurs to become extinct, or by studying the rise and fall of human societies and cultures. As well as investigation into ancient monuments, archaeological projects also study landscapes, buildings and the evidence left by previous environments. You may be studying the life of reindeer hunters in France; working on Roman, Anglo-Saxon or medieval sites in Britain; or uncovering the skeletons of bison killed thousands of years ago by Native Americans in the US.

Many projects welcome complete beginners but in some cases a more formal interest in history or a knowledge of archaeological techniques may be required. Experience is best first acquired on sites in your own country, after which you will find it easier to be accepted onto an excavation overseas. Archaeological work can be hard and may continue in all weathers, and participants should be prepared accordingly. Any relevant skills should be made clear when applying; those with graphic, topographic or photographic skills are often particularly welcome. Beginners will often receive board and lodging in return for their labours. Wages and/or travelling expenses may be offered to more experienced volunteers. Basic accommodation is normally provided, but volunteers may have to take their own tents and cooking equipment.

The minimum age is usually 18; those under 18 may be welcome provided they have a letter giving parental consent or are accompanied by a participating adult. Work may be available almost all year round, but owing to the nature of the work, projects are most often undertaken in the summer season. Participants are strongly advised to have an anti-tetanus injection beforehand.

AU PAIR/CHILDCARE

Working as an au pair is a practical and economic way to spend some time learning the language and experiencing the way of life in another country. It gives you a chance to widen your experience, particularly if you are taking a year out before starting college, university or a career, or if you fancy a break between job moves. Although au pair positions in most countries are now open to both sexes, many families stick to the traditional female au pair, and as agencies recruit accordingly, male applicants will find opportunities more limited. The term au pair means on equal terms, and this means an au pair should be treated as a member of a family, and not as a servant or domestic. In return for board, lodging and pocket money you will be expected to help with light household duties including simple cooking and the care of any children, for a maximum of 30 hours per week. This should allow you sufficient time to meet friends, go sightseeing and to take a part-time course in the language. Unfortunately, there is no absolute guarantee that these conditions will be met as arrangements depend almost totally on goodwill and cooperation between the host family and the au pair, so you should be aware of this and make sure working conditions are established before accepting a post. If an au pair post is found through a reputable agency such as those listed in *Working Holidays,* both family and au pair should be fully briefed. The agency or its representative should be able to intervene if problems arise and arrangements break down for any reason, but remember that a good working relationship will require goodwill and tolerance on both sides.

Au pair posts outside the UK are open to those aged 17-27/30; stays are usually for a minimum of six months. There may be a limited number of short-term summer stays of 2/3 months, depending on the country. The work involves general household chores such as ironing, bedmaking, dusting, vacuuming, sewing, washing up, preparing simple meals and taking the children to and from school, plus general childcare duties. A typical working day is of 5/6 hours, with 3/4 evenings babysitting in a 6 day week. The remainder of the evenings, 1 full day and 3 afternoons per week are usually free. In addition to board and lodging approx £30-£40 per week pocket money is provided. There is usually an agency service charge, and applicants are responsible for their travel and insurance costs, although most agencies can provide information and advice. In some cases, normally after a stay of 12 months or more, the host family will pay a single or return fare. Under current regulations au pair agencies in the UK must be licensed by the Department of Employment, and can charge up to a maximum of £40 (VAT may be added) for finding an au pair position provided that they use an agent abroad as an intermediary. This fee is payable only after the applicant has been offered and accepted a position. There is a growing demand for English-speaking au pairs to teach English informally to both children and parents of the host family. This is particularly the case in Scandinavia and in East/Central European countries.

Au pair programme in the United States is open to citizens of western European countries with at least a fair degree of fluency in English. Character references, medical certificate, childcare experience (such as babysitting) and driving licence required. Up to 45 hour week spread over a maximum of 5½ days, with 1 full weekend free each month. Involves active duties including feeding and playing with children, and passive supervision such as babysitting. Ages 18-25. The positions last 12 months. Return flight, approx $100 per week pocket money, board and accommodation, medical insurance, $300 for study course, 2 weeks holiday, and opportunities to travel are provided.

Au pair posts in Britain are open to those aged 17-27, unmarried and without dependants, who wish to learn English while living as a member of an English-speaking family. Only EEA nationals and nationals of Andorra, Bosnia-Herzegovina, Cyprus, the Czech Republic, the Faroes, Greenland, Hungary, Liechtenstein, Macedonia, Malta, Monaco, San Marino, the Slovak Republic, Slovenia, Switzerland and Turkey are eligible. As a general rule au pairs work up to 5 hours per day with 2 days per week free. They should have their own room and receive up to £35 per week pocket money.

The au pair agency should ensure that the correct arrangements are made for entry into the chosen country; however it is wise to check these requirements yourself with the relevant consulate, and details are given in this guide under the respective headings. Make sure you

know who is responsible for making travel arrangements and paying the fares; usually agencies will give advice on travel, but applicants make their own arrangements and pay the costs.
It is essential to have sufficient funds to pay the fare home in case of emergency.

Before leaving be sure you have a valid passport, a visa/work permit as necessary, and a letter of invitation from the host family, setting out details of the arrangements that have been made, including details of pocket money and any contributions that may be payable to national insurance or other schemes in the destination country.

Au pair posts should not be confused with regular domestic employment, posts as nannies or mother's helps, or posts advertised as demi-pair or au pair plus, which are covered by different employment and entry regulations. Nannies usually have to have formal training, such as NNEB qualifications. Mother's helps work alongside mothers, caring for children, and perhaps doing some cooking and housekeeping. They generally work a 8 hour day, 5/6 day week.

The Au Pair and Nanny's Guide to Working Abroad £8.95, is a guide for those considering au pair, nanny or domestic work. Published by Vacation Work, 9 Park End Street, Oxford OX1 1HJ ℅ Oxford (01865) 241978.

If you have an interest in working with children but are unavailable for the minimum periods of service of au pair and other childcare posts, or do not possess the relevant qualifications or experience, a variety of other opportunities exist, particularly in the areas of community work, courier work and working as leaders or monitors. Further details are given below and under the respective headings for each country throughout this guide.

COMMUNITY WORK & CHILDREN'S PROJECTS

There are many opportunities in Britain and abroad to take part in projects dedicated to providing service in the community or running schemes for children during the holidays. Such an experience can be very valuable, particularly if you are contemplating a career in social services, teaching, nursing or any of the caring professions. The work is classed as voluntary, but this does not necessarily mean that you work for nothing. Most of these volunteer placements provide board and lodging, and sometimes a small amount of pocket money to cover personal expenses. Projects run throughout the year and most of them will take you on for as long as you have the time to give.

Applicants should be aware that any type of **community work** involves a high degree of commitment. The ideas and attitudes of voluntary service which used to be expressed as *helping those less fortunate than ourselves* or as *giving benefit to people in need* are considered inappropriate and patronising in society today. Working to overcome the effects of poverty, homelessness, illiteracy, high unemployment, and discrimination against an immigrant population are worthwhile challenges in themselves. The work can be undertaken in a variety of forms; for example construction, carpentry, painting and decorating work in community centres and homes can be equal in value to helping directly in the care of homeless, disadvantaged or disabled members of society.

Typical projects include living and working alongside the residents of a community for people with learning difficulties, doing household chores, crafts, farming or gardening; providing round-the-clock support to help a severely physically handicapped person lead a more independent life; working in a day centre or night shelter for ex-drug addicts, alcoholics or the homeless; visiting and entertaining elderly patients at a hospital; taking wheelchair and bed-bound people on holidays abroad; or working within immigrant communities. Applicants for community work schemes will need a good command of the host language, but formal skills or experience are not always necessary. The minimum age is 18, although younger applicants may be accepted on the basis of interests, experience and individual maturity. Many community work projects can be particularly physically and emotionally draining, and potential applicants should read carefully all the literature provided on the project and consider their own strengths and weaknesses before formally applying. The ability to take initiatives within the framework of the project team, to cope with crises, and to maintain a sense of humour and perspective, is essential.

Playschemes and other **children's projects** are often run by charitable organisations or local authorities during the summer and occasionally at other times of the year, or all year round. They may cater especially for children who would otherwise be unable to have a holiday, or they may offer a break to the parents of children who have special needs and require constant personal care. Some projects bring together handicapped and able-bodied children in an effort to promote understanding of disabilities and reduce prejudice; others involve taking children from deprived inner-city areas or families under stress on holiday to the seaside or the countryside. Volunteers on such schemes have a very valuable contribution to make, in providing care, organising activities, and acting as supervisors. For some children, contact with the volunteers may be the only chance they have to meet people from outside their town or from another country.

If you're thinking of working on a children's project, bear in mind that unless it is a daily playscheme you will probably be in the company of children for 24 hours a day, which can be very demanding. A genuine love of children is essential, as is an unlimited supply of bright ideas on how to keep them occupied and entertained. You will also need an excellent knowledge of the host country's language in order to be able to relate well to the children, as well as enough self-confidence to be able to exert discipline without being authoritarian, and cope with being the target of children's jokes. Following the introduction of the 1989 Children Act, all those working in Britain with children under 8 (including volunteers) have to submit their details for police screening. Where volunteers from other countries are concerned, they will usually be required to submit references to the project organiser, or complete a declaration which is certified by a responsible member of their community.

CONSERVATION

The Earth is 4,600 million years old; over the last 150 years we have come ever closer to upsetting the ecological balance that has developed since the planet's creation. Earth's inhabitants have raided the planet for fuels, used the land, sea and air as rubbish tips, and caused the extinction of over 500 species of animals. The world is changing so rapidly that the environment left to us now may no longer be available to our children. If these threats to our natural and cultural heritage give you cause for alarm why not take positive action through volunteering?

Details are given below of the different types of project available. Relevant skills are always welcome, but many projects offer training in special techniques. The minimum age is usually 16 or 18 but can be as low as 13, depending on the project, and families with younger children will often be welcome. Basic accommodation will be provided on-site or in village halls, schools, farm buildings or hostels, depending on the situation. Food is usually provided on a self-catering basis, with volunteers taking it in turns to cook. Volunteers contribute towards the cost of food and pay their own travel costs. Work can be strenuous; all volunteers should be fit and are strongly advised to have an anti-tetanus injection before joining a project.

We learn more every day about the interconnectedness of nature and how ecosystems depend upon one another to form a living whole. The destruction of habitats threatens whole populations, and the extinction of a single species may put countless others at risk. In order to develop a strategy for planetary survival, we first need to discover as much as possible about different species, how they survive and how their behaviour affects others. For this reason, much of the work done by conservation volunteers involves detailed studying, surveying or monitoring to determine the current population levels, habits or optimum environment of a particular plant or animal species. Such work does not necessarily require you to have any knowledge of the species in question or experience in surveying techniques, as these can be learned on-the-job. However, you will need a lot of patience and attention to detail.

Conservation volunteers also work to solve or prevent problems caused by human or natural activity. For example, you may get involved in combating erosion, cleaning up pollution or protecting against encroachment by introduced species which pose a threat to native flora and fauna. There is also a need to promote growth in dwindling native populations through a programme of wildlife management - this may involve work such as digging ponds to create new habitats, collecting seeds for revegetation, or breeding animals in captivity for later release into the wild.

As well as hands-on work with nature, there are also plenty of opportunities to preserve the built or managed environment, including the restoration of railways, canals and other aspects of our industrial heritage; renovating churches, castles, stately homes and gardens; rebuilding abandoned hamlets; carrying out coppicing and hedge laying; and building drystone walls. This presents a real opportunity to learn about a region's history, culture and heritage and perhaps find out what ordinary life was really like in days gone by. In some cases you may be working alongside local craftspeople who can teach you traditional skills and techniques such as hedging, drystone walling, coppicing, basket making, masonry work, tiling or woodcarving. The human heritage is not necessarily destructive to nature - there are countless examples of areas such as railway cuttings, canals, managed woodlands, hedges, walls and meadows where plants and animals can flourish. Such environments need to be preserved and developed to encourage a diversity of wildlife, even in the most urban surroundings.

There is also a growing range of projects worldwide devoted to promoting sustainable living techniques and reducing the human impact on the environment. Examples of these include organic farms, communes, cooperatives and centres researching into alternative energy sources or sustainable development techniques - there is even an experimental eco-city being built in the Arizona desert. Unless you have a very high level of relevant skills or experience, work on such projects will be of a voluntary nature. There is a considerable demand for placements in this fascinating field of work, and volunteers will in many cases pay a fee to cover board, lodging and any training they may receive, although reductions are sometimes available for those on low incomes. Volunteers are placed in tasks according to the skills they have available and what requires doing at any particular time, so much of the work may be mundane, involving domestic chores, administration and general duties to enable the project to function effectively. Whatever work you will be doing, however, you will most probably be living amongst people who are dedicated to green living and who will be happy to pass on their skills, knowledge and enthusiasm.

One of the most important aspects of conservation work is to encourage others to take an interest in the world around them and to realise that parts of it are under threat. The range of tasks that this encompasses is quite considerable - for example, building a waymarked trail through a national park will encourage people to visit, and by keeping to the path they will reduce their impact on other areas. Working as a warden or environmental interpreter at a nature reserve will bring you into contact with both adults and children who are eager to find out more about the local environment. There are also a number of international workcamps devoted to campaigning and raising awareness about issues of conservation, pollution, waste recycling, energy use, nature protection and alternative lifestyles in general, in which volunteers can take part. Working holidays aside, environmental groups such as Friends of the Earth and Greenpeace are always looking for members who can devote time and energy to fundraising and campaigns. Your library should be able to give you the address of your local group.

Whatever type of project you choose it is always important to remember that we all have a part to play in caring for the environment. If you can accept some personal responsibility and resolve to reduce your own impact on the world around you, this is taking a step in the right direction. A good code to follow, wherever you travel, is to *take* nothing but photographs and *leave* nothing but footprints.

FARMWORK

The agricultural sector has long been a source of casual work opportunities due to the seasonal ripening of crops. Mechanisation has reduced but can never replace human labour: the slopes of a vineyard may be too steep, for example, and human hands and eyes will always be needed to judge whether fruit or vegetables are ripe for picking. To make farmwork pay you must be fit and ready to undertake whatever work may be required. The work is often very hard and patience is required; hours can be long and it is usually necessary to work every day, including weekends, to get the crop picked and processed. Working hours can be irregular, as the work is subject to weather conditions and market deadlines. You must be prepared to get up early and spend long periods standing, kneeling, crouching, bending, stretching or carrying heavy loads. You may also have to work all day in the blazing sun, the freezing cold or the stifling heat of a greenhouse.

Most picking jobs are paid at piecework rates; the more you pick the more you earn. Therefore bear in mind that bad weather can affect ripening, the amount of crops to be picked and thus the wages. In an average season, however, you should earn enough to cover food, accommodation and other charges and leave a small net gain, varying according to how efficiently you pick and the quality of the harvest. Self-catering accommodation may be provided but will be fairly basic and you will need a sleeping bag, if not a tent. Pack suitable clothing: a hat if you'll be working in the sun, woollies in autumn and winter, and waterproof clothing and footwear in case it rains or the fields are muddy. Check whether insurance cover is provided against accidents; you will also need to take out your own personal cover. As well as the paid opportunities given below, *Working Holidays 1995* also contains details of opportunities to work as a volunteer on organic farms and alternative farming projects; take part in schemes for young farmers; or work as a member of a farming family abroad.

The range of **opportunities abroad** can be as vast as the range of crops. You could pick peaches and pears in Australia, cut flowers in Holland, go maize-topping in France, harvest kiwifruit in New Zealand or gather olives and melons in Greece. There are also jobs available processing, such as peeling and packing bulbs, preparing cut flowers for transportation, or working in a canning or pickling plant. With a little bit of planning and organisation you may be able to work your way through Europe or even across the globe, following the crops as they ripen.

Grape picking in the south of France, tasting the product, living at the vineyard, taking *déjeuner sur l'herbe* with the grower and his family - all this may conjure up a colourful and idyllic scene. With proper planning a job in the grape harvest may live up to this standard. However the hours are long, you need to be very fit as the work is hard, involving lots of bending, stretching and carrying. The accommodation may be very basic and during bad weather only those hours actually worked will be paid. The decreasing need for manual labour together with the regular army of seasonal workers has also led to increased competition for jobs. Despite this the grape harvest can provide an enjoyable summer job, toiling away alongside locals and workers from all over the world. Details are given in the **Jobs Index**. The harvest dates should be regarded as approximate; they may vary by two weeks either way. Changes in the weather may also mean that if you apply from your home base you may be given as little as 48 hours notice before work is due to commence, and the quality and quantity of the harvests can vary enormously. Many EU farmers are taking advantage of subsidies to turn their land over to more lucrative forms of agriculture, and in France the total vineyard area has decreased from 3 million acres to 2.4 million in the last ten years. The net result, at least as far as summer workers are concerned, is that in France the quality areas such as Burgundy, Beaujolais and Bordeaux are where grape picking will prove to be most fruitful.

Summer farmwork in Britain includes general farm labouring as well as vegetable harvesting and fruit picking. The work is mainly in Scotland, East Anglia, the South, the West Country and Kent. Crops include raspberries, strawberries, blackcurrants, cherries, loganberries, blackberries, plums, gooseberries, apples, pears, potatoes, courgettes, beans and hops. A range of ancillary work such as strawing, weeding, irrigation, inspection, packing, indoor processing, tractor driving or working in oast houses may also be available. The work can be on individual, family-run farms, on smallholdings, with cooperatives, or on international farmcamps. The general number of hours worked are 40-45 per week for 5-6 days. The length of the season varies, depending on the crop, the weather and the location of the farm. The harvesting of **soft fruit** is normally undertaken between mid June and August, although in some areas picking may start as early as May. The picking of apples, pears and other crops runs from late August to October. Most soft fruit picking is a slow and painstaking job, and workers will often be required to pick to a very high standard. Poor weather at the time of setting or harvesting can mean that the number of pickers needed will be limited. In addition, the market competition of soft fruit from East Europe may well mean some decline in the number of farms, and consequently the number of opportunities available. **Hop picking** was traditionally undertaken as a working holiday by many of the families of London's East End and their counterparts in the Black Country, once England's industrial heart.

Although this tradition is still carried on today, the majority of seasonal workers in the hop fields of Hampshire, Kent, Sussex and Worcestershire are overseas students, local workers and travellers. At one time there were over 1,000 hop farms in southern England. However, since mainland Europe and the US began plantations to provide for most of their own needs, and since drinking fashion turned to lighter beers and lagers, the number of English hop producers has dwindled to around 260. Consequently the number of seasonal workers taken on is now substantially less. Manual labour is still essential, however, for drying the hops in the oast house and pressing them into bales. This may involve working long hours, as hops picked in the morning are dried in the afternoon and evening, then packed the following morning. Those picked in the afternoon are dried during the night and packed the following afternoon. There is also work available in gangs cutting down the taller bines. Pay is at an hourly rate, at the minimum laid down by the Agricultural Wages Board.

On **farmcamps** the emphasis is as much on living and working in an international community, with sports and social activities, as on earning money. The wages paid should be sufficient to cover food and accommodation costs and to provide a little pocket money. The facilities provided can include swimming pools, tennis courts, sports fields, games and television rooms, video, bars, discos and dances. The majority of workers will be aged 17-30, and families are often welcome. Work permits are not required by those from outside Britain wanting to work on approved farmcamps, but workers from outside the EEA subject to immigration control must be in full-time education abroad, aged 18-25 and have a Home Office card issued by an approved scheme operator. This card allows entry into Britain but does not entitle the visitor to take paid work of any other kind during the visit.

KIBBUTZIM/ MOSHAVIM

There are hundreds of kibbutzim and moshavim all over Israel, offering the opportunity to experience the challenge of living and working in a small, independent community. This in itself is potentially rewarding, as is living in a country whose society and culture are so different from one's own. The first **kibbutz** was established in 1909 by a group of pioneers who wanted to form a community where there was no exploitation and no drive to accumulate individual wealth. The desire to establish a just society is the basic principle guiding kibbutz life, together with a commitment to undertake tasks important to the development of Israel and the Jewish people. There are now some 270 kibbutzim throughout Israel. All the means of production are owned by the community as a whole, and all income generated is ploughed back into the community. The workforce consists of all members and any volunteers, who receive no wages but give their labour according to ability and in return receive in accordance with their needs. Kibbutzim welcome volunteers who are prepared to live and work within the community and abide by the kibbutz way of life. Volunteers share all communal facilities with kibbutz members, and should be capable of adapting to a totally new society. The work for volunteers may include farming, citrus, melon, soft fruit and vegetable harvesting, market gardening, haymaking, working in fishponds, cowsheds or chicken houses, and even light industry. In addition, everyone is expected to take their turn in doing household chores such as helping with cooking, cleaning and washing for the whole community. Volunteers work approx 8 hour day, 6 day week with Saturdays free and 2 additional days off at the end of each month. Additional work may be necessary at busy periods, such as the harvest. During the summer, work outdoors often starts at 05.00 with afternoons free to avoid the hottest part of the day. Volunteers live together in wood cabins, 2-4 to a room, males and females separated, with food provided in the communal area. **Moshavim** are collective settlements of from 10-100 individual smallholders. Each family works and develops its own area of land or farm while sharing the capital costs of equipment, marketing and necessary services. There are almost 1,000 moshavim where volunteers can live and work as a member of an Israeli family, mainly in the Jordan valley, the Arava and the western Negev. Most of the work is on the land, particularly in flower growing, market gardening, specialist fruit farming, chicken rearing or dairy farming. Kibbutzim or moshavim volunteers should be aged 18-32, in good physical and mental health, and will need references, a medical certificate and a special entry visa. Pregnant women or families with young children will not be accepted. Applicants should bear in mind that the work is often physically arduous, that conditions can be uncomfortable, the hours long, and understand that a serious attitude to work is required, as well as a genuine desire to become involved in the life of the community. Working holidays on kibbutzim and moshavim can last from 8 weeks upwards.

TEACHERS

There is a wide variety of teaching opportunities in many countries. Although teaching skills, qualifications and/or experience are a definite advantage, they are by no means essential for all opportunities. Millions of people around the world are eager to learn, practise and perfect their English-speaking ability. Teaching English as a Foreign Language (TEFL) is now a £6billion a year industry. Opportunities to teach English in eastern European countries are particularly on the increase. Due to the economic situation of these countries the teaching is in many cases done on a voluntary basis, with board and lodging provided; occasionally a small amount of pocket money in local currency will be paid. Teaching or TEFL qualification are not always essential for such posts; enthusiasm, motivation, commitment and English mother-tongue are the more vital requirements. More formal teaching jobs, such as those at private language schools abroad or those offered by state-run teacher recruitment programmes, will demand a higher level of qualifications and experience. The minimum requirement will be a degree, but a recognised teacher-training or TEFL qualification is often essential. A good way to gain experience after having obtained a TEFL qualification is to apply to work at a British summer school. Approximately half a million visitors to Britain take EFL courses each year; there are hundreds of summer schools and consequently a great demand for teachers. Contracts are usually for 1-2 months; salaries are modest but full board accommodation is often provided as part of the package. Even for posts that do not specify TEFL qualifications it is useful to have experience of working with children, teaching and a knowledge of another language. Alternatively, if you have specific skills and qualifications in a range of areas, from outdoor pursuits to performing arts, work at summer camps and activity centres can prove stimulating and challenging (see under **Travel & tourism** below).

Teach Abroad £8.99 offers information and advice to those wanting to teach in another country. In addition to a selective listing of English language schools abroad and centres in Britain offering RSA and Trinity TEFL courses, it also covers organisations recruiting for short and long-term teaching posts in a variety of subjects worldwide. Published by the Central Bureau for Educational Visits & Exchanges, Seymour Mews, London W1H 9PE ✆ 0171-725 9402.

TRAVEL & TOURISM

The travel and tourism industry is a vast business, and can provide a great number of seasonal work opportunities. The work can often be strenuous and stressful but what leisure time there is can be spent enjoying the sunshine, the skiing or a wide range of leisure activities. Each year some 500 million people travel on holiday, generating over £1 trillion and providing 130 million jobs. Around 14 million Britons annually take a package holiday overseas, 5 million of them in Spain. Many holiday companies employ **couriers** to escort groups on holiday, between holiday areas, or from Britain to destinations overseas, in both the winter and summer seasons, December-April and May-August/ September. Couriers are also required on a number of European campsites, acting as resident representatives, setting up and cleaning tents and mobile homes, responding to problems and emergencies, maintaining equipment, and arranging both children's and adult entertainment programmes.

Other **representatives** are needed at hotels and holiday centres in resorts worldwide, providing client information and looking after welfare and other needs. Requirements vary depending on the recruiting organisation, but in general, to do this type of work you will need to be at least 18, mature, reliable, and with a good knowledge of both the clients' and local languages. The ability to be adaptable, independent, efficient, sensible, tactful, patient and sociable is essential. Previous experience in either courier work or in dealing with the public in similar situations also desirable.

Many holiday operators will prefer to employ a courier or representative for the whole of the season, and consequently will give preference to those applicants available for long periods. Salaries and accommodation will vary according to qualifications, experience, resorts and seasons worked. There will usually be enough free time to make use of the hotel or centre's facilities, such as skiing or watersports. Hotels and holiday centres take on extra **domestic** staff, kitchen assistants, waiters, waitresses, bar staff, cleaners and chambermaids during the holiday seasons. Domestic work can be very hard with long, unsocial hours. The ability to work as part of a team is essential. Knowledge of the local language may be needed, particularly where contact with the public is made, and relevant skills or experience are an advantage. Salaries, living conditions, tips or bonuses vary according to placement. Often the facilities open to clients will be available for staff use during free time. The minimum age is usually 17, and those with experience or relevant qualifications are particularly sought, although there are posts such as kitchen assistants and porters where previous experience is not necessary. Preference will usually be given to those able to work the whole of either the winter or summer season, usually December-April/May and April/May-September respectively. There are also posts available in ski resorts for chalet staff, who take responsibility for shopping, budgeting, cooking meals and ensuring that chalets are clean and tidy. Chalet staff often need to be *cordon bleu* cooks with excellent organisational skills and an outgoing personality.

Leaders & guides A wide range of opportunities exist for those with organising and leadership skills. These may include leading adventure holidays and expeditions; organising sports and entertainment activities for groups of young people and adults on activity holidays; leading canoeing and hillwalking outings; and looking after children in holiday resorts, arranging entertainments, competitions and parties. Depending to some extent on the individual job, applicants will need at least some of the following qualities: to be energetic, reliable and mature, self-motivated, resourceful, adaptable, with good stamina, tolerance, flexibility, initiative and a sense of humour. Previous travel experience and a knowledge of foreign languages will be an advantage. The minimum age is normally 21, and the period of work from 8 weeks-6 months. It is often necessary to attend a short training course, and previous experience in working with children is a definite advantage.

Monitors/counsellors/children's couriers If you enjoy working with children you may like to consider working as a monitor on a residential holiday camp, activity centre or summer school. There are a wide range of opportunities both in Britain and in other European countries, as well as a special programme for camp counsellors to work during the summer on camps in Canada and the US. In general, the work involves being responsible for the care and supervision of a group of 8-10 aged 6-16. You will be expected to play and live with the children for 24 hours a day, supervising their activities and rest hours, helping to maintain a high level of morale, and organising entertainment. Posts are open to those aged 18/21+ who like and actively get on with children and are prepared to work intensively with them in an outdoor environment.

Instructors/specialist counsellors For those with some teaching or instructing experience and qualifications there are a number of posts in a wide range of countries. Most of the opportunities will require formal qualifications, although a number will be open to those with at least relevant experience. Posts available include those for ski instructors, usually with BASI or ASSI qualifications, working the winter season, December-April. Qualified sports, watersports and other activity instructors are also required in a number of countries, usually in the summer seasons, April/May-August/September. Instructors should be aged at least 21, and must have the ability to teach to a good basic level and impart their knowledge in an imaginative, interesting way, particularly as many of the posts involve work with children. In many centres the emphasis is on informality and enjoyment; safety, fun and participation is often the main aim, rather than just pure sports teaching. To this end the ability to manage and organise, and to work within a team, is as important as technical ability. Some activity centres will take on volunteer instructors who are perhaps unqualified but looking for experience. In this case, instructors will work in return for board and lodging, under the supervision of a qualified leader. They may also have the opportunity to take qualification exams at the centre where they are working.

Working in Tourism - The UK, Europe & Beyond £8.99 gives information for those looking for employment in the tourist industry, whether just for a summer season or as a career. Published by Vacation Work, 9 Park End Street, Oxford OX1 1HJ © Oxford (01865) 241978.

WORKCAMPS

International workcamps are a form of short-term voluntary service, providing an opportunity for people of different racial, cultural and religious backgrounds to live and work together on a common project of service to the community. By bringing together a variety of skills, talents and experiences from different nations, workcamps allow volunteers not only to provide a service to others but also to have an opportunity for personal growth and greater awareness of their responsibility to the society in which they live and work. Workcamp participants also find out about the history, culture and social conditions of the host community and become a part of it for a short time.

Workcamps generally run for periods of 2-4 weeks, April-October; some organisations also arrange camps at Christmas, Easter and at other times throughout the year. If you want to take part in a workcamp you need to be mature enough not to require adult supervision and prepared to take on some responsibility for the successful running of the work projects, group recreation activities and discussions that the workcamp will involve.

The minimum age is 17/18, with the exception of a number of youth projects, usually age 15+. Nearly all workcamp organisers will consider volunteers with disabilities providing the nature of the work and the terrain will allow their active participation.

The type of work undertaken varies considerably depending on both the area and the country in which the camp is being held. It is within the capacity of normally fit volunteers and can include building, gardening, painting and decorating, providing roads and water supplies to rural villages or constructing adventure playgrounds. There are also many workcamps where you can undertake conservation projects, help run children's playschemes, teach English at an informal level or work alongside people with learning difficulties or physical handicaps. Volunteers usually work a 7-8 hour day in a 5-6 day week. Most camps also have an informal study and discussion programme centred around the type of work that is being undertaken or dealing with wider international issues.

The first workcamp took place shortly after the First World War and involved volunteers building homes for refugees. It inspired the concept of promoting reconciliation and peace by bringing together young people from different countries. Peace camps continue to this day as a special type of workcamp, building upon these initial aims of preventing war and promoting peace. The work often involves the maintenance of Second World War concentration camps as monuments and warning symbols, and as a means of raising awareness of history. The camps also support peace information and activity centres, promote international discussion of the nuclear threat, alternative security policies and non-violence, and bring together peace movements in different countries. Volunteers should be aware that they may be confronted with disturbing reminders of war, and they should give a lot of thought to the subject of war and peace before participating. Equally, volunteers should also realise that each individual has the potential to make an important contribution to promoting peace, tolerance and justice. Discussion forums and educational and cultural activities form an integral part of all peace camp activities. Applicants should be interested in peace work, and have some knowledge of the political background of the host country.

Accommodation on workcamps is provided in a variety of buildings such as schools, community centres or hostels, and may sometimes be under canvas. Living conditions and sanitation vary considerably and can be very basic; in some cases running water may not be readily available. Food is generally provided, although it is often self-catering, with volunteers preparing and cooking meals together on a rota basis. In many camps food will be vegetarian. Most workcamps consist of 10-30 volunteers from several countries. English is in common use as the working language, especially in Europe; the other principal working language is French. A knowledge of the host country's language is sometimes essential, especially for community work. Most workcamp organisers operate on an exchange basis whereby volunteers are exchanged with volunteers sent by partner organisers in other countries. You may be expected to make a contribution towards the cost of board and lodging, and should take enough money to cover basic needs.

Although many organisations provide insurance cover for their volunteers, this is often solely against third party risks and accidents. You are strongly advised to obtain precise details on this and, where necessary, take out policies against illness, disablement and loss or damage to personal belongings. In addition to the vaccinations required for foreign travel, anyone joining a manual workcamp programme is strongly advised to have an anti-tetanus injection. It is quite usual for workcamp organisations to hold day or weekend orientation seminars prior to volunteers going abroad. In some cases, especially for workcamps held in eastern Europe or Third World countries, attendance at these seminars is essential. You will learn a lot about aspects of voluntary work in the relevant countries as well as gaining practical background information on the politics, culture and way of life.

Volunteering in the 90s lists voluntary workcamp organisations in a number of countries. *Book 1* covers Africa and Asia; *Book 2* covers Europe and North America. Each book costs FF6 or 6 IRCs. Also publish *Running a Workcamp*, a practical guide for workcamp coordinators. Cost FF25 or 25 IRCs. Add 20% for each order to cover postage. Published by the Coordinating Committee for International Voluntary Service, UNESCO, 1 rue Miollis, 75732 Paris Cedex 15, France.

Joining an international workcamp
For a workcamp in another country, you should apply through the organisation in your own country, **not** direct. The UK organisations that cooperate in recruiting volunteers are given at the end of each entry. Information on registration/membership fees is given below. **Only** if there is no cooperating organisation should you apply **direct**.

Service Civil International (SCI) is a major network of workcamp organisers. In **Britain**, apply to International Voluntary Service, Old Hall, East

Bergholt, Colchester, Essex CO7 6TQ. Membership fee £15 unwaged/low-waged/student, £25 waged. Registration fees: £25/£30 (camps in Britain); £60/£65 (camps in western Europe, Australia, United States); £100/£105 (camps in Eastern Europe). SCI branches in **other countries** are given below. Addresses of national branches and partner organisations can also be obtained from SCI European Secretariat, Draakstraat 37, 2018 Antwerp, Belgium.

Australia   IVP, 499 Elisabeth Street, Surry Hills, NSW 2010

Austria   SCI, Schottengasse 3a/1/59, 1010 Vienna

Bangladesh   SCI, GPO Box 3254, Dhaka 1000

Belgium   SCI, rue Van Elewijck 35, 1050 Brussels

VIA, Draakstraat 37, 2018 Antwerp

Denmark   SCI, Kyndbyvej 4, 3630 Jaegerspris

Finland   KVT, Rauhanasema, Veturitori, 00520 Helsinki 52

France   SCI, 2 rue Eugène Fournière, 75018 Paris

Germany   SCI, Deutscher Zweig eV, Blücherstraße 14, 5300 Bonn 1

Greece   SCI, Menandrou 55, 10437 Athens

Hungary   SCI, Thököly utca 27, 1076 Budapest

India   SCI, K5 Green Park, New Delhi 110016

Ireland   VSI, 30 Mountjoy Square, Dublin 1

Italy   SCI, via dei Laterani 28, 00184 Rome

Malaysia   SCI, c/o Ganesh Rasagam, 7 Jalan Taylor, 11600 Pinang

Mauritius   SVI, PO Box 153, Rose Hill

Nepal   SCI, PO Box 5730, Jyatha, Kathmandu

Netherlands   VIA, Pesthuislaan 25, 1054 RH Amsterdam

Northern Ireland   IVS, 122 Great Victoria Street, Belfast BT2 7BG

Norway   ID, Langesgate 6, 0165 Oslo

Slovenia   MOST, Breg 12, PP 279, 61101 Ljubljana

Spain   SCI-SCCT, Carrer del Carma 95, baixos 2a, 08001 Barcelona

SCI-Madrid, Calle Colón 14, 1er Piso, 28004 Madrid

Sri Lanka   SCI, 37 Mulgampola Road, Kandy

Sweden   IAL, Barnängsgatan 23, 11641 Stockholm

Switzerland   SCI, Geberngasse 21a, 3000 Bern 13

United States   SCI, Innisfree Village, Route 2, Box 506, Crozet, Virginia 22932

IVS also cooperates with a number of organisers in other countries, who are not members of SCI. Further details are given below, and in the **Jobs Index**.

Christian Movement for Peace (CMP) is another international network of workcamp organisers. Those wishing to take part in a workcamp abroad must apply through the CMP/MCP branch in their own country. In **Britain**, apply to CMP, 186 St Paul's Road, Balsall Heath, Birmingham B12 8LZ ✆ 0121-446 5704. Registration fee: £40-£50. CMP/MCP branches and associated groups in other

countries are given below. If there is no branch in your country, apply to the International/European headquarters, CMP/MCP Secrétariat, 3 avenue du Parc Royal, 1020 Brussels, Belgium.

Belgium   Carrefour Chantiers, 25 boulevard de l'Empereur, 1000 Brussels

Chile   CADESUR, Thompson 214, Castro

France   Solidarités Jeunesses/MCP, 38 rue du Faubourg St Denis, 75010 Paris

Germany   CFD, Rendelerstraße 9-11, 60385 Frankfurt

Hungary   Via Pacis, c/o Klauz Monika, Kollegium, #515 Budapest 1092, Ráday utca 43-45

Italy   MCP, Via Marco Dino Rossi 12/C, 00173 Rome

Latvia   CMP, c/o Latvijas Studentu Serviss, Jauniela 14, 226050 Riga

Malta   CMP, John XXIII Peace Lab, Hal Far

Netherlands   ICVD, MVB Bastiaansestratt 56, 1054 SP Amsterdam

Peru   MCP, c/o Tomas Astupina, Apartado Postal N33, Huaraz

Portugal   MCP, Plaça de Republica 18-3°, 3000 Coimbra

Romania   CMP Romania, Motilor Street 18, Cluj 3400

Switzerland   CFD, Falkenhöhleweg 8, 3001 Bern

Ukraine   SLU, Kosmanovta Komarova 1, 252058 Kiev

The British branch of CMP also cooperates with a number of organisers in other countries. Further details are given below, and in the **Jobs Index**.

International Building Companions (Internationale Bouworde - IBO)

organises workcamps, usually projects involving building, decorating and maintenance work. Has autonomous national branches in several countries, but none in the UK. Apply through your national branch, if there is one; in **Britain** you may apply direct. As well as the countries below, also recruits for workcamps in central/eastern Europe.

Austria Österreichischer Bauorden, Hörnesgasse 4, 1031 Vienna

Belgium (Flemish-speaking) Bouworde vzw, Tiensesteenweg 145, 3010 Leuven

(French-speaking) Compagnons Bâtisseurs, rue des Carmes 24, 6900 Marche-en-Famenne

France Compagnons Bâtisseurs, Maison de la Solidarité, 6 avenue Charles de Gaulle, 81100 Castres

Germany Internationaler Bauorden - Deutscher Zweig eV, PO Box 1438, 67504 Worms

Hungary Epito Baratok, Edina Boglary Mailath, Blathy Otto u 10, 1089 Budapest

Italy Soci Costruttori, Via Mazza 48, 20071 Casalpusterlengo

Netherlands Bouworde Nederland, Sint Annastraat 172, 6524 GT Nijmegen

Switzerland Internationaler Bauorden, J Feurer, Kirchweg 7, 9438 Lüchingen

The following British organisations recruit volunteers for workcamps in Britain and abroad:

Concordia (Youth Service Volunteers) Ltd (CYSV)

8 Brunswick Place, Hove, Sussex BN3 1ET ℗ Brighton (01273) 772086. Registration fee: £50-£70.

Quaker International Social Projects (QISP)

Friends House, Euston Road, London NW1 2BJ ℗ 0171-387 3601. Applicants for projects abroad must be over 18 with experience of similar projects or voluntary service. Registration fees: £9 unwaged, £17 low waged, £32 waged (UK camps) or £17/£24/£38 (overseas).

United Nations Association International Youth Service (UNA)

Temple of Peace, Cathays Park, Cardiff CF1 3AP ℗ Cardiff (01222) 223088. Registration fees: £45 (UK camps) or from £70 (overseas). Membership fees: £7.50 unwaged/student, £15 waged.

The workcamp organisers abroad together with their recruiting/partner organisations (**bold initials**) are:

Algeria ACAAEJ, Centre Culturel, Naciria 35250, W-Boumerdes **CMP QISP UNA**

Armenia HUJ, Korium Street 19A, Yerevan 375009 **IVS QISP UNA**

Australia ATCV, PO Box 423, Ballarat, Victoria 3353 **UNA**

CWA, PO Box K164, Haymarket, NSW 2000 **UNA**

Belarus ATM, PO Box 64, 220119 Minsk **CYSV IVS QISP UNA**

LYVS, Karl Marx Street 40, 220030 Minsk **UNA**

Belgium Compagnons Bâtisseurs, rue des Carmes 24, 6900 Marche-en-Famenne **CYSV QISP UNA**

Botswana BWA, PO Box 1185, Mochudi **UNA**

Bulgaria MAR, PO Box MAR, 1387 Sofia 87 **IVS QISP**

Canada CFS, 243 College Street, 5th floor, Toronto, Ontario M5T 2Y1 **UNA**

CJQ, 4545 avenue Pierre-de-Coubertin, CP1000, Succursale M, Montreal H1V 3R2 **UNA**

Côte d'Ivoire AICV, 04 BP 714, Abidjan **UNA**

Czech Republic INEX, Senovázne námesti 24, 116 47 Prague 1 **CYSV IVS QISP UNA**

KMC, Karolíny Svetlé 30, 110 00 Prague 1 **CYSV QISP UNA**

Denmark MS, Meslgade 49, 8000 Arhus **CMP IVS QISP UNA**

France Concordia, 38 rue du Faubourg St Denis, 75010 Paris **CYSV QISP UNA**

UNAREC, 3 rue des Petits Gras, 63000 Clermont-Ferrand **QISP UNA**

Gambia AFET, Brikama Town, Kombo Central Division, Western Division PMB **UNA**

Germany IBG, Schlosserstraße 28, 70180 Stuttgart **CYSV QISP UNA**

IJGD, Kaiserstraße 43, 53113 Bonn 1 **CYSV QISP UNA**

NIG, Am Vogenteich 13-15, 18057 Rostock **QISP UNA**

Pro International, Bahnhofstraße 26, 3550 Marburg/Lahn **CYSV**

VJF, Muggelstraße 22a, 10247 Berlin **IVS QISP UNA**

Ghana VOLU, PO Box 1540, Accra **UNA**

Greece ECVG, 41 Panepistimiou Street, 10564 Athens **QISP UNA**

Hungary UNIO, Nepszinhaz utca 24, 1081 Budapest **IVS QISP UNA**

India DEENA, C-6 Vikas Puri, New

Delhi 11018 **UNA**

Prepare, 4 Salthavar Street, Maggapair West, Padi, Madras 600 060 **UNA**

Italy OIKOS, Via Paolo Renzi 55, 00128 Rome **UNA**

Japan NICE, 501 Viewcity, 2-2-1 Shinjuku, Shinjuku-ku, Tokyo 160 **IVS QISP UNA**

Kenya KVDA, PO Box 48902, Nairobi **UNA**

Lesotho LWA, PO Box MS6, Maseru 100 **UNA**

Latvia LSV, Laeplesa 75/III-32, 1011 Riga **IVS UNA**

Lithuania Austeja, Pylimo 35, 2001 Vilnius **IVS**

CSA, K Donelaicio 73-113, Kaunas, LT-3006 **CYSV QISP UNA**

Mexico SEDEPAC, Huatusco No 39, Apartado Postal 27-054, CP 06760, Mexico DF **UNA**

VIMEX, Alfredo Elizando #69, CP 15450, Mexico DF **UNA**

Morocco CJM, BP 1351 Rabat RP, CP 1001, Rabat **QISP UNA**

CSM, BP 456, Rabat RP **UNA**

Netherlands SIW, Willemstraat 7, 3511 RJ Utrecht **IVS QISP UNA**

Poland FIYE, ul Nowy Swiat 18/20, 00 920 Warsaw **CMP CYSV IVS QISP UNA**

Portugal Instituto da Juventude, Avenida da Liberdade 194, 1200 Lisbon **QISP UNA**

Russian Federation/CIS YVS, 7/8 Bol Komsomolski per, Moscow 101846 **CYSV IVS UNA**

Senegal AJED, Parcelles Assaines Unité 10, No 143, BP 12035, Dakar **UNA**

Sierra Leone VWASL, PO Box 1205, Freetown **UNA**

Slovak Republic INEX, Prazská 11, 811 04 Bratislava **CYSV IVS QISP UNA**

Spain ICSJ, Calle de Calabria 147, 08015 Barcelona **UNA**

Instituto de la Juventud, José Ortega y Gasset 71, 28006 Madrid **CYSV QISP UNA**

Tanzania Umoja Wa Vijana, PO Box 199989, Dar es Salaam **UNA**

Tunisia ATAV, Maison du RCD, boulevard du 9 avril, La Kasbah, 1002 Tunis **CMP CYSV UNA**

Turkey Gençtur, Yerebatan Caddesi 15/3, Sultanahmet, 34410 Istanbul **CYSV IVS QISP UNA**

GSM, Yüksel Caddesi 44/6, 06420 Kizilay, Ankara **CMP CYSV QISP UNA**

Ukraine Forum, 10 Ternopolskaya Street, PO Box 10722, 290034 Lviv **QISP**

United States Cascadia Quest, 4649 Sunnyside Avenue North, Seattle, WA 98013 **UNA**

CIEE, 205 East 42nd Street, New York, NY 10017 **CYSV UNA**

VFP, 43 Tiffany Road, Belmont, Vermont 05730 **IVS UNA**

Working Holidays 1995 is published by the Central Bureau for Educational Visits & Exchanges, the UK national office for the provision of advice and information on all forms of educational visits & exchanges; the development and administration of a wide range of curriculum-related pre-service and in-service exchange programmes; the linking of educational establishments and local education authorities with counterparts abroad; and the organisation of seminars, workshops and conferences related to professional international experience.

Its information and advisory services extend throughout the educational field. Over 33,000 individual enquiries are answered each year; publications cater for the needs of people of all ages seeking information on the various opportunities available for educational contacts and travel abroad. The Central Bureau was established in 1948 by the British government and now forms part of the British Council. It is funded by the Departments of Education in the United Kingdom and by the European Union to promote international education through exchange and interchange. Registered charity number 209131.

Director   Tony Male

Seymour Mews
London W1H 9PE
0171-486 5101
0171-935 5741

3 Bruntsfield Crescent
Edinburgh EH10 4HD
0131-447 8024
0131-452 8569

1 Chlorine Gardens
Belfast BT9 5DJ
(01232) 664418
(01232) 661275

jOBS INDEX

aFRICA

INFO

Algerian Embassy
54 Holland Park, London WII 3RS
✆ 0171-221 7800

Kenya High Commission
45 Portland Place, London WIN 4AS
✆ 0171-636 2371/5

Lesotho High Commission
7 Chesham Place, London SWI 8HN
✆ 0171-235 5686

Nigeria High Commission
Nigeria House, 9 Northumberland
Avenue, London WC2N 5BX
✆ 0171-839 1244

Sierra Leone High Commission
33 Portland Place, London WIN 3AG
✆ 0171-636 6483-6

South African High Commission
South Africa House, Trafalgar Square,
London WC2N 5DP ✆ 0171-930 4488

Tunisian Embassy
29 Prince's Gate, London SW7 IQG
✆ 0171-584 8117

Uganda High Commission
Uganda House, 58/59 Trafalgar Square,
London WC2N 5DX ✆ 0171-839 5783

Zimbabwe High Commission
Zimbabwe House, 429 Strand, London
WC2R 0SA ✆ 0171-836 7755

Entry regulations Details of work
permits and entry requirements can be
obtained in Britain from the embassies/
high commissions above.

Travel Campus Travel offers low-cost
student/youth airfares to destinations
throughout Africa, and have offices
throughout the UK including a student
travel centre at 52 Grosvenor Gardens,
London SW1W 0AG (opposite Victoria
Station) ✆ 0171-730 8111 or ✆ 0131-
668 3303 for Scottish bookings.

Council Travel, 28A Poland Street, London W1V 3DB ✆ 0171-437 7767 (offices also in Paris, Nice, Lyon, Munich, Düsseldorf, Tokyo, Singapore and throughout the US) offers low-cost, student/youth airfares to destinations across Africa, plus travel insurance, guidebooks and travel gear.

North-South Travel, Moulsham Mill, Parkway, Chelmsford CM2 7PX ✆ Chelmsford (01245) 492882 arranges competitively priced, reliably planned flights to all parts of Africa. All profits given to projects in the developing world.

STA Travel, 86 Old Brompton Road, London SW7 3LQ/117 Euston Road, London NW1 2SX ✆ 0171-937 9962 (offices also in Birmingham, Bristol, Cambridge, Glasgow, Leeds, Manchester and Oxford) operates flexible, low-cost flights with open jaw facility, enter one country, leave by another to destinations throughout Africa. Internal flights, accommodation and tours also available.

Publications Lonely Planet's travel guides offer practical, down-to-earth information for people wanting to explore beyond the usual tourist routes. Titles include *Africa on a Shoestring* £16.95 for the low-budget independent traveller, and *Travel Survival Kits* to *Egypt & the Sudan* £10.95, *Kenya* £9.95, *Morocco, Algeria & Tunisia* £10.95, *South Africa, Lesotho & Swaziland* £10.95, *Zimbabwe, Botswana & Namibia* £10.95, *Central Africa* £10.95, *East Africa* £11.95 and *West Africa* £12.95.

Rough Guides provide comprehensive background information on cities and countries worldwide, plus details on getting there, getting around, places to explore and cheap places to stay. Titles include *Egypt* £10.99, *Kenya* £9.99, *Tunisia* £8.99, *West Africa* £12.99 and *Zimbabwe & Botswana* £10.99.

All the above are available from good bookshops and the larger travel chains.

CONSERVATION

EARTHWATCH EUROPE Belsyre Court, 57 Woodstock Road, Oxford OX2 6HU ✆ Oxford (01865) 516366
Aims to support field research in a wide range of disciplines including animal behaviour, archaeology, ornithology and nature conservation. Support is given to researchers as a grant and in the form of volunteer assistance. Recent projects involving **volunteers** have included pinpointing groundwater sites in Nigeria's drought-plagued Sahel region; studying the problem of a drop in the water level of Lake Navaisha, one of Kenya's largest freshwater lakes; monitoring the rhino population in Zimbabwe; and assisting at a paleontological excavation investigating human origins in Uganda.
⊕ Ages 16-80. No special skills required although each expedition may, because of its nature, demand some talent or quality of fitness. Volunteers should be generally fit, able to cope with new situations and work with people of different ages and backgrounds, and a sense of humour will help. 2-3 weeks, all year. Members share the costs of the expedition, from £340-£2,000, which includes meals, transport and field equipment, but not travel to the staging area, although assistance may be given with arrangements. Membership fee £25 entitles members to join an expedition, attend evening and weekend members' events, and receive magazines and newsletters providing all the information necessary to choose a project.
B D PH W depending on project.

COMMUNITY WORK

GLOBAL CITIZENS NETWORK 1931 Iglehart Avenue, St Paul, MN 55104, United States ✆ (1 612) 644 0960
Seeks to create a network of people who are committed to shared values of

peace, justice, tolerance, cross-cultural understanding and global cooperation. Sends teams of **volunteers** to rural communities in Kenya to assist in development, working on projects initiated by the community for the benefit of the community: building a health clinic, setting up a day care centre, teaching pre-school children and restoration work.

⊕ Ages 16+ unless accompanied. Teaching, health care and construction skills always in demand but not essential. Volunteers must be willing to experience and accept new cultures. Generally 5-6 hour day, 5 day week; weekends free. 2-3 weeks, all year. Full board accommodation in local homes or at community centre. Cost US$900-$1,300 includes board, accommodation, in-country travel, project materials, orientation manuals and pre-trip orientation meeting. Volunteers arrange and pay for own international travel and insurance. ✍ *Applications received 2 months in advance get $50 discount; late fee of $25 charged on applications received within 2 weeks of departure date.*

WORKCAMPS

AFRICA VOLUNTARY SERVICE OF SIERRA LEONE Private Mail Bag 717, Freetown, Sierra Leone

Aims to take part in development projects and to enhance international peace, understanding and cooperation. **Volunteers** are needed for agricultural or renovation work in rural areas. Previous experience not always necessary.

⊕ Ages 15+. Good spoken English essential. 35 hour week, end July-end August. Food and accommodation provided; some excursions and discussions organised. Volunteers pay own insurance and travel. Placement fee US$300. Medium and long-term placements (4-12 months) also available in the fields of medicine, civil engineering, construction work, carpentry, teaching and community

development for those with qualifications and/or experience. ✍ *Write for further details enclosing 3 IRCs and a self-addressed envelope.*

ASSOCIATION CULTURELLE DES ACTIVITÉS D'AMITIÉ ET D'ÉCHANGES ENTRE JEUNES (ACAAEJ) Centre Culturel, Naciria 35250, W-Boumerdes, Algeria

A national association grouping five regional organisations in Algeria with the aim of promoting volunteering and development, improving international cooperation and understanding, protecting the environment, combating illiteracy and encouraging humanitarian action. **Volunteers** are invited to take part in international workcamps. Recent projects have included tiling, painting and clearing work at an international peace centre in the Sidi-Ali-Bounab mountains; harvesting dates and working in a nature reserve on the edge of the Sahara; developing a village playground in the mountainous Kabylie region; and helping a humanitarian caravan distribute medicine and food to Tuareg refugees.

⊕ Ages 18+. Conversational level French or Arabic essential. 2-3 weeks, July-September. Insurance, food, and accommodation during workcamp provided. No fares or wages paid.

✍ *Apply through partner organisation in country of residence. In the UK: Christian Movement for Peace or Quaker International Social Projects. See page 30 for registration details and addresses.*

ASSOCIATION TUNISIENNE D'ACTION VOLONTAIRE (ATAV) Maison du RCD, boulevard 9 Avril 1938, La Kasbah, 1002 Tunis, Tunisia

Carries out voluntary work at local level throughout the year and also organises summer workcamps, involving participation from international **volunteers**. Recent projects have included restoring historic monuments, creating parks and children's playgrounds, and helping to construct or

renovate youth centres and schools in various towns throughout Tunisia. Study themes include youth participation in national development, peace and solidarity. Sports, cultural activities and excursions arranged.
⊕ Ages 18-35. Applicants must be in good health, with a good knowledge of French/Arabic and a background knowledge of Africa. Previous workcamp experience essential. 30 hour, 6 day week. Hours of work usually 0600/0700-1200. 2/3 weeks, June-September. Food, accommodation with basic facilities and insurance provided. No fares or wages paid.

≋ Apply through partner organisation in country of residence. In the UK: Concordia (Youth Service Volunteers) Ltd or United Nations Association International Youth Service. See page 30 for registration details and addresses.

CHRISTIAN STUDENTS' COUNCIL OF KENYA
Ufungamano House, State House Road, PO Box 52609, Nairobi, Kenya
Promotes cooperation and Christian unity, and organises workcamps, exchanges, afforestation, refugee awareness and women's programmes. Organises rural and urban projects providing an opportunity for **volunteers** to participate directly in the work of churches and social welfare agencies in an attempt to meet the needs and relieve the suffering of local people. Architects, agriculturists, poultry farmers, carpenters, nurses, counsellors and those with experience in building are especially needed. Knowledge of English necessary. 8 hour day, April, August and December. Visits arranged to self-sufficiency farms and tree nursery. Accommodation provided, but volunteers pay own travel and insurance. Also arrange exchange programmes, visits, language orientation, tours and travel programmes.
≋ Write for further details.

KENYA VOLUNTARY DEVELOPMENT ASSOCIATION
The Director, PO Box 48902, Nairobi, Kenya
Offers young people from Africa and overseas the opportunity to serve the country's rural or needy areas during their free time or holidays.
Volunteers work alongside members of the local community helping with rural development projects such as irrigation schemes, tree planting, food growing, tilling, goat and hen rearing; and the construction of schools and clinics, helping with roofing and foundation digging. Discussions, games and other entertainment arranged, often involving the community. Working languages are English and Swahili. Emergency projects also organised in times of catastrophe or disaster.
⊕ Ages 18+. Volunteers are expected to participate in all activities and adapt fully to the local way of life. 6 hour day, 6 day week. Each workcamp lasts 2-3 weeks, April, July, August and December. Food and accommodation in schools provided. No fares or wages paid.

≋ Apply through partner organisation in country of residence. In the UK: United Nations Association International Youth Service. See page 30 for registration details and addresses.

LESOTHO WORKCAMPS ASSOCIATION PO Box MS6, Maseru 100, Lesotho
International workcamps organised in rural areas throughout Lesotho, for which a small number of overseas **volunteers** are recruited to work alongside local people. Projects are in the field of rural development and involve manual work such as building roads, schools and clinics, tree planting, and laying water supplies. 40+ hours per week for 2-3 weeks, June-July (winter season) and December-January (summer season).
⊕ Ages 18+. Applicants must be physically fit; previous relevant experience preferred. Board and

lodging provided, but conditions can be quite primitive. No fares or wages paid. Excursions and entertainment organised. Registration fee payable.

🏛 *Apply through partner organisation in country of residence. In the UK: United Nations Association International Youth Service. See page 30 for registration details and addresses.*

NIGERIA VOLUNTARY SERVICE ASSOCIATION (NIVOSA)
General Secretary, GPO Box 11837, Ibadan, Nigeria
Brings together Nigerian and other nationals interested in promoting voluntary service. Organises international workcamps involving participation of **volunteers** and promotes understanding and cooperation among communities. Volunteers are drawn from secondary schools, colleges of education and universities. Projects include workcamps in the states of the Federation (Lagos, Oyo, Ogun, Osun and Ondo) involving the construction of hospitals, post offices, markets and schools.
Tasks include site clearance, making and laying blocks, plastering, carpentry and digging, all with the help of community artisans. Volunteers live and work in villages, cooking in groups.
⚘ Ages 18+. 6 hour day, 2 weeks, July-September. No fares or wages paid. Excursions, lectures and debates organised. Workcamps are usually preceded by 2/3 day leadership courses which include an orientation programme for new volunteers. Participation fee $5.
🏛 *Write for further details.*

ZIMBABWE WORKCAMPS ASSOCIATION PO Box CY 2039, Causeway, Harare, Zimbabwe
✆ **(263 4) 724859** 📠 **(263 4) 731902**
A recently-established workcamp organisation invites **volunteers** to work on a variety of development projects mainly in rural and remote areas of Zimbabwe. Work may involve brick-moulding, constructing buildings, digging wells, erecting toilets, conservation, reforestation or health programmes.
⚘ Ages 16-50. No experience necessary, but participants should be willing to work hard. English spoken on all projects. Approx 30 hour week for 2 weeks, August-December. US$150 participation fee covers food, accommodation, accident insurance and contribution to the work of the organisation. No fares or wages paid. Volunteers should take a sleeping bag.
🏛 *Completed applications to be received at least 2 weeks in advance.*

GENERAL

THE AFRICAN-AMERICAN INSTITUTE 833 United Nations Plaza, New York, NY 10017, United States
Can provide information on opportunities in Africa for employment in technical assistance positions, teaching posts and volunteer work experience.

See also opportunities under **Morocco** and **Worldwide**

INFO

Bangladesh High Commission
28 Queen's Gate, London SW7 5AJ
✆ 0171-584 0081

Embassy of the People's Republic of China
49-51 Portland Place, London W1N 3AH ✆ 0171-636 9375/5726

India High Commission
India House, Aldwych, London WC2B 4NA ✆ 0171-836 8484

Indonesian Embassy
38 Grosvenor Square, London W1X 9AD ✆ 0171-499 7661

Korean Embassy
4 Palace Gate, London W8 5NF
✆ 0171-581 0247

Royal Nepalese Embassy
12a Kensington Palace Gardens, London W8 4QU ✆ 0171-229 1594/6231

Pakistan High Commission
35-36 Lowndes Square, London SW1X 9JN ✆ 0171-235 2044

Philippines Embassy
9a Palace Green, London W8 4QE
✆ 0171-937 1600

Singapore High Commission
9 Wilton Crescent, London SW1X 8SA
✆ 0171-235 8315

Royal Thai Embassy
29-30 Queen's Gate, London SW7 5JB
✆ 0171-589 2944

Vietnamese Embassy
12-14 Victoria Road, London W8
✆ 0171-937 1912/8564

Entry regulations Details of work permits and entry requirements can be obtained in Great Britain from the embassies/high commissions above.

Travel SD Enterprises Ltd, 103 Wembley Park Drive, Wembley, Middlesex HA9 8HG ✆ 0181-903 3411 issues the Indrail Pass which allows unlimited travel on all trains throughout India, with no charge for night sleepers or reservations. Available for periods of 1, 7, 15, 21, 30, 60 or 90 days. Cost from $15. Also available from Campus Travel or the Government of India Tourist Office, see below.

Indian Airlines operate a youth fare scheme entitling those aged 12-30 to a discount of 25% off the normal fare, all year. Also Discover India scheme entitling the holder to unlimited air travel within India. 21 days, all year. Cost $400. Further information from the Government of India Tourist Office, 7 Cork Street, London W1X 1PB ✆ 0171-437 3677.

Campus Travel offers low-cost student/ youth airfares to destinations throughout Asia, and a range of rail passes. Offices throughout the UK including a student travel centre at 52 Grosvenor Gardens, London SW1W 0AG (opposite Victoria Station) ✆ 0171-730 8111 or ✆ 0131-668 3303 for Scottish telephone bookings.

Council Travel, 28A Poland Street, London W1V 3DB ✆ 0171-437 7767 (offices also in Paris, Nice, Lyon, Munich, Düsseldorf, Tokyo, Singapore and throughout the US) offers low-cost student/youth airfares to destinations in Asia, plus travel insurance, guidebooks and travel gear.

North-South Travel, Moulsham Mill, Parkway, Chelmsford CM2 7PX ✆ Chelmsford (01245) 492882 arranges competitively priced, reliably planned flights to all parts of Asia. All profits go to projects in the developing world.

STA Travel, 86 Old Brompton Road, London SW7 3LQ/117 Euston Road, London NW1 2SX ✆ 0171-937 9962 (offices also in Birmingham, Bristol, Cambridge, Glasgow, Leeds, Manchester, Oxford and across Asia) operates flexible, low-cost flights with open jaw facility - enter one country, leave by another - to destinations throughout Asia. Internal flights, accommodation and tours also available.

Trailfinders Travel Centre, 42-50 Earls Court Road, London W8 6EJ ✆ 0171-938 3366 and Trailfinders, 194 Kensington High Street, London W8 7RG ✆ 0171-938 3939 (also branches in Bristol, Glasgow and Manchester) operate low-cost flights between London and destinations throughout Asia. Also have a travellers' library and information centre, an immunisation centre for vaccinations, a travel goods shop, map/bookshop and visa service.

Publications Lonely Planet's travel guides offer practical, down-to-earth information for those wanting to explore beyond the usual tourist routes. Titles include *North East Asia on a Shoestring* £9.95 and *South East Asia on a Shoestring* £12.95 for the low-budget independent traveller. Also *Travel Survival Kits* to *Bali and Lombok* £7.95, *Bangladesh* £5.95, *Cambodia* £7.95, *China* £15.95, *Hong Kong, Macau & Canton* £8.95, *India* £14.95, *Indonesia* £14.95, *Kashmir, Ladakh & Zanskar* £6.95, *Korea* £6.95, *Laos* £7.95, *Malaysia, Singapore & Brunei* £10.95, *Myanmar (Burma)* £7.95, *Mongolia* £7.95, *Nepal* £8.95, *Pakistan* £9.95, *Philippines* £9.95, *Sri Lanka* £7.95, *Taiwan* £8.95, *Thailand* £10.95, *Tibet* £7.95 and *Vietnam* £9.95.

Rough Guides provide comprehensive background information plus details on getting there, getting around, places to explore and cheap places to stay. Titles include *Thailand* £8.99, *Nepal* £8.99, and *Hong Kong and Macau* £8.99.

Culture Shock! is a series of guides written for international travellers of any background. The reader is introduced to the people, customs, ceremonies, food and culture of a country, with checklists of dos and don'ts. All guides cost £6.95 and countries in the series include China, Hong Kong, India, Indonesia, Korea, Malaysia, Nepal, Pakistan, Philippines, Singapore, Sri Lanka, Taiwan and Thailand.

Vacation Work's *Travellers Survival Kit to the East* £6.95, is a practical guide to travelling between Turkey and Indonesia, following the overland route from Europe that remains accessible. Advice on preparation, transport, route planning, frontier regulations and medical facilities.

All the above are available from good bookshops and the larger travel chains.

COMMUNITY WORK

INDIAN VOLUNTEERS FOR COMMUNITY SERVICE
12 Eastleigh Avenue, South Harrow, Middlesex HA2 OUF
✆ **0181-864 4740**
Aims to educate the public in the UK about Indian culture and voluntary rural development. Operates a **Project Visitors' Scheme** open to anyone interested in involvement in rural development projects. 3 weeks' compulsory orientation in India before placements of up to 6 months. ⊕ Ages 18+. No special qualifications necessary. Basic board and vegetarian meals provided for £3 per day. Visitors pay their own travel expenses and insurance. No summer placements.
⊠ *Send SAE for more information and membership application form.*

YOUTH CHARITABLE ORGANISATION **20/14 Urban Bank Street, Yellamanchili 531 055, Visakhapatnam District, Andhra Pradesh, India** ✆ **(91 8924) 51122** ⌨ **(91 8924) 51131**
A secular, non-profit, non-political rural development agency working to improve the quality of life for the rural poor in India's Visakhapatnam district. Approx

40 **volunteers** required each year to work on conservation projects, community development programmes and computer and administrative activities.
⊕ Ages 18-60. Relevant experience welcome but not essential; volunteers must speak English. 40 hour week for 2+ weeks, all year except April-June. Full board accommodation provided; cost £100 per month. YCO will provide letter of invitation for volunteers to arrange own visa. No fares, wages or insurance paid. **B D**
⊠ *Apply 2 months in advance.*
UK applicants can get further information from Ruth McLeod, Director, Homeless International, 5 The Butts, Coventry, Warwickshire CV1 3GH ✆ *Coventry (01203) 632802* ⌨ *(01203) 632911.*

CONSERVATION

EARTHWATCH EUROPE **Belsyre Court, 57 Woodstock Road, Oxford OX2 6HU** ✆ **Oxford (01865) 516366**
Aims to support field research in a wide range of disciplines including animal behaviour, archaeology, ornithology, nature conservation and ecology. Support is given to researchers as a grant and in the form of volunteer assistance. Recent projects involving **volunteers** have included caring for baby orang-utans and tracking wild adults in the rainforest of Borneo; assessing the habitat needs of the endangered sloth bear in the lowlands of Nepal; saving a rare species of crane in Vietnam; and documenting the behaviour of macaque monkeys in Bali.
⊕ Ages 16-80. No special skills required although each expedition may, because of its nature, demand some talent or quality of fitness. Volunteers should be generally fit, able to cope with new situations and work with people of different ages and backgrounds, and a sense of humour will help. 2-3 weeks, all year. Members share the costs of the expedition, from £340-£2,000, which

includes meals, transport and all necessary field equipment, but not travel to the staging area, although assistance may be given with arrangements. Membership fee £25 entitles members to join expeditions, attend evening and weekend events, and receive magazines/ newsletters providing all the information necessary to choose a project. **B D PH W** depending on project.

FARMWORK

INTERNATIONAL FARM EXPERIENCE PROGRAMME
YFC Centre, N A C, Stoneleigh Park, Kenilworth, Warwickshire CV8 2LG ✆ **Coventry (01203) 696584**

Provides assistance to young **agriculturalists** and **horticulturalists** by finding places in farms/nurseries abroad enabling them to broaden their knowledge of agricultural and horticultural methods. Opportunities available on farms on the outskirts of Beijing, People's Republic of China. 1-3 months, beginning May or September. Board and lodging provided, plus 100 RMB pocket money per month. Optional 4-week course in Mandarin. Participants pay own fares and insurance; help given in obtaining visa. ⊕ Ages 18-28. Applicants must have at least 2 years' practical experience, one year of which may be at agricultural college, and intend to make a career in agriculture. Registration fee £85. ✍ *Apply at least 3 months in advance; UK nationals only.*

TEACHERS & INSTRUCTORS

English in Asia US$12.95 + $5 airmail is a useful guide for anyone interested in teaching English as a foreign language in Asia. Includes sections on teaching methods, common student errors, ideas for games and classroom activities,

together with the addresses of private English language schools in Japan, Korea and Taiwan, and tips on visas and living in these countries. Published by Global Press, 697 College Parkway, Rockville, MD 20850, United States and available in the UK from Vacation Work, 9 Park End Street, Oxford OX1 1HJ ✆ Oxford (01865) 241978, price £10.45.

INSIGHT NEPAL PO Box 6760, Kathmandu, Nepal
▭ **Kathmandu (977 1) 223515**

A recently-established organisation offering cultural tours and homestays in Nepal. Can arrange a very limited number of **volunteer placements** in both urban and remote areas of the country. Work involves teaching English, science and computer science in schools, ranging from primary to technical schools. ⊕ Ages 18-45. Applicants must be educated to at least A level or equivalent, preferably with some teaching experience. Skills in games, sports or art an advantage. 25 hour, 5-5½ day week for 1-4 months, beginning February and August. Other dates can be arranged on request. Half board accommodation provided. One week orientation includes language instruction, homestay and cross-cultural training. Tours and excursions arranged. Cost US$400 plus visa fee depending on length of work period. Application fee US$20. No fares or wages paid. ✍ *Completed application forms must be submitted at least 2 months in advance.*

WORKCAMPS

BANGLADESH WORK CAMPS ASSOCIATION (BWCA) 289/2 Work Camps Road, North Shahjahanpur, Dhaka 17, Bangladesh

Promotes international development and peace through voluntary activities, and organises international workcamps for **volunteers** in urban and rural areas of Bangladesh. Projects include

afforestation, construction work, digging canals, health education, literacy and community work. Working language is English.
⊕ Ages 18-45. 30 hour week, 1-6 weeks, October-February. Volunteers pay own insurance and travel. Participation fee US$20 per day.
☀ Apply at least 3 months in advance enclosing US$25 application fee.

JOINT ASSISTANCE CENTRE
G 17/3, DLF Qutab Enclave, Phase 1, Gurgaon, 122002 Haryana, India
✆ **(91 11) 835 2141**
A voluntary action group for disaster assistance invites **volunteers** to help in the office and join workcamps conducted throughout India. Projects include construction, environmental work, land reclamation, health and sanitation work, fundraising, teaching first aid, preparedness training for disasters and educational resource management. One month minimum stay. Year round opportunities include editing JAC newsletters, working in the library, teaching English, organising exhibitions and campaigns, helping with administration and working on a community development project on the outskirts of Delhi.
Also organises short visits/stays on projects all over India, with opportunities to meet and work with local people, and to learn yoga, nature cures and Hindi. Opportunities also exist for work with children, orphans and destitute women, often through institutions, including teaching English as a foreign language.
⊕ Ages 18+. All nationalities welcome, no experience necessary. Cost £70 (US$125) per month covers shared accommodation with self-catering facilities. Conditions primitive and the summer very hot. No travel, insurance or pocket money provided. Registration fee £10 (US$25/FF100/DM30) to be sent with the registration form.

☀ Apply to the following addresses for a registration form and other information

(enclose US$5 or equivalent for postage):

Friends of JAC, c/o 1 Ludgate Barns, Haytor, Newton Abbott, Devon TQ13 9XE (UK applicants, enclose £2 cheque payable to Friends of JAC)

Friends of JAC, c/o Krishna Gopalan, Post Box 14481, Santa Rosa, CA 95402, USA (North and South America applicants)

Simon Pierre Hamelin, 101 rue Condircet, 92410 Clamart, France (French applicants)

Applicants in all other countries should apply direct to JAC in India.

UNESCO YOUTH CENTRE
Korean National Commission for UNESCO, PO Box Central 64, Seoul, Korea 100 ✆ **(82 2) 776 4306**
🖷 **(82 2) 774 3956**
Organises an international youth camp with a work project prepared by the Work Committee during the camp period. Discussions, lectures and workshops held on international problems such as development and cultural identity. Recreational activities, including interaction with local villagers, organised. Campers learn about the history and culture of Korea through a 3 day study tour. Official language is English. Campers live in 6 camps of various nationalities. 10 days, end July. Accommodation, food, transport within Korea and medical expenses provided. Participation fee US$100.
☀ Apply by 31 May.

GENERAL

OMF INTERNATIONAL Belmont,
The Vine, Sevenoaks, Kent TN13 3TZ ✆ **Sevenoaks (01732) 450747**
🖷 **(01732) 456164**
Serve Asia offers the opportunity to observe/get involved in Christian activities in China, Hong Kong, Indonesia, Japan, Korea, the Philippines, Singapore, Taiwan or Thailand.
Volunteers work alongside expatriate

workers, local churches and local people. Also opportunities for **teachers** to teach English or work as relief teachers or hostel parents at mission schools, and for **medical or Bible school students** to gain hands-on experience. ⊕ Ages 18-30. Applicants must have a Christian commitment, be spiritually mature and in good health, with a serious interest in overseas missions. Normally 6-8 weeks, all year; longer terms possible. Participants are themselves responsible for airfare, board and administrative expenses, which can range from £1,000-£2,500 depending on the country and the length of stay. ✉ *Apply 3 months in advance.*

See also opportunities under **Japan** and **Worldwide**

APPLYING FOR A JOB

When writing to **any** organisation it is **essential** to mention **Working Holidays 1995** and enclose a **stamped, self-addressed A4 envelope**, or if in another country, an **addressed A4 envelope** and at least two **IRCs** (International Reply Coupons, available from post offices). Enquiries received without SAEs/IRCs are **unlikely** to be answered. **Before applying**, read carefully all the information given. Pay **particular** attention to:

✐ skills/qualifications/experience required

✐ the period of employment expected

✐ age limits or nationality restrictions

✐ application deadlines

✐ any other points, especially details of insurance cover, and other costs such as travel and accommodation.

When applying include the following:

✐ your name, address, date of birth, marital status, nationality, sex

✐ details of your education, qualifications, relevant experience, skills, languages spoken

✐ your period of availability for work

✐ a passport-size photo, particularly if you will be working with the public

✐ anything else recommended in the listing (such as a *cv*)

INFO

Australian High Commission
Australia House, Strand, London WC2B 4LA ✆ 0891 600333

British High Commission
Commonwealth Avenue, Yarralumla, Canberra, ACT 2600 ✆ (61 6) 270 6666

Tourist office
Australian Tourist Commission, Gemini House, 10-18 Putney Hill, Putney, London SW15 6AA ✆ 0181-780 1424

Youth hostels
Australian YHA, Level 3, 10 Mallett Street, Camperdown, New South Wales 2050

Youth & student information
Australian Union of Students, 97 Drummond Street, Carlton, Victoria 3053

Entry regulations A visa is required for a working holiday, and will be granted subject to certain conditions. The prime purpose of the visit must be a temporary stay for a holiday of specific duration and the applicant must have a return ticket, or sufficient funds to pay for this, plus sufficient funds to cover maintenance for a substantial part of the holiday period; employment must be incidental to the holiday and only to supplement holiday funds; employment in Australia must not be prearranged except on a private basis and on the applicant's own initiative; there should be reasonable prospects of obtaining temporary employment; full-time employment of more than 3 months with the same employer should not be undertaken; departure should be at the expiration of the authorised period of temporary entry; and applicants must meet normal health and character standards. If all these conditions are met the visa will be valid for a period of 13 months from the date of issue.

A period of up to 2 weeks should be allowed to obtain a working holiday visa and travel tickets should not be purchased before a visa is obtained. Applicants should be single people or married couples without children, aged 18-25 inclusive (exceptionally ages up to 30 will be considered) and holders of valid UK, Canadian, Dutch, Irish or Japanese passports. Visa applications should be made to the nearest Migration Office, together with passport and a processing fee of AU$130 (£65 in the UK). Offices in Britain are at Australia House, see above, and at the Australian Consulate, Chatsworth House, Lever Street, Manchester M1 2DL.

The objective of the working holiday scheme is essentially to provide young people with opportunities for cultural exchange, the work undertaken being part-time or of a casual nature. Personal qualities such as initiative, self-reliance, adaptability, resourcefulness and open-mindedness are the important attributes, enabling the participant to profit from the experience and to provide Australia with an insight into cultural differences.

Employment offices The Australian Government-run Commonwealth Employment Services (CES) offices are roughly equivalent to British job centres. Many CES offices have a noticeboard displaying current vacancies. Some specialise in different work areas such as temporary secretarial/clerical or casual labouring. They may also be able to provide information on seasonal farmwork. Australian citizens tend to be given priority but non-nationals may register provided they have a working holiday visa.

Travel Travellers are recommended to obtain relevant inoculations for their own personal protection during their journey to Australia depending on the route they take and the countries in which they stay.

Campus Travel offers competitive fares to destinations in Australia with open jaw facility, which allows travel out to one destination and return from another. Special student fares available to ISIC cardholders. Also offers bus, rail and air passes, stopovers in Asia en route to Australia, and a wide range of adventure tours. Offices throughout the UK including a student travel centre at 52 Grosvenor Gardens, London SW1W 0AG ℗ 0171-730 8111 or ℗ 0131-668 3303 for Scottish telephone bookings.

Council Travel, 28A Poland Street, London W1V 3DB ℗ 0171-437 7767 (offices also in Paris, Nice, Lyon, Munich, Düsseldorf, Tokyo, Singapore and throughout the US) offers low-cost student/youth airfares to destinations throughout Australia, and can issue rail and bus passes. Accommodation, tours, guidebooks, travel gear and travel insurance also available.

North-South Travel, Moulsham Mill, Parkway, Chelmsford CM2 7PX ℗ Chelmsford (01245) 492882 arranges competitively priced, reliably planned flights to all parts of Australia. All profits given to projects in the developing world.

STA Travel, 86 Old Brompton Road, London SW7 3LQ/117 Euston Road, London NW1 2SX ℗ 0171-937 9962 (offices also in Birmingham, Bristol, Cambridge, Glasgow, Leeds, Manchester, Oxford and throughout Australia) operates flexible, low-cost flights with open jaw facility to destinations across Australia. Internal flights, accommodation and tours also available.

The Australian Coachlines Bus-Pass offers unlimited bus travel on Australia's largest express route, with discounts on sightseeing, accommodation and car rental. Cost AU$343 (7 days) or AU$600 (15 days). Details from Greyhound International, Sussex House, London Road, East Grinstead, West Sussex RH19 1LD ℗ East Grinstead (01342) 317317 ▭ (01342) 328519, or from Long Haul Leisurail, see below.

Austrailpass entitles the holder to unlimited travel on Rail Australia. 14-90 days, cost from £218. Details from Long Haul Leisurail, PO Box 113, Bretton, Peterborough, Cambridgeshire PE3 8HY © Peterborough (01733) 335599.

Publications Budget Travel Australia is produced every 4 months and written with backpackers in mind. Contains information needed to plan a trip, including details on accommodation, working and getting around. Produced by Red Sky Publishing & Design, 70 Brunswick Street, Stockton-on-Tees, Cleveland TS18 1DW © Stockton-on-Tees (01642) 601694 ☎ (01642) 604309 (send large SAE and 2 first-class stamps). Also available free at various outlets including the Australian High Commission/Tourist Commission.

On arrival in Australia it is worth picking up For Backpackers By Backpackers, budget travellers' guidebooks to Sydney, Canberra & New South Wales; Melbourne, Victoria & Tasmania; Queensland; and The Outback (Northern Territory, South Australia & Western Australia). These are available free from airports, coach terminals, state tourism bureaux and hostels across Australia.

Australia - Traveller's Guide is a free annual booklet with all the facts to plan a trip: travel, where to stay, information on seasons, climate, health services, entry/ visa requirements and useful addresses. Available from the Australian Tourist Commission, see above.

Lonely Planet's guide Australia - A Travel Survival Kit £13.95 is an essential handbook for travellers in Australia, offering practical, down-to-earth information for people wanting to explore beyond the usual tourist routes.

The Rough Guide to Australia £12.99 provides comprehensive background information with details of getting there, getting around, places to explore and cheap places to stay.

Culture Shock! Australia £6.95 introduces the reader to the people, ceremonies, customs, food and culture of Australia, with checklists of dos and don'ts. ·

Travellers Survival Kit Australia & New Zealand £9.95, is a handbook for those going down under, giving information on travelling cheaply, local culture, pubs and restaurants, beaches and reefs, flora and fauna. Also Live & Work in Australia & New Zealand £8.95, a guide for those interested in finding work, starting a business or buying a home in the Antipodes. Both published by Vacation Work, 9 Park End Street, Oxford OX1 1HJ © Oxford (01865) 241978.

All the above guidebooks are available from good bookshops.

Accommodation Backpackers Resorts Australia, PO Box 1000, Byron Bay, NSW 2481 © (61 18) 66 6888 ☎ (61 66) 84 7100 is a leading hostel chain of over 100 independently owned and operated hostels catering for backpackers. They have a friendly and hospitable atmosphere, a minimum of restrictions and 24-hour access. Prices range between AU$10-AU$15 per night for a bed in a shared room. VIP card entitles the holder to a variety of savings including discount accommodation at hostels. Details in the UK from The Imaginative Traveller, 14 Barley Mow Passage, Chiswick, London W4 4PH © 0181-742 3113 ☎ 0181-742 3045.

CHILDCARE

ACADEMY AU PAIR AGENCY LTD 42 Cedarhurst Drive, Eltham, London SE9 5LP © **0181-294 1191** ☎ **0181-850 8932**
Can place **mothers' helps** and **au pairs**, all year. 12 months minimum. ⊕ Ages 18+. Applicants must have at least 6 months' childcare experience and full driving licence. Salary approx £40-£100 per week plus board and lodging provided. Travel, insurance and

visa costs paid by applicants.
Administration charge £40.

COMMUNITY WORK

**INVOLVEMENT VOLUNTEERS
ASSOCIATION INC PO Box 218,
Port Melbourne, Victoria 3207,
Australia** ☎/✉ **(61 3) 646 5504**
A not-for-profit organisation set up to
find unpaid **volunteer** placements in
community-based organisations involved
in social service programmes in Australia
and other countries. Volunteers of all
ages participate in individual placements,
assisting staff at rehabilitation institutes
or care organisations for disadvantaged
children or adults. Volunteers must be
able to speak English, arrange their own
visitor visas, and organise their own
international travel and insurance. Some
intinerant paid work can be found for
volunteers with suitable visas. Provides
advice, placements, itinerary planning,
meeting on arrival in Melbourne, initial
accommodation, introductions to
banking and taxation, discounted coach
travel, various activity courses, and a
communications base for mail. Cost
AU$400 and AU$35 placement fee. **B D**

✒ *In Europe, apply to Involvement
Volunteers-Deutschland, Postfach 110224,
37047 Göttingen, Germany* ☎ *(49 551)
33 765* ✉ *(49 551) 33 787*

✒ *In North America, apply to Involvement
Corps Inc, 15515 Sunset Boulevard, Suite
108, Pacific Palisades, CA 90272, United
States* ☎/✉ *(1 310) 459 1022.*

CONSERVATION

**AUSTRALIAN TRUST FOR
CONSERVATION VOLUNTEERS
National Director, PO Box 423,
Ballarat, Victoria 3350, Australia**
☎ **(61 53) 331 483**
A non-profitmaking, non-political,
community-based organisation
undertaking conservation projects such
as planting, erosion and salinity control,
seed collection of indigenous plants;
habitat restoration, noxious weed
eradication, endangered fauna and flora
protection. Echidna Package provides
opportunity for overseas **volunteers**.
Placements are at ATCV discretion;
projects take place in urban and rural
areas and in most states, although
limited in some states. Projects are
designed to perform the labour-
intensive work that the Australian
environment so urgently needs, and may
not necessarily involve direct contact
with endangered flora or fauna.
⊕ Ages 18+. Experience and
qualifications relating to the environment
welcome, but not essential. Applicants
should be fit, prepared to work in all
weather conditions and willing to mix
with people from many nations in teams
of 8-10. A sound knowledge of English
essential. Food, accommodation and
transport whilst working provided.
Cost AU$720 for 6 weeks. Applicants
pay their own airfares.
✒ *Write for further information enclosing 2
IRCs. Overseas volunteers welcome.*

**EARTHWATCH EUROPE Belsyre
Court, 57 Woodstock Road, Oxford
OX2 6HU** ☎ **Oxford (01865)
516366**
Aims to support field research in a wide
range of disciplines including
archaeology, nature conservation and
ecology. Support is given to researchers
as a grant and in the form of volunteer
assistance. Recent projects involving
volunteers have included studying the
tiny honey possum in Western Australia;
radio-tracking echidnas on Kangaroo
Island; and preserving coral reefs in
northern Queensland.
⊕ Ages 16-80. No special skills required
although each expedition may, because
of its nature, demand some talent or
quality of fitness. Volunteers should be
generally fit, able to cope with new
situations and work with people of
different ages and backgrounds, and a
sense of humour would help. 2-3
weeks, all year. Members share the

costs of the expedition, from £340-£2,000, which includes meals, transport and all necessary field equipment, but does not include the cost of travel to the staging area, although assistance may be given with arrangements. Membership fee £25 entitles members to join an expedition, attend evening and weekend events, and receive magazines and newsletters providing all the information necessary to choose a project. **B D PH W** depending on project.

INVOLVEMENT VOLUNTEERS ASSOCIATION INC PO Box 218, Port Melbourne, Victoria 3207, Australia ©/☎ **(61 3) 646 5504**
A not-for-profit organisation set up to find unpaid **volunteer** placements or team placements with community-based organisations involved in practical conservation activities in Australia or countries en route. Placements relate to conservation in urban or rural areas; farm tree planting programmes; marine archaeology or zoology research; bird observatory operations; researching, restoring or maintaining historic sites, gardens or covenanted areas; and developing national parks or wetlands. Placements available all year; 2-12 weeks. Volunteers must be able to speak English, arrange their own visitor visas, and organise their own international travel and insurance. Some itinerant paid work can be found for volunteers with suitable visas. Provides advice, placements, itinerary planning, meeting on arrival in Melbourne, initial accommodation, introductions to banking, taxation and a communications base for mail. Also discounted scuba diving courses on the Barrier Reef and other activities available, plus discounted coach travel. Cost AU$400 plus AU$35 placement fee. **B D**

🖳 *In Europe, apply to Involvement Volunteers-Deutschland, Postfach 37047, 110224 Göttingen, Germany* © *(49 551) 33 765* ☎ *(49 551) 33 787*

🖳 *In North America, apply to Involvement Corps Inc, 15515 Sunset Boulevard, Suite 108, Pacific Palisades, CA 90272, United States* ©/☎ *(1 310) 459 1022*

FARMWORK

There is a wide variety of farmwork, most of which is paid at piecework rates; good pickers can earn in the region of AU$300 per week after tax. As many farms are isolated it is advisable to have your own transport; a tent is also a good idea as accommodation is not always provided.

Commonwealth Employment Services (CES) offices may be able to provide details of farmwork available locally, and the following gives a general guide to what crops are harvested and when:

Year round
New South Wales: variety of harvesting opportunities outside the Sydney area. Queensland: pears, apples, grapes, beans, citrus fruit, courgettes, tomatoes and many other fruits and vegetables; main areas are Stanthorpe, Warwick, Bowen, Bundaberg and the Mary Valley. Western Australia: various crops in the southwest of the state; also tropical fruit in Carnarvon and bananas in Kununurra.

December-April
South Australia: oranges, apricots and dried fruit in Berri; grapes in the Barossa Valley and Adelaide Hills. Tasmania: Apples, grapes and hops; main areas are Launceston, Kingston and Glenorchy, but vacancies may be limited as there are experienced local pickers. New South Wales: grapes around Griffith. Victoria: grapes at Mildura and Swan Hill; tomatoes and pears in Shepparton; pears, peaches and apples in the Goulbourn/Murray Valley; tobacco in Wangaratta and Myrtleford.

June onwards
Variety of harvesting opportunities in

Riverland, South Australia.

October-January
Queensland: tobacco on the Atherton Plateau.
Western Australia: oats, wheat and barley around Geraldton, Merredin and Albany.

November-February
South Australia: strawberries in the Adelaide Hills.
Victoria: cherries in Lilyfield.

INTERNATIONAL AGRICULTURAL EXCHANGE ASSOCIATION YFC Centre, N A C, Stoneleigh Park, Kenilworth, Warwickshire CV8 2LG ✆ Coventry (01203) 696578

Provides opportunities for young people involved in **agriculture**, **horticulture** or **home management** to acquire practical work experience and improve their knowledge and understanding of the way of life in other countries. Types of farm include cattle and sheep; mixed (cattle, sheep and field crops); dairy; beef and crops; sheep and crops; plus a limited number of pig, horse and horticultural enterprises. Participants undertake paid work on the farm, approx 40 hours per week, and live as a member of the host family. Full board, lodging, insurance cover and minimum net weekly wage of £50-£60 provided. All programmes include 3/8 weeks unpaid holiday. 3 day orientation courses held at agricultural colleges and universities throughout Australia. Stopovers (2-3 days) in Singapore/Thailand arranged en route. ⚕ Ages 18-30. Applicants should be single and have good practical experience in the chosen training category, plus a valid driving licence. 9 months (departing April), 8 months (departing August), 7 or 9 months (departing September), 14 months - 7 in Australia plus 7 in Canada/US (departing September) or 14 months - 7 in New Zealand plus 7 in Australia (departing

August). Cost from £2,300 covers airfare, work permit, administration fee and orientation seminar, information meetings, insurance, supervision, placement with a host family and travel costs to placement. £200 deposit payable. **B D** if handicap is not severe. 🎓 *Apply at least 4 months in advance; UK or Irish passport holders only.*

Australian applicants requiring an exchange should apply to IAEA, 50 Oxford Street, Paddington, NSW 2021.

INTERNATIONAL FARM EXPERIENCE PROGRAMME YFC Centre, N A C, Stoneleigh Park, Kenilworth, Warwickshire CV8 2LG ✆ Coventry (01203) 696584

Provides assistance to young **agriculturalists** and **horticulturalists** by finding places in farms/nurseries abroad, enabling them to broaden their knowledge of agricultural and horticultural methods. Opportunities for placements in arable, sheep or dairy farming in Australia. Participants usually live and work with a farming family and the work is matched as far as possible with participant's requirements. Entails physical work and practical involvement. Basic wage plus board and lodging. 7-12 months, beginning March and July. ⚕ Ages 18-28. Applicants must have at least 2 years practical experience, one of which may be at agricultural college, and intend to make a career in agriculture/horticulture. Valid driving licence necessary. Participants pay own fares and insurance. Registration fee £70 plus programme fee. 🎓 *Apply 2-3 months in advance. UK nationals only.*

NORTHERN VICTORIA FRUITGROWERS' ASSOCIATION PO Box 394, Shepparton, Victoria 3630, Australia

VICTORIAN PEACH AND APRICOT GROWERS' ASSOCIATION PO Box 39, Cobram, Victoria 3644, Australia

Offer a variety of **fruit picking** jobs under the working holidaymakers scheme. The Associations represent the 500 orchards in the Goulburn/Murray Valley, Victoria. Season commences in late January with the harvesting of Bartlett pears, used mainly for canning, and continues into March and April when crops include other pear varieties, peaches, and apples. Piecework rates apply. Accommodation often available; participants may camp in the orchards if they take their own equipment. For latest details on availability of work, contact either of the below on arrival.

Addresses for personal callers:
Northern Victoria Fruitgrowers' Association Ltd, 21 Nixon Street, Shepparton, Victoria ℭ (058) 21 5844
Victorian Peach and Apricot Growers' Association, 21 Station Street, Cobram, Victoria ℭ (058) 72 1729.

WILLING WORKERS ON ORGANIC FARMS (WWOOF) W Tree, Buchan, Victoria 3885, Australia

A non-profitmaking organisation which aims to help organic farmers and smallholders whose work is often labour-intensive as it does not rely on the use of artificial fertilisers or pesticides. Offers placements whereby **volunteers** can gain first-hand experience of organic farming and gardening; approx 350 host farms all over Australia especially in the eastern and southern coastal areas. Volunteers learn by doing, working in exchange for their keep. All types of farmwork, field work, animal care and building. Placements of up to 6 months can be arranged for agricultural students.
⊕ Ages 17+. Full board and lodging provided in farmhouse or outbuildings; volunteers should take a sleeping bag. No fares or wages paid. Insurance and anti-tetanus vaccination recommended. Membership fee £10 includes accident insurance; more units can be added. **PH**

WORKCAMPS

CHRISTIAN WORKCAMPS AUSTRALIA PO Box K164, Haymarket, NSW 2000, Australia

Small group organising workcamps in Aborigine communities in Central Australia and Northern Territory. People of all religions or none invited to participate as **volunteers**; work involves constructing communal buildings.
⊕ Ages 18+. No special skills or experience required but applicants should be keen to learn, physically fit and open to Aborigine culture and society. Two camps in July and January. Cost AU$50 covers accommodation and food; volunteers may also be required to pay up to AU$250 to cover transport to workcamp site. No fares or wages paid.

Apply through partner organisation in country of residence. In the UK: United Nations Association International Youth Service. See page 30 for registration details.

INTERNATIONAL VOLUNTEERS FOR PEACE 499 Elizabeth Street, Surry Hills, NSW 2010, Australia

The Australian branch of Service Civil International, which promotes international reconciliation through work projects involving teams of **volunteers**. In recent projects volunteers have helped with building work, renovation, and the running of programmes at a farm for city children in Goulburn; and provided support and help with personal care for athletes at a wheelchair sports event in Sydney.
⊕ Ages 18+. Applicants should be highly motivated, preferably with previous workcamp or other voluntary experience, and prepared to work hard as part of a team. Workcamps generally last 2-4 weeks. Food, shared accommodation and work accident insurance provided. No fares or wages paid. **B D PH W** welcome.

Apply through partner organisation in country of residence. In the UK:

International Voluntary Service. See page 30 for registration details.

GENERAL

BRITISH UNIVERSITIES NORTH AMERICA CLUB (BUNAC)
16 Bowling Green Lane, London EC1R 0BD ✆ **0171-251 3472**
A non-profit, non-political educational student club venture which aims to encourage interest and understanding between students. Administers a **Work Australia** programme for those who want to work and travel. Jobs do not have to be organised in advance, but advice is offered to those wishing to do so. Orientation programmes on arrival give advice on job finding, income tax, obtaining a visa, accommodation, travel, food and budgeting.
⚐ Ages 18-25. Cost depends on route and stopovers. In order to obtain a visa, applicants must have evidence of £2,000 in personal funds. *UK, Irish, Canadian or Dutch nationals only.*

APPLYING FOR A JOB

When writing to **any** organisation it is **essential** to mention **Working Holidays 1995** and enclose a **stamped, self-addressed A4 envelope**, or if in another country, an **addressed A4 envelope** and at least two **IRCs** (International Reply Coupons, available from post offices). Enquiries received without SAEs/IRCs are **unlikely** to be answered. **Before applying**, read carefully all the information given. Pay **particular** attention to:

✐ skills/qualifications/experience required

✐ the period of employment expected

✐ age limits or nationality restrictions

✐ application deadlines

✐ any other points, especially details of insurance cover, and other costs such as travel and accommodation.

When applying include the following:

✐ your name, address, date of birth, marital status, nationality, sex

✐ details of your education, qualifications, relevant experience, skills, languages spoken

✐ your period of availability for work

✐ a passport-size photo, particularly if you will be working with the public

✐ anything else recommended in the listing (such as a *cv*)

INFO

Austrian Embassy
18 Belgrave Mews West, London SW1X
8HU ✆ 0171-235 3731

British Embassy
Jaurèsgasse 12, 1030 Vienna
✆ (43 1) 7131575/9

Tourist office
Austrian National Tourist Office,
30 St George Street, London W1R 9FA
✆ 0171-629 0461

Youth hostels
Österreichischer Jugendherbergs-
verband, Schottenring 28, 1010 Vienna

Youth & student information
Austrian Foreign Students' Service,
Rooseveltplatz 13, 1090 Vienna

Austrian Institute, 28 Rutland Gate,
London SW7 1PQ ✆ 0171-584 8653

Büro für Studentenreisen,
Schreyvogelgasse 3, 1010 Vienna

ÖKISTA (Austrian Committee for
International Educational Exchange),
Garnisongasse 7, 1090 Vienna

Entry regulations Work permits are
not required for nationals of EU/EEA
countries. All other nationals require
work permits for all kinds of
employment including au pair positions.
The number of work permits issued is
limited and a permit will only be granted
if there is no Austrian national to fill the
post; this applies particularly to clerical
and secretarial work. The work permit
or equivalent should be submitted to the
Consular Section of the Austrian
Embassy, together with a valid passport,
who will then issue the necessary visa.
All employed persons except au pairs
must contribute to the health and social
security scheme, which covers most
medical expenses.

Employment offices The Austrian Embassy, see above, can supply a list of provincial employment offices. When applying to one of the offices the following details should be supplied in a letter typed in German: name, address, date of birth, education, profession, type of present employment, knowledge of foreign languages, length of intended stay, and type of job required. Applications for au pair positions, however, cannot be accepted. Addresses of some provincial employment offices:

Landesarbeitsamt für das Burgenland, Permayerstraße 10, 7001 Eisenstadt

Landesarbeitsamt für Kärnten, Kumpfgasse 25, 9010 Klagenfurt

Landesarbeitsamt für Niederösterreich, Nohenstaufengasse 2, 1013 Vienna

Landesarbeitsamt für Oberösterreich, Gruberstraße 63, 4010 Linz

Landesarbeitsamt für Salzburg, Auerspergstraße 67a, 5021 Salzburg

Landesarbeitsamt für Steiermark, Babenbergerstraße 33, 8021 Graz

Landesarbeitsamt für Tirol, Schöpfstraße 5, 8010 Innsbruck

Landesarbeitsamt für Vorarlberg, Rheinstraße 32, 6903 Bregenz

Landesarbeitsamt für Wien, Weihburggasse 30, 1011 Vienna

For further information see *Working in Austria* available from the Austrian Embassy. Applications for work can also be made under the International Clearing of Vacancies scheme; for further details in the UK contact the Training Agency.

Job advertising Publicitas, 517/523 Fulham Road, London SW6 1HD ✆ 0171-385 7723 can accept job advertisements for a number of Austrian newspapers.

Travel Budget airfares are available from the Anglo-Austrian Society, 46 Queen Anne's Gate, London SW1H 9AU ✆ 0171-222 0366/2430.

Freedom Pass allows 3, 5 or 10 days unlimited travel in 1 month on the railways of Austria. Cost from £61 (under 26) or £76 (26+). Available from British Rail International Rail Centre, Victoria Station, London SW1V 1JY ✆ 0171-834 2345.

Campus Travel offers Eurotrain fares, Inter-rail and student/youth fares on travel by plane, train, boat and bus to destinations in Austria. Offices throughout the UK including a student travel centre at 52 Grosvenor Gardens, London SW1W 0AG (opposite Victoria Station) ✆ 0171-730 3402 or ✆ 0131-668 3303 for Scottish telephone bookings.

Council Travel, 28A Poland Street, London W1V 3DB ✆ 0171-287 3337 (offices also in Paris, Nice, Lyon, Munich, Düsseldorf, Tokyo, Singapore and throughout the US) offers Eurotrain under 26 reduced fares and student/youth airfares to destinations in Austria, plus travel insurance, guidebooks and travel gear.

Publications The Vienna Tourist Board publish a *Youth Scene* magazine which gives plenty of useful information for young visitors to the city. Available from the Vienna Tourist Board, 1025 Vienna, or from the Austrian National Tourist Office, see above.

Accommodation For accommodation in hotels, pensions and student hostels in Vienna, contact Büro für Studentenreisen, Schreyvogelgasse 3, 1010 Vienna.

ÖKISTA (Austrian Committee for International Educational Exchange), Garnisongasse 7, 1090 Vienna can provide all kinds of accommodation throughout Austria.

AU PAIR / CHILDCARE

Au pairs must be girls at least 18 years old, and can expect to receive board, lodging and a minimum of AS700 per week in exchange for looking after the children and helping with light housework and simple cooking. Au pairs do not pay income tax, and contributions to the health and social security scheme cannot be made, so it is essential to join a private health insurance scheme. Au pairs must give an undertaking to return home at the end of their stay, and prove that they have sufficient funds for the journey.

ACADEMY AU PAIR AGENCY LTD 42 Cedarhurst Drive, Eltham, London SE9 5LP ✆ 0181-294 1191 ℻ 0181-850 8932
Can place **au pairs**. ⚘ Ages 18-27. Some knowledge of German essential. Pocket money approx £35-£40 per week. Administration charge £40. **Nannies** and **mothers' helps** positions for those with qualifications/experience.

ARBEITSGEMEINSCHAFT AUSLANDS-SOZIALDIENST Au-Pair-Vermittlung, Johannesgasse 16/1, 1010 Vienna, Austria
Can place **au pairs** in Vienna and other areas. ⚘ Ages 18-25. Pocket money from AS700 per week. Registration fee AS600. Limited number of summer positions with families outside Vienna for 8+ weeks, without language classes.

BUNTERS AU PAIR & DOMESTIC AGENCY 17 Copper Street, Macclesfield, Cheshire SK11 7LH ✆ Macclesfield (01625) 614534
Can place **au pairs, demi pairs** and **mothers' helps**. 6-12 months all year or 10 weeks, summer. ⚘ Ages 18-27. Pocket money £35-£50 per week, depending on hours worked. Placement fee £40. ✍ Apply before May for summer placements.

HELPING HANDS AU PAIR & DOMESTIC AGENCY 39 Rutland Avenue, Thorpe Bay, Essex SS1 2XJ ✆ Southend-on-Sea (01702) 602067
Can place **au pairs** and **mothers' helps**. ⚘ Ages 18-27. Pocket money approx £35 per week for au pairs, higher for mothers' helps. Introduction fee £40 on acceptance of a family. UK nationals only.

INTERNATIONAL CATHOLIC SOCIETY FOR GIRLS (ACISJF) St Patrick's International Youth Centre, 24 Great Chapel Street, London W1V 3AF ✆ 0171-734 2156 ℻ 0171-287 6282
Arrange **au pair** posts for 9+ months. ⚘ Ages 18+. Mainly UK/Irish nationals.

LANGTRAIN INTERNATIONAL Torquay Road, Foxrock, Dublin 18, Ireland ✆ (353 1) 289 3876
Can place **au pairs** with Austrian families. ⚘ Ages 18+. Pocket money £30-£40 per week. Placement fee £60.

MONDIAL AGENCY 32 Links Road, West Wickham, Kent BR4 0QW ✆ 0181-777 0510
Can place **au pairs** in Vienna or the provinces. ⚘ Ages 18-27. Pocket money approx £35 per week. Service charge £40.

ÖKISTA (Austrian Committee for International Educational Exchange), Au Pair Department, Garnisongasse 7, 1090 Vienna, Austria
Can place **au pairs** in Vienna, main cities and country areas. ⚘ Ages 18-28. Pocket money approx AS700 per week. Registration fee AS600.

STUDENTS ABROAD LTD 11 Milton View, Hitchin, Hertfordshire SG4 0QD ✆ Hitchin (01462) 438909 ℻ (01462) 438919
Can place **au pairs** and occasionally **mothers' helps**. ⚘ Ages 18-27 for au pairs. Basic knowledge of German helpful but not essential. Pocket money

approx £35-£40 per week. Service charge £40.

COURIERS / REPS

BLADON LINES Personnel Department, 56-58 Putney High Street, London SW15 1SF
℃ 0181-785 2200
Opportunities for **representatives** to work in the ski resorts of St Anton or Lech. Work involves welcoming and looking after guests, providing information, helping with coach transfers, managing chalet staff and ensuring everything is running smoothly.
⊕ Ages 24+. Relevant experience an advantage, and good spoken German essential. Applicants must be prepared to work hard but will get time to ski. Season lasts December-May. Salary £50-£100 per week, depending on the size of the resort. Board, lodging, return travel, insurance, ski pass and ski hire provided. Small charge made for uniform. Training week held before departure.
Also a few places in each resort for **ski guides** who act as assistant reps and whose work involves showing guests around the slopes, helping with coach transfers and organising après ski.
⊕ Ages 22+ with good spoken German. Applicants should have good leadership qualities and be proficient skiers (minimum 20 weeks experience). Salary approx £50 per week. A week's training held in Val d'Isère before the season starts. EEA passport holders only.

CANVAS HOLIDAYS LTD
12 Abbey Park Place, Dunfermline, Fife KY12 7PD
Provides accommodation for holiday families in ready-erected fully equipped tents and mobile homes on campsites. Positions available as resident **campsite couriers**, **children's couriers** and **water sports couriers**.
The work involves a daily routine of tent cleaning as customers arrive and depart, providing information and advice on the

local attractions and essential services, helping to sort out problems that might arise and organising activities for the children and get-togethers for the families. 7 day week with no fixed hours; the workload varies from day to day. At the beginning and end of the season there is a period of physical work when tents are put up and prepared or taken down and stored for the winter. Other tasks include administration, book keeping and stock control. Working knowledge of German essential.
⊕ Ages 18-25. Applicants should be those with a year between school and further education, undergraduates or graduates. They need to be enthusiastic, practical, reliable, self-motivated, able to turn their hand to new and varied tasks, and with a sense of humour.
6 months, April-October. Return travel (dependent on successful completion of contract), accommodation in frame tents and bicycle for use on site provided. Salary £85 per week.
✉ Applications accepted anytime; interviews commence early November for the following season. UK nationals only.

CRYSTAL HOLIDAYS Crystal House, The Courtyard, Arlington Road, Surbiton, Surrey KT6 6BW
℃ 0181-241 5111
Tour operator arranging year-round air, rail, coach and self-drive holidays throughout Austria.
Representatives are required to meet and greet clients and be responsible for their welfare during their holiday.
Ski guides also needed during winter season.
⊕ Ages 22-35. Previous experience desirable and fluent German essential. Approx 60 hour, 7 day week, May-October and December-April. Basic salary plus commission; board, lodging, insurance, travel costs and uniform provided. One week training seminar held at beginning of each season.
✉ Apply January/February for summer season, April/May for winter season.

EUROCAMP Summer Jobs (Ref WH), PO Box 170, Liverpool L70 1ES ✆ Knutsford (01565) 625522

One of Europe's leading tour operators, specialising in providing quality camping and mobile home holidays for families throughout Europe.

Campsite couriers required. Work involves cleaning tents and equipment prior to the arrival of new customers; checking, replacing and making repairs on equipment; replenishing gas supplies; keeping basic accounts and reporting on a weekly basis to England. Couriers are also expected to meet new arrivals and assist holidaymakers with any problems that arise; organise activities and parties; provide information on local tourist attractions and maintain an information noticeboard. At the beginning and end of the season couriers are also expected to help in erecting and dismantling tents. Couriers need to be flexible to meet the needs of customers and be on hand where necessary; they will be able to organise their own free time as the workload allows.

⊕ Ages 18+. Applicants should be independent, adaptable, reliable, physically fit, have plenty of initiative and relish a challenging and responsible position. Good working knowledge of German also necessary. Preference given to those able to work the whole season, April-September/October; contracts also available for first half season, April-mid July and second half season, mid July-September/October.

Children's couriers also required, with the energy and enthusiasm to organise a wide range of exciting activities for groups aged 4-13. Experience of working with this age range essential, but language ability is not a requirement. ⊕ Ages 18+. Must be available for the whole season, May-September.

For both positions the salary is £95 per week. Training provided together with accommodation in frame tent with cooking facilities, insurance and return travel.

⚡ *Early application by telephone preferred; interviews start September/October. UK/EEA passport-holders only.*

SKIBOUND Olivier House, 18 Marine Parade, Brighton, East Sussex BN2 1TL

The largest independent group tour operator, specialising in winter sports tours for schools and adults, and in activity tours and excursions in spring/summer. **Area managers, representatives** and **hotel/chalet managers** required for the winter season, December-April in the Austrian Tirol. Posts involve a considerable amount of client contact; applicants must be presentable and keen to work hard. ⊕ Ages 21+. Good knowledge of German required for representatives and preferably for managers; previous experience an advantage. Insurance, travel and full board accommodation provided. Salary according to responsibility.

SKI TOTAL 10 Hill Street, Richmond, Surrey TW9 ✆ 0181-948 3535

Tour operator arranging skiing holidays in Austria. Opportunities for **ski resort managers**, to organise all aspects of clients' holidays, supervise staff and ensure standards are maintained with possible ski guiding up to 3½ days per week. Salary £70-£90 per week. ⊕ Ages 23+. Applicants must be hard working, resourceful, patient, outgoing, experienced resort managers, who get along with and can handle people well at all levels.

Ski guides/technicians/handymen/women also required. Duties include clearing snow, fitting gas bottles, unloading deliveries, maintenance, repairs and ski guiding approx 4 days per week. ⊕ Ages 21+. Applicants should be hard working, friendly, good skiers with some ski technician experience and a clean driving licence. Some German useful. Salary £50-£70 per week.

All staff work a 40-50 hour, 6 day week,

December-April. Full medical insurance, board accommodation and travel fares provided. I week pre-season training programme at resort. *UK nationals only.* ✍ *Apply from June onwards.*

DOMESTIC

BLADON LINES **Personnel Department, 56-58 Putney High Street, London SW15 1SF**
✆ **0181-785 2200**
Opportunities for **chalet girls** to work in the ski resorts of St Anton and Lech. Work involves cleaning chalets, making beds, caring for guests, shopping and preparing meals.
⊕ Ages 21+. Experience and/or qualifications in catering or domestic work essential.
Also positions for **hostesses** in larger chalets where no cooking experience is required.
Hours very variable; applicants must be prepared to work hard but will get time to ski. December-May. Salary approx £45 per week. Board, lodging, return travel, insurance, ski pass and ski hire provided. Small charge made for uniform. One day briefing in London held before departure. *EEA passport holders only.*

CRYSTAL HOLIDAYS **Crystal House, The Courtyard, Arlington Road, Surbiton, Surrey KT6 6BW**
✆ **0181-241 5111**
Tour operator arranging skiing holidays at resorts throughout Austria.
Chalet staff required to cook daily breakfast, afternoon tea and 3-course evening meal for clients, and keep chalets clean and tidy.
⊕ Ages 20-35. Catering qualifications or experience essential. Approx 60 hour, 6½ day week, December-April. Basic salary plus commission, board, lodging, insurance, travel costs and uniform provided. One week training seminar held at beginning of each season.
✍ *Apply April/May.*

SKIBOUND/TRAVELBOUND
Olivier House, 18 Marine Parade, Brighton, East Sussex BN2 1TL
The largest independent group tour operator, specialising in winter tours for schools and adults, and in activity tours and excursions in spring/summer. Staff are required for all grades of **hotel work** in the winter and spring/ summer seasons, December-April and May-August, in the Austrian Alps.
Posts involve client contact and applicants must be presentable and keen to work hard.
⊕ Ages 18+. Previous experience useful; catering experiece required for some posts. Insurance, travel and full board accommodation provided. Salary acccording to level of responsiblility.

SKI TOTAL 10 Hill Street, Richmond, Surrey TW9
✆ **0181-948 3535**
Tour operator arranging skiing holidays in Austria. Requires **chalet staff** to do catering, cleaning, washing up, bedmaking for 8-12 people in self-contained chalets. Salary £50 per week.
⊕ Ages 21+. Applicants should be experienced, capable, hard working with plenty of cooking experience. Sense of humour, patience and ability to get on with groups of people of varied ages and backgrounds essential, as is knowledge of German and a clean driving licence.
Cooks also required, to cater for 14-30 people per week, run a kitchen and supervise junior staff.
⊕ Ages 21+. Applicants must have experience and a proven record of cooking for large numbers of people. Driving licence and some German useful. Salary £60-£80 per week.
Opportunities for **chalet helpers/ assistant cooks** to do cooking, cleaning, washing up, making beds. Salary £40 per week.
⊕ Ages 19+. Applicants must have experience, an aptitude for hard work, enthusiasm, a sense of humour and an outgoing personality.
All staff work a 40-50 hour, 6 day week, December-April. Accommodation,

board, full medical insurance and travel costs provided. One week pre-season training programme at resort. 🕮 *Apply from June onwards. UK nationals only.*

FARMWORK

INTERNATIONAL FARM EXPERIENCE PROGRAMME
YFC Centre, N A C, Stoneleigh Park, Kenilworth, Warwickshire CV8 2LG ✆ Coventry (01203) 696584
Provides assistance to young **agriculturalists** and **horticulturalists** by finding places in farms/nurseries abroad, enabling them to broaden their knowledge of agricultural and horticultural methods. Opportunities for practical horticultural and agricultural work usually on mixed farms. Participants usually live and work with a farming family and the work is matched as far as possible with participant's requirements. Entails physical work and practical involvement. 8-10 hour day, 6 day week; every other weekend free. 3-12 months. Positions mostly available in spring and summer; some **au pair** positions for girls. Basic wage plus board and lodging.
⊕ Ages 18-28. Applicants must have at least 2 years practical experience, one of which may be at an agricultural college, and intend to make a career in agriculture/horticulture. Valid driving licence necessary. Participants pay own fares and insurance. Registration fee £85. *UK applications to IFEP; others via IFEP partners in home country.*

MONITORS & INSTRUCTORS

PGL SKI EUROPE Brentham House, 45c High Street, Hampton Wick, Kingston-upon-Thames, Surrey KT1 4DG ✆ 0181-977 7755
Operates holidays for groups and school parties. Part-time **ski instructors** required for winter sports centres in the Tyrol and Salzburgland. BASI or full foreign qualifications essential. Knowledge of foreign languages useful but not essential; fluent English a prerequisite. 6 hours teaching per day, 1-4 week periods over the New Year, February and April. Wages approx £90-£135 per week, according to qualifications. Full board hotel accommodation and ski pass plus travel from London/resort. Access to the same facilities as the clients.
🕮 *Interviews held May-November.*

VILLAGE CAMPS Chalet Seneca, 1854 Leysin, Switzerland
Organises American-style summer camps near Zell am See in the Austrian Alps for ages 8-18 from the international business and diplomatic communities. Opportunities for **counsellors, special activity counsellors, programme leaders, specialist instructors** and **nurses**. Staff live, work and play with the children and are responsible for their safety, health and happiness. **Counsellors** plan, organise and direct daytime and evening programmes, accompany campers on excursions and may be called upon to supervise other counsellors and take charge of a camper group. Evening activities include sports and games, films, competitions, fondues and discos. **Special activity counsellors**, having a high degree of proficiency, organise, execute and instruct specific programmes such as sports, arts and crafts, nature study and basic computer science. Counsellors with a substantial amount of leadership experience in recreational programmes can be appointed **programme leaders**, which includes running a camp programme and direction and supervision of adult counsellors. **Assistant** and **junior counsellors** are responsible for supporting counsellors in all activities and assisting with special activities at day camps as required. **Specialist instructors** should have 2 years' training and experience, and be able to instruct children of all ability

levels; they are responsible for the concentrated teaching of their subject at a speciality camp such as golf, tennis, computer science or French and English language. **Nurses** are responsible for the general health and welfare of campers and counsellors, attending to accidents and maintaining an infirmary. Compulsory pre-camp training course arranged for all staff.

⊕ Ages 21+, 26+ for programme leaders. Applicants must have training and/or experience of working with children and have an interest in children from many ethnic and religious backgrounds. English is the first language, but priority is given to applicants with additional French, Italian or German language skills. 45 hour week for 1+ months, June-August. 1½ days plus 3 evening free per 2 week session. Full board accommodation, accident and liability insurance provided, but not travel costs. Wages SF325 per 2 week session.

YOUNG AUSTRIA Alpenstraße 108a, 5020 Salzburg, Austria

Organises English language camps for Austrian and German children, for which **monitors** and **EFL teachers** are required. The camps are based at holiday centre chalets in the Salzburg region, and are organised for ages 10-19 who are studying English at school. The aim is to improve their knowledge of the English language and the British way of life. **Monitors** and teachers are responsible for the daily welfare of a group of approx 10-15 children, for the organisation of indoor and outdoor activities, including sports, music and crafts, excursions and for helping the children with English conversation. **Teachers** are responsible for the daily tuition (3½ hours) of English but also have to act as monitors. The language of the camps is English and a knowledge of German is not compulsory.

⊕ Ages 21-30. Applicants should be native English speakers and have experience in working with or teaching children. Qualified teachers will be given priority for teaching posts. Applicant's ability and organisational skills in sports, music and crafts will be taken into consideration. 3 or 6 weeks, end June-beginning September. Board, accommodation and insurance provided. Pay from AS4,800, monitors or AS5,800, teachers, per 3 week session, plus lump sum of AS2,000 for travel expenses. Compulsory interviews and briefing held in London in June. *UK residents preferred.* ✆ *Apply in February.*

WORKCAMPS

ÖSTERREICHISCHER BAUORDEN PO Box 149, Hörnesgasse 3, 1031 Vienna, Austria

Austrian branch of International Building Companions, an international volunteers' association with the aims of fighting misery and distress, and making a contribution towards a better understanding between nations. **Volunteers** are invited to work on international workcamps which take place throughout Austria. Projects have included construction, cleaning and renovation work at youth/social centres, churches, hostels, homes for the aged, kindergartens, schools, community centres and refugee resettlements; and housing for socially deprived families.

⊕ Ages 18+. Applicants should have previous workcamp experience. 40 hour week, 3-4 weeks, July and August. Food, prepared by volunteers, tent, family, school or centre accommodation, insurance and travel in Austria provided, but volunteers should take sleeping bags. Participation fee DM110. ✆ *Apply 2 months in advance.*

SERVICE CIVIL INTERNATIONAL Schottengasse 3a/1/59, 1010 Vienna, Austria

Service Civil International promotes international reconciliation through work projects involving international teams of **volunteers**. Recent projects have included working at a day care

centre and soup kitchen for homeless people in Vienna; organising workshops for disabled and abled teenagers in Graz; and helping with the harvest at an organic farm in Wartberg. Camps are linked to study themes. Workcamp languages are English and German.
⊕ Ages 18+. Applicants should be highly motivated, preferably with previous workcamp or other voluntary experience, and prepared to work hard as part of a team. 35-40 hour week, 2-4 weeks, June-September. Food, shared accommodation and work accident insurance provided. No fares or wages paid. **B D PH W** welcome.

🖎 *Apply through partner organisation in country of residence.*
In the UK: International Voluntary Service. See page 30 for registration details and addressees.

GENERAL

EUROYOUTH LTD
301 Westborough Road, Westcliff, Southend-on-Sea, Essex SS0 9PT
✆ **Southend-on-Sea (01702) 341434**
Holiday stays arranged where **guests** are offered board and lodging in return for an agreed number of hours English conversation with hosts or their children. Time also available for guests to practise German if desired.
⊕ Mainly ages 18-25, but there are sometimes opportunities for ages 13-16 and for older applicants. The scheme is open to anyone whose mother tongue is English and who is interested in visiting Austria and living with a local family. 2-3 weeks, June-August. Travel and insurance paid by applicants. Registration fee approx £70.
🖎 *Apply at least 12 weeks prior to scheduled departure date.*

APPLYING FOR A JOB

When writing to **any** organisation it is **essential** to mention **Working Holidays 1995** and enclose a **stamped, self-addressed A4 envelope**, or if in another country, an **addressed A4 envelope** and at least two **IRCs** (International Reply Coupons, available from post offices). Enquiries received without SAEs/IRCs are **unlikely** to be answered. **Before applying**, read carefully all the information given. Pay **particular** attention to:

✐ skills/qualifications/experience required

✐ the period of employment expected

✐ age limits or nationality restrictions

✐ application deadlines

✐ any other points, especially details of insurance cover, and other costs such as travel and accommodation.

When applying include the following:

✐ your name, address, date of birth, marital status, nationality, sex

✐ details of your education, qualifications, relevant experience, skills, languages spoken

✐ your period of availability for work

✐ a passport-size photo, particularly if you will be working with the public

✐ anything else recommended in the listing (such as a *cv*)

BALTIC STATES

INFO

Estonian Embassy 16 Hyde Park Gate, London SW7 5DG
✆ 0171-589 3428

Latvian Embassy 72 Queensborough Terrace, London W2 3SP
✆ 0171-727 1698

Lithuanian Embassy 17 Essex Villas, London W8 7BP ✆ 0171-938 2481

Entry regulations Details of work permits and entry requirements can be obtained in Britain from the embassies listed above.

Job advertising Frank L Crane (London) Ltd, International Press Representatives, 5/15 Cromer Street, London WC1H 8LS ✆ 0171-837 3330 can place job advertisements in leading newspapers in Latvia.

Travel Campus Travel offers low-cost student and youth fares to the Baltic States, plus rail passes for internal travel within the states. Offices throughout the UK including a student travel centre at 52 Grosvenor Gardens, London SW1W OAG (opposite Victoria Station) ✆ 0171-730 3402 or ✆ 0131-668 3303 for Scottish telephone bookings.

STA Travel, 86 Old Brompton Road, London SW7 3LQ/117 Euston Road, London NW1 2SX ✆ 0171-937 9921 (offices also in Birmingham, Bristol, Cambridge, Glasgow, Leeds, Manchester, and Oxford) operates flexible low-cost flights to Riga, Tallinn and Vilnius.

Publications Lonely Planet's *Scandinavian and Baltic Europe on a Shoestring* £10.95 and *Baltic States & Kaliningrad - A Travel Survival Kit* £9.95 offer practical, down-to-earth information for the low-budget, independent traveller in Estonia, Latvia and Lithuania.

WORKCAMPS

AUSTEJA Pylimo 35, 2001 Vilnius, Lithuania ✆ **(370 2) 61 17 10/62 61 38** ☎ **(370 2) 61 17 12**
A youth organisation running voluntary activities in Lithuania, invites **volunteers** to take part in international workcamps organised in town and country districts. Recent projects have included excavating a series of archaeological monuments in the ancient port of Klaipeda; helping to regenerate a 19th century botanical park in Palanga; and repair and maintenance work at a kindergarten for children with orthopaedic disorders in Vilnius.
Each workcamp has a study element on a social, ecological or archaeological theme, and excursions are arranged to local places of interest.
⊕ Ages 18+. Applicants should preferably have previous workcamp/ voluntary work experience, and be prepared to work hard as part of a team. 30 hour week, 2 weeks, July-August. Food and shared accommodation provided; volunteers arrange own travel and insurance. No fares or wages paid.

☙ *Apply through partner organisation in country of residence. In the UK: International Voluntary Service. See page 30 for registration details and addresses.*

CSA/SPEKTRAS Maironio 14-9, Kaunas 3000, Lithuania
Volunteers are invited to take part in international workcamps. Recent projects have included renovation work on the farm and repairing footpaths at the museum of folk architecture in Rumsiskes; coastal protection work and planting flowers at the seaside resort of Palanga; and organising a summer rock concert and other weekend performances at a youth centre near Lake Luksio. Discussion programmes and cultural excursions organised.
⊕ Ages 18-30. Applicants must be highly motivated and prepared to work hard as part of a team. 5 day week for 2-3 weeks, June-August. Food and accommodation provided, but volunteers pay their own travel and insurance costs.

☙ *Apply through partner organisation in country of residence. In the UK: Concordia (Youth Service Volunteers) Ltd, Quaker International Social Projects or United Nations Association International Youth Service. See page 30 for registration details and addresses.*

LATVIAN STUDENT CENTRE (LSV) Laeplesa 75/III - 32, 1011 Riga, Latvia ✆ **(371 2) 289496** ☎ **(371 8) 828303**
Volunteers are invited to take part in international workcamps organised throughout Latvia. Recent projects have included cleaning and tidying a Second World War cemetery for German soldiers in Liepaja; renovating an open-air museum at Jekabpils and restoring the Krustpils Castle; cleaning sand dunes on the Baltic sea shore; and painting and decorating work at a children's art school in Bauska. Each camp has a study theme and excursions are organised to places of interest.
⊕ Ages 18+. Applicants must be prepared to work hard as part of a team; previous workcamp experience useful. 2-3 weeks, July-September. Full board accommodation provided in local schools or youth hostels; volunteers should take out full insurance. The language on all camps is English. No fares or wages paid.

☙ *Apply through partner organisation in country of residence. In the UK: International Voluntary Service or United Nations Association International Youth Service. See page 30 for registration details and addresses.*

When writing to any organisation it is essential to mention Working Holidays 1995 and enclose a stamped, self-addressed A4 envelope, or if in another country, an addressed A4 envelope and at least two IRCs.

INFO

Belgian Embassy
103-105 Eaton Square, London SWIW
9AB ℂ 0171-235 5422

British Embassy
Rue d'Arlon 85, 1040 Brussels
ℂ (32 2) 287 6211

Tourist office
Belgian National Tourist Office, Premier
House, 2 Gayton Road, Harrow,
Middlesex HA1 2XU ℂ 0181-861 3300

Youth hostels
Centrale Wallonne des Auberges de la
Jeunesse, rue Van Oost 52, 1030 Brussels

Vlaamse Jeugdherbergcentrale, Van
Stralenstraat 40, 2008 Antwerp

Youth & student information
Centre National d'Information des Jeunes,
10 rue Jean Volders, 1060 Brussels

Nationaal Informatiecentrum voor
Jongeren, Prinsstraat 15, 2000 Antwerp

Caravanes de Jeunesse Belge, 216
chaussée d'Ixelles, 1050 Brussels

Accueil Jeunes, 79 rue Gillon, 1030
Brussels

Centre Jeunesse Liège, rue Ste Marguerite,
4000 Liège

Entry regulations UK citizens
intending to work in Belgium should
have a full passport. They must register
at the nearest town hall within 8 days
and bring along a certificate of good
conduct. UK/EEA nationals may stay in
Belgium for up to 3 months in order to
seek employment, though the number of
opportunities available to foreign
students is extremely limited.
The Belgian Embassy can supply a list
of job centres for temporary work
(T-Service).

Job advertising Advertisements for job vacancies, situations wanted, services offered and domestic help are included in the weekly news magazine for English-speaking residents in Belgium, *The Bulletin*, avenue Molière 329, 1060 Brussels ✆ (32 2) 343 99 09. On sale at all major news stands.

Publicitas Ltd, 517-523 Fulham Road, London SW6 1HD ✆ 0171-385 7723 can place job advertisements in Belgian newspapers and magazines.

Travel Belgian National Railways, 10 Greycoat Place, London SW1P 1SB ✆ 0891 51644 (calls charged at 39p/49p per minute off peak/other times), operates a scheme where a bike can be hired at one of 35 Belgian stations. Advisable to reserve bikes in advance; cost approx £5 per day (£3 for rail ticket holders).

The Benelux Tourrail Card entitles the holder to 5 days unlimited travel within a specified period of 1 month across the national rail networks of Belgium, Luxembourg and the Netherlands. Cost from £60 (under 26) or from £80 (26+). Details from Netherlands Railways, 25/28 Buckingham Gate, London SW1E 6LD ✆ 0171-630 1735.

Freedom Pass allows 3, 5 or 10 days unlimited rail travel in 1 month on the railways of Belgium. Cost from £31 (under 26) or from £38 (26+). Available from British Rail International Rail Centre, Victoria Station, London SW1V 1JY ✆ 0171-834 2345.

Campus Travel can arrange Eurotrain, Inter-rail and student/youth fares for travel by plane, train, boat and bus to destinations in Belgium. Offices throughout the UK including a student travel centre at 52 Grosvenor Gardens, London SW1W 0AG (opposite Victoria Station) ✆ 0171-730 3402 or ✆ 0131-668 3303 for Scottish telephone bookings.

Council Travel, 28A Poland Street, London W1V 3DB ✆ 0171-287 3337 (offices also in Paris, Nice, Lyon, Munich, Düsseldorf, Tokyo, Singapore and throughout the US) offers Eurotrain under 26 rail fares to all main destinations in Belgium, plus youth and student airfares, travel insurance, guidebooks and travel gear.

Information centres ACOTRA World, rue de la Madeleine 51, 1000 Brussels arranges youth and student travel and is able to give advice and make reservations for accommodation. Also books tours and excursions, cultural and activity holidays, and issues youth/student reduction and youth hostel cards. The ACOTRA Welcome Desk at Brussels airport provides information and reservations for accommodation and transport, including BIJ train tickets for those under 26.

Brussels Welcome Open Door, rue de Tabora 6, 1000 Brussels ✆ (32 2) 511 8178 or 511 2715 is a Catholic information service for visitors, residents, workers, immigrants, refugees and students, providing advice on education, language classes, social services, legal aid and religion. Free interpreting and translation service. Open Monday-Saturday, 10.00-18.00.

Centre National Infor Jeunes, impasse des Capucins 2/8, 5000 Namur ✆ (32 81) 22 08 72 is the head office of the youth information service that has 14 centres throughout Belgium. Information is available on legal rights, study, leisure, holidays, in fact anything that particularly affects young people.

Connections, 19-21 rue de Midi, 1000 Brussels and branches throughout Belgium (Campus Travel's sister organisation) arranges student and youth travel by rail, air and coach, and give information and advice.

Publications *The Rough Guide to Holland, Belgium and Luxembourg* £9.99

provides comprehensive background information on Belgium, plus details on getting there, getting around, places to explore and cheap places to stay. Available from good bookshops.

Live & Work in Belgium, the Netherlands & Luxembourg £8.95 is a guide for those interested in finding temporary or permanent work, starting a business or buying a home in the Benelux countries. Published by Vacation Work, 9 Park End Street, Oxford OX11HJ ✆ Oxford (01865) 241978.

Accommodation *Camping*, a leaflet listing by province all camping sites and their facilities, is available from the Belgian National Tourist Office, see above.

Le CHAB, Hôtel de Jeunes, rue Traversière 8, 1030 Brussels is an inexpensive international accommodation centre, with 1-8 bedded rooms or dormitories. Cost from BF300 for bed and breakfast plus BF100 linen charge. Garden, bar-restaurant, TV, left luggage lockers and laundry service. Walking tours organised in summer.

Rijksuniversiteit Gent, Mrs M Van Den Branden, Department of Guest Accommodation, Home A Vermeylen, Stalhof 6, 9000 Gent has cheap accommodation in single rooms in 3 halls of residence, 15 July-15 September. Bed and breakfast from BF500 per night. Restaurant available.

ARCHAEOLOGY

CENTRE STAVELOTAIN D'ARCHÉOLOGIE Association pour la Promotion de l'Archéologie de Stavelot et sa Région, Abbaye de Stavelot, 4970 Stavelot, Belgium ✆ **(32 80) 86 41 13**
Volunteers are invited to help with the excavation of an 11th century abbey church and a 16th century castle in Stavelot, eastern Belgium, with the aim

of gaining an introduction into archaeological methods and fieldwork. ✆ Ages 16+. Experience desirable but not essential; archaeological students and professionals welcome. 35 hour week for 1+ weeks, 3 July-8 September. Breakfast and lunch provided free by the Centre, plus accommodation in the abbey; participants should take a sleeping bag and air mattress. Site covered by work accident insurance. No fares or wages paid. ✉ *Apply as early as possible; deadline 31 May.*

AU PAIR / CHILDCARE

In Belgium, au pair posts are open to both sexes, ages 16-30. They are expected to work a maximum of 4 hours per day in return for pocket money, board and lodging, and must follow a language course in a recognised school. On arrival in Belgium au pairs who are EEA nationals must register with the local Communal Administration within 8 days, submitting proof of having enrolled at a language school. They must also ensure that they are adequately covered in case of accident or illness, either by being in possession of an *E111* form or by being included in the host family's health insurance scheme.

Prospective au pairs who are not EEA nationals must apply for an *authorisation de séjour provisoire* through the Belgian embassy in their country of residence, and on arrival in Belgium must apply for a work permit. The host family must also draw up and sign a contract of employment, to be approved by the local Communal Administration.

ACADEMY AU PAIR AGENCY LTD 42 Cedarhurst Drive, Eltham, London SE9 5PL ✆ **0181-294 1191** ⌨ **0181-850 8932**
Can place **au pairs**. ✆ Ages 18-27. Some knowledge of French or Dutch

essential. Pocket money approx £35-£40 per week. Administration charge £40. Positions as **nannies** and **mothers' helps** also available for those with qualifications/experience.

BUNTERS AU PAIR & DOMESTIC AGENCY 17 Copper Street, Macclesfield, Cheshire SK11 7LH
℗ **Macclesfield (01625) 614534**
Can place **au pairs**, **demi pairs** and **mothers' helps**. 6-12 months all year or 10 weeks, summer. ⊕ Ages 18-27. Pocket money £35-£50 per week depending on hours worked. Placement fee £40. ☜ *Apply before May for summer placements.*

HELPING HANDS AU PAIR & DOMESTIC AGENCY 39 Rutland Avenue, Thorpe Bay, Essex SS1 2XJ
℗ **Southend-on-Sea (01702) 602067**
Can place **au pairs** and **mothers' helps**. ⊕ Ages 18-27. Pocket money approx £35 per week for au pairs, higher for mothers' helps. Introduction fee £40 on acceptance of a family. *UK nationals only.*

INTERNATIONAL CATHOLIC SOCIETY FOR GIRLS (ACISJF) St Patrick's International Youth Centre, 24 Great Chapel Street, London W1V 3AF ℗ **0171-734 2156** ☐ **0171-287 6282**
Au pair posts arranged for 9+ months. ⊕ Ages 18+. *Mainly for UK and Irish nationals.*

JOLAINE AGENCY 18 Escot Way, Barnet, Hertfordshire EN5 3AN
℗ **0181-449 1334** ☐ **0181-449 9183**
Can place **au pairs** and **mothers' helps**. ⊕ Ages 18-27. Pocket money £40 per week (au pairs) or £50 (mothers' helps). Placement fee £40.

LANGTRAIN INTERNATIONAL Torquay Road, Foxrock, Dublin 18, Ireland ℗ **(353 1) 289 3876**
Can place **au pairs** in Belgian families. ⊕ Ages 18+. Pocket money approx £30-£40 per week. Placement fee £60.

PROBLEMS UNLIMITED AGENCY 86 Alexandra Road, Windsor, Berkshire SL4 1HU
℗ **Windsor (01753) 830101**
Can place **au pairs**. ⊕ Ages 18-27. Pocket money £30-£35 per week.

STUDENTS ABROAD LTD 11 Milton View, Hitchin, Hertfordshire SG4 0QD ℗ **Hitchin (01462) 438909** ☐ **(01462) 438919**
Can place **au pairs** and **mothers' helps**. ⊕ Ages 18-27 for au pairs. Basic knowledge of French preferred. Pocket money approx £35-£40 per week; higher for mothers' helps. Limited number of short-term summer placements for au pairs only. Service charge £40.

COMMUNITY WORK

ATD QUART MONDE Avenue Victor Jacobs 12, 1040 Brussels, Belgium ℗ **(32 2) 6479900**
An international voluntary organisation which brings together people from all walks of life in partnership with the most disadvantaged families, to support the efforts of the very poor in overcoming poverty and taking an active role in their community. Based on the commitment of those who have chosen to put their skills to the service of the very poor and learn from them, ATD's objectives are to reinforce cooperation between disadvantaged families and the community; develop a constructive public awareness of poverty; and encourage a fuller representation of poorest families in all areas of society. **Volunteers** are invited to take part in street workshops organised throughout the summer in different Belgian towns, sharing skills with parents, young people and children whose sense of creativity has never been challenged. The workshops are organised in very disadvantaged areas where holidays too often mean boredom and violence. ⊕ Ages 18+. No experience necessary but applicants should be interested in

better understanding the causes and effects of persistent poverty and willing to work hard with others as a team. Approx 40 hour week. Accommodation provided; applicants are asked to take a sleeping bag and to contribute towards living expenses. No fares or wages paid. ✆ Write for further details.

CONSERVATION

BRITISH TRUST FOR CONSERVATION VOLUNTEERS
Room IWH, 36 St Mary's Street, Wallingford, Oxfordshire OX10 0EU ✆ Wallingford (01491) 839766

The largest charitable organisation in Britain to involve people in practical conservation work. Following the success of the Natural Break programme in the UK, BTCV is now developing a series of international working holidays with the aim of introducing **volunteers** to practical conservation projects abroad. It is hoped that the British volunteers will adapt to and learn from local lifestyles as well as participate in the community. Projects last for 2-3 weeks and are based at the Château Braive. Work is on the management of the estate, a nature reserve being adapted for disabled access.

⊕ Ages 18-70. Cost from £60 per week includes transport from a pick-up point in Belgium, insurance, food and basic accommodation; everyone shares in domestic chores. Volunteers should take a sleeping bag. Membership fee £12. No fares or wages paid.

NATUUR 2000 Flemish Youth Federation for the Study of Nature & Environmental Conservation, Bervoetstraat 33, 2000 Antwerp, Belgium

Organises conservation activities such as management of nature reserves and smaller landscape elements, species protection, waste recycling, campaigns against sea pollution and runs solidarity campaigns on acid rain, tropical rain forests, pesticides and Arctic/Antarctic problems. Arranges nature study and conservation camps in Dutch-speaking areas of Belgium. **Volunteers**, preferably with experience in field biology are required to help lead the study camps which have recently included monitoring a bat reserve in an old fortress near Antwerp.

⊕ Ages 15+. Knowledge of Dutch, French or English needed. July and August. Food, accommodation, insurance and travel from Antwerp to site provided. Visas/work permits arranged if necessary. Cost from BF 1,000, depending on type of camp, duration and location. Help is also needed in the office, 40 hour week, all year. Experience preferred.

COURIERS/REPS

EUROCAMP Summer Jobs (Ref WH), PO Box 170, Liverpool L70 IES ✆ Knutsford (01565) 625522

One of Europe's leading tour operators, specialising in providing quality camping and mobile home holidays for families throughout Europe.

Campsite couriers required. Work involves cleaning tents and equipment prior to the arrival of new customers; checking, replacing and making repairs on equipment; replenishing gas supplies; keeping basic accounts and reporting on a weekly basis to England. Also to meet new arrivals and assist holidaymakers with any problems that arise; organise activities and parties; provide information on local tourist attractions and maintain a noticeboard. At the beginning and end of the season couriers are also expected to help in erecting and dismantling tents. Couriers need to be flexible to meet the needs of customers and be on hand where necessary; they will be able to organise their own free time as the workload allows.

⊕ Ages 18+. Applicants should be independent, adaptable, reliable, physically fit, have plenty of initiative and relish a challenging and responsible position. Good working knowledge of French/Dutch also necessary. Preference given to those able to work the whole season, April-September/October; contracts also available for first half season, April-mid July and second half season, mid July-September/October.

Children's couriers also required, with the energy and enthusiasm to organise a wide range of exciting activities for groups of children aged 4-13. Experience of working within this age range is essential, but language ability is not a requirement.

⊕ Ages 18+. Must be available for the whole season, May-September.

For both positions the salary is £95 per week. Training provided together with accommodation in frame tent with cooking facilities, insurance and return travel. *UK/EEA passport-holders only.*

🕮 *Early application by telephone preferred; interviews start September/October.*

FARMWORK

INTERNATIONAL FARM EXPERIENCE PROGRAMME YFC Centre, N A C, Stoneleigh Park, Kenilworth, Warwickshire CV8 2LG
✆ **(01203) 696584**

Provides assistance to young **agriculturalists** and **horticulturalists** by finding places in farms/nurseries abroad, enabling them to broaden their knowledge of agricultural and horticultural methods. Participants usually live and work with a farming family and the work is matched as far as possible with participant's requirements. Entails physical work and practical involvement. Basic wage plus board and lodging. 3-12 months, all year.

⊕ Ages 18-28. Applicants must have at least 2 years practical experience, one of which may be at agricultural college, and intend to make a career in agriculture/horticulture. Valid driving licence necessary. Participants pay own fares

and insurance. Registration fee £85.

🕮 *UK applications to IFEP. Other applications to IFEP partner in home country.*

TEACHERS

BELGIAN EMBASSY 103 Eaton Square, London SW1W 9AB
✆ **0171-235 5422**

Publish a list, *Posts for Foreign Teachers in Belgium,* giving the addresses of international English-speaking schools that may be able to offer **teaching posts**.

WORKCAMPS

BOUWORDE VZW Tiensesteenweg 145, 3010 Leuven, Belgium ✆ **(32 16) 25 91 44**
📠 **(32 16) 25 91 60**

Invites **volunteers** to take part in international workcamps, carrying out all types of construction work including painting, wallpapering, bricklaying, joinery, electrics and plumbing. Projects are aimed at providing aid for people in need.

⊕ Ages 18+. No experience necessary; volunteers work under the guidance of an experienced leader. Applicants should be prepared to participate in every aspect of workcamp life. Knowledge of English, French, Dutch or German essential. 40 hour week for 2-3 weeks, July-September; also 1 week projects at Christmas and Easter. Food and accommodation provided. Registration fee BF 1,500. No fares or wages paid. **D PH**

🕮 *Apply April-May, direct or through partner organisation in country of residence; see page 30 for addresses.*

CONTACT J-CARREFOUR CHANTIERS 25 boulevard de l'Empereur, 1000 Brussels, Belgium

An international movement open to all who share a common concern for lasting peace and justice in the world.

Volunteers are needed to work in international teams on projects aimed at offering a service in an area of need and promoting self-help within the community, international understanding and the discussion of social problems, and offering young people the chance to live as a group and take these experiences into the context of daily life. Recent projects have included painting and renovation work at a monastery dating back to the 13th century in Aubel; helping to produce a fresco on the facade of a youth centre in Nivelles; excavating the cemetery and dungeon of an old fortress in Nismes; and animating playschemes for 3-14 year-olds in Colfontaine.

⊕ Ages 18-30. Knowledge of French required on some camps. 3-6 hour day, 30-36 hour week. 2-4 weeks, July, August and September. Food, school, centre or tent accommodation and insurance provided; participants pay own travel costs.

⚛ *Apply through partner organisation in country of residence. In the UK: Christian Movement for Peace. See page 30 for registration details and addresses.*

COMPAGNONS BATISSEURS
24 rue des Carmes, 6900 Marche-en-Famenne, Belgium

Belgian branch of International Building Companions, an international volunteers association with the aims of fighting misery and distress and making a contribution towards a better understanding between nations. **Volunteers** are invited to take part in workcamps organised in the French-speaking part of Belgium. Recent projects have included renovating an old water mill at Chevilpont; building a house, farming and gardening at an institution for people with learning difficulties in Couvin; and fitting windows and cleaning machinery at a working industrial museum in Bois-du-Luc.

⊕ Ages 18-26 (some opportunities for ages 15-17). Applicants must be prepared to work hard as part of a team; previous workcamp experience useful. 2 weeks, July-September. Shared accommodation, food and work accident insurance provided. No fares or wages paid.

⚛ *Apply through partner organisation in country of residence.*
In the UK: Concordia (Youth Service Volunteers) Ltd, Quaker International Social Projects or United Nations Association International Youth Service. See page 30 for registration details and addresses.

SERVICE CIVIL INTERNATIONAL (SCI) rue Van Elewijck 35, 1050 Brussels, Belgium
VRIJWILLIGE INTERNATIONALE AKTIE (VIA) Draakstraat 37, 2018 Antwerp, Belgium

Service Civil International promotes international reconciliation through work projects. **Volunteers** are invited to work on workcamps organised by these two branches in Belgium. Recent projects organised by SCI have included preparing a school exhibition on waste and recycling, and performing street theatre at the end of an international bike tour in Brussels; facilitating and animating holidays for refugee children at a North-South village near Mons; and masonry and renovation work at the biological farm of Vévi Wéron. Recent projects organised by VIA have included preparing for an annual music festival featuring African and Latin American bands in Boechout; converting an old castle into an education centre for the long-term unemployed in Wilrijk; and working in the greenhouse, picking and selling fruit and vegetables at an organic farming centre for people with minor handicaps in Kortessem. Good knowledge of French/Dutch needed for some camps.

⊕ Ages 18+. Applicants should be highly motivated, preferably with previous workcamp or other voluntary experience, and prepared to work hard as part of a team. 35-40 hour week; 2-4 weeks, May-September. Food, shared accommodation and work accident insurance provided. No fares or wages paid. **B D PH W** depending on project.

📖 *Apply through partner organisation or SCI branch in country of residence. In the UK: International Voluntary Service. See page 30 for registration details and addresses.*

GENERAL

EUROYOUTH LTD
301 Westborough Road, Westcliff, Soiuthend-on-Sea, Essex SS0 9PT
🕾 **Southend-on-Sea (01702) 341434**
Holiday stays arranged where guests are offered board and lodging in return for an agreed number of hours English conversation with hosts or their children. Time also available for guests to practice the host language if desired.
🎖 Mainly ages 18-25, but sometimes opportunities for ages 13-16 and for older applicants. 2-3 weeks, June-August. Travel and insurance arranged by applicants. Registration fee approx £70. Number of places limited.
📖 *Apply at least 12 weeks prior to scheduled departure date. UK nationals only.*

APPLYING FOR A JOB

When writing to **any** organisation it is **essential** to mention **Working Holidays 1995** and enclose a **stamped, self-addressed A4 envelope**, or if in another country, an **addressed A4 envelope** and at least two **IRCs** (International Reply Coupons, available from post offices). Enquiries received without SAEs/IRCs are **unlikely** to be answered. **Before applying**, read carefully all the information given. Pay **particular** attention to:

✐ skills/qualifications/experience required

✐ the period of employment expected

✐ age limits or nationality restrictions

✐ application deadlines

✐ any other points, especially details of insurance cover, and other costs such as travel and accommodation.

When applying include the following:

✐ your name, address, date of birth, marital status, nationality, sex

✐ details of your education, qualifications, relevant experience, skills, languages spoken

✐ your period of availability for work

✐ a passport-size photo, particularly if you will be working with the public

✐ anything else recommended in the listing (such as a *cv*)

BULGARIA

INFO

Bulgarian Embassy
186-188 Queen's Gate, London SW7
5HL ✆ 0171-584 9400/9433

British Embassy
38 Boulevard Vassil Levski, Sofia
✆ (359 2) 885361/2

Tourist office
Bulgarian National Tourist Office,
18 Princes Street, London W1R 7RE
✆ 0171-499 6988

Youth hostels
Union Bulgare de Tourisme, Boulevard
Vassil Levski 18, Sofia 1000

Youth & student information
Orbita Chain for Youth Tourism,
Boulevard Alexander Stamboliski 45a,
Sofia

Entry regulations Details of entry
requirements can be obtained from the
Visa Section of the Bulgarian Embassy.
Organisations recruiting for work will
usually assist with arranging a visa.

Travel Freedom Pass allows 3, 5 or 10
days unlimited rail travel in 1 month oon
the railways of Bulgaria. Cost from £26
(under 26) or from £33 (26+). Available
from the British Rail International Rail
Centre, Victoria Station, London SW1V
1JY ✆ 0171-834 2345

Campus Travel offers Eurotrain under 26
fares and youth and student airfares to
Bulgaria. Offices throughout the UK,
including a student travel centre at 52
Grosvenor Gardens, London SW1 0AG
(opposite Victoria Station) ✆ 0171-730
3402 or ✆ 0131-668 3303 for Scottish
telephone bookings.

Information centres The Students
Labour Office, PO Box 504, Plovdiv
4000 ✆ (359 32) 226 756 is associated
with the Ministry of Labour and offers
paid and voluntary work to students in

Bulgaria. It also has information about entry and visa regualtions and can provide guides and interpreters for foreign students.

Publications Lonely Planet's *Eastern Europe on a Shoestring* £13.95 provides practical information on budget travel in Bulgaria and most other East European countries. *The Rough Guide to Bulgaria* £8.99 provides comprehensive background information on Bulgaria, plus details of getting there, getting around, places to explore and cheap places to stay. Both guides are available from good bookshops.

COURIERS/REPS

CRYSTAL HOLIDAYS Crystal House, The Courtyard, Arlington Road, Surbiton, Surrey KT6 6BW
✆ 0181-241 5111
Tour operator arranging skiing holidays in Borovets and Pamporova.
Representatives are required to meet and greet clients and be responsible for their welfare during their holiday.
Ski guides and **chalet staff** also required.
⊕ Ages 22-35. Previous experience and fluent Bulgarian desirable. Chalet staff must have catering qualifications and experience. Approx 60 hour, 6½ or 7 day week, December-April. Basic salary plus commission, board, lodging, insurance, travel costs and uniform provided. One week training seminar held at beginning of each season.
✉ *Apply April/May.*

FARMWORK

INTERNATIONAL FARM EXPERIENCE PROGRAMME YFC Centre, N A C, Stoneleigh Park, Kenilworth, Warwickshire CV8 2LG
✆ **(01203) 696584**
Provides assistance to young **agriculturalists** and **horticulturalists** by finding places in farms/nurseries abroad, enabling them to broaden their knowledge of agricultural and horticultural methods. Participants usually live and work with a farming family and the work is matched as far as possible with participant's requirements. Entails physical work and practical involvement. Basic wage plus board and lodging. 3 months, during the summer.
⊕ Ages 18-28. Applicants must have at least 2 years practical experience, one of which may be at agricultural college, and intend to make a career in agriculture/horticulture. Valid driving licence necessary. Participants pay own fares and insurance. Registration fee £85.
✉ *UK applications to IFEP. Other applications to IFEP partner in home country.*

WORKCAMPS

MAR Bulgarian Youth Alliance for Development, 1387 Sofia 87, Bulgaria
Organises international workcamps with more than 250 **volunteers** from over 40 countries. Recent projects have included archaeological excavations in Devetaki cave, Lovetch; social work in Bulgaria's largest school for blind children in Sofia; construction work at a hospital in the Kardjali area of southern Bulgaria; and work in botanical gardens in the town of Baltchik.
⊕ Ages 18-30. Previous workcamp/community work experience useful. Knowledge of English, Russian or German helpful. 6 hour day, 5 day week. 2-3 weeks, July and August. Board, lodging and working clothes provided. No fares or wages paid.

✉ *Apply through partner organisation in country of residence.*
In the UK: International Voluntary Service or Quaker International Social Projects.
See page 30 for registration details and addresses.

CANADA

INFO

Canadian High Commission
Macdonald House, I Grosvenor Square,
London WIX 0AB ℰ 0171-258 6600

Immigration Section: 38 Grosvenor
Street, London WIX 0AA
ℰ 0171-258 6527

British High Commission
80 Elgin Street, Ottawa, Ontario
KIP 5K7 ℰ (I 613) 237 1530

Tourist office
Tourism Program, Canadian High
Commission, Macdonald House,
I Grosvenor Square, London WIX OAB
ℰ 0171-839 2299

Youth hostels
Canadian Hostelling Association,
National Office, 33 River Road, Tower
A-3, Vanier, Ottawa, Ontario KIL 8H9

Youth & student information
Association of Student Councils
(Canada), 171 College Street, Toronto,
Ontario M5T IP7

Canadian Bureau for International
Education, 220 Laurier Avenue West,
Suite 1100, Ottawa, Ontario KIP 5Z9

Tourbec (1979) inc, 1178 Avenue
Cartier, Quebec City, Quebec GIR 2S7

Entry regulations A limited number
of foreign students are admitted to
Canada each year under an international
student summer employment
programme. Under this programme,
authorisation is granted to students who
have been offered employment in
Canada, without the vacancy first having
been advertised to Canadian nationals.
Applicants must obtain an offer of
employment by their own means and
having done so, produce written proof
of the offer, showing position, salary, and
working conditions. Authorisation is
issued only for the job specified in the

application, and is normally valid for a maximum period of 1 year. UK applicants must produce written proof that they are British citizens, and bona fide full-time students of British or Irish universities or similar institutions (including students who have been accepted for admission in the current year), and that they will be returning after the vacation period to continue their course of study.

A number of organisations in the UK operate Exchange Visitor Programmes which help students to find employment. As the number of places is limited, applications should be made as early as possible. An additional student programme is now available whereby an offer of prearranged employment is not required, but evidence of funds and student status needs to be produced. Applications for other types of employment should be made by post to the Immigration Section, Canadian High Commission. Authorisation cannot be issued until the prospective employer has obtained certification from a Canadian employment centre to say that no qualified Canadian citizen or landed immigrant is available to fill the job in question. An Authorisation only becomes valid when stamped at the port of entry. Employment opportunities for visitors are therefore extremely restricted.

Those travelling to Canada and planning to remain there for an extended period may be required to prove at the time of entry that they have sufficient means to maintain themselves and have evidence of onward reservations. Those under 18 not accompanied by an adult should have a letter from a parent/guardian giving them permission to travel to Canada. Those wishing to work or study in Canada should contact the High Commission for further information before seeking admission.

Travel Campus Travel offers flexible airline tickets and student/youth fares for travel by plane, train, boat and bus to destinations throughout Canada, plus specialist tours and treks. Offices throughout the UK, including a student travel centre at 52 Grosvenor Gardens, London SW1W OAG (opposite Victoria Station) ✆ 0171-730 2101 or ✆ 0131-668 3303 for Scottish telephone bookings.

Council Travel, 28A Poland Street, London W1V 3DB ✆ 0171-437 7767 (offices also in Paris, Nice, Lyon, Munich, Düsseldorf, Tokyo, Singapore, and throughout the US) offers low-cost student/youth airfares to destinations in Canada and issues rail and bus passes. Accommodation, tours, travel insurance, guidebooks and travel gear also available.

North-South Travel, Moulsham Mill, Parkway, Chelmsford CM2 7PX ✆ Chelmsford (01245) 492882 arranges competitively priced, reliably planned flights to all parts of Canada. All profits given to projects in the developing world.

STA Travel, 86 Old Brompton Road, London SW7 3LQ/117 Euston Road, London NW1 2SX ✆ 0171-937 9971 (offices also in Birmingham, Bristol, Cambridge, Glasgow, Leeds, Manchester and Oxford), operates flexible, low-cost flights to destinations throughout Canada. Also air and coach passes.

Greyhound Lines of Canada offers unlimited travel passes for use on all their coach services. Prices start from £92 for 7 days. All tickets must be purchased in the UK. Details from Greyhound International, Sussex House, London Road, East Grinstead, West Sussex RH19 1LD ✆ East Grinstead, (01342) 317317 🖷 (01342) 328519, or from Long-Haul Leisurail, see below.

The Canrailpass provides unlimited travel at a fixed cost over the entire rail network or over any of 3 designated territories. Cost from Can$220, 30 days nationwide. Greyhound Bus passes also available from £75 (7 days low season). Details from Long-Haul Leisurail, PO Box 113, Bretton, Peterborough, Cambridgeshire PE3 8HY ✆ Peterborough (01733) 335599. Also available from Campus Travel and Council Travel, see above.

Publications Lonely Planet's *Canada - A Travel Survival Kit* £12.95 offers practical, down-to-earth information for independent travellers wanting to explore beyond the usual tourist routes.

The Rough Guide to Canada £10.99 provides comprehensive background information on Canada plus details on getting there, getting around, places to explore and cheap places to stay.

Culture Shock! Canada £6.95 introduces the reader to the people, customs, ceremonies, food and culture of Canada, with checklists of dos and don'ts.

Travellers Survival Kit USA and Canada £9.95, is a down-to-earth, entertaining guide for travellers to North America. Describes how to cope with the inhabitants, officialdom and the way of life. Also *Live & Work in the USA & Canada* £8.95, a guide for those interested in finding temporary or permanent work, starting a business or buying a home in North America. Both published by Vacation Work Publications, 9 Park End Street, Oxford OX1 1HJ ✆ Oxford (01865) 241978.

All the above are available from good bookshops.

Canada Travel Information provides helpful practical hints covering health, climate, travel and accommodation. Available from Tourism Programme, Canadian High Commission, see above.

North America Rail & Bus Guide is an essential handbook for budget travellers in Canada and the US, including timetables, details of passes and maps, street plans and practical advice.

Available from Thomas Cook Publications, PO Box 227, Peterborough, Cambridgeshire PE3 6SB ✆ Peterborough (01733) 505821/ 268943, price £7.75 including UK postage.

The Moneywise Guide to North America £11.10 including postage, provides essential information for anyone travelling on a budget in Canada, the US and Mexico, with useful information on getting around, where to stay, what to eat and places to visit. Published by BUNAC, 16 Bowling Green Lane, London EC1R OBD ✆ 0171-251 3472.

Information centres The Canadian Bureau for International Education, 220 Laurier Avenue West, Suite 1100, Ottawa, Ontario K1P 5Z9 provides information and publications on international work, study and exchange, and a reception service for incoming students at airports, August/September.

Accommodation Backpackers Hostels Canada, c/o Thunder Bay International Hostel, Longhouse Village, RR #13, Thunder Bay, Ontario P7B 5E4 ✆ (1 807) 983 2042 ▭ (1 807) 983 2914 is a network of independently owned and operated hostels across Canada catering for backpackers at budget rates. They have in common a friendly and hospitable atmosphere, a minimum of restrictions and 24-hour access, as well as fully-equipped kitchens, showers, phones, TV and general facilities. Prices range from Can$11-Can$20 per bednight. Some are associated with Backpackers Resorts Australia and honour their VIP cards (see Australia section for details).

No-frills accommodation available in a hostel in the heart of Old Quebec. Cost Can$14.75-$19.75 per night, plus membership fee. Dormitories of 10 beds or more, washing facilities, TV lounge and baggage check-in. Cafeteria on premises. No age limits. Apply to Centre International de Séjour de

Quebec, 19 rue Ste-Ursule, Quebec GIR 4EI. **PH W**

Ys Way International, 244 East 47th Street, New York, NY 10017, United States offers inexpensive accommodation at YMCAs in major cities in Canada and the US. Average cost US$40 per night includes use of sports facilities. Details in Britain from Travel Cuts UK, 295A Regent Street, London WIR 7YA ✆ 0171-637 3161.

CHILDCARE

At present there is no au pair scheme in Canada, although similar employment for foreign nationals exists under the Live-in Caregiver Program. To qualify, applicants must have completed the equivalent of Canadian secondary school plus 6 months' full-time training in caregiving work, or be able to prove they have at least 12 months' experience as caregivers, including a minimum of 6 months continuous employment with one employer. Applications for temporary entry into Canada under the Program must be made to the Immigration Section of the Canadian High Commission once an offer of employment has been made. Applicants may have to attend an interview, and a medical examination is required, after which applications take 4-6 weeks to process. Processing fee Can$125.

LANGTRAIN INTERNATIONAL Torquay Road, Foxrock, Dublin 18, Ireland ✆ **(353 1) 289 3876** Can arrange **childcare posts**. ⚤ Ages 18+. Salary Can$550 per month. 8-10 hour day plus 2 evenings babysitting and 2 days free per week. Minimum stay one year. Placement £60.

NANNIES UNLIMITED INC 350-604 - 1 St SW, Calgary, Alberta T2P IM7, Canada Can place **nannies** in Calgary, Edmonton, Saskatchewan and the North West Territories.

⚤ Ages 18+. Applicants must speak English or French and have six months related childcare/elderly training, 5 GCSEs or equivalent, or one year's related experience. 47½ hour week. Salary from Can$614 per month and accommodation with family in own room. Minimum 1 year. Medical insurance available at nominal cost. Assistance given with obtaining a visa.

STUDENTS ABROAD LTD 11 Milton View, Hitchin, Hertfordshire SG4 0QD ✆ **Hitchin (01462) 438909** ✉ **(01462) 438919** Can place qualified **nannies** for a minimum of 1 year. ⚤ Ages 18+. Applicants should be NNEB qualified or equivalent. Excellent references and driving licence essential. Board and lodging provided. Salary, dependent on age, qualifications and experience. Medical examination required. Applicants pay their own fare. Allow 2-3 months to obtain work permit. 🔖 *Applicants should be resident in the UK, available for interview. EEA passport holders only.*

CONSERVATION

PARKS CANADA National Volunteer Coordinator, 25 Eddy Street, Hull, Quebec KIA 0M5, Canada ✆ **(1 819) 994 5127** The federal agency responsible for protected examples of Canada's natural and cultural heritage. Aims to encourage public understanding, appreciation and enjoyment of this heritage in ways which will leave it unimpaired for future generations. Limited numbers of international **volunteers** are placed in national parks, historic sites and canals across Canada. Voluntary positions exist to assist and enhance new programmes in natural resource management, cultural resource management, interpretation, visitor services and maintenance. Volunteers may serve as assistants interpreting or animating the history of a park, hosting in a campground, collecting data on flora and fauna, maintaining or building trails, designing posters, photographing historic artefacts or wildlife, or keeping library files. ⊕ No age restrictions. Experience essential for applicants from outside Canada; degrees desirable for some positions. Working languages English and French; bilingual applicants particularly welcome. Fluency in Japanese or German also an advantage. 2-40 hour week, depending on project. Direct expenses reimbursed and general liability insurance provided. Volunteers pay travel, accommodation, food costs. *Apply before January for summer and autumn; before July for winter and spring.*

FARMWORK

CANADIEN NATIONAL Mme Deschamps, 1 rue Scribe, 75009 Paris, France ℰ (33 1) 47 42 76 50 ✉ (33 1) 47 42 24 39
French subsidiary of the Canadian National Railway Company. Requires **tobacco harvesters** in the fields of south-western Ontario. Work may involve picking leaves, sewing them on sticks, hanging them in the kiln and removing cured tobacco from the kiln. Help with irrigation and other tasks may also be required. ⊕ Ages 18+. Male applicants only. Applicants must be healthy, willing to work hard and have a knowledge of English. Agricultural experience particularly welcome but not essential. Up to 70 hours a week; August-mid September. Participants should be prepared to work until end of harvest. Full board accommodation in bunkhouse or other building provided. Wages Can$67.50 per day. Participants are advised to take a sleeping bag. Cost FF4,350 covers accommodation airfare, transportation with escort from airport, administration fee and insurance. Local agent on site will deal with any problems. *Apply early in the year. UK, Belgian and French nationals only.*

INTERNATIONAL AGRICULTURAL EXCHANGE ASSOCIATION YFC Centre, N A C, Stoneleigh Park, Kenilworth, Warwickshire CV8 2LG ℰ Coventry (01203) 696578
Operates opportunities for young people involved in **agriculture**, **horticulture** or **home management** to acquire practical work experience, and to strengthen and improve their knowledge and understanding of the way of life in other countries. Participants are given an opportunity to study practical methods on approved training farms, and work as trainees, gaining further experience in their chosen field. Types of farm include mixed (grain production and livestock); grain; dairy and crop; beef; poultry; plus a limited number of bee, horse and horticultural enterprises. Participants undertake paid work on the farm, approx 40 hours per week, and live as a member of the host family. Full board, lodging, insurance cover and minimum net weekly wage of £50-£60 provided. All programmes include 3/4 weeks unpaid holiday. 4 day orientation seminar held at agricultural colleges and universities throughout Canada. Stopovers (2-4 days) in the South Pacific arranged for participants en route for the 14 month programme. ⊕ Ages 18-30. Applicants should be single, and have good practical experience in the chosen training category, plus a valid driving licence. 9 months (departing February); 7 months (departing April); 14 months - 7 in Australia/New Zealand plus 7 in Canada (departing September). Cost from £1,600 covers airfare, work permit, placement with a host family, travel costs to placement, administration fee, orientation seminar, information meetings, and supervision. £200 deposit payable. *Apply at least 4 months in advance. UK or Irish passport-holders only.*

Canadian applicants requiring an exchange should apply to IAEA, 206-1501-17 Avenue SW, Calgary, Alberta T2T 0E2.

INTERNATIONAL FARM EXPERIENCE PROGRAMME YFC Centre, N A C, Stoneleigh Park, Kenilworth, Warwickshire CV8 2LG ✆ Coventry (01203) 696584

Provides assistance to young **agriculturalists** and **horticulturalists** by finding places in farms/nurseries abroad, enabling them to broaden their knowledge of agricultural and horticultural methods. Opportunities for placements in arable, sheep or dairy farming in Canada. Participants usually live and work with a farming family and the work is matched as far as possible with participant's requirements. Entails physical work and practical involvement. Basic wage plus board and lodging. 7-12 months, beginning March and July. ⊕ Ages 18-28. Applicants must have at least 2 years practical experience, one of which may be at agricultural college, and intend to make a career in agriculture/ horticulture. Valid driving licence necessary. Participants pay own fares and insurance. Registration fee £70 plus programme fee. ✍ *Apply 2-3 months in advance. UK nationals only.*

WILLING WORKERS ON ORGANIC FARMS (WWOOF CANADA) RR 2, Carlson Road S18 C9, Nelson, British Columbia V1L 5P5, Canada

Aims to help organic farmers and smallholders whose work is often labour intensive. Offers 1 week-3 month placements whereby **volunteers** can gain first hand experience of organic farming and gardening on over 100 host farms throughout Canada, on homesteads on the east coast (Nova Scotia, Prince Edward Island and New Brunswick), in Quebec, Ontario, Alberta and many in British Columbia on the west coast. The work can include weeding, milking, apple picking and cleaning out stalls. Members receive a detailed farm description and address list of places needing help. ⊕ Ages 16+. Hours vary from one farm to another. Integration into the farm family is valued, including recreational

possibilities. Work available all year but especially between early spring and late autumn. Full board and lodging in own room, cabin or tent provided, but volunteers should take a sleeping bag. Excellent opportunity to see Canada and meet Canadians. Insurance and anti-tetanus vaccination recommended. Membership fee Can$25 (single) or Can$30 (couple) plus 2 IRCs. *EEA nationals only.*

MONITORS & TEACHERS

BRITISH UNIVERSITIES NORTH AMERICA CLUB (BUNAC) 16 Bowling Green Lane, London EC1R 0BD ✆ 0171-251 3472

A non-profit, non-political educational student club which aims to encourage interest and understanding between students in Britain and North America. Through its camp counsellor programme, BUNACAMP, a small number of opportunities available for young people to work on summer camps in Canada. The camps are permanent sites and cater for 40-600 children at a time. Camps can be organised privately, by the YMCA, Girl Scouts or Salvation Army, or they can be institutional camps for the physically, socially or mentally handicapped. Work involves living, working and playing with groups of 3-8 children aged 6-16. **General counsellors** are responsible for the full-time supervision of their group, ensuring that the children follow the set routine and providing counsel and friendship. They must therefore have fairly general experience and aptitude in the handling of children. **Specialist counsellors** must have a sporting/craft interest, qualifications or skills plus ability and enthusiasm to organise or teach specific activities. These include sports, watersports, music, arts and crafts, science, pioneering, entertainments and dance. **Counsellors with secretarial skills** also needed for office work.

⊕ Ages 19½ (by I July) -35. Applicants must be resident in the UK, single, hard working as hours are long, with a genuine love of children and relevant experience. They should be able to show firm, fair leadership and be flexible, cooperative, energetic, conscientious, cheerful, patient, positive, able to adapt to new situations, and to function enthusiastically in a structured setting. 8/9+ weeks, with I day off most weeks, mid June-end August, followed by 1-6 weeks free for travel after the camp. Return flight, overnight hostel accommodation, transfer to camp, orientation and training, guide to North America plus board and lodging at the camp provided. Counsellors live with the children in log cabins or tents. BUNACAMP registration fee £59 (1994). Insurance fee approx £85. Salary approx US$390 (US$430 for ages 21+). Suitable for students, teachers, social workers and those with other relevant qualifications. Interviews held throughout the UK, mid November-early May. Compulsory orientation programme held at Easter. Membership fee £3.50. ✎ *Early application advisable; places limited.*

Irish applicants should apply to USIT, Aston Quay, O'Connell Bridge, Dublin 2
℗ *Dublin (353 1) 6778117*

WORKCAMPS

FRONTIERS FOUNDATION INC Operation Beaver, 2615 Danforth Avenue, Suite 203, Toronto, Ontario M4C 1L6, Canada
℗ **(1 416) 690 3930** ▭ **(1416) 690 3934**
Frontiers Foundation is a community development voluntary service organisation which works in partnership with requesting communities in low-income, rural areas across Canada.
Volunteers are invited to take part in helping to provide and improve adequate housing, training and recreational

activities in developing regions.
⊕ Ages 18+. Volunteers must be available for a minimum of 12 weeks. Skills in carpentry, plumbing and electrical work preferred for construction projects; previous social service and experience with children preferred for recreation projects. Projects run all year; new volunteers recruited between April and November. All food, accommodation and travel inside Canada provided. Travel outside Canada paid by applicants. Long-term projects of up to 18 months available, provided the volunteer's work is satisfactory after the initial 12 weeks.
✎ *Application kits and forms available upon request.*

GENERAL

BRITISH UNIVERSITIES NORTH AMERICA CLUB (BUNAC) 16 Bowling Green Lane, London EC1R 0BD ℗ **0171-251 3472**
Aims to encourage interest and understanding between students in Britain and North America; a non-profit, non-political educational student club which has enabled many thousands of students to enjoy self-financing working vacations in North America. As well as arranging employment on children's summer camps, BUNAC can also assisit with an unlimited variety of jobs through their **Work Canada** programme organised in cooperation with the Canadian Federation of Students. The job does not have to be organised in advance, and participants are able to change jobs once in Canada if necessary. Those who wish to organise jobs before arrival will be offered advice on how to do so, and may use BUNAC's own job directory. Also places outside the summer season, for year out students. The summer programme involves a compulsory orientation in Britain, return flight, one night's accommodation followed by an orientation in Canada, work authorisation papers, a guidebook and the services of BUNAC and CFS in

North America. In order to obtain a visa, applicants must have evidence of student status, an orientation course certificate and proof of round-trip transportation. They must also provide evidence that they can support themselves whilst in canada in one of the following three ways: definite evidence of a job, plus proof that they are taking at least Can$500 with them; definite evidence of sponsorship, plus proof that they are taking at least Can$1000 with them and can thus support themselves with their own funds until they get a job. ⊕ Ages 18-29. 8/9+ weeks-6 months. Registration fee £79 (1994), return flight £370-£460, insurance fee £86. Medical in Britain may be necessary at participants expense. Membership fee £3.50. Full British passport-holders only. 🖎 *Apply from October/November; closing date end April. Job directory available from January.*

INTERNSHIP CANADA PROGRAMME Council on International Educational Exchange (CIEE), 33 Seymour Place, London WIH 6AT ✆ 0171-706 3008 ☎ 0171-724 846

Enables students to complete a period of **work experience** of 6 months-1 year.
⊕ Ages 18+. Applicants must be enrolled in full time further or higher education (HND level or above) on a course where practical experience forms an integral part. They must find their own work placement and, either through payment by their employer or through other means, finance their own visit to Canada. Participants must pay an administration fee of £125 (1994), and have insurancce cover for the length of their stay. Official documentation and assistance with visa application procvided, as are orientation materials covering issues such as taxes, housing, Canadian culture and transportation; plus 24-hour emergency assistance with any problems whilst in Canada.
🖎 *Apply all year round, at least 2 months in advance.*

APPLYING FOR A JOB

When writing to **any** organisation it is **essential** to mention **Working Holidays 1995** and enclose a **stamped, self-addressed A4 envelope**, or if in another country, an **addressed A4 envelope** and at least two **IRCs** (International Reply Coupons, available from post offices). Enquiries received without SAEs/IRCs are **unlikely** to be answered. **Before applying**, read carefully all the information given. Pay **particular** attention to:

🖋 skills/qualifications/experience required

🖋 the period of employment expected

🖋 age limits or nationality restrictions

🖋 application deadlines

🖋 any other points, especially details of insurance cover, and other costs such as travel and accommodation.

When applying include the following:

🖋 your name, address, date of birth, marital status, nationality, sex

🖋 details of your education, qualifications, relevant experience, skills, languages spoken

🖋 your period of availability for work

🖋 a passport-size photo, particularly if you will be working with the public

🖋 anything else recommended in the listing (such as a *cv*)

CIS / RUSSIA

INFO

Armenian Embassy
25 Cheniston Gardens, London W8 6TG
✆ 0171-938 5435

Belarussian Embassy
1 St Stephen's Crescent, London W2
5QT ✆ 0171-225 4568

Russian Federation Embassy
13 Kensington Palace Gardens, London
W8 4QX   ✆ 0171-229 3628

Consular section: 5 Kensington Palace
Gardens, London W8 4QS
✆ 0171-229 8027

Ukraine Embassy
78 Kensington Park Road, London W11
2PL ✆ 0171-727 6312

Entry regulations The organisations
listed here will all assist participants on
their programmes to obtain the
necessary visa for entry into Russia and/
or the republics of the Commonwealth
of Independent States. Visas are
required for all visitors; completed
applications should be submitted to the
relevant embassy/consulate at least two
weeks in advance.

Job advertising Frank L Crane
(London) Ltd, International Press
Representatives, 5/15 Cromer Street,
London WC1H 8LS ✆ 0171-837 3330
can place job advertisements in leading
Russian newspapers and English language
magazines.

Travel Campus Travel offers student/
youth airfares to Moscow and St
Petersburg and can also book internal
travel within Russia including the
Trans-Siberian Railway. Offices
throughout the UK including a student
travel centre at 52 Grosvenor Gardens,
London SW1W 0AG (opposite Victoria
Station) ✆ 0171-730 3402 or ✆ 0131-
668 3303 for Scottish telephone
bookings.

Council Travel, 28A Poland Street, London WIV 3DB ✆ 0171-437 7767 (offices also in Paris, Nice, Lyon, Munich, Düsseldorf, Tokyo, Singapore and throughout the US) offers low-cost student/youth airfares to Moscow and St Petersburg, plus travel insurance, guidebooks and travel gear.

STA Travel, 86 Old Brompton Road, London SW7 3LQ/117 Euston Road, London NW1 2SX ✆ 0171-937 9921 (offices also in Birmingham, Bristol, Cambridge, Glasgow, Leeds, Manchester and Oxford) operates flexible, low-cost flights to Moscow, Kiev and St Petersburg.

Publications Lonely Planet's *USSR - A Travel Survival Kit* £13.95 offers practical, down-to-earth information for independent and group travellers wanting to explore beyond the usual routes.

The Rough Guide to St Petersburg £8.99 provides comprehensive information, with details of getting there, getting around, places to explore and cheap places to stay.

Vacation Work's *The Travellers Survival Kit Russia & the Republics* £9.95 offers a complete guide to where to eat and stay, how to travel and what to see and do, for any travellers to Russia and the republics of Armenia, Azerbaijan, Belarus, Estonia, Georgia, Kazakhstan, Kirkhiziam, Latvia, Lithuania, Moldova, Tajikistan, Turkmenistan, the Ukraine and Uzbekistan.

All the above guides are available from good bookshops.

Accommodation Russian Youth Hostels was established in spring 1992 with the goal of opening independent youth hostels throughout Russia. Can arrange visa support and processing, supply train tickets and give travel advice as well as offering accommodation in the centrally located, 50-bed St Petersburg

International Hostel, 3rd Sovetskaya Street 28, St Petersburg 193312 ✆ (7 812) 277 0569 or 329 8018 �📠 (7 812) 277 5102 or 329 8019. Facilities include hot showers, a TV room, kitchens and a safe for storage of valuables.
Also books the Moscow Travellers Guest House, Bolshaya Pereyaslavkaya Ulitsa 50, Floor 10, Moscow ✆ (7 095) 971 4059. Reservations can be made by contacting the St Petersburg Hostel or in person at the YHA Travel Shop, 14 Southampton Street, London WC2E 7HY. Reservations can also be made by contacting the North American representative at 409 N Pacific Coast Highway, Building 106, Suite 390, Redondo Beach, CA 90277 ✆ (1 310) 379 4316 �📠 (1 310) 379 8420.

TEACHERS

MIR-V-MIG PO Box 1085, 310168 Kharkov, Ukraine
📠 **Kharkov (7 0572) 653141**
Can arrange placements for **English teachers** at secondary schools and universities in the Ukrainian towns of Kharkov and Kiev, and also in some areas of Russia. 8-10 hour week for 3+ months, September-June.
⊕ Ages 18+. Applicants should be students, postgraduates or qualified teachers. Some knowledge of Russian or Ukrainian and previous teaching experience desirable. Teachers are paid at local rates with accommodation in local families. **Au pair** posts also arranged all year. Placement fee £40 payable on arrival. Applicants pay own travel and insurance costs.
🖋 *Write enclosing cv. Native English speakers only.*

WORKCAMPS

ATM PO Box 64, 220119 Minsk, Belarus
The Belarussian Association of International Youth Work invites **volunteers** to take part in international

workcamps 70% of the radioactive material produced by Chernobyl was deposited in Belarus, affecting some 800,000 children. Many ATM projects are related to this, including some based at a children's residential centre in Zubrionok, a rural, non-irradiated area; work may involve constructing play facilities, gardening, decorating the centre and animating children's activities. Other recent projects have included restoration work on the St Nikolay Cathedral in Mogilev; and river cleaning and forestry work at a sports centre near Minsk.

⊕ Ages 18+. Applicants should have previous workcamp or other voluntary experience, and be motivated to work hard as part of a team. 2-3 weeks, June-September. Food and accommodation provided; volunteers cover their own travel, insurance and personal expenses.

⚑ Apply through partner organisation in country of residence.
In the UK: Concordia (Youth Service Volunteers) Ltd, International Voluntary Service, Quaker International Social Projects or United Nations Association International Youth Service. See page 30 for registration details and addresses.

FORUM 10 Ternopolskaya Street 10/33, PO Box 10722, 290034 Lviv, Ukraine ©/🖿 (7 322) 422003
A non-profitmaking, non-political organisation aimed at stimulating cooperation between Ukraine and other European countries. Invites **volunteers** to take part in international workcamps. Recent projects have included an archaeological dig in cooperation with the Lviv Picture Art Gallery Association; an environmental project in the Carpathian Mountains; a holiday scheme with children; and a social project in a psychiatric hospital.
⊕ Ages 18+. Applicants must be highly motivated and prepared to work hard and contribute to team life. Knowledge of Russian or Ukrainian very useful. 2-3 weeks, June-August. Food and accommodation provided; volunteers pay

their own travel and insurance costs.

⚑ Apply through partner organisation in country of residence. In the UK: Quaker International Social Projects. See page 30 for registration details and addresses.

HUJ (ARMENIAN STUDENT BRIGADES) Korium Street 19a, Yerevan 375009, Armenia
Volunteers are invited to take part in international workcamps in Armenia. Recent projects have included organising an international music group to play to local people in Yerevan and Dilijan; building a kindergarten in the earthquake-damaged region of Spitak; and researching into alternative energy sources in Yerevan to help fight the chronic fuel shortage.
⊕ Ages 18+. Applicants should have previous workcamp or other voluntary experience, and be motivated to work hard as part of a team. 2 weeks, July-September. Projects are dependent on western funding; volunteers will need to cover their own travel, insurance and personal expenses and may also have to pay for food and accommodation.

⚑ Apply through partner organisation in country of residence.
In the UK: International Voluntary Service, Quaker International Social Projects or United Nations Association International Youth Service. See page 30 for registration details and addresses.

LEAGUE OF YOUTH VOLUNTARY SERVICE Karl Marx Street 40, 220030 Minsk, Belarus
Invites **volunteers** to take part on international workcamps in Belarus. Projects may include working with children, some of whom have been affected by the Chernobyl distaster; or doing environmental work such as ecological monitoring. Camp languages include Russian, English and German.
⊕ Ages 18+. Applicants should have previous workcamp or other voluntary experience, and be motivated to work hard as part of a team. 3-4 weeks,

May-October. Food and accommodation provided; volunteers cover their own travel, insurance and personal expenses.

🕮 *Apply through partner organisation in country of residence. In the UK: United Nations Association International Youth Service. See page 30 for registration details and addresses.*

SLAVONIC CENTRE 16 Pipska, 252021 Kiev, Ukraine

An independent organisation founded in 1989 under the umbrella of the Ukrainian Culture Foundation to preserve Slavic cultural heritage and traditions. Invites **volunteers** to take part on international workcamps in Ukraine. Recent projects have included working with children from Russia and Ukraine at a holiday centre in the Carpathian mountains; renovating the historical gardens of Kiev; and working alongside monks doing renovation work at the 300 year-old Mgary Monastery in eastern Ukraine. Language courses available; visits arranged to places of interest.
⊕ Ages 18+. Applicants should have previous workcamp or other voluntary experience, and be motivated to work hard as part of a team. 2-5 weeks, June-July. Food and accommodation provided; volunteers cover their own travel, insurance and personal expenses.

🕮 *Apply through partner organisation in country of residence. In the UK: United Nations Association International Youth Service. See page 30 for registration details and addresses.*

YOUTH VOLUNTARY SERVICE (YVS) 7/8 Bol Komsomolski per, Moscow 103982, Russia

Volunteers are invited to take part in international workcamps organised mainly in Russia but there are also some in Ukraine. Recent projects have included restoration work and creating exhibitions at the museum of the Peter and Paul Fortress in St Petersburg;

caring for horses and cleaning out the stables at a hippodrome in Smolensk; plastering and whitewashing to restore old stone and wooden churches in Irkutsk; and cleaning caves and forestry work in Alushta, a mountainous region near the Black Sea. Study and discussion programmes related to camp themes; visits organised to local places of interest.
⊕ Ages 18+. Applicants must be highly motivated and prepared to work hard as part of a team. Previous workcamp experience useful. 35-40 hour week. 2 weeks, June-August. Food and accommodation provided, but volunteers must pay their own travel and insurance costs. Camp language usually Russian, sometimes English.

🕮 *Apply through partner organisation in country of residence. In the UK: Concordia (Youth Service Volunteers) Ltd, International Voluntary Service or United Nations Association International Youth Service. See page 30 for registration details and addresses.*

When applying to any organisation it is essential to mention Working Holidays 1995 and enclose a stamped, self-addressed A4 envelope, or if in another country, an addressed A4 envelope and at least two IRCs (International Reply Coupons, available from post offices). Enquiries received without SAEs/IRCs are unlikely to be answered.

CZECH & SLOVAKIA REPUBLIC

INFO

Czech Embassy
26 Kensington Palace Gardens, London
W8 4QY ✆ 0171-243 1115
Visa section: 28 Kensington Palace
Gardens, London W8 4QY
✆ 0171-243 7942/3

British Embassy
Thunovská 14, 125 50 Prague
✆ (42 2) 533 347/8/9

Slovak Embassy
25 Kensington Palace Gardens, London
W8 4QY ✆ 0171-243 0803

British Embassy
Grösslingova 35, 811 09 Bratislava
✆ (42 7) 364 459

Youth & student information
Czech Youth and Students Travel Bureau
(KMC), Zitna ulice 12, 12105 Prague 2

Slovak Academic Information Agency,
Hviezdoslavovo námestie 14, 214 29
Bratislava

Entry regulations UK and Irish
nationals, and nationals most other
European countries do not require a visa
to enter the Czech Republic or Slovakia.
US nationals do not need a visa for a
stay of up to 30 days. Other nationals
should check visa requirements and
procedures with the relevant embassy.

Travel Freedom Pass allows 3, 5 or 10
days travel in 1 month on the railways of
the Czech Republic or Slovakia. Cost
from £30, Czech Republic (under 26) or
from £39 (26+). Cost from £22,
Slovakia (under 26) or from £29 (26+).
Available from British Rail International
Rail Centre, Victoria Station, London
SW1V 1JY ✆ 0171-834 2345.

Campus Travel can arrange Eurotrain,
Inter-rail and student/youth fares on all
travel to destinations in the Czech
Republic and Slovakia. Special summer

student charter flights to Prague. Also offer internal rail passes and book accommodation. Offices throughout the UK including a student travel centre at 52 Grosvenor Gardens, London SW1W 0AG (opposite Victoria Station) ℰ 0171-730 3402 or ℰ 0131-668 3303 for Scottish telephone bookings.

Council Travel, 28A Poland Street, London W1V 3DB ℰ 0171-437 7767 (offices also in Paris, Nice, Lyon, Munich, Düsseldorf, Tokyo, Singapore and throughout the US) offers Eurotrain under 26 fares and student/youth airfares to the Czech Republic and Slovakia, plus travel insurance, guidebooks and travel gear.

STA Travel, 86 Old Brompton Road, London SW7 3LQ/117 Euston Road, London NW1 2SX ℰ 0171-937 9921 (offices also in Birmingham, Bristol, Cambridge, Glasgow, Leeds, Manchester and Oxford) operates flexible, low-cost flights to Prague.

Publications Lonely Planet's *Eastern Europe on a Shoestring* £13.95 provides practical information on budget travel in the Czech Republic and Slovakia. *The Rough Guide to the Czech and Slovak Republics* £8.99 and *The Rough Guide to Prague* £7.99 provide comprehensive background information, details on places to explore and cheap places to stay. All available from good bookshops.

CONSERVATION

BRONTOSAURUS MOVEMENT
Rada Brontosaura CR, Bubenská 6, 170 00 Prague 7, Czech Republic
ℰ/☎ **(42 2) 6671 0245**
An independent movement open to anyone wishing to improve the state of the environment. **Volunteers** are invited to take part in workcamps throughout the Czech Republic. Projects include nature conservation and the restoration of historic monuments. ⊕ Age limits and other details vary

depending on camp. No experience required. 1-3 weeks, during the summer. Board and lodging provided in return for approx 28 hours work per week. Volunteers pay own travel expenses and insurance. ✴ *Apply April-May.*

INEX Senovázné námestí 24, 116 47 Prague 1, Czech Republic
ℰ **(42 2) 24 10 25 51** ☎ **(42 2) 24 21 48 60**
INEX SLOVAKIA Prazská 11, 81104 Bratislava, Slovakia
ℰ **(42 7) 49 62 49** ☎ **(42 7) 49 88 89**
Organisation aimed at promoting international understanding, cooperation and leisure activities through exchange; split into two independent parts with the division of Czechoslovakia in 1993. **Volunteers** are invited to take part in international workcamps which contribute to environmental and historical conservation. Recent projects organised by the Czech branch have included replanting trees in a forest damaged by air pollution in the Jizersk Mountains; preparing for the annual wine festival in Bzenec; working in the grounds of a Gothic castle in Chanovice; and clearing undergrowth from the Jewish cemetery in the old town of Trebic. Recent projects organised by the Slovak branch include preparing for the 750th anniversary celebrations in the village of Vistuk; repairing the forest railway of Cierny Balog; gardening and maintenance work at an arboretum in Vieska nad Zitavou; and rebuilding a medieval castle in Trencin. ⊕ Ages 18+. Working language is English. 2 weeks, July-August. Food and accommodation in schools, tents or dormitories provided; volunteers pay own travel and insurance. **B D PH**

✴ *Apply through partner organisation in country of residence. In the UK: Concordia (Youth Service Volunteers) Ltd, International Voluntary Service, Quaker International Social Projects or United Nations Association International Youth Service. See page 30 for registration details and addresses.*

FARMWORK

INTERNATIONAL FARM EXPERIENCE PROGRAMME YFC Centre, N A C, Stoneleigh Park, Kenilworth, Warwickshire CV8 2LG
© (01203) 696584

Provides assistance to young **agriculturalists** and **horticulturalists** by finding places in farms/nurseries abroad, enabling them to broaden their knowledge of agricultural and horticultural methods. Opportunities for practical agricultural or horticultural work in the Czech Republic. Participants usually live and work with a farming family and the work is matched as far as possible with participant's requirements. Entails physical work and practical involvement. Basic wage plus board and lodging. 3 months, summer. ⊕ Ages 18-28. Applicants must have at least 2 years practical experience, one of which may be at agricultural college, and intend to make a career in agriculture/ horticulture. Valid driving licence necessary. Participants pay own fares and insurance. Registration fee £85.
※ UK applications to IFEP; others to IFEP partner in home country.

TEACHERS

CZECHPOINT GB CLUB
56 Wandsworth Road, Hampton, Middlesex TW12 1ER

Opportunities for **teachers** to teach English to students of different ages and abilities on activity camps.
⊕ Ages 21+. Applicants must speak perfect English and preferably have TEFL or similar qualification. 30-40 hour week, 2 weeks minimum, summer months in particular. Accommodation and travel costs provided. Salary approx £160 per month paid in Czech currency. £5 processing and administration fee.
※ Apply at least 2 months in advance for summer posts. UK nationals only.

PRIVATE SCHOOL OF ENGLISH PROGRAM ul Fredry 7, Poznan, Poland

Volunteers required to teach English and organise activities for groups of 10-12 children on camps in Slovakia. ⊕ Ages 21-35. Applicants should be enthusiastic and creative, preferably with experience of working with children. 24-hour day; four 2-week camps, June-August. Full board accommodation and pocket money provided.
※ Apply by 30 August. Native English speakers only.

WORKCAMPS

KLUB MALDYCH CESTOVATELU (KMC) Karolíny Svetlé 30, 110 00 Prague 1, Czech Republic
©/✉ (42 2) 24 23 0633

Volunteers are invited to take part in international workcamps concerned with conservation, construction and agricultural work. Recent projects have included maintaining the grounds of a castle at Nachod; helping with the harvest at a cooperative farm in Bohemia; teaching English to children at summer camps near Pisek; and working on the renovation of an historic brewery in Prague. Also work/study/peace camps. Excursions, lectures and discussions linked to projects, meetings with youth groups and visits to local places of interest arranged.
⊕ Ages 18+. Previous workcamp or similar voluntary work experience useful. 40 hour, 5 day week. 2-3 weeks, June-September. Full board and simple accommodation provided. Anti-tetanus injection required. No fares or wages paid except for English teaching, where pocket money is provided. Working language usually English. **B D**

※ Apply through partner organisation in country of residence. In the UK: Concordia (Youth Service Volunteers) Ltd, Quaker International Social Projects or United Nations Association. See page 30 for registration details and addresses.

INFO

Royal Danish Embassy
55 Sloane Street, London SW1X 9SR
✆ 0171-333 0200

British Embassy
Kastelsvej 36/38/40, 2100 Copenhagen
✆ (45) 35 26 46 00

Tourist office
Danish Tourist Board, 55 Sloane Street,
London SW1X 9SR ✆ 0171-259 5959
(open 1100-1600)

Youth hostels
Landsforeningen Danmarks Vandrerhjem,
Vesterbrogade 39, 1620 Copenhagen V

Youth & student information
Danmarks Internationale
Studenterkomite, Skindergade 36, 1159
Copenhagen K

Informationskontoret/Huset, Vester Alle
15, 8000 Århus C

Entry regulations A UK citizen
intending to work in Denmark should
have a full passport. UK/EEA nationals
may stay for up to 3 months in order to
seek employment. If employment is
obtained within this period, the
residence permit will be granted
automatically on application. To qualify
for a residence permit the job must fulfil
certain conditions such as working
hours, salary and membership of an
employment fund.
Once a job has been found and a
residence permit has been obtained it is
necessary to obtain a personal
registration number and social security
certificate within 5 days by taking
personal identification and a statement
from the employer to the nearest
Folkeregisteret. This entitles the
employee to use the national health
service.
There are no Danish offices operating
exclusively as labour exchanges for
foreigners; it is practically impossible to

get a job without some knowledge of Danish, unless the work is in a restaurant or hotel where English is usually required. Permission to stay for more than 3 months must be obtained from the Department for Supervision of Aliens; for EEA citizens this is a formality if they have a job.

Job advertising Frank L Crane (London) Ltd, International Press Representatives, 5/15 Cromer Street, Grays Inn Road, London WC1H 8LS ℗ 0171-837 3330 can place job advertisements in the Danish newspapers *Berlingske Tidende* and *Metropol.*

Travel Freedom Pass allows 3, 5 or 10 days unlimited travel in 1 month on the railways of Denmark. Cost from £42 (under 26) or from £60 (26+). Available from British Rail International Rail Centre, Victoria Station, London ℗ 0171-834 2345.

The ScanRail Pass is a flexible rail pass for Scandinavia, valid for unlimited travel during 5 days within 15 days, 10 days within 1 month and 1 month consecutive. Cost from £94 (ages under 25) or from £125 (25+) for 5 days. Discounts offered on certain ferry and bus routes. Available from Norwegian State Railways, 21-24 Cockspur Street, London SW1Y 5DA ℗ 0171-930 6666.

Campus Travel can arrange Eurotrain, Inter-rail and student/youth fares for travel by plane, train, boat and bus to destinations in Denmark. Offices throughout the UK including a student travel centre at 52 Grosvenor Gardens, London SW1W 0AG (opposite Victoria Station) ℗ 0171-730 3402 or ℗ 0131-668 3303 for Scottish telephone bookings.

Council Travel, 28A Poland Street, London W1V 3DB ℗ 0171-287 3337 (offices also in Paris, Nice, Lyon, Munich, Düsseldorf, Tokyo, Singapore and throughout the US) offers Eurotrain

under 26 fares and youth and student airfares to Denmark, plus travel insurance, guidebooks and travel gear.

Publications Lonely Planet's *Scandinavian and Baltic Europe on a Shoestring* £10.95 offers practical, down-to-earth information for the low-budget, independent traveller in Denmark and the Faroe Islands.

The Rough Guide to Scandinavia £10.99 provides comprehensive background information on Denmark and the Faroe Islands, with details on getting there, getting around, places to explore and cheap places to stay.

Michael's Guide to Scandinavia £10.95 is detailed and concise, providing invaluable practical advice for all kinds of travellers. Published by Inbal Travel.

Vacation Work's *Live & Work in Scandinavia* £8.95 is a guide for those interested in finding temporary or permanent work, starting a business or buying a home in Denmark, Finlamnd, Sweden, Norway or Iceland.

All the above guides are available from good bookshops.

Map and General Travel Information leaflet provides information on travel, Customs and entry formalities, residence and employment, the health service and other practical information. Available from the Danish Tourist Board, see above, price £2.50.

Information centres The Use-It Youth Information Centre Copenhagen, Radhusstraede 13, 1466 Copenhagen K ℗ (45) 33 15 65 18 issues an information pack including *Working and Residence in Denmark*, a leaflet outlining help in looking for employment. Also produces *Playtime*, a newspaper intended as an alternative guide to Copenhagen for low-budget visitors, with advice on travel, food and accommodation, cultural attractions, practical information and a list of alternative organisations. Also provides poste restante and travel help/hitch hiking link services, plus free locker facilities. Open 0800-1900 (mid June-mid September) and 1000-1600 (mid September-mid June).

Accommodation The Danish Tourist Board, see above, publish *Camping, Youth and Family Hostels*, a list of officially approved campsites and hostels.

Bellahoj Camping, Hvidkildevej 66, 2400 Copenhagen NV is a campsite 5 km from Copenhagen, open 1 June-1 September, cost DKr40 per night. A camping pass is required on all campsites in Copenhagen, obtainable from campsite wardens, price DKr24 and valid all year.

The Use-It Youth Information Centre Copenhagen, see above, publishes *Housing in Copenhagen* giving information on private rooms for rent, flats, bedsits, student halls and communes.

Copenhagen Sleep-In, Per Henrik Lings Alle 6, 2100 Copenhagen 0, is a hostel with 452 beds in 4-bedded rooms. Free hot showers. Open July and August. Cost DKr95 per night, bed and breakfast; take your own sleeping bag.

A hostel within walking distance from Central Station is Vesterbro Ungdomsgard, Absalonsgade 8, 1658 Copenhagen V, ☎ (45) 31 31 20 70 ⌨ (45) 31 23 51 75 with 209 beds; cost DKr110 per night, bed and breakfast. Open 5 May-end August.

AU PAIR / CHILDCARE

ACADEMY AU PAIR AGENCY LTD 42 Cedarhurst Drive, Eltham, London SE9 5LP ☎ 0181-294 1191 ⌨ 0181-850 8932
Can place **au pairs**. ⚜ Ages 18-27. Some knowledge of Danish useful.

Pocket money approx £35-£40 per week. Administration charge £40. Positions as **nannies** and **mothers' helps** also available for those with qualifications/experience.

HELPING HANDS AU PAIR & DOMESTIC AGENCY 39 Rutland Avenue, Thorpe Bay, Essex SS1 2XJ ☎ **Southend-on-Sea (01702) 602067**
Can place **au pairs** and **mothers' helps**. ⚜ Ages 18-27. Pocket money approx £35 per week for au pairs, higher for mothers' helps. Introduction fee £40 on acceptance of a family. *UK nationals only.*

LANGTRAIN INTERNATIONAL Torquay Road, Foxrock, Dublin 18, Ireland ☎ **(353 1) 289 3876**
Can place **au pairs** in Danish families. ⚜ Ages 18+. Pocket money approx £35-£40 per week. Placement fee £60.

COURIERS/REPS

EUROCAMP Summer Jobs (Ref WH), PO Box 170, Liverpool L70 1ES ☎ **Knutsford (01565) 625522**
One of Europe's leading tour operators, specialising in providing quality camping and mobile home holidays for families throughout Europe.
Campsite couriers required. Work involves cleaning tents and equipment prior to the arrival of new customers; checking, replacing and making repairs on equipment; replenishing gas supplies; keeping basic accounts and reporting on a weekly basis to England. Couriers are also expected to meet new arrivals and assist holidaymakers with any problems that arise; organise activities and parties; provide information on local tourist attractions and maintain an information noticeboard. At the beginning and end of the season couriers are also expected to help in erecting and dismantling tents. Couriers need to be flexible to meet the needs of customers and be on hand where necessary; they will be able to

organise their own free time as the workload allows.
⊕ Ages 18+. Applicants should be independent, adaptable, reliable, physically fit, have plenty of initiative and relish a challenging and responsible position. Good working knowledge of Danish necessary. Preference given to those able to work the whole season, April-September/October; contracts also available for first half season, April-mid July and second half season, mid July-September/October.
Children's couriers also required, with the energy and enthusiasm to organise a wide range of exciting activities for groups aged 4-13. Experience of working with this age range essential, but language ability is not a requirement.
⊕ Ages 18+. Must be available for the whole season, May-September.
For both positions, salary £95 per week. Training provided together with return travel, insurance and accommodation in frame tent with cooking facilities,
✎ Early application by telephone preferred; interviews start September/October. UK/EEA passport-holders only.

FARMWORK/ FRUIT PICKING

ALSTRUP FRUGT EXPORT
Alstuprej 1, 8305 Samso, Denmark
ℂ **(45) 86 59 13 38**
Fruit pickers are needed to pick strawberries, 5-6 weeks, mid June-end July. 36 hour week. Wages DKr300-DKr500. Camping area provided.
⊕ Ages 18+. Applicants must speak English. No travel or insurance provided.
✎ Apply by 1 May. EEA nationals only.

BIRKHOLM FRUGT & BÆR APS
v/ Bjarne Knutsen, Hornelandevej 2 D, 5600 Faaborg, Denmark
ℂ/▭ **(45) 62 60 22 62**
Strawberry pickers required.
40 hour, 6 day week starting 0500 for 2+ weeks, mid June-mid August.
Piecework rates apply.

⊕ Ages 18+. Campsite available with toilet, shower and cooker provided. Pickers should take camping equipment, raincoat and boots.
✎ Apply by 1 June. EEA nationals only.

GRAEVLERUPGAARD FRUGTPLANTAGE Egsgyden 38, Horne, 5600 Fåborg, Denmark
ℂ **(45) 62 60 22 31**
Fruit pickers are needed to pick strawberries, 3-4 weeks, June-July. 30-40 hour week. Piecework rates paid.
⊕ Ages 18+. Pickers should take their own food and camping equipment; insurance and travel not provided.
✎ Apply by 1 May. EEA nationals only.

INTERNATIONAL FARM EXPERIENCE PROGRAMME
YFC Centre, N A C, Stoneleigh Park, Kenilworth, Warwickshire CV8 2LG ℂ **Coventry (01203) 696584**
Provides assistance to young **agriculturalists** and **horticulturalists** by finding places in farms/nurseries abroad enabling them to broaden their knowledge of agricultural and horticultural methods. Participants live and work with a farming family and the work is matched as far as possible with participant's requirements. Entails physical work and practical involvement. 3-12 months, all year. Basic wages plus board and lodging.
⊕ Ages 18-28. Applicants must have at least 2 years practical experience, 1 year of which may be at agricultural college, and intend to make a career in agriculture. Valid driving licence necessary. Participants pay own fares and insurance. Registration fee £85.
✎ UK applications to IFEP; others to IFEP partner organisation in home country.

VI HJAELPER HINANDEN
Inga Nielsen, Asenvej 35, 9881 Bindslev, Denmark ℂ **(45) 98 93 86 07**
A non-profitmaking organisation which aims to help organic farmers and smallholders whose work is often

labour-intensive as it does not rely on artificial fertilisers or pesticides. Provides **placements** whereby volunteers can gain first-hand experience of organic farming and gardening, and a chance to spend some time in the country. Places exist on organic farms, smallholdings and gardens throughout Denmark.

⊕ Ages 16+. 3-4 hours per day; 3+ days, all year. Full board and lodging provided in the farmhouse or outbuildings; volunteers should take a sleeping bag. No wages paid, and helpers must pay their own travel costs. Insurance and anti-tetanus vaccination recommended.

An address list giving details of people who require help can be obtained by sending a large self-addressed envelope plus Dkr50/£5 or equivalent. Most people on the list speak English.

WORKCAMPS

MELLEMFOLKELIGT SAMVIRKE (Danish Association for International Coooperation), Meslgade 49, 8000 Århus, Denmark

Mellemfolkeligt Samvirke international workcamps gather young people from different countries to cooperate as **volunteers** on a project which benefits the local community. This provides an opportunity to come into contact with the social problems found in every society and to help volunteers become more actively involved in the creation of a more just society. Recent projects have included organising drama and musical activities and other entertainments for 7-14 year olds in Aalborg; building a playground and a sheltered area in a public park in Kokkedal; practical preparation for a rock festival in Skanderborg; and living and working in an Iron Age village in Odense. Projects are also run in Greenland and have included reconstructing a Viking village and building a playground.

⊕ Ages 18+. Applicants should be highly motivated, preferably with previous workcamp or voluntary experience, and prepared to work hard as part of a team. 30 hour week. 2-3 weeks, June-September. Food, shared accommodation and work accident insurance provided. No fares or wages paid. Physically handicapped volunteers welcome on most camps, but camps on Greenland cannot take wheelchairs; places also available for families. **B D PH**

Apply through partner organisation in country of residence.
In the UK: Christian Movement for Peace, International Voluntary Service, Quaker International Social Projects or United Nations Association International Youth Service. See page 30 for registration details and addresses.

When applying to any organisation it is essential to mention Working Holidays 1995 and enclose a stamped, self-addressed A4 envelope, or if in another country, an addressed A4 envelope and at least two IRCs (International Reply Coupons, available from post offices). Enquiries received without SAEs/IRCs are unlikely to be answered.

fiNLAND

INFO

Finnish Embassy
38 Chesham Place, London SW1W
8HN ✆ 0171-235 9531

British Embassy
Itainen Puistotie 17, 00140 Helsinki
✆ (358 0) 661293

Tourist office
Finnish Tourist Board, 66/68 Haymarket,
London SW1Y 4RF ✆ 0171-839 4048
✇ 0171-321 0696

Youth hostels
Suomen Retkeilymajajärjestö SRM,
Yrjönkatu 38B15, 00100 Helsinki 10
✆ (358 0) 693 1347 ✇ (358 0) 693
1349

Youth & student information
Travela-FSTS, Mannerheimintie 5C,
00100 Helsinki 10

City of Helsinki Youth Department,
Hietaniemenkatu 9B, 00100 Helsinki

Entry regulations UK/EU/EEA
nationals wishing to visit Finalnd do not
need a visa, nor do they require a work
permit in order to take up employment.
They are, however, required to register
with the local police within 3 months of
entry in order to receive a residence
permit, which is normally issued for 5
years. All other nationals wishing to
work in Finland require a work permit.
Applications for a permit may not be
made until an offer of work has been
received and the prospective employer
has provided a certificate giving details of
salary, type and duration of work, plus
personal information and a letter of
recommendation. Once this has been
received, a Labour Permit Application
form, available from Finnish embassies,
should be completed and returned,
together with the certificate. These will
be sent to the Office of Alien Affairs of
the Finnish Ministry of the Interior in
Helsinki who will consult the Ministry of

Labour and reject or accept the application accordingly; this takes about 4 weeks. The applicants will then be notified of the decision by the Embassy. A work permit is only valid for the specific job for which it has been issued. It is usually granted for 3 months, after which it may or may not be extended.

A booklet entitled *Working in Finland* outlining legal aspects of employment in Finland is available from Finnish embassies.

Job advertising Frank L Crane (London) Ltd, International Press Representatives, 5/15 Cromer Street, Grays Inn Road, London WC1H 8LS ℰ 0171-837 3330 can place job advertisements in *Aamulehti* (Tampere regional daily) and *Turun Sanomat* (Turku regional daily).

Travel Freedom Pass allows 3, 5 or 10 days unlimited travel within 1 month on the railways on Finland. Cost from £49 (under 26) and £64 (26+). Available from British Rail International Rail Centre, Victoria Station, London SW1V 1JY ℰ 0171-834 2345.

The Finnrailpass entitles the holder to unlimited travel on Finnish State Railways, cost from £61 for 3 days. Available from Finlandia Travel, 227 Regent Street, London W1R 7DB ℰ 0171-409 7334.

The ScanRail Pass is a flexible rail pass for Scandinavia, valid for unlimited travel during 5 days within 15 days, 10 days within 1 month and 1 month consecutive. Cost from £94 (ages under 25) or from £125 (ages 25+) for 5 days. Discounts offered on certain ferry and bus routes. Available from Norwegian State Railways, 21-24 Cockspur Street, London SW1Y 5DA ℰ 0171-930 6666.

Campus Travel can arrange Eurotrain, Inter-rail and student/youth fares for travel by plane, train, boat and bus to destinations in Finland. Offices throughout the UK including a student travel centre at 52 Grosvenor Gardens, London SW1W 0AG (opposite Victoria Station) ℰ 0171-730 3402 or ℰ 0131-668 3303 for Scottish telephone bookings.

Council Travel, 28A Poland Street, London W1V 3DB ℰ 0171-287 3337 (offices also in Paris, Nice, Lyon, Munich, Düsseldorf, Tokyo, Singapore and throughout the US) offers Eurotrain under 26 fares and student/youth airfares to destinations in Finland, plus insurance, guidebooks and travel gear.

Information centres Kompassi, Simonkatu 1, 00100 Helsinki ℰ (358 0) 6121 863 ℤℤ (358 0) 6121 905 is an advice and information centre providing assistance and counselling for young people in difficulties, as well as information on events, public transport, places to go, clubs, youth activities or festivals. Open Mondays-Thursdays 1100-1800 and Fridays 1100-1600.

Lighthouse, Porthaninkatu 2, 00530 Helsinki ℰ/ℤℤ (358 0) 7099 25 91 is an international meeting point for young travellers in Helsinki, providing information about accommodation, cultural events and festivals, concerts and sights. Left luggage facility; TV, video, laundry and dryer. Open early June-mid August, Monday-Friday 0730-1900 and weekends 0730-1100.

The Youth Centre, Nuorisokeskus, Kauppakatu 44, 70110 Kuopio is an international meeting place in the centre of Kuopio. Provides tourist information and facilities including rest room, showers, left luggage, washing machine, dryer and cafe. Open end June-mid August, Monday-Friday 0900-2200.

Publications Lonely Planet's *Finland - A Travel Survival Kit* £9.95 and *Scandinavian and Baltic Europe on a Shoestring* £10.95 offer practical, down-to-earth information for the low-budget independent traveller in Finland.

The Rough Guide to Scandinavia £10.99 provides comprehensive background information on getting around Finland, with details on getting there, places to explore and cheap places to stay.

Michael's Guide to Scandinavia £10.95 is detailed and concise, providing invaluable practical advice for all kinds of travellers. Published by Inbal Travel.

Vacation Work's *Live & Work in Scandinavia* £8.95 is a guide for those interested in finding temporary or permanent work, starting a business or buying a home in Finland, Denmark, Sweden, Norway or Iceland.

All the above guidebooks are available from good bookshops.

Finland Facts and Map covers travel to and within Finland, accommodation, customs and other useful information. Available from the Finnish Tourist Board, see above.

Accommodation The Finnish Tourist Board, see above, publish *Budget Accommodation* listing hostels, campsites and B&B establishments with their facilities and a map, and also directories of *Holiday Villages* and *Hotels*.

The Kallio Youth Hostel, Porthaninkatu 2, 00530 Helsinki ✆ (358 0) 7099 2590 is located close to the city centre and offers accommodation in one 15-bed room for men and three 5-bed rooms for women. Also has showers, self-service kitchen, TV room, laundry and dryer, and safety deposit boxes. Cost FIM50 per night including sheets. Open early June-mid August.

When writing to any organisation it is essential to mention Working Holidays 1995 and enclose a stamped, self-addressed A4 envelope, or if in another country, an addressed A4 envelope and at least two IRCs (International Reply Coupons, available from post offices).

AU PAIR / CHILDCARE

FINNISH YOUTH COOPERATION ALLIANCE Stadion, Eteläkaare, 00250 Helsinki, Finland ✆ **(358 0) 348 2422** ✍ **(358 0) 491 290**
Can place **au pairs** with families in various parts of Finland. 30 hour week, 6-12 months or 2-3 months, June-August. Board and accommodation provided, pocket money FIM1,100 per month, plus possibility of studying a language course.
⚜ Ages 18-30. Applicants must be female, with childcare experience; at least one childcare reference required. Native speakers of English, French, German or Spanish particularly needed.
✍ *Apply 2 months in advance.*
All nationalities welcome.

DOMESTIC

FINNISH FAMILY PROGRAMME Centre for International Mobility, PB 343, 00531 Helsinki, Finland ✆ **(358 0) 7747 7033** ✍ **(358 0) 7747 7064**
Offers native speakers of English, French or German an opportunity to get acquainted with the Finnish way of life, living as a member of a family whilst speaking their own language. Host families include both farming and urban or suburban families who may move into the country for the summer. Applicants are expected to help with household chores and/or childcare. On farms the work also involves helping with milking, fruit picking, hay making and gardening.
⚜ Ages 18-23. 1-12 months, mostly June-August. Approx 25 hour, 5 day week. Board, lodging plus pocket money provided. ✍ *Applications for summer positions by 28 February; for other positions apply at least 3 months in advance.*

UK applications to Central Bureau for Educational Visits & Exchanges, Seymour week. Board, lodging plus pocket money provided. ✎ *Applications for summer positions by 28 February; for other positions apply at least 3 months in advance.*

UK applications to Central Bureau for Educational Visits & Exchanges, Seymour Mews House, Seymour Mews, London W1H 9PE ✆ 0171-486 5101.

FARMWORK

INTERNATIONAL FARM EXPERIENCE PROGRAMME
YFC Centre, N A C, Stoneleigh Park, Kenilworth, Warwickshire CV8 2LG ✆ **Coventry (01203) 696584**
Provides assistance to young **agriculturalists** and **horticulturalists** by finding places in farms/nurseries abroad, enabling them to broaden their knowledge of agricultural and horticultural methods. Participants usually live and work with a farming family and the work is matched as far as possible with the participant's requirements. 3-12 months, all year. Basic wages plus board and lodging. ⊕ Ages 18-28. Applicants must have at least 2 years practical experience, one of which may be at agricultural college, and intend to make a career in agriculture. Participants pay own fares and insurance. Registration fee £85. ✎ *Apply at least 3 months in advance; UK applications to IFEP. Other applications to IFEP partner organisation in home country.*

WORKCAMPS

KANSAINVÄLINEN VAPAAEHTOISTYÖ RY (KVT)
Rauhanasema, Vetuitori, 00520 Helsinki 52, Finland
KVT is the Finnish branch of Service Civil International which promotes international reconciliation through work projects. **Volunteers** are invited to work in international teams on workcamps organised throughout Finland. The workcamps aim to make people realise their responsibility and to work for constructive changes in the unjust areas of society. Projects are of a combined manual and social nature, supporting communities either in remote depressed areas or those practising alternative methods with handicapped or underprivileged people. Recent projects have included reconstruction of the sailing vessel *Estelle* at Turku to carry fair trade cargo; repairing and painting old bikes at an Emmaus camp in Jokioinen to send to Chile; renovating a villa on an island near Helsinki for use as a youth centre; haymaking and gardening at an old farmhouse with disabled and able-bodied people; and cleaning up surroundings and making nature paths with the Keep Lapland Clean Association on wilderness camps in Saariselka and Lokka. Most of the camps have a study element, which involves the discussion of questions and folk traditions relevant to the community and work for peace. The main language of the camps is English. ⊕ Ages 18+. Applicants should be highly motivated, preferably with previous workcamp or other voluntary experience, and prepared to work hard as part of a team. 35-40 hour week. 2-4 weeks, June-September. Food, shared accommodation in schools, barns, tents or log cabins and work accident insurance provided. No fares or wages paid. Places also available for families. **B D PH W** depending on project.

✎ *Apply through partner organisation in country of residence. In the UK: International Voluntary Service or Quaker International Social Projects. See page 30 for registration details and addresses.*

GENERAL

CENTRE FOR INTERNATIONAL MOBILITY **PB 343, 00531 Helsinki,**

forestry, horticulture or environmental protection; work in the service outlets such as hotels, restaurants, tourist offices and travel agencies; social work, nursing and youth work; trainee positions in commerce and retail; or teaching one's native language (usually English, German or French) in a private family, kindergarten, school or firm.

✤ Ages 18-30. Applicants must be students or graduates in a relevant subject; the type of work offered will depend on applicants' own interests and amount of work experience. 1-3 months, usually May-August; longer placements for graduates. Minimum salary covers living costs.

🕮 *Applications should reach the Centre by 28 February. In the UK further information and application forms are available from the Central Bureau for Educational Visits & Exchanges, Seymour Mews House, Seymour Mews, London W1H 9PE* ✆ *0171-486 5101.*

MONASTERY OF VALAMO
79850 Uusi - Valamo, Finland

An ancient Eastern Orthodox religious community, whose history dates back to the 12th century. A popular pilgrimage site, it also serves as a meeting place for Christians of differing traditions and nationalities.

Volunteers are invited to help with different tasks such as working in the monastery kitchen and garden; collecting brushwood, mushrooms and berries in the forest; and other common domestic chores which community living involves.

✤ Ages 18+. 42 hour week, all year. There is ample time for relaxation, traditional recreations such as sauna, and daily worship. Full board and hostel accommodation provided, but no fares or wages paid. *All nationalities welcome.*

APPLYING FOR A JOB

When writing to **any** organisation it is **essential** to mention **Working Holidays 1995** and enclose a **stamped, self-addressed A4 envelope**, or if in another country, an **addressed A4 envelope** and at least two **IRCs** (International Reply Coupons, available from post offices). Enquiries received without SAEs/IRCs are **unlikely** to be answered. **Before applying**, read carefully all the information given. Pay **particular** attention to:

✐ skills/qualifications/experience required

✐ the period of employment expected

✐ age limits or nationality restrictions

✐ application deadlines

✐ any other points, especially details of insurance cover, and other costs such as travel and accommodation.

When applying include the following:

✐ your name, address, date of birth, marital status, nationality, sex

✐ details of your education, qualifications, relevant experience, skills, languages spoken

✐ your period of availability for work

✐ a passport-size photo, particularly if you will be working with the public

✐ anything else recommended in the listing (such as a *cv*)

*f*RANCE

INFO

French Embassy
58 Knightsbridge, London SW1X 7JT
✆ 0171-201 1000
Visa Section: Consulate General,
6A Cromwell Place, London SW7 2EW
✆ 0171-838 2050
Long Stay Visa Section: ✆ 0171-838 2049

British Embassy
35 rue du Faubourg St Honoré, 75383
Paris Cedex 08 ✆ (33 1) 42 66 91 42

Tourist office
French Government Tourist Office,
178 Piccadilly, London W1V 0AL
✆ 0891 244123

Youth hostels
Fédération Unie des Auberges de
Jeunesse, 27 rue Pajol, 75018 Paris

Ligue Française pour les Auberges de la
Jeunesse, 38 boulevard Raspail, 75007
Paris

Youth & student information
Accueil des Jeunes en France, 12 rue des
Barres, 75004 Paris

Centre d'Information et de
Documentation Jeunesse (CIDJ), 101
quai Branly, 75740 Paris Cedex 15

Organisation pour le Tourisme
Universitaire, 39 avenue Georges
Bernanos, 75005 Paris

Entry regulations UK citizens
intending to work in France should have
full passports. UK/EEA nationals may
stay for up to 3 months to find a job;
once a job has been found a residence
permit, *carte de séjour*, must be applied
for. Application forms are available from
the Prefecture de Police in Paris, or
from the local police station or town
hall elsewhere. The permit is valid for
the period of employment, if this is less
than 12 months. Those under 18 should
have written parental consent and are

not allowed to work in bars. Details of particular regulations applying to **au pair** posts and seasonal **agricultural work** are given under the respective headings in this section.
Non-EEA nationals are not allowed to take up any form of employment in France unless they have been granted a permit before arrival.
Several agreements exist between France and some African and South East Asian countries, Poland and Lebanon, and nationals of these countries are allowed to work in specific cases. Those studying in France can work after their first year.

Employment offices The French equivalent of a British Jobcentre is the Agence Nationale pour l'Emploi (ANPE). There are ANPE offices throughout France and EEA nationals can use their services. A list of all regional offices can be obtained from the head office, ANPE, 4 rue Galilee, 93198 Noisy-le-Grand or from the Social Service at the Consular Section of the French Embassy.
The Consulate issues a leaflet, *Employment in France of British nationals and nationals of other EC countries,* available from the Long Stay Visa Section, PO Box 57, 6A Cromwell Place, London SW7 2EW.

Job advertising The French Publishing Group, 4 Wendle Court, 131-137 Wandsworth Road, London SW8 2LL ℭ 0171-498 2333 ℳ 0171-498 2514 can place advertisements in most French newspapers and magazines.

Travel Rent-a-bike scheme available at 53 stations, bookable in advance; FF1,500 deposit, cost FF55 per day, decreasing as the number of rental days increases. Carrismo card available in France only for ages 12-25 offers up to 50% reduction on 4 or 8 journeys, valid 1 year. Holiday Return (Séjour) Ticket gives concession of 25% if the journey covers more than 1,000 km; valid two months. Further information from the Rail Shop ℭ 0891 515477 (39p/49p per minute off peak/other times). For bookings ℭ 0345 300003.

Freedom Pass allows 3, 5 or 10 days unlimited rail travel in 1 month on the railways of France. Cost from £95 (under 26) or £114 (26+). Available from British Rail International Rail Centre, Victoria Station, London SW1V 1JY ℭ 0171-834 2345.

Campus Travel can arrange Eurotrain, Inter-rail and student/youth fares for travel by plane, train, boat and bus to destinations throughout France. Offices throughout the UK including a student travel centre at 52 Grosvenor Gardens, London SW1W 0AG (opposite Victoria Station) ℭ 0171-730 3402 or ℭ 0131-668 3303 for Scottish bookings.

Council Travel, 28A Poland Street, London W1V 3DB ℭ 0171-287 3337 (offices also in Paris, Nice, Lyon, Munich, Düsseldorf, Tokyo, Singapore and throughout the US) offers flexible student/youth charter flights to destinations throughout France. Also Eurotrain under 26 fares, travel insurance, guidebooks and travel gear.

STA Travel, 86 Old Brompton Road, London SW7 3LQ/117 Euston Road, London NW1 2SX ℭ 0171-937 9921 (offices also in Birmingham, Bristol, Cambridge, Glasgow, Leeds, Manchester and Oxford) operates flexible, low-cost flights to destinations across France.

Information centres Accueil des Jeunes en France, 119 rue St Martin, 75004 Paris and 139 boulevard St Michel, 75005 Paris offers a general information and advisory service for young travellers. Can provide vouchers for low-cost hotels and arrange cheap accommodation, see below, and also supply cheap air, rail and coach tickets.

Centre d'Information et de Documentation Jeunesse (CIDJ), 101 quai Branly, 75740 Paris Cedex 15 provides a comprehensive information service for young people, with branches throughout France. Practical help can be provided in finding work. Information is also available on accommodation, social, cultural, artistic, scientific and sports facilities, activities and holidays plus practical information on staying, travelling and studying in France and facilities for the disabled. The centre also acts as the local branch of the ANPE and career advice/social security office. Publish a wide range of booklets and information sheets including *Recherche d'un Job; Séjour et Emploi des Étudiants Étrangers en France; Entrée, Séjour et Emploi des Étrangers en France* and *Réductions de Transports pour les Jeunes.* **PH**

Usit Voyages, 6 rue de Vaugirard, 75006 Paris and branches throughout France (Campus Travel's sister organisation) arrange student/youth travel and give information and advice.

Publications Lonely Planet's *France - A Travel Survival Kit* £13.95 offers practical, down-to-earth information for budget travellers wanting to explore beyond the usual tourist routes.

Rough Guides provide comprehensive background information plus details on getting there, getting around, places to explore and cheap places to stay. Titles include *France* £9.99, *Paris* £9.99, *Brittany and Normandy* £7.99, *Corsica* £8.99 *Provence and the Côte d'Azur* £8.99 and *Pyrenées* £8.99.

Culture Shock! France £6.95 introduces the reader to the people, customs, ceremonies, food and culture of France, with checklists of dos and don'ts.

All the above are available from good bookshops.

Emplois d'Été en France 1995 lists thousands of vacancies including waiting and bar staff, au pairs, sports instructors, receptionists, work in factories, shops, language schools and offices and on farms and children's summer camps. Also includes special information for foreign students, with details of authorisation on working in France. Published by Vac-job, 4 rue d'Alesia, 75014 Paris. Distributed in the UK by Vacation Work, 9 Park End Street, Oxford OX1 1HJ © Oxford (01865) 241978, price £7.95. Vacation Work also publish *Live and Work in France* £8.95, a guide for those interested in finding temporary or permanent work, starting a business or buying a home in France.

1,000 Pistes de Jobs FF110 including postage, is a comprehensive guide giving 1,000 ideas and different ways of finding a holiday job, with practical advice and useful addresses. Although the book is primarily a guide for young French people, it is an invaluable source of reference for anyone wanting to work in France, providing that they speak fluent French. Available from L'Étudiant, 27 rue du Chemin Vert, 75011 Paris.

Accommodation Centre d'Information et de Documentation Jeunesse (CIDJ), 101 quai Branly, 75740 Paris Cedex 15 publish information sheets providing addresses of reasonable accommodation in youth centres, university halls and pensions, mainly in the Paris region: *Centres d'Hébergement Temporaires Paris et Région Parisienne; Hôtels Bon Marché à Paris; Logement des Jeunes Travailleurs;* and *Le Logement de L'Étudiant.*

Accueil des Jeunes en France is a central booking office with access to 11,000 beds in the summer. Guarantee to find any young traveller decent, cheap accommodation in Paris, with immediate reservation. Cost approx FF105 per night. Contact AJF Beaubourg, 119 rue St-Martin, 75004 Paris; AJF Quartier Latin, 139 boulevard Saint-Michel, 75005 Paris; or AJF Gare du Nord, 75010 Paris.

Accommodation available for young people at a modern residential centre.

Facilities include cafeteria, bar, TV rooms and a night club. Maximum 2 weeks, all year. Cost from FF124 per night, bed and breakfast; meals available from FF59. Advance reservations possible. FIAP Jean Monnet, L'Espace Accueil de Paris, 30 rue Cabanis, 75014 Paris ℂ (33 1) 45 89 89 15 ☎ (331) 45 81 63 91. **PH**

UCRIF, 72 rue Rambuteau, 75001 Paris ℂ (33 1) 40 26 57 64 ☎ (33 1) 40 26 58 20 has 63 international accommodation centres for young people throughout France, with some 11,000 beds. Each centre is open the year round and is comfortably equipped, offering sightseeing and cultural programmes with the emphasis on international friendship.

ARCHAEOLOGY

ASSOCIATION DE RECHERCHES ET D'ÉTUDES D'HISTOIRE RURALE Serge Grappin, Maison du Patrimoine, 21190 Saint-Romain, France

Excavations in the Burgundy village of Saint-Romain require **volunteers**. Previous digs have revealed 16 layers of occupation dating back to Neolithic times. ⊕ Ages 18+. No experience necessary, but volunteers should be able to speak French. 40 hours per week, 15+ days, July/August. No fares or wages paid. Food and village accommodation provided for FF20 per day; volunteers should take a sleeping bag. FF20 fee covers registration and insurance. Weekly visits to local museums and sites of archaeological interest; conferences, courses and training organised on site.

ASSOCIATION POUR LE DÉVELOPPEMENT DE L'ARCHÉOLOGIE URBAINE A CHARTRES 16 rue Saint Pierre, 28000 Chartres, France

Organises urban rescue excavation work on sites in Chartres, for which **volunteers** are required. The project is a long-term research programme on the archaeological and historical development, covering the economic, cultural and social evolution from Roman to medieval times. Sites include Gallo-Roman buildings and constructions including amphitheatre, roads, houses, metal and pottery workshops, plus sites dating from the High Middle Ages. Talks/slides will be given on a variety of related subjects during June-September. Volunteers should be prepared for hard, physical work in all weathers. Punctuality is expected. Volunteers also work in the laboratory, washing, classifying, repairing and drawing finds. ⊕ Ages 18+. Previous experience desirable and if possible applicants should enclose an archaeological cv. 8 hour day, 5 day week, with weekends free. 3+ weeks, preferably 4+, June-September. Food, accommodation and insurance provided, but no fares or wages paid. Volunteers should take sleeping bags. Registration fee FF200. ⌛ Apply 4 weeks in advance.

CENTRE DE DECOUVERTE 16190 Aubeterre, France ℂ (33) 45 98 50 40

Environmental centre in the Charente region organising an annual summer workshop for young Europeans. Projects include building a large Gallo-Roman style pottery kiln; experimenting with casting in a bronze furnace; building Gallic style huts thatched with chestnut and heather; creating artificial archaeological digs to teach excavation techniques; investigating the ruins of local water mills and researching written and oral information about the locality's history. ⊕ Ages 18+. No experience necessary, but participants should be prepared to live and work as a team. 30-35 hour. 6 day week, with swimming, archery, fencing and canoeing in spare time, plus visits to local places of interest. 3 weeks, July. Cost FF1,300 covers food, accommodation and insurance; cultural visits cost extra. No fares or wages paid. **B D PH W** ⌛ Apply early; limited places.

CENTRE DE RECHERCHES ARCHÉOLOGIQUES F Audouze, Centre National de la Recherche Scientifique, 1 place Aristide Briand, 92195 Meudon Cedex, France

Experienced **volunteers** required for the excavation of the Upper Palaeolithic site of Verberie on the river Oise, 80km north of Paris. The excavation aims to study the everyday life of Magdalenian reindeer hunters. Work involves the digging of a living floor covered with flint tools and chips, bones and stones, plus mapping and restoring artefacts. ⚥ Ages 18+. Some knowledge of French preferred. 8 hour day, 6 day week, 1 July-15 August. Food, camping accommodation and insurance provided. No fares or wages paid. Occasional visits to places of interest in the Oise area may be arranged. ☎ *Apply by end May.*

CHANTIERS D'ÉTUDES MEDIÉVALES 4 rue du Tonnelet Rouge, 67000 Strasbourg, France

Organise international workcamps devoted to the study, restoration and maintenance of monuments or sites dating back to the Middle Ages. **Volunteers** are invited to help with restoration and excavation work on various sites throughout Alsace, including medieval castles and houses. Teams of specialists in history, ceramics, architecture and archaeology accompany participants on both restoration and excavation projects. Opportunities to study finds and draw conclusions; excavation techniques taught. ⚥ Ages 16+; under 18s require parental consent. Applicants accepted from all countries, as long as they are fit and willing to adapt to a community lifestyle. 36 hour, 6 day week. 12/15 days, July-September. Cost from FF500 includes food and very basic accommodation in schools, houses, barracks, tents or hostels with self-catering facilities, plus insurance. Participants should take sleeping bags and work clothes. ☎ *Apply by May; applications may take several weeks to process.*

DEPARTMENT OF PREHISTORY & ARCHAEOLOGY Prof J Collis, The University, Sheffield, South Yorkshire S10 2TN

Volunteers are required for excavating, processing finds and surveying at Iron Age-Roman sites near Mirefleurs, Clermont-Ferrand, in conjunction with the Service des Fouilles Historiques de l'Auvergne. Long-term project studying the impact of urbanisation on a rural settlement, 2nd century BC and 2nd century AD. Experience not necessary. 16 weeks, mid June-September. Campsite accommodation with meals provided at a nearby house. Cost approx FF40 per day. No fares or wages paid. ☎ *Apply by 31 March.*

ÉQUIPE DE RECHERCHE ARCHÉOLOGIQUE N° 12, CNRS, 3 rue Michelet, 75006 Paris, France

Volunteers are needed for excavation work in the Vallée de l'Aisne. The project, organised in conjunction with the Université de Paris, involves the rescue of sites threatened by urban expansion, and the study of changes in settlement, subsistence and material culture within the valley over a 5,000 year period. Recent work has been undertaken on a number of Neolithic and early Iron Age settlement sites. ⚥ Ages 18+. Archaeology students or experienced excavators preferred. 2+ weeks, late June-early September. Good food, dormitory accommodation in old farm buildings or camping space and hot showers provided, but no fares or wages paid. ☎ *Apply to the Director by 15 June.*

FRÉDÉRIC SURMELY 3 rue Grégoire de Tours, 63000 Clermont-Ferrand, France ☎ (33) 73 41 27 69

Invites **volunteers** to help excavate an early Mesolithic hunter's camp in the volcanic mountains of the Cantal region, with the possibility of prospecting for further sites in surrounding cliffs. ⚥ Ages 18-65. Experience not essential, but volunteers should be well-motivated and eager to work as part of a team.

2-4 weeks, July. Food and campsite accommodation provided. Participation fee FF165.

GROUPE ARCHÉOLOGIQUE DU MEMONTOIS M Louis Roussel, Directeur des Fouilles, Mairie de Malain, 21410 Pont-de-Pany, France

Excavation work at Malain on the Côte d'Or requires **volunteers**. The site consists of the Gallic and Roman town as well as a medieval castle and prehistoric earthworks. The object is to study the development of the town from its origins and explore its later development. The camp is based on a collective lifestyle, and volunteers share in supervising digs, discussions on finds, taking charge of exhibitions and preparing meals. Work involves documenting, classifying, washing, collecting, drawing and photographing finds, and restoration work on ruins. Lectures and excursions organised. 7 hour day, 5½ day week. 4 weeks, July-August. Camping accommodation provided; food at a cost of FF100 per week. Volunteers should preferably be experienced, and can take their own camping equipment. No wages or fares paid. 📖 *Apply by May*. **D**

LABORATOIRE D'ANTHROPOLOGIE PRÉHISTORIQUE Université de Rennes I, Campus de Beaulieu, 35042 Rennes Cedex, France

Volunteers required for excavations on prehistoric and protohistoric remains in Brittany.
⚜ Ages 18+. 3-4 weeks, summer. Food and campsite accommodation provided but volunteers must take their own camping equipment. No fares or wages paid. 📖 *Apply in April for further details*.

MINISTERE DE LA CULTURE Service Régional de l'Archéologie de Bretagne, 6 rue du Chapitre, 35044 Rennes Cedex, France

Volunteers are needed to work on archaeological sites all over Brittany, ranging from Palaeolithic to medieval periods. Recent projects have included work on megalithic monuments and sites in Locmariaquer, St Laurent sur Oust and Monteneuf; the excavation of a Gallic/Gallo-Roman site prior to the building of a new road near Rennes; work on Iron Age and Dark Ages sites; and uncovering the ancient area of shops near the site of the forum in the Gallo-Roman capital at Corseul.
⚜ Ages 18+. Volunteers should be prepared for hard physical work. Archaeological experience useful but not essential; basic French necessary. Approx 40 hour week. 1+ weeks, April-September. Board and lodging provided, varying from campsites to university halls of residence depending on the location. Cost FF50 per week plus travel to site. Participants should take a sleeping bag. Insurance provided. Anti-tetanus vaccination required. Excursions sometimes arranged.
📖 *Detailed list of sites available in March*.

MUSÉE DES SCIENCES NATURELLES ET D'ARCHÉOLOGIE Service Archéologique du Musée de la Chartreuse, 191 rue St-Albin, 59500 Douai, France ✆ (33) 27 96 90 60 📠 (33) 27 96 90 75

Beginners and experienced **volunteers** required to help with urban rescue excavation in an area of Douai. The object is to trace the origins and development of the town from the 11th-16th century, concentrating on the medieval houses. There is also another excavation of a Merovingian abbey in Wandignies-Hanage (near Douai).
⚜ Ages 18+. Preference given to those sufficiently experienced to take over sections of the excavation. Knowledge of French useful but not essential. 7½ hour day. 2+ weeks, July-September. Food and accommodation provided. No fares paid, but wages may be offered to specialists. Participants should take their own sleeping bag. Anti-tetanus vaccination compulsory. Registration fee FF150 covers insurance. 📖 *Apply by 15 June to Pierre Demolon, Conservateur*.

MUSEUM NATIONAL D'HISTOIRE NATURELLE

Laboratoire de Préhistoire, Institut de Paléontologie Humaine, Professeur Henry de Lumley, 1 rue René Panhard, 75013 Paris, France
Volunteers required to work on various sites and caves in south east and south west France. Projects include investigating Acheulian and Tayacian industries, fauna, pre-Neanderthal human remains and dwelling structures at the Grotte du Lazaret in Nice and at Tautavel near Perpignan; studying and recording protohistoric rock engravings at a research centre in the Vallée des Merveilles in Tende; excavation at the Palaeolithic site of La Baume Bonne, Alpes de Haute Provence and at Les Eyzies, Dordogne. Opportunities to study finds. Specialists and amateurs welcome. 15+ days in March/April or 1 month, June-August. Board provided at local campsites, but participants should take their own tents and equipment. No fares or wages paid.

REMPART (Union des Associations pour la Réhabilitation et l'Entretien des Monuments et du Patrimoine Artistique), 1 rue des Guillemites, 75004 Paris, France

Aims to improve the way of life through a better understanding of and a greater respect for the archaeological, architectural and natural heritage and environment through the restoration of endangered buildings and monuments. Consists of a grouping of more than 140 local, departmental or regional associations, providing a wide variety of projects. **Volunteers** are needed for archaeological work on sites in Auvergne, Centre, Ile de France, Languedoc-Roussillon, Lorraine, Midi-Pyrénées, Normandie, Poitou-Charentes, Provence-Alpes-Côte d'Azur and Corsica. Sites include medieval towns and villages, châteaux, fortresses, abbeys and churches, prehistoric and Gallo-Roman towns, early Christian sites, amphitheatres and villas, and post-medieval fortresses and castles. Work involves excavation, cleaning and restoration. Participants are usually accompanied by experienced archaeologists and are involved in carrying out surveys, drawing plans, technical photography and learning archaeological methods and site history. Opportunities for swimming, tennis, riding, cycling, rambling, exploring the region, crafts and taking part in local festivities.
⊕ Ages 14/18+. There is no upper age limit, anyone feeling young is welcome. Some knowledge of French needed. 30-35 hour week. 2-4 weeks, Easter and June-September; a few camps are open throughout the year. Cost approx FF45 per day includes food and accommodation in huts, old buildings and tents, with self-catering facilities; a few camps are free. Volunteers help with camp duties, pay their own fares, and should take a sleeping bag. Applicants can choose which project they would like to work on in the workcamp programme and contact addresses are given. Registration fee FF200 includes insurance. Also arrange archaeology courses. **D PH**
🖂 Write for further information and application form enclosing 3 IRCs.

SERVICE ARCHÉOLOGIQUE - VILLE D'ARRAS Alain Jacques, 22 rue Paul Doumer, 62000 Arras, France

Excavation in Arras including the remains of the Roman town of Nemetacum and a 4th century barracks requires **volunteers**. No experience necessary. ⊕ Ages 18+. 40 hour week, 15+ days, July and August. No fares or wages paid, but food, accommodation and insurance provided. Registration fee FF25.
🖂 Apply by 30 May.

SERVICE DEPARTEMENTAL D'ARCHÉOLOGIE DU CALVADOS 28 rue Jean Eudes, 14000 Caen, France ℰ (33) 31 86 26 61

Volunteers needed for archaeological work on sites in Calvados, Normandy.

Two excavations concerning the Roman period will be carried out in 1995: an artisanal production centre (kilns and workshop) and a theatre. Work involves excavation, cleaning and restoration and archaeological drawing. 35-40 hour, 5-6 day week, mid June-October. Board and accommodation provided.

⊕ Ages 18+. Archaeological experience an advantage but not essential; basic French useful. Training provided in basic archaeological techniques. No fares or wages paid. ✆ *Apply May/June.*

UNIVERSITÉ DU MAINE
Annie Renoux, Département d'Histoire, Avenue Olivier Messiaen, BP 535, 72017 Le Mans, France

Excavation at the site of the Château Comtal at Chavôt, Epernay, Champagne, requires **volunteers**. Recent work has concentrated on the 10th-13th century castle of the Count of Champagne and involves excavating, cleaning, marking and recording finds. Lectures on excavation techniques.

⊕ Ages 18+. Experience not necessary. 8 hour day, 5½ day week. 15+ days, July and August. Lunch and accommodation in stone building provided, but no fares or wages paid. Volunteers should take a sleeping bag. Qualified volunteers staying more than 3 weeks may be offered full expenses.
✆ *Early application advisable.*

AU PAIR/ CHILDCARE

Certain conditions apply to anyone working as an au pair in France, regardless of the organisation through which they apply. Both sexes can apply, and must be aged between 18 and 30. Work is for a minimum of 3 months and a maximum of 12 months, with the possibility of an extension to 18 months. As a rule applicants should reach an agreement with the host family before leaving for France. It is then up to the host family or the organisation which arranged the placement to obtain, from the Direction Départementale du Travail et de l'Emploi (in Paris: Service de la Main-d'Oeuvre Etrangère, 80 rue de la Croix-Nivert, 75732 Paris Cedex 15), the form *Accord de placement au pair d'un stagiaire aide-familial*. This has to be signed by the family and returned together with a certificate of registration at a school in France specialising in teaching foreign students, proof of academic studies, and a current medical certificate. If the Direction Départementale are satisfied with the information supplied, they will stamp the *Accord de placement* and a copy will be sent to the applicant.

On arrival in France, an au pair from an EEA country must obtain a *carte de séjour* from the local Commissariat de Police. Non-EEA passport-holders must apply for a long stay visa from the French Consulate in their country of residence before going to France, and on arrival must obtain a *carte de séjour* and *autorisation provisoire de travail* from the Direction Départementale, on production of the *Accord de placement.* The host family must register the au pair with the national insurance scheme and pay quarterly contributions which cover the au pair for accidents at work, sickness and maternity. Au pairs can expect to live as a member of the family and to have sufficient free time for recreation and to attend language classes. Work involves light household tasks including simple cooking, hand washing, cleaning, washing up, shopping, helping to prepare simple meals and childcare for up to 5 hours a day, plus 2 nights' babysitting per week. At least 1 day per week free, including at least 1 Sunday per month. Pocket money average FF1,300 per month.

An information sheet, *Au Pair Posts in France,* giving details of conditions and formalities is available from the Long Stay Visa Section of the French Consulate.

Placement Au Pair en France (Stagiaire Aide-Familial) is an information sheet including details of regulations and formalities, a list of organisations placing au pairs, plus addresses of Préfectures de Police in Paris. Also *Garde d'Enfants Temporaire et Baby-Sitting (Paris et Région Parisienne)*. Both published by the Centre d'Information et de Documentation Jeunesse (CIDJ), 101 quai Branly, 75740 Paris Cedex 15.

ACADEMY AU PAIR AGENCY LTD 42 Cedarhurst Drive, Eltham, London SE9 5PL ℰ 0181-294 1191 ℳ 0181-850 8932
Can place **au pairs**. ⊕ Ages 18-27. Some knowledge of French essential. Pocket money approx £35-£40 per week. Administration charge £40. Positions as **nannies** and **mothers' helps** also available for those with qualifications/experience.

ANGLO PAIR AGENCY 40 Wavertree Road, Streatham Hill, London SW2 3SP ℰ 0181-674 3605
Can place **au pairs** and au **pairs plus**. ⊕ Ages 18-27. Pocket money £30-£50 per week. Also placements for experienced **nannies** and **mothers' helps**; salary up to £100 per week. Agency fee £40.

AVALON AGENCY Thursley House, 53 Station Road, Shalford, Guildford, Surrey GU4 8HA ℰ Guildford (01483) 63640
Can place **au pairs**. ⊕ Ages 18-30. Basic knowledge of French needed. Pocket money equal to £30-£35 per week usually paid monthly. Fee £40 for placement and use of French agent. Summer holiday placements June-August only. Long-term 6 month-2 year vacancies to start any time.

BUNTERS AU PAIR & DOMESTIC AGENCY 17 Copper Street, Macclesfield, Cheshire SK11 7LH ℰ Macclesfield (01625) 614534
Can place **au pairs, demi pairs** and

mothers' helps. 6-12 months all year or 10 week summer placements. ⊕ Ages 18-27. Pocket money £35-£50 per week depending on hours worked. Placement fee £40. ✉ *Apply before May for summer placements.*

HELPING HANDS AU PAIR & DOMESTIC AGENCY 39 Rutland Avenue, Thorpe Bay, Essex SS1 2XJ ℰ Southend-on-Sea (01702) 602067
Can place **au pairs** and **mothers' helps**. ⊕ Ages 18-27. Pocket money approx £35 per week for au pairs, higher for mothers' helps. Introduction fee £40. *UK nationals only.*

HOME FROM HOME Walnut Orchard, Chearsley, Aylesbury, Buckinghamshire HP18 0DA ℰ/ℳ Aylesbury (01844) 208561
Can place **au pairs**. ⊕ Ages 18+. Reasonable level of French essential. Pocket money £35 per week. Placement fee £40. *UK nationals only.*

INTER-SÉJOURS 179 rue de Courcelles, 75017 Paris, France ℰ (33 1) 47 63 06 81
Can place **au pairs** in Paris and the provinces; 3 month placements in summer, otherwise 6-12 months. ⊕ Ages 18-26. Pocket money FF1,500 per month. Registration fee FF670.

INTERNATIONAL CATHOLIC SOCIETY FOR GIRLS (ACISJF) St Patrick's International Youth Centre, 24 Great Chapel Street, London W1V 3AF ℰ 0171-734 2156 ℳ 0171-287 6282
Au pair posts arranged for 9+ months or 3 month summer placements. ⊕ Ages 18+. *Mainly UK/Irish nationals.*

JOLAINE AGENCY 18 Escot Way, Barnet, Hertfordshire EN5 3AN ℰ 0181-449 1334 ℳ 0181-449 9183
Can place **au pairs** and **mothers' helps**. ⊕ Ages 18+. Weekly pocket money approx £40 (au pairs) or £50 (mothers' helps). Placement fee £40.

JUST THE JOB (NOTTINGHAM)
32 Dovedale Road, West Bridgford, Nottingham NG2 6JA © 0115-945 2482
Can place **au pairs**, **mothers' helps** and **nannies**. 6+ months; no short-term placements. ⊕ Ages 18+. Weekly pocket money £32-£40 (au pairs). *UK nationals only.*

LANGTRAIN INTERNATIONAL
Torquay Road, Foxrock, Dublin 18, Ireland © (353 1) 289 3876
Can place **au pairs** in French families. ⊕ Ages 18+. Pocket money approx £35-£40 per week. Placement fee £60.

MONDIAL AGENCY 32 Links Road, West Wickham, Kent BR4 0QW © 0181-777 0510
Can place **au pairs** in Paris or Nice. ⊕ Ages 18-27. Pocket money approx £35 per week. Service charge £40.

PROBLEMS UNLIMITED AGENCY 86 Alexandra Road, Windsor, Berkshire SL4 1HU
© Windsor (01753) 830101
Can place **au pairs**. ⊕ Ages 18-27. Pocket money £30-£35 per week.

SÉJOURS INTERNATIONAUX LINGUISTIQUES ET CULTURELS
32 Rempart de l'Est, 16022 Angoulême, France © (33) 45 97 41 00
Can place **au pairs** all over France. ⊕ Ages 18+. Pocket money approx FF350 per week. Registration fee FF850.
Apply by April for summer placements, by end July for placements starting September.

STUDENTS ABROAD LTD
11 Milton View, Hitchin, Hertfordshire SG4 0QD © Hitchin (01462) 438909 ⅏ (01462) 438919
Can place **au pairs**, **mothers' helps** and **nannies**. ⊕ Ages 18-27 for au pairs. Basic knowledge of French preferred. Pocket money approx FF1,600 per month; higher for mothers' helps and nannies. Service charge £40.

Apply early for short-term summer placements and winter ski resort positions (au pairs only).

COMMUNITY WORK

APF ÉVASION (Association des Paralysés de France), 17 boulevard Auguste-Blanqui, 75013 Paris, France
A non-profitmaking organisation recruiting **volunteers** to help physically handicapped adults on holiday all over France. Participants give aid and share their time with the handicapped as appropriate, so there are no fixed hours of work. July and August.
⊕ Ages 18+. Males in greater demand; no experience necessary, but knowledge of French essential. Full board youth centre accommodation, insurance and travel expenses from the French border provided. Social activities/excursions arranged are available to the volunteers.
Written applications in French.

PAX CHRISTI JEUNES 58 avenue de Breteuil, 75007 Paris, France ⅏ (33 1) 44 49 02 15
An international Catholic movement for peace, organising centres for international encounters during the summer which attempt to encourage dialogue between different nations, races and religions, to give a living witness that peace is possible.
Volunteers are needed to work in Lourdes. Hostels are set up in school buildings, to provide meals and accommodation. The aim is for the volunteers to form a lively international community. Work involves reception duties, cleaning, shopping, laundry, publicity and the setting up and dismantling of beds. Volunteers also invite the visitors to join them in reflection, dialogue and prayer.
The work is hard but often rewarding. Duties and free time are allocated on a rota basis as far as possible so that everyone shares menial as well as more enjoyable aspects of the work.

⊕ Ages 18-30. Volunteers must speak French and have a real commitment to peace. 2 weeks, July-early September, or 1+ months, early April-mid October. Food, accommodation and insurance provided. No fares or wages paid.

CONSERVATION

LES ALPES DE LUMIERE
Prieuré de Salagon, Mane, 04300 Forcalquier, France
Arranges conservation workcamps for **volunteers** throughout Haute-Provence. Recent projects have included renovating medieval fortifications in Castellane; restoring the tower of a castle in Selonnet; tidying up the site of the ruined village of Méthamis; and preserving local architecture with historical or archaeological value, such as churches, castles and fountains.
⊕ Ages 18+. 15+ days, July-September, approx 30 hour week with afternoons free for leisure activities. Countryside excursions arranged. Volunteers should take a sleeping bag, working clothes, rucksack and walking shoes. Food, camping accommodation and insurance provided. Volunteers pay own travel and FF400-FF500 registration fee depending on length of stay. **D PH**

ASSOCIATION CHANTIERS HISTOIRE ET ARCHITECTURE MEDIÉVALES (CHAM) 5 & 7 rue Guilleminot, 75014 Paris, France
Founded in 1980 with the aim of rescuing and restoring historic French medieval buildings and monuments. **Volunteers** are required for workcamps organised at sites in Brittany, Centre, Nord-Pas de Calais, Pays-de-Loire and Upper Normandy for groups of 15-40 volunteers. The work involves clearing sites, improving, rebuilding and stabilising, restoration work on masonry and archaeological excavations. Recent projects have included clearing the subterranean vaults of a 12th century château in Morbihan and repairing the masonry of a Roman abbey in Ille-et-

Vilaine. Visits arranged to local sites of historic interest, and talks are given on medieval history and architecture.
⊕ Ages 16+. No experience necessary, but volunteers must be fit, motivated and able to adapt to communal life. Good knowledge of French needed. Approx 35 hour week, 1-10 weeks, July-August. Cost FF60 per day covers food and camping accommodation. Volunteers take turns to prepare food, pay their own travel expenses and should take a sleeping bag, practical clothes and sturdy footwear. Registration fee FF100 includes insurance. Also run training courses in restoration techniques.
D PH depending on ability.

ASSOCIATION DROMOISE CHANTIERS ANIMATION ET VIE LOCALE (ADCAVL) Secrétariat International, 39 rue Pêcherie, 26100 Romans, France ℂ (33) 75 02 39 45
An association organising workcamps in villages throughout the region of Drôme-Ardèche. **Volunteers** are invited to take part in projects aimed at restoring and allowing access to sites of historic and cultural interest. Recent projects have included restoration work on a castle in the medieval village of Poët-Célard; creating a walk along the banks of the Isère in the town of Romans; renovating a fountain in the Provençal village of Buis-les-Baronnies; restoring the dungeon in Mornans; and repaving steep and narrow streets in the mountain village of Bourdeaux.
⊕ Ages 18+. No experience necessary, but knowledge of French helpful. 25 hour week for 2-3 weeks, April-September. Afternoons are devoted to sports such as rock climbing, river walking or horse riding; or craft workshops such as pottery, theatre or painting. Also French conservation/ grammar classes combined with excursions. Cultural activities, walks and excursions organised at weekends, with opportunities to attend local festivals. Insurance, food and basic

accommodation in tents, schools or village halls provided, with volunteers taking turns to cook. Tools and materials provided, but volunteers should take work clothes, walking boots, rucksack and sleeping bag. All-inclusive participation fee FF1,050 or FF1,250. No fares or wages paid. ✏ *UK applications direct, in English or French.*

In Belgium, apply through VZW Mooss, Diestsesteenweg M 104, 3010 Kessel-Lo

In Germany, apply through Pro International, Bahnhofstraße 26B, 35037 Marburg/Lahn

In the Netherlands, apply through Activity International, Bieslookstraat 31, 9731 HH Groningen

ASSOCIATION LE MAT Le Viel Audon, Balazuc, 07120 Ruoms, France

Volunteers needed to help in restoring a village in the Ardèche, developing its resources to create new jobs. Twenty years of workcamps have resulted in the creation of a farm and a youth hostel, and educational courses are also held. Work involves masonry, carpentry, cooking, baking bread and general care of the environment. Sports and social activities can also be organised.
⊕ Ages 17-25. 6 hour day. Easter, July and August. Basic accommodation and communal meals provided. FF46 per day covers board. Volunteers pay own travel costs. Registration fee FF70 includes insurance.

ASSOCIATION POUR LA PARTICIPATION A L'ACTION RÉGIONALE (APARE) 41 cours Jean Jaurès, 84000 Avignon, France

Offers participants the opportunity to discover Provence through projects involving **volunteers** in protecting the region's environment and heritage. Recent projects have included restoring two 16th century mills in Régusse; cleaning up the rivers Recluse and Pesquier; helping to preserve cultivated

terraces north of Avignon; and repairing a Roman bridge in Var.
⊕ Ages 18+. 3 or 4 weeks, July-October. Approx 30-35 hour week, with afternoons and weekends free for discovering the region on foot, by bike or canoe. Opportunities to attend local festivals, plays and poetry workshops. Volunteers should take a sleeping bag, working clothes, rucksack and walking shoes. Accommodation, food and insurance provided. Volunteers pay own travel. FF600 registration fee, payable on sending completed application form. Also organises special youth camps for ⊕ ages 15-17; FF2,000 registration fee.

BRITISH TRUST FOR CONSERVATION VOLUNTEERS Room 1WH, 36 St Mary's Street, Wallingford, Oxfordshire OX10 0EU ℭ Wallingford (01491) 839766

The Trust is Britain's leading organisation for the promotion of practical conservation work for protecting the environment. Since 1983 **volunteers** have worked alongside French environmental groups to carry out conservation tasks. Recent projects have included restoring traditional stone farm buildings in the Pyrénées; constructing a badger hide in the Ravine de Valbois, near Besançon; helping with organic gardening at an alternative technology centre near Grenoble; and fencing work at a tortoise village built to protect the Hermanns Tortoise in Corsica. 1-2 weeks June-September.
⊕ Ages 18-70. Cost from £60 includes transport from a suitable pick-up point in France, insurance, food and basic accommodation. Everyone shares in the cooking. Volunteers should take a sleeping bag. Membership fee £12. No fares or wages paid.

CENTRE PERMANENT D'INITIATION A LA FORET PROVENÇALE (ASSODEF) Hôtel de Ville, Chemin du Loubatas, 13860 Peyrolles, France

Each year large areas of forest in the

south of France, Greece, Italy and Portugal fall victim to forest fires, due to carelessness and ignorance. For 10 years ASSODEF has been teaching young people about the dangers of forest fires and involving them in forest protection work. **Volunteers** are invited to take part in summer workcamps. Recent projects have included helping to build a forest information centre based on solar energy; setting up observation posts and information boards; building a concrete tank to hold rainwater in case of fire; footpath maintenance, coppicing, clearing undergrowth, and working to prevent forest fires.
✦ Ages 18+. No special skills or techniques required, but knowledge of French essential. 1/3 weeks, July-early September. Approx 30 hour week, with afternoons free for arranged leisure activities. Accommodation, food and insurance provided. Volunteers pay own travel and FF550 registration fee. **PH**

CENTRE SOCIAL ET CULTUREL DU MARAIS 3 place de la Coutume, 79510 Coulon, France ✆ (33) 49 35 99 90

Volunteers are invited to take part in a European youth workcamp in an area of the Marais Poitevin known as Venise Verte, 50km from La Rochelle. Work involves cleaning canals and clearing brushwood. 2 weeks, August. Full board accommodation provided in families. Programme includes visits to La Rochelle, coastal islands, archaeological sites and monuments; canoe and kayak excursions; social evenings and events.
✦ Ages 17-25. No experience necessary; knowledge of English/French essential. Cost FF400; volunteers pay own travel and insurance.
⚜ *Apply by 25 July.*

CLUB DU VIEUX MANOIR 10 rue de la Cossonnerie, 75001 Paris, France ✆ (33 1) 45 08 80 40

A national movement which brings together young people willing to work as **volunteers** to help with the restoration and upkeep of historic and

endangered monuments and sites and with the protection of the natural environment. Recent projects have included restoring 18th century fortresses and village sundials at Briançon in the Hautes-Alpes; helping with archaeological work at Philippe le Bel's 13th century château in Oise; and restoring a 16th century wooden coaching inn with dovecotes at Casteljaloux in the Lot-et-Garonne. Three permanent sites at Guise, Argy and Pontpoint serve as centres for an introduction to the environment, architectural heritage and for specialised research and instruction on materials, techniques and tools. Some sites also run special programmes/festivals. All volunteers receive manual and technical tuition in archaeology, building techniques, restoration of buildings, architecture, history and handicrafts.
✦ Ages 14/15+, depending on site chosen. Minimum age for specialised instruction, 16. 15+ days, Easter, July-September, Christmas and during the year. Simple self-catering tent accommodation (summer) or under shelter (winter). Participants share in the day-to-day organisation of the camp, and discipline is strict. Cost FF65 per day includes board and lodging. Participants should take a sleeping bag. Volunteers aged 17+ staying for an extended period, other than during the summer, receive free board and lodging after a trial period of 15 days. Registration fee FF80 covers membership and insurance. No fares or wages paid.

LES COMPAGNONS DU CAP Pratcoustals, Arphy, 30120 Le Vigan, France ✆ (33) 67 81 82 22

Volunteers are invited to help restore the abandoned village of Pratcoustals, situated high above the Arphy valley in the Cévennes region. Every summer workcamps help make the site into a permanent centre, adding a museum and restaurant to existing facilities. Work involves re-roofing with traditional tiles,

masonry, drystone walling, rebuilding steps and general improvements to the village. There is also environmental work in the surrounding chestnut forest and the chance to do research into the village's history. Weekend and evening activities include hiking, mountain-biking, swimming in mountain streams, sports, social and musical events.
⊕ Ages 18+. No experience necessary, but volunteers should be able to speak French and be interested in living and working as a group. 2 weeks, June–September. Approx 30 hours work per week. FF58 per day covers dormitory/tent accommodation and meals; volunteers should take a sleeping bag. Registration fee FF70 covers accident insurance. **D**

CONCORDIA 38 rue du Faubourg St Denis, 75010 Paris, France
Volunteers are needed on approx 60 international workcamps which aim to help in the development of small communities in mountainous and isolated rural areas including Alpes, Alsace, Auvergne, Burgundy, Franche-Comté, Languedoc-Roussillon, Limousin, Midi-Pyrénées and Picardy, giving participants the chance to get to know their natural, political, economic and social environment. Typical conservation projects include restoring houses, churches, feudal châteaux and forts, fountains and wells in villages and abandoned hamlets; clearing and signposting footpaths and hiking tracks; creating gardens and green spaces, observatories and bird hides; repairing traditional bread ovens, sheepfolds and mountain huts; restoring paintings and frescoes; and environmental protection in the Parc Naturel de la Vanoise. Volunteers are taught traditional building techniques by local craftsmen. Sports, crafts, theatre, festivals and other cultural and social activities arranged.
⊕ Ages 18+. Good knowledge of French needed for some camps. Applicants should preferably have workcamp experience. 35 hour week. 2-3 weeks, all year; majority of projects

during the summer. Also camps for ⊕ ages 15-17; July and August. 25 hour week, 2-3 weeks. Work accident insurance and full board in schools, huts or community buildings provided. No fares or wages paid. **B D PH**

🏕 *Apply through partner organisation in country of residence. In the UK: Christian Movement for Peace, Concordia (Youth Service Volunteers) Ltd, Quaker International Social Projects or United Nations Association International Youth Service. See page 30 for registration details and addresses.*

ENFANTS ET AMIS DE BEAUCHASTEL Marie-Jeanne Grandclere, rue de la Brèche, 07800 Beauchastel, France
Volunteers are needed to help in the restoration of an abandoned medieval village in the Ardèche, developing its resources to create new jobs. Work involves masonry, carpentry, roof and floor tiling, paving and cooking.
⊕ Ages 18+. No experience necessary, but knowledge of French useful. Approx 30 hour week, 1-15 August. Accommodation in village schoolhouse and meals provided; sports and social activities organised. Volunteers pay own travel costs. Cost FF400 for 2 weeks includes insurance. Anti-tetanus vaccination advisable.

ÉTUDES ET CHANTIERS INTERNATIONAL (UNAREC) Délégation Internationale, 3 rue des Petits Gras, 63000 Clermont-Ferrand, France
A national federation of regional associates working to encourage and promote the participation of young people and adults in the redevelopment of rural communities, the conservation of the environment and the rehabilitation of old town areas.
Volunteers are invited to take part in workcamps organised in many areas of France. The work includes clearing silt and debris from rivers and streams, stabilising banks and clearing vegetation;

clearing and maintaining footpaths and constructing new ones to give access to rural sites; restoring old buildings and converting them into meeting or sports centres; rebuilding villages or buildings which have been abandoned or fallen into disrepair; and creating environmental education centres in existing green spaces or laying out playgrounds in towns. Technical help and advice given by local craftsmen. Sports and social activities include festivals, concerts, exhibitions, evenings with the villagers, discovery of the region, crafts, sailing and windsurfing.

⚘ Ages 13-19 (25 hour week) and 19+ (35 hour week). Food and lodging in gîtes, tents or schools provided. Cost FF100 per day for ages 13-17, free for ages 17+. Volunteers prepare their own food and help with chores and pay their own travel costs. Registration fee FF800. Long-term work also available.

🕮 *Apply through partner organisation in country of residence. In the UK: Quaker International Social Projects or United Nations Association International Youth Service. See page 30 for registration details and addresses.*

JEUNESSE ET RECONSTRUCTION 10 rue de Trévise, 75009 Paris, France
✆ **(33 1) 47 70 15 88**
Aims to provide short-term practical aid towards the redevelopment of small rural communities, the understanding of the environment and to encourage local inhabitants to continue with the work. Recent projects involving **volunteers** have included clearing brushwood and cleaning riverbanks, repaving village streets, restoring ancient ramparts, castles and churches in Drôme; restoring a Roman road and medieval tower in Hautes-Alpes; restoring a 14th century château, a watermill and a bread oven in Haute-Loire; and thatching a summer house, cleaning and renovating a stone bridge, replanting grass on ski slopes and clearing rivers in Puy-de-Dome. Tasks involve masonry,

woodwork, carpentry, painting, electrical work, roofing and other manual work. Discussions held in the evenings and at weekends, centring on environmental problems. Camps are run on a democratic basis; volunteers decide how to go about the project, when to work, rest, shop and cook.

⚘ Ages 17-35. Parental consent needed for those under 18. Applicants should preferably have previous workcamp experience. 7 hour day, 5 day week. 2/3+ weeks, April-September. Basic accommodation provided in schools, dormitories, tents, mills or barns. Volunteers should take a sleeping bag. Food, prepared by the volunteers, and insurance provided. Volunteers pay their own travel costs. Registration fee FF425. 🕮 *UK applicants may apply through the British Trust for Conservation Volunteers, Room IWH, 36 St Mary's Street, Wallingford, Oxfordshire OX10 0EU ✆ Wallingford (01491) 839766.*

KLAUS & JEAN ERHARDT Bardou, 34390 Olargues, France
✆ **(33) 67 97 72 43**
The village of Bardou is a living museum of medieval farming life and a retreat for artists and writers. **Volunteers** are required to help in the restoration of 16th century stone houses, plus farm maintenance and the care of a flock of 200 prizewinning Bizet sheep.

⚘ Ages 20+. No experience necessary. 16 hour week. May-June and September-November. French useful but not essential. Accommodation in the village and social activities provided. Volunteers pay own food, insurance and travel costs.

REMPART (Union des Associations pour la Réhabilitation et l'Entretien des Monuments et du Patrimoine Artistique), 1 rue des Guillemites, 75004 Paris, France
Aims to improve the way of life through a better understanding of and a greater respect for the archaeological, architectural and natural heritage and environment through the restoration of

endangered buildings and monuments. A grouping of over 140 autonomous associations, providing a wide variety of projects involving **volunteers** in the restoration of medieval towns, cities, châteaux, fortresses, religious buildings, farms, ancient villages, roads, forges, walls, wind/watermills, Gallo-Roman amphitheatres and baths, churches and post-medieval fortresses, houses, villages and castles, old industrial sites plus contemporary murals, ramparts, churches, underground passages, paths, ski runs and steam engines. Work includes masonry, woodwork, carpentry, roofing, interior decorating, restoration and clearance work, plus carrying out surveys, technical photography and filing. Opportunities for sports, exploring the region, crafts, music, cinema and taking part in local festivities.

⊕ Ages 14/18+. There is no upper age limit, anyone feeling young is welcome, and some camps accept families. Previous experience not necessary. Some knowledge of French needed. 30-35 hour week. 2-4 weeks, Easter and June-September; a few camps are open throughout the year.

Cost approx FF45 per day for food and accommodation in huts, old buildings or tents, with self-catering facilities; a few camps are free. Volunteers help with camp duties, pay their own fares, and should take a sleeping bag. Applicants can choose which project they would like to work on from the workcamp programme and contact addresses are given. Registration fee FF200 includes insurance. Also arranges courses in restoration techniques, artistic activities and environmental studies. **D PH**

🖎 Write for further information and application form enclosing 3 IRCs.

RESTANQUES ET MURETS DE VENASQUE Mairie, 84210 Venasque, France

Volunteers required for workcamps with an environmental theme in the village of Venasque, near Avignon. Work involves environmental management and the restoration of ancient monuments.

⊕ Ages 18+. No experience necessary. 25-30 hours per week, July-August, with work taking place in the mornings and afternoons devoted to leisure activities. Board, lodging and insurance provided, and excursions arranged to local places of interest. Cost FF400-FF500 covers membership fee and registration. No fares or wages paid. 🖎 Apply by 30 June.

LA SABRANENQUE CENTRE INTERNATIONAL rue de la Tour de l'Oume, 30290 Saint Victor la Coste, France

A small, non-profitmaking organisation that has been working since 1969 to preserve, restore and reconstruct abandoned rural sites, and bring them back to life. Aims to give **volunteers** the chance to discover the pleasure of working directly on genuine rural restoration projects while being part of a cooperative team. After completing the reconstruction of the medieval village of Saint Victor la Coste, 25km north of Avignon, La Sabranenque now works on several sites in nearby villages. Volunteers work in small teams, learning traditional construction techniques on-the-job from experienced leaders. Work can include masonry, stone cutting, floor or roof tiling, interior restoration, drystone walling, path paving and planting trees. 1 day per session spent visiting the region, which is rich in ancient monuments.

⊕ Ages 18+. No experience necessary. 2+ weeks, 1 June-30 August. Cost FF100 per day includes full board accommodation in restored houses. Registration fee FF200.

SOLIDARITÉS JEUNESSES 38 rue du Faubourg St Denis, 75010 Paris, France

An international movement open to all who share a common concern for lasting peace and justice in the world. **Volunteers** are required to work in international teams on summer projects aimed at offering a service in an area of need and promoting self-help within the community; promoting international

understanding and the discussion of social problems; and offering young people the chance to live as a group and take these experiences into the context of daily life. Volunteers are needed to help in small rural communities, preserving their heritage by carrying out restoration and salvage work on old buildings and the environment. Recent projects have included restoring the ruins of a monument and organising a sound and light show to display the tower during a village festival; clearing and repairing footpaths, and restoring an old village in the Drôme region; renovating medieval castles, churches, chapels and traditional country houses; clearing moats; renovating an old train and railway in the Gironde; clearing canals in the Cévennes, and repairing the banks of the river Hérault; studying the medicinal and nutritional values of forgotten plants, and creating a nature reserve. Sports, social activities and village festivities organised.
⊕ Ages 15-17 and 18+. 6 hour day, 30 hour week. 3 weeks, July-August. Food, accommodation in tents or barns and work accident insurance provided. No fares or wages paid. **D PH**

🐝 *Apply through partner organisation in country of residence. In the UK: Christian Movement for Peace or United Nations Association International Youth Service. See page 30 for registration details and addresses.*

COURIERS / REPS

BELLE FRANCE Bayham Abbey, Lamberhurst, Kent TN3 8BG
✆ **Lamberhurst (01892) 890885**
Organise bicycle and walking holidays in Provence, the Loire Valley, the Dordogne and the Auvergne. Limited number of positions available for **representatives**. Applicants must have a thorough knowledge of French, good manual dexterity, a clean driving licence and two years driving experience. Training given.
⊕ Ages 21+. 2½-3 months minimum,

mid May-end September. Salary £300 per calendar month. Accommodation in caravan, personal insurance and return travel costs from London provided. Applicants should note that areas are very rural and there is likely to be little in the way of night life. Interviews held prior to appointment. *UK nationals only.*

BLADON LINES Personnel Department, 56-58 Putney High Street, London SW15 1SF
✆ **0181-785 2200**
Opportunities for **representatives** to work in ski resorts. Work involves helping with coach transfers, looking after guests, providing information, and ensuring everything is running smoothly.
⊕ Ages 24+. Relevant experience an advantage; fluent French essential. Applicants must be prepared to work hard but will get time to ski. Season lasts December-May. Salary £50-£100 per week, depending on size of resort. Board, lodging, return travel, insurance, ski pass and ski hire provided. Small charge for uniform. Training course held in London before departure.

**CANVAS HOLIDAYS LTD
12 Abbey Park Place, Dunfermline, Fife KY12 7PD**
Provides accommodation for families in ready-erected fully equipped tents and mobile homes. Positions available as **resident couriers, children's couriers** and **watersports couriers**. The work involves a daily routine of cleaning as customers arrive and depart, providing information and advice on the local attractions and essential services and helping to sort out any problems that might arise. 7 day week job with no fixed hours; the workload varies from day to day. At the beginning and end of the season there is a period of physical work when tents are put up and prepared for the customers or taken down and stored for the winter. Other tasks include administration, book-keeping and stock control. Children's couriers are responsible for a number of children during various

periods of the day or evening, and are expected to organise a variety of games, activities and competitions within the limitations of the campsite, and be flexible to cope with the weather, varying numbers and limited preparation time. Applicants should have previous experience with children, through nursing, teacher training or group playschemes, and be able to use their initiative to develop ideas for activities. ⊕ Ages 18-25. Applicants are normally those with a year between school and further education, undergraduates or graduates. They need to be enthusiastic, practical, reliable, self-motivated, able to turn their hand to new and varied tasks, and with a sense of humour. 6 months, April-October. Return travel, dependent on successful completion of contract, accommodation in frame tents and bicycle for use on site provided. Salary £85 per week. 🐿 *Applications accepted anytime; interviews commence November for the following season.*

CARISMA HOLIDAYS
Bethel House, Heronsgate Road, Chorleywood, Hertfordshire WD3 5BB ✆ **Chorleywood (01923) 284235**
Organises holidays in tents and mobile homes on beach sites along the west coast of France. **Managers** and **couriers** required to be responsible for client families. Work involves welcoming families, providing information and advice, cleaning and maintaining tents and mobile homes, and babysitting. ⊕ Ages 18+. Applicants should have a helpful and friendly disposition and experience of dealing with people. Good spoken French and English essential. Working hours vary; couriers are expected to work early May-end September or late June-early September. Salary £65-£90 per week depending on responsibility and experience. Self-catering accommodation provided in tents or mobile homes. Full training given on site at start of season. Travel costs paid. *EEA nationals only.*

CLUB CANTABRICA HOLIDAYS LTD **Overseas Department, Holiday House, 146-148 London Road, St Albans, Hertfordshire AL1 1PQ**
Organises camping holidays, providing fully equipped tents, caravans and mobile homes. Vacancies exist for **couriers** and **maintenance staff** to work the whole summer season, early May-early October, in Port Grimaud, Antibes, Presqu'ile and Canet. 6 day week. ⊕ Ages 21+. Salary from £55 per week, plus bonus at end of season. Experience an advantage, as is a good knowledge of French. Self-catering accommodation in tents or caravans, travel costs from Watford and insurance provided. 🐿 *Apply enclosing cv and SAE/IRCs. EEA nationals only.*

CRYSTAL HOLIDAYS **Crystal House, The Courtyard, Arlington Road, Surbiton, Surrey KT6 6BW** ✆ **0181-241 5111**
Tour operator arranging year-round holidays throughout France, and winter skiing holidays in the French Alps. **Representatives** are required to meet and greet clients and be responsible for their welfare during the holiday. **Ski guides** also needed during winter. ⊕ Ages 22-35. Previous experience desirable and fluent French essential. Approx 60 hour, 7 day week, May-October and December-April. Basic salary plus commission; board, lodging, insurance, travel costs and uniform provided. One week training seminar at beginning of each season. 🐿 *Apply January/February for summer season, April/May for winter season.*

ESPRIT HOLIDAYS LTD **Oaklands, Reading Road North, Fleet, Hampshire GU13 8AA** ✆ **Fleet (01252) 625177**
Organises winter ski holidays in the French Alps. Requires **resort representatives** to deal with most aspects of a guest's holiday: dealing with ski hire, lift passes, ski schools and any immediate problems arising from chalet

operations or guests' requirements. Hours vary; 6 day week, December-April. Board and accommodation provided. Pocket money plus lift pass, skis, boots and ski jacket. Full medical insurance cover; travel costs paid if season completed.
⊕ Ages 23+. Applicants must speak French, should have a minimum parallel skiing standard and able to work on own initiative. Experience of working in service industry desirable. 6 day training programme in France in December. Also summer **resort representatives** to work in Morzine. Similar duties but more involvement in running hotel.
⊕ Ages 23+. Applicants should be French-speaking, preferably with some catering ability. Programme runs late June-early September.
☜ *Apply June/July for winter season; February/March for summer season. EEA nationals only.*

EUROCAMP Summer Jobs (Ref WH), PO Box 170, Liverpool L70 IES ✆ **Knutsford (01565) 625522**
One of Europe's leading tour operators, specialising in providing quality camping and mobile home holidays for families throughout Europe.
Campsite couriers are required: work involves cleaning tents and equipment prior to the arrival of new customers; checking, replacing and making repairs on equipment; replenishing gas supplies; keeping basic accounts and reporting on a weekly basis to England. Couriers are also expected to meet new arrivals and assist holidaymakers with any problems that arise; organise activities and parties; provide information on local tourist attractions and maintain an information noticeboard. At the beginning and end of the season couriers are also expected to help in erecting and dismantling tents. Couriers need to be flexible to meet the needs of customers and be on hand where necessary; they will be able to organise their own free time as the workload allows.
⊕ Ages 18+. Applicants should be independent, adaptable, reliable,

physically fit, have plenty of initiative and relish a challenging and responsible position. Good working knowledge of French also necessary. Preference given to those able to work the whole season, April-September/October; contracts also available for first half season, April-mid July and second half season, mid July-September/October.
Children's couriers also required, with the energy and enthusiasm to organise a wide range of exciting activities for ages 4-13. Experience of working within this age range essential, but language ability is not a requirement.
⊕ Ages 18+. Children's couriers must be available for the whole season, May-September.
For both positions the salary is £95 per week. Training is provided together with accommodation in frame tent with cooking facilities, insurance and return travel. ☜ *Early application by telephone preferred; interviews start September/ October. UK/EEA passport-holders only.*

FRENCH COUNTRY CAMPING Assistant Operations Manager, 126 Hempstead Road, Kings Langley, Hertfordshire WD4 8AL ✆ **Watford (01923) 261316**
Operates self-drive family holidays providing fully furnished and equipped tents and mobile homes. Vacancies exist for **operations team members** plus a limited number of **campsite couriers**. Operations teams consist of 3-5 members and a supervisor travelling around France, responsible for setting up or closing down campsites. 3-4 days are spent at each site and the work involves long car journeys and heavy lifting work so applicants must be fit and capable of working long hours, maybe in poor weather. They will be expected to show initiative and an ability to work without supervision. 3-4 weeks, May or September, depending on unpredictable factors such as weather. Applicants should have sound organisational ability and a mature, outgoing personality. French language ability essential for courier posts, useful for other positions.

End May-beginning September.
Work as campsite couriers entails
preparing tents or mobile homes,
welcoming clients, occasionally
organising social activities, and dealing
with any problems which may arise. Mid
May-mid July or mid July-mid September.
⊕ Ages 19+ (operations team members)
or 21+ (couriers). Salary approx £95
per week. Accommodation in tents with
cooking facilities and insurance provided.
Travel expenses paid, provided company
transport is used when available.
EEA nationals only.

**FRENCH LIFE MOTORING
HOLIDAYS Overseas Personnel
Manager, 26 Church Road,
Horsforth, Leeds LS18 5LG**
✆ 0113-239 0077
Organises self-drive holidays with fully
equipped tents and caravans on
campsites, and requires **site
representatives**.
Work involves welcoming clients and
looking after them during their holiday,
cleaning and maintaining tents and
caravans, organising excursions, caring
for and entertaining children, providing a
babysitting service, and running evening
entertainment activities such as
barbecues, wine and cheese and fancy
dress parties. Representatives on call
24 hours a day, usually 6 days a week.
⊕ Ages 21+. Applicants should have
experience of dealing with people, and
be used to hard physical work. They
should be dynamic, reliable, hard
working, conscientious and loyal with
the ability to work as part of a team,
plus the staying power to last the whole
season. Working knowledge of French
essential. All applicants must be available
from end April-end September.
Accommodation in shared frame tents
with own bedroom area, self-catering
cooking facilities and return travel
provided. Salary approx £85 per week.
All staff are required to take part in a
training programme in April.
✎ *Early application advisable - recruitment
starts December, interviews commence
mid-January. UK or French nationals only.*

**HAVEN EUROPE Northney
Marina, Northney Road, Hayling
Island, Hampshire PO11 0NH**
Tour operator organising self-drive
package holidays, with accommodation in
luxury mobile homes and tents.
Seasonal **park managers** required to
work on parks in coastal and inland
regions. Work involves preparing
accommodation, welcoming guests and
dealing with any problems that arise.
Tiger Club couriers also required, to
work with children and organise
entertainment. Experience preferred
but not essential, as training is given.
Knowledge of French essential.
⊕ Ages 18+. 40+ hour week, although
hours vary. May-September. Salary
according to workload. Accommodation
provided in self-catering mobile homes
or tents. Personal insurance and travel
expenses provided. *UK nationals only.*

**KEYCAMP HOLIDAYS 92-96 Lind
Road, Sutton, Surrey SM1 4PL**
✆ 0181-395 8170
One of the UK's largest self-drive
camping and mobile home tour
operators, offering holidays on over
100 campsites in Europe.
Campsite couriers required to work
for 3-6 months in an outdoor
environment. Main duties include
providing clients with information,
organising social and sporting activities,
cleaning mobile homes and tents, and
providing activities for children.
⊕ Ages 18+. Knowledge of French
desirable. March-July or July-September.
Accommodation, uniform, training
provided. Competitive salary.
✎ *Application requests by postcard to
above address. UK/EEA nationals only.*

**LOTUS SUPERTRAVEL Alpine
Operations Department, Hobbs
Court, 2 Jacob Street, London SE1
2BT** ✆ 0171-962 9933
Arranges skiing holidays in the alpine
resorts of Méribel, Courchevel and Val
d'Isère. Opportunities for **resort
representatives**, responsible for
looking after guests and supervising staff.

⊕ Ages 24+. Work involves travelling to the airport each weekend to welcome guests; organising their ski passes, ski hire and ski school; informing them of local events; overseeing the work of chalet girls and ensuring that chalets are kept in perfect running order. Applicants must be available for the whole season, early December-end April. Approx 40+ hours per week. Board, lodging, ski pass, insurance, ski and boot hire and return travel provided; also uniform in return for approx £50 contribution. Salary £55-£85 per week, paid in local currency. Training course held in London before departure, plus individual session to learn about the resort. *UK/EEA passport holders only.*

MATTHEWS HOLIDAYS LTD
8 Bishopsmead Parade, East Horsley, Surrey KT24 6RP
✆ **East Horsley (01483) 284044**
Operates holidays in mobile homes on campsites mainly in Normandy, Brittany and on the Atlantic coast. **Representatives** required to work on sites, welcoming clients, maintaining good relations, providing information and advice and cleaning mobile homes. No experience necessary, but fluent French essential.
⊕ Ages 20+. 35 hour week; reps are expected to work the whole season, early May-end September. Salary FF850 per week. Self-catering accommodation in caravans/mobile homes, medical insurance and travel costs provided. *British nationals only.*

PGL YOUNG ADVENTURE LTD
Personnel Department, Alton Court, Penyard Lane (878), Ross-On-Wye, Herefordshire HR9 5NR
✆ **Ross-on-Wye (01989) 767833**
Organises outdoor adventure holidays for young people and adults in the Ardèche and on the Mediterranean. Activities include canoeing, sailing and windsurfing. **Couriers/group leaders** are required, accompanying children aged 12-17, starting and finishing in Manchester, Birmingham and London. The position involves complete responsibility for the group whilst travelling and at the centre, dealing with pocket money, illness and general coordination, including lights out, and helping with the evening programme.
⊕ Ages 21+. Applicants should have a strong sense of responsibility, total commitment, enjoy the company of young people, be self-motivated, tolerant, flexible, positive, mature, with vitality, a good sense of humour, stamina, energy, enthusiasm, and a fairly extrovert personality. Good spoken French essential; experience in working with groups of young people, preferably abroad, in informal or formal settings, and ability to cope with demands on one's time needed. July-September. Couriers accompany groups on 10-day trips, and usually take 2/3 trips during the season. Return travel from the UK, full board accommodation in frame tents and health insurance provided. Sports and social facilities available, plus participation in programmed activities. Pocket money from £75 per 10-day trip. *Applications should ideally be made November-April.*

SIMPLY SKI Chiswick Gate,
598-608 Chiswick High Road, London W4 5RT ✆ **0181-742 2541**
Organises winter ski holidays in the French Alps. **Representatives** required to liaise with clients and provide ski guidance. 54 hour week; 20 weeks, December-April. Fully comprehensive insurance, board and accommodation provided. Salary £60 per week.
⊕ Ages 22-40. Applicants should be able skiers and speak fluent French. Training provided. *Apply as soon as possible.*

SKI TOTAL 10 Hill Street,
Richmond, Surrey ✆ **0181-948 3535**
Tour operator arranging skiing holidays in France. Opportunities for **ski resort managers**, to organise all aspects of clients' holidays, supervise staff and ensure standards are maintained with possible ski guiding up to 3½ days per

week. Salary £70-£90 per week.

⚕ Ages 23+. Applicants must be hard working, resourceful, patient, outgoing, experienced resort managers, who get along with and can handle people well at all levels. **Ski guides/technicians/handymen/women** also required. Duties include clearing snow, fitting gas bottles, unloading deliveries, repairs, maintenance and ski guiding approx 4 days per week.

⚕ Ages 21+. Applicants should be hard working, friendly, good skiers with some ski technician experience and clean driving licence. Some French useful. Salary £50-£70 per week.

All staff work a 40-50 hour, 6 day week, December-April. Board, accommodation, full medical insurance and travel fares provided. One week pre-season training programme at resort. ✉ *Apply from June onwards. UK nationals only.*

SKIBOUND/TRAVELBOUND Olivier House, 18 Marine Parade, Brighton, East Sussex BN2 1TL
The largest independent group tour operator, specialising in winter sports tours for schools and adults, and in activity tours and excursions. **Area managers, hotel/chalet managers** and **representatives** required for the winter and spring/summer seasons, December-April and May-August in the French Alps. Posts involve a considerable amount of client contact, and applicants must be presentable and keen to work hard.

⚕ Ages 21+. Good knowledge of French required for representatives and preferably for managers; previous experience an advantage. Insurance, travel and full board accommodation provided. Salary according to level of responsibility.

SKIWORLD 41 North End Road, West Kensington, London W14 8SQ ✆ **0171-602 4826**
Opportunities for **representatives** to work in French ski resorts. Work

involves meeting guests, dealing with guests' queries, arranging transfers and ski packs.

⚕ Ages 20-35. Applicants should speak French and be able to ski. Vacancies from December onwards; 7 day week for approx 17 weeks, hours vary. Accommodation provided. Salary £50 per week plus commission. £30 deposit on accepting position. Training and briefing sessions provided.
✉ *Apply May onwards. EEA nationals only.*

SNOWTIME LTD 96 Belsize Lane, London NW3 5BE ✆ **0171-433 3336**
Organises luxury winter skiing holidays in Méribel. Requires **representatives** to ensure that high standards are maintained, that clients enjoy their holiday, and to liaise with local companies, agents and suppliers.

⚕ Ages 24+. Ideal applicants will be fluent in French, outgoing and cheerful with strong organisational and communication skills. Must be available December-May. Salary from £45 per week, plus accommodation and food, ski equipment, ski pass, return travel from London and insurance. **B D PH**

SOLAIRE INTERNATIONAL HOLIDAYS 1158 Stratford Road, Hall Green, Birmingham B28 8AF ✆ **0121-778 5061**
Organises camping and mobile home holidays in Normandy, Paris, Brittany, the Loire and Vendée, Dordogne, southwest France and on the Mediterranean. **Seasonal staff** are required to prepare tents and mobile homes at the beginning of the season in May and then close down at the end of the season in September/October. During the season staff act as couriers, ensuring the smooth running of the camps, and undertake some maintenance work. **Children's couriers** also required.

⚕ Ages 18+. No previous experience necessary. Fluency in French preferable but not essential. No fixed hours. Wages £55-£80 per week. Accommodation in tents or mobile homes, insurance and travel provided.

SUSI MADRON'S CYCLING FOR SOFTIES 2 & 4 Birch Polygon, Rusholme, Manchester M14 5HX ✆ 0161-248 8282

Organises a variety of cycling holidays in the regions of Beaujolais & Jura, Cognac & Charente, Dordogne & Garonne, Loire, Mayenne & Sarthe, Provence & Camargue, Rhône, Tarn and Venise Verte. Vacancies exist for **regional assistants**. The work includes maintaining cycles to a high standard, welcoming holiday makers, helping in emergencies and providing on the spot information about the region. 2-3 months, 1 May-1 August, 1 June-1 August, 23 July-28 September. ⊕ Ages 20+. Applicants should be mature, self-confident and adaptable; able to liaise with diverse groups from guests to hoteliers. Fluent English and French essential. Hours variable with one day off per week. Salary £75 per week plus bonus. Self-catering flat or house accommodation, travel and insurance provided. Full training given in all aspects of the job before work commences, and high level of support in place. ✎ Apply November-January.

VENUE HOLIDAYS 21 Christchurch Road, Ashford, Kent TN23 1XD

Small family company offering self-drive holidays with fully-equipped tents on campsites near Canet Plage in Roussillon and in the Dordogne. **Representatives** required to clean and maintain accommodation, sort out customers' problems and organise social events for adults and children. At beginning and end of season representatives assist with the setting up and dismantling of the operation. No fixed hours; workload varies from day to day. Season lasts April-October, with minimum requirement to work all July and August. ⊕ Ages 18-30. Previous experience of working with the public desirable, as is a working knowledge of French. Applicants should be fit, able to work in hot conditions, mentally alert and practical, with a pleasant, easygoing personality. Salary approx £60 per week, with possibility of bonuses. Tented accommodation, insurance and return fare provided. ✎ Postal applications only.

DOMESTIC

ACORN VENTURE LTD Personnel Department, 137 Worcester Road, Hagley, Stourbridge DY9 0NW

An activity holiday company catering for school groups at camping centres in Pas de Calais, Normandy and the Ardèche. Experienced **catering staff** required. Fluency in French an advantage. ⊕ Ages 18+. Minimum 50 hour, 6 day week. Applicants are expected to work the full season, May-September. Salary approx £40-£45 per week. All meals and accommodation in tents provided, as well as insurance and cost of return travel from ferry ports. **PH** ✎ Apply in writing with cv by end of February. If no reply within 28 days assume application unsuccessful.

ALPOTELS AGENCY PO Box 388, London SW1X 8LX

Carries out aptitude tests at the request of hotels for 40 winter and 20 summer jobs as **waitresses** and **chambermaids** or **night porters**, **waiters** and **dishwashers**. ⊕ Ages 18+. Good knowledge of French needed. All jobs involve long hours and hard work as part of a professional team of French workers. 8 hour day with 1 day free per week. December-April or June-September. Pay approx £150 per week; board, lodging and insurance provided. Interview fee £1 plus subscription to JITA Club (£30 plus £15 per week). ✎ Closing dates for interviews: 30 September (winter), 30 April (summer). EEA nationals only.

BLADON LINES Personnel Department, 56-58 Putney High Street, London SW15 1SF ✆ 0181-785 2200

Opportunities for **chalet girls** to work in ski resorts. Work involves cleaning

chalets, making beds, looking after guests, shopping and preparing meals. **Chefs**, **handymen** and **cleaners** also needed. Limited amount of work also available in Corsica, May-October.
⊕ Ages 21+. Experience and/or qualifications in catering or domestic work essential. Hours are very variable; applicants must be prepared to work hard but will get time to ski. Season lasts December-May. Salary from approx £40 per week. Board, lodging, return travel, insurance, ski pass and ski hire provided. Small charge made for uniform. One-day training course in London held before departure.
EEA nationals only.

CRYSTAL HOLIDAYS Crystal House, The Courtyard, Arlington Road, Surbiton, Surrey KT6 6BW
Ⓒ **0181-241 5111**
Tour operator arranging skiing holidays at resorts throughout the French Alps. **Chalet staff** required to cook daily breakfast, afternoon tea and 3-course evening meal for clients, and keep chalets clean and tidy.
⊕ Ages 20-35. Catering qualifications or experience essential. Approx 60 hour, 6½ day week, December-April. Basic salary plus commission, board, lodging, insurance, travel costs and uniform provided. 1 week training seminar held at beginning of each season.
🦉 *Apply April/May.*

DISCOVER LIMITED Timbers, Oxted Road, Godstone, Surrey RH9 8AD Ⓒ **Godstone (01883) 744392**
Organises field trips and adventure holidays for young people. Small number of vacancies available for **cooks**, **assistant cooks** and **general assistants** at field study/activity centre in Mont Lozère. Experience useful but not essential; knowledge of French helpful. Nonsmokers preferred.
⊕ Ages 18+. No fixed hours, April-October. Full board accommodation provided and travel costs paid. Salary £30-£65 per week. Friendly and relaxed

working environment. Staff can usually take part in excursions with visiting groups. *UK nationals only.*

ESPRIT HOLIDAYS LTD Oaklands, Reading Road North, Fleet, Hampshire GU13 8AA
Ⓒ **Fleet (01252) 625177**
Organises winter ski holidays in the French Alps. Requires **chalet staff** to shop, cook, clean and host guests. **Nannies** also required to run in-chalet crèches and Snowclub, caring for children aged 4 months to 8 years.
⊕ Ages 18+. Chalet staff should have City and Guilds 706 or equivalent qualification. Nannies should be NNEB, BTEC or RGN qualified. Hours will vary; 6 day week, December-April. Board and accommodation provided plus pocket money, lift pass, skis, boots and ski jacket. Full medical insurance cover; travel costs paid if season completed. French useful but not essential.
4 day training programme provided in December.
Also requires **chalet cook** and several **nannies** for summer season in Morzine. Cook should have commercial catering experience; nannies should be NNEB, BTEC or RGN qualified.
⊕ Ages 20+. French useful, but flexibility and enthusiasm more important. Programme runs late June-early September. 🦉 *Apply June/July for winter season; February/March for summer season. EEA nationals only.*

EUROPEAN WATERWAYS 25 Kingswood Creek, Wraybury, Staines, Middlesex
Operates floating holidays on French canals. Vacancies exist for *cordon bleu* **chefs** to work on hotel barges in Burgundy, Alsace-Lorraine and the Midi area of southern France. Experience, driving licence and some knowledge of French or German essential.
⊕ Ages 25+. 50+ hours per week. 6+ months, throughout the year; peak season April-October. Salary £90-£150 per week, depending on experience. On-board accommodation, food and

travel expenses provided, but not insurance. *UK nationals only.*

LOTUS SUPERTRAVEL Alpine Operations Department, Hobbs Court, 2 Jacob Street, London SE1 2BL ✆ 0171-962 9933

Arranges skiing holidays in the alpine resorts of Méribel, Courchevel and Val d'Isère. Opportunities for **chalet staff** responsible for looking after guests and keeping chalet clean and tidy.
⊕ Ages 21+. Work involves cooking, cleaning, acting as host/hostess, sitting down to dinner with guests, advising them on skiing areas and keeping them up to date with events in the resort. Chalet staff must work to a budget and account for expenditure. Applicants must have cooking experience and preferably qualifications, be capable of running a chalet of approx 8 guests and have an outgoing and helpful personality. Applicants must be available for the whole season, early December-end April. Approx 40+ hours per week. Board, lodging, ski pass, insurance, ski and boot hire and return travel provided; also uniform in return for approx £50 contribution. Salary £60 per week, paid in local currency. Training course held in London before departure. *UK/EEA passport holders only.*

PGL YOUNG ADVENTURE LTD Personnel Department, Alton Court, Penyard Lane (878), Ross-on-Wye, Herefordshire HR9 5NR ✆ Ross-on-Wye (01989) 767833

Organises outdoor adventure holidays for young people and adults in the Ardèche and on the Mediterranean. Activities include canoeing, sailing and windsurfing. **Kitchen assistants, housemaids, caterers/cooks, chalet maids, bar/shop staff** and **organisers** required.
⊕ Ages 20+. Applicants should have relevant experience and be energetic and enthusiastic, reliable and mature, adaptable, friendly and efficient, with a sense of humour. May-September. Jobs are usually for approx 8 week periods

but sometimes for the whole season. Staff also recruited for very short periods over the Spring Bank Holiday. Return travel from Dover, full board accommodation in frame tents and health insurance provided. 1 day free per week. Pocket money per week approx FF330 (housemaids, kitchen assistants, chalet maids, bar/shop staff and bar/shop organisers), or from £80 (cooks). Sports and social facilities available, plus participation in programmed activities.
☞ *Applicants available in May have a greater chance of selection. Applications should ideally be made November-April.*

SILVER SKI HOLIDAYS Conifers House, Grove Green Lane, Maidstone, Kent ME14 5JW

Couples required to **staff ski chalets**. Work involves hosting and running a fully catered chalet programme; providing breakfast, afternoon tea and dinner as well as a ski guiding service.
⊕ Ages 23/25-40. Applicants must be able to demonstrate some catering/housekeeping experience and should preferably run their own home in the UK. They should be skiers of above average ability with an outgoing personality. French language useful but not essential. Hours will vary; 6 day week, for approx 20 weeks, December-May, must work whole season. Board, accommodation and pocket money plus commission provided. Two week training programme. ☞ *Apply May-October. UK nationals only.*

SIMPLY SKI Chiswick Gate, 598-608 Chiswick High Road, London W4 5RT ✆ 0181-742 2541

Organises winter ski holidays in the Savoie area of the French Alps. **Chalet girls** and **nannies** required. Chalet girls cook and clean; applicants should have catering qualification. Nannies care for infants aged 6+ months; applicants should have a NNEB or equivalent qualification.
⊕ Ages 18-40. 54 hour week; 20 weeks, December-April. Fully comprehensive insurance, board and accommodation

provided. Salary £45 per week (chalet girls); £48 per week (nannies). **Handymen** also required, with experience of mechanics, carpentry, electrics and basic all-round work. Salary £60 per week. All applicants should speak French. Training provided. 🖎 *Apply as soon as possible.*

SKI ENTERPRISE (CHALET HOLIDAYS) Owners Abroad Overseas Recruitment, Astral Towers, Betts Way, Crawley, West Sussex RH10 2GX ℗ Crawley (01293) 588222

Arranges chalet holidays in the Alps. **Chalet hosts** required to work in ski resorts. Work involves keeping chalets clean and tidy, making beds, cooking meals and acting as host/hostess. ⊕ Ages 21+. *Cordon bleu* cookery qualification and/or extensive experience of catering essential. Applicants should also have a basic knowledge of accounts/ budgeting, conversational French, German or Italian, outgoing, friendly personality with the ability to put people at their ease. They also need stamina and a sense of humour. Hours variable; applicants must be prepared to work hard. 6 days per week, December-May. Pay up to £75 per week. Board, lodging, return travel, medical insurance, seasonal ski pass, skis and boots provided. *EEA nationals only.*

SKI TOTAL/FRENCH GOLF COTTAGES 10 Hill Street, Richmond, Surrey ℗ 0181-948 3535

Tour operator arranging skiing holidays in France. Requires **chalet staff** to do catering, cleaning, washing up, bedmaking for 8-12 people in self-contained chalets. Also **golf chalet girls** required for summer months. Salary £50 per week. ⊕ Ages 21+. Applicants should be capable and hard working with plenty of cooking experience. A sense of humour, patience and the ability to get on with groups of people of varied ages and backgrounds essential, as is a knowledge of French and a clean driving licence.

Cooks also required, to cater for 14-30 people per week, run a kitchen and supervise junior staff. ⊕ Ages 21+. Applicants must have experience and a proven record of cooking for large numbers of people. Salary £60-£80 per week. Driving licence and some French useful. Opportunities for **chalet helpers/ assistant cooks** to do cooking, cleaning, washing up, making beds. ⊕ Ages 19+. Salary £40 per week. Applicants must have experience, an aptitude for hard work, enthusiasm, a sense of humour and an outgoing personality.

All staff work a 40-50 hour, 6 day week, December-April. Accommodation, board, full medical insurance and travel costs provided. 1 week pre-season training programme at resort. 🖎 *Apply from June onwards. UK nationals only.*

SKIBOUND/TRAVELBOUND Olivier House, 18 Marine Parade, Brighton, East Sussex BN2 1TL

The largest independent group tour operator, specialising in tours for schools and adults, and in activity tours and excursions. Staff required for all grades of **hotel work** in the winter and spring/summer seasons, December-April and May-August, in the French Alps and Normandy. Posts involve client contact and applicants must be presentable and keen to work hard. ⊕ Ages 18+. Previous experience useful; catering experience required for some posts. Insurance, travel and full board accommodation provided. Salary according to level of responsibility.

SKIWORLD 41 North End Road, West Kensington, London ℗ 0171-602 4826

Opportunities for **chalet girls** to work in French ski resorts. Work involves cooking and cleaning for guests. ⊕ Ages 20-35. Vacancies from December onwards; 6 day week, approx 17 weeks, hours vary. Applicants should be outgoing, hardworking and have some catering experience. Salary £35 per week plus commission. £30 deposit required on accepting position. Accommodation, training and briefing sessions provided. **Chefs** and **cleaners** also needed. ☃ *Apply May onwards.* *EEA nationals only.*

SNOWTIME LTD 96 Belsize Lane, London NW3 5BE ✆ **0171-433 3336**
Organises luxury winter skiing holidays in Méribel. **Chalet girls** required to run chalets single-handed. Duties include cooking to a high standard, shopping, budgeting, housekeeping and acting as hostess.
⚘ Ages 18+. Applicants must have experience of cooking in a professional environment/for private dinner parties, preferably holding a recognised cooking qualification. Must also be outgoing and cheerful, willing to work hard and able to organise themselves. Salary from £35 per week plus benefits below.
Hotel girls also required to work in 2-star chalet hotels. Work involves cleaning, housekeeping, waitressing, reception work, some cooking (cakes and biscuits) and washing up.
⚘ Ages 18+. Cooking skills not essential, but experience in catering industry and basic French an advantage. Outgoing personality and willingness to work hard essential. Salary from £35 per week plus benefits below.
Waitresses and **bar people** required.
⚘ Ages 18+. Applicants should be conversant in French with cheerful and outgoing personality, willing to work hard and able to work quickly and efficiently. Experience in catering industry preferred. Salary from £35 per week plus benefits below.
Head and **assistant chefs** required.
⚘ Ages 18+. Previous experience essential (7061/2 preferred); working knowledge of French an advantage. Salary from £50 per week, plus benefits below.
Nannies required to run creche facilities.
⚘ Ages 18+. Applicants must be NNEB qualified, well-organised with basic cooking skills. Salary approx £100 per week plus benefits below.

For all positions applicants must be available December-May inclusive. Staff receive salary, accommodation, food, ski equipment, ski pass (except nannies), return travel from London and insurance. **B D PH**

SOLAIRE INTERNATIONAL HOLIDAYS 1158 Stratford Road, Hall Green, Birmingham B28 8AF ✆ **0121-778 5061**
Organises camping and mobile home holidays, and requires a **receptionist**, **bar staff** and **cleaners** to work on owned campsite in south Brittany.
⚘ Ages 18+ (20+ for bar staff). Fluency in French and English essential for receptionist and bar staff; other languages an advantage. 35-45 hour week. Wages £60-£80 per week; accommodation in tent, insurance and travel provided.

YSE LIMITED The Business Village, Broomhill Road, London SW18 4JQ ✆ **0181-871 5117**
Opportunities for **chalet girls** to work in ski resorts in the Val d'Isère. Work involves cooking, cleaning and acting as hostess. **Cooks** also required.
⚘ Ages strictly 21-40. Chalet girls should have relevant qualifications/experience. Cooks must have City & Guilds 706 1 & 2 or equivalent, as well as experience of cooking for 80+ people. French an advantage. 6 day, 35-40 hour week, late November-early May. Full board, travel costs, third party and medical insurance provided.
Also opportunities for **ski guides** who must be excellent skiers. One week pre-season training programme provided. Wages on application.
☃ *Apply from May. EEA nationals only.*

When applying to any organisation it is essential to mention Working Holidays 1995 and enclose a stamped, self-addressed A4 envelope, or if in another country, an addressed A4 envelope and at least two IRCs (International Reply Coupons, available from post offices).

FARMWORK /
GRAPE PICKING

A variety of seasonal farmwork is available, May-October. However those seeking this type of work will be competing against a large number of students as well as regular seasonal workers. This, added to the number of unemployed looking for work and to the decreasing need for manual labour due to mechanisation, often makes it difficult to find employment. Seasonal agricultural workers receive the national minimum wage, le SMIC, approx FF30 per hour. Accommodation and food not always provided; workers should take their own camping/cooking equipment.

The **grape harvest** takes place between approx 20 September and 30 October in the Alsace, Aquitaine, Beaujolais, Bordeaux, Burgundy, Champagne, the Loire Valley, Languedoc and Midi-Pyrénées regions. Three types of work are available: picking the grapes, collecting the baskets, or emptying baskets for which 20% more is paid. Work is generally for 8 hours a day and may include Sundays. Wages are usually slightly higher than SMIC rates, with board and lodging provided and deducted from gross earnings. Workers generally pay their own travel costs.

All agricultural work is physically demanding and can involve working long hours in all-weather conditions; accommodation may be very basic. See under the **Farmwork/Grape picking** heading in the **Work Profiles** section for further information. Those without a prearranged job are strongly advised to take enough money to cover the cost of their stay in France and their return fare, should they be unable to find work. Applications for employment can be made to the organisations listed below, or to the local national employment agency (ANPE) in the relevant areas, listed at the end of this section.

Applications should be written in French and sent a few months before work is due to start. Applicants should state the type of work they are willing to undertake and the period for which they will be available. Due to the heavy demand for this type of work, many ANPEs may be reluctant to enter into correspondence. Applicants can call in person at an ANPE a few days before work is due to start, but the chances of finding employment at this stage are limited. All applicants should have a working knowledge of French and a full passport. A birth certificate may be required by some employers in order for affiliation to the national insurance scheme.

Those interested in working on **organic farms** should check the classified section of the French bi-monthly review Nature et Progrès. They also publish Les Bonnes Addresses de la Bio, cost FF60 including postage, which lists opportunities for work on organic farms. Contact Nature et Progrès, Service Librairie, BP6, 69921 Oullins.

Seasons With adjustments depending on the weather, the following periods represent the best opportunities for agricultural work and grape picking.

Mid May-late June
Cherries and strawberries in the Rhône Valley, Central France and Perigord

June-August
Haymaking all over France

July-September
Gherkins and raspberries in Brittany the Centre, Southwest, the Auvergne and Aquitaine
Maize topping in the Auvergne and the Southwest

August-September
Tomatoes and tobacco in the Southwest, East and the Paris Basin
Mid-September-end October
Apples in Brittany, Normandy, the

Dordogne, Languedoc and Centre
Plums in Brittany, Dordogne and Médoc
Pears in the Rhône and Loire Valleys and
the Paris Basin.
Grapes in the Beaujolais, Bordeaux and
Languedoc regions

Throughout October
Grapes in the Pays de la Loire, Alsace,
Centre, Burgundy, Aquitaine and
Champagne regions

November-December
Chestnuts in the South, Ardèche and
Corsica

FERME APICOLE DE SABLE
**Joseph Barale, 47400 Grateloup,
France** ℰ **(33) 53 88 80 23** (evenings
only)
Farm devoted to the production of bees
and honey, situated in the heart of the
Aquitaine region, 100km from Bordeaux.
Currently open to visitors, tourists and
school groups. Can offer **placements**
to those with a genuine interest in
working with bees.
✦ Ages 18+. Applicants must be
nonsmokers, with good spoken French,
fit and healthy, willing to work very hard;
must not be allergic to bee stings.
Full board accommodation provided,
plus payment to be agreed according to
work undertaken. ✎ *Write for further
information.*

INTERNATIONAL FARM
EXPERIENCE PROGRAMME
**YFC Centre, N A C, Stoneleigh
Park, Kenilworth, Warwickshire
CV8 2LG** ℰ **Coventry (01203)
696584**
Provides assistance to young
agriculturalists and **horticulturalists**
by finding places in farms/nurseries
abroad enabling them to broaden their
knowledge of agricultural and
horticultural methods. Participants
usually live and work with a farming
family, the work being matched as far as
possible with the participant's
requirements. Entails physical work and

practical involvement. Basic wages plus
board and lodging.
✦ Ages 18-28. Applicants must have a
minimum of 2 years' practical
experience, of which at least one may be
at agricultural college, and intend to
make a career in agriculture or
horticulture. Valid driving licence
necessary. Participants pay own fares
and insurance. Registration fee £85.
✎ *UK applications to IFEP; others to IFEP
partner in home country.*

JEUNESSE ET
RECONSTRUCTION
**10 rue de Trévise, 75009 Paris,
France** ℰ **(33 1) 47 70 15 88**
Offers a large number of places on
grape picking camps in Beaujolais,
Champagne, Chablis, and Côte d'Or.
✦ Ages 16-30; applicants under 18 must
have parental consent. All participants
must supply a medical certificate. Up to
9 hour day, 7 day week. Applicants
should be free to work anytime, for at
least 8-10 days, and good harvests last
15-20 days, September and October.
As little as 48 hours' notice may be given
before work starts; applicants must be
prepared to leave for France at any time.
Food and basic accommodation usually
provided on the farm but participants
should take a sleeping bag. Wages
FF200-FF250 per day, from which board,
lodging and national insurance are
deducted. Participants arrange and pay
their own travel. Membership fee FF150.
✎ *Enclose IRCs to the value of FF10.*

ANPEs IN THE WINE
PRODUCING AREAS

Aquitaine Tour 2000, terrasse Front-
du-Médoc, 33706 Bordeaux Cedex

Bourgogne 7 rue des Corroyeurs,
21033 Dijon Cedex

6 rue Claude Debussy, 71000 Macon

Centre 3 passage des Albanais, 45000
Orléans

Cité Administrative, Champ Girault, PO Box 2510, 37025 Tours Cedex

Languedoc-Roussillon 44 avenue de Grande-Bretagne, 66000 Perpignan

Midi-Pyrénées 16 allée de Bellefontaine, 31081 Toulouse Cedex

16 rue Lavedan, 81004 Albi Cedex

Pays de la Loire 3 rue Celestin Frenet, 44000 Nantes Cedex

Square Lafayette, 49000 Angers

Poitou-Charentes 14 boulevard Chasseigne, Poitiers Cedex

Provence-Cote d'Azur 65 avenue Cantini, 13298 Marseille Cedex

Rhône-Alpes 87 rue de Seze, 69451 Lyon Cedex

ANPEs IN OTHER AGRICULTURAL AREAS

Alsace 8 rue de l'Auge, 68021 Colmar Cedex

18 rue Auguste-Larney, 67005 Strasbourg

Aquitaine Residence A Fallières, rue Diderot, 47015 Agen Cedex

2 rue Henri-Farbos, 4000 Mont-de-Marsan

45 rue Emile Guichene, 64016 Pau Cedex

17 rue Louis Blanc, 24016 Perigueux Cedex

Auvergne 70 rue Blatin, 63000 Clermont-Ferrand

Languedoc-Roussillon 76 allée d'Iéna, 11002 Carcassone

25 boulevard Renouvier, 34000 Montpellier

80 Avenue Jean-Jaurès, 30040 Nîmes Cedex

Rhône-Alpes 98/100 rue Boileau, 69455 Lyon Cedex 3

14 rue du Jeu de Paume, 26001 Valence Cedex

MONITORS & LEADERS

There are 23,000 *centres de vacances*, all over France, recruiting camp counsellors or monitors to supervise young people using the facilities during the summer holidays. Applicants must speak good French and will need to acquire a *Brevet d'aptitude aux fonctions d'animateur* (BAFA) certificate by undertaking a week's study of theory, a 50 hour specialisation course, and a week of practical application in a *centre*. The two training courses will cost approx FF4,200, although in some cases the potential employer will offer reimbursement, but payment will be made for the practical training work. The training associations usually act as placement agencies. As a certified monitor the pay is approx FF4,000 per month plus board and accommodation. Work is also available during other school holidays, and on Wednesdays during term time in *centres de loisirs*. The following three organisations offer preparation courses for the BAFA:

CENTRE D'ENTRAINEMENT AUX MÉTHODES D'ÉDUCATION ACTIVE (CEMEA) 76 boulevard de la Villette, 75019 Paris, France ✆ (33 1) 40 40 43 43

ORGANISME PROTESTANT DE FORMATION 47 rue de Clichy, 75311 Paris Cedex 09, France ✆ (33 1) 42 80 06 99

UNION FRANÇAISE DES CENTRES DE VACANCES (UFCV)
19 rue Dareau, 75014 Paris, France
℄ (33 1) 45 65 27 00

CLUB CANTABRICA HOLIDAYS LTD Overseas Department, Holiday House, 146-148 London Road, St Albans, Hertfordshire AL1 1PQ
Organises camping holidays, providing fully equipped tents, caravans and mobile homes. **Kiddies representatives** are required for the summer season, early May-early October, in Port Grimaud, Antibes, Presqu'ile and Canet.
⚘ Ages 21+. 6 day week. Wages from £55 per week, plus bonus at end of the season. Nursing, teaching or NNEB qualifications and experience an advantage. Self-catering accommodation in tents or caravans, travel costs from Watford and insurance provided.
🕮 Apply enclosing cv and SAE/IRCs. EEA nationals only.

PGL YOUNG ADVENTURE LTD
Personnel Department, Alton Court, Penyard Lane (878), Ross-on-Wye, Herefordshire HR9 5NR
℄ Ross-on-Wye (01989) 767833
Organises outdoor adventure holidays for young people and adults in the Ardèche and on the Mediterranean. Activities include canoeing, sailing and windsurfing. Group and entertainment organisers required. **Group organisers** are responsible for group welfare and for contributing to the entertainments programme when not participating in the main sports activities. They greet the group of approx 45 on its arrival and are responsible for them until their departure 3/4 days later. **Entertainment organisers** are responsible for the organisation and running of all evening activities and entertainments including discos, games, talent contests and competitive events for ages 12-18. Applicants should be energetic and enthusiastic, reliable and mature, self-motivated, with leadership

qualities, stamina, tolerance, flexibility, initiative and a sense of humour. Experience in working with children and handling young people at leisure preferable.
⚘ Ages 20+. May-September. Jobs are usually for 8 week periods. Staff are also recruited for very short periods over the Spring Bank Holiday. Return travel from Dover, full board accommodation in frame tents and health insurance provided. Sports and social facilities available, plus participation in programmed activities. 1 day free per week. Pocket money approx FF360 per week.
🕮 Applications should ideally be made between November and April.

VILLAGE CAMPS Chalet Seneca, 1854 Leysin, Switzerland
Organises American-style summer camps near Vallon Pont d'Arc in the Ardèche region for ages 10-17 from the international business and diplomatic communities. Opportunities for **counsellors, special activity counsellors, programme leaders, special instructors** and **nurses**. Staff live, work and play with the children and are responsible for their safety, health and happiness. **Counsellors** plan, organise and direct daytime and evening programmes, accompany campers on excursions and may be called upon to supervise other counsellors and take charge of a camper group. Evening activities include sports and games, films, competitions, fondues and discos. **Special activity counsellors**, having a high degree of proficiency, organise, execute and instruct specific programmes such as sports, arts and crafts, nature study and basic computer science. Counsellors with a substantial amount of leadership experience in recreational programmes can be appointed **programme leaders**, which includes running a camp programme and direction and supervision of adult counsellors. **Assistant** and **junior counsellors** are responsible for supporting counsellors in

all activities and assisting with special activities at day camps as required. **Specialist instructors** should have 2 years' training and experience, and be able to instruct children of all ability levels; they are responsible for the concentrated teaching of their subject at a speciality camp such as golf, tennis, computer science or French and English language. **Nurses** are responsible for the general health and welfare of campers and counsellors, attending to accidents and maintaining an infirmary. ✤ Ages 21+, 26+ for programme leaders. Applicants must have training and/or experience of working with children and have an interest in children from many ethnic and religious backgrounds. English is the first language, but priority is given to applicants with additional French, Italian or German language skills. 45 hour week for 1+ months, June-August. 1½ days plus 3 evening free per 2 week session. Compulsory pre-camp training course arranged for all staff. Full board accommodation, accident and liability insurance provided, but not travel costs. Wages SF325 per 2 week session.

TEACHERS & INSTRUCTORS

ACORN VENTURE LTD Personnel Department, 137 Worcester Road, Hagley, Stourbridge, West Midlands DY9 0NW
An activity holiday company catering for school groups at camping centres in Pas de Calais, Normandy and the Ardèche. **Instructors** required to supervise activities such as watersports, target sports, climbing, abseiling, orienteering, caving and gorge walking. Previous experience and qualifications such as BCU/RYA essential. Fluency in French a distinct advantage.
✤ Ages 18+. Minimum 50 hour, 6 day week. Applicants are expected to work the full season, May-September. Salary approx £40-£45 per week. All meals

and accommodation in tents provided, as well as insurance and cost of return travel from ferry ports. **PH**
✍ Apply in writing with cv by end February. If no reply within 28 days assume application unsuccessful.

CENTRE DE VOILE DE L'ABER WRAC'H BP4, 29870 Landeda, France
Vacancies exist for qualified **instructors** to teach sailing and windsurfing at the centre in a small fishing village.
✤ Ages 19+. Knowledge of French essential. 40 hour week, June-September. Board, lodging and insurance provided. Salary FF660 per week. Excursions to surrounding areas.

HEADWATER HOLIDAYS 146 London Road, Northwich, Cheshire CW9 5HH ✆ **Northwich (01606) 48699**
Operates activity holidays involving cycling, walking and Canadian canoeing throughout France.
Requires **canoeing instructors** and **cycling representatives** with some experience of bicycle maintenance. Work includes briefing clients at the start of the holiday, helping with any queries or problems and canoe or bicycle familiarisation.
✤ Ages 21+. Hours vary according to client's needs. Mid May-beginning October. Driving licence and fluent French essential. Salary approximately £105 per week plus expenses, self-catering accommodation in village, travel and insurance provided. Training weekend in UK before start of season.

PGL SKI EUROPE Brentham House, 45c High Street, Hampton Wick, Kingston-upon-Thames, Surrey KT1 4DG ✆ **0181-977 7755**
Operates holidays for groups and school parties. Part-time **ski instructors** required for winter sports in Savoie, Vanoise and Hautes-Alpes. Work involves 6 hours teaching per day. BASI or full foreign qualifications essential, together with a high level of teaching

skill. A knowledge of foreign languages useful but not essential; fluent English is a prerequisite. 1-2 week periods over Christmas, New Year, in February and April. Instructors receive full board hotel accommodation and ski pass plus travel expenses London/resort, and have access to the same facilities as the clients. Wages approx £90-£135 per week, depending on qualifications.

🐾 *Interviews take place May-November.*

PGL YOUNG ADVENTURE LTD
Personnel Department, Alton Court, Penyard Lane (878), Ross-on-Wye, Herefordshire HR9 5NR
✆ **Ross-on-Wye (01989) 767833**
Organises outdoor adventure holidays for young people and adults in the Ardèche and on the Mediterranean. Activities include canoeing, sailing and windsurfing. Experienced or qualified Canadian canoeists, sailors and windsurfers required as **instructors** and **river leaders** at the centres. River leaders, senior sailors and their teams assist with the care and welfare and evening entertainment of the group, including total responsibility for their safety and enjoyment, as well as canoeing/sailing instruction.
⊕ Ages 20+, occasionally 18+ with relevant qualifications and experience. Applicants should ideally have considerable experience, hold a RYA or BCU Certificate, and have worked as an instructor. A good basic level of skill is important as well as the ability to impart to others with enthusiasm and interest. Applicants should also be able to adhere to strict safety standards, have the foresight to deal with emergencies, and recognise the limitations of each learner. The emphasis is on informality and enjoyment; the ability to manage and organise a team of staff is essential. Applicants should be fit, energetic and enthusiastic, reliable and mature, with leadership qualities, initiative and a sense of humour; experience of working with young people preferable.
May-September; jobs are usually for 8 week periods but are sometimes for the whole season.
Staff are also recruited for short periods over the Spring Bank Holiday. Return travel from Dover, full board accommodation in frame tents and health insurance provided. Sports and social facilities available, plus participation in programmed activities. Pocket money per week from FF360 (canoeists, sailors and windsurfers), from FF460 (river leaders), and from £70 (senior watersports instructors in sailing, windsurfing and senior canoeists).
🐾 *Applicants available in May and early June have a greater chance of selection. Applications should ideally be made between November and April.*

SKI ARDMORE 11-15 High Street, Marlow, Buckinghamshire SL7 1AU
✆ **Marlow (01628) 890060**
Organise skiing holidays for school groups in Serre Chevalier, Montgenevre, Megève and Pelvoux.
Ski representatives/leaders required to supervise groups of up to 10 children, organise and run evening activities and generally ensure a good trip.
⊕ Ages 20+. Experience of working with youngsters, some skiing experience and First Aid qualification desirable. Hours flexible, approx 60 hours per week. 1-8 weeks, December-April. Wages from £45+ per week, plus full board accommodation, insurance and travel costs. Training day held in December.

WORKCAMPS

CENTRE ALPIN DE VALORISATION POUR L'AUTONOMIE (CAVA)
Le Foreston, route de Réallon, 05160 Savines-le-Lac, France
A self-sufficiency training centre on the edge of the Ecrins national park in the Hautes-Alpes region. **Volunteers** are invited to take part in organic farming, gardening and building houses.
⊕ Ages 18+. Volunteers must speak English, French or German. Experience

useful but not essential. Work may involve roof and window fitting, ceiling and wall insulation, raw clay brick making, plumbing and electrics, harvesting, haymaking, irrigation maintenance, gardening and dry stone walling. 30-36 hour, 5-6 day week for 3 weeks, July-end August. Cost FF50 per day covers application fee, board and accommodation in farm house, insurance and leisure activities. Volunteers should bring own sleeping bag/sheets and towels. Training courses in making and using raw clay bricks, traditional and solar house building. No fares or wages paid. ✍ *Apply by 15 June.*

CENTRE D'INFORMATION ET DE DOCUMENTATION JEUNESSE (CIDJ) 101 Quai Branly, 75740 Paris Cedex 15, France

Publishes an information sheet, *Chantiers de Travail Volontaire*, which gives details on workcamps with a list of addresses, type of work and dates.

CHANTIERS DE JEUNES PROVENCE-COTE D'AZUR 7 avenue Pierre de Coubertin, 06150 Cannes La Bocca, France

Arranges workcamps for young people to work as **volunteers** all year round and especially during the summer. Recent projects have included environmental protection programmes and converting buildings to create outdoor pursuits centres or meeting places for young people, including the restoration of a 17th century fort on the Ile Sainte-Marguerite.
⚘ Ages 14-18. 2 weeks, July and August. Nature walks and watersports arranged. Volunteers pay own travel and approx FF2,200 to cover membership, food, accommodation and insurance. Volunteers must have written parental consent, a medical certificate and a good knowledge of French. ✍ *Write in French to request further information.*

COLLÈGE LYCÉE CÉVENOL INTERNATIONAL Camp International de Travail, 43400 Le Chambon sur Lignon, France ✆ (33) 71 59 72 52 ▭ (33) 71 65 87 38

An international school situated in 40 acres of wooded grounds high up in the heart of the Massif Central. The school was built through the help of **volunteers**, and an international workcamp is held every year to carry out renovation, decoration and repairs. Work is both indoor and outdoor, involving tasks such as painting, landscaping and paving. Evenings are time for discussion or relaxation. No experience necessary, but applicants should be fit for strenuous work.
⚘ Ages 16-30. 30 hour week. 3 weeks, July-August. Full board accommodation provided, but no fares or wages paid. Participation fee FF855. Volunteers may take part, at a reduced rate, in a discovery trip around France organised at the end of the workcamp.

CONCORDIA 38 rue du Faubourg St Denis, 75010 Paris, France

Volunteers are invited to work on a choice of approx 60 international workcamps which aim to help in the development of small communities in mountainous and isolated rural areas including Alpes, Alsace, Auvergne, Burgundy, Franche-Comté, Languedoc-Roussillon, Limousin, Midi-Pyrénées and Picardy, giving participants a chance to get to know their natural, political, economic, and social environment. Typical projects involve constructing community centres for use by villagers, children or handicapped people, and renovating or converting agricultural buildings, abbeys and schools. Work includes masonry, carpentry, flooring, painting, roofing, tiling, woodwork, plumbing, electrical and insulation work. Also equipping mountain huts with water and electricity, building rest *gîtes*, demolition, repair or maintenance work. Volunteers are taught traditional building techniques by local craftsmen. The

camps provide an opportunity to discover a region, its traditions and inhabitants, and to become involved in the life of a village community. Sports, crafts, dance, music, theatre and other cultural activities arranged.
⊕ Ages 18+. Good knowledge of French needed for some camps. Applicants should preferably have previous workcamp experience. 35 hour week. 2-3 weeks, all year with majority of projects during the summer.
⊕ Also camps for ages 15-17; 25 hours per week for 2-3 weeks, July and August. Full board, accommodation in schools, huts or community buildings and work accident insurance provided. No fares or wages paid. **B D PH**

🎓 *Apply through partner organisation in country of residence.*
In the UK: Concordia (Youth Service Volunteers) Ltd, Quaker International Social Projects or United Nations Association International Youth Service. See page 30 for registration details and addresses.

FÉDÉRATION UNIE DES AUBERGES DE JEUNESSE (FUAJ) Chantiers et Rencontres Internationales, 27 rue Pajol, 75018 Paris, France

French youth hostelling organisation invites **volunteers** to take part in international workcamps. Work generally involves renovation, repair and maintenance of hostels, many of which are old, traditional buildings or situated in picturesque parts of the country. All projects include opportunities to discover the locality and take part in outdoor activities such as hiking, climbing, canoeing, horse-riding or mountain biking.
⊕ Ages 18-25. Applicants should have some knowledge of French and be prepared to work as part of a team. 1-3 weeks, April-October. Cost from FF350 per week covers accommodation and activities. No fares or wages paid.

FOURTH WORLD YOUTH TRAINING CENTRE 29 rue du Stade, 77720 Champeaux, France ✆ (33) 60 66 91 28 ☏ (33) 60 69 97 17

Part of the ATD Fourth World Movement which aims to protect the fundamental rights of the poorest and most disadvantaged and excluded families, which constitute the Fourth World. These rights include the right to family life, to education and training, and to representation. **Volunteers** are invited to take part in workcamps organised at the youth centre, involving construction, carpentry, electrical installation, painting, gardening, office work and cooking. Evenings are reserved for discussions and the exchange of ideas about the fight against poverty, as well as sharing knowledge between young people of different social backgrounds.
⊕ Ages 16-25. Volunteers should be concerned by persistent poverty and social exclusion. 30 hours of manual work each week. 6-7 days, February-November. Full board accommodation provided. Volunteers pay their own travel and insurance. Cost FF50 per day.

INTERNATIONAL MOVEMENT ATD FOURTH WORLD 107 avenue du Général Leclerc, 95480 Pierrelaye, France

An international voluntary organisation which supports the efforts of the very poor in overcoming poverty and taking an active role in the community.
Volunteers are invited to take part in workcamps organised at the international centre at Méry Sur Oise where training sessions take place. Work involves construction, carpentry, electrical installation, painting, plumbing, gardening, office work and cooking. Evenings are reserved for discussions and the exchange of ideas about the fight against poverty.
⊕ Ages 18-35. Volunteers should be concerned by persistent poverty and social exclusion. All nationalities accepted. Knowledge of French helpful

but not essential. 7 hour day.
2 weeks, July-September. Full board
accommodation provided in tents and
bungalows. Volunteers should take a
sleeping bag and work clothes. Cost
FF450, 14 days. Volunteers pay their
own travel costs. **B D**

NEIGE ET MERVEILLES
**La Minière de Vallauria, 06430 Saint
Dalmas de Tende, France**
Arranges sports, leisure and cultural
activities, and youth meetings.
Volunteers are invited to take part in
workcamps organised in the mountain
hamlet where the centre is based.
Recent projects have included rebuilding
a mountain shelter surrounded by
Bronze Age rock carvings; constructing a
road; chopping and gathering wood;
and conservation work on the site of a
nearby fort.
⊕ Ages 18+. 35 hour week. 2 weeks,
April-September. Mountain walks and
excursions arranged. Volunteers pay
own travel and FF360 fee to cover costs.

SERVICE CIVIL INTERNATIONAL
**2 rue Eugène Fournière, 75018
Paris, France**
Service Civil International promotes
international reconciliation through
work projects. **Volunteers** are invited
to take part in international workcamps
organised throughout France. Recent
projects have included accompanying
mentally handicapped people on a
holiday to Normandy; working with
children from disadvantaged
backgrounds on a summer adventure
playground project in Lille; repairing the
leaky basement of a Cistercian abbey in
Aveyron; and building a hen house and
organic landscaping work in Perluc near
Rennes. Projects are linked to study
themes. Good knowledge of French
needed on some camps. Walking
holidays in the mountains also arranged,
which provide fundraising and a
workcamp atmosphere for those unable
to attend other projects.
⊕ Ages 18+. Applicants should be highly
motivated, preferably with previous

workcamp or other voluntary work
experience, and prepared to work hard
as part of a team. 35-40 hour week.
2-4 weeks, July-September. Food,
shared accommodation, and work
accident insurance provided. No fares
or wages paid. **B D PH**

⚖ *Apply through partner organisation in
country of residence.*
*In the UK: International Voluntary Service.
See page 30 for registration details and
addresses.*

SOLIDARITÉS JEUNESSES **38 rue
du Faubourg St Denis, 75010 Paris,
France**
An international movement open to all
who share a common concern for
lasting peace and justice in the world.
Volunteers are needed to work in
international teams on summer projects
aimed at offering a service in an area of
need and promoting self-help within the
community, promoting international
understanding and the discussion of
social problems, and offering young
people the chance to live as a group and
take these experiences into the context
of daily life. Recent projects have
included constructing a centre for
meetings and group activities; building a
new workshop in an educational centre;
converting an old school into a rest
centre in the Hautes-Alpes; restoring a
12th century chapel for use as a
museum on provincial history and
traditions; and converting a 16th century
chapel into a hiker's shelter. Sports and
social activities organised. International
seminars also arranged.
⊕ Ages 15-17 and 18+. 6 hour day, 30
hour week. 3 weeks, July-September.
Food, accommodation and work
accident insurance provided. No fares
or wages paid. **D PH**

⚖ *Apply through partner organisation in
country of residence.*
*In the UK: Christian Movement for Peace or
United Nations Association International
Youth Service. See page 30 for registration
details and addresses.*

GENERAL

ACORN VENTURE LTD Personnel Department, 137 Worcester Road, Hagley, Stourbridge, West Midlands DY9 0NW

An activity holiday company catering for school groups at camping centres in Pas de Calais, Normandy and the Ardèche. **Site managers** required to make sure groups have all they need, organise evening entertainments and coordinate activities. **General maintenance staff** and qualified **nurses** also required. Applicants should have some previous experience and fluency in French.
⊕ Ages 18+. Minimum 50 hour, 6 day week. Applicants are expected to work the full season, May-September. Salary £40-£80 per week according to position. All meals and accommodation in tents, insurance and cost of return travel from ferry ports provided. **PH** ☙ *Apply in writing with cv by end February. If no reply within 28 days assume unsuccessful.*

CENTRE D'INFORMATION DE DOCUMENTATION JEUNESSE (CIDJ) 101 Quai Branly, 75740 Paris Cedex 15, France

Issues an information sheet listing offices throughout France which act as local branches of the Agence National pour l'Emploi. **Temporary jobs** for young EEA nationals, usually in offices, working with children, or as monitors in holiday camps, are put on the noticeboards.

DOMAINE DU SURGIE 46100 Figeac, France ✆ (33) 65 34 59 00 ☎ (33) 65 34 20 80

A holiday village in the Quercy region of south central France, with camping, mobile home, self-catering and hotel accommodation plus a wide range of leisure and watersports facilities. Seasonal staff are required, including **reception staff, bar and restaurant staff** and **activity monitors**.
⊕ Ages 18+. Relevant experience in the tourist and/or catering industry preferred; knowledge of French, English

and Dutch required. 40-50 hour week for 6-8 weeks, July-August. Board and lodging provided, plus a salary of FF1,500-FF2,000 per month.
☙ *Apply November-April.*

EURO DISNEY SCA Service du Recrutement-Casting, BP 110, 77777 Marne-la-Vallée Cedex 4, France ✆ (33 1) 49 31 19 99

Euro Disneyland Paris (consisting of 5,200 hotel rooms, a theme park, 47 restaurants, 45 shops and 40 attractions) is situated 30km east of Paris. **Seasonal jobs** are available March-October. The majority of the opportunities are in food and beverage, housekeeping and custodial.
⊕ Ages 18+. Applicants must be able to communicate well in French and English. A friendly, cheerful and outgoing personality is essential as the work will involve a lot of contact with visitors. Approx 39 hour week. Monthly gross salary FF6,010. Staff covered by French social security and health insurance. No accommodation or travel costs provided. *EEA nationals or those authorised to work in France only.*

EUROPEAN WATERWAYS 25 Kingswood Creek, Wraysbury, Staines Middlesex

Operates floating holidays on canals, using hotel barges. Vacancies exist for **barge crews** in Burgundy, Alsace-Lorraine and the Midi area of southern France. Crews consist of 4 members, including an experienced bargemaster, and positions range from deckhand to mechanic. **Stewardesses** also required.
⊕ Ages 25+. 6+ months, throughout the year; peak season April-October. Crews work long hours, 50-80 per week, and must be fit. Previous experience of similar work preferred. Driving licence and some knowledge of French and German essential. Salary £70-£125 per week, depending on experience; on-board accommodation and travel expenses provided. Applicants pay own insurance costs. *EEA nationals only.*

EUROYOUTH LTD
301 Westborough Road, Westcliff, Southend-on-Sea, Essex SS0 9PT
C **Southend-on-Sea (01702) 341434**
Holiday guest stays are arranged whereby **guests** are offered board and lodging in return for an agreed number of hours' English conversation with hosts or their children. Time also available for guests to practise French if desired.
⊕ Mainly ages 18-25, but sometimes opportunities for older applicants. Open to anyone whose mother tongue is English and who is interested in visiting France and living with a local family for a short time. 2-3 weeks, June-August. Insurance and travel arranged by applicants, but tickets at reduced rates on request. Registration fee approx £80.
⚲ *Apply at least 12 weeks prior to scheduled departure date. Limited places.*

FÉDÉRATION UNIE DES AUBERGES DE JEUNESSE (FUAJ)
27 rue Pajol, 75018 Paris, France
Variety of short-term work available at those youth hostels that organise sporting, cultural and educational activity programmes. Positions include **cooks, dishwashers, kitchen assistants, receptionists, activity leaders** and **sports monitors.**
⊕ Ages 18+. Good knowledge of French essential. Terms and conditions of work as agreed with employing hostel. FUAJ produce a guide to youth hostels in France which is available to personal callers; those interested must apply to individual hostels direct. Alternatively, addresses can be found in the *International Youth Hostel Handbook Vol I*; see **Worldwide Info** section for further details.

FRENCH COUNTRY CAMPING
Assistant Operations Manager, 126 Hempstead Road, Kings Langley, Hertfordshire WD4 8AL
C **Watford (01923) 261316**
Operates self-drive family holidays providing fully furnished and equipped tents and mobile homes.

Vacancies exist for **drivers** and **assistant drivers** to deliver equipment and to help with the setting up and closing down of campsites immediately before and after the summer season. Applicants must have driving experience, preferably overseas and/or using vans. Good command of French desirable. Mid April-mid May or during September.
⊕ Ages 21+. Salary approx £95 per week. Accommodation on sites, transport and insurance provided.
EEA nationals only.

HAVEN EUROPE
Northney Marina, Northney Road, Hayling Island, Hampshire PO11 ONH
Tour operator organising self-drive package holidays, with accommodation in luxury mobile homes and tents. Requires various seasonal staff to work on two parks owned by Haven on the Atlantic coast and near Montpellier. Opportunities for **reception, bar work, lifeguards, entertainment** and general **cleaning** duties. Reasonable knowledge of French necessary for positions with client contact.
⊕ Ages 18+. 45 hour, 6 day week, May-September. Salary according to workload. Accommodation provided in shared mobile homes. Personal insurance and travel expenses provided.
UK nationals only.

HORIZON HPL LTD
Southbank House, Black Prince Road, London SE1 7SJ *C* **0171-735 8171**
A training organisation that can place candidates in hotels and companies throughout France in order to gain professional experience. Responsibilities depend on language level, ranging from **general duties, waiter/waitress, reception** and **secretarial training** to **marketing placements.**
⊕ Ages 18-35. Experience not essential, but applicants must be highly motivated and have at least a basic knowledge of French. Courses in French (5 students per class) and computer training organised in Paris; special courses for the hotel and catering industry

organised in London. Hotel trainees receive FF1,600 per month and hotel/family accommodation; company trainees receive pocket money and family accommodation. Cost £240-£300 covers training, administration, follow-up and accommodation. Support provided by Paris office to ensure progress during placement and help with any problems. 🕮 *Apply 2-3 months in advance. EEA nationals only.*

NSS RIVIERA HOLIDAYS
199 Marlborough Avenue, Hull HU15 3LG

Owns 30 chalets, cottages and mobile homes on a holiday village situated in wine-growing countryside halfway between St Tropez and Cannes.

Active couples required who can offer a variety of high-standard DIY skills such as joinery, plumbing, electrics, building, gas fitting and decorating.

⊕ Ages 45+; enthusiastic, self-motivated, self-taught, disciplined adults required, preferably nonsmokers, owning a reliable car, with a pension or private income. 3 day week for 4-7 weeks, spring and autumn or May-September. Self-contained, fully furnished accommodation provided with own patio and private parking; all electricity, gas, water, local rates, local taxes and site fees paid.

🕮 *Apply in writing to Lilian Jordan, with full background details for each person, a recent photo and copies of references if available, indicating preferred dates.*

PGL YOUNG ADVENTURE LTD
Personnel Department, Alton Court, Penyard Lane (878), Ross-on-Wye, Herefordshire HR9 5NR
🕾 Ross-on-Wye (01989) 767833

Organises outdoor adventure holidays for young people and adults in the Ardèche and on the Mediterranean. Activities include canoeing, sailing and windsurfing. Staff required at the centres include **nurses**, mainly responsible for the treatment of minor ailments, maintaining a medicine stock and also helping in administration and

welfare; **driver, site and stores assistants**, responsible for collecting and delivering food and equipment, ensuring tidiness and keeping a close check on all the equipment; **general maintenance assistants**, painting, labouring, carpentry, gardening, driving and errands, unloading and delivering goods; **fibreglassers/canoe leaders** to repair and maintain fibreglass canoes and accompany canoe pick-up trips; **LGV drivers**, responsible for delivering and collecting canoes; **administrative assistants** required for office work, public relations, costings, ordering, petty cash, wages, stock and giving information to the centres.

⊕ Ages 20+. Applicants should be responsible, self-motivated, flexible, positive, energetic, and enthusiastic, reliable and mature, with a sense of humour; supplies and services staff also need to be very fit. Staff working with guests should preferably have experience of working with children.

May-September; jobs are usually for 8 week periods but are sometimes for the whole season. Staff are also recruited for short periods over the spring bank holiday. Fibreglassers, LGV drivers and general maintenance staff work March-October. Return travel from Dover, full board accommodation in frame tents and health insurance provided. Sports and social activities. One day free per week. Pocket money FF330-FF600 per week according to qualifications and position.

🕮 *Applicants available in May have a greater chance of selection. Applications should ideally be made November-April.*

QUICK Direction d'Exploitation
Paris, 3 avenue du Général Galliéni, 93100 Montreuil, France
🕾 (33) 48 59 61 16

Fast food chain in Paris recruiting **staff** on a part-time contractual basis, particularly during holiday periods.

⊕ Ages 18-25. Food, uniform and *le SMIC*, the national minimum wage provided.

SNOWTIME LTD 96 Belsize Lane, London NW3 5BE ✆ **0171-433 3336**
Organises luxury winter skiing holidays in Méribel. Requires **hotel, restaurant** and **bar managers**.

✤ Ages 24+ preferred. These positions involve a great deal of responsibility, client contact and administration. Previous experience in the hotel and catering industry and a good command of French essential, as well as a friendly, outgoing personality and good organisational skills. Salary from £45 per week, plus benefits below.

Handymen/drivers also required.

✤ Ages 25+. Applicants must have clean current driving licence and plenty of experience. Must also be practically/ mechanically minded with some knowledge of electrics (eg lighting fuses), plumbing and general building maintenance. Salary from £45 per week plus benefits below.

Also require **ski guides**.

✤ Ages 24+. Applicants must be competent skiers with 15-29 weeks experience, comfortable leading groups, of cheerful disposition and willing to turn their hand to other things when required. Salary from £35 per week plus benefits below.

For all positions applicants must be available from December-May inclusive. Staff receive salary plus accommodation and food, ski equipment, ski pass, return travel from London and insurance.

B D PH

SUNSAIL The Port House, Port Solent, Portsmouth PO6 4TH ✆ **Portsmouth (01705) 214330** ▱ **(01705) 219827**
Crew members are required to work aboard cruising yachts flotilla sailing off Corsica and Sardinia. Vacancies for RYA qualified and experienced **skippers**, responsible for the wellbeing of up to 13 cruising yachts and 60 holidaymakers, giving daily briefings on navigation and providing sailing assistance where necessary.

Also qualified **diesel mechanics** needed, responsible to the skipper for maintaining the marine diesel engines and repairing any other items aboard.

Hostesses are also required to look after laundry, accounting and cleaning of boats, advising holidaymakers on shops and restaurants, and organising social events and barbecues.

✤ Ages 21-35 for all posts. Relevant qualifications and experience essential; sailing experience desirable and conversational French/German advantageous. All staff should be prepared for very hard work and long hours. 45-50 hour, 6 day week plus social hours in evenings. Staff must work the full season, mid March-November. Salary £55-£95 per week, depending on position. Accommodation on board, return travel and medical insurance provided.

🕮 *Apply December-March.*

When writing to any organisation it is essential to mention Working Holidays 1995 and enclose a stamped, self-addressed A4 envelope, or if in another country, an addressed A4 envelope and at least two IRCs (International Reply Coupons, available from post offices). Enquiries received without SAEs/IRCs are unlikely to be answered.

INFO

Embassy of the Federal Republic of Germany
23 Belgrave Square, 1-6 Chesham Place, London SW1X 8PZ
✆ 0171-235 5033/824 1300
Visa information service ✆ 0891 331166

British Embassy
Friedrich-Ebert-Allee 77, 53113 Bonn
✆ (49 228) 91 67-70

Tourist office
German National Tourist Office, Nightingale House, 65 Curzon Street, London W1Y 7PE ✆ 0171-495 3990

Youth hostels
Deutsches Jugendherbergswerk, Bismarckstraße 8, PO Box 1455, 32756 Detmold

Youth & student information
Artu Berliner Gesellschaft für Studenten und Jugendaustausch GmbH, Hardenbergstraße 9, 10623 Berlin (Charlottenburg)

Youth Information Centre, Paul-Heyse-Straße 22, 80336 Munich

Entry regulations A UK citizen intending to work in Germany should have a full passport. UK/EEA nationals may stay in Germany for up to 3 months in order to seek employment; a person intending to stay longer than 3 months or who is taking up employment must obtain a residence permit from the local *Ausländerbehörde*, no later than 3 months after entry. Non-EEA nationals wishing to enter Germany require an entry visa which has to have the approval of the destination's *Ausländerbehörde*. This must be obtained prior to entering and applicants should be resident in an EEA country for 12 months before their application can be considered. Application forms are obtainable from the German embassy in the country where they are staying. Clearance may take 6 weeks or more. If employment is intended, written confirmation of the job offer is required before an entry visa will be granted.

The Bundesverwaltungsamt, PO Box 680169, 50728 Cologne distributes an information booklet for non-resident workers and emigrants returning to Germany, containing background notes and details on all aspects of working including entry requirements, employment regulations, social security and taxation. The German Embassy publishes a leaflet, *Residence and Work in Germany,* providing information likely to be needed upon taking up employment.

Job advertising The Axel Springer Publishing Group, Unit 2, Princeton Court, 53/55 Felsham Road, London SW15 1BY ℘ 0181-789 4929 is the UK office of a leading German publishing group which can place paid job advertisements in *Die Welt, Welt am Sonntag, Bild, Bild am Sonntag, Hamburger Abendblatt, Berliner Morgenpost, BZ* and approx 20 other national and local newspapers and magazines.

Publicitas Ltd, 517/523 Fulham Road, London SW6 1HD ℘ 0171-385 7723 can place job advertisements in *Rheinische Post, Stuttgarter Zeitung, Süddeutsche Zeitung, Der Tagesspiegel* and *Frankfurter Neue Presse.*

Travel Freedom Pass allows 3, 5 or 10 days unlimited rail travel in 1 month on the railways of Germany. Cost from £94 (under 26) or £125 (26+). Available from DER Travel Service, 18 Conduit Street, London W1R 9TD ℘ 0171-290 1116 or from British Rail International Rail Centre, Victoria Station, London SW1V 1JY ℘ 0171-834 2345.

Campus Travel can arrange Eurotrain, Inter-rail and student/youth travel by plane, train, boat or bus to destinations in Germany. Offices throughout the UK including a student travel centre at 52 Grosvenor Gardens, London SW1W

0AG (opposite Victoria Station) ℘ 0171-730 3402 or ℘ 0131-668 3303 for Scottish telephone bookings.

Council Travel, 28A Poland Street, London W1V 3DB ℘ 0171-287 3337 (offices also in Paris, Nice, Lyon, Munich, Düsseldorf, Tokyo, Singapore and throughout the US) offers Eurotrain under 26 fares and student/youth airfares to Germany, plus travel, insurance, guidebooks and travel gear.

STA Travel, 86 Old Brompton Road, London SW7 3LQ/117 Euston Road, London NW1 2SX ℘ 0171-937 9921 (offices also in Birmingham, Bristol, Cambridge, Glasgow, Leeds, Manchester and Oxford) operates flexible, low-cost flights between London and destinations throughout Germany.

Information centres Campus Travel's sister organisation in Germany has branches at Usit/Connections, Ladengalerie, Bockenheimer Warte, Adalbertstraße 8, 6000 Frankfurt 90, and at Univers Tours, Grolmanstraße 16a, 100 Berlin 12. They arrange student/youth travel by air, rail and coach, and give information and advice.

Publications *Young People's Guide to Munich* is an indispensable guide containing notes on where to stay, eating and drinking, public transport, maps, entertainment, places of interest, where to meet young people, special events and other useful information. Published by the Tourist Office of the City of Munich, Sendlinger Straße 1, 80331 Munich 2, and available at tourist offices.

International Youth Meetings in Germany 1994/95 lists services offered by German organisations to young visitors, and includes information on international workcamps, environmental protection programmes, youth work, language courses and social services. Available from Studienkreis für Tourismus, Dampschiffstraße 2, PO Box 1653, 82306 Starnberg.

Vacation Work's *Live and Work in Germany* £8.95 is a guide for those interested in finding temporary or permanent work, starting a business or buying a home in Germany.

Rough Guide to Germany £11.99 and *Rough Guide to Berlin* £8.99 provide comprehensive background information on Germany and its capital, plus details on getting there, getting around, places to explore and cheap places to stay.

Culture Shock! Germany £6.99 introduces the reader to the people, customs, food and culture of Germany, with checklists of dos and don'ts.

All the above guides are available from good bookshops.

Accommodation *Camping in Germany* lists over 400 campsites with a map indicating the locations. Available from the German National Tourist Office, see above, who can also supply a comprehensive list of youth hostels.

Christlicher Verein Junger Menschen, Jugend-Gästehaus, Landwehrstraße 13, 80336 Munich ✆ (49 89) 552 1410 ☎ (49 89) 550 4282 offers YMCA accommodation in 1-3 bedded rooms at a Christian centre situated close to station. Cost from DM38 per night includes breakfast and shower. **D PH**

Haus International, Elisabethstraße 87, 80797 Munich offers cheap, short-stay accommodation in 1-5 bedded rooms with shower and WC. Facilities include swimming pool, games room, bar and restaurant. Cost from DM40 includes breakfast. Reservations in advance. **PH**

Jugendlager am Kapuzinerhölzl, In den Kirschen, 8000 Munich 19 is a large sleeping tent with space for 420, cooking area, canteen, showers, information bureau and recreation tent. Ages up to 27. Cost DM13 per night includes bedding and breakfast. Up to 5 nights, end June-early September. Details from

Kreisjugendring München, Paul-Heyse-Straße 22, 8000 Munich 19.

The International Stuttgart Camp, Wiener Straße 317, 70469 Stuttgart Feuerbach ✆ (49 711) 81 77 476 is a dormitory 15 minutes from the central station with room for up to 200 young people. Special section for women. Free showers and washrooms; cafeteria and self-catering facilities. Ages 16-27. Cost DM8 per night includes bedding. Maximum stay 3 nights, no reservation, late June-early September.

AU PAIR / CHILDCARE

Both males and females can be placed as au pairs with families provided they have experience of housework and childcare. Ages 18-25; 17 year old A level German students also accepted. Applicants must be single and without dependants and should get board and lodging, their own room, DM200-DM300 per month pocket money, plus a travel ticket in order to attend language classes. EEA nationals should register with the local immigration office, *Ausländermeldeamt,* during the first 3 days of their stay. A 3 month residence permit will be granted which can later be extended to the whole length of the stay. Non-EEA nationals must obtain a visa before entry from the German Consulate responsible for their place of residence, on production of their current passport and a letter of invitation from the host family. Applications for visas take 2-3 months to process, so early application is advisable. On arrival the au pair must register at the local *Ausländeramt* within 3 days and will be issued with a 4 week residence permit. During this time they are required to undergo a medical examination at the local health department, *Gesundheitsamt,* the fee being paid by the host family. After a satisfactory medical the residence permit will be extended for one year, and a work permit will be issued by the labour exchange. Before returning to their own country, all au pairs must inform the local *Ausländeramt*. The host family insures the au pair against illness and accident, but this only covers 50% of dental fees and does not cover chronic illness. It is customary for au pairs to have a fortnight off after a 6 month stay.

ACADEMY AU PAIR AGENCY LTD 42 Cedarhurst Drive, Eltham, London SE9 5LP ℰ 0181-294 1191 ℤ 0181-850 8932

Can place **au pairs**. ⊕ Ages 18-27. Some knowledge of German essential. Pocket money approx £35-£40 per week. Administration charge £40. Positions as **nannies** and **mothers' helps** also available for those with qualifications/experience.

ANGLO PAIR AGENCY 40 Wavertree Road, Streatham Hill, London SW2 3SP ℰ 0181-674 3605

Can place **au pairs** and **au pairs plus** for 6+ months. ⊕ Ages 17-27. Pocket money £30-£50 per week. Also placements for experienced **nannies** and **mothers' helps**; salary up to £100 per week. Agency fee £40.

AVALON AGENCY Thursley House, 53 Station Road, Shalford, Guildford, Surrey GU4 8HA ℰ Guildford (01483) 63640

Can place **au pairs**. ⊕ Ages 18-24. Basic knowledge of German needed. Pocket money equal to £30-£35 per week, usually paid monthly. Fee £40 for placement and use of German agent. Summer holiday placements June-August only. Long-term, 6 month-2 year, vacancies to start any time.

BUNTERS AU PAIR & DOMESTIC AGENCY 17 Copper Street, Macclesfield, Cheshire SK11 7LH ℰ Macclesfield (01625) 614534

Can place **au pairs**, **demi pairs** and

mothers' helps. 6-12 months all year or 10 week summer placements. ⊕ Ages 18-27. Pocket money £35-£50 per week depending on hours worked. Placement fee £40. ⚞ *Apply before May for summer placements.*

HELPING HANDS AU PAIR & DOMESTIC AGENCY 39 Rutland Avenue, Thorpe Bay, Essex SS1 2XJ ℰ Southend-on-Sea (01702) 602067

Can place **au pairs** and **mothers' helps**. ⊕ Ages 18-27. Pocket money approx £35 per week for au pairs, higher for mothers' helps. Introduction fee £40. *UK nationals only.*

IN VIA Katholische Mädchensozialarbeit, Deutscher Verband e V, Ludwigstraße 36, 79104 Freiburg, Germany

Can place **au pairs** throughout Germany. ⊕ Ages 18-25. Knowledge of German essential. Pocket money DM350 per month. Branch offices in 26 towns in Germany. ⚞ *Enclose 4 IRCs.*

INTERNATIONAL CATHOLIC SOCIETY FOR GIRLS (ACISJF) St Patrick's International Youth Centre, 24 Great Chapel Street, London W1V 3AF ℰ 0171-734 2156 ℤ 0171-287 6282

Au pair posts arranged for 9+ months. ⊕ Ages 18+. *Mainly UK/Irish nationals.*

JOLAINE AGENCY 18 Escot Way, Barnet, Hertfordshire EN5 3AN ℰ 0181-449 1334 ℤ 0181-449 9183

Can place **au pairs** and **mothers' helps**. ⊕ Ages 18-30. Weekly pocket money approx £40 (au pairs) or £50 (mothers' helps). Placement fee £40.

JUST THE JOB (NOTTINGHAM) 32 Dovedale Road, West Bridgford, Nottingham NG2 6JA ℰ 0115-945 2482

Can place **au pairs**; 6+ months, no short-term placements. ⊕ Ages 18+. Weekly pocket money £30-£40. *UK applicants only.*

LANGTRAIN INTERNATIONAL
Torquay Road, Foxrock, Dublin 18,
Ireland © **(353 1) 289 3876**
Can place **au pairs** in families
throughout Germany. ✤ Ages 18+.
Pocket money approx £25-£40 per
week. Placement fee £60.

PROBLEMS UNLIMITED
AGENCY 86 Alexandra Road,
Windsor, Berkshire SL4 1HU
© **Windsor (01753) 830101**
Can place **au pairs**. ✤ Ages 18-27.
Pocket money £30-£35 per week.

STUDENTS ABROAD LTD
11 Milton View, Hitchin,
Hertfordshire SG4 0QD © **Hitchin**
(01462) 438909 ☎ **(01462) 438919**
Can place **au pairs**. ✤ Ages 18-27.
Basic knowledge of German helpful but
not essential. Pocket money approx
£35-£40 per week. Service charge £40.

VEREIN FÜR INTERNATIONALE
JUGENDARBEIT EV German
YWCA, 39 Craven Road, London
W2 3BX © **0171-723 0216**
Can place **au pairs** of both sexes in
families all over Germany.
✤ Ages 18-24. Reasonable knowledge of
German essential. Pocket money
DM350 per month.

COMMUNITY WORK

ATD VIERTE WELT Eisenhartstraße
15, 81245 Munich, Germany
An international voluntary organisation
which develops a human rights approach
to overcoming poverty. Brings together
people from all walks of life in
partnership with the most disadvantaged
families, to support the efforts of the
very poor in overcoming poverty and
taking an active role in their community.
Based on the commitment of those who
have chosen to put their skills to the
service of the very poor and learn from
them, ATD's objectives are to reinforce
cooperation between disadvantaged
families and the community; develop a

constructive public awareness of
poverty; and encourage a fuller
representation of poorest families in all
areas of society. **Volunteers** are invited
to take part in street workshops
organised in Munich, sharing skills with
parents, young people and children
whose sense of creativity has never been
challenged. Workshops are organised in
very disadvantaged areas where holidays
too often mean boredom and violence.
✤ Ages 18+. No experience necessary
but applicants should be interested in
better understanding the causes and
effects of persistent poverty and willing
to work hard with others as a team.
Approx 40 hour week for 1 week, July.
Accommodation provided; applicants are
asked to take a sleeping bag and to
contribute towards living expenses.
No fares or wages paid.
✎ Write for further details.

CAMPHILL SCHOOLS
Heimsonderschule Brachenreuthe,
88662 Überlingen-Bodensee,
Germany © **(49 7551) 80070**
Aims to provide a new and constructive
way of life for mentally handicapped
children, assisting them to achieve
individual independence and social
adjustment within Camphill Trust
communities.
Volunteers are needed to work
alongside the residents in every aspect
of life and also as helpers in school
classes. As many of the children have
severe handicaps they are in need of
care such as bathing, dressing and other
personal tasks. Volunteers must be
willing to help wherever needed, and are
encouraged not only to share in the
responsibilities of living and working
with the handicapped but also to
participate in the recreational, cultural
and social aspects of community life.
✤ Ages 19+. 60-70 hours per week, all
year round. Full board accommodation
in single or double rooms and insurance
provided, plus DM350 pocket money
per month. Applicants pay their own
travel expenses. Knowledge of German
essential. Participants staying for one

year have an opportunity to take part in the first year of a training course in curative education. **D PH**
Overseas applicants accepted.

INTERNATIONALE JUGENDGEMEINSCHAFTSDIENSTE EV (IJGD) Kaiserstraße 43, 53113 Bonn, Germany

A society for international and political education, involving **volunteers** on approx 120 international workcamps each year. Recent projects have included helping to build a village of peace in Storkow, enabling refugees and German families to live together; and assisting on a circus playscheme in Bertingen, organizing workshops on circus skills, setting up a marquee and designing costumes. Time for preparation and evaluation must be added to the normal 6 hour day on playschemes.
⊕ Ages 16-26. Good knowledge of German may be needed. 30 hour, 5 day week. 3 weeks, June-September. Simple accommodation provided in schools, youth centres, boarding houses, tents or barns. A budget for food, cooking facilities and insurance is provided for each group of volunteers. Excursions arranged to sites of interest. Registration fee DM150. No fares or wages paid. **B D PH**

📖 *Apply through partner organisation in country of residence.*
In the UK: Concordia (Youth Service Volunteers) Ltd, Quaker International Social Projects or United Nations Association International Youth Service. See page 30 for registration details and addresses).

CONSERVATION

BRITISH TRUST FOR CONSERVATION VOLUNTEERS Room IWH, 36 St Mary's Street, Wallingford, Oxfordshire OX10 0EU ℂ Wallingford (01491) 839766

The largest charitable organisation in Britain to involve people in practical conservation work. Following the success of the Natural Break programme in the UK, BTCV is now developing a series of international working holidays with the aim of introducing **volunteers** to practical conservation projects abroad. It is hoped that the British volunteers will adapt to and learn from local lifestyles as well as participate in the community. Projects last for 2-3 weeks and are based at the Ammersee Lake reserve, south of Munich. Work involves harvesting hay meadows, coppicing and creating pools for breeding birds and amphibians.
⊕ Ages 18-70. Cost from £175 includes transport from suitable pick-up point in Germany, insurance, food and basic accommodation with everyone sharing domestic chores. Volunteers should take a sleeping bag. Membership fee £12. No fares or wages paid.

CHRISTLICHER FRIEDENS-DIENST EV Rendelerstraße 9-11, 60385 Frankfurt, Germany ℂ (49 69) 459071-72

An international movement open to all who are concerned about violence, exploitation and injustice in society. **Volunteers** are needed to work in international teams. Recent projects have included building an environmental education centre in the hills above Tharndt, near Dresden; restoring an old half-timbered house in Seifhennersdorf, in the mountains bordering the Czech Republic; and restoring a baroque stately home situated in Luskow, near the Baltic coast. Volunteers share in discussions centring on the host community and world problems.
⊕ Ages 18+. 6 hour day, 30-36 hour week. 2-3 weeks, July-September. Food, accommodation and work accident insurance provided. No fares or wages paid. Registration fee DM150. **B D PH**

📖 *Apply through partner organisation in country of residence. In the UK: Christian Movement for Peace. See page 30 for registration details and addresses.*

INTERNATIONALE BEGEGNUNG IN GEMEINSCHAFTSDIENSTEN EV (IBG) Schlosserstraße 28, 70180 Stuttgart, Germany

Founded in 1965 to organise work projects of benefit to the community and to promote better international understanding. **Volunteers** are needed on international workcamps; each camp is made up of 15-20 participants from 6-8 countries. Recent projects have included working to preserve a threatened juniper heath in Hayingen; restoring an old city wall near Kassel; reconstructing an ore-mining railway track and wagons in the Harz nature reserve; and renovating a 12th century castle alongside local unemployed people in Wulmersen.

⊕ Ages 18+. 30 hour week with weekends free. 3 weeks, June-October. Food, simple accommodation in schools, youth hostels, empty buildings, forest or mountain huts with self-catering facilities and work accident insurance provided. No fares or wages paid. Participants should take a sleeping bag. Registration fee DM140.

Apply through partner organisation in country of residence. In the UK: Concordia (Youth Service Volunteers) Ltd, Quaker International Social Projects or United Nations Association International Youth Service. See page 30 for registration details and addresses.

INTERNATIONALE JUGENDGEMEINSCHAFTSDIENSTE EV (IJGD) Kaiserstraße 43, 53113 Bonn, Germany

A society for international and political education, involving **volunteers** on approx 120 international workcamps each year. Recent projects have included building nesting facilities for birds in the Duingen nature reserve south of Hannover; reconstructing a 9th century village near Neubrandenburg; helping to excavate an early Celtic tumulus in Landshut, southern Bavaria; and planting marram grass and setting up fences to catch sand and prevent wind and wave

erosion on the North Sea islands of Wangerooge and Borkum.

⊕ Ages 16-26. Basic knowledge of German may be needed, and previous workcamp experience preferable. 30 hour, 5 day week for 3 weeks, during April and June-October. Simple accommodation provided in schools, youth centres, boarding houses, tents or barns. A budget for food, cooking facilities and insurance is provided for each group of volunteers. Excursions arranged to sites of interest. Registration fee DM150. No fares or wages paid. Also arrange youth workshops linked to workcamp tasks on ecology themes. **B D PH**

Apply through partner organisation in country of residence. In the UK: Concordia (Youth Service Volunteers) Ltd, Quaker International Social Projects or United Nations Association International Youth Service. See page 30 for registration details and addresses.

SERVICE CIVIL INTERNATIONAL Deutscher Zweig eV, Blücherstraße 14, 5300 Bonn 1, Germany

Service Civil International promotes international reconciliation through work projects. **Volunteers** are invited to work in international teams on environmental and ecological workcamps. Recent projects have included building a compost loo and a water purification system at an environmental centre near Passau; harvesting hay and environment management work in the wine-growing area of the Kaiserstuhl; exploring alternative energy techniques at a youth education centre in Emlichheim; restoring old railway vehicles at an industrial railway museum in Cologne; and conservation work studying ecological systems in the damaged alpine forests of Burgberg/Allgau. Opportunities to meet local members of ecological movements. All camps have a strong study element, linked to pollution, nature protection and ecological problems. Ecology cycle tours also arranged. Knowledge of German needed on some camps.

⊕ Ages 18+. No experience necessary, but applicants should be highly motivated, preferably with previous workcamp or other voluntary experience and prepared to work hard as part of a team. 35-40 hour week. 2-4 weeks, April-October. Food, shared accommodation and work accident insurance provided. No fares or wages paid. **B D PH**

☙ *Apply through partner organisation in country of residence. In the UK: International Voluntary Service. See page 30 for registration details and addresses.*

COURIERS / REPS

CANVAS HOLIDAYS LTD
12 Abbey Park Place, Dunfermline, Fife KY12 7PD

Holiday company providing accommodation for families in ready-erected, fully equipped tents and mobile homes on campsites in Germany. Requires **resident couriers**, **children's couriers** and **watersports couriers**. Work involves a daily routine of tent cleaning as customers arrive and depart, providing information and advice on the local attractions and essential services, helping to sort out problems that might arise, and organising activities for the children and get-togethers for the families. Seven day week job with no fixed hours; the workload varies from day to day. At the beginning and end of the season there is a period of physical work when tents are put up and prepared for the customers or taken down and stored for the winter. Other tasks include administration, book keeping and stock control. Working knowledge of German essential.

⊕ Ages 18-25. Applicants are normally those with a year between school and further education, undergraduates or graduates. They need to be enthusiastic, practical, reliable, self-motivated, able to turn their hand to new and varied tasks,

and with a sense of humour. 6 months, April-October. Return travel, dependent on successful completion of contract, accommodation in frame tents, and bicycle for use on site provided. Salary £85 per week. ☙ *Applications accepted anytime; interviews commence early November for the following season.*

EUROCAMP Summer Jobs (Ref WH), PO Box 170, Liverpool L70 1ES ✆ **Knutsford (01565) 625522**

One of Europe's leading tour operators, specialising in providing quality camping and mobile home holidays for families throughout Europe. **Campsite couriers** required: work involves cleaning tents and equipment prior to the arrival of new customers; checking, replacing and making repairs on equipment; replenishing gas supplies; keeping basic accounts and reporting on a weekly basis to England. Couriers are also expected to meet new arrivals and assist holidaymakers with any problems that arise; organise activities and parties; provide information on local tourist attractions and maintain an information noticeboard. At the beginning and end of the season couriers are also expected to help in erecting and dismantling tents. Couriers need to be flexible to meet the needs of customers and be on hand where necessary; they will be able to organise their own free time as the workload allows.

⊕ Ages 18+. Applicants should be independent, adaptable, reliable, physically fit, have plenty of initiative and relish a challenging and responsible position. Good working knowledge of German also necessary. Preference given to those able to work the whole season, April-September/October; contracts also available for first half season, April-mid July and second half season, mid July-September/October. **Children's couriers** also required, with the energy and enthusiasm to organise a wide range of exciting activities for groups of children aged 4-13. Experience of working with children within this age range essential, but language ability is not a requirement. ⊕ Ages 18+. Children's couriers must be available for the whole season, May-September. For both positions the salary is £95 per week. Training is provided together with accommodation in frame tent with cooking facilities, insurance and return travel. *Early application by telephone preferred; interviews start September/ October. UK/EEA passport-holders only.*

D O M E S T I C

ALPOTELS AGENCY PO Box 388, London SW1X 8LX
Carries out aptitude tests at the request of hotels for 20 winter and 40 summer jobs mainly as **chambermaids** or **kitchen helpers**. ⊕ Ages 18+. Some knowledge of German useful but not essential. All jobs involve long hours and hard work in a professional team. 8 hours per day, with 2 days free per week. Jobs are available during two long seasons, December-May or June-November. Pay approx £120 per week. Board, lodging and insurance provided. Interview fee £1 plus subscription to JITA Club (£30 plus £15 per week). ✎ *Closing dates for interviews: 30 September (winter) or 30 March/April (summer). EEA nationals only.*

F A R M W O R K

Since farms in Germany tend to be small and highly mechanised, the opportunities for seasonal agricultural work are limited. The main crops are flour and feed grains, potatoes, sugar beet, vegetables, fruit and wine. The *Altes Land*, a flat, irrigated area to the south of the Elbe between Hamburg and Stade is a major fruit-growing region with opportunities for cherry-picking during the summer and apple picking in September. Another important area for apples and other fruit is the *Bergstraße*, on the eastern side of the Rhine Valley, between Darmstadt and Mannheim.

There are also opportunities in the major wine growing areas of south western Germany, especially along the Rhine and Mosel valleys. Grapes take longer to ripen in Germany than other countries; the grape harvest begins in mid-October and can carry on through November into December for the famous *Eiswein*.

INTERNATIONAL FARM EXPERIENCE PROGRAMME
YFC Centre, N A C, Stoneleigh Park, Kenilworth CV8 2LG
✆ Coventry (01203) 696584
Provides assistance to young **agriculturalists** and **horticulturalists** by finding places in farms/nurseries abroad enabling them to broaden their knowledge of agricultural and horticultural methods. Participants usually live and work with a farming family and the work is matched as far as possible with the participant's requirements. Entails physical work and practical involvement. 8-10 hour day, 6 day week, every other weekend free. 3-12 months throughout the year. Basic wage plus board and lodging. ⊕ Ages 18-28. Applicants must have a minimum 2 years' practical experience, of which 1 year may be at agricultural college, and intend to make a career in agriculture/horticulture. Valid driving licence necessary. Participants pay own fares and insurance. Registration fee £85. ✎ *UK applications to IFEP. Other applications to IFEP partner in home country.*

WILLING WORKERS ON ORGANIC FARMS (WWOOF-DEUTSCHLAND) Stettiner Straße 3, 35415 Pohlheim, Germany
A non-profitmaking organisation which aims to help organic farmers and smallholders whose work is often labour-intensive as it does not rely on the use of artificial fertilisers or pesticides. Provides unskilled **volunteers** with first hand experience of organic farming and gardening and a

chance to spend some time in the country. Places exist on 100 farms throughout Germany. Work outside includes working in the fields, in the stable or on the market stall; indoor work includes spinning, weaving, cheesemaking, pottery and woodwork. Members receive a quarterly newsletter which details farms needing help. ⊕ Ages 16+. 1+ weeks, all year. Full board and lodging provided in the farmhouse or in outbuildings; volunteers should take a sleeping bag. No wages paid, although long-term volunteers may receive small payment as arranged with host. Helpers pay own travel costs. Insurance and anti-tetanus vaccination recommended. Families welcome. Membership fee DM20.

PEACE CAMPS

SERVICE CIVIL INTERNATIONAL
Deutscher Zweig eV, Blücherstraße 14, 5300 Bonn 1, Germany
Service Civil International promotes international reconciliation through work projects. **Volunteers** are needed to work in international teams on peace camps run to support peace information and activity centres, to promote international discussion of the nuclear threat, alternative security policies and nonviolence, and to bring together peace movements in different countries. Camps are linked to peace study themes and opportunities to meet local peace groups. Also organise anti-Fascist camps, helping to maintain concentration camps as monuments, warning symbols and means of raising awareness of history. Volunteers should be interested in and have some knowledge of the political background of this theme. Recent projects have included building a playground at an anti-war house near Hannover; working in the archives and talking to eye-witnesses at the Reiherhorst evacuation camp; reconstructing the living and working spaces at the former labour/ concentration camp of Neuengamme,

near Hamburg, which has been turned into a documentation centre by former Resistance fighters; and gardening in the memorial grounds at Dachau. Study themes include history of the concentration camp and anti-Fascist resistance. Also organise cycle and sailing tours for peace. ⊕ Ages 18+. Applicants should be highly motivated, committed to the camp theme and prepared to work hard as part of a team. Previous workcamp or other voluntary experience desirable. Some camps require a knowledge of German. 35-40 hour week, 2-4 weeks, June-September, Christmas and Easter. Food, shared accommodation and work accident insurance provided. No fares or wages paid. **B D PH**

🌀 *Apply through partner organisation in country of residence. In the UK: International Voluntary Service. See page 30 for registration details and addresses.*

WORKCAMPS

CHRISTLICHER FRIEDENS-DIENST EV **Rendelerstraße 9-11, 60385 Frankfurt, Germany**
✆ **(49 69) 459071-72**
An international movement open to all who share a common concern for lasting peace and justice in the world. **Volunteers** are required to work in international teams on summer projects aimed at offering a service in an area of need and promoting self-help within the community; promoting international understanding and the discussion of social problems; and offering young people the chance to live as a group and take these experiences into the context of daily life. Recent projects have included helping with agricultural and construction work at a Franciscan farm community in Leuwitz; repairing bicycles and building a roofed site for campfires at a young people's free time centre south of Hamburg; and working on a memorial for victims of war in Sassnitz, on the Baltic island of Rugen. All camps

have a strong study element.
⊕ Ages 18+. Some camps require a
basic knowledge of German. 30-36
hour week, 2-4 weeks, July-September.
Food, accommodation and work
accident insurance provided. No fares
or wages paid. Registration fee DM150.
B D PH

📃 *Apply through partner organisation in
country of residence. In the UK: Christian
Movement for Peace. See page 30 for
registration details and addresses.*

INTERNATIONALE BEGEGNUNG IN GEMEINSCHAFTSDIENSTEN EV (IBG) Schlosserstraße 28, 70180 Stuttgart, Germany

Founded in 1965 to organise work
projects of benefit to the community
and to promote better international
understanding. **Volunteers** are needed
on international workcamps; each camp
is made up of 15-20 participants from
6-8 countries who work together on
common projects which have recently
included maintaining a bicycle trail and
building a barbecue hut in Wehrheim;
taking part in an Indian Game to teach
children about South American Indian
culture at a playscheme in Schramberg;
working in the reception and café/bar of
a tent city for young travellers in
Stuttgart; and helping with the harvest at
a village rebuilt as it was 200 years ago
in an open-air museum of Wackershofen.
⊕ Ages 18+. 30 hour week with free
weekends. 3 weeks, June-October.
Food, simple accommodation in schools,
youth hostels, empty buildings, clubs or
forest/mountain huts with self-catering
facilities, and work accident insurance
provided. No fares or wages paid.
Registration fee DM140.

📃 *Apply direct or through partner
organisation in country of residence.
In the UK: Concordia (Youth Service
Volunteers) Ltd, Quaker International Social
Projects or United Nations Association
International Youth Service. See page 30
for registration details and addresses.*

INTERNATIONALE JUGENDGEMEINSCHAFTSDIENSTE EV (IJGD) Kaiserstraße 43, 53113 Bonn, Germany

A society for international and political
education, involving **volunteers** on
approx 120 international workcamps
each year. Recent projects have included
renovating an information centre on the
Third World in Berlin Kreuzberg;
gardening and building a footbridge at an
artists' conference home in Schildow;
renovating a former potash works in
Hannover, which has been converted
into a tram museum, and cleaning and
painting the trams; building a skittle alley
and designing a mural at a youth centre
in Halle; and creating a playground at a
small community school in Mecklenburg.
Basic craftsmanship skills are taught for
all projects. Parent/children and women
only camps organised. Work/study
camps also arranged on themes including
Third World, peace and anti-Fascism.
Excursions arranged.
⊕ Ages 16-26. Basic knowledge of
German needed. 30 hour, 5 day week.
3 weeks, during April and June-
September. Simple accommodation
provided in schools, youth centres, flats,
stations, boarding houses, tents or
barns. A budget for food, cooking
facilities and insurance is provided for
each group of volunteers. Registration
fee DM150. No fares or wages paid.

📃 *Apply through partner organisation in
country of residence.
In the UK: Concordia (Youth Service
Volunteers) Ltd, Quaker International Social
Projects or United Nations Association
International Youth Service. See page 30
for registration details and addresses.*

INTERNATIONALER BAUORDEN-DEUTSCHER ZWEIG EV PO Box 1438, 67504 Worms, Germany

An international volunteers association
with the aims of fighting misery and
distress and making a contribution
towards a better understanding between
nations. **Volunteers** are needed to

work in international teams for and together with the socially, mentally, economically and physically underprivileged. Recent projects have included painting and renovating an old people's home in Kirchheim; converting old houses into homes for young families and thereby saving them from the bulldozer in Halberstadt; converting an old factory in Leuna into a workplace for severely handicapped adults; converting an old railway station into a leisure centre in Hasel; and renovating a Jewish cemetery in the eastern part of Berlin.
⊕ Ages 18+. Some knowledge of German essential. 40 hour, 5 day week, 2-4 weeks. Easter and June-September. Food prepared by volunteers, tent, school or barrack accommodation and insurance provided, but volunteers should take a sleeping bag. No fares or wages paid.

Apply 1 month in advance, either direct or through partner organisation in country of residence. See page 30 for registration details and addresses.

NORDDEUTSCHE JUGEND IM INTERNATIONALEN GEMEINSCHAFTSDIENST (NIG) Am Vögenteich 13-15, 18057 Rostock, Germany

A non-profitmaking organisation founded in 1990 by students of Rostock University with the aim of supporting important and urgent projects in north eastern Germany. **Volunteers** are invited to take part in international workcamps. Projects include reconstruction and renovation work, organising children's activities at holiday centres, construction work, gardening and work in Jewish cemeteries.
⊕ Ages 18-30. English is usually the working language, although conversational German may be necessary on some projects. 30 hour, 5 day week for 2-3 weeks, February-March and July-September. Participants have the chance to find out about everyday life in that part of Germany, on

excursions and through contact with local people. Food, accommodation and insurance provided; volunteers pay their own travel costs. **B D PH**

Apply direct or through partner organisation in country of residence. In the UK: Quaker International Social Projects or United Nations Association International Youth Service. See page 30 for registration details and addresses.

NOTHELFERGEMEINSCHAFT DER FREUNDE EV Secretariat General, PO Box 101510, 52349 Düren, Germany

A fellowship founded on the conviction that peaceful coexistence is only possible if prejudices and differences between peoples are overcome. Aims to improve the situation of the needy and works for better understanding and reconciliation between peoples. **Volunteers** are needed to help on projects which include manual and social work in homes for children, the elderly and the mentally handicapped, and in hospitals. Recent projects have included construction work, gardening and domestic work at centres for mentally handicapped people; path construction, farming and gardening at Camphill Village community farms for the handicapped; and repair work, painting and looking after elderly people at different homes throughout Germany.
⊕ Ages 18-30. Junior camps arranged for ages 16-18. Volunteers must be willing to work hard, show tolerance, initiative and enthusiasm, and be prepared to participate in discussions and seminars during their free time. Good knowledge of German needed on some camps. 30-35 hour week, 3/4 weeks, March, April, May-December. Self-catering accommodation, food and insurance provided. Registration fee DM140. *Apply by mid May.*

PRO INTERNATIONAL Bahnhofstraße 26A, 35037 Marburg/Lahn, Germany

Founded after the Second World War; aims to promote cooperation and understanding between people from all over the world by providing opportunities for them to meet and work together as **volunteers**. The accent is on learning new skills and gaining experience in a practical field. Recent projects have included restoring an old railway carriage for a museum; renovating and gardening at homes for the handicapped and at youth centres; renovating and clearing paths, playgrounds and parks; looking after and playing with children; and coastal protection work, stabilising dunes and planting grass on the East Frisian Islands. ⊕ Ages 16-26. Previous workcamp experience preferable; knowledge of German useful. 30-35 hour, 5 day week. 2-3 weeks, Easter, and June-October. Board and accommodation provided in schools, old houses, youth hostels or tents. Volunteers help prepare meals and should take a sleeping bag. Travel extra. Registration fee DM100 includes insurance.

⚞ Apply through partner organisation in country of residence. In the UK: Concordia (Youth Service Volunteers) Ltd. See page 30 for registration details and addresses.

SERVICE CIVIL INTERNATIONAL Deutscher Zweig eV, Blücherstraße 14, 5300 Bonn 1, Germany
Service Civil International promotes international reconciliation through work projects. **Volunteers** are needed to work in international teams on social/ manual projects in a variety of fields such as Third World solidarity and with self-help groups organised by young people facing long-term unemployment. Recent projects have included fitting out rooms in the attic of a community farm for handicapped and non-handicapped adults near the North Sea coast; making toys and relocating an adventure playground in Stuttgart; installing organically made insulation material at an ecology centre converted from an old water-mill on the outskirts of Leipzig; assisting at an environment education festival in Magdeburg; and organising a

holiday programme at a camp for refugee and German children in Solingen. Solidarity camps also organised, supporting Third World countries, helping organisations and projects involved in social, medical and educational work, by a combination of practical and educational assistance which includes providing materials for refugee camps and supporting self-reliant development and human rights. All camps include strong study element. ⊕ Ages 18+. Applicants should be highly motivated, preferably with previous workcamp or other voluntary experience and prepared to work hard as part of a team. Good German needed for some camps. 40 hour week, 2-3 weeks, July-September. Food, shared accommodation and work accident insurance provided. No fares or wages paid.

⚞ Apply through partner organisation in country of residence. In the UK: International Voluntary Service. See page 30 for registration details and addresses.

VEREINIGUNG JUNGER FREIWILLIGER Müggelstraße 22a, 10247 Berlin, Germany
Founded as a voluntary service organisation in 1990 in what was then the GDR. Aims to promote solidarity, humanitarian and environmental action, and to combat racism and Fascism. **Volunteers** are invited to join international workcamps to help with a variety of construction and social projects. Recent projects have included putting on a musical about understanding and tolerance at a youth education centre in Gräfenheinichen; working with mentally handicapped people in the gardens of Gamig Castle, near Dresden; and repairing gravestones and gardening at a Jewish cemetery in Berlin which was recently partly destroyed by vandalism. Opportunities to meet ordinary people and talk about life in eastern Germany before and after unification. ⊕ Ages 18-30. No experience

necessary but applicants must be prepared to work hard and contribute to team life. Working languages are English and German. 4-6 hour day, 5 day week. 2-3 weeks, July-September. Food, shared accommodation and work accident insurance provided. No fares or wages paid. **B D PH**

🕮 Apply through partner organisation in country of residence. In the UK: Concordia (Youth Service Volunteers) Ltd, International Voluntary Service, Quaker International Social Projects or United Nations Association International Youth Service. See page 30 for registration details and addresses.

GENERAL

EUROYOUTH LTD
301 Westborough Road, Westcliff, Southend-on-Sea, Essex SS0 9PT ✆ **Southend-on-Sea (01702) 341434**
Holiday guest stays are arranged where **guests** are offered board and lodging in return for an agreed number of hours English conversation with hosts or their children. Time also available for guests to practise German if desired.
✦ Mainly ages 18-25, but sometimes opportunities for older applicants. 2-3 weeks, June-August. Travel and insurance paid by applicants. Registration fee approx £70.
🕮 Apply at least 12 weeks prior to scheduled departure date; number of places limited. UK nationals only.

INVOLVEMENT VOLUNTEERS-DEUTSCHLAND Postfach 110224, 37047 Göttingen, Germany ✆ (49 551) 33 765 🖷 (49 551) 33 787
Works in association with the Involvement Volunteers Association Inc network to find unpaid **volunteer** activities in Germany and Europe. Placements relate to conservation in urban or rural areas; bird breeding/training operations; biological research; restoring or maintaining historic sites or gardens; developing national parks; and

assisting at special schools for disabled children. Volunteers must be able to speak English (German in special cases), arrange their own visitor visas where necessary, and organise their own international travel and insurance. Involvement Volunteers-Deutschland provides advice, placements, itinerary planning, introductions to banking, and a communications base in Germany. Cost DM400. **B D**

🕮 In Australia, New Zealand and the Asia Pacific region, apply to Involvement Volunteers Association Inc, PO Box 218, Port Melbourne, Victoria 3207, Australia ✆/🖷 (61 3) 646 5504.

In North America, apply to Involvement Corps Inc, 15515 Sunset Boulevard, Suite 108, Pacific Palisades, CA 90272, United States ✆/🖷 (1 310) 459 1022.

TOC H National Projects Office, 1 Forest Close, Wendover, Aylesbury, Buckinghamshire HP22 6BT ✆ Aylesbury (01296) 623911
Requires **volunteers** for a variety of short-term projects throughout Germany. Projects may include working with people having different disabilities; work with underprivileged children; playschemes and camps; conservation and manual work.
✦ Ages 18+. Programmes giving further details of projects and application procedures are published in March and September. **B D PH** depending on project. 🕮 Early application advised.

ZENTRALSTELLE FÜR ARBEITSVERMITTLUNG DER BUNDESANSTALT FÜR ARBEIT Postfach 17 05 45, 60079 Frankfurt, Germany
The central placement office of the federal employment services. Concerned with the recruitment of foreign workers, including the free placement of foreign students for **temporary jobs** of at least 2 months.
✦ Ages 18+. Applicants must speak German.

GREAT BRITAIN

INFO

Tourist offices
British Tourist Authority, Thames Tower, Black's Road, Hammersmith, London W6 9EL ✆ 0181-846 9000. Offices in 19 countries and a network of information centres throughout Britain.

Scottish Tourist Board, 23 Ravelston Terrace, Edinburgh EH4 3EU
✆ 0131-332 2433
London office: 19 Cockspur Street, London SW1Y 5BL ✆ 0171-930 8661-3

Wales Tourist Board, Brunel House, 2 Fitzalan Road, Cardiff CF2 1UY
✆ Cardiff (01222) 499909
London office: 12 Lower Regent Street, London SW1 ✆ 0171-409 0969

Youth hostels
YHA, Trevelyan House, 8 St Stephen's Hill, St Albans, Hertfordshire AL1 2DY

SYHA, 7 Glebe Crescent, Stirling FK8 2JA

Youth & student information
National Union of Students, 461 Holloway Road, London N7 6LJ
✆ 0171-272 8900

UK Council for Overseas Students (UKCOSA), 60 Westbourne Grove, London W2 5SH ✆ 0171-229 9268

Entry regulations EU/EEA (Austria, Belgium, Denmark, Finland, France, Germany, Gibraltar, Greece, Iceland, Ireland, Italy, Luxembourg, the Netherlands, Norway, Portugal, Spain and Sweden) nationals do not need a work permit to take up or seek employment in Britain. Other nationals subject to immigration control need a work permit and will be refused entry if one cannot be produced at the port of entry. A work permit is not required for au pair posts or temporary employment at approved farmcamps, but an au pair must have a letter of invitation from the family and seasonal agricultural workers must be between the ages of 18 and 25 years inclusive, in full-time education and have a Home Office card issued by an approved scheme operator. Neither the letter of invitation nor the Home Office card provides entitlement to any other kind of paid work. Permits are not usually required for temporary voluntary work on international workcamps or other voluntary opportunities with charitable organisations, but it is advisable to obtain prior entry clearance from a British diplomatic post abroad. Overseas students studying in Britain who wish to take paid work in their free time or during vacations do not require work permits but they must first obtain the consent of the Department of Employment through the local Jobcentre or employment office and provide evidence from their college that employment will not interfere with their studies.

Further information on work permits may be obtained from the Department of Employment, Overseas Labour Service, W5 Moorfoot, Sheffield S1 4PQ ℗ 0114-259 4074 or in leaflets *WP1/5 Notes* or *WP2/5 Notes for the Training and Work Experience Scheme* obtainable by phoning ℗ 0117-924 4780.

Commonwealth citizens with proof of a grandparent's birth in the UK and islands who wish to take up or seek employment in the UK will be granted entry clearance for that purpose. They do not need a work permit and will be admitted for a period of 4 years. Other Commonwealth citizens aged 17-27 inclusive may enter Britain for up to 2 years during which they can take work incidental to their holiday, provided they obtain prior entry clearance from a British diplomatic post abroad. They must have the means to pay for their return journey and not fall a charge on public funds. Further information on concessions for Commonwealth citizens of UK ancestry, the provisions for Commonwealth working holidaymakers

and immigration requirements generally may be obtained from the Home Office, Lunar House, Wellesley Road, Croydon, Surrey CR9 2BY ℗ 0181-686 0688.

Nationals from countries needing a visa to come to the UK must obtain one before travelling, whether coming for a temporary or longer stay. Applications for visas must be made to a British diplomatic post overseas.

Job advertising Most newspapers in Britain carry classified advertising. There are several daily newspapers with national distribution and hundreds of local newspapers published on a daily or weekly basis.

A daily evening newspaper circulating in London only is the *Evening Standard,* Classified Advertising, Northcliffe House, 2 Derry Street, London W8 5TT ℗ 0171-938 3838. As well as accepting paid advertisements, also advertises many short-term job opportunities, especially the Tuesday edition.

Time Out is a weekly magazine aimed at young people in London, giving details of events in the capital; to advertise contact Classified Advertising, Time Out, London WC2E 7HA ℗ 0171-836 5131.

Travel Anyone under 24 or a full-time student in the UK can buy a British Rail Young Person's Railcard, entitling the holder to 30% reduction on many tickets. Cost £15, valid 1 year. Further details and application forms available from principal British Rail stations or most student travel offices. British Rail also offer a variety of discount tickets depending on age, time of day and distance to be travelled. Further information can be obtained from British Rail offices or agents in other countries, and from any British Rail station.

National Express operate extensive coach services to most major towns and cities throughout the UK. Full-time students can buy a Student Coach Card entitling them to approx 30% reduction on standard fares. Cost £6, valid 1 year. For further information contact National Express © 0181-770 7770.

Both the Young Persons Railcard and Student Coach Card are available from Campus Travel, who have offices throughout Britain on university campuses, within YHA Adventure shops, and on the high street. London office is at 52 Grosvenor Gardens, London SW1W 0AG (opposite Victoria Station) © 0171-730 3402.

Information centres The National Association of Volunteer Bureaux, St Peter's College, College Road, Saltley, Birmingham B8 3TE © 0121-327 0265 was set up to serve and represent Britain's volunteer bureaux and to promote volunteering in general. Does not recruit volunteers, but can put enquirers in touch with their local volunteer bureau, who will be able to advise them of the entire range of voluntary work available locally. The majority of local volunteering opportunities do not provide accommodation and bureaux are unable to help in finding accommodation.

The National Youth Agency, 17-23 Albion Street, Leicester LE1 6GD © 0116-247 1200 can provide information on community involvement and young volunteer organisations in England and Wales.

The Scottish Community Education Council (SCEC), Rosebery House, 9 Haymarket Terrace, Edinburgh EH12 5EZ © 0131-313 2488 promotes community involvement and service by young people in Scotland. Although it does not recruit volunteers or find placements for them, it provides an information sheet giving details of volunteer projects in Scotland, including conservation work, workcamps, community projects, playschemes and some opportunities for long-term volunteers.

Publications *Directory of Summer Jobs in Britain 1994* £7.95, lists opportunities all over Britain with details of wages, conditions of work, and qualifications required. Published by Vacation Work, 9 Park End Street, Oxford OX1 1HJ © Oxford (01865) 241978.

Accommodation The International Friendship League, Peace Haven, 3 Creswick Road, Acton, London W3 9HE works to promote a spirit of mutual respect and friendship among the peoples of the world. Offers accommodation at a residential centre in London all year from £10.50 per night, bed and breakfast. Also offers a hospitality service throughout Britain of households prepared to provide accommodation at a reasonable charge and take visitors to places of interest. *Apply at least 8 weeks in advance enclosing 4 IRCs.*

Hackney Camping, Millfields Road, London E5 © 0181-985 7656 is a campsite for those taking their own tents/equipment. Open mid June-end August. Cost £4 per night, includes the use of hot showers, shop, snack bar and baggage store. From September-May contact Tent City, see address below. © 0171-415 7143. **B D PH**

Tent City, Old Oak Common Lane, East Acton, London W3 7DP © 0181-743 5708 offers camping accommodation for young travellers at a football pavilion and park, with 450 beds in 14 large mixed or single sex tents. Bedding available; also space for those taking their own tents. Open early June-late September. Cost £5 per night; hot showers, snack bar and baggage store. **B D PH**

When writing to any organisation it is essential to mention Working Holidays 1995 and enclose a stamped, self-addressed A4 envelope, or if in another country, an addressed A4 envelope and at least two IRCs (International Reply Coupons, available from post offices).

ARCHAEOLOGY

Work on archaeological digs is unpaid and you will also be expected to pay for food and/or accommodation.

ARBEIA ROMAN FORT & MUSEUM Baring Street, South Shields, Tyne & Wear NE33 2EY
℃ 0191-455 4406 ⅲ 0191-427 6862
Volunteers are required for the excavation of a 1st-2nd century Roman fort at South Shields. Features currently under investigation include an extensive Iron Age horizon with a roundhouse rich in carbonised grain and plant materials; this is overlain by a vast levelled area of stones and clay, possibly used as a parade ground; and two periods of barracks where excavations have revealed doorways, passages, plastered walls, burnt hearths and cooking areas. Students will gain experience in excavating complex stratigraphy, written recording sheets, site planning, surveying, photography, preparing drawings and plans, and processing finds. 37 hour week, 1-2+ weeks, mainly April-October. No fares or wages paid; insurance cover provided. ⊕ Ages 16+. Applicants should have enthusiasm for the work and a good level of English. On-site training and tours of site provided. Volunteers should take with them a 100mm drop-forged pointing trowel, waterproofs and stout footwear in case of bad weather. ⚆ Apply as far in advance as possible; last minute applications accepted subject to available places.

COUNCIL FOR BRITISH ARCHAEOLOGY Bowes Morrell House, 111 Walmgate, York YO1 2UA ℃ York (01904) 671417 ⅲ (01904) 671384
Works to promote the safeguarding of Britain's historic environment, to provide a forum for archaeological opinion, and to improve public knowledge of Britain's past. Operates a British archaeological information service which gives details on how volunteers can assist in archaeological excavations. Opportunities in all parts of Britain; hours and payment vary. Details published in CBA Briefing, a supplement to British Archaeological News, published five times a year; available through membership of the CBA (£18 for individuals, £10 for students). Lists sites requiring volunteer helpers, giving details of location, type and accommodation.

THISTLE CAMPS National Trust for Scotland (NTS), 5 Charlotte Square, Edinburgh EH2 5DU ℃ 0131-226 5922 ext 257
Founded to promote the permanent preservation of the countryside and buildings of historic interest or natural beauty. Thistle Camps are residential work projects organised by NTS and now include archaeological digs that volunteers may join. Recent projects have included the excavation and examination of a Bronze Age barrow at House of Dun on Scotland's east coast. ⊕ Ages 16-70. Up to 2 friends can be placed together. Volunteers should be fit for hard, practical work. 8 hour day, 5 day week for 1-2 weeks, June. Participants should take old clothes, waterproofs, a sleeping bag and boots or wellingtons. Contribution £12.50 or £25 depending on circumstances. ⚆ Apply by March to be sure of a place. Overseas volunteers with good English welcome.

UNIVERSITY OF WALES Dr C J Arnold, Gregynog, Newton, Powys SY16 3PW ℃ Newton (01686) 650715
Volunteers are required to work on an archaeological excavation in Wales. ⊕ Ages 16+. English useful, no experience necessary. 30 hour, 6 day week, end July-end August. Campsite accommodation, personal and third party insurance provided. Food cost £30 per week. Training provided plus alternate evenings visiting related archaeological sites. No fares or wages paid. ⚆ Apply by 22 July.

UPPER NENE ARCHAEOLOGICAL SOCIETY

Toad Hall, 86 Main Road, Hackleton, Northampton NN7 2AD ✆ Northampton (01604) 870312

Limited number of **volunteers** required to assist in the excavation of a large Romano-British villa. Work involves trowelling, digging, drawing, surveying, assisting with photography, processing and recording finds. ⊕ Ages 17+. Relevant qualifications and experience welcome but not essential. 50 hours per week. 3 weeks, August, and Sundays all year. Campsite available nearby, cost approx £10 for 2 weeks; or bed and breakfast arranged with local families, cost from approx £8 per night. Approx £20 fee for 2 weeks covers site running costs and refreshments. Insurance provided, but no fares or wages paid. Occasional talks and excursion to local excavation or place of interest arranged. **D PH**

AU PAIR / CHILDCARE

Au pair placements are intended only for unmarried people aged 17-27, without dependants, wishing to visit Britain to learn English while living as a member of an English-speaking family and having appropriate opportunities to study. As a general rule au pairs can expect to work up to 5 hours per day with 2 days per week free. They should have their own room and receive up to £35 per week pocket money. They may be asked to do light housework, childcare and occasional evening babysitting. Only nationals of Andorra, Bosnia-Herzegovinia, Cyprus, the Czech Republic, the Faroes, Greenland, Hungary, Liechtenstein, Macedonia, Malta, Monaco, San Marino, the Slovak Republic, Slovenia, Switzerland and Turkey are eligible, and may spend no more than a total of 2 years in Britain as an au pair. EEA nationals are also free to take up au pair posts with no limit on how long they stay. On arrival non-EEA national au pairs should provide the immigration officer with a letter of invitation from the host family, giving precise details of the arrangements, including the amount of pocket money, accommodation, free time, details of the host family, house and household, and exact nature of assistance expected. They may also be required to produce a return ticket or evidence of sufficient funds to pay for return travel. Those entering the UK in another capacity (eg as a visitor) will not be allowed to remain as an au pair. Au pair posts should not be confused with regular childcare employment; nannies and au pair plus posts usually fall into this category. Further information and advice on immigration matters can be obtained from British Embassies, Consulates and High Commissions or from the Home Office, Lunar House, Wellesley Road, Croydon CR9 2BY ✆ 0181-686 0688.

ACADEMY AU PAIR AGENCY LTD

42 Cedarhurst Drive, Eltham, London SE9 5LP ✆ 0181-294 1191 ⌨ 0181-850 8932

Can place **au pairs**. ⊕ Ages 18-27. Some knowledge of English essential. Pocket money approx £35-£40 per week. Positions as **nannies** and **mothers' helps** also available for those with qualifications/experience.

ANGLO PAIR AGENCY

40 Wavertree Road, Streatham Hill, London SW2 3SP ✆ 0181-674 3605

Can place **au pairs** and **au pairs plus** in London. ⊕ Ages 17-27. Weekly pocket money £30+ (au pairs) or £40+ (au pairs plus).

AVALON AGENCY

Thursley House, 53 Station Road, Shalford, Guildford, Surrey GU4 8HA ✆ Guildford (01843) 63640

Can place **au pairs, au pairs plus**, and **mothers' helps**. ⊕ Ages 18-35 depending on position. Pocket money from £30 per week. 6-24 months to start any time.

BELAF STUDY HOLIDAYS
Banner Lodge, Cherhill, Calne, Wiltshire SN11 8XR ℂ Calne (01249) 812533 ☎ (01249) 821533
Can place summer **holiday helps** and **au pairs** throughout the year in Berkshire, Surrey, Hampshire, Somerset and Gloucestershire. ⊕ Ages 18-25. Pocket money £25-£40 per week. Language classes available. *Initial application by telephone.*

BUNTERS AU PAIR & DOMESTIC AGENCY 17 Copper Street, Macclesfield, Cheshire SK11 7LH ℂ Macclesfield (01625) 614534
Can place **au pairs**, **demi pairs**, **mothers' helps** and **au pairs plus** throughout the UK. 6-12 months all year or 10 weeks, summer. ⊕ Ages 18-27. Pocket money £35-£50 per week depending on hours worked. ✍ *Apply before May for summer placements.*

EUROYOUTH LTD
301 Westborough Road, Westcliff, Southend-on-Sea SSO 9PT ℂ Southend-on-Sea (01702) 341434
Can place **au pairs**. ⊕ Ages 18+. Knowledge of English desirable. Pocket money from £30 per week. Also **mothers' helps** and **holiday helps**. Short-term placements early February-end May. ✍ *Apply 9 weeks in advance.*

HELPING HANDS AU PAIR & DOMESTIC AGENCY 39 Rutland Avenue, Thorpe Bay, Essex SS1 2XJ ℂ Southend-on-Sea (01702) 602067
Can place **au pairs**, **demi pairs**, **au pairs plus** and **mothers' helps** in all areas including London suburbs, major towns, country areas and coastal towns. ⊕ Ages 17-27. Pocket money £20-£70 per week depending on position.

HOME FROM HOME Walnut Orchard, Chearsley, Aylesbury, Buckinghamshire HP18 0DA ℂ/☎ Aylesbury (01844) 208561

Can place **au pairs** throughout Britain. ⊕ Ages 18+. Pocket money £35 per week.

INTERNATIONAL CATHOLIC SOCIETY FOR GIRLS (ACISJF) St Patrick's International Youth Centre, 24 Great Chapel Street, London W1V 3AF ℂ 0171-734 2156 ☎ 0171-287 6282
Au pair posts arranged mostly for 9+ months. ⊕ Ages 18+.

JOLAINE AGENCY 18 Escot Way, Barnet, Hertfordshire EN5 3AN ℂ 0181-449 1334 ☎ 0181-449 9183
Can place **au pairs**, **demi pairs** and **mothers' helps** with families in the London area, on the coast and in the country. ⊕ Ages 17+. Pocket money £12-£80 per week, depending on position.

JUST THE JOB (NOTTINGHAM) 32 Dovedale Road, West Bridgford, Nottingham NG2 6JA ℂ 0115-945 2482
Can place **au pairs** and **au pairs plus** in Aberdeen, Blackpool, Cardiff, Derby, Glasgow, Leeds, Leicester, London, Manchester, Newcastle, Norwich, Nottingham and Sheffield. ⊕ Ages 18+. 6+ months; no short-term placements. Weekly pocket money £34 (au pairs) or £50 (au pairs plus).

MONDIAL AGENCY 32 Links Road, West Wickham, Kent BR4 0QW ℂ 0181-777 0510
Can place **au pairs** with families in the south of London and the Home Counties. ⊕ Ages 18-27. Pocket money £32-£35 per week.

PROBLEMS UNLIMITED 86 Alexandra Road, Windsor, Berkshire SL4 1HU ℂ Windsor (01753) 830101
Can place **au pairs**, **au pairs plus** and **mothers' helps** mainly in the south east, also Scotland and Wales. ⊕ Ages 18-27 (au pairs), 18+ (mothers' helps). Basic conversational English and

some experience in housework essential. Weekly pocket money £30-£35 (au pairs), £40 (au pairs plus), £80-£100 (mothers' helps). *EEA nationals only.*

STUDENTS ABROAD LTD
11 Milton View, Hitchin, Hertfordshire SG4 0QD ℰ **Hitchin (01462) 438909** ☎ **(01462) 438919**
Can place **au pairs** and **mothers' helps** with families in the London area and throughout the UK. ⊕ Ages 18-27 for au pairs. Basic knowledge of English preferred. Pocket money £35-£45 per week; higher for mothers' helps.

CHILDREN'S PROJECTS

Work on community children's projects is tiring but fun. There will sometimes be a small amount of pocket money, but in most cases the work is unpaid. However, on residential projects food and accommodation will be provided.

AFASIC Overcoming Speech Impairments, 347 Central Markets, Smithfield, London EC1A 9NH
ℰ **0171-236 6487/3632**
Works to improve educational provision for children and young people with speech and/or language impairments, and gives support and advice to parents and professionals. Arranges adventure weeks for those aged 8-25, covering a wide range of outdoor pursuits and indoor activities. The adventure weeks are held in centres in the countryside or at the seaside; recent venues have included Kendal, Whitby, Bournemouth and Northampton. Committed **volunteers** with fluent English are needed, to spend a week devoting time and energy. Work involves being a friend and constant companion on a 1:1 basis throughout the week, helping to stimulate and give supportive help to children and young adults with communication disabilities.

⊕ Ages 18+. Volunteers accepted for one 1-week project only. Full board accommodation in hostel or youth centre provided, but help towards cost welcomed. No wages or travel paid. **B D PH** depending on ability.

BIRMINGHAM PHAB CAMPS
Sally Rate, 60 Christchurch Lane, Lichfield WS13 8AN
ℰ **Lichfield (01543) 262858**
PHAB camps are week-long holidays at outdoor pursuits centres, integrating equal numbers of disabled and able bodied young people, looked after by a team of 18 volunteers including an experienced leader and nurse. Activities range from sailing, canoeing and riding to outings, barbecues and discos.
Volunteers are needed to take on 24-hour care involving everything from feeding, dressing and toileting to arranging games and activities.
⊕ Ages 17+ (21+ for minibus drivers). Applicants should have imagination, initiative and enthusiasm, they must be utterly dependable and willing to work really hard even when they don't get much sleep. Most of all they need to enjoy children and be prepared to dedicate themselves to children's needs 24 hours a day. No formal experience or qualifications needed although talents of all sorts are valuable - sporting, musical, driving - and a sense of humour. Training day provides opportunity for volunteers to be fully briefed on the disabilities they will meet and discuss their role with the camp leader and experienced volunteers. 7 days, July and August. Board and lodging provided. Insurance and travel between Birmingham and holiday centre arranged.

BIRMINGHAM YOUNG VOLUNTEERS ADVENTURE CAMPS 4th Floor, Smithfield House, Digbeth, Birmingham B5 6BS ℰ 0121-622 2888
Organises holidays on the Pembrokeshire coast, in Tywyn, in the Malvern Hills and in Atherstone for disadvantaged children from the

Birmingham area. One week, July-September. **Volunteer** helpers needed to encourage close personal contact, allowing development of personalities through new relationships and experiences. Experience of drama, art, games, music or cooking useful. ⊕ Ages 17+. Also opportunities for minibus drivers, ages 21+. Training available on a number of topics relating to the work. Full board hostel or camping accommodation, insurance cover and travel costs from Birmingham to the holiday provided. *Overseas applicants welcome, but as camps are only one week long they need to be already resident in Britain.*

THE BLACKIE Duty Officer, Great Georges Project, Great George Street, Liverpool L1 5EW
✆ 0151-709 5109

The Great Georges Community Cultural Project, known locally as The Blackie, is a centre for experimental work in the arts, sports, games and education of today. Housed in a former church in an area typical of the modern inner-city: multi-racial, relatively poor, with a high crime rate and a high energy level, sometimes a lot of fun. **Volunteers** are needed to work with children/adults on playschemes, special projects and outdoor events. The work of running the Project is shared as fairly as possible, with everyone doing some administration, repairs, building work, cleaning, talking to visitors and playing games with the children. ⊕ Ages normally 18+, although younger volunteers may be accepted. Applicants should have a good sense of humour, stamina, a readiness to learn, and a willingness to work hard and to share any skills they may have. The children and young people who visit the Project are tough, intelligent, friendly and regard newcomers as a fair target for jokes, so the ability to exert discipline without being authoritarian is essential. 12 hour day, 5½ day week, 4+ weeks; volunteers particularly needed at Christmas, Easter and summer. Accommodation provided

in shared rooms at staff house; volunteers should take a sleeping bag. Vegetarian breakfast and evening meal provided, cooking on a rota basis. Those who can afford to, contribute approx £17.50 per week to cover food and housekeeping. *Overseas applicants welcome; good working knowledge of English required.*

CHRISTIAN MOVEMENT FOR PEACE 186 St Pauls Road, Balsall Heath, Birmingham B12 8LZ
✆ 0121-446 5704

An international movement open to all who share a common concern for lasting peace and justice in the world. **Volunteers** are required to work in international teams on summer projects aimed at offering a service in an area of need and promoting self-help within the community; promoting international understanding and the discussion of social problems; and offering young people the chance to live as a group and take these experiences into the context of daily life. Recent projects have included running playschemes in Leicester, Dudley and County Durham, involving fundraising, arts and craft activities, music and movement, sports, camping and bus trips. Participants encouraged to become involved in the life of the host community. ⊕ Ages 17+, or 18+ for overseas volunteers, who must have good English. Volunteers must enjoy working with children, be able to contribute their own ideas to the schemes, show initiative in organising indoor and outdoor activities and be prepared to take a full part in all aspects of the project. 30-35 hour week. 2-3 weeks, July and August, and sometimes at Easter. Board, lodging and insurance provided, but participants pay their travel costs. Registration fee £42. Membership fee £18 (waged) or £8 (unwaged).

⚱ *Apply through partner organisation in country of residence; for further information see page 30. UK applicants should enclose £1 in stamps to cover postage.*

COMMUNITY ACTION PROJECTS Camp Organiser, Goodricke College, University of York, Heslington, York YO1 5DD

℗ York (01904) 433133
✉ (01904) 433724

Organises an annual camp for those with additional needs aged 6-13, who might not otherwise get a holiday; **volunteers** are needed to help out. Many of the children are emotionally disturbed, hyperactive or come from unsettled backgrounds. The camp takes about 30 children per week and is usually held on the North Yorkshire Moors. Activities include drama, arts/crafts, horse-riding, ice-skating, going to the beach, excursions, games, shows and walks. Duties include supervising tents, playing with and looking after the children, dealing with emotional problems, taking responsibility for situations as they arise, driving the minibus, cooking and sharing camp duties/chores. 1-3 weeks during school summer holidays. The work is physically and emotionally tiring; maximum stay as a volunteer 3 weeks, 2 weeks as a driver.

✣ Ages 18+; drivers must be over 21 with 1 year's clean driving licence. Volunteers should have initiative, enthusiasm, a sense of humour, lots of energy, the ability to take responsibility and participate fully in all camp activities, plus a liking for children, friendliness and tolerance. Skills in games, arts/crafts, cookery, wildlife, sports or first aid are very useful, as well as the ability to drive a minibus. References required. Smaller camps, catering for up to 20, also run at Easter, based in village schools or similar buildings. Accommodation and food provided. Venture weeks run for 14-16 year olds in August, involving backpacking, canoeing, rock climbing, abseiling, setting up camp, orienteering and problem solving. Experience of camping and working with teenagers useful. Training day arranged the day before each camp begins to give volunteers the opportunity to meet one another and discuss the running of the camp. **B D PH** depending on ability.

Overseas volunteers with a working knowledge of English accepted.

FLYSHEET CAMPS SCOTLAND The Resident Organiser, Finniegill, Lockerbie, Dumfriesshire DG11 2LP

A remote farmstead situated high in the hills of southwest Scotland, providing wilderness camps for children, mainly from families in need. The aim is to provide a setting where people of all ages and backgrounds can come together and experience living and working in ways that are different from their everyday life. All aspects of a simple lifestyle are explored, and the experience is as important as the end-product. There is no telephone, no electricity and no amenities for 15 miles. Flysheet is a small, 100% voluntary organisation, locally based, poor, but well established. A limited number of dedicated **volunteers** are needed.

✣ Ages 18+. 2-3+ weeks, July-August. Tent accommodation and insurance provided. Volunteers pay their own travel costs and contribute to the cost of food. The camps are of special interest to anyone training for, interested or involved in social work or education. **D PH**

🕿 No telephone enquiries. Overseas applicants accepted; fluent English required.

INTERNATIONAL VOLUNTARY SERVICE Old Hall, East Bergholt, Colchester, Essex CO7 6TQ

IVS is the British branch of Service Civil International which promotes international reconciliation through work projects. **Volunteers** are needed to work in international teams running children's projects throughout Britain. Recent projects have included involving local children in a water safety project on a canal in Glasgow; working on a holiday playscheme at a community school in Glastonbury; developing play activities for refugee children in east London; and working among children with mental and physical disabilities in Rotherham, South Yorkshire.

⊕ Ages 18+. 35-40 hour week, 2-4 weeks, June-September, Christmas and Easter. Overseas volunteers must speak good English. Experience in working with children an advantage. Volunteers must be prepared to work hard and contribute actively to the work and team life. Food, accommodation in village halls, houses, schools, homes, hospitals or community centres with self-catering facilities provided. No fares or wages paid. Registration fee £30 (students/unwaged £25) Membership fee £25 (students/unwaged £15). **B D PH**

🗺 *Apply through partner organisation in country of residence; for further information see page 30.*

JOINT HOLIDAY PROJECT
(National Eczema Society/National Asthma Campaign) c/o National Eczema Society, 4 Tavistock Place, London W1H 9RA ✆ **0171-388 4097**
Volunteers are needed to help with and participate in sporting activities with those aged 7-17 who are suffering from varying degrees of asthma and eczema. Activities include canoeing, sailing, archery, pioneering and climbing. Volunteers take responsibility for a group of 4-5 children who share a room. They provide practical care and supervision at the beginning and end of each day and occasionally at night. During the day volunteers work with another member of staff and a group of participants supporting and encouraging them through a range of activities, with qualified instructors to do the teaching.
⊕ Ages 18-60. 1 week minimum. Approx 12 hour day, July/August. Full board accommodation provided. Volunteers may be fully-qualified doctors/nurses or general helpers who are interested in working with young people. Life saving and first aid qualifications an advantage. Training weekend for volunteers covering asthma and eczema treatments usually takes place in April. All nationalities welcome; volunteers must speak English.
🗺 *Apply January-April.*

LEICESTER CHILDREN'S HOLIDAY HOME Quebec Road, Mablethorpe, Lincolnshire LN12 1QX ✆ Mablethorpe (01507) 472444
Holiday home which provides the poorest and most deserving children aged 7-11 from Leicester and its neighbourhood with a fortnight's holiday. Situated on the sandhills, the children have their own path to the beach.
Seasonal staff required; work includes looking after the children, playing, taking them to the beach, and perhaps making beds and a little housework.
⊕ Ages 18+. 1+ months, May-August. Preference given to applicants able to work the whole season. Board and lodging provided plus a salary of £49 per week. *UK nationals only.*

LIVERPOOL CHILDREN'S HOLIDAY ORGANISATION Wellington Road School, Wellington Road, Liverpool L8 4TX ✆ 0151-727 7330
Volunteers are needed to help run holidays for Merseyside children, particularly those from low income families who would not otherwise be able to afford one, at centres throughout Britain. Volunteers are responsible for looking after the happiness and safety of groups of 4-6 children aged 7-9 and 9-11, providing them with a wide range of entertaining and stimulating activities.
No experience necessary but volunteers must have plenty of energy and enthusiasm for being with children, and are on call 24 hours per day.
All volunteers will be interviewed before attending a 1 week training course.
⊕ Ages 18+. Holidays last 8 or 11 days. Full board dormitory accommodation shared with the children, expenses covered during the holiday period, and basic insurance and return travel from Liverpool to centre provided. Pocket money approx £30 per week.
Participants pay nominal fee for training course. **PH** *UK residents only; preference given to those living in Merseyside.*

LONDON CHILDREN'S CAMP
Recruitment Officer, 105 Bevan Street West, Lowestoft, Suffolk NR32 2AF

Organises a holiday for underprivileged children from London on a campsite in Suffolk, for which **volunteers** are required. Leaders have pastoral care for a group of approx 6 children, aged 8-14, and are involved in inventing and organising different activities and in the day-to-day running of the camp.
⊕ Ages 18+. 11-13 days, July-end August. Applicants should be energetic, prepared to work 16-17 hours per day, have a sense of humour, be innovative, fairly thick-skinned, tolerant, able to listen, confident, willing to keep order and cope with the children who are sometimes difficult and hard to motivate. Camping accommodation provided plus washing facilities, leaders' hut and a large dining room. Pocket money £25+ per camp. **B** if accompanied **D PH**
☙ Apply by end December.
UK nationals only.

MANSFIELD DISTRICT COUNCIL
Play Officer, Leisure & Community Services, Civic Centre, Chesterfield Road, Mansfield, Nottinghamshire NG19 9BT ✆ **Mansfield (01623) 656656 ext 3372**

Playleaders and **assistants** required to work at various venues throughout the Mansfield area. Work involves organising a variety of play activities for both able-bodied and disabled children aged 5-14. Applicants must have previous experience of working with groups of children in a play environment (eg playschemes, school groups).
⊕ Ages 18+. 2 weeks, Easter and 4 weeks, summer. Pay £3.88 per hour (leaders), £3.46 per hour (assistants).
☙ Applicants **must** be UK residents living in the Mansfield area.

SCRIPTURE UNION 130 City Road, London EC1V 2NJ
✆ **0171-782 0013**

Organises Christian activity holidays in the UK. **Volunteers** are needed to help run holidays for children and young people aged 8-18. Hours can be long; 3-10 days, Easter/summer.
⊕ Ages 18+. Volunteers must be physically fit, committed Christians. No experience necessary but qualifications in outdoor activities, sports, working with disabled people, catering, first aid or life saving helpful. Training provided.
☙ Apply from December onwards to the Activities Secretary.

TADWORTH COURT CHILDREN'S SERVICES Tadworth Court Trust, Tadworth, Surrey KT20 5RU ✆ Burgh Heath (01737) 357171

Requires **volunteers** to work on residential summer schemes for profoundly disabled children, who normally live at home. The services are provided in a children's hospital and at a residential school. Work involves acting as a friend to the children, carrying out basic personal care, organising games, encouraging them to take an active part in daily activities, escorting them on outings and organising evening activities. Previous experience with children or handicapped people preferable, but not essential. Creative skills, handicraft or musical ability welcomed. The work is very rewarding but can also be physically and emotionally tiring.
⊕ Ages 18+. 9 hour day, worked in shifts; 2 days off per week. 4+ weeks, mid July-mid September. Lodging and meal allowance of £42 per week. Travel expenses within England can be reimbursed. **D PH** depending on ability.
☙ Apply to Rachel Turner, Voluntary Services Organiser, by 31 March.

UNITED NATIONS ASSOCIATION International Youth Service, Temple of Peace, Cathays Park, Cardiff CF1 3AP ✆ Cardiff (01222) 223088

Aims to assist in community development by acting as a means to stimulate new ideas and projects, and encouraging the concept of voluntary work as a force in the common search for peace, equality, democracy and social justice. **Volunteers** are needed for community work on summer workcamps in various parts of Wales. Recent projects have included helping run playschemes in the south Wales valleys, organising indoor and outdoor activities for children, some of whom are mentally and physically handicapped; and taking groups of deprived or socially handicapped children on holiday, including walks, sports and excursions. ⊕ Ages 18+. Volunteers are expected to join in local community activities and to create a happy and effective project. 40 hour week, 2-4 weeks, July-August. Accommodation in church halls, youth hostels, schools or community centres, food and insurance provided. Volunteers share the cooking, pay their own travel costs and should take a sleeping bag. Good command of English essential. No fares or wages paid. Registration fee £45. **B D PH** on some projects.

🐾 *Apply through partner organisation in country of residence; for further information see page 30.*

COMMUNITY WORK

Opportunities may include providing personal care and friendship to people with physical and mental disabilities; working to overcome homelessness, poverty or discrimination; or helping people who are disadvantaged in some way. The work is mostly unpaid but board and accommodation are often provided, and on longer projects, a small amount of pocket money. Applicants must have a high degree of commitment; overseas volunteers will need a good command of English.

Opportunities for Volunteers on Holiday Projects free on receipt of SAE/IRC and published annually, gives details of organisations needing volunteers to help physically disabled people on holiday. Published by RADAR (Royal Association for Disability and Rehabilitation), 12 City Forum, 250 City Road, London EC1V 8AF ✆ 0171-250 3222, which works to remove the barriers which separate disabled people from society.

Student Community Action (SCA) is a network of over 100 groups of volunteers based in colleges and universities throughout Britain, working in cooperation with community-based projects, or on their own projects in response to the needs of the local area. Projects include playschemes, work in women's refuges, caring for the elderly or disabled, and campaigning on welfare rights and homelessness. The SCA Development Unit (SCADU) provides information on summer volunteering opportunities from May/June each year, and can give details of local SCA groups. 🐾 *Write, stating where in Britain you would like to volunteer, to SCADU, Oxford House, Derbyshire Street, London E2 6HG.*

ASHRAM HOUSE AND ASHRAM ACRES 23/25 Grantham Road, Sparkbrook, Birmingham B11 1LU ✆ 0121-773 7061
A community and development project in a multi-racial, inner city area, working for social, economic and environmental change. Activities include organic gardening on derelict land, a legal advice bureau and a Credit Union. **Volunteers** are invited to help with horticulture, domestic tasks, work with children and general administration, as well as helping at stalls and various events.
⊕ Ages 21+. No experience necessary. Hours negotiable; usually 0900-1700. Insurance and accommodation provided in residential community on site, with opportunities to join in social events. Volunteers pay travel and board and lodging as far as possible. **B D PH** *Overseas applicants welcome.*

ATD FOURTH WORLD The General Secretary, 48 Addington Square, London SE5 7LB ✆ 0171-703 3231
An international voluntary organisation which develops a human rights approach

to overcoming poverty. Brings together people from all walks of life in partnership with the most disadvantaged families, to support the efforts of the very poor in overcoming poverty and taking an active role in their community. Based on the commitment of those who have chosen to put their skills to the service of the very poor and learn from them, ATD's objectives are to reinforce cooperation between disadvantaged families and the community; develop a constructive public awareness of poverty; and encourage a fuller representation of poorest families in all areas of society. **Volunteers** are invited to take part in street workshops organised in different areas of Britain, sharing skills with parents, young people and children whose sense of creativity has never been challenged. Also working alongside full-time volunteers on international workcamps.

⊕ Ages 18+. No experience necessary but applicants should be interested in better understanding the causes and effects of persistent poverty and willing to work hard with others as part of a team. Approx 40 hour week for 1-2 weeks, July-September. Accommodation provided; applicants are asked to take a sleeping bag and to contribute towards living expenses. No fares or wages paid. *Write for further details.*

BREAK Mr G M Davison, 20 Hooks Hill Road, Sheringham, Norfolk NR26 8NL ℂ Sheringham (01263) 823170
Provides holidays and respite for unaccompanied mentally, physically and emotionally handicapped children and adults from pre-school age upwards, and for socially deprived children. Holiday and special care opportunities also exist for mentally handicapped adults and families with special needs.
Volunteers are needed as care assistants for residential work at two holiday homes at Sheringham and Hunstanton. Work involves helping with the personal welfare of the guests, their recreational programme and with

essential domestic duties. Placements involving work discussions and assessments can be arranged for those seeking practical experience prior to or as part of an educational course.

⊕ Ages 17/18+. Applicants should be stable, conscientious, patient and understanding. The work is physically and emotionally demanding. 40 hour week. 1-6 months, all year. Board, lodging and £23 per week pocket money provided, plus travel expenses within Britain. *Overseas volunteers accepted.*

CAMPHILL VILLAGE TRUST Loch Arthur Village Community, Beeswing, Dumfries DG2 8JQ ℂ Kirkgunzeon (0138 776) 687
Aims to provide a new and constructive way of life for adults with a mental handicap, assisting them to achieve individual independence and social adjustment within Trust communities. Loch Arthur Community provides a home, work, further education and general care for approx 30 adults with a handicap, and consists of 6 houses, a farm and an estate of 500 acres.
Volunteers are needed to work alongside the residents in every aspect of life and main areas of work are on the farm and in the garden, houses and workshops. As many of the adults have fairly severe handicaps they are also in need of care such as bathing, dressing and other personal tasks.

⊕ Ages 18+. Volunteers must be willing to help wherever needed, and are encouraged not only to share in the responsibilities of living and working with the handicapped but also to participate in the cultural, recreational and social aspects. 6 weeks minimum stay; 6-12 months preferred. Food and accommodation provided, plus pocket money for long-term volunteers. *Overseas applicants accepted.*

CARE FOR PEOPLE WITH A MENTAL HANDICAP 9 Weir Road, Kibworth, Leicester LE8 0LQ
Volunteers needed to live and work alongside people with a learning

disability at communities in Devon, Kent, Lancashire, Leicestershire, Shropshire, Northumberland, Sussex and Wiltshire. ⊕ Ages 18+. No experience necessary; applicants must speak English. 40 hour, 5 day week all year. Board, accommodation and full insurance provided, plus £25 per week pocket money. *UK nationals only.*

HELP THE HANDICAPPED HOLIDAY FUND Holiday Organiser, 147A Camden Road, Tunbridge Wells, Kent TN1 2RA ✆ Tunbridge Wells (01892) 547474

Provides large group holidays for physically handicapped people from the age of 11 upwards. Able-bodied **volunteers** required to provide help and care during holiday visits in Dorset, Kent, Cornwall, Lancashire and Sussex. Tasks include washing, dressing, feeding and taking the guests on outings. ⊕ Ages 18+. No experience necessary. Most holidays in the summer and last 1 week; volunteers have 1 afternoon off during the week. Hours depend on the guests' needs and level of care. Helpers must provide their own pocket money and a small contribution towards the cost of accommodation and insurance.

HERTFORDSHIRE ASSOCIATION FOR THE DISABLED The Woodside Centre, The Commons, Welwyn Garden City, Hertfordshire AL7 4DD ✆ Welwyn Garden City (01707) 324581 ☎ (01707) 371297

Volunteers are needed to accompany disabled guests on holiday at a hotel in Clacton. Duties on a rota basis in pairs include pushing guests in wheelchairs to shops, seafront, market, church; escorting guests on outings; helping guests with dressing and undressing; transferring from wheelchair to bed; or in the bathroom. ⊕ Ages 18+. No experience necessary; applicants must have good spoken English, be fit, healthy, cheerful and compassionate. 6 day week, work available all year. Full board accommodation provided in twin rooms.

Assistance may be given for UK travel costs. No wages or insurance provided. ✍ *Apply in writing 3 months in advance enclosing 2 character references to the Manageress, Hertford House Hotel, Clacton-on-Sea, Essex CO15 1BJ.*

INDEPENDENT LIVING ALTERNATIVES Fulton House, Fulton Road, Wembley Park, Wembley, Middlesex HA9 0TF ✆ 0181-902 8998 ext 270

A non-profitmaking charity run by people with direct experience of disability, designed to promote independence to people disabled. **Volunteers** are needed to provide physical support (for example cooking, washing, driving) in the form of a full-time partnership with a person with a physical disability. ⊕ Ages 21+. Applicants must have a clean driving licence. 5 day week. Food, accommodation and £56 per week plus expenses provided. Training given on placement. **B D PH** depending on ability. *Overseas volunteers completely fluent in English welcome.*

INDEPENDENT LIVING SCHEMES (ILS) Kenneth Smith & Dorothy Kendrick, Lewisham Social Services, Dartmouth Road, Forest Hill, London SE23 3YE ✆ 0181-699 0111 ext 247/248 ☎ 0181-291 5720

Aims to enable severely disabled people, all wheelchair users, to live in the community with help from **volunteers**, who will assist in personal care, including toileting and lifting, shopping, social and community activities. ⊕ Ages 18-50, no experience necessary. Two 24 hour shifts per week, sleeping in. Weekly allowances: £20 pocket money and £35 for food (total £55 per week); £15 per month for clothing and leisure. Shared accommodation provided and household bills paid. 6 month placement period preferred but other lengths can be negotiated. Obligatory interview in London; UK travel costs reimbursed. **B D PH** depending on ability. ✍ *Write or telephone for application form* and information pack. Overseas applications can only be accepted from those who have right of entry into the UK or who require no sponsorship; please apply when in the UK. Cannot help with work permits or visas.

INTERNATIONAL VOLUNTARY SERVICE Old Hall, East Bergholt, Colchester CO7 6TQ

The British branch of Service Civil International, which promotes international reconciliation through work projects. **Volunteers** needed for community work on international workcamps. Recent projects have included gardening and decorating for elderly and handicapped people and single parent families in Croydon, south London; caring for patients with various degrees of mental disability at a hospital in Birmingham; living with a community of mentally handicapped adults in Danby, North Yorkshire, doing fruitpicking, weeding and gardening; and renovating the library at a home for people with cerebral palsy in Beaconsfield. There are approx 80 international workcamps involving groups of 6-18 volunteers. ⊕ Ages 18+. Volunteers must be prepared to work hard and contribute actively to the work and team life. 35-40 hour week, 2-4 weeks, June-September, and Christmas and Easter. Food, insurance and accommodation in village halls, houses, schools, homes, hospitals or community centres with self-catering facilities provided. No fares or wages paid. Registration fee £30 (students/unwaged £25). Membership fee £25 (students/unwaged £15). Overseas volunteers must speak fluent English. **B D PH**

🔉 Apply through partner organisation in country of residence; for further information see page 30.

KITH & KIDS c/o Irish Centre, Pretoria Road, London N17 8DX
✆ 0181-801 7432
A self-help group providing support for the families of children who have a

physical or learning disability. **Volunteers** are required to take part in social training schemes, working on a 2:1 basis with learning-disabled children and young adults, helping them with everyday skills and experiences within the community. No experience necessary, just enthusiasm. ⊕ Ages 16+. 2 consecutive weeks, August or 1 week, Christmas and Easter. Hours 0930-1700 daily. Lunch provided and travel expenses within Greater London area paid. 2 days training provided before each project. No accommodation available so volunteers should be based in or around London. Also 1 week camping holiday, late August, where accommodation is provided. **PH** depending on ability.

THE LEONARD CHESHIRE FOUNDATION Personnel Secretary, Leonard Cheshire House, 26/29 Maunsel Street, London SW1P 2QN
✆ 0171-828 1822
Runs over 80 Homes throughout the UK, mostly in country areas, for the care of severely handicapped people, mainly physically disabled adults. Cheshire Homes offer the affection and freedom of family life, and the residents are encouraged to lead the most active lives that their disabilities permit. **Volunteers** are needed in many Homes to assist with general care of residents who require help in personal matters, such as washing, dressing and feeding, as well as hobbies, letter writing, driving, going on outings or holidays and other recreational activities. ⊕ Ages 18-30. Preference generally given to those planning to take up medical or social work as a career. Volunteers must be adaptable, dedicated, hard working, punctual and willing to undertake a wide variety of tasks. Up to 37½ hour, 5 day week, for 3-12 months. Board, lodging and at least £27 per week pocket money provided. Travel costs paid by volunteers. Overseas applicants must have a good working knowledge of English.

MENCAP (Royal Society for Mentally Handicapped Children and Adults), Holiday Services Office, 119 Drake Street, Rochdale, Lancashire OL16 1PZ
℃ **Rochdale (01706) 54111**
Volunteer helpers are needed on adventure, guest house and special care holidays throughout England and Wales for unaccompanied people with a mental handicap. Involves being responsible for the personal care of each guest, including washing, feeding and other essential tasks as well as stimulating and interesting them in activities, communicating and being a friend. Duties shared on a rota basis include cooking, cleaning, making beds and night duty. Time is also spent playing, talking and planning activities.
⚜ Ages 18+. No experience necessary, but volunteers need energy, enthusiasm and an interest in people with a mental handicap. Qualified nurses welcome. Maximum 14 hours work per day. 1-2 weeks, Easter-September. Board and accommodation provided. Travelling expenses up to £20 reimbursed. **PH** *Applications from outside Britain welcome.*

NANSEN SOCIETY (UK) LTD Redcastle Station, Muir-of-Ord, Ross-shire IV6 7RX ℃ **Muir-of-Ord (01463) 871255** ☎ **(01463) 870258**
A non-political, non-religious humanitarian organisation inspired by the humanistic work of the Arctic explorer Fridtjof Nansen. Much of its work is concerned with helping young people with emotional and behavioural difficulties to gain greater control over their own lives and contribute more positively to others.
Runs a farm community in the Scottish Highlands where **volunteers** are required to live together with permanent staff and youngsters with special needs. The farm demonstrates a self-sustaining, clean and non-exploitative agricultural system, combined with alternative energy generation and conservation. Much of the work is of an environmental nature, including conservation work and renovation.
⚜ Ages 21+. Previous experience of social work desirable; good spoken English essential. Volunteers pay own travel and insurance. 8 hour day, 40 hour week on a shift system. 1+ months, all year. Full board accommodation provided, plus £25 per week pocket money for volunteers staying at least 3 months.

QUEEN ELIZABETH'S FOUNDATION FOR THE DISABLED Holiday Organiser, Lulworth Court, 25 Chalkwell Esplanade, Westcliff-on-Sea, Essex SS0 8JQ ℃ **Southend-on-Sea (01702) 431725**
Volunteers are required to help give lively informal holidays to severely physically disabled people at a holiday home on the seafront at Westcliff-on-Sea. Work involves assisting nursing staff to look after guests, many of whom are confined to wheelchairs and need complete help with all aspects of personal care as well as escorting on outings, shopping, theatre and pub trips. The work is hard but rewarding, requiring some heavy lifting. A sense of humour helps.
⚜ Ages 18+. 1-2 weeks, all year except Christmas. Accommodation and full board provided, and contribution of £15 per week made towards travel expenses. *Overseas volunteers with a good working knowledge of English accepted.*

THE RICHARD CAVE MULTIPLE SCLEROSIS HOLIDAY HOME The Matron, Servite Convent, Leuchie House, North Berwick, East Lothian EH39 5NT
℃ **North Berwick (01620) 892864**
Volunteers are needed at a holiday home for persons of all ages with multiple sclerosis. Male and female applicants accepted, though there are twice as many female guests as males. No nursing qualifications necessary.
⚜ Ages 18-30. Board, accommodation plus pocket money provided.

RIDING FOR THE DISABLED ASSOCIATION Avenue R, National Agricultural Centre, Kenilworth, Warwickshire CV8 2LY
℡ Coventry (01203) 696510

Provides the opportunity of riding for disabled people who might benefit in their general health and wellbeing. **Voluntary helpers** are sometimes needed for riding holidays in the summer; a list is produced in January detailing the holidays available.
⊕ Ages 17+. Experience with horses or disabled people useful. No set hours of work; volunteers will be expected to work a full week. Board and lodging plus travel expenses may be provided subject to the holiday organiser's discretion; helpers may be asked to contribute. No wages provided.

RITCHIE RUSSELL HOUSE The Churchill Hospital, Headington, Oxford OX3 7LJ
℡ Oxford (01865) 225482/0

A purpose-built unit designed for disabled adults, the majority of whom suffer from chronic or progressive neurological diseases, such as multiple sclerosis, cerebro-vascular accidents or the effects of head or spinal injury. Patients are intermittently resident or attend daily, in a secure, lively and relaxed environment where patients and staff work together to improve the quality of life. Tries to give each patient the opportunity of an annual holiday and **volunteers** are needed, responsible with the help of staff for the total care of patients on a 1:1 basis, including washing, dressing, toileting and feeding.
⊕ Ages 18+, fluent English necessary. Experience useful but not essential. All prospective carers are interviewed. 12 hours per day, summer, client holidays usually a week long. Half board accommodation, usually in hotel or chalet, insurance and some travel provided. Volunteers are asked to contribute £35-£40. Volunteers are also utilised within the unit. Applicants must attend an interview and should be aware that no accommodation is available.

SENSE 11-13 Clifton Terrace, Finsbury Park London N4 3SR
℡ 0171-272 7774 ℻ 0171-272 6012

The national deaf-blind and rubella association, providing services, advice, support and information. Requires **volunteers** to help out on holidays for deaf-blind children and young adults at various places, including activity centres, cottages and caravans. Each holiday is managed by one or more experienced leaders backed by a team of volunteers who act as befrienders and help holidaymakers participate in activities, assist with daily care and also help out with tasks such as cooking or driving.
⊕ Ages 18+. Volunteers should have positive attitudes towards people with disabilities, a commitment to making holidays a good experience for all, and a sense of fun. No experience necessary, but knowledge of sign language and ability to drive useful. 1 week, end July-early September. Introduction and awareness day held during June/July to meet leaders and other volunteers, and build a team. All expenses during holiday covered, including food, accommodation and transport. No wages paid. ✍ *Apply to Holiday Officer before end March. UK residents only.*

SHAD Support and Housing Assistance for People with Disabilities, Sue Denney, Winkfield Resource Centre, 33 Winkfield Road, London N22 5RP
℡ 0181-365 8528

Enables people with physical disabilities to live in their own homes, with full control over their lives. **Volunteers** required to assist with all aspects of daily living, including personal care, cooking, housework and going out. Experience not necessary; volunteers will receive instruction. Driving licence useful.
⊕ Ages 18-30. 3+ months, all year. Volunteers work full-time with one person, as part of a team of 2-3 volunteers on a rota basis. Pocket money £50 per week, fares, other expenses, separate accommodation and insurance provided. 4 days per fortnight

and regular long weekends off. *Limited number of overseas applications accepted; EEA nationals only.*

SHAD (ISLINGTON) Project Worker, c/o Manor Gardens Centre, 6-9 Manor Gardens, Holloway Road, London N7 6LA

Run for and by people with disabilities to promote and support independent living. **Volunteers** required to enable people with severe physical disabilities live independently in their own home. Tasks cover all aspects of personal care, domestic work, assisting at work and leisure activities, wheelchair pushing, usually car driving and for some users interpreting their speech to others. ⚘ Ages 19+. No previous care experience necessary; training provided. For most vacancies a driving licence is necessary and driving experience, especially in London, desirable. Approx 168 hours, spread over 3 weeks. 4 month placements preferred. Volunteers must be fluent in English; clear writing and the ability to take dictated notes necessary for some vacancies. Pocket money £22 per week, food allowance £26.50 per week and accommodation provided. ✍ *Apply 2 months in advance. All nationalities welcome; applicants must be available for interview in London (travel expenses paid for inland travel only).*

SHAD WANDSWORTH c/o The Nightingale Centre, Balham Hill, London SW12 9EA ℭ 0181-675 6095

Offers the opportunity of independence, self-determination and freedom of choice to people with severe physical disabilities. **Volunteers** needed to enable people with severe disabilities to live independently in their own homes. ⚘ Ages 18-30. No experience necessary but volunteers should be physically fit, with a good standard of English. 2-3, 24-hour shifts per week, for minimum 4 months. Vacancies available all year. Accommodation and training provided. Salary £51 per week plus expenses. *All nationalities welcome, applicants from abroad must pay own*

travel expenses and will need to be interviewed before placement.

ST EBBA'S HOSPITAL Hook Road, Epsom, Surrey KT19 8QJ ℭ Epsom (01372) 722212

Cares for the mentally/physically handicapped, with about 350 adult residents, and aims to give the extra care and attention needed, and so help them lead a more contented life. **Volunteers** are needed to help in various departments: sports, music and drama, physiotherapy, gardening, training, and with general care. ⚘ Ages 16+. 32 hour week. No experience necessary, just a sensible, caring nature. Work available for different periods, all year. No wages paid. *Local applicants preferred as accommodation is very limited.*

ST PANCRAS HOSPITAL Voluntary Services Organiser, 4 St Pancras Way, London NW1 0PE ℭ 0171-387 4411 ext 368

A hospital specialising in elderly care and psychiatric rehabilitation. **Volunteers** are required to befriend elderly patients and assist with outings, shopping trips and home visits as well as spending time chatting, listening, playing games and other activities. Volunteers also needed to help run trolley shop and library trolley, as well as to assist in groups run for patients by the voluntary services and occupational therapy departments. ⚘ Ages 18+. 1000-1630, 3 days a week for 6+ weeks. Experience not necessary, just enthusiasm and a liking for the elderly. Volunteers should be punctual, reliable and able to converse in English. Insurance and local travel costs provided. No accommodation available, but meal vouchers provided.

THE SUE RYDER FOUNDATION Administration Officer, Sue Ryder Home, Cavendish, Sudbury, Suffolk CO10 8AY ℭ Glemsford (01787) 280252

A charity with over 80 homes all over the world, primarily for the disabled and incurable but also admitting those who, on discharge from hospital, still need care and attention. Aims to provide residents with a family sense of being, each with something to contribute to the common good. Seeks to render personal service to those in need and to give affection to those who are unloved, regardless of age, race or creed. **Volunteers** needed at headquarters and in 24 homes in the UK. Work includes helping with patients; office work; assisting in the kitchen, garden, museum, coffee and gift shop; general maintenance and other work arising. Experienced volunteers also needed for secretarial work and nursing. ⊕ Ages 16+. Applicants should be flexible and adaptable. Keen interest in caring work desirable. Qualifications or experience not essential but an advantage; preference given to students or graduates. Doctor's certificate required. 2+ months, all year; more volunteers required in summer. 2 week trial period. On-the-job instruction provided. Board and lodging provided, plus approx £10 pocket money per week. *Overseas volunteers with good command of spoken English accepted.*

UNIVERSITY COLLEGE LONDON HOSPITALS NHS TRUST Voluntary Services Department, Rockefeller Nurses' Home, Huntley Street, London WC1E 6AU ✆ **0171-388 6866**
Volunteers welcome to assist in wards befriending patients and helping to offer a variety of services. No qualifications or experience necessary except a genuine interest in people. ⊕ Ages 17+. 24 hour week, 6+ weeks, all year. Insurance and local travel costs provided, but no accommodation. Meals provided, depending on hours worked. *Fluent English essential.*

WINGED FELLOWSHIP TRUST Recruitment Officer, Angel House, 20-32 Pentonville Road, London N1 9XD ✆ **0171-833 2594**
Aims to provide 1/2 week holidays for as many severely physically disabled people as possible, to give their families a break. Runs 5 holiday centres in Surrey, Essex, Hampshire, Nottinghamshire and Merseyside, each providing holidays for 30-36 disabled adults at a time. **Volunteers** needed to provide help, companionship and entertainment. This includes washing, dressing and feeding the guests, helping them to bed, writing postcards, playing cards, accompanying them on outings, plus a certain amount of domestic work. Some volunteers may also be asked to help on night duty. Special fortnights include music, drama, craft, fishing and photography; volunteers with these skills particularly welcome. Opportunity to take part in country day trips. The atmosphere at the centres is informal and friendly. ⊕ Ages 16+. 1 or 2 weeks, almost all year round. Board and lodging provided and fares withing the UK to centres refunded. Volunteers also required to help on overseas trips and adventure holidays for which a small contribution towards costs in required. *Overseas volunteers with a good standard of spoken English accepted.*

WOODLARKS CAMP SITE TRUST Honorary Secretary, Kathleen Marshall House, Tilford Road, Lower Bourne, Farnham, Surrey GU10 3RN ✆ **Farnham (01252) 716279**
Organises summer camps for severely physically handicapped adults and children at a 12 acre site of pinewoods and grassland on the Surrey/Hampshire border; **volunteers** are required. Emphasis is placed on the participants trying to do things they would not otherwise have the opportunity to do, and accomplishing things they had always thought impossible. Each week a different group goes to the camp from hospitals, special schools or private homes. Usually one volunteer for each disabled person, and they remain partners for the duration of the camp. Facilities include heated swimming pool, sports equipment, dining/recreation

room and open wood fires for cooking.
1+ weeks, mid May-mid September.
⊕ Ages 12+. No experience needed,
but commitment essential. A nominal
fee is charged to help cover food costs.
Camping equipment supplied. **B D PH**
Overseas volunteers accepted.

YOUNG DISABLED ON HOLIDAY
33 Longfield Avenue, Heald Green,
Cheadle, Cheshire SK8 3NH
Organises holidays for young physically
disabled people. Requires **volunteers**
to help; activities include sightseeing,
shopping expeditions, theatre visits,
discos, and other adventure pastimes.
⊕ Ages 18-35. Applicants should have a
sense of fun and adventure. Each
disabled person has at least 1 helper.
1 week, April-October. Volunteers
expected to contribute 25% of holiday
costs.

CONSERVATION

Conservation projects can involve
volunteers in practical action to protect
vulnerable flora and fauna; restore old
buildings and urban heritage; encourage
public interest in the environment; or
promote alternative technologies for
more sustainable living. The work is
mostly unpaid and volunteers may also
be required to make a small contribution
to cover board and accommodation.

BRITISH TRUST FOR
CONSERVATION VOLUNTEERS
Room WH, 36 St Mary's Street,
Wallingford, Oxfordshire OX10
0EU *✆ Wallingford (01491) 839766*
A charity promoting practical
conservation work by volunteers;
organises numerous conservation
working holidays on sites including
nature reserves, country estates and
National Parks. **Volunteers** are given a
chance to contribute in a practical way
to the conservation of rural and urban
areas. Over 600 projects are organised
each year, and recent projects have
included conserving the sensitive coastal

habitats of orchids, natterjack toads and
sand lizards on Merseyside; clearing
reeds from a medieval moat in
Worcestershire; excavating a secret
water garden in Wales; and conserving
floating acid bogs in Staffordshire.
Instruction is given in the use of tools
and equipment, traditional techniques
and other conservation skills. Also
provide slide shows, guided tours and
talks on the conservation value of the
work. Approx 12 volunteers on each
project with an experienced leader.
Beginners welcome.
⊕ Ages 16-70. Overseas volunteers
must be over 18, and speak reasonably
good English. 1 or 2 weeks, all year. 1
day off per week to explore surrounding
area. Food and accommodation in
centres, youth hostels, estate cottages,
village halls, farm buildings or basecamps
provided. Volunteers should take a
sleeping bag, waterproofs, boots and
working clothes. Cost from £28 includes
food and accommodation, with everyone
taking turns to prepare food. Two
friends can apply to work on the same
project. Travel paid by volunteers. Anti-
tetanus vaccination essential. Projects
qualify under the Duke of Edinburgh's
Award Scheme. Weekend courses in
practical conservation skills and
leadership arranged. Membership fee
£12; £6, unwaged, students or retired;
£17, families; and £20, overseas
volunteers. 🕮 *Full programme available*
by Easter.

CATHEDRAL CAMPS Shelley Bent,
Booking Secretary, 16 Glebe
Avenue, Flitwick, Bedfordshire
MK45 1HS *✆ Flitwick (01525)*
716237
Aims to preserve, conserve, restore and
repair cathedrals and Christian buildings
of the highest architectural significance.
Volunteers can expect both
spectacular and routine work,
maintenance work, cleaning roof voids,
towers, spiral staircases, wall memorials,
traceried woodwork and drain culverts,
vacuum-cleaning nave walls, washing
floors, painting iron railings, plus

gardening and renewing path areas, all under guidance of craftsmen. At some cathedrals volunteers are also able to work with professional conservators on projects concerning external stonework, internal marble pillars and memorials. 36 hour week, 08.30-17.00 each day with Saturday afternoon, Sunday and evenings free. Food and self-catering accommodation provided, sometimes in hostels, often in the cathedral hall; volunteers should take a sleeping bag. ⊕ Ages 16-30. Volunteers should be willing to do a fairly hard day's work, contribute to the social life of the camp, and help with domestic duties on a rota. Each camp is run by a leader and 2 assistants. Letter of recommendation required from anyone attending a camp for the first time; 2 friends may apply to work in the same camp. Anti-tetanus vaccination advised. Camps are held at different cathedrals and churches for 1 week, mid July-early September. Travel and optional personal insurance paid by volunteers. Projects qualify under the Duke of Edinburgh's Award Scheme. All volunteers receive admission card valid for 1 year for most English cathedrals. Camp fee £36 per week.

CENTRE FOR ALTERNATIVE TECHNOLOGY Machynlleth, Powys SY20 9AZ ✆ Machynlleth (01654) 702400

A display and education centre offering practical ideas and information on environmentally sound practices. Open 7 days a week, the Centre is visited by over 90,000 people each year. 40 acre site has working displays of wind, water and solar power, low-energy buildings and organic growing. **Volunteer** programme offers opportunity to work on site; tasks vary depending on weather and what is most urgent at the time, but may include gardening, landscaping, building, digging holes, moving rocks, fixing leaks, cooking, cleaning or typing; flexible attitude essential. No formal training but participants can learn through working, talking to staff and consulting information material.

⊕ Ages 16+. No experience necessary; knowledge of English important. 32 hour, 5 day week; 1-2 weeks, February-September. Work is unpaid; hostel-style board and accommodation provided at cost of £5.75 (waged) or £4 (low-waged/claimants) per day. Volunteers advised to take sleeping-bag, torch, strong work clothes, wellington boots and waterproof clothing. ⚲ *Early booking recommended; places limited.*

THE CRAFT CENTRE St George's Island, Looe, Cornwall PL13 2AB ✆ (01836) 522919

St George's Island lies one mile off the south Cornish coast, and has been opened to day visitors as a non-commercial, non-profitmaking project to conserve its unspoilt natural beauty and develop it as a nature reserve. **Helpers** required to meet and assist day visitors, serve in the craft shop, help with gardening, track and beach clearing and plotting nature trails. ⊕ Ages 16+ for unaccompanied volunteers; families also welcome. No experience necessary. Approx 40 hour week. 1+ weeks, April-end September, weather permitting. Self-catering accommodation provided in chalet, cottage and huts. £20 booking fee covers gas/electricity charges and insurance. Volunteers pay own travel costs and must take a sleeping bag, sensible clothing and adequate supplies for several days, as tides and weather restrict trips to the mainland and there are no shops on the island. Opportunities to learn organic gardening, recycling, shell and flower craft and other crafts. **B D PH** welcome, but difficult terrain and access. ⚲ *Send SAE/IRCs for details and application form.*

DERBYSHIRE INTERNATIONAL YOUTH CAMP Derby Youth House, Mill Street, Derby DE1 1DY ✆ Derby (01332) 345538

Organises an International Youth Camp in Derbyshire with conservation projects taking place at Elvaston Castle

Country Park and work with the local Groundwork Trust. Also work on children's summer playschemes. Aims to develop understanding between young people from different countries whilst they are working as **volunteers** to improve the environment. Extensive social programme includes art, sport, video, canoeing and climbing. ⊕ Ages 16-21. 1-2 weeks, late July-mid August. Accommodation provided in a residential centre with all meals included. Qualified supervisors available at all times. Cost approx £50 per week or £25 for Derbyshire residents. Qualifies under the Duke of Edinburgh's Award Scheme. **B D PH** ✎ *Apply by end April.*

DYFED WILDLIFE TRUST Islands Booking Officer, 7 Market Street, Haverfordwest, Dyfed SA61 1NF ✆ **Haverfordwest (01437) 765462**
Skomer Island is a 720 acre national nature reserve, renowned for the finest seabird colonies in the south west, with fulmars, guillemots, kittiwakes, oystercatchers, puffins, razorbills, large gulls and over 100,000 pairs of Manx shearwaters. In addition there are many land birds including buzzards, choughs, owls, skylarks, ravens and pheasants. **Voluntary assistant wardens** required to help with a variety of tasks; the main work concerns the day visitors, helping to meet the boats, collect landing fees and giving general information and advice. Also patrolling the island to ensure visitors keep to the footpaths, and possibly assisting with various management tasks such as repair and maintenance work, path clearance, driftwood collecting, and surveys and scientific work. Applicants should be fit and prepared for hard work and long hours. Experience useful but not essential. 1+ weeks, mid April-September. Boat passage to Skomer and simple bunk bed accommodation with cooking facilities provided. Volunteers should take a sleeping bag and food. ✎ *Apply in September to be sure of place.*

FESTINIOG RAILWAY COMPANY Volunteer Officer, Harbour Station, Porthmadog, Gwynedd LL49 9NF ✆ **Porthmadog (01766) 512340**
Volunteers are required to help in the maintenance and running of the 150 year old narrow gauge railway. Wide variety of work available. Traffic & Commercial Department: working in booking offices, guard's vans, buffet cars, shops, cafes and small sales outlets. Locomotive Operating Department: cleaning locomotives, working on the footplate. Mechanical Department: turning, welding, machining, steam fitting, sheet metal work, joinery, upholstery and paintwork. Permanent Way/Civil Engineering Department: working on winter track relaying projects and summer siding work, helping to repair fences, bridges, culverts and heavy walling. The Active Parks and Gardens Department needs skilled and unskilled assistance, improving the appearance of the station surrounds and picnic areas. Qualified and experienced electricians and builders also needed. Training given where necessary. Qualifies under the Duke of Edinburgh's Award Scheme. ⊕ Ages 16+, unless in a supervised party. All volunteers must be fit. All year. Limited hostel accommodation for regular volunteers, for which a small charge is made; food extra. Camping space and list of local accommodation also available. *Overseas volunteers with a good understanding of, and ability to speak clear English accepted.*

GREAT WESTERN SOCIETY Didcot Railway Centre, Didcot, Oxfordshire OX11 7NJ ✆ **Didcot (01235) 817200**
A society dedicated to preserving the history of the Great Western Railway. Runs a 16 acre working museum housing restored locomotives, rolling stock and other exhibits of a vanished age. **Volunteers** are invited to help out with restoration projects, each year there being new projects to work on. Work may involve track work, maintenance of locomotives and coaches, gardening,

signalling, painting, cleaning small relics or catering. No experience necessary as training or guidance is given. ⊕ Ages 14+ unless accompanied by an adult. Work available weekends all year, or midweek April-October. Also 1 week during August when board and lodging is provided in train compartments. No fares or wages paid, but third party insurance cover provided. **B D PH**

INTERNATIONAL VOLUNTARY SERVICE Old Hall, East Bergholt, Colchester, Essex CO7 6TQ

The British branch of Service Civil International invites **volunteers** to join international teams working on various conservation projects. Recent projects have included conserving Sherwood Forest and attempting to return it to its former state; digging ponds and laying footpaths on the Devon coast; repairing dry stone walls and protecting wildlife and trees on the Orkney island of Rousay and on the Out Skerries, Shetland; and building a cycle path in Edinburgh, in cooperation with a charity providing sustainable transport links. ⊕ Ages 18+. Applicants should be prepared to work hard and contribute actively to team life. 35-40 hour week. 2-4 weeks, June-September. Food, accommodation and insurance provided. No fares or wages paid. Registration fee £30 (students/unwaged £25). Membership fee £25 (students/unwaged £15). **B D PH**

🐾 *Apply through partner organisation in country of residence; for further information please see page 30.*

IRONBRIDGE GORGE MUSEUM TRUST Volunteer Organiser, The Wharfage, Ironbridge, Telford, Shropshire TF8 7AW © Ironbridge (01952) 433522

Conserves, restores and interprets the rich industrial heritage of the Gorge, the birthplace of the Industrial Revolution. The Museum comprises six main sites and a number of smaller ones, and has been created around a unique series of industrial monuments concentrating on the iron and pottery industries, and spread over some 6 square miles. **Volunteers** are needed to work on various sites involving research, documentation, interpretation of exhibits and general site duties. At Blists Hill Open Air Museum demonstrators in Victorian costume are sometimes needed to explain the site and its shops, works and houses to visitors. Training, costume, equipment and supervision provided as appropriate. Opportunities for talking to the public; those with good language skills particularly welcome. ⊕ Ages 18+. 36 hour week, March-October. Self-catering hostel accommodation on site or youth hostel 3 miles away. Daily food allowance at Blists Hill. Insurance provided. Own transport, bicycle or car, usually essential. Participants can enter sites free. *Overseas volunteers must have excellent standard of spoken English.*

THE MONKEY SANCTUARY Looe, Cornwall PL13 1NZ © Looe (01503) 262532

Has received worldwide recognition as the first place where a natural colony of woolly monkeys has survived and bred outside the South American rainforests. A centre both for conservation and for the education of the public, who visit at Easter and during the summer months. **Volunteers** are required to help with various jobs including preparation of monkey foods; cleaning and maintenance of monkey enclosures and grounds; attending to visitors in the summer; and general maintenance work during the winter. Summer volunteers with appropriate skills and an interest in conservation may contribute in talking with visitors and educational work. ⊕ Ages 18+. No experience necessary, but applicants should have an interest in the field, and practical skills are always welcome. 2-4 weeks, all year. Full board accommodation provided, but volunteers pay their own travel. Food is usually vegetarian, and volunteers share accommodation with the Sanctuary team. Those with musical instruments should bring them along. Subsistence may be available to long-term volunteers. **B D PH W** applications considered on an individual basis. 🕮 Apply at least 4 months in advance.

NATIONAL TRUST WORKING HOLIDAYS PO Box 538, Melksham, Wiltshire SN12 8SU

🕾 Melksham (01225) 790290
The Trust was formed at the end of the 19th century for the preservation of places of historic interest and natural beauty. It owns and protects houses and gardens, parks and estates, mountains, moors, coastline, farms and nature reserves. Working holidays are organised at NT properties throughout England, Wales and Northern Ireland, providing an opportunity to carry out conservation work and to encourage an active and practical interest in the Trust's work. **Volunteers** carry out essential tasks on estates which could not otherwise be done. Recent projects include improving and widening coastal footpaths, barn construction, botanical surveying, the repair of drystone walling; fenland conservation work, erosion control and scrub clearance to improve downland ecology; and archaeological digs. Majority of the work done outdoors, but there are occasionally wet weather tasks such as clearing out old buildings or cleaning, restoring or painting agricultural implements. ⊕ Mainly ages 17-30, 18+ for overseas volunteers. Special projects for the over 35s and over 50s. Instruction given by experts. 8 hour day, 5½ day week, evenings free. 1+ weeks, all year. Accommodation provided in NT hostels, village halls, stable blocks, farmhouses, cottages or converted barns. Volunteers should take sleeping bags and contribute approx £37 per week towards the cost of food and accommodation. Help with kitchen duties expected; travel costs paid by volunteers. Projects qualify under the Duke of Edinburgh's Award Scheme. Two friends may apply to work on same project. Anyone completing a full week's work qualifies for 1 year's free admission to NT properties. 🕮 Application forms and brochure available from January; send 36p in stamps or 5 IRCs.

OPERATION OSPREY
The Royal Society for the Protection of Birds, c/o Richard Thaxton, Grianan, Nethy Bridge, Inverness-shire PH25 3EF

🕾 **Boat of Garten (01479) 831694**
Volunteer wardens and **cooks** are needed at Loch Garten, part of the Abernethy Forest Nature Reserve in the ancient Caledonian Forest, Strathspey. Teams of **volunteer wardens** keep a 24 hour watch from the hide and are expected to maintain a log of the ospreys' activities and to spend time talking to visitors (around 60,000 a year) about the RSPB's work at Loch Garten. Volunteers work on a shift basis, with every third day free, and also help with camp chores. Own transport useful. Interest in ornithology preferable. **Volunteer cooks** are responsible for preparing meals for up to 18 people; after initial supervision they will be expected to cope on their own on a day on/day off basis. ⊕ Ages 18+. 1+ weeks, 25 March-2 September. Full board and camping or caravan accommodation, washing facilities, kitchen/dining area and common room provided for nominal charge of £20 per week. Volunteers should take sleeping bag, warm clothing and walking boots. Volunteer cooks who stay 1 week will have single fare paid; for 2+ weeks return travel paid. Overseas volunteer cooks have rail fare paid, London-Aviemore.

THE ROYAL SOCIETY FOR THE PROTECTION OF BIRDS
Sandra Manners, Reserves Management Department, The Lodge, Sandy, Bedfordshire SG19 2DL 🕾 Sandy (01767) 680551

Protects wild birds and their threatened habitat by giving them a haven of 130 nature reserves all over Britain, publicising and enforcing bird protection laws, guarding rare breeding birds, studying environmental effects, protecting migratory birds, producing films, publications, lectures and displays. **Volunteer wardens** are needed on 30 nature reserves, assisting the wardens by carrying out physical management work, helping to escort visitors around the reserve, helping in information centres and dealing with enquiries and keeping records of birds. Volunteers usually work in teams of 2-4.

⊕ Ages 16+. An interest in conservation and knowledge of birds an advantage. 1+ weeks, all year. Accommodation in chalets or cottages. Cooking facilities provided, but volunteers are responsible for their own food and transport, and should take a sleeping bag. *EEA nationals only; good English essential.*

THE SCOTTISH CONSERVATION PROJECTS TRUST Director, Balallan House, 24 Allan Park, Stirling FK8 2QG
℗ **Stirling (01786) 479697**
A charity promoting the practical involvement of **volunteers** working to improve the quality of Scotland's environment. Work is carried out throughout Scotland, including the Western Isles, Orkney and Shetland. Recent projects have included marram grass planting at Gairloch, Wester Ross; footbridge construction at Duchess Wood, Strathclyde; drystane dyking on North Berwick Law, East Lothian; rhododendron clearance at Ernest's Wood, Stirlingshire; and tree planting on Beinn Eighe National Nature Reserve, Wester Ross. Instruction is given in the use of tools and equipment, traditional techniques and other conservation skills. Also slide shows, guided tours and talks on the conservation value of the work. Approx 12 volunteers work on each project; beginners welcome.

⊕ Ages 16-70. Some projects are more physically demanding than others and volunteers must be prepared to cope with working on remote and exposed sites. 8 hour day, 1 day off per week.

1-2 weeks, March-November. Food, insurance and accommodation in centres, tents, huts, youth hostels, cottages, village halls, farm buildings or basecamps provided. Volunteers should take a sleeping bag, waterproof clothing, boots and midge repellent. Anti-tetanus vaccination advisable. Everyone helps to prepare food, and volunteers contribute £5 per day (£4 for students/unwaged) towards food and accommodation costs. Two friends can apply to work on the same project. Projects qualify under the Duke of Edinburgh's Award Scheme. Weekend training courses in practical conservation skills and leadership arranged. Membership fee £15; £8 if unwaged or student, £20 for family, £5 supplement for overseas members. **PH** depending on ability.

THISTLE CAMPS National Trust for Scotland, 5 Charlotte Square, Edinburgh EH2 4DU
℗ **0131-226 5922 ext 257**
Founded to promote the permanent preservation of countryside and buildings of historic interest or natural beauty. Thistle Camps are residential work projects organised by NTS where **volunteers** can help in the conservation and practical management of properties in the care of the Trust. Recent projects have included sand dune stabilisation and conserving historic marble quarrying machinery on the Isle of Iona; woodland management around the country park at Brodick Castle on the Isle of Arran; building maintenance and habitat surveys on the Isle of Canna; rhododendron clearance in Torridon; and upland footpath maintenance at Glencoe. Work parties on Fair Isle, Britain's most remote inhabited island, help the islanders repair buildings, maintain the airstrip and help with all kinds of croft work such as fencing, drystane dyking, painting, crop-cleaning, ditching and haymaking.

⊕ Ages 16-70. Up to 2 friends can be placed together. Volunteers should be fit for hard, practical work. 8 hour day, 5 day week. 1-2 weeks, March-October.

Similar weekend projects are carried out by local Conservation Volunteers groups on NTS properties in their area. An experienced leader and/or a Trust Ranger Naturalist supervises all practical work, and gives instruction in the safe use of tools. One day free for recreation and exploration in the area. Insurance, hostel-type or basecamp accommodation and food provided, but volunteers help with catering arrangements and other chores. Old clothes, waterproofs, a sleeping bag and boots or wellingtons should be taken to all camps. Qualifies under the Duke of Edinburgh's Award Scheme. Participants pay their own way to a central pick-up point, and make a contribution, either £12.50 or £25 depending on their circumstances. ✍ *Apply by March at the latest to be sure of a place. Overseas volunteers with good English welcome.*

UNITED NATIONS ASSOCIATION International Youth Service, Temple of Peace, Cathays Park, Cardiff CF1 3AP ✆ Cardiff (01222) 223088

Volunteers are needed to work in international teams on conservation workcamps in various parts of Wales. Recent projects have included working with young people to clear a pond in Caerphilly; improving public access on the Pembrokeshire coast path, with training in the traditional rural craft of hedgebanking; and constructing footpaths and footbridges in the Afan Valley Country Park, West Glamorgan. Volunteers share in discussions centring on the host community and world problems, and are expected to take an active part in all aspects of the project. ⊕ Ages 18+. 40 hour week. 2 weeks, June-August. Accommodation, food and insurance provided. Volunteers share the cooking, and should take a sleeping bag. Registration fee £45. No fares or wages paid. **B D PH**

✍ *Apply through partner organisation in country of residence; for further information please see page 30.*

THE WATERWAY RECOVERY GROUP Neil Edwards, 114 Regents Park Road, London NW1 8UQ ✆ 0171-586 2510 ✉ 0171-722 7213

The national coordinating body for voluntary labour on the inland waterways of Britain, promoting and coordinating local societies and travelling groups involved in restoring derelict waterways to a navigable state.

Volunteers are needed on workcamps to help with this work. There are over 30 active restoration projects which encompass excavating and laying foundations for a new bridge, building retaining walls, dredging and banking, clearing vegetation, bricklaying and demolition work. Canals currently being restored include the Huddersfield, Montgomery, Wey and Arun, Droitwich, Hereford and Gloucester, Wiltshire and Berkshire, and Pocklington.

⊕ Ages 17+. Parental consent required for those under 18. Work is unpaid and mostly unskilled, although there is suitable work available for those with skills who wish to use them, and who are made especially welcome. Full training given and work is directed by local experts. Volunteers should be reasonably fit and willing to work hard in all weathers, with enthusiasm, a sense of humour and the ability to live harmoniously in fairly close contact with approx 20 volunteers at each camp. 1+ weeks, February-October and over the Christmas/New Year holiday. 8 hour day. Basic accommodation provided in village halls, schools and youth centres, plus 3 good meals a day at charge of approx £28 per week. Volunteers should take a sleeping bag and old clothes and be prepared to help with domestic chores, although a camp cook is normally resident. Insurance provided. Qualifies for the residential qualification under the Duke of Edinburgh's Award Scheme. Publish *Navvies* a bi-monthly journal which provides details of all activities. *Overseas volunteers with good command of English accepted.*

COURIERS / REPS

BUTLIN'S Wonderwest World, Heads of Ayr, KA7 4LB, Scotland BUTLIN'S Southcoast World, Bognor Regis, West Sussex PO21 1JJ BUTLIN'S Somerwest World, Minehead, Somerset TA24 5SH BUTLIN'S Starcoast World, Pwllheli, Gwynedd LL53 6HX, North Wales BUTLIN'S Funcoast World, Skegness, Lincolnshire PE25 1NJ Provides family holidays and leisure facilities, encompassing accommodation, retailing, catering, amusement parks, professional entertainment and conferences, all on the same site. Vacancies exist for Redcoats, **hosts/ hostesses** responsible for entertainments and organising children's programmes, at centres in Ayr, Bognor Regis, Minehead, Pwllheli and Skegness. Short and long term positions available virtually all year round, exact dates depending on each centre. ⊕ Ages 18+. Experience not normally necessary as training provided. 37½-45 hour week. Applicants should have enthusiasm, tact, attention to detail and the ability to integrate into a team. Salary, according to individual centres, accommodation in single or shared rooms, meals and uniform provided. Insurance and travel paid by applicants. Staff entertainment programmes, use of leisure facilities plus many of guest facilities, and holiday discounts available. ▣ Apply direct to the preferred centre, EEA nationals only:

DOMESTIC

This section lists numerous opportunities for paid work such as cleaning, cooking, barwork, serving food or general maintenance in Britain's hotels, resorts and holiday centres. Before applying, those from outside the EEA should note that for any paid work they will need a valid work permit. A reasonable knowledge of English is also essential.

ACORN VENTURE LTD Personnel Department, 137 Worcester Road, Hagley, Stourbridge, West Midlands DY9 0NW An activity holiday company catering for school groups at camping centres in Tal-y-Bont and Shell Island in North Wales. Experienced **catering staff** required. ⊕ Ages 18+. Minimum 50 hour, 6 day week. Applicants are expected to work the full season, May-September. Salary approx £40-£45 per week. All meals accommodation in tents and insurance provided. ▣ Apply in writing with cv by end February. If no reply within 28 days assume application unsuccessful.

BUTLIN'S Wonderwest World, Heads of Ayr, KA7 4LB, Scotland BUTLIN'S Southcoast World, Bognor Regis, West Sussex PO21 1JJ BUTLIN'S Somerwest World, Minehead, Somerset TA24 5SH BUTLIN'S Starcoast World, Pwllheli, Gwynedd LL53 6HX, North Wales BUTLIN'S Funcoast World, Skegness, Lincolnshire PE25 1NJ Provides family holidays and leisure facilities, encompassing accommodation, retailing, catering, amusement parks, professional entertainment and conferences, all on the same site. **Catering** and **bar staff, waiters/ waitresses**, qualified **chefs** and **cooks, cleaners** and **porters** required at centres in Ayr, Bognor Regis, Minehead, Pwllheli and Skegness. Short and long term positions available virtually all year round, exact dates depending on each centre. Experience not normally necessary as training provided. ⊕ Ages 16+, local applicants, 18+ others. Applicants should have enthusiasm, tact, attention to detail and the ability to integrate into a team. Salary according to individual centres, accommodation, meals and uniform provided. 37½ hour week. Insurance and travel paid by applicants. Staff entertainment programmes, use of leisure facilities plus many of guest facilities, and holiday discounts available. 🕮 *Apply direct to the preferred centre, EEA nationals only:*

CAMP BEAUMONT LTD Recruitment Department, Bridge House, Orchard Lane, Huntingdon, Cambridgeshire PE18 6QT
✆ Huntingdon (01480) 456123
Organises a wide range of children's activity holidays throughout England. Opportunities for **caterers/head cooks, kitchen assistants, cleaners.** ⚲ Ages 18+. All staff must enjoy working enthusiastically with children. Season runs mid July-end August; some permanent positions available. Wages £40-£100 per week; board and accommodation provided.

FRIENDLY HOTELS PLC Premier House, 10 Greycoat Place, London SW1P 1SB ✆ 0171-222 8866
Hotel group requires **waitresses, room attendants** and **porters** in hotels in Birmingham, Burnley, Eastbourne, Hull, London, Milton Keynes, Newcastle-under-Lyme, Newcastle-upon-Tyne, Nottingham, Walsall, Welwyn and in Scotland. ⚲ Ages 18+. Experience useful but not essential. Work available all year round, minimum 4 months. 39 hour week. Salary approx £100 per week. Accommodation available in single or shared rooms, in or outside hotel. **PH** limited opportunities.

HF HOLIDAYS LTD Recruitment & Training Department, Redhills, Skirsgill Park, Penrith, Cumbria CA11 0DT ✆ Penrith (01768) 899988 📠 (01768) 899323
Holiday company specialising in walking and special interest holidays. Provides guest house accommodation throughout Great Britain and requires **general assistants, kitchen porters** and **cooks.** ⚲ Ages 18-35. Cooks should have some experience; no experience necessary for other posts. All applicants must have a

good knowledge of English. 39 hour week, March-November. Full board accommodation provided. Salary approx £71 per week depending on post. Staff are free to join guests in walking and social activities when off duty. 🕮 *Apply all year round. EEA and US nationals only.*

HATTON HOTELS GROUP SERVICES LTD Hatton Court, Upton Hill, Upton St Leonards, Gloucester GL4 8DE
✆ Gloucester (01452) 617412
A small, privately owned company running hotels in the English Cotswolds. **Restaurant staff, bar staff** and **chambermaids** required. Preference given to those with catering experience. ⚲ Ages 18+. 45 hour, 5 day week. Wages £75-£100 per week depending on position; full board/lodging provided.

HOTHORPE HALL Christian Conference Centre, Theddingworth, near Lutterworth, Leicestershire LE17 6QX
✆ Market Harborough (01858) 880257
Provides conference facilities for groups of up to 140 people, mainly church groups. **Volunteers** required to undertake a variety of duties, including kitchen assistance, serving and washing up, and general domestic work. Gardening and maintenance work also involved. ⚲ Ages 18+. Volunteers should have a Christian commitment, willingness to join in as a member of the community, and a responsible attitude to their work. 6 day week. 6+ weeks, all year. No experience necessary. Pocket money £15 per week for first 4 weeks, then £21 per week. Accommodation in shared rooms and all meals provided. *Overseas applicants with good spoken English accepted.*

HUNTSHAM COURT Huntsham Village, Near Tiverton, Devon EX16 7NA ✆ Clayhanger (0139 86) 365
Staff required all through the year at country house hotel in the heart of

Devon. Offers the opportunity to learn aspects of catering and hotel management in a warm, friendly atmosphere. Work is varied and interesting, and includes acting as **waiter/waitress, catering** and **cleaning.** ⊕ Ages 19+. Willingness to learn more important than experience, though cooks require qualifications. Knowledge of English necessary. 15-40 hour week. Pay from £60 per week, plus full board accommodation and insurance. ✍ *Write for details. EEA nationals only.*

THE IONA COMMUNITY
Staff Coordinator, Isle of Iona, Argyll, Strathclyde PA76 6SN ✆ **Iona (0168 17) 404**
An ecumenical Christian community seeking new and radical ways of living the Gospel in today's world. On Iona the Community runs two centres, each welcoming up to 50 guests to a common life of work, worship, meals and recreation. **Kitchen assistants** and **housekeeping assistants** required at both centres. Kitchen assistants help provide up to 90 meals, often vegetarian. Cooking skills not essential, but a willingness to learn is. Housekeeping assistants help with cleaning, washing and ironing, as well as supervising guests in household chores.
Also require **assistants** to work in the Coffee House, baking, preparing food, serving, clearing tables and keeping the place clean and tidy. On the nearby Island of Mull the Camas Centre welcomes up to 16 guests each week, mainly unemployed or disadvantaged young people, to a common life of work, worship, arts, crafts and outdoor activities. Requires a competent **cook** to provide up to 25 meals over the summer months.
⊕ Ages 18+. Most important is a willingness to join fully in the Community life, which includes worship and social activities as well as work. The work is demanding but rewarding, and the hours flexible. 6 day week, February-December. Shared

accommodation, full board, pocket money £17 per week and assistance with travel expenses within mainland Britain provided. ✍ *Applications received before 31 December given priority.*

KNOLL HOUSE HOTEL Staff
Manager, Studland, Dorset BH19 3AH ✆ **Studland (0192 944) 251**
Country house hotel with 80 rooms and 100 acres of gardens and grounds adjoining the beach. **Chefs** (must have previous experience), **waiters, waitresses** and **general staff** required for Easter and summer vacations and May-September. Willingness to learn and happy disposition more important than experience.
⊕ Ages 17+. 39 hour week, 2 days free. Pay approx £94 per week, live-in, all found. *UK nationals only.*

LEICESTER CHILDREN'S
HOLIDAY HOME Quebec Road, Mablethorpe, Lincolnshire LN12 1QX ✆ **Mablethorpe (01507) 472444**
Seasonal **domestic staff** required at a holiday home which provides the poorest and most deserving children aged 7-12 from Leicester and its neighbourhood with a fortnight's holiday. The home is situated on the sandhills and the children have their own path to the beach. Positions include **cooks** and **kitchen assistants, catering staff** and **dining room attendants** to supervise children at mealtimes.
⊕ Ages 18+. 1+ months, May-August. Preference given to applicants able to work the whole season. Board and lodging provided plus a salary of approx £49 per week. *UK nationals only.*

LONDON HOSTELS
ASSOCIATION LTD Personnel Manager, 54 Eccleston Square, London SW1V 1PG ✆ **0171-834 1545** ✉ **0171-834 7146**
Part-time residential domestic work available in 10 London houses run mainly for young people in full-time employment or students. Female staff

are employed as **dining room assistants**, serving meals, clearing tables and using washing up machines; also as **junior housekeepers**, involving normal housekeeping duties, cleaning public and residential rooms, changing linen and general evening duties once a week. Male staff are employed as **kitchen** or **house porters**, assisting in the preparation of food, cleaning the kitchen catering area and public utility rooms, washing up, and other manual duties. ⊕ Ages 17+. 6+ months, possibly 3-4 months in summer, all year. 30-40 hour week. Working hours vary from house to house. Board, accommodation and insurance provided. Salary approx £39-£53 per week, according to hours worked. *EEA nationals only.*

MAYDAY STAFF SERVICES
21 Great Chapel Street, London W1V 3AQ ℂ **0171-439 3009**
An employment agency recruiting temporary and permanent catering staff of a high standard throughout central London and surrounding area. Can place **chefs**, **waiting** and **bar staff**, as well as **kitchen porters** and **general catering assistants**. **Catering assistants**' work includes food preparation, serving food at counter, washing up, clearing tables, and general kitchen duties. **Kitchen porters**' work includes washing up both manually and with a machine, cleaning and vegetable preparation. 25-40 hour week, all year. ⊕ Ages 16+. Catering assistants and kitchen porters wages £3.20-£3.60 per hour. Meals usually available when on duty and public liability insurance provided. **D PH** limited opportunities.
🏠 *Applicants must have accommodation, references and work permit where applicable. UK and US nationals only.*

MONTPELIER EMPLOYMENT AGENCY 34 Montpelier Road, Brighton, Sussex BN1 2LQ
ℂ **Brighton (01273) 778686**
Introduces **staff of all categories** to hotels throughout Britain. Previous experience essential. Applicants must be

free of any work permit restrictions and already resident in Britain. ⊕ Ages 18+. Approx 39 hour week. Minimum 12 weeks during summer period. Salary approx £80-£100 including accommodation; varies according to area, type of job, previous experience and whether accommodation is provided.

PGL YOUNG ADVENTURE LTD
Personnel Department, Alton Court, Penyard Lane (878), Ross-on-Wye, Herefordshire HR9 5NR
ℂ **Ross-on-Wye (01989) 767833**
Organises outdoor adventure holidays for young people and families in England, Scotland and Wales.
Catering and **domestic assistants**, **cooks** and **assistant cooks** required. Most centres run a self-service system with cooked breakfast, packed lunch and full evening meal.
⊕ Ages 18+. Applicants should be fond of children, responsible, flexible, patient, energetic and enthusiastic, reliable and mature, with a sense of humour and have the ability to cooperate with others as part of a team contributing fully to the life of the centre. 4+ weeks, February-September. Staff are also recruited for short periods at peak times such as Easter and the Spring Bank Holiday. Catering staff generally work a split shift, with the middle hours of the day free. 1 day off per week. Full board accommodation provided. Pocket money £30-£42 per week depending on qualifications, responsibility and length of stay. Travel expenses paid by applicants. All staff can join in the activities during free periods and are encouraged to take part in evening activities with the guests. Staff may sometimes be asked to help out in areas other than their own.
🏠 *Early application advisable; the majority of positions are filled by end June.*

PORTH TOCYN HOTEL
Abersoch, Gwynedd LL53 7BU
ℂ **Abersoch (0175 881) 2966**
A country house hotel, requiring **staff** for all aspects of **front of house** hotel

work. No experience necessary, but languages an advantage.
⊕ Ages 18+. Easter-November, hours variable. Salary £9.50-£10.50 per shift, accommodation in staff cottage, food, liability insurance, use of hotel facilities including tennis courts, swimming pool, windsurfers, provided. *UK nationals only.*

SCATTERGOODS AGENCY
Thursley House, 53 Station Road, Shalford, Guildford, Surrey GU4 8HA ℂ **Guildford (01483) 33732**
Arranges posts in hotels, restaurants and public houses as **chambermaids, plongeurs, barpersons, waiting staff, cooks, kitchen assistants, porters** and **general assistants**. Relevant experience preferable.
⊕ Ages 18+. 40-50 hour week; 6 months minimum. Wages £75+ per week. Board, lodging and insurance provided. *EEA nationals only.*

SCOTTISH FIELD STUDIES ASSOCIATION LTD Kindrogan
Field Centre, Enochdhu, Blairgowrie, Perthshire PH10 7PG
ℂ **Strathardle (01250) 881286**
Aims to create a greater awareness and understanding of the Scottish countryside. The Centre is a large country house in the Highlands and provides accommodation, laboratories and library for up to 80 people with opportunities for all aspects of field studies. **Seasonal staff** are needed for domestic duties such as **cleaning, washing up, general maintenance** and **gardening**.
⊕ Ages 18+. No experience needed. 37 hour week, all year. Wages £74 per week. Accommodation and meals provided. Participants pay own travel and insurance costs. Staff may participate in field study courses when possible. *EEA nationals only.*

SUSSEX BEACH HOLIDAY VILLAGE Andy Barnsdale, Operations Manager, Earnley, Chichester, West Sussex PO20 7JP
Large private holiday village in West Sussex. Opportunities for **waiters/ waitresses, bar staff, counter assistants, kitchen assistants** and **cleaners**.
⊕ Ages 16+. No experience necessary; full training given. All staff must be good time keepers, have a mature attitude and smart appearance. 39 hour week, mainly during summer months. Shared accommodation and 3 meals a day provided plus £1.95 per hour wages. **D**
🏛 *Apply March-June. EEA nationals only.*

UNIVERSAL AUNTS PO Box 304, London SW4 0NN ℂ 0171-738 8937
Vacancies are available for resident and non-resident **housekeepers, nannies** and **mothers' helps**.
Also opportunities for **cooks, washers up, waitresses, cleaners** and **drivers**.
⊕ Ages 18+. Permanent and temporary positions, all year. Salary according to qualifications.

FARMWORK / FRUIT PICKING

Summer farmwork in Britain includes general farm labouring as well as vegetable harvesting and soft fruit picking, often on international farmcamps. The work is mainly in Scotland, East Anglia, the South, the West Country and Kent, where it includes the traditional English working holiday of hop picking. Other crops to be picked include cherries, raspberries, strawberries, blackcurrants, loganberries, blackberries, plums, gooseberries, apples, pears, potatoes, courgettes and beans. A range of ancillary work such as strawing, weeding, irrigation, fruit inspection, packing, indoor processing, tractor driving or working in oast houses may also be available.

The work can be on individual, often family-run farms, on smallholdings or with cooperatives, or on international farmcamps. The general number of hours worked are 40-45 per week for 5-6 days. The length of the working season varies, depending on the crop being harvested, the weather and the location of the farm. The harvesting of soft fruit is normally undertaken between mid June and August, although in some areas picking may start as early as May. The picking of hops, apples and other crops runs from late August to October.

On farmcamps the emphasis is as much on living and working in an international community, with sports and social activities, as on earning money. The wages paid may only be sufficient to cover food and accommodation costs and to provide a little pocket money. The social and sports facilities provided can include swimming pools, tennis courts, games fields, games and television rooms, video, bars, discos and dances. The majority of workers will be in the 17-30 age range; families are often welcome. On some camps English language tuition may be available for overseas workers during free time. In order to be eligible to work on farmcamps in Britain, applicants from countries outside the EEA subject to immigration control must be in full-time education abroad, between the ages of 18 and 25 and have a Home Office card issued by an **approved scheme operator** such as Concordia, Harvesting Opportunity Permit Scheme, International Farm Camp (Tiptree) and R & JM Place (all listed below). This card allows entry into Britain but does not entitle the visitor to take paid work of any other kind during the visit.

Most fruit picking jobs are paid at piecework rates. Bad weather can affect the ripening and amount of crops to be picked, and while effort is made to provide full-time employment, on occasion work may be temporarily limited. It is therefore essential that workers have enough money to cover living expenses throughout their stay.

ADRIAN SCRIPPS LTD Moat Farm, Five Oak Green, Tonbridge, Kent TN12 6RR
✆ **Paddock Wood (01892) 832406**
Apple, pear and **hop pickers** required on four farms in Kent. No experience necessary, but good English required. ⊕ Ages 18+. 50+ hours per week, September-October. Wages approx £140 per week for hop pickers; piecework rates paid to fruit pickers. Self-catering accommodation provided; workers should take sleeping bag and working clothes. ✉ *Apply mid June (not before). Non-EEA nationals must have valid work permit.*

ASHRAM HOUSE AND ASHRAM ACRES 23/25 Grantham Road, Sparkbrook, Birmingham B11 1LU
✆ **0121-773 7061**
A multi-purpose community and development project in a multi-racial, inner-city area, working for social, economic and environmental change. **Volunteers** are invited to help with a land use project, Ashram Acres, which grows vegetables organically on previously derelict land. Asian vegetables are a speciality, and various animals are kept. Work involves organic gardening, caring for animals, building and maintenance work. ⊕ Ages 21+. No experience necessary, training is usually given where required. Hours negotiable; usually 0900-1700, all year. Insurance and accommodation in residential community provided with opportunities to join social events. Volunteers pay own travel, and are expected to pay as far as possible for board and lodging. **B D PH**

S C & J H BERRY LTD Gushmere Court Farm, Selling, Faversham, Kent ME13 9RF
✆ **Canterbury (01227) 750205**
Assistance needed with the **harvest of hops**: loading and unloading kilns and pressing hops in oast house. ⊕ Ages 18+. Basic 39 hour week plus up to 20 hours overtime. End August-mid September. Wages approx £190 per

week. Accommodation with facilities available; workers buy and cook own food. Take own sleeping bag and towel. Assistance also needed with **apple picking**. Piecework rates paid. Up to 8 hours per day; dates variable, usually 2 weeks, early September. Campsite with WC and showers. Own tent, cooking facilities and waterproofs essential. *Apply enclosing SAE/IRCs. EEA nationals only.*

CAWLEY FARMS Ashton Fruit Farm, Ashton, Leominster, Herefordshire HR6 0DN
Brimfield (01584) 711401
Fruit pickers needed.
Ages 16+. Hours variable, end June-early August. Piecework rates paid. Campsite provided, but workers should take their own food and camping equipment. *EEA nationals only.*

CONCORDIA (Youth Service Volunteers) Ltd, Recruitment Secretary, 8 Brunswick Place, Hove, Sussex BN3 1ET
Brighton (01273) 772086
Aims to bring together the youth of all nations throughout the world, to promote a better understanding between them of their ideas, beliefs and ways of living. Can place overseas applicants on international farmcamps in the UK: **hop picking** in Kent; **soft fruit picking** in Scotland, Kent, Lincolnshire, Oxfordshire, Herefordshire, Sussex and Devon; **apple picking** in Hampshire and Kent; and **vegetable picking** in Cambridgeshire, Devon, Kent and Somerset. Applicants must be prepared to work hard when and where required. Every effort will be made to find alternative work in the event of bad weather or crop failure, but it should be stressed that work cannot be guaranteed.
Ages 19-25. Season runs May-October. Wages are either piecework or at rates laid down by the Agricultural Wages Board. Accommodation usually provided in huts, caravans or farm cottages but workers are expected to take own food, sleeping bag, tents and cooking equipment. Registration fee payable. Travel paid by applicants.
Apply September-December stating age and student status. Programmes and application forms distributed in January.

FIVEWAYS FRUIT FARM Fiveways, Stanway, Colchester, Essex CO3 5LR
Colchester (01206) 330244
Strawberry and **apple pickers** required on 80-acre farm; semi-skilled **orchard work** also available after picking.
Ages 18+. No experience necessary. 40+ hours per week, May-October. Piecework rates paid. Campsite for tents and recreational caravan provided with showers, toilets, TV and cooking facilities; £9 per week charge payable in advance.

FORDE ABBEY FRUIT GARDENS c/o Alice Roper, Forde Abbey, Chard, Somerset TA20 4LU
South Chard (01460) 220231
Fruit pickers required to work in fields belonging to Forde Abbey, Dorset. Work is mainly strawberry picking, with possibly administrative or supervisory work. No experience necessary.
Ages 18+. 30-40 hours per week; 4+ weeks, mid June-mid August. Piecework/Agricultural Wages Board rates paid. Camping facilities provided free of charge. Self-contained cottages or caravans for early applicants, cost £2.50 per night. *Apply in writing enclosing SAE/IRCs and photo. Early application advised.*

FRIDAY BRIDGE INTERNATIONAL FARMCAMP LTD The Manager, March Road, Friday Bridge, Wisbech, Cambridgeshire PE14 0LR
Wisbech (01945) 860255 (May-November) or Norwich (01603) 662052 (November-May)
A cooperative set in the heart of the Fen Country with local growers and farmers, needs **seasonal workers** to

harvest its crops. Work involves weeding and strawing, and also picking gooseberries, strawberries, plums, apples, blackberries, pears, potatoes, courgettes and beans. Campers are collected from and returned to the camp daily by the farmer for whom they are working.
⊕ Ages 16-30. 1+ weeks, approx 30 May-23 October. Hourly and piecework rates normally paid. Indoor processing work also available. Many social and sports facilities available including swimming pool, tennis courts, games field, games/TV room, bar, discos and dances. Other facilities include hot showers, drying rooms and camp shop. Cost approx £58 per week covers full board accommodation in huts and facilities. Registration fee £35.
EEA nationals only.

GREAT HOLLANDEN FARM
Mr B R Brooks, Mill Lane, Hildenborough, near Sevenoaks, Kent TN15 0SG
✆ **Hildenborough (01732) 832276**
Fruit pickers and **agricultural workers** needed to pick and pack all types of soft fruit to a very high standard. Work is also available harvesting and pruning raspberries at the end of the season.
⊕ Ages 18+. Pickers are trained and should be hard working and conscientious. 3+ weeks, mid May-end October. Hours 0600-1500 with opportunities for evening work. Piecework rates paid. Accommodation available in mobile homes, cost £11 per week; or those with tents may use campsite. Charge of £5 per week for use of facilities such as kitchens, mess room, showers. Group outings, discos and barbecues organised. Farm shop offering food on site, English lessons given 2 nights per week. Easy access to London (by train 38 minutes).
✍ Early booking advised; notification of acceptance early March. Replies only to those enclosing SAE/IRCs.

GREENS OF DEREHAM
Norwich Road, Dereham, Norfolk
✆ **Dereham (01362) 692014**
Fruit pickers required throughout July to pick strawberries.
⊕ Ages 17+. Work may take place until 1600. Workers are paid in cash daily. Camping area provided. Applicants pay own insurance and travel costs.
UK nationals only.

HARVESTING OPPORTUNITY PERMIT SCHEME (GB)
YFC Centre, N A C, Stoneleigh Park, Kenilworth, Warwickshire CV8 2LG ✆ **Coventry (01203) 696589** ✉ **(01203) 696559**
Finds employment on **fruit**, **vegetable** and **hops farms** throughout Britain for full-time university students from Europe. Limited number of work permits available for students from central and eastern Europe.
⊕ Students must have been born in the years 1970-1974 and able to speak English. Preference given to agriculture students. No experience necessary, but the work is physically hard. British agricultural casual wage rates.
✍ Apply giving personal details for information and application form after 1 August. Completed forms with £40 fee accepted November-January.

HAYGROVE FRUIT Redbank, Ledbury, Hertfordshire HR8 2JL
✆ **Ledbury (01531) 633659**
Fruit pickers required, mainly for strawberries, also a few experienced **supervisors** and **drivers**.
⊕ Ages 19-35. All applicants should have some knowledge of English. 50 hour, 6 day week for 1+ months, May-October. Campsite available with toilets, showers, kitchen and TV room; cost from £7 per week. Salary approx £20 per day fruit pickers; £35 per day supervisors and drivers. Weekend day trips and English language tuition available. Applicants must arrange own travel, insurance and work permits; and take own camping equipment and sleeping bag. **D**
✍ Apply from February.

HILLTOP FRUIT FARM Ledbury, Herefordshire HR8 1LN
Ⓒ Ledbury (01531) 632630
⌥ (01531) 631996
Fruit pickers needed.
✤ Ages 18+. Approx 8 hour day, 5 day week, June-mid October. Piecework rates for strawberries and plums; hourly rate for apples and pears. All rates as laid down by the Agricultural Wages Board. Campsite area with hot showers, toilets and canteen area with sinks, tables and benches provided; cost £1.60 per person per day, 80p when full hours worked. Pickers must take own tents, groundsheets, sleeping bags, cooking and eating utensils. Warm clothing, rubber boots and waterproofs also essential. Parking available for caravans. Third party insurance provided. Applicants should speak English.
☙ Non-UK/EEA nationals must apply through Concordia or Harvesting Opportunity Permit Scheme (see above).

HUDSON FARMS Badliss Hall, Ardleigh, Colchester, Essex
Ⓒ Colchester (01206) 230306
Soft fruit production and plant raising farm; work includes **picking** and **planting strawberries, raspberries** and **vegetables**. June-October. 30 hour week, Monday-Friday with occasional weekend work.
✤ Ages 18+. Piecework/Agricultural Wages Board rates paid. Work not guaranteed in bad weather and no wet weather equipment provided. Campsite facilities with cooking areas available, £8.50 per week; workers must take their own sleeping bags/tents.
UK/EEA students only.

INTERNATIONAL FARM CAMP
The Organiser, Hall Road, Tiptree, Colchester, Essex CO5 0QS
Ⓒ Tiptree (01621) 815496
Fruit picking work available.
✤ Ages 18-25. 35 hour, 5 day week. 2+ weeks, early June-mid July; few places available mid July-end August. Facilities include hot showers, drying and ironing rooms, shop, table tennis and TV.

Piecework rates paid. Cost approx £40 per week includes full board accommodation in huts. Workers must help with kitchen duties for at least 1 day during their stay. £25 deposit, £15 of which is refundable on completion of booked stay. *Students only; non-EEA must not be in final year.*

MARK DAVIDSON Ploddy House, Newent, Gloucestershire
Ⓒ Newent (01531) 820240
Farm workers required for planting, picking and packing salad and some other horticultural crops.
✤ Ages 18+. Experience useful but not essential. Approx 45 hour week, early May-end October. Agricultural and piecework rates paid. Limited accommodation available for small fee. On-the-job training. Language tuition available according to demand. No fares paid. *☙ Early application advised. Non-EEA nationals must arrange own visa/ work permit.*

OAK TREE FARM
Mr R E S Stephenson, Hasketon, Woodbridge, Suffolk IP13 6JH
Ⓒ Grundisburgh (01473) 735218
Strawberry pickers needed.
✤ Ages 18+, women and couples only. 8 hour day, 6 day week excluding Saturday. 3+ weeks, approx 25 June-25 July. Piecework rates paid. Self-catering hostel or camping accommodation approx £3 per week. Campers should take their own tents and equipment. *Apply by mid-March.*

A P & S M PARRIS Cutliffe Farm, Sherford, Taunton, Somerset TA1 3RQ *Ⓒ* Taunton (01823) 253808
Farm close to Exmoor National Park requires **pickers** for strawberries, raspberries, currants, runner beans and other harvesting jobs. Work also available **packing fruit** for markets.
✤ Ages 18+. No experience necessary as training given. 45-50 hour week, beginning 0530-0600 during busy periods. 6-8 weeks, early June-August. Piecework rates paid. Self-catering

accommodation in caravans for small weekly charge, or pickers can take their own tents.
🐝 *Apply by February. Can only accept EEA nationals or those already with work permits through approved scheme.*

R & J M PLACE LTD International Farm Camp, Church Farm, Tunstead, Norwich, Norfolk NR12 8RQ ✆ **Smallburgh (01692) 536337**
Strawberry, raspberry and **blackberry pickers** and **agricultural workers** needed. Other work, such as **crop irrigation, fruit inspection** or **packing**, may also be available.
⚘ Ages 17-25. 8 hour day, 5/6 day week. I May-28 October. Piecework rates paid. Bed and breakfast provided from £37 per week in converted farm buildings; the remaining meals are self-catering. Workers should take a sleeping bag and cooking utensils, and help with essential camp duties. Facilities include kitchen, dining hall, bar, showers, shop, laundry room, pool tables, table tennis, darts, volleyball, football and canoeing instruction. Registration fee £25 includes membership of social club. **D** *Overseas applicants accepted.*

SEGGAT FARMS Seggat, Auchterless, Turriff, Aberdeenshire AB53 8DL ✆ **Auchterless (01888) 511223** 📠 **(01888) 511434**
Strawberry pickers and **packers** needed. No experience necessary.
⚘ Ages 17+. 45 hour week, early July-mid August. Piecework rates paid. Self-catering accommodation in dormitory; workers should take own sleeping bags. Space for tents also available. Pickers pay own travel costs and insurance. *All nationalities welcome; non-EEA nationals must have work permit.*

SPELMONDEN ESTATE CO LTD The Director, Spelmonden Farm, Goudhurst, Kent TN17 IHE
Hop and **apple/pear pickers** required from I September.
⚘ Ages 18+. 50 hour week; pay approx £152. Self-catering accommodation in

2/3/4 bedrooms, plus TV room, showers etc; cost £8 per week. *EEA nationals only.*

G & B WALKER STRAWBERRY GROWERS Newton of Lewesk, Old Rayne, Insch, Aberdeenshire AB52 6SW
✆ **Old Rayne (014645) 250**
Pickers wanted for strawberry season on farm in Scotland.
⚘ Ages 16+. No experience required. 36 hour week for 4-6 weeks, July-August. Piecework rates. Self-catering dormitory accommodation on site. Workers pay for food, laundry and travel costs. *All nationalities welcome.*

WASPBOURNE MANOR FARM Sheffield Park, near Uckfield, East Sussex TN22 3QT
✆ **Uckfield (01825) 723414**
Strawberry pickers required.
⚘ Ages 18+. English speakers preferred. 40 hour, 5-7 day week for 6+ weeks, May-July. Piecework rates paid. Public liability insurance and excursions provided. Accommodation provided in caravans; cost £15 per week. No fares paid. **D PH** 🐝 *Apply November-May. Early application advised. Non-EEA nationals must have work permit.*

WWOOF (WORKING FOR ORGANIC GROWERS) 19 Bradford Road, Lewes, Sussex BN7 IRB
A non-profitmaking organisation which aims to help organic farmers and smallholders whose work is often labour-intensive as it does not rely on the use of artificial fertilisers or pesticides. Unskilled **voluntary workers** can gain first-hand experience of organic farming and gardening, and get a chance to spend an energetic weekend in the country. Working weekends are organised on organic farms, smallholdings and gardens throughout Britain. The work can include hedging, haymaking, fruit, vegetable and dairy work, beekeeping, sheep shearing, rearing kids and ducklings, building renovation, peat

cutting, hooking and scything, seaweed spraying and compost making. Members receive a bi-monthly newsletter which details places needing help on specific weekends, and also lists job opportunities in the organic movement. After completing 2 scheduled weekends members may apply for their own copy of the complete list of WWOOF places, including some overseas, so that independent arrangements for longer periods can be made.
⊕ Ages 16+. Families welcome on some farms. Opportunities to learn crafts. 8 hour day, weekends all year. Full board and lodging provided in the farmhouse or outbuildings; volunteers should take a sleeping bag. No wages paid, and helpers must pay their own travel costs. Insurance and anti-tetanus vaccination recommended. Membership fee £8. **D** 🏊 *Send SAE/IRCs for further information.*

MONITORS, LEADERS & INSTRUCTORS

THE ABBEY COLLEGE
Wells Road, Malvern Wells, Worcestershire WR14 4JF
ⓒ **Malvern (01684) 892300**
Residential **sports coaches, activity leaders**, and **social organisers** required.
⊕ Ages 18 +. Sports coaches should have some sports qualifications/ experience. 40 hour week; 4+ weeks, mid June-end August. Full board accommodation plus £25 travel costs. Salary £90-£180 per week. 🏊 *Apply 3 months in advance. UK nationals only.*

ACADEMIC TRAVEL
(LOWESTOFT) LTD The Briar School of English, 8 Gunton Cliff, Lowestoft, Suffolk NR32 4PE
ⓒ **Lowestoft (01502) 573781**
Aims to provide an educational and cultural experience for young people from overseas, providing sports, visits and social activities in addition to English lessons. Requires experienced **teachers** and **instructors** to teach English and sports. Appropriate qualifications necessary: TEFL English, LTA tennis, RYA sailing and BCU kayak/ canoe. Knowledge of French, German, Italian and Spanish useful. End June-end August, average 25 hours per week. ⊕ Ages 18+. Salaries according to position; insurance provided. *UK nationals only.*

ACORN VENTURE LTD Personnel Department, 137 Worcester Road, Hagley, Stourbridge, West Midlands DY9 0NW
An activity holiday company catering for school groups at camping centres in Tal-y-Bont and Shell Island in North Wales. **Instructors** required to supervise activities such as watersports, target sports, climbing, abseiling, orienteering, caving and gorge walking.
⊕ Ages 18+. Previous experience and qualifications such as BCU/RYA essential. Minimum 50 hour, 6 day week. Applicants are expected to work the full season, May-September. Salary approx £40-£45 per week. All meals and accommodation in tents plus insurance provided. 🏊 *Apply in writing with cv by end February. If no reply within 28 days assume application unsuccessful.*

ACTION HOLIDAYS LTD
Robinwood, Jumps Road, Todmorden, Lancashire OL14 8HJ
ⓒ **Todmorden (01706) 814554**
Runs children's multi-activity holidays at centres in Cheshire, Lancashire, Surrey and Staffordshire. Requires **supervisors** and **instructors** with considerable previous experience of working with children. Enthusiasm for the job and enjoyment of sports activities essential. Specialist activities include archery, go-karting and performing arts. 50+ hour week with 1 day off. Salary £45-£100 per week, depending on responsibility, all meals, and shared accommodation provided.

Participants pay their own travel expenses and insurance. *Overseas applicants must arrange own work permit.*

ADVENTURE & COMPUTER HOLIDAYS LTD PO Box 183, Dorking, Surrey RH5 6FA
ℂ Dorking (01306) 730716
Adventure holiday **camp leaders** required for day and residential courses at centres in Surrey and Cornwall.
⊕ Ages 21+ for Surrey day camps; must have own accommodation in London or Surrey.
⊕ Ages 25+ for residential courses in Cornwall; must have full, clean driving licence.
Experience of working with children essential; preference given to teachers, student teachers and those with NNEB qualifications. 5-6 weeks, May-August, with busiest period July-August. 35+ hour week. Full board and lodging provided on residential courses. Weekly salary £120 (day courses) or £150 (residential courses).

ANGLO-CONTINENTAL
Director of Studies, 33 Wimborne Road, Bournemouth BH2 6NA
ℂ Bournemouth (01202) 557414
An English language school which, as part of a wide range of programmes, organises junior holiday courses for those aged 8-16, combining English language and creative leisure.
Staff required for **sports coaching** and **residential supervision**, with additional responsibility for recreational and social activities. The posts involve careful supervision in and out of school hours. Opportunities to teach and organise sports, lead excursions and to conduct activities such as computer programming, arts and crafts and give talks on British life, literature and institutions. A number of **administrative posts** also available in the areas of travel and social activities. Applicants should have organising ability, drive and enthusiasm plus wide sporting and cultural interests. Irregular working hours including evening activities.

6 day week, June-August. Staff may be required to attend brief training seminars in the week prior to the arrival of students. Residential accommodation provided at most centres in return for extra duties. Weekly salaries, paid according to qualifications and experience. All applicants must attend for interview; travel expenses refunded for successful candidates.

ARDMORE ADVENTURE
11-15 High Street, Marlow, Buckinghamshire SL7 1AU
ℂ Marlow (01628) 890060
Organises activity holidays for young people at residential and day centres in south east England. **Group leaders** with qualifications/relevant experience required to lead archery, arts and crafts, excursions, karaoke, performing arts, pottery, rifle shooting and tennis.
⊕ Ages 20+. Lifesavers and first aiders particularly required. Applicants should preferably have experience of working with children. 2/3+ weeks, mid June-August. day centres 40 hours per week, residential 60 hours per week. Wages from £45 per week, depending on position. Full board, single or shared accommodation and insurance provided, but no travel. **B D PH** depending on ability. *UK nationals only.*

BEARSPORTS OUTDOOR CENTRES Personnel Department, Windy Gyle, Belford, Northumberland NE70 7QE
ℂ Belford (01668) 213289
Voluntary and paid **outdoor pursuits instructors** required to lead a wide variety of activities including canoeing, rock climbing, windsurfing, hill walking, orienteering, cycling and wilderness survival. **Domestic assistants** also required. Applicants must be experienced and proficient in outdoor pursuits; for paid positions a clean driving licence and recognised qualifications are essential.
⊕ Ages 17-35 (voluntary) or 21-35 (paid). 6 day week, with long hours of rewarding, enjoyable work.

Appointments made at various times throughout the year. Full board accommodation provided. Salary for paid positions from £25-£50 per week depending on age and qualifications. Staff entitled to discounts on RYA, BCU and MLTB qualification courses run at the centres.

CAMP BEAUMONT Recruitment Department, Bridge House, Orchard Lane, Huntingdon, Cambridgeshire PE18 6QT
℘ Huntingdon (01480) 456123
Organises a wide range of holidays for children in American-style day and residential camps throughout the country. Opportunities for **group leaders, monitors, specialist instructors, nurses** and **nursery nurses**. Staff are chosen for their experience with children and their activity or sports skills. Activities include field sports and games, arts, crafts, computers, drama, motorsports, watersports and outdoor pursuits. Specialists are recruited for shooting, archery, judo, fencing, kayaking and TEFL, and must be qualified. Monitors on day camps should live within the Greater London area. Specialists assume total responsibility for the safety of both children and staff during the activity. Monitors and group leaders are responsible for the supervision and welfare of a group of 12-20 children. All staff liaise with the camp director. Residential staff are involved with the evening entertainments and night-time supervision. All staff must genuinely enjoy working with children, possess leadership ability, and be willing to work a long, hard exhausting day enthusiastically in a structured setting where regulations apply to all.
⚜ Ages 18+. Staff must be available for whole season: mid July-end August, and for compulsory staff training/orientation session prior to camp opening. 1-2 days off per week, and alternate evenings off. Wages £30-£90 per week.

CAMP WINDERMERE Low Wray, Ambleside, Cumbria LA22 0JJ
℘ Ambleside (0153 94) 32163
A full-time training centre for school parties and youth groups with the emphasis on training, safety and enjoyment. Recognised as an approved establishment by the Mountain Leadership Training Board, the British Canoe Union and the Royal Yachting Association. Volunteer **assistant outdoor pursuits instructors** needed to teach walking, canoeing, sailing, camping and other activities.
⚜ Ages 18+. Experience useful but not essential. 24 hour day, 7 day week, May-September. Full training to national standards in canoeing, sailing and walking, tent accommodation and catering provided.

DORSET ADVENTURE HOLIDAYS High Street, Wool, Wareham, Dorset BH20 6BP
℘ Wareham (01920) 405176
Organise activity holidays in Dorset, Hampshire and Wiltshire for adults, families, unaccompanied children and teenagers. Require **group leaders, play scheme workers, instructors**.
⚜ Ages 18+. Applicants must be bright, active, good humoured, hardworking, outgoing and caring, preferably with some experience of working with 8-15 age group. Instructors must have national qualifications in outdoor activities. Variable hours, May-October and during school holidays. Full board accommodation in tent or caravan on residential holidays. Salary £25-£150 per week according to position and experience. ▨ Apply by 1 April. EEA and US nationals only.

EDINBURGH SCHOOL OF ENGLISH (Junior Courses), 271 Canongate, The Royal Mile, Edinburgh EH8 8BQ
℘ 0131-557 9200
Organise residential and non-residential English language classes for young people at schools in Edinburgh, Aberdeen, Dundee and Strathallan.

Activity monitors required to supervise groups of up to 10 students and help organise their leisure programme of sports, cultural visits and social outings. Applicants must be fit, active, keen on sports, with a friendly, outgoing personality and a sound knowledge of the locality they will be working in. Experience of working with young people an advantage.
⊕ Ages 21+. 3-12 weeks, Easter and mid June-September. Hours by agreement. Wages £100 per week. Full board university or school accommodation provided only if course is residential. One day briefing provided at start of course. *UK nationals only.*

EXTRAMURAL CENTRE Atlantic College, St Donats, Llantwit Major, South Glamorgan CF61 1WF
℃ (01446) 792711
Requires **instructors** to teach a variety of outdoor activities including canoeing, climbing, swimming and archery, on courses for disadvantaged young people.
⊕ Ages 18-25. Previous experience highly desirable, and national awards in the relevant sport an advantage. June-August. Salary £42 per week; on-the-job training, board and dormitory accommodation provided. ✍ *Apply by mid February. EEA nationals only.*

HOTROCKS 97 Swineshead Road, Wyberton Fen, Boston, Lincolnshire PE12 7JG
℃ **Boston (01205) 359909**
Organises activity courses for school groups at centres in Derbyshire, Snowdonia and north Devon. Qualified and experienced **instructors** required to teach a variety of activities including canoeing, hillwalking, climbing, archery and watersports. Unqualified applicants also considered for **kitchen** and **maintenance duties**.
⊕ Ages 18-30. Approx 50 hours per week, May-September. Staff training, full board and lodging provided, plus salary of approx £45 per week, depending on experience and qualifications.
✍ *Apply by end April.*

HYDE HOUSE ACTIVITY HOLIDAY CENTRE
c/o 6 Kew Green, Richmond, Surrey
℃ 0181-940 7782
Situated on a 50 acre estate 9 miles from Poole, organising outdoor multi-activity holidays and courses for schools and groups. Sports include windsurfing, water skiing, dinghy and longboat sailing, snorkelling, canoeing, climbing, abseiling, orienteering, riding and archery. Full and part-time **instructors** required; qualifications preferred. 6 day week. 8+ weeks, March-October. Full board accommodation provided. Salary £50 per week.

THE IONA COMMUNITY Staff Coordinator, Isle of Iona, Argyll, Strathclyde PA76 6SN
℃ Iona (0168 17) 404
An ecumenical Christian community seeking new and radical ways of living the Gospel in today's world. On Iona the Community runs two centres, each welcoming up to 50 guests to a common life of work, worship, meals and recreation. **Volunteers** required to help run the children's programme for those staying at the centres. Some experience of working with children, flexibility and organisation essential, as is the willingness to work as part of a team. Also require **guides** to offer guided tours of the Abbey, a rebuilt Benedictine monastery, for guests and visitors, often many hundreds each day in the summer months. Duties include keeping the Abbey clean, preparation for worship and welcoming people to services. An interest in history, meeting people and worship essential. On the nearby island of Mull the Camas Centre welcomes up to 16 guests each week, mainly unemployed or disadvantaged young people, to a common life of work, worship, arts, crafts and outdoor activities. Requires **programme workers** and **general assistants** with experience and, if possible, qualifications in one or more of the following: outdoor skills (canoeing, walking, camping, abseiling), arts and crafts,

working with groups of sometimes very demanding teenagers, games, driving and maintenance.

✣ Ages 18+. All the work is demanding but rewarding, but most important is a willingness to join fully in the community life, which includes worship and social activities as well as work. 6 day week, February-December. Full board, shared accommodation, pocket money of £17 per week and assistance with travel expenses within mainland Britain provided. ✤ Applications received before 31 December given priority.

KIDS KLUB The Gardens, Great Finborough, near Stowmarket, Suffolk IP14 3EF ✆ Stowmarket (01449) 675907 ☎ (01449) 771396 Provides activity holidays for ages 6-15 at four centres. Requires **activity instructors** to organise and play with the children. Qualifications and experience in outdoor pursuits and sports essential. Staff chosen for their enthusiasm and energy. **Activity assistants** also required to help instructors and for general supervision of children in free time. Various jobs available.

✣ Ages 18+. European languages an asset but not essential. 50 hour week, March-September. Wages £50 per week. Excursions available; full board accommodation provided. Participants pay own travel and insurance costs.

MILLFIELD SCHOOL Village of Education, Street, Somerset BA16 0YD ✆ Street (01458) 45823 An independent school organising a range of special interest holidays for children and adults, with over 100 different activities and 350 courses to choose from. **Instructors** needed to teach a wide variety of outdoor pursuits, sports, arts, crafts and cookery courses, plus EFL. Facilities include sports halls, games fields, swimming pool, dance/health studios and technology centre.

✣ Ages 20+. Degree or teaching qualifications and/or relevant sports

coaching qualifications essential. 25 hour week. 4 weeks, July and August. Wages approx £100 per week. Small group accommodation and catering provided in exchange for evening or weekend supervisory duties. Staff pay own travel and insurance costs. **PH**

MOUNTAIN VENTURES LTD 120 Allerton Road, Liverpool L18 2DG ✆ 0151-734 2477 Jobs at **Bryn Du, Ty Du Road, Llanberis, Gwynedd** ✆ Llanberis (01286) 870454 **Assistant instructors** required to work on a voluntary basis at a centre in Snowdonia running activity and adventure holidays for children and school groups, and outdoor development training programmes for young adults. Wide range of activities are covered, including watersports, hill walking, rock climbing, target sports, orienteering, campcraft and expeditions.

✣ Ages 17+. Previous experience and outdoor pursuits qualifications welcome but not essential; motivation and enthusiasm for outdoor activities are considered more important. Approx 40 hour week, June and July. Pocket money from £10 per week. Full board accommodation and insurance provided; volunteers can also take part in in-house training programmes when available. **D** *Overseas volunteers should have a good command of English.*

NANSEN SOCIETY (UK) LTD Redcastle Station, Muir-of-Ord, Ross-shire IV6 7RX ✆ Muir-of-Ord (01463) 871255 ☎ (01463) 870258 A non-political, non-religious humanitarian organisation inspired by the humanistic work of the Arctic explorer Fridtjof Nansen. Much of its work is concerned with helping young people with emotional and behavioural difficulties to gain greater control over their own lives and contribute more positively to others. **Monitors** and **instructors** required to work on a voluntary basis at a farm community in the Scottish highlands, living together with permanent staff and youngsters with special needs. The farm demonstrates a self-sustaining, clean and non-exploitative agricultural system, combined with alternative energy generation and conservation.

⊕ Ages 21+. Applicants must be experienced in teaching young people with special needs, or in teaching outdoor education or conservation/farmwork. Good spoken English required. Volunteers pay own travel and insurance. 8 hour day, 40 hour week on a shift basis. 1+ months, all year. Full board accommodation provided, plus £25 per week pocket money for volunteers staying at least 3 months.

NORD-ANGLIA INTERNATIONAL LTD 10 Eden Place, Cheadle, Cheshire SK8 1AT ✆ 0161-491 4191

Organises children's summer day camps in north west England, and English language courses for overseas students at centres throughout Britain. **Social activity monitors** needed for supervision and courier duties, to liaise with the course director and help with the organisation/animation of sports.

⊕ Ages 18+. No formal teaching qualifications required. Mostly 5 afternoons per week. 2-10 weeks, Easter and July/August. Most courses last 3 weeks, July. Wages £50-£105 per week depending on duties.

Activity directors also required, to take responsibility for planning, organising and running social programme. Suitable candidates should be older with organisational skills. Salary £110-£195. Successful applicants are expected to attend 1-day training/ information session before starting. Applicants must arrange own board, accommodation, travel and insurance. *Native speakers of English only.*

PGL YOUNG ADVENTURE LTD Personnel Department, Alton Court, Penyard Lane (878), Ross-on-Wye, Herefordshire HR9 5NR ✆ Ross-on-Wye (01989) 767833

Organises outdoor adventure holidays in England, Wales and Scotland.

Instructors are needed for sailing, windsurfing, pony trekking, canoeing, hill walking, orienteering and archery. Staff are also needed with particular interest and skills in swimming, campcraft, caving, basketball, American football, aerobics, tennis, squash, badminton, volleyball, judo, fencing, cycling, drama, field studies, climbing, abseiling, assault courses, nature trails and arts and crafts. At some centres instructors are needed who are proficient in a number of activities.

⊕ Ages 18+. Instructors should ideally have a qualification or previous experience of teaching with a good basic level of skill, but consideration will be given to candidates who are competent in the given activity. Training is given. Enthusiasm and stamina essential, plus the ability to adhere to strict safety standards, and the foresight to deal with emergency situations and recognise the limitations of each child.

Group leaders also required to take charge of a group of young people, joining in the activities and developing group identity, as well as planning and organising the evening activities. They are responsible for looking after the welfare of the group and must expect to be fully involved with them throughout their stay, with the prime task of ensuring guests enjoy their holiday and get the most out of their experience.

⊕ Ages 20+. Applicants should have a strong sense of responsibility and total commitment, enjoy the company of young people, be self-motivated, tolerant, flexible, positive, mature, with vitality and a good sense of humour. 4+ weeks, February-September. Staff are also recruited for short periods such as Easter and the Spring Bank Holiday. 1 day off per week. Full board accommodation provided. Pocket money from £32-£47 per week, depending on qualifications and length of stay. Senior activity instructors receive from £65 per week; senior watersports instructors and canoeists receive £60-£100 per week. Applicants pay own travel expenses. All staff are encouraged to take part in evening activities with the guests, and may sometimes be asked to help out in areas other than their own. *Early application advisable; majority of positions filled by end June.*

PILGRIM ADVENTURE
120 Bromley Heath Road, Downend, Bristol BS16 6JJ
A Christian-based, ecumenical organisation running an annual programme of pilgrim journeys through areas such as Snowdonia, the Scottish Highlands and Islands and the Lake District. A small number of **volunteer team members** are required to help lead groups of 10-25 people and assist with worship and camp chores. Ages 18+. Applicants must have an interest in and experience of outdoor activities, especially hillwalking. Must be able to work the whole season, early July-mid September; additional help occasionally required at other times of year. Each journey lasts 5-15 days; 2-3 days in between may be taken as leave. Full board accommodation provided on trips, plus £12 per week pocket money. Induction provided during first few days of service. *Early applications advised.*

PRIME LEISURE ACTIVITY HOLIDAYS LTD **The Manor Farm House, Dunstan Road, Old Headington, Oxford OX3 9BY**
Oxford (01865) 750775
Organise multi-activity holiday camps for children aged 4-14 at day centres in the south of England.
Monitors are required to coach and supervise groups of up to 16 children in activities such as tennis, trampolining, football, swimming, archery, and art and craft. Previous experience of teaching or working with children preferred, and applicants should have relevant awards or professional qualifications. Ages 18+. 50 hour week. 2-6 weeks during Easter and summer school holidays. Wages £60-£200 per week, plus full board accommodation on site. No travel costs provided.

ROB HASTINGS ADVENTURE LTD **25 Southcourt Avenue, Leighton Buzzard LU7 7QD**
Leighton Buzzard (01525) 379881
Operate adventure, activity and creative holidays for all ages at a centre in north Wales. Wide range of activities organised including sailing, white water canoeing, golf, archery, fencing, mountain biking, racquet sports, walking, horse riding, rock climbing, arts and crafts.
Instructors required to supervise and teach activities, help out with domestic duties and contribute to evening entertainment. Ages 18+. Specialist qualifications desirable and experience essential. Driving licence and experience of driving minibuses required for some positions. Applicants need to be outgoing and enthusiastic, enjoy challenges, working in a team and doing a job well. Tolerance, flexibility, stamina, and a sense of fun combined with a responsible attitude also important. 6 day week, 6 weeks, July and August. Salary from £43 per week according to the type of job. Full board accommodation provided. All staff take part in on-site training programme. **PH** *Write enclosing* cv. *UK nationals or experienced/qualified instructors from overseas only.*

ROCKLEY POINT SAILING SCHOOL **Hamworthy, Poole, Dorset BH15 4LZ** *Poole (01202) 677272*
Teaches sailing to individuals and groups in dinghies and yachts, and requires **instructors** with RYA qualifications. Those with the ability to achieve RYA qualifications within a short time may also apply. Some posts for **house mothers**, to look after the children when not sailing. Ages 18+. 40 hour week, March-October. Wages dependent on experience. Accommodation provided.

SPORTS EXPERIENCE **86 Dorset Road, Merton Park, London SW19**
0181-715 5434
Organises multi-activity day and

residential camps for children in London and south east England. **Monitors** are required to assist in the supervision of both sporting and non-sporting activities. Relevant sports qualifications and experience of working with children desirable but not essential; applicants should be young, enthusiastic people who have a positive ability to get on with children. Qualifications in first aid, swimming or outdoor pursuits particularly useful. Good spoken English essential.
⊕ Ages 18+. Hours variable, mid July-end August. Salary £40-£75 per week depending on responsibility, qualifications and experience. Accommodation can be arranged. *EEA nationals only.*

SUPERCHOICE Personnel Department, 191 Freshfield Road, Brighton, East Sussex BN2 2YE
℗ **Brighton (01273) 676467**
Operates adventure-based educational activity holidays for school groups and unaccompanied young people aged 8-17 at Pontins centres throughout England and Wales. **Multi activity instructors** required.
⊕ Ages 18-30. Experience in outdoor pursuits useful but not essential as full training given. Applicants must be dedicated, enthusiastic sports people who are keen to work with children in a residential outdoor environment. They should be energetic and out-going with a good sense of humour. 60 hour week, February-October; part season options available. Full board accommodation provided for resident staff plus £40 per week wages and free use of all sports and leisure facilities. Intensive training programme and assessment period prior to work. Staff are given opportunity to gain nationally recognised qualifications.
⧖ Apply January-May. *UK nationals only.*

TASIS ENGLAND Coldharbour Lane, Thorpe, Surrey KT20 8TE
℗ **Chertsey (01932) 565252**
Counsellors required to work at an American-style international summer school for 12-18 year-old students.

Counsellors act as teacher aides, sports coaches, evening activity organisers, excursion chaperons and also have some residential/dormitory duties.
⊕ Ages 19+. Applicants should be students who have completed at least one year in higher education.
An interest in sports and some relevant experience also desirable. 40 hour week. 8 weeks, end June-end August. Salary approx £1,000 for 8 weeks. Full board dormitory accommodation provided. No travel costs paid. *EEA and US nationals only.*

TIGHNABRUAICH SAILING SCHOOL Tighnabruaich, Argyll PA21 2BD
Instructors are needed to teach sailing and windsurfing to high standards in a relaxed holiday atmosphere. Appropriate sailing or windsurfing qualifications required.
⊕ Ages 18+. Approx 36 hour week, June-September. Salary £60 per week and self-catering youth hostel accommodation provided.

TRIG POINT 49 Paul Findlay, Activities Coordinator, 80 Staithes Lane, Staithes, Saltburn TS13 5AH
℗ **Saltburn (01947) 840757**
⧢ **(01947) 840274**
Offers multi activity holidays for school and college groups, unaccompanied children, adults, people with special needs, and women's groups.
Carers, assistants and **instructors** required to help run holidays. Activities include canoeing, kayaking, climbing, abseiling, orienteering, rope/assault courses, expeditions, bivouac, archery, teamwork challenges, raft building, racing, mountain biking and pony trekking.
⊕ Ages 18+. All applicants should have an outgoing personality and must speak English. Recognised qualifications an advantage. Hours vary; work available all year round. Dormitory accommodation and employer's liability insurance provided. Salary negotiable.
B D PH W

VILLAGE CAMPS Chalet Seneca, 1854 Leysin, Switzerland
Organises American-style summer camps at Hurstpierpoint College, West Sussex for those aged 8-18 from the international business and diplomatic communities. Opportunities for counsellors, special activity counsellors, programme leaders, special instructors and nurses. Staff live, work and play with the children and are responsible for their safety, health and happiness. **Counsellors** plan, organise and direct daytime and evening programmes, accompany campers on excursions and may be called upon to supervise other counsellors and take charge of a camper group. Evening activities include sports and games, films, competitions, fondues and discos. **Special activity counsellors**, having a high degree of proficiency, organise, execute and instruct specific programmes such as sports, arts and crafts, nature study and basic computer science. Counsellors with a substantial amount of leadership experience in recreational programmes can be appointed **programme leaders**, which includes running a camp programme and direction and supervision of adult counsellors. **Assistant** and **junior counsellors** are responsible for supporting counsellors in all activities and assisting with special activities at day camps as required. **Specialist instructors** should have 2 years' training and experience, and be able to instruct children of all ability levels; they are responsible for the concentrated teaching of their subject at a speciality camp such as golf, tennis, computer science or French and English language. **Nurses** are responsible for the general health and welfare of campers and counsellors, attending to accidents and maintaining an infirmary. ⊕ Ages 21+, 26+ for programme leaders. Applicants must have training and/or experience of working with children and have an interest in children from many ethnic and religious backgrounds. English is the first language, but priority is given to applicants with additional French, Italian or German language skills. 45 hour week for 1+ months, June-August. 1½ days plus 3 evening free per 2 week session. Full board accommodation, accident and liability insurance provided, but not travel costs. Wages SF325 per 2 week session. Compulsory pre-camp training course arranged for all staff.

THE WOODSIDE ADVENTURE CENTRE c/o 6 Kew Green, Richmond, Surrey ✆ 0181-940 7782
The Centre is situated in Bideford and organises outdoor activity holidays and courses for all ages and levels. Sports include water skiing, canoeing, sailing, surfing, riding, abseiling, sand yachting, climbing, snorkelling, coastal/hill walking, orienteering, skate sailing, grass slope skiing and archery. Full or part-time **instructors** required. Qualifications essential. 36 hour, 6 day week. 8+ weeks, March-October. Salary £50 per week. Full board centre accommodation provided.

TEACHERS

Seasonal jobs for teachers are available at English language summer schools throughout Britain. Applicants generally have to be graduates with English mother tongue; in many cases TEFL qualifications and experience will be required.

THE ABBEY COLLEGE Wells Road, Malvern Wells, Worcestershire WR14 4JF ✆ Malvern (01684) 892300
TEFL teachers required to teach English to international students aged 8 to adult. ⊕ Ages 18+. Applicants must be qualified TEFL teachers. 40 hour week; 4+ weeks, mid June-end August. Full board accommodation plus £25 travel costs provided. Salary £180-£250 per week. ✍ *Apply 3 months in advance. UK nationals only.*

ANGLO EUROPEAN STUDY TOURS LTD 8 Celbridge Mews, London W2 6EU ℂ 0171-229 4435

Runs EFL summer courses for foreign teenagers at approximately 30 locations throughout Britain including London, Edinburgh, Plymouth, St Andrews, Leicester and Tunbridge Wells. Graduate **teachers** with recognised TEFL qualification (RSA/UCLES or Trinity College London Certificate) required. Applicants must be native English speakers and either be EC nationals or have a valid work permit. Vacancies mid June-end August. Salary up to £200 per week for 17 contact hours. Accommodation not normally available. Also a small number of vacancies for suitably qualified/experienced **activity leaders** to organise and run the students' sports and leisure programme. Accommodation included.

ANGLO-CONTINENTAL Director of Studies, 33 Wimborne Road, Bournemouth BH2 6NA ℂ Bournemouth (01202) 557414

A group of schools providing English language courses for overseas students. Qualified **teachers** and **university graduates**, preferably with EFL experience, required at international vacation centres (ages 14+) and at an international school for juniors (ages 8-16). English is taught at 6 levels, with emphasis on oral English; maximum class size 15. Junior school staff will also be expected to take part in out-of-class activities, including excursions, sports and social activities, and general student welfare. 30-40 hour week, June-August. Staff may be required to attend brief training seminars in the week prior to the arrival of the students. Residential accommodation provided in return for extra duties at junior school, but at some centres staff have to arrange their own accommodation. Weekly salary according to qualifications/experience. Vacation course teachers are carefully chosen for their skill, enthusiasm and a lively, interesting and entertaining approach. Applicants must attend for interview and successful candidates will have travelling expenses refunded.

BUCKSWOOD INTERNATIONAL SUMMER SCHOOL Uckfield, East Sussex TN22 3PU ℂ Uckfield (01825) 761666

Residential summer schools situated in Kent, Surrey and Sussex. **Teachers** required to provide EFL tuition to 7-16 year olds. ⊕ Ages 21-45, TEFL experience preferred. Programme includes full day outings and sports activities; applicants should have relevant skills/qualifications. Hours may vary, 3-8 week contracts, July/August. Accommodation provided. Salary £100-£250 per week plus bonus, depending on qualifications and experience. *All nationalities welcome; must be English speakers.*

CAMP BEAUMONT Recruitment Department, Bridge House, Orchard Lane, Huntingdon, Cambridgeshire PE18 6QT ℂ Huntingdon (01480) 456123

Organises a wide range of children's activity holidays, including English language holidays throughout Britain. **TEFL teachers** and **coordinators** required for residential camps. ⊕ Ages 21+. Full season only; mid July-end August. 6 day week. Salary £40-£100 per week; board and accommodation provided.

EASTBOURNE SCHOOL OF ENGLISH 8 Trinity Trees, Eastbourne, East Sussex BN21 3LD

Non-profit making educational trust, providing courses for students and teachers of English. Qualified and experienced **TEFL teachers** required to teach adults. ⊕ Ages 23+. 25 hour day, 5 day week, July/August. Staff arrange own accommodation. Salary £250+ per week, depending on qualifications. Applicants should have RSA/Cambridge CTEFLA and must be of English mother tongue. Pre-course induction day provided. *Apply January-April.*

ELIZABETH JOHNSON ORGANISATION

Education Department, West House, 19/21 West Street, Haslemere, Surrey GU27 2AE ℰ Haslemere (01428) 652751
Arranges short-term holiday courses in English for young students, particularly from mainland Europe, the Middle East and Japan. Qualified and experienced **TEFL teachers** are needed at more than 35 centres in the areas around Brighton, Bristol, Farnham, Reading, Southampton, Bournemouth, Portsmouth, Guildford, Cambridge and Chertsey. Applicants must be native speakers of English. Work normally involves 4 mornings teaching per week, accompanying students on excursions and supervising activities in the afternoons and sometimes in the evenings; occasionally escorting between course centre and arrival/departure point. Weekends normally free, although some programmes involve weekend activities. Vacancies on some courses for those with qualifications to **teach art, drama, riding, tennis** and **indoor sports**. Flexibility and enthusiasm essential. All applicants should be capable of carrying out programmes in a lively and responsible way as a full-time commitment. 2-3 weeks, Easter and 2-8 weeks, June-September. Salary according to programme. No accommodation provided; preference given to local applicants. All new teachers attend 1 day briefing workshop.

EMBASSY STUDY TOURS

44 Cromwell Road, Hove, East Sussex BN3 3ER ℰ Hove (01273) 207481 ☎ (01273) 208527
Organises residential English language summer courses for 10-16 year-olds at schools, colleges and universities in the south, south east and south west of England. Courses combine practical language learning with activities and excursions. Requires **EFL teachers** and **activity staff** to teach English and organise a variety of afternoon, evening and weekend activities.
⚐ Ages 20-30. Applicants with summer school/camp experience preferred. Teachers must be qualified and/or experienced; activity staff should ideally have sports coaching qualifications/ experience, but not essential. All applicants must have English mother tongue, a lively personality, be decisive, hardworking, flexible and able to work under pressure. 6 day week for 3 weeks, end June-early July. Longer contracts available. Full board accommodation provided. Salary £120-£150 per week EFL teachers; £90 per week activity staff. *Apply March/April. UK nationals and native speakers of English only.*

EURO-ACADEMY

77A George Street, Croydon, Surrey CR0 1LD ℰ 0181-681 2905/6
Teachers required for 15 centres in the south of England, London and the Home Counties, to provide EFL tuition to classes of up to 15 students, supervise sports and accompany them on excursions. Applicants should be graduates with English as their mother tongue; TEFL RSA Preparatory certificate essential. 3 hours teaching per morning, plus afternoon and Saturday excursions, March-April and July-August. Wages £160-£190 per week depending on experience and qualifications. No insurance, travel costs or accommodation provided.

EUROYOUTH LTD

301 Westborough Road, Westcliff, Southend-on-Sea, Essex SS0 9PT ℰ Southend-on-Sea (01702) 341434
Organises stays for overseas students which can be combined with language and activity courses. Part-time **TEFL teachers** required for English language courses for students aged 14-17.
⚐ Ages 20+. 12 hour week, 3 weeks, Easter and July-August. TEFL training or experience desirable, and knowledge of foreign languages useful. Salary approx £7 per hour depending on qualifications or experience. No accommodation provided. *Apply giving personal*

particulars, experience, qualifications and availability dates. UK nationals only.

INTERLINK SCHOOL OF ENGLISH 126 Richmond Park Road, Bournemouth, Dorset BH8 8TH ✆ Bournemouth (01202) 290983 ▭ (01202) 291141
Requires experienced **teachers** with degree and preferably TEFL qualification, to teach English to overseas students. ⊕ Ages 21+. 20-30 hour week, July-August. Salary £160-£188 per week. Applicants must arrange their own accommodation.

LTC INTERNATIONAL COLLEGE OF ENGLISH Compton Park, Compton Place Road, Eastbourne, East Sussex BN21 1EH
✆ Eastbourne (01323) 27755
Residential college with junior courses for 10-16 year olds during June-August. Experienced **teachers** required to teach English, supervise students and organise extracurricular activities.
⊕ Ages 22+. Applicants must be native English speakers with a degree and initial qualification in TEFL. Residential shared accommodation, full board and National Insurance provided. Salary £700 per month. One-day induction programme. Also residential or non-residential vacancies for social **programme organisers** and **welfare staff** with appropriate qualifications/experience. **PH** 🐾 *Apply after 1 February; all staff must be available for interview in Eastbourne.*

NORD-ANGLIA INTERNATIONAL LTD 10 Eden Place, Cheadle, Cheshire SK8 1AT ✆ 0161-491 4191
Organises holidays, based on English language courses, for overseas students at up to 50 centres throughout Britain. Staff required to **teach** English and supervise social/cultural activity sessions. ⊕ Ages 21+. Applicants must be graduates, preferably with TEFL experience. 15+ hours teaching, plus up to 5 afternoon or evening activity sessions per week. 2-10 weeks, Easter

and July/August; most courses 3 weeks, July. Teachers are expected to arrange own accommodation except in a few circumstances where courses are residential and teachers have responsibility for supervising students in the evenings. Salary from £125 per week, depending on hours worked and accommodation. Successful applicants expected to attend 1 day training and information session before commencing employment. Applicants arrange own travel and insurance. *Native English speakers only.*

RICHARD LANGUAGE COLLEGE 43-45 Wimborne Road, Bournemouth, Dorset BH3 7AB ✆ Bournemouth (01202) 555932
Graduates required to **teach** EFL to groups of 12-14 adults. Duties include teaching, correction of homework, and some participation in the extracurricular sports/social programme. Applicants should have a degree in English, French or German, and preferably RSA Cambridge TEFL Certificate.
⊕ Ages 22+. Average 30 x 45 minute lessons per week. Late June-mid September. Salary according to qualifications and experience. Employer's public liability insurance and interview travel expenses provided.

STUDIO SCHOOL OF ENGLISH 6 Salisbury Villas, Station Road, Cambridge CB1 2JF ✆ Cambridge (01223) 69701
Vacancies for high calibre EFL **teachers**. Applicants should have a degree/PGCE, and ideally a TEFL qualification. 15-45 hour week, June/July-August. Wages according to qualifications and experience. Board and accommodation not provided. *Native English speakers only.*

YORKSHIRE INTERNATIONAL SCHOOL 21 St Helens Gardens Leeds LS1 8BT53 ✆ 0113-261 1603 ▭ 0113-261 3794
Requires fully qualified **teachers** to teach English to overseas students. ⊕ Ages 30-55. Applicants should have a

degree in English, a teaching qualification and 3 years teaching experience and must be native English speakers.
3 weeks, July; 18 hour week (4 mornings plus day excursion). Accommodation available at £50 per week. Salary £420 for 3 weeks. ✎ *Apply by 1 June. UK nationals only.*

WORKCAMPS

ATD FOURTH WORLD
The General Secretary, 48 Addington Square, London SE5 7LB ✆ **0171-703 3231**
Strives to protect the fundamental rights of the poorest, most disadvantaged and excluded families, which constitute the Fourth World. These rights include the right to family life, to education and training and to representation.
Volunteers are invited to take part in workcamps at the Family Centre at Frimhurst in Surrey. They are needed to help repair and maintain the house and the work involves construction, carpentry, electrical installation, painting, plumbing, gardening, office work and cooking. Evenings are reserved for discussions and the exchange of ideas about the fight against poverty, as well as sharing knowledge between young people of different social backgrounds. ⊕ Ages 18-35. Volunteers should be concerned by persistent poverty and social exclusion. All nationalities accepted. 7 hour day for 2 weeks, August. Full board accommodation provided. Volunteers should take a sleeping bag and work clothes. Cost approx £50; volunteers pay their own travel costs.

CHRISTIAN MOVEMENT FOR PEACE 186 St Pauls Road, Balsall Heath, Birmingham B12 8LZ ✆ 0121-446 5704
An international movement open to all who share a common concern for lasting peace and justice in the world.
Volunteers are invited to work in international teams on summer projects

aimed at offering a service in an area of need; promoting international understanding and the discussion of social problems; and offering young people the chance to live as a group and take these experiences into the context of daily life. Recent projects have included working on a children's mural project on the theme of One World, One Race; organising a holiday for children of Somali refugees; helping on a mobile playbus on council estates and outside benefit offices; and helping to organise One World Week in a community centre in Birmingham.
⊕ Ages 17+ (18+ for overseas volunteers). Volunteers with community/ social work experience particularly welcome. Volunteers must be prepared to take a full part in all aspects of the camp. Overseas volunteers must have good English. 30-35 hour week.
2 weeks, usually during the summer. Board, lodging and insurance provided but volunteers pay their own travel costs and sometimes contribute towards living expenses. Registration fee £42. Membership fee £18 or £8 for students/ unwaged. **B D PH**

✎ *Apply through partner organisation in country of residence; for further information see page 30. UK applicants should enclose £1 in stamps to cover postage.*

INTERNATIONAL VOLUNTARY SERVICE Old Hall, East Bergholt, Colchester, Essex CO7 6TQ
IVS is the British branch of Service Civil International, which promotes international reconciliation through workcamps. **Volunteers** are needed to work in international teams on various projects, often combining manual and social work. Recent projects have included carpentry, painting and gardening to finish off a self-build nursery in Islington, north London; organising and running a One World Week festival in Dewsbury, west Yorkshire; helping crofters with weeding, drystone walling, fencing and cleaning ditches on Fair Isle; and cleaning,

sharpening and renovating tools in Southampton to send to communities in the Third World. Work/study camps also organised on specific themes such as anti-racism, Third World solidarity and East-West cooperation. Approx 80 international workcamps all over Britain involving groups of 6-18 volunteers. ⊕ Ages 18+. Volunteers must be fit and prepared to work hard, contributing actively to the work and team life. Overseas volunteers must speak fluent English. 35-40 hour week, 2-4 weeks, June-September. Food, accommodation and insurance provided. No fares or wages paid. Registration fee £30 (students/unwaged £25). Membership fee £25 (students/unwaged £15). **B D PH**

⚫ *Apply through partner organisation in country of residence; for further information see page 30.*

QUAKER INTERNATIONAL SOCIAL PROJECTS Volunteer Administrator, Friends House, Euston Road, London NW1 2BJ Volunteers are invited to work on a variety of projects aimed at making life more positive for members of a community. Projects bring together 8-20 people of different nationalities, backgrounds and countries to work on a common task. Previous volunteers have been involved in organising general activities, crafts, sports and music on various children's playschemes; redecorating and painting a mural designed by volunteers and residents at a centre for people with head injuries in Cambridge; and establishing a permaculture garden and a water recycling scheme at an eco-park in Islington, north London. Work/study projects also organised on East-West relations. Most projects have a study element relevant to work undertaken. ⊕ Ages 18+; 16+ on some projects. 1-3 weeks, mainly during the summer. Volunteers of all backgrounds/abilities welcome. Foreign volunteers should have good English. Accommodation,

food and insurance provided. No fares or wages paid. Registration fee £17 (unwaged), £24 (low waged), £38 (waged). **B D PH** welcome.

⚫ *Apply through partner organisation in country of residence; for further information see page 30.*

UNITED NATIONS ASSOCIATION International Youth Service, Temple of Peace, Cathays Park, Cardiff CF1 3AP ℂ **Cardiff (01222) 223088** Aims to assist in community development by acting as a means to stimulate new ideas and projects, encouraging the concept of voluntary work as a force in the common search for peace, equality, democracy and social justice. **Volunteers** are invited to take part on international workcamps. Recent projects have included constructing a children's play area at a city farm in Cardiff; preparing for a village carnival in Betws; helping at the Llangollen International Eisteddfod; and looking after handicapped children on holiday in Mid Glamorgan. ⊕ Ages 18+. Volunteers are expected to join in the the local community activities, and to create a happy and effective project. 40 hour week. 2-4 weeks, July-August. Accommodation in church halls, hospitals, homes or community centres, food and insurance provided. Some camps are self-catering. Volunteers share the cooking, and should take a sleeping bag. Registration fee £45. No fares or wages paid. **B D PH**

⚫ *Apply through partner organisation in country of residence; for further information see page 30.*

GENERAL

ACORN VENTURE LTD Personnel Department, 137 Worcester Road, Hagley, Stourbridge DY9 0NW Activity holiday company catering for school groups at camping centres in Tal-

y-Bont and Shell Island in North Wales. **Site managers** required to coordinate activities, organise evening entertainments and make sure groups have all they need. **General maintenance staff** and qualified **nurses** also required.
⊕ Ages 18+. Applicants should have some previous experience. Minimum 50 hour, 6 day week. Applicants are expected to work the full season, May-September. Salary approx £40-£80 per week according to position. All meals, accommodation in tents, and insurance provided. ☙ *Apply in writing with cv by end February. If no reply within 28 days assume application unsuccessful.*

ARDMORE ADVENTURE LTD 11-15 High Street, Marlow, Buckinghamshire SL7 1AV
✆ **Marlow (01628) 890060**
Organises activity holidays for young people at residential and day centres in the south east of England. **Centre directors** and **senior group leaders** required.
⊕ Ages 20+. Applicants should be English speakers, preferably with experience of working with children. 2/8+ weeks, mid June-August. Day centres 40 hour week, residential centres 60 hour week. Wages £45+ per week, depending on position. Full board, single or shared accommodation and insurance provided, but not travel. **B D PH** depending on ability. *UK nationals only.*

BAPTIST UNION TF8 Coordinator, Baptist House, PO Box 44, Didcot, Oxfordshire OX11 8RT ✆ **Didcot (01235) 512077 Volunteers** with a Christian commitment are invited to join summer programme working in small Baptist churches throughout England and Wales, in both rural and inner-city areas. Opportunities for involvement in children's holiday clubs, outreach, drama, music and practical work.
⊕ Ages 16+. No experience necessary, simply enthusiasm and a willingness to serve God and share the Gospel. 6 day week; 1-2 weeks, July-September. Work is unpaid but accommodation is provided. Application fee £75. Travel costs and 20% of fee are paid for by volunteer's home church. Training day held in June. ☙ *Apply by end April.*

BUTLIN'S Wonderwest World, Heads of Ayr KA7 4LB BUTLIN'S Southcoast World, Bognor Regis, West Sussex PO21 1JJ BUTLIN'S Somerwest World, Minehead, Somerset TA24 5SH BUTLIN'S Starcoast World, Pwllheli, Gwynedd, North Wales LL53 6HX BUTLIN'S Funcoast World, Skegness, Lincolnshire PE25 1NJ
Provides family holidays and leisure facilities, encompassing accommodation, retailing, catering, amusement parks, professional entertainment and conferences, all on the same site. Vacancies exist in the **retail** and **leisure areas**, and for **lifeguards, nurses, nursery nurses, entertainers, security staff, electricians** and **technicians** at centres in Ayr, Bognor Regis, Minehead, Pwllheli and Skegness. Relevant qualifications such as RGN, NNEB useful. Short and long term positions almost all year, exact dates varying according to centre.
⊕ Ages 16+, local applicants, 18+ others. 37½ hour week. Salary dependent on individual centres, accommodation, meals, uniform and staff entertainment programme provided. Use of the leisure and guest facilities and holiday discounts available. Applicants pay own insurance and travel costs.
☙ *Apply direct to the preferred centre; EEA nationals only*

CAMP BEAUMONT Recruitment Department, Bridge House, Orchard Lane, Huntingdon, Cambridgeshire PE18 6QT
✆ **Huntingdon (01480) 456123**
Organises a wide range of activity holidays for children in American-style day and residential camps. Staff are

recruited for 10 day and 8 residential camps. Opportunities for **administration staff, transport coordinators** and **drivers**.
⊕ Ages 18+. All staff must genuinely enjoy working with children, possess leadership ability, and be willing to work a long, hard, exhausting day enthusiastically in a structured setting where regulations apply. English must be spoken as first language. Season from mid-July-end August; some permanent positions available. Salary £30-£150 per week; some posts provide accommodation and board.

CHESSINGTON WORLD OF ADVENTURES Leatherhead Road, Chessington, Surrey KT9 2NE
ℂ **Epsom (01372) 729560**
A zoo and theme park, requiring seasonal staff as **catering assistants, cashiers, ride operators, cleaners, gardeners** and **shop assistants**.
⊕ Ages 16+. No experience necessary as training given, but staff must be enthusiastic and enjoy working as part of a team. 40 hour week, March-October. Salary £3-£4 per hour, employers' liability insurance and staff canteen. Accommodation not provided. *Overseas applicants with work permits and good English welcome.*

COUNCIL ON INTERNATIONAL EDUCATIONAL EXCHANGE (CIEE) Work Exchanges Department, 205 East 42nd Street, New York NY 10017, United States
Work in Britain/Student Exchange Employment Programme enables **American students** to have an educational and cultural experience through a period of work in Britain of up to 6 months. Programme participants may enter Britain at any time of year, and work in any type of employment; most students work in the service industries, although many undertake career-oriented jobs.
⊕ Ages 18+. Students must be residing and studying in the US at the time of application and enrolled as a

matriculating student at an accredited college or university, taking at least 8 credit hours, or enrolled full-time. Applicants may either find a job before leaving the US or look for one on arrival. Advice on accommodation, travel, administrative procedures and finding a job provided prior to departure and at orientation session on arrival. The *Work in Britain Handbook* includes information contacts for employment and a regional employment guide. Administration fee $160 (1994).
B D PH W

CUFFLEY CAMP OUTDOOR CENTRE Carbone Hill, Cuffley, Hertfordshire EN6 4PR ℂ **Cuffley (01707) 872632** ✉ **(01707) 875705**
A well established outdoor education centre set in 90 acres of woodland. Provides residential and day courses for schools, teachers and other special interest groups.
Opportunities for **caretaking staff, general assistants, kitchen staff, clerical staff** and **tutors**.
⊕ Ages 20+. Experience depending on post; tutors should preferably have teaching qualifications and experience. Approx 39 hour week for 3-6 months, April-October. Full board accommodation provided for tutors, lunch for other staff. Salary for tutors £100 per week; other staff £3-£4 per hour. 🖳 *Apply January-March.*

THE GRAIL CENTRE 125 Waxwell Lane, Pinner, Middlesex HA5 3ER
ℂ **0181-866 2195**
The Centre, set in 10 acres of gardens and wooded grounds, is home to a Christian lay community of women. Conferences and courses are organised and the Centre is always open to friends and strangers alike. **Volunteers** are required, mainly to assist with household tasks and garden maintenance; possibility of other types of work such as administration, reception duties, office work, sewing and artwork. Any particular skills or experience volunteers

may have are put to good use. Applicants are likely to be motivated by a desire to experience community life and offer service to the wider community.
⊕ Ages 20+. Basic knowledge of spoken English necessary for volunteers to gain from their experience. 35-40 hour week, with 1½ days free. 3+ months, all year, except summer, where 2 month stay is acceptable for students whose vacation time is limited. £12-£15 pocket money per week and full board accommodation in Centre provided. **D** ✎ *Apply 6 months in advance if possible.*

HORIZON HPL 17 rue Pache, 75011 Paris, France ✆ (33 1) 40 24 09 31 ▥ (33 1) 40 24 09 53
A training organisation that can place French candidates in hotels and companies throughout Britain in order to gain professional experience. Responsibilities depend on language level, ranging from **general duties**, **waiter/waitress**, **reception** and **secretarial training** to **marketing placements.**
⊕ Ages 18-35. Experience not essential, but applicants must be highly motivated and have at least a basic knowledge of English. English tuition provided to classes of 5 students. Hotel trainees receive monthly salary and hotel/family accommodation; company trainees receive pocket money and family accommodation. Cost £240-£300 covers training, administration, follow-up and accommodation. Support provided to ensure progress during placement and help with any problems.
✎ *Apply 2-3 months in advance. French nationals only.*

THE IONA COMMUNITY Staff Coordinator, Isle of Iona, Argyll, Strathclyde PA76 6SN
✆ **Iona (0168 17) 404**
An ecumenical Christian community seeking new and radical ways of living the Gospel in today's world. On Iona the Community runs two centres, each welcoming up to 50 guests to a common life of work, worship, meals and recreation.
Volunteers are needed to work in the Abbey shop. The work involves contact with a large number of people and includes till work, serving, stocking shelves and cleaning. The ability and willingness to serve and work quickly under pressure for prolonged periods is essential. Also require a **driver/ general assistant** to take luggage and provisions between the centres and the jetty. A full driver's licence is required, as is a willingness to work responsibly, often alone. An interest in meeting people is useful: the driver comes into contact with many staff, guests, day villagers and islanders.
⊕ Ages 18+, 21+ for drivers. Most important is a willingness to join fully in the Community life, which includes worship and social activities as well as work. The work is demanding but rewarding, and the hours flexible. 6 day week, February-December. Full board, shared accommodation, pocket money of £17 per week and assistance with travel expenses within mainland Britain provided. ✎ *Applications received before 31 December given priority.*

LONDON ZOO Personnel Department, Regent's Park, London NW1 4RY
Seasonal staff required to work as **cashiers, first aid attendants, groundspeople, gardeners, sales assistants** and **toilet attendants**.
⊕ Ages 18+. Cashiers must have 3 years fast cash handling experience and recent 3 year working reference. Groundspeople must hold a current driving licence. First Aid at Work Certificate essential for first aid attendants. All posts require good communication and customer care skills, and a good standard of written and spoken English. Full-time and part-time hours; March-September. Salary according to position. Third party insurance, induction and training provided. ✎ *Apply by February.*
All nationalities welcome.

MADHYAMAKA BUDDHIST CENTRE Kilnwick Percy Hall, Pocklington, York YO4 2UF

© **Pocklington (01759) 304832** (1130-1300 and 1400-1700)

A residential Buddhist community of lay and ordained people living and working together. Based in a Georgian hall situated in 40 acres of woodland, lakes and parkland. **Volunteers** are invited to help with the upkeep of the building and grounds, in return for board and lodging. Up to 6 volunteers required at a time. ⊕ Ages 16+. No experience necessary, but volunteers should speak some English. The work is varied and can include sewing, cleaning, painting and decorating, gardening, plastering, joinery and electrical work. 35 hour, 5 day week, usually for 1 or 2 weeks, all year. Opportunity to learn about Buddhist thought by attending free teaching and meditation sessions. Volunteers pay own travel costs and are asked to abide by the Centre's simple code of discipline while on the premises. **B D PH**
✎ *US applications to Saraha Buddhist Centre, 44 Fairview Plaza, Los Gatos, California 95030.*

MANJUSHRI MAHAYANA BUDDHIST CENTRE Conishead Priory, Ulverston, Cumbria LA12 9QQ *©* **Ulverston (01229) 584029** (during office hours)

A residential Buddhist community of 100 people studying and working together. The Priory is a listed large Victorian building situated near the Lake District on the shores of Morecambe Bay, and has over 70 acres of grounds and woodlands. **Volunteers** are invited to help with building repairs, restoration work, painting, cleaning and other tasks. Work will begin shortly on building a meditation hall to seat over 1,000. ⊕ Ages 18+. No particular skills or experience required, except a willingness to work hard, although DIY skills or building qualifications are very welcome. 35 hour, 5 day week. 1 week stay, starting Mondays, all year except during annual summer festival.

Dormitory accommodation and vegetarian food provided. Opportunity to spend free time attending the Centre's teachings, meditation classes and other activities. Volunteers pay their own travel expenses and should take a sleeping bag. Visitors requested not to smoke or take intoxicants on the property. ✎ *Apply well in advance as places are limited. Brochure on request.*

NORTH YORK MOORS HISTORICAL RAILWAY TRUST Volunteer Liaison Officer, c/o Pickering Station, Pickering, North Yorkshire YO18 7AJ

A busy preserved steam railway built in the 1930s operating between Pickering and Grosmont near Whitby. Largely operated by **volunteers**, work includes engineering, the operating of trains, booking offices, shops, refreshment trolleys, tea rooms, signalling, and gardening. ⊕ Ages 16+. All applicants must speak English; type of work allocated according to qualifications and experience. Varying hours, work available all year. Basic self catering accommodation and general employers' insurance provided in return for each full day worked. No fares or wages paid. Small fee charged to cover accommodation plus £10 annual membership fee. ✎ *Applications to be received at least 2 weeks in advance.*

PAX CHRISTI 9 Henry Road, London N4 2LH *©* **0181-800 4612**

Promotes international exchanges, forming an international community spirit to spread the church's teaching on peace, and encourages Christian participation in social and political life. **Volunteers** are needed to work in international summer youth hostels in London and possibly other cities, usually set up in school buildings, and providing bed and breakfast and light refreshment in the evenings. Each hostel is run by a team of 15 volunteers; approx two-thirds are from overseas. The aim is for the volunteers to form a lively international community to provide a welcoming and friendly atmosphere. Work involves reception duties, cleaning, cooking, shopping, laundry, publicity, accounts and the setting up and dismantling of beds, and is hard but rewarding. Duties and free time allocated on a rota basis so that everyone shares the menial as well as the more enjoyable aspects. Free time activities include picnics, sightseeing, sports, parties, theatre and cinema trips. ⊕ Ages 19+. Approx 40 hour week. 4/5 weeks, July/August. Food, dormitory accommodation with self-catering facilities and insurance provided. Volunteers pay their own travel costs.

PGL YOUNG ADVENTURE LTD Personnel Department, Alton Court, Penyard Lane (878), Ross-on-Wye, Herefordshire HR9 5NR ✆ Ross-on-Wye (01989) 767833 Organises outdoor adventure holidays in England, Wales and Scotland. Activities include pony trekking, sailing, canoeing, archery, hill walking, tennis, squash, arts and crafts, fencing, judo, rifle shooting, cycling, grass skiing, badminton and many others. Staff are required for the following service and supplies positions. **Administrative assistants**, generally acting as assistants to the manager and responsible for petty cash, staff wage sheets, lost property, programme schedules, reception, telephone enquiries and correspondence; **Stores** and **site maintenance staff**, responsible for the general appearance and cleanliness of the centre, with duties including litter control, maintaining tents and equipment, cutting grass, cleaning, painting, looking after stores, and maintenance and repair work, carpentry, plumbing, electrical experience welcome; **Nurses**, preferably RGN/EGN qualified, with a driving licence and experience in child nursing; **Drivers**, including PCV and LGV, responsible for looking after passengers and maintenance of vehicles; **Gardeners**, with horticultural interest and ability; **Coffee bar/tuck shop staff**,

responsible for cleaning and organising the shop, displaying and selling the goods, stocktaking and taking charge of the money. ⊕ Ages 18+, 21+ for drivers. Applicants should be fond of children, responsible, flexible, energetic and enthusiastic, patient, reliable and mature with a sense of humour, capable of working on their own initiative, and have the ability to cooperate with others as part of a team, contributing fully to the life of the centre. 4+ weeks, February-September. Staff are also recruited for short periods at Easter and the Spring Bank Holiday. 1 day off per week. Full board accommodation provided. Pocket money from £34-£42 per week for general positions, from £75 for nurses and LGV/PCV drivers. Travel expenses paid by applicants. All staff can join in the activities during free periods and are encouraged to take part in evening activities with the guests. Staff may sometimes be asked to help out in areas other than their own. *Early application advisable; majority of positions filled by end June.*

TENT CITY Old Oak Common Lane, East Acton, London W3 7DP Tent City and Hackney Camping offer tented accommodation and or/campsite facilities to young visitors during the summer. Each site requires **volunteers** for the whole season, June-September, for a variety of tasks including cleaning, erecting and dismantling tents; helping in the snack bar and reception; general maintenance work and cooking for fellow volunteers. 8 hour day, 5 day week. Full board accommodation and £30 per week provided. Ideal opportunity to live, work and interact with people from different countries and cultures. *Apply to M Lambert, early in the year.*

TOC H National Projects Office, 1 Forest Close, Wendover, Aylesbury, Buckinghamshire HP22 6BT ✆ Aylesbury (01296) 623911 Requires **volunteers** for a variety of short-term residential projects throughout Great Britain. Projects include working with people having different disabilities; work with underprivileged children; playschemes and camps; conservation and manual work.

⊕ Ages 16+. Programmes giving further details of projects and application procedures are published in March and September. **B D PH W** depending on project. ⚑ *Early application advised.*

TRIDENT TRANSNATIONAL
Saffron Court, 14b St Cross Street, London EC1N 8XA ✆ **0171-242 1515** ⊡ **0171-430 2975**

A registered charity allied to the Trident Trust, which has over 20 years' experience working with schools, teachers and businesses.

Offers young people from overseas the opportunity to gain work experience in the UK. Placements exist in a wide range of business areas, including sales and marketing, hotel and catering, manufacturing, research and development, import/export, travel and tourism, engineering, electronics and agriculture.

⊕ Ages 17½-26. No experience necessary, but good knowledge of English required. 3 weeks-6 months, all year. Placements are generally unpaid, although fares and luncheon vouchers may be provided. Small allowance may be paid for placements in excess of 3 months. Accommodation can be organised with families near the workplace, or in self-catering hostels for placements in central London.

All placements are carefully monitored and supervised, and trainees are awarded a certificate validated by Cambridge University on completion. Placement fee from £120 for 3-4 weeks.

⚑ *EEA nationals should apply 6-8 weeks in advance. Non-EEA nationals should apply at least 3 months in advance; additional £35 fee payable to cover administration of Trainee Work Experience Scheme permit.*

WELSHPOOL & LLANFAIR LIGHT RAILWAY **The Station, Llanfair Caereinion, Welshpool, Powys SY21 0SF**
✆ **Welshpool (01938) 810441**

Volunteers required for maintenance and operation of a preserved 8-mile narrow gauge steam railway in Wales.

⊕ Ages 16+. No experience necessary; training and supervision given, but all volunteers must speak English. Approx 40 hour week, all year; most work carried out during winter when railway is closed. Limited basic accommodation available in old sleeping car for small fee. Volunteers must provide their own food and pocket money and bring overalls, waterproofs, strong boots, heavy duty gloves, pillow, sleeping bag and blankets. Employers liability insurance provided. No fares or wages paid.

⚑ *Apply 2-4 weeks in advance.*

When writing to any organisation it is essential to mention Working Holidays 1995 and enclose a stamped, self-addressed A4 envelope, or if in another country, an addressed A4 envelope and at least two IRCs (International Reply Coupons, available from post offices). Enquiries received without SAEs/IRCs are unlikely to be answered.

INFO

Greek Embassy
1a Holland Park, London W11 3TP
℡ 0171-221 6467

British Embassy
1 Ploutarchou Street, 106 75 Athens
℡ (30 1) 7236 211

Tourist office
National Tourist Organisation of Greece,
4 Conduit Street, London W1R 0DJ
℡ 0171-734 5997

Youth hostels
Greek YHA, 4 Dragatsaniou Street,
Athens

Youth & student information
British Travel and Student Service,
10 Stadiou Street, Athens

International Student and Youth Travel,
11 Nikis Street, Syntagma Square,
105 57 Athens

Entry regulations A UK citizen
intending to work in Greece should have
a full passport. UK/EEA nationals may
stay for up to 3 months in order to look
for or take up employment, after which
a residence permit will be required.
To obtain a residence permit applicants
should go to the Aliens' Department of
the Ministry of Public Order in Athens,
or outside Athens to the local police
station. Citizens of non-EEA countries
require a work permit and a temporary
residence permit, which should be
applied for by the prospective employer
from the local prefecture. Applicants
will be notified once permission has
been granted, and should take their
passport to the Greek consulate in their
home country to be stamped.
This entitles the applicant to obtain a
residence permit from the Aliens'
Department and a work permit from
the local prefecture, on arrival in
Greece. During the time of this
procedure the applicant should not be

resident in Greece. Job opportunities are extremely limited and permits are only issued in cases where the work necessitates the employment of a foreigner, and in some professions of special interest. It is against immigration regulations to enter Greece as a tourist to seek and/or take up employment, and any persons so doing risk refusal of leave to enter Greece and/or deportation. An information sheet *Residence and Employment,* is available from the Labour Counsellor Office at the Greek Embassy.

Travel Freedom Pass allows 3, 5, or 10 days unlimited rail travel in 1 month on the railways of Greece. Cost from £34 (under 26) or £44 (26+). Available from British Rail International Rail Centre, Victoria Station, London SW1V 1JY ✆ 0171-834 2345.

Campus Travel can arrange Eurotrain, Inter-Rail and student/youth fares for travel by plane, train, boat or bus to destinations throughout Greece. Offices throughout the UK including a student travel centre at 52 Grosvenor Gardens, London SW1W 0AG (opposite Victoria Station) ✆ 0171-730 3402 or ✆ 0131-668 3303 for Scottish telephone bookings.

Council Travel, 28A Poland Street, London W1V 3DB ✆ 0171-287 3337 (offices also in Paris, Nice, Lyon, Munich, Düsseldorf, Tokyo, Singapore and throughout the US) offers student/youth airfares and charter flights to Athens, plus Eurotrain under 26 fares, travel insurance, guidebooks and travel gear.

STA Travel, 86 Old Brompton Road, London SW7 3LQ/117 Euston Road London NW1 2SX ✆ 0171-937 9921 (offices also in Birmingham, Bristol, Cambridge, Glasgow, Leeds, Manchester and Oxford) operates flexible low-cost flights between London and Greece.

Information centres International Student & Youth Travel Service (ISYTS/ Eurotrain), 11 Nikis Street, 2nd Floor,

Syntagma Square, 105 57 Athens ✆ (30 1) 322 1267/323 3767 ⌨ (30 1) 322 1531 is the official student and youth travel service specialising in tickets for air, sea and land travel, plus information on tours, cruises, festivals and cheap hotel accommodation. Also issues student cards and provides free welcome and poste restante service. Cannot offer information on job opportunities. Open Monday-Friday, 0900-1700 and Saturday, 0900-1300.

Usit, Campus Travel's sister organisation in Greece, have branches at Filelinon 1, Syntagma Square, Athens 105 57 and at 15 Ippodromiou Street, Thessaloniki. They arrange student/youth travel by air, rail and coach (including student charter flights from Athens and Thessaloniki) and give information and advice.

Publications Lonely Planet's *Greece - A Travel Survival Kit* £10.95 offers practical, down-to-earth information for budget travellers wanting to explore beyond the usual tourist routes.

The Rough Guide to Greece £9.99 and *The Rough Guide to Crete* £6.99 provide comprehensive background information on Greece and Crete, plus details on getting there, getting around, places to explore and cheap places to stay.

All the above guidebooks are available from good bookshops.

Accommodation National Tourist Organisation of Greece, see above, issues *Camping,* a book listing sites run by them, situated by the sea and equipped with modern facilities.

Young Women's Christian Association of Greece, 11 Amerikis Street, 106 72 Athens offers accommodation at Heliopolis YWCA centre near Athens airport for females only. Can also provide bed and breakfast hostel accommodation in single and double bedded rooms for females only travelling through Athens.

AU PAIR/ CHILD CARE

There are no special regulations governing the employment of au pairs. EEA nationals must obtain a medical certificate, and apply for a residence permit if staying for longer than 3 months.

GALENTINAS EUROPEAN NANNIES & AU PAIRS
PO Box 51181, 145 10 Kifissia, Greece ✆/☎ (30 1) 808 1005
Can place **nannies, au pairs**, and **mothers' helps**. Females only.
⚜ Ages 18-35. Pocket money Drs90,000-Drs250,000 depending on experience. *EEA nationals, Australians and South Africans only.*

STUDENTS ABROAD LTD
11 Milton View, Hitchin, Hertfordshire SG4 0QD ✆ Hitchin (01462) 438909 ☎ (01462) 438919
Can place **au pairs, mothers' helps,** and **nannies**.
⚜ Ages 18-27 for au pairs. Knowledge of Greek not essential. Pocket money from £40 per week; higher for other positions. 1 year stay preferred for nannies. Service charge £40.

CONSERVATION

EUROPEAN CONSERVATION VOLUNTEERS IN GREECE
41 Panepistimiou Street, 145 62 Athens, Greece
A non-profitmaking, non-governmental organisation promoting intercultural exchanges and conservation.
Volunteers are invited to take part in international workcamps. Projects have a strong emphasis on Greek culture and tend to take place in very remote areas. Recent projects have included signposting and repairing footpaths through the spectacular Samaria Gorge, southwest Crete; repairing cobbled pavements in a small village on the Albanian border; and restoring an old mansion in the forest area of Pelion, for use as a folk art museum.
⚜ Ages 18-28. Applicants must be highly motivated to make each project a success. 2-3 weeks, July-August. Food, shared accommodation and work accident insurance provided. No fares or wages paid. **B D PH**

🏆 *Apply through partner organisation in country of residence. In the UK: British Trust for Conservation Volunteers, 36 St Mary's Street, Wallingford, Oxfordshire OX10 0EH ✆ Wallingford (01491) 839766 or through Quaker International Social Projects or United Nations Association International Youth Service. See page 30 for registration details and addresses.*

FARMWORK

Greece has a wide range of crops and harvesting opportunities may exist all year round. The following gives some idea of the seasons for different crops. It is very difficult to arrange work from outside of Greece; most of the recruitment is done on a casual basis.

January-April
Oranges and other citrus fruits in western Crete
Olives in the central Peloponnese

April-June
Tomatoes in southern Crete
Apricots around Návplion, in the eastern Peloponnese
Cherries and pears between Argos and Tripolis in the central Peloponnese
Cherries to the west of Thessaloniki, Macedonia

June-October
Watermelons around Patras
Tobacco to the west of Thessaloniki, Macedonia
Grapes, especially in the central Peloponnese, on Crete and on Rhodes

Apples to the west of Thessaloniki, Macedonia and in the central Peloponnese
Apples, pears, nuts and soft fruit on the Pílion peninsula, west of Vólos

November-February
Olives on Rhodes
Oranges in the eastern Peloponnese

AMERICAN FARM SCHOOL
Summer Work Activities Programme, PO Box 23, 55 102 Kalamaria, Thessaloniki, Greece
✆ **(30 31) 471 803/471 825**
An independent, not-for-profit agricultural school in northern Greece operating a Summer Work Activities Programme, which aims to give college-aged individuals from around the world an intense period of hands-on practical experience and the opportunity to become familiar with the geography, culture and customs of Greece.
Agricultural placements available, working in dairy herd management and milk processing, poultry farming, fielding crops, haymaking, greenhouse production, irrigation, landscaping, house painting, building, tractor maintenance and repair. 45 hour, 5 day week for 30 days, mid June-early August.
⊕ Ages 19-35. Relevant experience preferred. Accommodation plus approx US$20 per day wages provided. Small fee charged for 3 meals a day. Cost US$500 includes weekend trips, Greek language and dance lessons, access to swimming pool and sports facilities and use of laundry and TV/video room. Participants arrange own travel and insurance. **D** 🐾 *Apply in the autumn.*

INTERNATIONAL FARM EXPERIENCE PROGRAMME
YFC Centre, N A C, Stoneleigh Park, Kenilworth CV8 2LG
✆ **Coventry (01203) 696584**
Provides assistance to young **agriculturalists** and **horticulturalists** by finding places in farms/nurseries abroad, enabling them to broaden their

knowledge of agricultural and horticultural methods. Participants usually live and work with a farming family and the work is matched as far as possible with participant's requirements. Entails physical work and practical involvement. Basic wage plus board and lodging. 3-12 months, all year.
⊕ Ages 18-28. Applicants must have at least 2 years practical experience, 1 year of which may be at agricultural college, and intend to make a career in agriculture/horticulture. Valid driving licence necessary. Participants pay own fares and insurance. Registration fee £85. 🐾 *UK applications to IFEP. Other applications to IFEP partner in home country.*

WORKCAMPS

SERVICE CIVIL INTERNATIONAL
55 Menandrou Street, 104 37 Athens, Greece
Service Civil International promotes international reconciliation through work projects. **Volunteers** are needed to work in international teams on various workcamps. Recent projects have included opening a path leading to a bird observatory in a village in the Gulf of Amvarakikos; helping in the kitchen and with the entertainment at a summer camp for young disabled people in Leptokarya; and construction work in a small chapel and an open air theatre on the northern coast of Crete.
⊕ Ages 18+. Applicants should be highly motivated, preferably with previous workcamp or other voluntary work experience, and prepared to work hard as part of a team. 35-40 hour week, 2-4 weeks, July-August. Food, shared accommodation and work accident insurance provided. No fares or wages paid. **B D PH**

🐾 *Apply through partner organisation in country of residence.*
In the UK: International Voluntary Service.
See page 30 for registration details and addresses.

GENERAL

DORA STRATOU DANCE THEATRE 8 Scholiou Street, Plaka, 105 58 Athens, Greece
✆ (30 1) 324 4395
Founded as a living museum for Greek dance, with a troupe of 50 dancers and a collection of some 2,500 traditional costumes from all regions of Greece. Evening performances held during the summer at an open-air theatre on Philopappou Hill, Athens. **Volunteer assistants** required to help with costume maintenance, theatre administration and stage management. ⊕ Ages 18+. Knowledge of Greek not necessary, but good English or French essential. Preference given to those wishing to gain experience in arts/theatre management or in traditional culture. 20-30 hour, 5 day week, May-October. No food or accommodation, but some pocket money provided. Opportunity to attend dance courses, lectures and workshops. ✑ *Apply at least 1 month in advance.*

EUROYOUTH LTD
301 Westborough Road, Westcliffe, Southend-on-Sea, Essex SSO 9PT
✆ Southend-on-Sea (01702) 341434
Arranges holiday stays where **guests** are offered board and lodging in return for an agreed number of hours English conversation with hosts or their children. Time also available to practise Greek if desired.
⊕ Mainly ages 18-25, but sometimes opportunities for older applicants. 2-3 weeks, June-August. Travel and insurance paid by applicants. Registration fee £70. ✑ *Apply at least 12 weeks prior to scheduled departure. UK nationals only.*

PIONEER TOURS Working Holiday, 11 Nikis Street, Syntagma Square, 105 57 Athens, Greece
✆ (30 1) 32 24 321/32 55 168
Organises a variety of working holidays all over Greece, including **hotel work** and **au pair** positions.

⊕ Ages 18+. Relevant experience sometimes required, also knowledge of English. 8 hour day, 6 day week. Work available mainly in summer. Pay from Dr1,500 per day, plus food and accommodation. Travel paid from Athens to place of work; return fare to Athens paid after 1+ month's work. Registration fee £20. *EEA nationals only.*

SUNSAIL The Port House, Port Solent, Portsmouth PO6 4TH
✆ Portsmouth (01705) 214330
✉ (01705) 219827
Crew members required to work aboard cruising yachts sailing in flotillas around the Greek islands. Vacancies for RYA qualified and experienced **skippers**, responsible for the wellbeing of up to 13 cruising yachts and 60 holidaymakers, giving daily briefings on navigation, and providing sailing assistance where necessary. Qualified **diesel mechanics** also needed, responsible to the skipper for maintaining the marine diesel engines and repairing other items aboard. **Hostesses** also required to look after laundry, accounting, and cleaning of boats, advising holidaymakers on shops and restaurants, and organising social events and barbecues. Vacancies for qualified and experienced **hotel managers, chefs, cooks, bar staff, receptionists** and **windsurfing instructors** at watersports clubs across Greece; and NNEB qualified **nannies/nurses** to look after children in the day. ⊕ Ages 21-35 for all posts. Relevant qualifications and experience essential; sailing experience desirable; conversational French/German an advantage. Staff should be enthusiastic, hardworking, loyal and honest, with an outgoing personality. 45-50 hour, 6 day week plus social hours in evenings. Staff must work the full season, March/April-October/November. Salary £55-£95 per week, depending on position. Accommodation provided on board yachts in flotillas; in hotels with meals for club staff. Return travel and 50% insurance paid. ✑ *Apply December-March.*

INFO

Hungarian Embassy
35 Eaton Place, London SW1X 8BY
℃ 0171-235 4048/7179
Consular section: ℃ 0171-235 2664

British Embassy
Harmincad Utca 6, Budapest V
℃ (36 1) 226 2888

Tourist office
Hungarian National Tourist Board,
PO Box 4336, London SW18 4XE
℃/℻ 0181-871 4009

Youth hostels
Hungarian YHA, Semmelweis utca 4,
1395 Budapest V

Youth & student information
International Bureau for Youth Tourism &
Exchange (BITEJ), Ady E utca 19, 1024
Budapest
Postal address: PO Box 147, 1389
Budapest

Express Youth & Student Travel Bureau,
Szabadság tér 16, 1395 Budapest.

Entry regulations British and other
European and North American nationals
do not need a visa to visit Hungary or to
take up voluntary work there. All other
nationalities should check visa
requirements with Hungarian embassies/
consulates. Those wishing to take up
paid work in Hungary must get their
prospective employer to apply for a
work permit. With the exception of
British nationals, a work visa must also
be applied for: applicants must complete
a visa form at the Hungarian embassy
and submit their passport, 2 photos and
their work permit (forwarded by the
prospective employer), after which the
visa should take 24 hours to process.

Travel Freedom Pass allows 3, 5 or 10
days unlimited rail travel in 1 month on
the railways of Hungary. Cost from £29

(under 26) or £36 (26+). Available from British Rail International Travel Centre, Victoria Station, London SW1V 1JY ✆ 0171-834 2345.

Campus Travel can arrange Eurotrain, Inter-Rail and student/youth fares for travel by plane, train, boat and bus to destinations in Hungary. Offices throughout the UK, including a student travel centre at 52 Grosvenor Gardens, London SW1W 0AG (opposite Victoria Station) ✆ 0171-730 3402 or ✆ 0131-668 3303 for Scottish bookings.

Council Travel, 28A Poland Street, London, W1V 3DB ✆ 0171-437 7767 (offices also in Paris, Nice, Lyon, Munich, Düsseldorf, Tokyo, Singapore and throughout the US) offer Eurotrain under 26 fares and student/youth flights to Budapest, plus travel insurance, guidebooks and travel gear.

Publications Lonely Planet's *Hungary - A Travel Survival Kit* £9.95 and *Eastern Europe on a Shoestring* £13.95 provide practical information on budget travel in Hungary.

The Rough Guide to Hungary £7.99 provides comprehensive background information on Hungary, plus details on getting there, getting around, places to explore and cheap places to stay.

Michael's Guide to Hungary £9.95 is detailed and concise, providing invaluable practical advice for all kinds of travellers. Published by Inbal Travel.

All the above are available from good bookshops.

Accommodation Danube Travel Ltd, 6 Conduit Street, London W1R 9TG ✆ 0171-493 0263 can help with accommodation bookings including Strawberry Youth Hostels Ltd, a chain offering budget accommodation in Budapest.

The Hungarian National Tourist Board,

see above, can supply a booklet listing campsites in Hungary.

CONSERVATION

BRITISH TRUST FOR CONSERVATION VOLUNTEERS Room IWH, 36 St Mary's Street, Wallingford, Oxfordshire OX10 0EU ✆ Wallingford (01491) 839766
The largest charitable organisation in Britain to involve people in practical conservation work. Following the success of the Natural Break Programme in the UK, BTCV is now developing a series of international working holidays with the aim of introducing **volunteers** to conservation projects abroad. It is hoped that British volunteers will adapt to and learn from local lifestyles as well as participate in the community. Recent projects in Hungary have included protecting the great bustard and erecting nesting platforms for red-footed falcons on the Great Hungarian Plain; and wetland management in the Bükk National Park. ⊕ Ages 18-70. 10-14 days, June-September. Cost from £125 includes transport from a suitable pick-up point in Hungary, insurance, food and basic accommodation, with everyone sharing in domestic chores. Volunteers should take a sleeping bag. Membership fee £12. No fares or wages paid.

FARMWORK

BIOKULTURA ASSOCIATION Mr Szabolcs Seléndy, President, 1204 Budapest, Rezeda u 3, Hungary
The Hungarian Association of Organic Growers may be able to help find placements for **volunteers** on organic farms and gardens in Hungary. Work can include weeding, animal husbandry and helping with the harvest. Participants receive food, lodging and educational experience, but normally no

pocket money. 8-10 hours per day, 5 days per week for 1-2 weeks, April-October.
⊕ Ages 18+. Applicants must speak German or English; Russian useful. Insurance and anti-tetanus vaccination recommended.
🕮 Contact address for farmworkers: Ifjúságy Iroda/WWOOF, Gödöllö ATE, 2103 Práter Károly u1, Hungary © (36 28) 310 200 ⊞ (36 28) 310 804.

INTERNATIONAL FARM EXPERIENCE PROGRAMME
YFC Centre, N A C, Stoneleigh Park, Kenilworth CV8 2LG
© (01203) 696584
Provides assistance to young **agriculturalists** and **horticulturalists** by finding places in farms/nurseries abroad, enabling them to broaden their knowledge of agricultural and horticultural methods. Participants usually live and work with a farming family and the work is matched as far as possible with participant's requirements. Entails physical work and practical involvement. Basic wage plus board and lodging. 3 months, during the summer.
⊕ Ages 18-28. Applicants must have at least 2 years practical experience, one of which may be at agricultural college, and intend to make a career in agriculture/ horticulture. Valid driving licence necessary. Participants pay own fares and insurance. Registration fee £85.
🕮 UK applications to IFEP. Other applications to IFEP partner in home country.

MONITORS & TEACHERS

CENTRAL BUREAU FOR EDUCATIONAL VISITS & EXCHANGES
Seymour Mews House, Seymour Mews, London W1H 9PE © 0171-725 9411
Teachers and **sixth formers** are required at English language summer schools, the main objective of which is to provide Hungarian pupils, aged 16-17, with the opportunity of practising English learnt in school, and by spending 3 weeks in the company of a group of British teachers and young people to acquire a deeper awareness of the British way of life. Duties include helping to teach English as a foreign language, running conversation classes and organising sporting, musical and social activities such as drama, folk dancing and singing workshops.
⊕ Ages 16-45. Applicants should be native English speakers, sixth formers or those aged 16-19 and willing to assist the staff; or teachers qualified in the teaching of any discipline: EFL or ESL qualifications an advantage. Applicants should have a sense of responsibility, organisational skill, adaptability, sociable nature and an ability and interest in sports and/or drama and music, plus experience in working with or teaching children. Participants must fully commit themselves to teaching English and the organising various educational, outdoor and social activities. 3 weeks, July/ August. Board and accommodation provided at school, sharing with the pupils, plus honorarium in Hungarian currency towards pocket money. Excursions and visits to places of interest arranged by the host school and 3 day trip to visit places of interest on the return to Budapest. Applicants pay group travel cost of approx £250 including insurance. One day briefing session held in June. Organised by the Hungarian Ministry of Education under the auspices of the Hungarian Commission for UNESCO.
🕮 Completed application forms should be submitted by mid April.

WORKCAMPS

UNIO YOUTH WORKCAMPS ASSOCIATION
International Relations Department, Nepszinhaz u 24, 1081 Budapest, Hungary
Volunteers are invited to take part in international workcamps at various

locations in Hungary. Recent projects have included renovating a stable and clearing the surrounding parkland of a 14th century monastery in Szecseny; harvesting cherries, peaches and plums at a village in central Hungary; working in the corn and wheatfields of southern Hungary alongside Romanian and Slovakian students; and signposting a path in the picturesque village of Velem, at the foot of the Hungarian Alps. Leisure activities also arranged.

⊕ Ages 17-30. Applicants should be highly motivated with previous workcamp or voluntary experience and prepared to work hard as part of a team. Camp language is English, but German also useful. 2-3 weeks, June-August. Food and accommodation provided in schools, huts or tents. Participants pay own insurance and travel costs.

Apply through partner organisation in country of residence. In the UK: Quaker International Social Projects. See page 30 for registration details and addresses.

GENERAL

EUROYOUTH LTD
301 Westborough Road, Westcliff, Southend-on-Sea, Essex SS0 9PT
✆ **Southend-on-Sea (01702) 341434**
Holiday guest stays arranged where guests are offered board and lodging in return for an agreed number of hours English conversation with hosts or their children. Time also available for guests to practise the host language.

⊕ Mainly ages 17-25, but sometimes open to older applicants. Open to anyone whose mother tongue is English, and interested in visiting Hungary and living with a local family for a short time. 2-3 weeks and occasionally 1-2 months, mainly July and August, but also during the year. Travel and insurance arranged by applicants. Registration fee approx £70. *Apply at least 12 weeks prior to scheduled departure date.*

APPLYING FOR A JOB

When writing to **any** organisation it is **essential** to mention **Working Holidays 1995** and enclose a **stamped, self-addressed A4 envelope**, or if in another country, an **addressed A4 envelope** and at least two **IRCs** (International Reply Coupons, available from post offices). Enquiries received without SAEs/IRCs are **unlikely** to be answered. **Before applying**, read carefully all the information given. Pay **particular** attention to:

✐ skills/qualifications/experience required

✐ the period of employment expected

✐ age limits or nationality restrictions

✐ application deadlines

✐ any other points, especially details of insurance cover, and other costs such as travel and accommodation.

When applying include the following:

✐ your name, address, date of birth, marital status, nationality, sex

✐ details of your education, qualifications, relevant experience, skills, languages spoken

✐ your period of availability for work

✐ a passport-size photo, particularly if you will be working with the public

✐ anything else recommended in the listing (such as a *cv*)

iCELAND

INFO

Icelandic Embassy
1 Eaton Terrace, London SW1W 8EY
✆ 0171-730 5131/2

British Embassy
Laufasvegur 49, 101 Reykjavik
✆ (354 1) 15883

Tourist office
Icelandair, 172 Tottenham Court Road,
London W1P 9LG ✆ 0171-388 5599

Youth hostels
Icelandic YHA, Bandalag Islenzkra
Farfugla, Sundlaugavegur 34, PO Box
1045, 121 Laufasvegur Reykjavík
✆ (354 1) 38110 ☎ (354 1) 679201

Youth & student information
Iceland Tourist Board, Laufasvegur 3, 101
Reykjavík

Entry regulations EEA nationals may
work in Iceland without a work permit
and are entitled to stay for up to 3
months in order to seek work, provided
they can support themselves during this
time. If employment is found they may
apply for a residence permit, which is
issued for a period of up to 5 years.
Other foreign nationals may not seek or
accept employment in Iceland after their
arrival in the country unless they have a
prior working permit. This must be
applied for from the Ministry of Social
Affairs by the prospective employer on
behalf of the foreign national, and the
employer must show sufficient proof
that the foreign national will fill a
position for which no skilled Icelander is
presently available.

British nationals do not need a visa to
visit Iceland as a tourist or volunteer,
but must be in possession of a return
travel ticket, have a re-entry permit into
their country of origin, and show
sufficient funds for their support during
their intended stay. Provided these

requirements are met, they may stay in Iceland for a period of up to 3 months; extensions may be granted by the nearest police authority.

Travel Campus Travel offers low-cost, flexible student/youth fares to Reykjavík. Offices throughout the UK including a student travel centre at 52 Grosvenor Gardens, London SW1W OAG (opposite Victoria Station) ✆ 0171-730 3402 or ✆ 0131-668 3303 for Scottish telephone bookings.

Information centres Dick Phillips Specialist Icelandic Travel Service, Whitehall House, Nenthead, Alston, Cumbria CA9 3PS ✆ Alston (01434) 381440 can give details on the physical environment and general advice, and stocks maps and most of the relevant English language publications including guides and books on Icelandic life, environment and history. Hostelling, walking, riding and motorised tours of Iceland organised. Can also book travel by ferry from Aberdeen, from £142 single, June-August. 25% reduction to holders of ISIC cards.
⚜ *Personal callers welcome October-June.*

Publications Lonely Planet's *Iceland, Greenland and the Faroe Islands - A Travel Survival Kit* £8.95 offers practical, down-to-earth information for the low-budget, independent traveller in Iceland.

The Rough Guide to Scandinavia £10.99 provides comprehensive background information on getting around Iceland, with details on getting there, places to explore and cheap places to stay.

Live & Work in Scandinavia £8.95 is a guide for those interested in finding work, starting a business or living in Iceland, Denmark, Finland, Sweden or Norway. Published by Vacation Work, 9 Park End Street, Oxford OX1 1HJ ✆ Oxford (01865) 241978.

All the above are available from good bookshops.

CONSERVATION

BRITISH TRUST FOR CONSERVATION VOLUNTEERS Room 1WH, 36 St Mary's Street, Wallingford, Oxfordshire OX10 0EU ✆ **Wallingford (01491) 839766**
The largest charitable organisation in Britain to involve people in practical conservation work. Since 1983 Trust members have been assisting the Icelandic Nature Conservancy Council with footpath maintenance work in the Skaftafell National Park, and more recently in the spectacular Jökulsá Canyon. **Volunteers** work alongside locals, and should be prepared for hard physical work. The constant daylight means that there are plenty of opportunities for walking, climbing and exploring the spectacular land and ice scape.
⊕ Ages 18-70. 14-16 days, June-July. Cost from £380 includes food and flight. Camping accommodation, cooking facilities and insurance provided. No wages paid.

When writing to any organisation it is essential to mention Working Holidays 1995 and enclose a stamped, self-addressed A4 envelope, or if in another country an addressed A4 envelope and at least two IRCs (International Reply Coupons, available from post offices). Enquiries received without SAEs/IRCs are unlikely to be answered.

iRELAND

INFO

Irish Embassy
17 Grosvenor Place, London SW1X
7HR ✆ 0171-235 2171

British Embassy
31/33 Merrion Road, Dublin 4
✆ (353 1) 269 5211

Tourist office
Irish Tourist Office, Ireland House,
150 New Bond Street, London W1Y
0AQ ✆ 0171-493 3201

Youth hostels
An Oige Irish YHA, 61 Mountjoy Street,
Dublin 7 ✆ (353 1) 304555
⚏ (353 1) 305808

Youth & student information
Union of Students in Ireland, 16 North
Great Georges Street, Dublin 1
✆ (353 1) 878 6366

Union of Students in Ireland Travel
Service (USIT), Aston Quay, O'Connell
Bridge, Dublin 2 ✆ (353 1) 677 8117

National Youth Council of Ireland, 3
Montague Street, Dublin 2
✆ (353 1) 784122

Entry regulations UK citizens
intending to work in Ireland do not need
a passport, but should produce evidence
of their place of birth; those born in
Northern Ireland may claim Irish
nationality. Citizens of other member
states of the EEA do not require work
permits. Those already in Ireland should
consult the nearest office of FAS,
Ireland's Training and Employment
Authority, or consult recruitment
advertisements in local newspapers.
Those in the UK seeking work in Ireland
can get details from the Overseas
Placing Unit, Employment Services,
Sheffield, or from their local Jobcentre.

Travel Freedom Pass allows 3, 5 or 10
days unlimited travel in 1 month on the

railways of Ireland. Cost from £36 (under 26) or from £38 (26+). Available from British Rail International Rail Centre, Victoria Station, London SW1V 1JY ✆ 0171-834 2345.

Campus Travel can arrange student/youth fares for travel by plane, train, boat and bus to destinations throughout Ireland. Also issues a £8 travelsave stamp for ISIC cards, entitling holders to 50% discount on Irish rail, ferry and coach travel. Offices throughout the UK including a student travel centre at 52 Grosvenor Gardens, London SW1W 0AG (opposite Victoria Station) ✆ 0171-730 3402 or ✆ 0131-668 3303 for Scottish telephone bookings.

Council Travel, 28A Poland Street, London W1V 3DB ✆ 0171-287 3337 (offices also in Paris, Nice, Lyon, Munich, Düsseldorf, Tokyo, Singapore and throughout the US) offers student/youth airfares, student coach fares and Eurotrain under 26 fares. Student/youth ferry fares for car travel also available, plus travel insurance, guidebooks and travel gear.

Information centres Community and Youth Information Centre, Sackville House, Sackville Place, Dublin 1 ✆ (353 1) 8786844 offers information on a wide range of subjects including youth affairs, education, employment agencies, welfare rights, sports, travel and accommodation.

Publications Lonely Planet's *Ireland - A Travel Survival Kit* £11.95 offers practical, down-to-earth information for budget travellers wanting to explore beyond the usual tourist routes.

The Rough Guide to Ireland £9.99, provides comprehensive background information on Ireland, with details of getting there, getting around, places to explore and cheap places to stay.

Both the above guidebooks are available from good bookshops.

Accommodation Kinlay House, Christchurch, 2-12 Lord Edward Street, Dublin ✆ (353 1) 679 6644 offers high quality, low-cost accommodation in Dublin city centre. 2-4 and 6 bedded rooms from £7 per person per night, including continental breakfast. Similar facilities in Kinlay House, Shandon, Cork ✆ (353 21) 508 966 and Kinlay House, Eyre Square, Galway ✆ (353 91) 65244.

AU PAIR / CHILDCARE

LANGTRAIN INTERNATIONAL Torquay Road, Foxrock, Dublin 18, Ireland ✆ (353 1) 289 3876
Can place **au pairs** in Irish families. 30 hour week with one full day and some evenings off. Time off to attend language classes 2-3 mornings or afternoons per week. Experience desirable but not essential. 6+ months. ⊕ Ages 18+. £25-£40 per week pocket money, full board, lodging and insurance provided. Travel paid by applicants. Placement fee £60.

COMMUNITY WORK

SIMON COMMUNITY (NATIONAL OFFICE) PO Box 1022, Dublin 1, Ireland ✆ (353 1) 671 1606/1319
A voluntary body offering support and accommodation to the long-term homeless at residential houses and night shelters in Cork, Dublin, Dundalk and Galway. Full-time **volunteers** required to work on a residential basis, living-in and sharing food with residents, taking responsibility for household chores and working to create an atmosphere of trust, acceptance and friendship by talking, listening and befriending. ⊕ Ages 18-35; older volunteers considered. No experience or qualifications necessary, but applicants should be mature, responsible individuals with an understanding of, and empathy

for homeless people. Tolerance and an ability to get on with people and work as part of a team also essential qualities. 3-12 months, recruitment throughout the year; first month probationary. Volunteers work 3 days on, 2 days off, with 2 weeks holiday entitlement every 3 months. A flat away from the project is provided for workers on their days off. Allowance of IR£34 per week and insurance provided, but not travel costs. Training given by project leaders; formal training courses in aspects such as first aid may also be provided. *All nationalities welcome; overseas applicants must have a good standard of spoken English.*

VOLUNTARY SERVICE INTERNATIONAL 30 Mountjoy Square, Dublin 1, Ireland Ⓒ (353 1) 855 1011 ⬚ (353 1) 855 1012

The Irish branch of Service Civil International, which promotes international reconciliation through work projects. **Volunteers** are needed to work in international teams on various community workcamps. Recent projects have included helping to run the Navan Travellers Summer Project in Co Meath, with the aim of improving facilities, organising sports, arts/crafts, games and outings for the children and youth with talks on their life and culture; helping staff and local people run holiday activities for children in Dublin; and doing manual work alongside the young residents of Camphill Communities in Wexford, Kilkenny and Tipperary. ⊕ Ages 18+. Overseas volunteers should have good English. Volunteers must be highly motivated preferably with previous workcamp or other voluntary experience, and prepared to work hard as part of a team. 35-40 hour week, 2-4 weeks, June-September. Food, shared accommodation and work accident insurance provided. No fares or wages paid. **B D PH**

🕮 *Apply through partner organisation in country of residence. In the UK: International Voluntary Service. See page 30 for registration details and addresses.*

CONSERVATION

BRITISH TRUST FOR CONSERVATION VOLUNTEERS Room 1WH, 36 St Mary's Street, Wallingford, Oxfordshire OX10 0EU Ⓒ Wallingford (01491) 839766

The largest charitable organisation in Britain to involve people in practical conservation work. Following the success of the Natural Break Programme in the UK, BTCV is now developing a series of international working holidays with the aim of introducing **volunteers** to conservation projects abroad. It is hoped that British volunteers will adapt to and learn from local lifestyles as well as participate in the community. Projects last 2 weeks, July-September and are run in conjunction with Conservation Volunteers Ireland. Recent projects have included repairing a stone wall surrounding the gardens of Shankhill Castle near Kilkenny and restoring a Victorian pond in Co Cork. ⊕ Ages 18-70. Cost from £70 includes transport from Dublin, insurance, food and accommodation, with everyone sharing in domestic chores. Volunteers should take a sleeping bag. Membership fee £12. No fares or wages paid.

FARMWORK

INTERNATIONAL FARM EXPERIENCE PROGRAMME YFC Centre, N A C, Stoneleigh Park, Kenilworth, Warwickshire CV8 2LG Ⓒ (01203) 696584

Provides assistance to young **agriculturalists** and **horticulturalists** by finding places in farms/nurseries abroad, enabling them to broaden their knowledge of agricultural and horticultural methods. Participants usually live and work with a farming family and the work is matched as far as possible with participant's requirements. Entails physical work and practical

involvement. Basic wage plus board and lodging. 3-12 months, all year.
⊕ Ages 18-28. Applicants must have at least 2 years practical experience, one of which may be at agricultural college, and intend to make a career in agriculture/horticulture. Valid driving licence necessary. Participants pay own fares and insurance. Registration fee £85.
🦅 UK applications to IFEP; others to IFEP partner in home country.

WILLING WORKERS ON ORGANIC FARMS (WWOOF)
c/o Annie Sampson, Tulla PO, Tulla, Clare, Ireland
A non-profitmaking organisation which aims to help organic farmers and smallholders whose work may be labour-intensive as it does not rely on the use of artificial fertilisers or pesticides. Provides unskilled volunteers with first hand experience of organic farming and gardening, and a chance to spend some time on small or large holdings throughout Ireland. The work can include working with horses, cows, goats, sheep, pigs and fowl; all aspects of organic gardening, cutting turf, preserving fruit and vegetables; making cheeses and yoghurt, stone walling, hedging and renovating.
⊕ Ages 16+. Members receive a current list of holdings together with a short description of each one. Length of stay can be weekend, week, month or longer by arrangement. Opportunities to learn crafts. Full board lodging provided in the farmhouse and outbuildings; volunteers should take a sleeping bag. No wages paid, and helpers must pay their own travel costs. Insurance and anti-tetanus vaccination recommended. Membership fee £6 and 2 IRCs.

TEACHERS

ANGLO EUROPEAN STUDY TOURS LTD 8 Celbridge Mews, London W2 6EU ℗ 0171-229 4435
Runs EFL summer courses for foreign teenagers at centres in Dublin.

Graduate teachers with recognised EFL qualification (minimum RSA/UCLES or Trinity College London Certificate or equivalent). Applicants must be native English speakers and either be EEA nationals or have a valid work permit for Ireland. Vacancies mid June-end August. Salary up to £200 per week for 17 contact hours. Accommodation is not normally available. Also a small number of vacancies for suitably qualified/experienced activity leaders to run the students' sports and leisure programme. Accommodation included.

WORKCAMPS

VOLUNTARY SERVICE INTERNATIONAL 30 Mountjoy Square, Dublin 1, Ireland ℗ (353 1) 855 1011 ✉ (353 1) 855 1012
The Irish branch of Service Civil International, which promotes international reconciliation through work projects. Volunteers are needed to work in international teams on various workcamps. Recent projects have included planting trees in the provinces of Ulster, Munster, Leinster and Connaught as part of a symbolic peace forest around Ireland; working with community activists in the west of Ireland, and area devastated by the 1845 famine, to map out deserted villages and famine graves; and planting reeds to establish a reed bed sewage system at an organic farming community in Wexford.
⊕ Ages 18+. Overseas volunteers should speak good English. Volunteers must be highly motivated preferably with previous workcamp or other voluntary experience, and prepared to work hard as part of a team. 35-40 hour week, 2-4 weeks, June-September. Food, shared accommodation and work accident insurance provided. No fares or wages paid. B D PH

🦅 Apply through partner organisation in country of residence. In the UK: International Voluntary Service. See page 30 for registration details and addresses.

iSRAEL

INFO

Israeli Embassy
2 Palace Green, London W8 4QB
© 0171-957 9500

British Embassy
192 Hayarkon Street, Tel Aviv 63405
© (972 3) 524 9171/8

Tourist office
Israel Government Tourist Office,
18 Great Marlborough Street, London
WIV IAF © 0171-434 3651

Youth hostels
Israel Youth Hostels Association, Youth
Travel Bureau, PO Box 1075, 3 Dorot
Rishonim Street, Jerusalem © (972 2)
221 648

Youth & student information
Israel Students' Tourist Association,
109 Ben Yehuda Street, Tel Aviv 63401

The Public Council for Exchange of
Youth and Young Adults, 67 Pinsker
Street, Tel Aviv

Entry regulations A work permit is
required for employment in Israel, and
this should be obtained by the
prospective employer on application to
the Ministry of the Interior, who will
then authorise the issue of a visa.
It is important that a permit is obtained
before leaving for Israel. Volunteers on
archaeological digs, kibbutzim or
moshavim will receive their visas on
arrival. Applicants should be aware that
it is now more difficult to find a place on
a kibbutz, and are strongly advised not
to travel to Israel hoping to be accepted
if they have not arranged a place prior
to departure. Immigration officials are
making it very difficult for one-way ticket
holders to enter the country; kibbutz
and moshav volunteers should be able to
produce a return or open ticket plus
proof of sufficient means of support
whilst in the country, at the port of
entry. The cost of living is high and no

volunteer should leave for Israel with less than £100 spending and emergency money. Employment opportunities are limited and a work permit will only be granted if a vacancy cannot be filled by local manpower.

British Visitors Passports are not accepted for entry into Israel. All passports must be valid for 6+ months from the date of intended departure from Israel.

Travel Campus Travel offers low-cost, flexible student/youth fares to Tel Aviv and Eilat. Offices throughout the UK including a student travel centre at 52 Grosvenor Gardens, London SW1W OAG (opposite Victoria Station) ✆ 0171-730 3402 or ✆ 0131-668 3303 for Scottish telephone bookings.

Council Travel, 28A Poland Street, London, W1V 3DB ✆ 0171-287 3337 (offices also in Paris, Nice, Lyon, Munich, Düsseldorf, Singapore, Tokyo and throughout the US) offers low-cost student/youth airfares to Tel Aviv, plus travel insurance, guidebooks and travel gear.

North-South Travel Ltd, Moulsham Mill, Parkway, Chelmsford CM2 7PX ✆ Chelmsford (01245) 492882 arranges competitively priced, reliably planned flights to Israel. From the profit made from each ticket £5 is donated to Third World charities through a special plan.

STA Travel, 86 Old Brompton Road, London SW7 3LQ/117 Euston Road, London NW1 2SX ✆ 0171-937 9921 (offices also in Birmingham, Bristol, Cambridge, Glasgow, Leeds, Manchester and Oxford) operates flexible low-cost flights between London and Tel Aviv.

Publications Lonely Planet's *Israel - A Travel Survival Kit* £10.95 offers practical, down-to-earth information for independent travellers wanting to explore beyond the usual tourist routes.

Culture Shock! Israel £6.95 introduces the reader to the people, customs, ceremonies, food and culture of Israel, with checklists of dos and don'ts.

The above guides are available from good bookshops.

Accommodation *Kibbutz Inns Guest Houses* lists 25 inns offering board and accommodation; facilities include private beaches, pools and tennis courts. *Christian Hospices* lists approx 40 hospices offering accommodation and board, indicating denomination and prices. Both available from the Israel Government Tourist Office, see above.

ARCHAEOLOGY

DEPARTMENT OF CLASSICAL STUDIES Professor M Gichon, Division of Archaeology, Yad Avner, Ramat Aviv, 69978 Tel Aviv, Israel Volunteers required for excavations of town fortifications and public buildings at two sites at Horvat Eqed and Emmaus, dating from the Hellenistic to the Roman and Byzantine period. ⊕ Ages 16+. 1+ weeks, June-September. 6½ hour day with 1 hour rest. Accommodation provided at a cost of US$30 per day. No charge for senior students, postgraduates in archaeology or experienced diggers, provided arrangements are made in advance. No fares, insurance or wages paid. Lectures in history, archaeology and geography provided as well as trips and recreational activities. Also opportunities for volunteers to work on processing of archaeological finds, under supervision, November-June. **PH** accepted under certain circumstances.

THE HEBREW UNIVERSITY OF JERUSALEM The Director, Institute of Archaeology, Mount Scopus, Jerusalem 91905, Israel Conducts excavations all over Israel, concerned with the prehistoric, Biblical and classical periods. Current excavations include a dig at Hazor in Galilee, with Bronze and Iron Age remains; a large Iron Age site at Miqne/ Ekron, one of 5 Philistine capital cities; and Persian, Iron Age, Hellenistic and Roman period remains at Tel Dor. **Volunteers** are invited to work 2-6 weeks, June-August. Lectures on Biblical archaeology and visits to other sites. 7-9 hour day, starting early in the morning. Accommodation provided for small fee. Volunteers pay own travel and insurance. ✍ *Volunteers should write, indicating the period and vicinity they are interested in, and the times and dates when they will be available.*

ISRAEL ANTIQUITIES AUTHORITY PO Box 586, Rockefeller Museum, Jerusalem 91004, Israel ✆ (972 2) 292607 ⌨ (972) 292628

Volunteers are needed to help on excavations dating from the prehistoric era through to Crusader times. Recent excavations carried out at over 30 sites include a major port on the Mediterranean coast dating to the late Hellenistic and Islamic periods; a Roman water system near the Sea of Galilee; a castle and village with Crusader, Mamluk and Ottoman remains; remains of a Roman-Byzantine city near Nazareth; Bronze Age remains of a fortified city near Naharriya; a Chalcolithic village in the Negev desert; a sanctuary of Pan-Hellenistic temples and grotto; and a prehistoric site in the northern Jordan Valley. Work includes digging, shovelling, and hauling baskets, with cleaning and sorting pottery in the afternoons. ⚜ Ages 18+. Experience not needed, but volunteers should be highly motivated, fit and able to work long hours in very hot weather. Excavations are conducted throughout the year, but the main season is May-September. 2+ weeks. The Authority also conducts rescue excavations and emergency surveys throughout the year on short notice. On some sites volunteers may have to pay a fee and provide a medical certificate. Insurance obligatory. Travel to Israel paid by volunteers. *Archaeological Excavations* published annually in January, gives details of digs arranged.

JEWISH NATIONAL FUND Eli Shenhav, 11 Zvi Shapira Street, Tel Aviv 64538, Israel

Volunteers required to help excavate a Shuni Roman theatre at Binyamina. ⚜ Ages 17+. 1+ weeks, July-August. Cost US$20 per day includes medical and accident insurance, meals and accommodation in tents. Lectures arranged. 5 day week. Hours of work 0600-1300; other work 1700-1900. Volunteers pay own travel costs and should take a sleeping bag.

PROJECT 67 LTD 10 Hatton Garden, London EC1N 8AH ✆ 0171-831 7626

Organises digs for **volunteers** at various sites in cooperation with the Antiquities Authority. The work consists of clearing away debris, shovelling, hauling baskets, cleaning fragments of pottery and other artefacts. ⚜ Ages 18+; no maximum limit. Previous experience not necessary, but volunteers should be fit, enthusiastic and prepared for hard work in a hot climate. Hours of work 0500-1230. Afternoons usually free. Evening lectures and trips to nearby sites and museums. 2 weeks, all year. Cost from £350 covers return flight, full board and insurance.

UNIVERSITY OF PENNSYLVANIA 119 Meyerson Hall, Philadelphia PA 19104-6311, United States ✆ (1 215) 898 4909 ⌨ (1 215) 898 9215

Volunteers are invited to help excavate the ruins of a magnificent palace built by King Herod the Great at Caesara Maritima, on the Mediterranean coast between Tel Aviv and Haifa. Previous excavations have revealed a luxurious mosaic-floored dining room and a huge swimming pool extending several hundred feet into the sea. 5 weeks, late June-early August; preference given to those who can come for full season.

5 day week, with weekend tours available to other sites of interest. ⊕ Ages 18-50+. No experience necessary; knowledge of Hebrew helpful but not essential. Cost US$1,750 for 5 week session covers local transportation and room, board and laundry in beach-side kibbutz. Volunteers arrange own travel and insurance. No fares or wages paid. ✍ *Apply to Dr Kathryn Gleason, Project Director at least 2 months in advance.* **D PH**

AU PAIR / CHILDCARE

AU PAIR INTERNATIONAL
2 Desler Street, Bnei Brak 51507, Israel ℂ **(972 3) 6190423**
Can place **mothers' helps, nannies** and **housekeepers**. 1 year contract. Approx 40 hour, 5 day week. Board and accommodation provided. Salary US$500-US$600 per month. ⊕ Ages 19-45. Experience preferable but not essential; English language preferred. Applicants must have full health insurance.

STAR AU PAIRS INTERNATIONAL
16 Michal Street, Tel Aviv 63261, Israel ℂ/▱ **(972 3) 291 748**
Can place **au pairs, mothers' helps** and **nannies** throughout Israel. 4+ months. ⊕ Ages 22-38. Previous childcare experience preferred but not essential. Knowledge of English and driving licence an advantage. Pocket money US$600-US$900 per month. Return fare paid after completing 1 year's contract.

KIBBUTZIM

A kibbutz is a communal society in which all the means of production are owned by the community as a whole, and all income generated is ploughed back into the community. Members do not receive wages or salaries but give their labour in return for the provision of their basic needs. Kibbutzim welcome volunteers who are prepared to live and work within the community, abide by the kibbutz way of life and are capable of adapting to a totally new society. The work may be based indoors or outdoors and may include farming, fruit and vegetable picking, market gardening and even light industry. In addition, everyone is expected to take their turn in doing household chores such as helping with cooking, cleaning and washing for the whole community. Volunteers work approx 8 hour day, 6 day week, with Saturdays free and 2 additional days off at the end of each month. Additional hours' work may be necessary at busy periods, such as the harvest. During the summer, work often starts at 0500, with afternoons free to avoid the heat of the day. Volunteers live together in wood cabins or stone houses with food provided in the communal dining area. Male and female volunteers generally sleep in separate 2-4 bedded rooms. Laundry, toilet requisites, entertainment, medical care and other basic needs, such as stamps and cigarettes, usually available as required, and some kibbutzim have bars and discos. A small amount of pocket money, approx £20 per month, may also be provided. There are now fewer kibbutz placements than there were previously, due to a variety of factors: increased efficiency, cheap labour and an unfavourable economic climate have all exerted an influence. Applicants should therefore realise that a serious attitude towards the work is required, as well as a genuine desire to become involved in kibbutz life. Kibbutzim should not be regarded as holiday bases; volunteers can make arrangements for sightseeing at the end of their work period.

Kibbutz Volunteer £5.95 describes kibbutzim and how they function, conveying the atmosphere of the communities and explaining what to expect when working in one. There are details of 200 kibbutzim plus a map showing locations and how to apply. Published by Vacation Work, 9 Park End Street, Oxford OX1 1HJ ✆ Oxford (01865) 241978.

KIBBUTZ REPRESENTATIVES
Volunteer Coordinator,
1a Accommodation Road, London
NW11 8ED ✆ **0181-458 9235**
Operates a working visitor scheme throughout the year. **Volunteers** spend 8-12 weeks on a kibbutz.
⊕ Ages 18-32. Volunteers pay their own travel costs and must be in possession of a return ticket or adequate funds for the return journey. Applicants must supply a medical certificate and 2 character references, and attend an orientation interview. Registration fee £45.
✍ *Limited places during July and August; apply before Easter.*

PROJECT 67 LTD 10 Hatton
Garden, London EC1N 8AH
✆ **0171-831 7626**
Arranges **kibbutz volunteer** placements for 8+ weeks, all year.
⊕ Ages 18-32. Cost from £249 covers return flight and registration fee.
Tel Aviv office assists with queries and onward travel and can also be used as mailing address, message board plus left luggage facility. *All nationalities welcome.*

MOSHAVIM

A moshav is a collective of individual smallholders, based on the family unit. Each family works and develops its own plot of land/farm while sharing the capital costs of equipment and marketing. Moshavim are different from kibbutzim in that each family lives in its own house and makes its own living; there are some communal buildings and facilities such as a club house, post office, supermarket and swimming pool. Volunteers on moshavim live and work as a member of an Israeli family and are expected to share in the social and cultural activities of the family and village. In some cases a small group of

2-3 volunteers may live in their own bungalow, but they will each be 'adopted' by the family for whom they are working. Most of the work is on the land, with emphasis on flower growing, market gardening, specialist fruit farming, chicken rearing or dairy farming. It should be stressed that work on a moshav is tougher and more demanding than on a kibbutz, and working hours may be long. Volunteers are expected to develop close relationships with the family, which demands a far greater personal effort than in the communal life of a kibbutz. In return for working a basic 8 hour, 6 day week, volunteers receive board and lodging plus wages of approx £200 per month, more than the pocket money given on a kibbutz. Lectures, cultural activities and excursions may be arranged.

PROJECT 67 LTD 10 Hatton
Garden, London EC1N 8AH
✆ **0171-831 7626**
Arranges moshav **volunteer** placements in families. 2+ months, all year.
⊕ Ages 21-35. Wages approx £200 per month. Cost to participants from £235 covers return flight and registration fee. *All nationalities welcome.*

GENERAL

FRIENDS OF ISRAEL
EDUCATIONAL TRUST
25 Lyndale Avenue, London NW2
2QB ✆ **0171-435 6803**
Volunteers required to work in Jerusalem's 60-acre botanic garden, in the grounds of the Hebrew University. Work involves digging, weeding and seed maintenance.
⊕ Ages 18+. Horticultural qualifications preferred; volunteers must have previous experience of long hours of manual work. 30-40 hours per week. 2 weeks, March and October. Cost £450 covers half-board hotel accommodation and travel, but not insurance. Tours and lectures organised for volunteers. **D** *UK nationals only.*

INFO

Italian Embassy
14 Three Kings Yard, Davies Street,
London WIY 2EH ✆ 0171-312 2200

British Embassy
Via XX Settembre 80A, 00187 Rome
✆ (39 6) 482 5441/5551

Tourist office
Italian State Tourist Board (ENIT),
1 Princes Street, London WIR 8AY
✆ 0171-408 1254

Youth hostels
Associazione Italiana Alberghi per la
Gioventù, via Cavour 44, 3rd floor,
00184 Rome

Youth & student information
Centro Turistico Studentesco et
Giovanile CTS (Student Travel), via
Nazionale 66, 00184 Rome

Student Travel Service Florence, via
Zannetti 18, 50123 Florence

Intercultura, Piazza San Pantaleo 3,
I-00186 Rome

Entry regulations UK citizens
intending to work in Italy should have
full passports. Police registration is
required within 3 days of entering Italy.
UK/EEA nationals may stay for up to 3
months, and those wishing to stay longer
must obtain an extension from the
police. When status changes from
visitor to employee the individual must
immediately apply for a work permit.

Job advertising The Italian Publishing
Group, 4 Wendle Court, 131-137
Wandsworth Road, London SW8 2LL
✆ 0171-498 0900 ⌨ 0171-498 2514
can place advertisements in most Italian
newspapers and magazines.

Publicitas Ltd, 517/523 Fulham Road,
London SW6 1HD ✆ 0171-385 7723
can place job advertisements in a

number of Italian newspapers and magazines including *Il Giorno* (Milan daily); *Il Gazzettino* (Venice daily); *Il Tempo* (leading Rome newspaper); *La Sicilia* (leading Sicilian newspaper), plus a great number of trade, technical and general interest magazines.

Travel CIT (England) Ltd, 3-5 Landsdowne Road, Croydon, Surrey CR9 1LL ✆ 0181-686 0677 issues a Kilometric ticket valid for 3,000 km (maximum 20 journeys) which can be shared by up to 5 people, the 3,000 km being divided by the number of passengers. Valid 2 months; cost £90. A Travel at Will ticket entitles the holder to unlimited travel on the Italian rail network. Valid for up to 30 days; cost from £88 (8 consecutive days).

Freedom Pass allows 3, 5 or 10 days unlimited rail travel in 1 month on the railways of Italy. Cost from £79 (under 26) or £105 (26+) for 3 days. Available from British Rail International Rail Centre, Victoria Station, London SW1V 1JY ✆ 0171-834 2345.

Campus Travel can arrange Eurotrain, Inter-rail and student/youth fares for travel by plane, train, boat and bus to destinations throughout Italy. Offices throughout the UK, including a student travel centre at 52 Grosvenor Gardens, London SW1W 0AG (opposite Victoria Station) ✆ 0171-730 3402 or ✆ 0131-668 3303 for Scottish bookings.

Council Travel, 28A Poland Street, London, W1V 3DB ✆ 0171-287 3337 (offices also in Paris, Nice, Lyon, Munich, Düsseldorf, Tokyo, Singapore and throughout the US) offers Eurotrain under 26 fares and low-cost student/ youth airfares to Italy, plus travel insurance, guidebooks and travel gear.

STA Travel, 86 Old Brompton Road, London SW7 3LQ/117 Euston Road, London NW1 2SX ✆ 0171-937 9921 (offices also in Birmingham, Bristol, Cambridge, Glasgow, Leeds, Manchester

and Oxford) operates flexible, low-cost flights between London and destinations throughout Italy.

Information centres Servizio Turistico Sociale, Youth and Student Travel Service, via Zannetti 18, 50123 Florence provides a reception and information service and can arrange accommodation plus discount travel. Also gives information on tours, Italian courses and events. **B D PH**

Publications Lonely Planet's *Italy - A Travel Survival Kit* £11.95 offers practical, down-to-earth information for budget travellers wanting to explore beyond the usual tourist routes.

Rough Guides provide comprehensive background information, plus details on getting there, getting around, places to explore and cheap places to stay. Titles include *Italy* £12.99, *Sicily* £8.99, *Tuscany and Umbria* £8.99, and *Venice* £8.99. All are available from good bookshops.

Vacation Work's *Live and Work in Italy* £7.95 is a guide for those interested in finding temporary or permanent work, starting a business or buying a home in Italy.

Culture Shock! Italy £6.95 introduces the reader to the people, customs, ceremonies, food and culture of Italy, with checklists of dos and don'ts.

All the above guides are available from good bookshops.

Italy, Travellers Handbook is a free booklet containing useful information for visitors with notes on accommodation, culture and leisure, sports and travel. Also includes general information, and the addresses of provincial and local tourist boards. Available from the Italian State Tourist Board, see above.

Accommodation Federazione Italiana del Campeggio e del Caravanning, via V Emanuele 11, PO Box 23, 50041

Calenzano, Florence ℂ (39 55) 882391 operates an international campsite booking centre and publishes a list of member campsites which can accept bookings, with details of costs, opening dates and facilities. 🐾 *Apply by 15 May.* Also publishes a map of all Italian campsites, available on receipt of 3 IRCs.

AU PAIR / CHILDCARE

Au pair posts are open to males and females, ages 18-30, for a maximum of 12 months. A written agreement must specify duties, which should not involve more than 5-6 hours of light housework per day, with two days and 2-3 evenings free each week. The host family must provide full board accommodation, private accident/health insurance and at least L50,000 pocket money per week.

ACADEMY AU PAIR AGENCY LTD 42 Cedarhurst Drive, Eltham, London SE9 5LP ℂ 0181-294 1191 𝄐 0181-850 8932
Can place **au pairs**. ⊕ Ages 18-27. Some knowledge of Italian essential. Pocket money approx £30-£40 per week. Administration charge £40. Positions as **nannies** and **mothers' helps** also available for those with qualifications/experience.

ANGLO PAIR AGENCY 40 Wavertree Road, Streatham Hill, London SW2 3SP ℂ 0181-674 3605
Can place **au pairs** and **au pairs plus**. ⊕ Ages 18-27. Pocket money £30-£50 per week. Also placements for experienced **nannies** and **mothers' helps**; salary up to £100 per week. Agency fee £40.

AU PAIRS-ITALY 46 The Rise, Sevenoaks, Kent TN13 1RJ
Can place **au pairs, mothers' helps, nannies** and **governesses** in families

throughout Italy, including Sicily and Sardinia. Usual length of stay 6-12 months, but some shorter vacancies, and summer holiday posts for 2-3 months. ⊕ Ages 18+. Applicants must supply 3 references, a medical certificate and photos. Monthly pocket money approx £140 (au pairs), £230 (mothers' helps), £300-£800 (nannies and governesses). *EEA nationals only.*

AVALON AGENCY Thursley House, 53 Station Road, Shalford, Guildford, Surrey GU4 8HA ℂ Guildford (01483) 63640
Can place **au pairs**. ⊕ Ages 18-30. Basic knowledge of Italian needed. Pocket money equal to £30-£35 per week, usually paid monthly. Summer holiday placements June-August only. Long-term 6 month-2 year vacancies to start any time.

BUNTERS AU PAIR & DOMESTIC AGENCY 17 Copper Street, Macclesfield, Cheshire SK11 7LH ℂ Macclesfield (01625) 614534
Can place **au pairs, demi pairs** and **mothers' helps**. 6-12 months all year or 10 week summer placements. ⊕ Ages 18-27. Pocket money £35-£50 per week depending on hours worked. Placement fee £40. 🐾 *Apply before May for summer placements.*

HELPING HANDS AU PAIR & DOMESTIC AGENCY 39 Rutland Avenue, Thorpe Bay, Essex SS1 2XJ ℂ Southend-on-Sea (01702) 602067
Can place **au pairs** and **mothers' helps**. ⊕ Ages 18-27. Pocket money approx £35 per week for au pairs, higher for mothers' helps. Introduction fee £40. *UK nationals only.*

HOME FROM HOME Walnut Orchard, Chearsley, Aylesbury, Buckinghamshire HP18 0DA ℂ/𝄐 Aylesbury (01844) 208561
Can place **au pairs**. ⊕ Ages 18+. Basic knowledge of Italian essential. Pocket money £35 per week. Placement fee £40. *UK nationals only.*

JOLAINE AGENCY 18 Escot Way, Barnet, Hertfordshire EN5 3AN ☎ 0181-449 1334 ⊡ 0181-449 9183
Can place **au pairs, mothers' helps** and **nannies**. ⊕ Ages 18-27. Pocket money from £40 per week. Placement fee £40.

JUST THE JOB (NOTTINGHAM) 32 Dovedale Road, West Bridgford, Nottingham NG2 6JA ☎ 0115-945 2482
Can place a**u pairs, mothers' helps** and **nannies** for 6+ months; no short-term placements. ⊕ Ages 18+. Weekly pocket money £32-£40 (au pairs), £75-£140 (other positions). *UK nationals only.*

LANGTRAIN INTERNATIONAL Torquay Road, Foxrock, Dublin 18, Ireland ☎ (353 1) 289 3876
Can place **au pairs** with Italian families. ⊕ Ages 18+. Pocket money £25 per week. Placement fee £60.

STUDENTS ABROAD LTD 11 Milton View, Hitchin, Hertfordshire SG4 0QD ☎ Hitchin (01462) 438909 ⊡ (01462) 438919
Can place **au pairs, au pairs plus, mothers' helps** and **nannies**. 1 year stay preferred for mothers' helps and nannies; short-term summer placements available for au pairs. ⊕ Ages 18-27, au pairs. Basic knowledge of Italian useful but not essential. Pocket money from approx £35 per week, au pairs; higher for other positions. Service charge £40. ☀ *Apply early for summer positions.*

COMMUNITY WORK

SERVIZIO CIVILE INTERNAZIONALE via dei Laterani 28, 00184 Rome, Italy
Service Civil International promotes international reconciliation through work projects. **Volunteers** needed to work in international teams on various community workcamps. Typical projects include working at social centres for people with problems such as ex-drug addicts or ex-offenders; organising activities for disadvantaged children and teenagers; and organising anti-racist/anti-Fascist workcamps alongside refugees or other immigrants.
⊕ Ages 18+. Knowledge of Italian necessary for some camps. Applicants should be highly motivated, preferably with previous workcamp or other voluntary experience, and prepared to work hard as part of a team. 35-40 hour week. 1-3 weeks, June-September. Food, shared accommodation and work accident insurance provided. No fares or wages paid. **B D PH**

☀ *Apply through partner organisation in country of residence. In the UK: International Voluntary Service. See page 30 for registration details and addresses.*

CONSERVATION

BRITISH TRUST FOR CONSERVATION VOLUNTEERS Room IWH, 36 St Mary's Street, Wallingford, Oxfordshire OX10 0EU ☎ Wallingford (01491) 839766
The largest charitable organisation in Britain to involve people in practical conservation work. Following the success of the Natural Break programme in the UK, BTCV is now developing a series of international working holidays with the aim of introducing **volunteers** to practical conservation projects abroad. It is hoped that the British volunteers will adapt to and learn from local lifestyles as well as participate in the community. Projects last for 2-3 weeks and take place throughout Italy. Work is often in conjunction with WWF Italy on the management of their reserves. Recent projects have included reed cutting, fencing and footpath work at a wetland reserve in the Bay of Trieste.
⊕ Ages 18-70. Cost from £145 includes transport from a pick-up point in Italy, insurance, food and accommodation, with everyone sharing in domestic

chores. Volunteers should take a sleeping bag. Membership fee £12. No fares or wages paid.

MOVIMENTO CRISTIANO PER LA PACE via Marco Dino Rossi 12/C, 00173 Rome, Italy

Volunteers are invited to work in international teams on summer projects aimed at offering a service in an area of need and promoting self-help within the community; promoting international understanding and the discussion of social problems; and offering young people the chance to live as a group and take these experiences into the context of daily life. Recent projects have included working with local groups to prevent fires in an area south of Rome; creating footpaths in the Monte Prenestini Park; and assisting with the creation of a national park on Mount Tancia.
⊕ Ages 18-26. A knowledge of Italian may be required. 6 hour day, 30-36 hour week. 2-4 weeks, July-August. Food and shared accommodation provided, but participants pay own travel costs, and should take out full insurance.

🕮 *Apply through partner organisation in country of residence. In the UK: Christian Movement for Peace or United Nations Association International Youth Service. See page 31 for registration details and addresses.*

LA SABRANENQUE CENTRE INTERNATIONAL rue de la Tour de l'Oume, 30290 Saint Victor la Coste, France

A small, non-profitmaking organisation that has been working since 1969 to preserve, restore and reconstruct abandoned rural sites, and bring them back to life. Aims to give volunteers the chance to discover the interest and pleasure of working directly on genuine rural restoration projects while being part of a cooperative team.
In collaboration with Italian preservation organisations, La Sabranenque supervises several conservation projects.

Volunteers are needed in small teams in Gnallo, a hamlet in northern Italy, learning traditional construction techniques on-the-job from experienced leaders. Work includes masonry, stone cutting, floor or roof tiling, interior restoration, drystone walling, paving and planting trees.
⊕ Ages 18+. No experience necessary. 3 weeks, August. Cost L15,000 per day includes full board accommodation. Registration fee FF200.

SERVIZIO CIVILE INTERNAZIONALE via dei Laterani 28, 00184 Rome, Italy

Service Civil International promotes international reconciliation through work projects. Volunteers are invited to take part in international workcamps on various conservation projects, which have recently included completing bicycle tracks along the Addo and Brembo rivers near Bergamo; restoring farmed terraces and renovating the medieval part of a village in Imperia; building a structure to support a centuries-old oak tree in Bologna; and cleaning bathing beaches in the Capaci area of Palermo.
⊕ Ages 18+. Applicants should be highly motivated, preferably with previous workcamp or other voluntary experience, and prepared to work hard as part of a team. 40 hour week. 2-4 weeks, June-September. Food, shared accommodation and work accident insurance provided. No fares or wages paid. B D PH

🕮 *Apply through partner organisation in country of residence. In the UK: International Voluntary Service. See page 30 for registration details and addresses.*

COURIERS / REPS

BLADON LINES Personnel Department, 56-58 Putney High Street, London SW15 1SF
✆ 0181-785 2200

Opportunities for **representatives** to work in the ski resorts of Courmayeur,

Selva or La Thuile.
⊕ Ages 24+. Relevant experience an advantage, and fluent Italian essential. Applicants must be prepared to work hard but will get time to ski. December-May. Salary approx £50-£70 per week, board, lodging, return travel, insurance, ski pass and ski hire provided. Small charge made for uniform. Training course held in London before departure. *EEA nationals only.*

CANVAS HOLIDAYS LTD
12 Abbey Park Place, Dunfermline, Fife KY2 7PD
Resident **couriers, children's couriers, nannies** and **watersports couriers** needed to work on campsites for a holiday company providing accommodation for families in ready-erected fully equipped tents and mobile homes. Work involves a daily routine of tent cleaning as customers arrive and depart, providing information and advice on the local attractions and essential services, helping to sort out problems that might arise, and organising activities for the children and get-togethers for the families. 7 day week with no fixed hours; workload varies from day to day. At beginning and end of season there is a period of physical work when tents are put up and prepared for customers or taken down and stored for the winter. Other tasks include administration, book keeping and stock control.
⊕ Ages 18-25. Working knowledge of Italian essential. Applicants are normally those with a year between school and further education, undergraduates or graduates. They need to be reliable, self-motivated, able to turn their hand to new and varied tasks, and with a sense of humour. 6 months, April-October. Return travel, dependent on successful completion of contract, and accommodation in frame tents provided. Salary £85 per week. *Applications accepted anytime; interviews commence early November. UK nationals only.*

CLUB CANTABRICA HOLIDAYS LTD **Personnel Department, Holiday House, 146-148 London Road, St Albans, Hertfordshire AL1 1PQ** ✆ St Albans (01727) 833141
Organises holidays providing fully equipped tents and caravans. Requires **couriers** and **maintenance staff** to work from early May-early October.
⊕ Ages 21+. Previous experience an advantage, as is a good knowledge of Italian. 6 day week. Salary from £55 per week with bonus at end of the season. Self-catering accommodation in tents or caravans, travel costs from Watford and insurance provided. *Apply enclosing cv and SAE/IRCs. EEA nationals only.*

CRYSTAL HOLIDAYS **Crystal House, The Courtyard, Arlington Road, Surbiton, Surrey KT6 6BW** ✆ 0181-241 5111
Tour operator arranging air, rail and self-drive holidays to the Italian Lakes and winter skiing holidays in the Italian Alps. **Representatives** required to meet and greet clients and be responsible for their welfare during their holiday. **Ski guides** also needed during winter season.
⊕ Ages 22-35. Previous experience desirable and fluent Italian essential. Approx 60 hour, 7 day week, May-October and December-April. Basic salary plus commission, board, lodging, insurance, travel costs and uniform provided. 1 week training seminar held at beginning of each season.
Apply January/February for summer season, April/May for winter season.

EUROCAMP **Summer Jobs (Ref WH), PO Box 170, Liverpool L70 1ES** ✆ Knutsford (01565) 625522
One of Europe's leading tour operators, specialising in providing quality camping and mobile home holidays for families throughout Europe. **Campsite couriers** are required: work involves cleaning tents and equipment prior to the arrival of new customers; checking, replacing and making repairs on equipment; replenishing gas supplies; keeping basic accounts and reporting on

a weekly basis to England. Couriers are also expected to meet 'new arrivals and assist holidaymakers with any problems that arise; organise activities and parties; provide information on local tourist attractions and maintain an information noticeboard. At the beginning and end of the season couriers are also expected to help in erecting and dismantling tents. Couriers need to be flexible to meet the needs of customers and be on hand where necessary; they will be able to organise their own free time as the workload allows.

⊕ Ages 18+. Applicants should be independent, adaptable, reliable, physically fit, have plenty of initiative and relish a challenging and responsible position. Good working knowledge of Italian also necessary. Preference given to those able to work the whole season, April-September/October; contracts also available for first half season, April-mid July and second half season, mid July-September/October.

Children's couriers also required, with the energy and enthusiasm to organise a wide range of exciting activities for groups of children aged 4-13. Experience of working with this age range essential, but language ability is not a requirement. ⊕ Ages 18+. Must be available for whole season, May-September.

For both positions the salary is £95 per week. Training provided together with accommodation in frame tent with cooking facilities, insurance and return travel. 🕮 *Early application by telephone preferred; interviews start September/October. UK/EEA passport-holders only.*

HAVEN EUROPE Northney Marina, Northney Road, Hayling Island, Hampshire PO11 0NH
Tour operator organising self-drive package holidays, with accommodation in luxury mobile homes and tents.
Seasonal park managers required to work on parks in coastal and inland regions. Work involves preparing accommodation, welcoming guests and dealing with problems that may arise.
Tiger Club couriers also required to work with children and organise entertainment.
⊕ Ages 18+. Experience preferred but not essential as training is given. Knowledge of Italian essential. 40+ hour week, although hours vary. May-September. Salary according to workload. Accommodation provided in self-catering mobile homes or tents. Personal insurance and travel expenses provided. *UK nationals only.*

KEYCAMP HOLIDAYS 92-96 Lind Road, Sutton, Surrey SM1 4PL
✆ 0181-395 8170
One of the UK's largest self-drive camping and mobile home tour operators, offering holidays on over 100 campsites in Europe. **Campsite couriers** required to work in an outdoor environment. Main duties include providing information, organising social and sporting activities, cleaning mobile homes and tents, and providing activities for children.
⊕ Ages 18+. Knowledge of Italian desirable. March-July or July-September. Accommodation, uniform, training and competitive salary provided.
🕮 *Application requests by postcard. UK/EEA nationals only.*

SKIBOUND/TRAVELBOUND Olivier House, 18 Marine Parade, Brighton, East Sussex BN2 1TL
The largest independent group tour operator, specialising in winter sports tours for schools and adults, and in activity tours and excursions in spring/summer. **Area managers, hotel/chalet managers** and **representatives** required, December-April and May-August, in the Italian Alps. Posts involve a considerable amount of client contact; applicants must be presentable and keen to work hard.
⊕ Ages 21+. Good knowledge of Italian required for representatives and preferably for managers; previous experience an advantage. Insurance, travel and full board accommodation provided. Salary according to level of responsibility.

SIMPLY SKI Chiswick Gate,
598-608 Chiswick High Road,
London W4 5RT ✆ 0181-724 2541
Organises ski holidays in the Dolomites.
Representatives required to liaise with
clients and provide ski guidance.
⚜ Ages 22-40. Applicants should be able
skiers and speak fluent Italian. 54 hour
week; 20 weeks, December-April. Fully
comprehensive insurance, board and
accommodation provided. Salary £60
per week. Training provided. ✍ *Apply
as soon as possible.*

VENUE HOLIDAYS
21 Christchurch Road, Ashford,
Kent TN23 1XD
Small family company offering self-drive
holidays with fully-equipped tents,
caravans and chalets at campsites in
Tuscany and on the Venetian Riviera.
Representatives required to clean and
maintain accommodation, sort out
customers' problems and organise social
events for adults and children. At the
beginning and end of season reps assist
with the setting up and dismantling of
the operation. No fixed hours; workload
varies from day to day. Season lasts
April-October; minimum requirement to
work all of July and August.
⚜ Ages 18-30. Previous experience of
working with the public desirable, as is a
working knowledge of Italian or
German. Applicants should also be
physically fit, able to work in hot
conditions, mentally alert and practical,
with a pleasant, easy-going personality.
Salary approx £60 per week, with
possibility of bonuses. Tented
accommodation, insurance and return
fare provided. ✍ *Postal applications only.*

DOMESTIC

BLADON LINES Personnel
Department, 56-58 Putney High
Street, London SW15 1SF
✆ 0181-785 2200
Opportunities for **chalet girls** to work
in the ski resorts of Courmayeur, Selva
or La Thuile. The work involves cleaning
chalets, making beds, caring for guests,
shopping and preparing meals.
⚜ Ages 21+. Experience and/or
qualifications in catering or domestic
work essential, as is the ability to cook
well. Hours are very variable; applicants
must be prepared to work hard but will
get time to ski. Season lasts December-
May. Salary approx £45 per week,
board, lodging, return travel, insurance,
ski pass and ski hire provided. Small
charge made for uniform. One day
briefing held in London before
departure. *EEA nationals only.*

CRYSTAL HOLIDAYS Crystal
House, The Courtyard, Arlington
Road, Surbiton, Surrey KT6 6BW
✆ 0181-241 5111
Tour operator arranging winter skiing
holidays in the Italian Alps. **Chalet staff**
required to cook daily breakfast,
afternoon tea and 3-course evening
meal, and keep chalets clean and tidy.
⚜ Ages 20-35. Catering qualifications or
experience essential. Approx 60 hour,
6½ day week, December-April. Basic
salary plus commission; board, lodging,
insurance, travel costs and uniform
provided. 1 week training seminar held
at beginning of each season.
✍ *Apply April/May.*

FARMWORK

Seasonal farmwork is available through
local agricultural cooperatives, at *Ufficio
di Collocamento* (job centres) or by
applying direct to farms. Information on
local cooperatives, job centres and farms
is available by calling in person at *Centri
Informazione Giovani* (youth information
centres) in most major towns.
The harvesting seasons are:

May-August
Strawberries, cherries, peaches and
plums in Emilia Romagna

September-October
Apples and pears in Emilia Romagna,
Piemonte and Trentino

Grapes in Emilia Romagna, Lazio, Piemonte, Puglia, Trentino, Veneto and Toscana

November-December
Olives in Puglia, Toscana, Liguria, Calabria and Sicilia
Flowers in Liguria, Toscana, Lazio, Puglia
Tobacco in Umbria, Puglia and Campania

INTERNATIONAL FARM EXPERIENCE PROGRAMME
YFC Centre, N A C, Stoneleigh Park, Kenilworth, Warwickshire CV8 2LG ✆ (01203) 696584
Provides assistance to young **agriculturalists** and **horticulturalists** by finding places in farms/nurseries abroad, enabling them to broaden their knowledge of agricultural and horticultural methods. Participants usually live and work with a farming family and the work is matched as far as possible with participant's requirements. Entails physical work and practical involvement. Basic wage plus board and lodging. 3-12 months, all year.
⊕ Ages 18-28. Applicants must have at least 2 years practical experience, one of which may be at agricultural college, and intend to make a career in agriculture/ horticulture. Valid driving licence necessary. Participants pay own fares and insurance. Registration fee £85.
✍ *UK applications to IFEP; others to IFEP partner in home country.*

MONITORS, LEADERS & INSTRUCTORS

CLUB CANTABRICA HOLIDAYS LTD Overseas Department, Holiday House, 146-148 London Road, St Albans, Hertfordshire AL1 1PQ ✆ St Albans (01727) 833141
Organises camping holidays, providing fully equipped tents, caravans and mobile homes. **Kiddies club staff** are required

for the summer season, early May-early October.
⊕ Ages 21+. Nursing, teaching or NNEB qualifications and experience an advantage. 6 day week. Salary from £55 per week, plus bonus at end of season. Self-catering accommodation in tents and caravans, travel costs from Watford and insurance provided.
✍ *Apply enclosing cv and SAE/IRCs. EEA nationals only.*

PGL SKI EUROPE Brentham House, 45c High Street, Hampton Wick, Kingston-upon-Thames, Surrey KT1 4DG ✆ 0181-977 7755
A company with its own ski school operating holidays for groups and school parties. Part-time **ski instructors** required for winter sports in Piemonte. Work involves 6 hours teaching per day. BASI or full foreign qualifications essential, together with a high level of teaching skill. Knowledge of foreign languages useful but not essential; fluent English a prerequisite. 1-2 week periods over Christmas and the New Year, February and April. Instructors receive full board accommodation and ski pass plus travel expenses London/resort, and have access to the same facilities as the clients. Wages approx £90-£135 per week, depending on qualifications.
✍ *Interviews take place May-November.*

SKI ARDMORE 11-15 High Street, Marlow, Buckinghamshire SL7 1AU ✆ Marlow (01628) 890060
Organises skiing holidays for school groups in Bardonecchia.
Ski representatives/leaders required to help supervise groups of up to 10 children, organise and run evening activities and generally ensure a good trip. Experience of working with youngsters, some skiing experience and first aid qualifications preferable.
⊕ Ages 20+. Hours flexible; approx 60 hours per week. 1-8 weeks, December-April. Wages from £45 per week plus full board accommodation, insurance and travel costs. Training day held in December.

SUMMER CAMPS (British Institutes), via Matteotti 34, 18038 San Remo, Italy
©/⌨ (39 184) 50 60 70
Organises English language courses combined with multi-activity holidays for Italian children under 16 at summer camps in the pine forests and mountain areas of northern Italy.
Teaching staff are needed to teach English, develop creative thinking and stimulate appreciation of the natural environment. As well as teaching and supervising, work involves organising evening entertainment, a gala day and participating in camp duties. Activities include hill walking, sports, excursions, handicrafts and drama.
⊕ Ages 19+. Applicants should have English as their mother tongue, a genuine interest in children, be fun loving, energetic and have high moral standards. Experience of working with children necessary. TEFL qualifications and knowledge of Italian useful.
Also opportunities for **actors** and **sports/survival instructors**.
65-75 hours per week, mid June-end August. Salary £350 per month, plus full board accommodation and insurance.

WORKCAMPS

EMMAUS ITALIA Segretariato Campi Lavoro, via Castelnuovo 21/B, 50047 Prato, Italy
Volunteers are needed to join international workcamps in various towns throughout Italy, organised by individual Emmaus communities which are self-supporting through recycling raw materials and old items. This involves collecting, sorting and selling paper, books, clothes, furniture, household apparatus, ironware and metals. Proceeds from the sale of items is often directed to development projects in the Third World. The camps aim to create a community in each place.
⊕ Ages 18+. Volunteers should be committed to community living and solidarity. 8 hour day, 6 day week.

3+ weeks, June-September. Board, accommodation and accident insurance provided, but volunteers pay their own travel costs and should take a sleeping bag and work clothes.

MOVIMENTO CRISTIANO PER LA PACE via Marco Dino Rossi 12/C, 00173 Rome, Italy
Volunteers are invited to work in international teams on summer projects aimed at offering a service in an area of need and promoting self-help within the community; promoting international understanding and the discussion of social problems; and offering young people the chance to live as a group and take these experiences into the context of daily life. Recent projects have included organising and animating a festival in an isolated Calabrian village; staging anti-racist theatrical performances in Rome; and working alongside handicapped young people on an organic farm in Reggio Emilia.
⊕ Ages 18-26. Knowledge of Italian may be required. 6 hour day, 5/6 day week. 2-4 weeks, July-August. Food and shared accommodation provided, but participants pay own travel costs, and should take out full insurance.

📝 *Apply through partner organisation in country of residence. In the UK: Christian Movement for Peace or United Nations Association International Youth Service. See page 30 for registration details and addresses.*

SERVIZIO CIVILE INTERNATIONALE via dei Laterani 28, 00184 Rome, Italy
Service Civil International promotes international reconciliation through work projects. **Volunteers** are needed to work in international teams on various workcamps usually combining work of a manual and social nature. Recent projects have included working in Taranto to collect information and raise awareness about human rights abuses in East Timor; painting murals on the theme of peace in Cagliari; and helping

with preparations for an African theatre festival in Ferrara. Most camps include a study element on ecology, peace and disarmament.

⊕ Ages 18+. Applicants should be highly motivated, preferably with previous workcamp or other voluntary work experience, and prepared to work hard as part of a team. Knowledge of Italian useful. 40 hour week. 2-4 weeks, June-September. Food, shared accommodation and work accident insurance provided. No fares or wages paid. **B D PH** depending on project.

🕮 *Apply through partner organisation in country of residence.*
In the UK: International Voluntary Service. See page 30 for registration details and addresses.

SOCI COSTRUTTORI via Mazza 48, 20071 Casalpusterlengo (MI), Italy

An international volunteers association with the aims of fighting misery and distress and making a contribution towards a better understanding between nations. **Volunteers** are needed on workcamps; projects involve living and working in small communities, often rural, which are socially or economically underprivileged. Recent projects have included renovating a country school in Ferrara for use as workshops for young disabled people; turning an old hamlet near Perugia into a reception centre for Third World refugees; and laying a footpath and building a play area at a holiday centre for children with handicaps in Gubbio. Importance is given to volunteers understanding the significance and purpose of each project and realising the importance of their personal contribution.

⊕ Ages 18+. 40-48 hour, 5 day week. 3 weeks, July-September. Food, prepared by the volunteers, and tent, family, school or centre accommodation provided, but volunteers should take sleeping bags. No fares or wages paid. Registration fee payable.
🕮 *Apply 2 months in advance.*

GENERAL

COMUNITA' DI AGAPE Centro Ecumenico, Segreteria, 10060 Prali, Torino, Italy

An international ecumenical community centre in a remote part of the Italian Alps, used for national and international conferences, study camps, courses and other meetings on ecological, peace, Third World, political, cultural, theological and women's issues.
An international service group made up of **volunteers** works alongside the resident community during the summer months. The work is varied and can include kitchen duties, housework, cleaning, working in the coffee bar or laundry, babysitting, maintenance, construction or repair work. There are opportunities for volunteers to take part in the conferences. Applicants should be willing to make a contribution to the collective life of the community.
⊕ Ages 18+. Knowledge of at least basic Italian useful. 36 hour, 6 day week. 1+ months, June-September. Volunteers are sometimes taken on outside the summer period. Insurance and full board accommodation and insurance provided. Volunteers pay own travel costs. Anti-tetanus vaccination advised.
🕮 *Apply February/March. Only 7-8 places per month.*

EUROYOUTH LTD
301 Westborough Road, Westcliff, Southend-on-Sea SS0 9PT
✆ Southend-on-Sea (01702) 341434

Holiday stays arranged where **guests** are offered board and lodging in return for an agreed number of hours English conversation with hosts or their children. Time also available for guests to practise Italian if desired.
⊕ Mainly ages 18-25, but there are sometimes opportunities for older applicants. 2-3 weeks, mainly July/August. Travel and insurance paid by applicants. Registration fee approx £70.
🕮 *Apply at least 12 weeks prior to scheduled departure. UK nationals only.*

jAPAN

INFO

Japanese Embassy
101-104 Piccadilly, London W1V 9FN
✆ 0171-465 6500

British Embassy
1 Ichiban-cho, Chiyoda-ku, Tokyo 102
✆ (81 3) 3265 6340

Tourist office
Japan National Tourist Organisation,
167 Regent Street, London W1R 7FD
✆ 0171-734 9638

Youth hostels
Japan Youth Hostel Association, 3F
Hoken Kaikan Honkan Building, 1-2,
khigaya-Sadoharacho, Shinjuku-Ku, Tokyo
162 ✆ (81 3) 3269 5831

Youth & student information
International Student Association of
Japan, Tokyo Chapter, c/o Kokusai
Kyoiku, Shinko-kai, 1-21 Yotsu Ya,
Shinjuku-ku, Tokyo 160

Entry regulations A visa is required
for all types of employment. This can
only be obtained once a job has been
secured and application must be made
from outside Japan. Before granting a
visa the Japanese Embassy will require
various documents, including the
applicant's valid passport; a completed
and signed Visa Application Form; a
passport-sized photograph; and a
Certificate of Eligibility issued by the
Ministry of Justice in Japan and provided
by the future employer or sponsor. In
certain cases additional support
documents may be required.

If entering Japan by the Polar Route via
Moscow no vaccinations are necessary;
however, if any countries on the
Southern Hemisphere Route have been
visited, vaccination against cholera is
strongly recommended. For further
details, contact the Consular Section of
the Embassy.

Job advertising Publicitas Ltd, 517/523 Fulham Road, London SW6 1HD ✆ 0171-385 7723 can place job advertisements in *Nihon Keizai Shimbun*, the leading financial business daily.

Travel Campus Travel can arrange low-cost, flexible student/youth fares to Tokyo. Offices throughout the UK, including a student travel centre at 52 Grosvenor Gardens, London SW1V 0AG (opposite Victoria Station) ✆ 0171-730 8111 or ✆ 0131-668 3303 for Scottish telephone bookings.

Council Travel, 28A Poland Street, London W1V 3DB ✆ 0171-437 7767 (offices also in Paris, Nice, Lyon, Munich, Düsseldorf, Tokyo, Singapore and throughout the US) offers low-cost student/youth airfares to Tokyo, plus travel insurance, guidebooks and travel gear.

North-South Travel Ltd, Moulsham Mill, Parkway, Chelmsford CM2 7PX ✆ Chelmsford (01245) 492882 arranges competitively priced, reliably planned flights to Japan. All profits given to projects in the developing world.

The Japan Rail pass provides first class or economy travel passes throughout the Japanese rail network. Available for 7, 14 or 21 days; cost from £172, economy. Details from Long-Haul Leisurail, PO Box 113, Bretton, Peterborough, Cambridgeshire PE3 8HY ✆ Peterborough (01733) 335599.

Publications Lonely Planet's guide *Japan - A Travel Survival Kit* £13.95, is an essential handbook for travellers, offering practical, down-to-earth information for people wanting to explore beyond the usual tourist routes.

Culture Shock! Japan £6.95 introduces the reader to the people, customs, ceremonies, food and culture of Japan, with checklists of dos and don'ts.

Both available from good bookshops.

Your Guide to Japan is a 35 page booklet containing notes on climate, currency accommodation, travel to and within Japan, places of interest, what to do, including festivals, arts and traditional sports plus general information. Available from the Japan National Tourist Organisation, see above. Maps, guides/ pamphlets and a variety of other tourist literature also available.

Making It In Japan £8.95 is a guide to every aspect of working in Japan including makingpreparations, job hunting and finding accommodation, with essential background information on Japanese culture and way of life. Available from Vacation Work, 9 Park End Street, Oxford OX1 1HJ ✆ Oxford (01865) 241978.

Jobs in Japan US$14.95 + $5 airmail has information and advice for English-speakers wishing to work in Japan. Most opportunities are in the teaching field, but details of other possibilities are also given. Appendix includes list of employment sources, private English language schools, international schools and survival Japanese. Published by Global Press, 697 College Parkway, Rockville, MD 20850, United States. Available in the UK from Vacation Work, see above.

FARMWORK

INTERNATIONAL AGRICULTURAL EXCHANGE ASSOCIATION YFC Centre, N A C, Stoneleigh Park, Kenilworth, Warwickshire CV8 2LG ✆ Coventry (01203) 696578 Operates opportunities for young people involved with **agriculture**, **horticulture** or **home management** to acquire practical work experience in the rural sector, and to strengthen and improve their knowledge and understanding of the way of life in other countries. Participants are given an opportunity to study practical methods on approved training farms and work as trainees, gaining further experience in their chosen field. Types of farm include pig, dairy or beef farms, horticulture in apple orchards, or enterprises growing mixed vegetables or cucumbers. Participants undertake paid work on the farm, approx 48 hours per week, and live as a member of the host family. Full board and lodging, insurance cover and a minimum net weekly wage of £80 provided. All programmes include at least 3-4 weeks unpaid holiday. 10 day orientation seminar held at the beginning of each programme.

⊕ Ages 18-30. Applicants should be single, have good practical experience in the chosen training category, plus a valid driving licence. 4, 8 and 12 months (departing April). Cost from £2,400 covers airfare, administration fee, work permit, orientation seminar, information meetings, insurance, supervision, placement with a host family and travel to placement. £200 deposit payable.

Apply at least 6 months in advance. UK or Irish passport-holders only.

Japanese applicants requiring an exchange should apply to IAEA Japan, Doeru Aoyagi II-203 Aoyagi 521, Maebashi Gunma 371.

T E A C H E R S

English in Asia US$12.95 + $5 airmail is a useful guide for TEFL teachers, including sections on English teaching methods, common student errors, ideas for games and classroom activities, together with the addresses of private English language schools in Japan and other Asian countries, and tips on visas and living in these countries. Published by Global Press, 697 College Parkway, Rockville, MD 20850, United States and available in the UK from Vacation Work, 9 Park End Street, Oxford OX1 1HJ ✆ Oxford (01865) 241978, price £8.95 plus £1.50 postage.

JAPAN EXCHANGE AND TEACHING (JET) PROGRAMME

JET Programme Desk, Council on International Educational Exchange, 33 Seymour Place, London W1H 6AT ✆ 0171-224 8896

Seeks to promote mutual understanding between Japan and other countries, and foster international perspectives by promoting international exchange at local levels and foreign language education in Japan. Conducted under the co-sponsorship of local government authorities and the Ministries of Foreign Affairs, Education and Home Affairs. Vacancies for **Assistant Language Teachers**, to assist in English lessons taught by Japanese foreign language teachers, prepare teaching materials and participate in extracurricular activities, under the guidance of Japanese academic staff. Placements are mostly in lower and upper secondary schools. Teaching experience or training not required. Knowledge of Japanese not essential, but candidates are expected to devote some effort to learning the language before they leave for Japan and whilst they are there. Before departure successful candidates receive written materials on the programme and on basic Japanese and attend pre-departure orientation; further orientation provided in Tokyo. British nationals only, in principle aged ⊕ under 35 and holding at least a Bachelor's degree. One year contracts commencing mid/late July; may be renewed for up to 2 further years in certain circumstances by mutual consent. Salary ¥3,600,000 per year, usually tax free; approx 12 days' paid leave plus Japanese national holidays. Average 40 hour week. Return air ticket provided. Assistance given in finding accommodation.

Application forms available late September. Closing date early December; interviews January/February in London or Edinburgh. Nationals of Ireland, Canada, France, Germany, United States, Australia, New Zealand, China and Korea should apply to the Japanese Embassy in their country.

SHIN SHIZEN JUKU Tsurui-Mura, Akan Gun, Hokkaido 085 12, Japan
℗ (81 154) 64 28 21

A small organic farm community recruiting a limited number of **volunteers** to work on the farm and to teach conversational English in surrounding towns and villages. ⊕ Ages 18+. No qualifications necessary, although teaching skills are a bonus. Volunteers should be English-speaking and open to cultural exchange. Knowledge of Japanese helpful. Volunteers pay own travel and insurance costs, and work approx 5-6 hours per week teaching and 50 hours per month helping on the farm, in return for accommodation and ¥10,000 monthly allowance. Plenty of free time for sightseeing and learning about Japanese language and culture.
🕮 Apply at least 1 month in advance.

No fares or wages paid. **B D PH W**

🕮 Apply through partner organisation in country of residence.
In the UK: International Voluntary Service, Quaker International Social Projects or United Nations Association International Youth Service. See page 30 for registration details and addresses.

WORKCAMPS

NEVER-ENDING INTERNATIONAL WORKCAMPS EXCHANGE (NICE) 501 Viewcity, 2-2-1 Shinjuku, Shinjuku-ku, Tokyo 160, Japan

A relatively new workcamp organisation, established by young Japanese who have participated in projects in Europe and the United States over the past few years. **Volunteers** are invited to take part in international workcamps. Recent projects have included helping with haymaking and flower cultivation in Yuri; building small boats to be used in a sea cleaning exercise in Numazu; living and working in a Buddhist temple and organising a summer festival in Hikama; helping with litter control on Mount Fuji; and working in the rice fields at an eco-village in Miasa. ⊕ Ages 18+. 2-3 weeks, August and September. Food and accommodation provided, but volunteers may have to contribute US$50 towards the cost of each project, in addition to any registration fee levied by the organisation through which they apply.

When writing to any organisation it is essential to mention Working Holidays 1995 and enclose a stamped, self-addressed A4 envelope, or if in another country, an addressed A4 envelope and at least two IRCs (International Reply Coupons, available from post offices). Enquiries received without SAEs/IRCs are unlikely to be answered.

LATIN AMERICA & CARIBBEAN

INFO

Argentine Embassy
53 Hans Place, London SW1X 0LA
℡ 0171-584 6494

Belize High Commission
10 Harcourt House, 19a Cavendish
Square, London W1M 9AD
℡ 0171-499 9728

Bolivian Embassy
106 Eaton Square, London SW1W 9AD
℡ 0171-235 4248/2257

Brazilian Embassy
32 Green Street, Mayfair, London W1Y
4AT ℡ 0171-499 0877

Chilean Embassy
12 Devonshire Street, London W1N
2DS ℡ 0171-580 6392

Costa Rica Embassy
2nd Floor, 36 Upper Brook Street,
London W1Y 1PE ℡ 0171-495 3985
Consular Section: Flat 2, 38 Redcliffe
Square, London SW10 ℡ 0171-373
7973

Cuban Embassy
167 High Holborn, London WC1V 6PA
℡ 0171-240 2488

Ecuador Embassy
Flat 3b, 3 Hans Crescent, Knightsbridge,
London SW1X 0LS ℡ 0171-584 1267

Grenada High Commission
1 Collingham Gardens, London SW5
0AW ℡ 0171-373 7808/9

Jamaican High Commission
1-2 Prince Consort Road, London SW7
2BZ ℡ 0171-823 9911

Mexican Embassy
42 Hertford Street, Mayfair, London
W1Y 7TF ℡ 0171-499 8586

Nicaraguan Embassy
8 Gloucester Road, London SW7 4PP
℡ 0171-584 4365

Paraguay Embassy
Braemar Lodge, Cornwall Gardens,
London SW7 4AQ ✆ 0171-937 1253

Peruvian Embassy
52 Sloane Street, London SW1X 9SP
✆ 0171-235 1917/2545/3802

Entry regulations Details of work
permits and entry requirements can be
obtained in Britain from the embassies
listed above.

Job advertising Frank L Crane
(London) Ltd, International Press
representatives, 5/15 Cromer Street,
Grays Inn Road, London WC1H 8LS
✆ 0171-837 3330 can place job
advertisements in the *Buenos Aires
Herald*, Latin America's leading English
daily; also in a variety of Brazilian
newspapers and magazines.

Travel Campus Travel offers flexible low
cost student/youth fares to various
destinations in Latin America. Also offer
internal flights, air passes and tours.
Offices throughout the UK, including 52
Grosvenor Gardens, London SW1W
OAG ✆ 0171-730 8111 or ✆ 0131-668
3303 for Scottish telephone bookings.

Council Travel, 28A Poland Street,
London W1V 3DB ✆ 0171-437 7767
(offices also in Paris, Nice, Lyon, Munich,
Düsseldorf, Tokyo, Singapore and
throughout the US) offers low cost
student/youth airfares to destinations
throughout Latin America plus travel
insurance, guidebooks and travel gear.

North-South Travel Ltd, Moulsham Mill,
Parkway, Chelmsford CM2 7PX
✆ Chelmsford (01245) 492882 arranges
competitively priced, reliably planned
flights to all parts of Latin America. All
profits given to projects in the
developing world.

STA Travel, 86 Old Brompton Road,
London SW7 3LQ/117 Euston Road,
London NW1 2SX ✆ 0171-937 9962
(offices also in Birmingham, Bristol,

Cambridge, Glasgow, Leeds, Manchester
and Oxford) operates flexible, low-cost
flights between London and destinations
throughout Latin America. Internal
flights, accommodation and tours also
available.

Publications *Latin America: a guide to
employment and opportunities for young
people* offers advice and contacts for
those seeking long and short term
teaching posts, office work, voluntary
work, expeditions and cheap travel.
Available from the Hispanic & Luso
Brazilian Council, Canning House,
2 Belgrave Square, London SW1X 8PJ
✆ 0171-235 2303. Price £3 (free to
members).

Lonely Planet's travel guides offer
practical, down-to-earth information for
people wanting to explore beyond the
usual tourist routes. Titles include *South
America on a Shoestring* £16.95, *Central
America on a Shoestring* £10.95, *Travel
Survival Kits* to *Argentina, Uruguay &
Paraguay* £10.95, *Bolivia* £10.95, *Brazil*
£10.95, *Chile & Easter Island* £9.95,
Colombia £7.95, *Costa Rica* £8.95,
Ecuador & the Galapagos Islands £10.95,
Guatemala, Belize and Yucatan £10.95,
Mexico £12.95 and *Peru* £8.95.

Rough Guides provide comprehensive
background information on cities and
countries worldwide, plus details on
getting there, getting around, places to
explore and cheap places to stay. Titles
include *Brazil* £7.95, *Guatemala & Belize*
£9.99, *Mexico* £10.99 and *Peru* £7.95.

Vacation Work's *The Traveller's Survival Kit
Central America* £8.95, and *The Traveller's
Survival Kit South America* £12.95 are
detailed handbooks containing
information on where it's safe to go,
budget travel and accommodation, eating
and drinking. *The Travellers Survival Kit
Cuba* £9.95 gives full information for
visitors on how to get there, eating out,
where to stay, how to get around, what
to see and what to do, and includes a set
of 20 maps.

Michael's Guide to South America £15.95, is detailed and concise, providing invaluable practical advice for all kinds of travellers. Smaller *Michael's Guides* to various areas of Latin America also available, price £9.95. Each guide is illustrated throughout with colour photographs and maps. Published by Inbal Travel.

All the above are available from good bookshops and the larger travel chains.

ARCHAEOLOGY

EARTHWATCH EUROPE Belsyre Court, 57 Woodstock Road, Oxford © Oxford (01865) 516366
Aims to support field research in a wide range of disciplines including ornithology, animal behaviour, archaeology, nature conservation and ecology. Support is given to researchers as a grant and in the form of volunteer assistance. Recent projects involving **volunteers** have included finding evidence of Jamaica's renegade Maroons; discovering how the Incas ruled an area in Argentina; and excavating ancient Mayan architecture in Belize.
✦ Ages 16-80. 2-3 weeks, all year. No special skills required although each expedition may, because of its nature, demand some talent or quality of fitness. Volunteers should be generally fit, able to cope with new situations and work with people of different ages and backgrounds, and a sense of humour will help. Members share the costs of the expedition, from £340-£2,000, which includes meals, transport and necessary field equipment, but does not include the cost of travel to the staging area, although assistance may be given in arranging it. Membership fee £25 entitles members to join an expedition, attend evening and weekend events, and receive magazines and newsletters providing all the information necessary to choose a project. **B D PH W** depending on project.

COMMUNITY WORK

AMERICAN FRIENDS SERVICE COMMITTEE Human Resources Department, 1501 Cherry Street, Philadelphia, PA 19102, United States
A Quaker organisation undertaking programmes of relief, service and education. **Volunteers** are needed for manual and educational work on community service projects in villages in Mexico and occasionally other Latin American countries, living and working with the community, cooperating with local organisations in projects involving constructing and repairing schools, irrigation systems, clinics and roads. Other work includes reforestation, gardening, nutrition and health. Projects follow the patterns of village life, and volunteers must fit into and respect local customs. Groups consist of about 15 volunteers; half of the leaders and volunteers are Mexican. Participants live as a group, sharing in work and tasks such as cooking, carrying water and weekly market trips. Work can be physically and psychologically strenuous. Each unit responds to its situation with creativity and flexibility; projects develop from the participants' initiatives/skills.
✦ Ages 18-26. Applicants should be fluent in Spanish, healthy, willing to adapt to group living, prepared to respond positively to the unexpected and have had some workcamp or community experience. Construction, gardening, arts, crafts, childcare or recreation experience useful. 7 weeks, July-August. Cost approx US$750 includes orientation conferences, food, accommodation in schools or unused buildings and insurance. Travel and pocket money not provided. Registration fee US$75. Limited scholarships available. ✎ *Apply by 1 March.*

Also organises a 3-week summer programme in Cuba, where participants help on small farms near Havana, planting and tending sugar and food crops, with evenings devoting to music, cultural and discussion programmes. ⊕ Ages 18-28. Applicants must be mature, open-minded, fluent in Spanish, with community or church activist experience. Participation fee US$300 does not include round-trip travel. ✎ Apply by mid March.

AMIGOS DE LAS AMERICAS
5618 Star Lane, Houston, TX 77057, United States
An international non-profitmaking, private voluntary organisation that provides leadership development opportunities for young people, improved community health for the people of Latin America and better cross-cultural understanding on both American continents. **Volunteers** are needed to work in teams in schools, health clinics and house-to-house in countries including Brazil, Mexico, Costa Rica, the Dominican Republic, Ecuador, Honduras and Paraguay. In addition to providing technical knowledge and supplies, volunteers assume leadership roles as health educators. Projects include animal health and rabies inoculation; human immunisation; oral rehydration therapy; community sanitation and dental hygiene. ⊕ Ages 16+. Volunteers must complete a training programme. One year of secondary school Spanish required. 4-8 weeks, mid June-mid August. Volunteers live with families or in schools or clinics; food provided by the community. Cost US$2,300-$2,900, depending on the region, includes international travel between US and Latin America, board, lodging, in-country travel, supplies and training materials. Volunteers arrange and pay for domestic travel to point of departure, and are advised to take out health insurance.

GLOBAL CITIZENS NETWORK
1931 Iglehart Avenue, St Paul, MN 55104, United States
℅ (1 612) 644 0960
Seeks to create a network of people committed to shared values of peace,

justice, tolerance, cross-cultural understanding and global cooperation, and sends teams of **volunteers** to rural communities in Belize, Guatemala and St Vincent to assist in development. Volunteers work on projects initiated by the community for the benefit of the community: building a health clinic, setting up a day care centre, teaching pre-school children and restoration work. Generally 5-6 hour day, 5 day week with weekends free; 2-3 weeks, all year. Full board accommodation provided in local homes or centres. ⊕ Ages 16+ unless accompanied. Teaching, health care and construction skills always in demand but not essential. Volunteers must be willing to experience and accept new cultures. Knowledge of Spanish an advantage. Cost US$900-$1,300 includes board, accommodation, in-country travel, project materials, and orientation. Volunteers arrange and pay for own international travel and insurance. ✎ Applications received 2 months in advance get $50 discount; late fee of $25 charged on applications received within 2 weeks of departure date.

CONSERVATION

ARTEMIS CLOUDFOREST PRESERVE Apdo 937, 2050 San Pedro, Montes de Oca, Costa Rica
℅ (506) 253 7243
A recently established, private cloudforest preserve in the Talamanca mountains of Costa Rica. Situated at an elevation of 8,800 feet, comprises 25 hectares of primary forest and home to a great diversity of trees, flowers, birds and insects. The owners wish to protect the forest and open it up to visitors. **Volunteers** required to build a trail system, help with the reafforestation of cleared areas and share in maintenance, and gardening tasks. ⊕ Ages 18+. No experience necessary but relevant skills welcome and fluent English or Spanish essential. 6 hour day, 5 day week or 10 days followed by 4 days off. 1+ months, all year.

Contribution of US$125 per week to cover meals, accommodation and laundry. Vegetarians and non-vegetarians catered for. Volunteers must take their own sleeping bag, wellingtons or hiking boots, warm clothing and waterproofs, and pay own travel and insurance.
🕮 *Apply enclosing US$125 returnable deposit at least 2 months in advance.*

CORAL CAY CONSERVATION LTD The Ivy Works, 154 Clapham Park Road, London SW4 7DE
Established in 1986 to assist the Belize Government in managing and protecting coastal resources threatened by recent booms in tourism and fisheries.
Volunteers are required to assist scientific expeditions in surveying the Belize Barrier Reef, which is unique in the western hemisphere as regards its size and variety of reef types and pristine corals.
⊕ Ages 16+. No scientific background required; training in survey techniques given. Volunteers must be members of the British Sub-Aqua Club or have proof of diving ability through another recognised training agency. Approx 60 hour week, 4-12 weeks all year. Subject to weather conditions, two survey dives take place per day under the supervision of qualified marine scientists. Expedition members also share responsibility for organising dive teams, preparing and maintaining equipment, and domestic tasks. Some weekends free for recreational diving, watersports or visits to rainforests, Mayan ruins or jaguar and howler monkey reserves. Cost from £1,725 for 4 weeks includes return flight, transit accommodation, full board basic accommodation on site and scientific training. Volunteers must take adequate medical precautions and supply own diving kit.

EARTHWATCH EUROPE Belsyre Court, 57 Woodstock Road, Oxford
✆ **Oxford (01865) 516366**
Aims to support field research in a wide range of disciplines including archaeology, ornithology, animal behaviour, conservation and ecology. Support is given to researchers as a grant and in the form of volunteer assistance. Recent expeditions involving **volunteers** have included recording the behaviour of katydids in the Amazon rainforests of Peru; monitoring sea turtles in Brazil; and studying red howler monkeys in Venezuela.
⊕ Ages 16-75. No special skills required although each expedition may, because of its nature, demand some talent or quality of fitness. Volunteers should be generally fit, able to cope with new situations, work with people of different ages and backgrounds, and a sense of humour will help. 2-3 weeks, all year. Members share costs of from £340-£2,000, which includes meals, transport and all necessary field equipment, but does not include cost of travel to staging area, although assistance may be given. Membership fee £25 entitles members to join an expedition, attend evening and weekend events, and receive magazines and newsletters providing all information necessary to choose a project. **B D PH W** depending on project.

GENESIS II - TALAMANCA CLOUD FOREST Apdo 655, 7.050 Cartago, Costa Rica
Volunteers are needed to help with new trail routing, construction, maintenance and upgrade work on existing trails, in a rare tropical white oak cloud forest in the mountains of Costa Rica. The forest is situated at a height of 2,360m and is being preserved for academic research and recreational activities such as bird-watching.
⊕ Ages 21+. Experience preferred, but not essential as training can be given. All nationalities welcome; some knowledge of Spanish helpful. 30 hour week, for 4+ weeks, all year. Volunteers contribute US$125 per week to cover dormitory style accommodation, all meals and laundry facilities, but make own travel and insurance arrangements.
🕮 *Only fully fit and dedicated people need apply; competition for places is strong.*

NICARAGUA SOLIDARITY CAMPAIGN The Red Rose Club, 129 Seven Sisters Road, London N7 7QG ℂ 0171-272 9619

An organisation set up in 1978, dedicated to building support for the FSLN (Sandinista party) and popular organisations in Nicaragua. **Volunteers** are invited to join environmental brigades organised by NSC and the Environmental Network for Nicaragua. Work involves planting trees, terracing and soil conservation. Skills in ecology or biology welcome but not essential. ⊕ Ages 18+. Volunteers must be fit, ready to learn and prepared to adapt to living and working in very basic conditions. They should also be committed to supporting the work being done in Nicaragua on their return. Activists in the labour/environmental movements and people from ethnic minorities particularly encouraged to apply. 30 hour week. Two brigades each summer, 4 weeks, July/August; and one in winter, 4 weeks, December/January. 3 day programme of visits and talks included. Cost approx £1,100 covers air fare, insurance, local transport, food and accommodation. Advice given on fundraising and/or sponsorship. **B D PH** accepted, depending on ability. ▧ Apply 3 months in advance. UK residents only.

LEADERS & GUIDES

TAMBOPATA JUNGLE LODGE Inversiones Maldonado SA, Casilla 454, Cusco, Peru ℂ (51 84) 22 57 01 ▭ (51 84) 23 89 11

Jungle lodge located in the rainforest of southern Peru. Operates short trails and longer nature programmes. **Trail guides** needed to guide groups of guests on their various day and night activities; some trail maintenance work also involved. ⊕ Ages 22-65. Background in botany, biology, zoology or similar is useful, as is previous guiding experience. General information and reading lists sent to participants in advance. Applicants should be outgoing, enjoy outdoor activities and speak English, German or Spanish. Approx 50 hour week, 20 day month with 10 days free; minimum 90 days. Work available all year round. Board and accommodation provided plus US$150 per month spending money, and return domestic airfare from Lima or Cusco. Applicants must make own arrangements regarding international travel, insurance and visas. ▧ Apply as early as possible; summer positions fill up very quickly.

WORKCAMPS

CUBA SOLIDARITY CAMPAIGN The Red Rose Club, 129 Seven Sisters Road, London N7 7QG ℂ 0171-263 6452

Offers western Europeans a unique way of seeing life in Cuba and of learning how the people have organised their society since the revolution in 1959. **Volunteers** needed for agricultural and construction work in the Caimito area of Havana province. As well as tending and picking fruit, the Campaign has contributed to the construction of a polytechnic, housing for textile workers and a college for building workers. ⊕ Ages 17+. Volunteers must be fit. 4½ day, 35 hour week, July or September-October. Participants work for 2 weeks and spend the final week travelling around. If possible, 2 days per week are spent visiting factories, schools, hospitals, industry, agriculture and seeing Havana and its surroundings. Full programme of activities organised including lectures, concerts and films. Applications encouraged from those who have undertaken active political work within ethnic groups, the women's movement, industry, the Labour movement and solidarity organisations. Cost to participants approx £700 covers airfare, food, hostel accommodation, insurance and travel within Cuba, allowing approx £100 for pocket money. Compulsory orientation weekends organised. **B D** ✉ *Apply by end March.*

GENERAL

BRITISH UNIVERSITIES NORTH AMERICA CLUB (BUNAC)
16 Bowling Green Lane, London
ECIR OBD ✆ **0171-251 3472**
A non-profit, non-political educational student club venture which aims to encourage interest and understanding between students in Britain and the Americas. Operates a small programme in Jamaica for adventurous people for whom the unique experience gained is more important than the money earned. The programme is open to **full-time degree/HND students**
⚭ Ages 18+. Work is available for the summer months, from end June onwards. Orientation programmes held throughout Britain give advice on finding and choosing a job, obtaining a visa, income tax, accommodation, travel food and budgeting. Cost approx £1,000, depending on departure date, includes administration fees, insurance and round trip flight to Montego Bay. Applicants will need to show proof of purchase of £250 travellers cheques.
✉ *Application forms available January; apply by 30 April. EEA nationals only.*

APPLYING FOR A JOB

When writing to **any** organisation it is **essential** to mention **Working Holidays 1995** and enclose a **stamped, self-addressed A4 envelope**, or if in another country, an **addressed A4 envelope** and at least two **IRCs** (International Reply Coupons, available from post offices). Enquiries received without SAEs/IRCs are **unlikely** to be answered. **Before applying**, read carefully all the information given. Pay **particular** attention to:

✍ skills/qualifications/experience required

✍ the period of employment expected

✍ age limits or nationality restrictions

✍ application deadlines

✍ any other points, especially details of insurance cover, and other costs such as travel and accommodation.

When applying include the following:

✍ your name, address, date of birth, marital status, nationality, sex

✍ details of your education, qualifications, relevant experience, skills, languages spoken

✍ your period of availability for work

✍ a passport-size photo, particularly if you will be working with the public

✍ anything else recommended in the listing (such as a *cv*)

LUXEMBOURG

INFO

Luxembourg Embassy
27 Wilton Crescent, London SW1X
8SD ℅ 0171-235 6961

British Embassy
14 boulevard Roosevelt, 2450
Luxembourg ℅ (352) 22 98 64/65/66

Tourist office
Luxembourg Tourist Office, 122 Regent
Street, London W1R 5FE
℅ 0171-434 2800

Youth hostels
Centrale des Auberges de Jeunesse
Luxembourgeoises, 18 place d'Armes,
2346 Luxembourg ℅ (352) 25588

Youth & student information
Centre Information Jeunes asbl,
76 boulevard de la Petrusse, 2320
Luxembourg

Union Nationale des Étudiants
Luxembourgeois, 20 avenue
Marie-Thérèse, 2132 Luxembourg

Entry regulations UK citizens
intending to work in Luxembourg should
have full passports. UK/EEA nationals
may stay in Luxembourg for up to 3
months; those wishing to stay longer
must apply to the local police for a
residence permit. Non-EEA nationals
must have a job and a work permit
(*Déclaration Patronale*), and have *Permis
de Séjour* stamped in their passport
before entering Luxembourg. French
and German, in addition to
Letzeburgesch, are commonly used in
business and industry, and anyone
seeking employment should have a good
knowledge of at least one of these.

Job advertising *Lëtzebuerger Journal*,
rue A Fischer 123, PO Box 2101, 1251
Luxembourg is a leading daily newspaper
which will accept job advertisements.

Luxemburger Wort, rue Christophe-

Plantin, 2988 Gasperich-Luxembourg is the largest Luxembourg daily newspaper accepting job advertisements.

Travel Freedom Pass allows 3, 5 or 10 days unlimited rail travel in 1 month on the railways of Luxembourg. Cost from £11 (under 26) or £14 (26+). Available from British Rail International Rail Centre, Victoria Station, London SW1V 1JY © 0171-834 2345.

Campus Travel can arrange Eurotrain, Inter-Rail and student/youth fares for travel to Luxembourg. Offices throughout the UK including a student travel centre at 52 Grosvenor Gardens, London SW1W 0AG (opposite Victoria Station) © 0171-730 3402 or © 0131-668 3303 for Scottish bookings.

Council Travel, 28A Poland Street, London W1V 3DB © 0171-287 3337 (offices also in Paris, Nice, Lyon, Munich, Düsseldorf, Tokyo, Singapore and throughout the US) offers Eurotrain under 26 fares and youth/student airfares to Luxembourg plus travel insurance, guidebooks and travel gear.

The Benelux Tourrail Card entitles holders to 5 days unlimited travel, within a specified period of 1 month, on the national railway networks of Luxembourg, Belgium and the Netherlands and on the Luxembourg CFL/CRL country buses. Cost from £60 (under 26) or from £80 (26+). Details from Netherlands Railways, 25/28 Buckingham Gate, London SW1E 6LD © 0171-630 1735.

Publications *The Rough Guide to Holland, Belgium and Luxembourg* £9.99 provides comprehensive information plus details on getting around, places to explore and cheap places to stay.

Vacation's *Live & Work in Belgium, The Netherlands & Luxembourg* £8.95 is a guide for those interested in finding temporary or permanent work, starting a business or buying a home.

All the above guidebooks are available from good bookshops.

Grand Duchy of Luxembourg contains practical information for visitors covering entry requirements, climate, accommodation, transport, outdoor activities, museums, special events and places of interest. Available from the Luxembourg Tourist Office, see above.

Accommodation The Luxembourg Tourist Office, see above, can provide a booklet listing accommodation throughout the country. Also a leaflet listing authorised camping sites together with facilities available.

AU PAIR / CHILDCARE

There is no special agency for au pairs in Luxembourg; positions may be found through general employment agencies, advertisements in the local press or through the government employment bureau, Administration de l'Emploi, see the **General** section, below.
The employer must obtain from the bureau an *Accord Placement Au Pair*, an agreement specifying the conditions and obligations governing the stay. This agreement must be filled in by the host family and forwarded to the au pair for signature. The agreement is then submitted to the Administration de l'Emploi for approval, who forwards copies to the parties concerned. This contract must be concluded before the au pair leaves her/his country of residence, especially in the case of non-EEA nationals, for whom the contract serves as a work permit. The agreement stipulates that the host family is required to affiliate the au pair to all branches of the Luxembourg Social Security system. If the au pair falls ill, the host family must continue to provide board and lodging and guarantee all appropriate treatment until necessary arrangements have been made.

CONSERVATION

BRITISH TRUST FOR CONSERVATION VOLUNTEERS
Room IWH, 36 St Mary's Street, Wallingford, Oxfordshire OX10 0EU ✆ Wallingford (01491) 839766

The largest charitable organisation in Britain to involve people in practical conservation work. Following the success of the Natural Break programme in the UK, BTCV is now developing a series of international working holidays with the aim of introducing **volunteers** to practical conservation projects abroad. It is hoped that the British volunteers will adapt to and learn from local lifestyles as well as participate in the community. Recent projects in Luxembourg have included footpath construction, hedge laying and planting willow, alongside people from a local special needs group. Projects last 2-3 weeks.

⚱ Ages 18-70. Cost from £120 includes transport from suitable pick-up in Luxembourg, insurance, food and basic accommodation with everyone sharing domestic chores. Membership fee £12. No fares or wages paid.

COURIERS/REPS

EUROCAMP Summer Jobs (Ref WH), PO Box 170, Liverpool L70 1ES ✆ Knutsford (01565) 625522

One of Europe's leading tour operators, specialising in providing quality camping and mobile home holidays for families throughout Europe.

Campsite couriers required. Work involves cleaning tents and equipment prior to the arrival of new customers; checking, replacing and making repairs on equipment; replenishing gas supplies; keeping basic accounts and reporting on a weekly basis to England. Couriers are also expected to meet new arrivals and assist holidaymakers with any problems that arise; organise activities and parties; provide information on local tourist attractions and maintain an information noticeboard. At the beginning and end of the season couriers are also expected to help in erecting and dismantling tents. Couriers need to be flexible to meet the needs of customers and be on hand where necessary; they will be able to organise their own free time as the workload allows.

⚱ Ages 18+. Applicants should be independent, adaptable, reliable, physically fit, have plenty of initiative and relish a challenging and responsible position. Good knowledge of local languages also necessary. Preference given to those able to work the whole season, April-September/October; contracts also available for first half season, April-mid July and second half season, mid July-September/October.

Children's couriers also required, with the energy and enthusiasm to organise a wide range of exciting activities for groups aged 4-13. Experience of working with this age range essential, but language ability is not a requirement.

⚱ Ages 18+. Must be available for the whole season, May-September.

For both positions the salary is £95 per week. Training, accommodation in frame tent with cooking facilities, insurance and return travel provided.

✉ *Early application by telephone preferred; interviews start September/October. UK/EEA passport-holders only.*

DOMESTIC

LUXEMBOURG EMBASSY
27 Wilton Crescent, London SW1X 8SD ✆ 0171-235 6961

Can supply a booklet *Hotels, Auberges, Restaurants, Pensions*, published annually, which includes detailed listings of establishments all over Luxembourg which often need seasonal staff.

✉ *Available free on receipt of an A4 SAE. Those outside the UK should contact the Luxembourg Embassy in their country.*

FARMWORK

INTERNATIONAL FARM EXPERIENCE PROGRAMME
YFC Centre, N A C, Stoneleigh Park, Kenilworth, Warwickshire CV8 2LG ✆ (01203) 696584
Provides assistance to young **agriculturalists** and **horticulturalists** by finding places in farms/nurseries abroad, enabling them to broaden their knowledge of agricultural and horticultural methods. Participants usually live and work with a farming family and the work is matched as far as possible with participant's requirements. Entails physical work and practical involvement. Basic wage plus board and lodging. 3-12 months, all year.
⊕ Ages 18-28. Applicants must have at least 2 years practical experience, one of which may be at agricultural college, and intend to make a career in agriculture/ horticulture. Valid driving licence necessary. Participants pay own fares and insurance. Registration fee £85.
✍ *UK applications to IFEP. Other applications to IFEP partner in home country.*

TEACHERS

LUXEMBOURG EMBASSY
27 Wilton Crescent, London SW1X 8SD ✆ 0171-235 6961
Publishes an information sheet listing English-speaking schools, language and secretarial schools, *lycées*, and *collèges d'enseignement* which may have vacancies for teachers. Opportunities in private schools, as only Luxembourg nationals only can teach in state schools.
✍ *Available free on receipt of an A4 SAE. Those outside the UK should contact the Luxembourg Embassy in their country.*

GENERAL

ADMINISTRATION DE L'EMPLOI
38a rue Philippe II, BP 23, 2010 Luxembourg City, Luxembourg ✆ (352) 47 68 55-1
The government employment office dealing with all employment enquiries, can provide information on the availability of work in Luxembourg.

AIDA LUXEMBOURG
70 Grand'rue, 1660 Luxembourg City, Luxembourg
Can provide information on temporary jobs for students.

LUXEMBOURG EMBASSY
27 Wilton Crescent, London SW1X 8SD ✆ 0171-235 6961
Can provide lists for those interested in working in Luxembourg; one gives the addresses of British and American firms, the other lists major companies classified according to activity.
✍ *Available free on receipt of an A4 SAE. Those outside the UK should contact the Luxembourg Embassy in their country.*

MANPOWER-AIDE TEMPORAIRE
19 rue Glesener, 1631 Luxembourg City, Luxembourg
Can provide information on temporary jobs in all professions.

OFFICENTER 25 boulevard Royal, 2449 Luxembourg City, Luxembourg
Can provide information on temporary office jobs for students.

When writing to any organisation it is essential to mention Working Holidays 1995 and enclose a stamped, self-addressed A4 envelope, or if in another country, an addressed A4 envelope and at least two IRCs (International Reply Coupons, available from post offices). Enquiries received without SAEs/IRCs are unlikely to be answered.

INFO

Malta High Commission
16 Kensington Square, London W8 5HH
© 0171-938 1712/6

British High Commission
7 St Anne Street, Floriana
© (356) 233134-7

Tourist office
Malta National Tourist Organisation,
Mappin House, 4 Winsley Street,
London W1N 7AR © 0171-323 0506

Youth hostels
Malta Youth Hostels Association, 17
Tal-Borg Street, Pawla © (356) 693957

Youth & student information
Youth Service Organisation, c/o
Director of Education, Floriana

NSTS, Student and Youth Travel,
220 St Paul Street, Valletta

Entry regulations Foreign nationals
may not seek or accept employment in
Malta after arrival unless they have a
prior work permit. These must be
applied for by the employer on behalf of
the foreign national; the employer must
show sufficient proof that the foreign
national will fill a position for which no
skilled Maltese national is available.
British nationals do not need a visa to
stay in Malta for up to 3 months.

Travel *Malta and its Islands* is an
information sheet giving brief details of
history, climate, health, accommodation,
food, shopping, places of interest, sport,
festivals and other events. Available free
from the Malta National Tourist
Organisation, see above.

Campus Travel can arrange low-cost,
flexible student/youth flights to Malta.
Offices throughout the UK, including 52
Grosvenor Gardens, London SW1W
0AG © 0171-730 3402 or © 0131-668
3303 for Scottish telephone bookings.

GENERAL

BRITISH UNIVERSITIES NORTH AMERICA CLUB (BUNAC)
16 Bowling Green Lane, London EC1R 0BD ✆ 0171-251 3472
A non-profit, non-political educational student club which aims to encourage interest and understanding between students. Administers a Work Malta programme for **catering students** who wish to gain course-related experience. Participants spend 3-6 months in accredited Maltese hotels or restaurants, April-October. Students and their tutors are encouraged to set out work experience criteria so that a suitable position can be arranged. Cost £395 includes placement, working visa, round-trip flight, pre-booked accommodation for 2 nights and orientation on arrival, assessment (optional) and support from cooperators. Applicants must be British nationals, enrolled in a full-time course of HND level or above in catering or hotel administration at a recognised college or university in the UK.
Organised in cooperation with NSTS Malta.

MALTA YOUTH HOSTELS ASSOCIATION 17 Triq Tal-Borg, Pawla PLA 06 ✆/☎ (356) 693957
Volunteers motivated to help and work hard to develop Malta's tourist industry are needed. This will mainly involve support work in Malta and Gozo's youth hostels and youth centres, including office work and administration, renovation and construction work such as painting, plastering, building walls and roofing. ♠ Ages 16-50; those under 18 must provide a letter giving parental consent. 21 hours per week. for 2-12 weeks, all year, commencing the 1st and 15th of each month. Accommodation provided; volunteers prepare own meals. Participants pay own travel and insurance costs. Good faith deposit of £25 every 2 weeks is required, returnable on completing work.
All nationalities welcome; must have good knowledge of English.

APPLYING FOR A JOB

When writing to **any** organisation it is **essential** to mention **Working Holidays 1995** and enclose a **stamped, self-addressed A4 envelope**, or if in another country, an **addressed A4 envelope** and at least two **IRCs** (International Reply Coupons, available from post offices). Enquiries received without SAEs/IRCs are **unlikely** to be answered. **Before applying**, read carefully all the information given. Pay **particular** attention to:

✐ skills/qualifications/experience required

✐ the period of employment expected

✐ age limits or nationality restrictions

✐ application deadlines

✐ any other points, especially details of insurance cover, and other costs such as travel and accommodation.

When applying include the following:

✐ your name, address, date of birth, marital status, nationality, sex

✐ details of your education, qualifications, relevant experience, skills, languages spoken

✐ your period of availability for work

✐ a passport-size photo, particularly if you will be working with the public

✐ anything else recommended in the listing (such as a *cv*)

INFO

Moroccan Embassy
49 Queen's Gate Gardens, London SW7
5NE ℂ 0171-581 5001/4
Consular Section: Diamond House,
97/99 Praed Street, London W2
℃ 0171-724 0719

British Embassy
17 boulevard de la Tour Hassan, BP45,
Rabat ℃ (212 7) 209 05/06

Tourist office
Moroccan Tourist Office, 205 Regent
Street, London W1R 7DE
℃ 0171-437 0073

Youth hostels
Fédération Royale Marocaine des
Auberges de Jeunesse, avenue Oqba Ibn
Nafii, Meknes ℃ (212 5) 24698

Entry regulations British nationals
require a full passport and a work
permit before taking up employment.
This will be applied for by the
prospective employer and issued by the
Ministry of Labour. British passport
holders are free to travel without a visa,
but their passport must be valid for 6+
months on their day of entry. Those
wishing to stay over 3 months must
register with the police, justifying their
stay with a valid work permit.
An information sheet, *Employment in
Morocco,* is available from the Moroccan
Consulate.

Travel Freedom Pass allows 3, 5 or 10
days unlimited rail travel in 1 month on
the railways of Morocco. Cost from £26
(under 26) or £27 (26+). Available from
British Rail International Rail Centre,
Victoria Station, London SW1V 1JY
℃ 0171-834 2345.

Campus Travel can arrange Inter-Rail and
low cost student flights to various
destinations in Morocco. Offices
throughout the UK, including
52 Grosvenor Gardens, London SW1W

0AG ✆ 0171-730 8111 or ✆ 0131-668 3303 for Scottish telephone bookings.

Council Travel, 28A Poland Street, London W1V 3DB ✆ 0171-437 7767 offers low-cost student/youth fares to destinations in Morocco, plus travel insurance, guidebooks and travel gear.

Publications Lonely Planet's *Morocco, Algeria & Tunisia - A Travel Survival Kit* £10.95 offers practical, down-to-earth information for travellers wanting to explore beyond the usual tourist routes. *The Rough Guide to Morocco* £9.99 provides background information plus details on getting around, places to explore and cheap places to stay. Both are available from good bookshops.

WORKCAMPS

LES AMIS DES CHANTIERS INTERNATIONAUX DE MEKNES (ACIM) PO Box 8, Meknes, Morocco

Volunteers are invited to take part in international workcamps. Projects generally include archaeological digs, agricultural and construction work. Excursions and social evenings arranged.
⊕ Ages 18+. Applicants should have previous workcamp or voluntary work experience. 30-35 hour week, afternoons and weekends free. 3 weeks, July/August. Board, lodging and insurance provided, but no pocket money. Travel costs paid by volunteers.

CHANTIERS JEUNESSE MAROC BP 1351, Rabat RP, Morocco

Volunteers invited on international workcamps concerned with economic, social and cultural development. Recent projects have included restoring the historical gates of Essaouira; gardening and landscaping in the parks of Agadir; helping in the reconstruction of a youth centre in Ahfir; and helping out with children at an orphanage in Casablanca.
⊕ Ages 18+. 35 hour week. 3 weeks, July and August. Basic accommodation, sometimes with no running water, food and some insurance cover provided, but not travel. Applicants should have previous workcamp or voluntary work experience. Knowledge of French or Arabic an advantage.
🕮 *Apply through partner organisation in country of residence. In the UK: Quaker International Social Projects or United Nations Association International Youth Service. See page 30 for registration details.*

CHANTIERS SOCIAUX MAROCAINS PO BOX 456, Rabat RP, Morocco

Volunteers required to work on manual and community projects. Recent projects have included building a playground in Safi; renovating historic monuments in Fes; and using traditional materials to lay a path in Chefchaouen. Volunteers share in discussions centring on the host community and world problems and are expected to take a full part in all aspects of the camp.
⊕ Ages 18+. 35 hour week. 2-3 weeks, July and August. Food, accommodation in schools, centres or rural communes and insurance provided. Participants share chores and should take a sleeping bag. No fares or wages paid.
🕮 *Apply through partner organisation in country of residence. In the UK: United Nations Association International Youth Service. See page 30 for registration details.*

PENSÉE & CHANTIERS BP 1423, Rabat RP, Morocco

Volunteers are needed for a variety of workcamps aimed at helping community schemes. Projects include work on schools, youth clubs, social centres and green spaces, involving construction, restoration, painting and gardening tasks.
⊕ Ages 17+. All nationalities accepted. 5 hour day, 6 day week. 3 weeks, July and August. Food, accommodation and insurance provided, but participants should take a sleeping bag and work clothes. Social and cultural activities organised, including excursions and discussions. No fares or wages paid.
🕮 *Write for further details.*

NETHERLANDS

INFO

Royal Netherlands Embassy
38 Hyde Park Gate, London SW7 5DP
© 0171-584 5040

British Embassy
Lange Voorhout 10, 2514 ED
The Hague © (31 70) 364 5800

Tourist office
Netherlands Board of Tourism, 25-28
Buckingham Gate, London SW1E 6LD
Postal address: PO Box 523, London
SW1E 6NT © 0891 200 277

Youth hostels
Stichting Nederlandse Jeugdherberg
Centrale, Prof Tulpplein 4, 1018 GX
Amsterdam © (31 20) 551 3133

Youth & student information
EXIS, Prof Tulpstraat 2, 1018 HA
Amsterdam/PO Box 15344,
1001 MH Amsterdam

Foreign Student Service, Oranje
Nassaulaan 5, 1075 AH Amsterdam
© (31 20) 671 5915

Entry regulations UK citizens
intending to work in the Netherlands
should have a full passport. UK/EEA
nationals may stay for up to 3 months;
those wishing to stay longer should
contact the local police within 8 days of
arrival in order to apply for a residence
permit. Citizens of non-EEA countries
must possess a work permit, which can
be applied for by the employer. Visitors
may be asked to prove that they have
adequate means of self-support for the
duration of their proposed stay and that
the cost of the return journey can be
covered. Further details of the
regulations governing temporary
employment in the Netherlands, plus
useful information for those seeking a
job, are contained in an information
sheet, *Information about working and
residence in the Netherlands*, available
from the Netherlands Embassy.

Job advertising Frank L Crane (London) Ltd, International Press Representation, 5/15 Cromer Street, Grays Inn Road, London WC1H 8LS ✆ 0171-837 3330 can place job advertisements in the Dutch newspapers *Het Parool, De Volkskrant and Trouw.*

Publicitas Ltd, 517/523 Fulham Road, London SW6 1HD ✆ 0171-385 7723 can place job advertisements in *De Telegraaf* (largest morning daily) and numerous magazines.

Travel NBBS Travel, Informatiecentrum, Schipholweg 101, PO Box 360, 2300 AJ Leiden is the national office for youth and student travel. It administers 40 travel offices including 7 in Amsterdam, and can arrange cheap travel and hotel accommodation.

7 Day Rover offers unlimited travel for 7 consecutive days on the Netherlands Railways network; cost from £56. A Public Transport Link Rover, in conjunction with the Rover, offers unlimited travel on all town and country buses and on the Amsterdam and Rotterdam metro systems. Cost £10 for 7 days. Summer Tour Rover allows 2 people unlimited rail travel for 3 days within a 10 day period. Cost from £40.50. Summer Tour Rover Plus includes buses, trams and metros; cost from £49.50. Both available June-August. Teenage Rover is available for 4 days within a period of 10 days, June-August, to those aged 18 and under; cost £24. Teenage Rover Plus includes buses, trams and metros; cost £30. The Benelux Tourrail Card entitles the holder to 5 days unlimited travel, within a specified period of 1 month, on the national railway networks of the Netherlands, Belgium and Luxembourg, March-October; cost from £60 (under 26) or from £80 (26+). Bicycle hire at reduced rates for rail ticket holders at many stations. Details on all of these from Netherlands Railways, 25/28 Buckingham Gate, London SW1E 6LD ✆ 0171-630 1735.

Freedom Pass allows 3, 5, or 10 days unlimited rail travel in 1 month on the railways of the Netherlands. Cost from £24 (under 26) or £31 (26+). Available from Netherlands Railways, see above, or British Rail International Rail Centre, Victoria Station, London SW1V 1JY ✆ 0171-834 2345.

Campus Travel can arrange Eurotrain, Inter-Rail and student/youth fares for travel to destinations in the Netherlands. Offices throughout the UK including 52 Grosvenor Gardens, London SW1W 0AG (opposite Victoria Station) ✆ 0171-730 3402 or ✆ 0131-668 3303 for Scottish telephone bookings.

Council Travel, 28A Poland Street, London W1V 3DB ✆ 0171-287 3337 (offices also in Paris, Nice, Lyon, Munich, Düsseldorf, Tokyo, Singapore and throughout the US) offers Eurotrain under 26 fares and youth/student flights to destinations in the Netherlands, plus travel insurance, guidebooks and travel gear.

Publications Netherlands Board of Tourism, see above, produces an annual guide *Holland Traveller* which has a wealth of information on the Netherlands.

The Rough Guide to Holland, Belgium, and Luxembourg £9.99 and *The Rough Guide to Amsterdam* £7.99 provide comprehensive background information on the Netherlands and Amsterdam plus details on getting there, getting around, places to explore and cheap places to stay.

Vacation Work's *Live & Work in Belgium, The Netherlands & Luxembourg* £8.95 is a guide for those interested in finding temporary or permanent work, starting a business or buying a home in the Benelux countries.

The above guides are available from good bookshops.

Information centres EXIS, PO Box 15344, 1001 MH Amsterdam/Prof

Tulpstraat 2, 1018 Amsterdam provides information and advice, mainly to young Dutch people, on holidays, vacation work, au pair placements, language courses and exchanges.

Accommodation Hans Brinker Hotel, Kerkstraat 136-138, 1017 GR Amsterdam has budget accommodation in a variety of rooms from singles to dormitories of up to 12 beds. Facilities include restaurants, cafe, bar and tourist information. Open all year. Cost from Dfl 23 bed and breakfast, summer.

AU PAIR / CHILDCARE

Au pair posts are open to both males and females, aged 18-30. In return for light housework and looking after children au pairs get board, lodging, insurance, minimum of Dfl 500 per month and the opportunity to attend a language course. Posts generally for a minimum of 6 months, maximum 1 year.

ACADEMY AU PAIR AGENCY 42 Cedarhurst Drive, Eltham, London SE9 5LP ✆ **0181-294 1191** ☎ **0181-850 8932**
Can place **au pairs**. ⊕ Ages 18-27. Applicants should have some knowledge of Dutch. Pocket money approx £30-£40 per week. Administration charge £40. Positions also available as **nannies** and **mothers' helps** for those with qualifications/experience.

AVALON AGENCY Thursley House, 53 Station Road, Shalford, Guildford, Surrey GU4 8HA ✆ **Guildford (01483) 63640**
Can place **au pairs**. ⊕ Ages 18-30. Pocket money equal to £30-£35 per week, usually paid monthly. Fee £40 for placements and use of Dutch agent. Summer holiday placements June-August only. Long-term 6 month-2 year placements to start any time.

HELPING HANDS AU PAIR & DOMESTIC AGENCY 39 Rutland Avenue, Thorpe Bay, Essex SS1 2XJ ✆ **Southend-on-Sea (01702) 602067**
Can place **au pairs** and **mothers' helps**. ⊕ Ages 18-27. Pocket money approx £35 per week for au pairs, higher for mothers' helps. Introduction fee £40 on acceptance of a family. *UK nationals only.*

HOME FROM HOME Walnut Orchard, Chearsley, Aylesbury, Buckinghamshire HP18 0DA ✆/☎ **Aylesbury (01844) 208561**
Can place **au pairs**. ⊕ Ages 18+. Pocket money £35 per week. Placement fee £40.

JUST THE JOB (NOTTINGHAM) 32 Dovedale Road, West Bridgford, Nottingham NG2 6JA ✆ **0115-945 2482**
Can place **au pairs** on 6+ month placements only. ⊕ Ages 18+. Weekly pocket money £32-£40. *UK nationals only.*

LANGTRAIN INTERNATIONAL Torquay Road, Foxrock, Dublin 18, Ireland ✆ **(353 1) 289 3876**
Can place **au pairs** with families. ⊕ Ages 18+. Pocket money £25-£40 per week. Placement fee £60.

PROBLEMS UNLIMITED AGENCY 86 Alexandra Road, Windsor, Berkshire SL4 1HU ✆ **Windsor (01753) 830101**
Can place **au pairs**. ⊕ Ages 18-27. Pocket money £30-£35 per week.

STUDENTS ABROAD LTD 11 Milton View, Hitchin, Hertfordshire SG4 0QD ✆ **Hitchin (01462) 438909** ☎ **(01462) 438919**
Can place **au pairs** for 6+ months. ⊕ Ages 18-27. Knowledge of Dutch not essential. Pocket money approx £30-£35 per week. Service charge £40.

CONSERVATION

SIW INTERNATIONALE VRIJWILLIGERS-PROJEKTEN
Willemstraat 7, 3511 RJ Utrecht, Netherlands
Volunteers are invited to work in international teams on conservation projects. Recent projects have included mowing grass and clearing ditches in the fenland nature reserve of the Maarsseveense Plassen; making hay and cutting trees to maintain peat moors and reed beds in Vreeland; and conservation work in the wetland nature reserve of Guisveld. Study elements include environmental education, pollution and nature protection.
⊕ Ages 18-30. Applicants should be highly motivated, preferably with previous workcamp or other voluntary experience, and prepared to work hard as part of a team. 30 hour, 5 day week, with weekends free. 2/3 weeks, May-August. Food, shared accommodation and work accident insurance provided. No fares or wages paid. **B D PH**

✍ *Apply through partner organisation in country of residence. In the UK: International Voluntary Service, Quaker International Social Projects or United Nations Association International Youth Service. See page 30 for registration details and addresses.*

COURIERS / REPS

EUROCAMP Summer Jobs (Ref WH), PO Box 170, Liverpool L70 1ES ✆ Knutsford (01565) 625522
One of Europe's leading tour operators, specialising in providing quality camping and mobile home holidays for families throughout Europe.
Campsite couriers required. Work involves cleaning tents and equipment prior to the arrival of new customers; checking, replacing and making repairs on equipment; replenishing gas supplies; keeping basic accounts and reporting on

a weekly basis to England. Couriers are also expected to meet new arrivals and assist holidaymakers with any problems that arise; organise activities and parties; provide information on local tourist attractions and maintain an information noticeboard. At the beginning and end of the season couriers are also expected to help in erecting and dismantling tents. Couriers need to be flexible to meet the needs of customers and be on hand where necessary; they will be able to organise their own free time as the workload allows.
⊕ Ages 18+. Applicants should be independent, adaptable, reliable, physically fit, have plenty of initiative and relish a challenging and responsible position. Good working knowledge of Dutch also necessary. Preference given to those able to work the whole season, April-September/October; contracts also available for first half season, April-mid July and second half season, mid July-September/October.
Children's couriers also required, with the energy and enthusiasm to organise a wide range of exciting activities for groups aged 4-13. Experience of working with this age range essential, but language ability is not a requirement.
⊕ Ages 18+. Must be available for the whole season, May-September.
For both positions the salary is £95 per week. Training provided together with accommodation in frame tent with cooking facilities, insurance and return travel. ✍ *Early application by telephone preferred; interviews start September/October. UK/EEA passport-holders only.*

KEYCAMP HOLIDAYS 92-96 Lind Road, Sutton, Surrey SM1 4PL ✆ 0181-395 8170
One of the UK's largest self-drive camping and mobile home tour operators, offering holidays on 100 campsites in Europe. **Campsite couriers** required to work for 3-6 months in an outdoor environment. Main duties include providing clients with information, organising social and sporting activities, cleaning mobile

homes and tents, and providing activities for children. Period of employment March-July/July-September. ⚘ Ages 18+. Knowledge of French/German/Spanish/Italian desirable. Uniform, training and accommodation provided. Competitive salary. ▣ *Application requests by postcard. UK/EEA nationals only.*

PGL YOUNG ADVENTURE LTD Personnel Department, Alton Court, Penyard Lane (878), Ross-on-Wye, Herefordshire HR9 5NR ℂ Ross-on-Wye (01989) 767833 Couriers required to escort groups of young people on barge holidays, starting and finishing in London. Couriers are totally responsible for the welfare of their group, and for giving them an enjoyable holiday. The barge provides accommodation for up to 34 guests, and each group has 2 couriers. Holidays run for 10 days and the itinerary allows for frequent stops at centres of interest within easy access of the moorings. ⚘ Ages 21+. Applicants should have skill and experience of working with children, and in controlling groups of teenagers aged 12-15 and 16-18. They should be committed, tolerant, enthusiastic, flexible and have stamina, energy and a sense of humour. Fairly demanding job; preference given to those with maturity, resourcefulness, strong personality and a previous knowledge of the area. 1 or 2 trips, July-September. Pocket money £4 per day plus expenses (approx £78 in total per 10 day trip).

FARMWORK

Flower bulbs are big business in the Netherlands. Fields along the coastal strip from Leiden to Haarlem glow with colour for a brief springtime burst of glory, until the flower heads are cut off to preserve the bulbs' growing power. Bulbs are then dug up, peeled, sorted, counted and packed during June-October. Hyacinths, tulips, daffodils, carnations, chrysanthemums, roses and lilies are grown for auction and export, and jobs are available outdoors and in greenhouses where work involves cutting and packing flowers.

There are also seasonal vacancies harvesting fruit and vegetables, packing produce for transport to market, and working in food-processing factories. Working hours can be irregular, as the work is subject to weather conditions and market deadlines. Applicants must be prepared to get up early, get their hands filthy, and spend long periods standing, kneeling, crouching, or carrying crates. They may also have to work all day in the stifling heat of a greenhouse. The Arbeidsburo, PO Box 183, 2160 AD Lisse can send a list of factories in early June, to which you can apply direct. Alternatively try turning up in person at farms, greenhouses, bulb factories, nurseries or food-processing plants. The main farming areas are:

Bulbs and flowers
Coastal Noord-Holland and Zuid-Holland, especially the towns and villages between Leiden and Haarlem. Also the Noordostpolder and some areas of Friesland and Groningen.

Cucumbers, peppers, lettuce, tomatoes, strawberries
Glass City is another name for the many greenhouses in the Westland province of Zuid-Holland, the area between Den Haag, Rotterdam and Hoek van Holland.

Apples, pears, cherries
Area known as *De Betuwe* between the Rhine and Waal rivers, including the towns of Buren and Culemborg. Also in the southern province of Limburg.

INTERNATIONAL FARM EXPERIENCE PROGRAMME YFC Centre, N A C, Stoneleigh Park, Kenilworth CV8 2LG ℂ Coventry (01203) 696584 Provides assistance to young **agriculturalists** and **horticulturalists** by finding places in farms and nurseries abroad, enabling them to broaden their knowledge of agricultural methods. Participants usually live and work with a farming family and the work is matched as far as possible with participant's requirements. Entails physical work and practical involvement. Basic wage plus board and lodging. 3-12 months, all year.

✠ Ages 18-28. Applicants must have at least 2 years practical experience, one of which may be at an agricultural college, and intend to make a career in agriculture or horticulture. Valid driving licence necessary. Participants pay own fares and insurance. Registration fee £85. ⚅ *UK applications to IFEP; other applications to IFEP partner in home country.*

MONITORS & INSTRUCTORS

VILLAGE CAMPS Chalet Seneca, 1854 Leysin, Switzerland
Organises American-style summer day camps at the American School of The Hague for children aged 4-13 from the international business and diplomatic communities. Opportunities for counsellors, special activity counsellors, programme leaders, special instructors and nurses. Staff live, work and play with the children and are responsible for their safety, health and happiness. **Counsellors** plan, organise and direct daytime programmes, accompany campers on excursions and may be called upon to supervise other counsellors and take charge of a camper group. **Special activity counsellors**, having a high degree of proficiency, organise, execute and instruct specific programmes such as sports, arts and crafts, nature study and basic computer science. Counsellors with a substantial amount of leadership experience in recreational programmes can be appointed **programme leaders**, which includes running a camp programme and direction and supervision of adult counsellors. **Assistant** and **junior**

counsellors are responsible for supporting counsellors in all activities and assisting with special activities as required. **Specialist instructors** should have 2 years' training and experience, and be able to instruct children of all ability levels; they are responsible for the concentrated teaching of their subject at a speciality camp such as golf, tennis, computer science or French and English language. **Nurses** are responsible for the general health and welfare of campers and counsellors, attending to accidents and maintaining an infirmary.

✠ Ages 21+, 26+ for programme leaders. Applicants must have training and/or experience of working with children and have an interest in children from many ethnic and religious backgrounds. Compulsory pre-camp training course arranged for all staff. English is the first language, but priority is given to applicants with additional French, Italian or German language skills. 45 hour week for 1+ months, June-August. Full board accommodation, accident and liability insurance provided, but not travel costs. Wages SF150 (junior counsellors), SF225 (assistant counsellors) or SF275 (counsellors, special activity counsellors and nurses) per 10 day session.

WORKCAMPS

ICVD MvB Bastiaansestratt 56, 1054 SP Amsterdam, Netherlands
Volunteers are needed to work in international teams on projects aimed at offering a service in an area of need and generating self-help within the community; promoting international understanding and the discussion of social problems; and offering young people the chance to live as a group and take these experiences into the context of daily life. Recent projects have included renovation work and gardening at a peace and Third World solidarity centre in Boxmeer; restoring old lifeboats and building a boathouse at a

maritime museum on the island of Texel; and collecting and recycling waste materials in Amsterdam to produce a recycled art exhibition.

⊕ Ages 18+. 6 hour day, 30-36 hour week. 2-3 weeks, June-August. Food, shared accommodation and work accident insurance provided. No fares or wages paid.

🦑 *Apply through partner organisation in country of residence. In the UK: Christian Movement for Peace. See page 30 for registration details and addresses.*

SIW INTERNATIONALE VRIJWILLIGERS-PROJEKTEN
Willemstraat 7, 3511 RJ Utrecht, Netherlands

Volunteers are invited to work in international teams on construction and social projects. Recent projects have included putting up marquees and doing other jobs in preparation for a World Festival in Gemert; creating a garden for people with special needs in Eindhoven; and constructing a Bronze Age farm and making canoes out of tree trunks at an open-air museum in Enkhuizen. All camps include a related study theme. Excursions and films arranged.

⊕ Ages 18-30. Applicants should be highly motivated, preferably with previous workcamp or other voluntary work experience, and prepared to work hard as part of a team. 30-35 hour, 5 day week, with weekends free. 2/3 weeks, August. Food, shared accommodation and work accident insurance provided. No fares or wages paid. **B D PH**

⊕ *Apply through partner organisation in country of residence. In the UK: International Voluntary Service, Quaker International Social Projects or United Nations Association International Youth Service. See page 30 for registration details and addresses.*

VRIJWILLIGE INTERNATIONALE AKTIE
Pesthuislaan 25, 1054 RH Amsterdam, Netherlands

VIA is the Dutch branch of Service Civil International which promotes international reconciliation through work projects. **Volunteers** are invited to take part in international workcamps. Recent projects have included collecting, sorting and recycling discarded goods at the Haarzuilens Emmaus community; making paintings to brighten up the neighbourhood, working alongside young people from the deprived Amsterdam suburb of Bijlmer; and working in the garden of a permaculture centre in Friesland. Study themes include Third World problems, human rights, peace, apartheid systems, women and violence.

⊕ Ages 18+. Applicants should be highly motivated, preferably with previous workcamp or other voluntary work experience, and prepared to work hard as part of a team. 35-40 hour week. 2-4 weeks, June-September. Food, shared accommodation and work accident insurance provided. No fares or wages paid. **B D PH W**

🦑 *Apply through partner organisation in country of residence.*
In the UK: International Voluntary Service. See page 30 for registration details and addresses.

GENERAL

ROYAL NETHERLANDS EMBASSY
38 Hyde Park Gate, London SW7 5DP ✆ **0171-584 5040**
Can provide a list of **labour exchanges** in some major towns in the Netherlands, as well as information sheets on social security and income tax.

When writing to any organisation it is essential to mention Working Holidays 1995 and enclose a stamped, self-addressed A4 envelope, or if in another country, an addressed A4 envelope and at least two IRCs (International Reply Coupons, available from post offices). Enquiries received without SAEs/IRCs are unlikely to be answered.

NEW ZEALAND

INFO

New Zealand High Commission
Immigration Service: New Zealand
House, Haymarket, London SW1Y 4TE
✆ 0891 200288

British High Commission
44 Hill Street/PO Box 1812,
Wellington 1 ✆ (64 4) 472 6049

Tourist office
New Zealand Tourism Board, 7th floor,
New Zealand House, 80 Haymarket,
London SW1Y 4TE ✆ 0171-973 0360

Youth hostels
YHA of New Zealand Inc, PO Box
68-149, Auckland ✆ (64 9) 309 20802
📠 (64 9) 373 5083

Youth & student information
New Zealand University Students
Association, Student Travel Bureau,
PO Box 6368, Te Aro, Wellington

Entry regulations UK citizens may
visit for up to 6 months without a visa;
EEA nationals and nationals of most
western European countries, the US and
Canada may stay for up to 3 months.
In these cases a visitors permit will be
issued on arrival. A work visa is
required for all types of employment.
Those entering temporarily for full-time
and pre-arranged employment, as
distinct from working on a casual basis,
should apply to the Immigration Service
at New Zealand House, see above, at
least 4 weeks before the intended date
of departure. An application for a work
visa must be supported by an offer of
employment from an employer. Those
who have been accepted under an
approved exchange scheme or whose
prospective employer has been given
permission to recruit by the Immigration
Service may also be considered. The
Working Holiday Scheme enables UK
citizens aged 18-30 to travel to New
Zealand for a working holiday of up to
12 months. The Scheme opens each

year on 1 May, and 500 places are available on a first come, first served basis. Applicants must supply their passport, a completed *Application for Work Visa* form, the correct fee, evidence of sufficient funds for a return ticket and evidence of at least NZ$4,200 to cover living expenses. Those interested in working on a casual basis may also apply for a work permit when they are in the country itself. They should approach the nearest office of the Immigration Service with a written offer of employment; the Immigration Service will check that the work offered cannot be undertaken by local jobseekers and will not restrict employment opportunities. There is no guarantee that applicants will be able to secure permission to work. Applicants must have a passport valid for at least 3 months beyond the last day of their proposed stay, a fully paid return or onward ticket, plus proof that they will have a minimum of NZ$1,000 per month of stay or have made prior arrangements for their support while in the country. Permits granted for initial period of 3 months, 6 months for UK passport-holders. 9 months is the maximum period of stay for visitors.

Travel Campus Travel can arrange flexible, low-cost student/youth fares, internal air passes and adventure tours. Offices throughout the UK, including at 52 Grosvenor Gardens, London SW1W 0AG ✆ 0171-730 8111 or ✆ 0131-668 3303 for Scottish telephone bookings.

Council Travel, 28A Poland Street, London W1V 3DB ✆ 0171-437 7767 (offices also in Paris, Lyon, Nice, Munich, Düsseldorf, Tokyo, Singapore and throughout the US) offers low-cost student/youth airfares plus travel insurance, guidebooks and travel gear.

Long-Haul Leisurail, PO Box 113, Bretton, Peterborough, Cambridgeshire PE3 8HY ✆ Peterborough (01733) 335599 issue a Travelpass providing unlimited travel on trains, buses and ferry. Cost from £133.

Publications Lonely Planet's *New Zealand - A Travel Survival Kit* £11.95 offers practical, down-to-earth information for travellers wanting to explore beyond the usual routes. Vacation Work's *Travellers Survival Kit Australia & New Zealand* £9.95 gives information on travelling, local culture, restaurants, beaches and reefs. Also *Live & Work in Australia & New Zealand* £8.95, a guide for those interested in finding work or starting a business. All available from good bookshops.

Accommodation The New Zealand Tourism Board, see above, can provide leaflets on various types of accommodation, including *New Zealand Backpackers Accommodation,* a booklet listing over 100 independent hostels. Prices from NZ$8-NZ$16 per day.

Backpackers Resorts of New Zealand Ltd, Box 991, Taupo, New Zealand ✆/▭ (64 7) 377 1157 is a chain of 66 hostels catering for backpackers. Prices from NZ$10 per night, shared room.

FARMWORK

There is a wide range of seasonal work. Hostel noticeboards may list local jobs, or farmers may recruit directly. The following gives a general guide:

January-April
Tobacco, apples, pears and peaches around Blenheim, Nelson and Motueka
Apples, pears and grapes around Hawkes Bay
Plums, apricots, apples and pears in central Otago
Apples, peaches, berries, other fruit and potatoes around Christchurch

April-July
Kiwifruit in Northland, the Bay of Islands, south of Auckland and around the Bay of Plenty
October-December
Strawberries in Northland
Citrus fruit around the Bay of Plenty

December-January
Cherries and grapes in the Wairau Valley
Berries around Nelson
Peaches and apricots around the Bay of
Islands

INTERNATIONAL AGRICULTURAL EXCHANGE ASSOCIATION YFC Centre, N A C, Stoneleigh Park, Kenilworth, Warwickshire CV8 2LG ✆ Coventry (01203) 696578

Operates opportunities for young
people involved with **agriculture**,
horticulture or **home management**
to acquire practical work experience in
the rural sector, and to strengthen and
improve their knowledge and
understanding of the way of life in other
countries. Participants are given an
opportunity to study practical methods
on approved training farms, and work as
trainees, gaining further experience in
their chosen field. Types of farm include
dairy, sheep, cropping or mixed farms
(crops plus dairy/sheep/beef/deer);
sheep and beef; limited horticultural
enterprises. Participants undertake paid
work on the farm, approx 45 hours per
week, and live as a member of the host
family. Full board and lodging, insurance
cover and a minimum net weekly wage
of £50-£60 provided. All programmes
include 3/4 weeks unpaid holiday and 4
day orientation seminar. Stopovers (2-4
days) in Singapore/Thailand (on direct
programmes) or South Pacific (for 14
months programme) arranged en route.
✦ Ages 18-30. Applicants should be
single, have good practical experience in
the chosen training category, plus a valid
driving licence. 8 months (departing
August); 6 months (departing
September); 14 months - 7 in New
Zealand plus 7 in Australia (departing
August). Cost from £2,325 covers
airfare, work permit, administration fee,
orientation, insurance, supervision,
placement with a host family and travel
to placement. £200 deposit payable. **B
D** if handicap is not severe.
✎ *Apply at least 4 months in advance.
UK or Irish passport-holders only.*

*New Zealand applicants seeking an
exchange should apply to IAEA, Parklane
Arcade, The Strand, PO Box 328,
Whakatane, North Island.*

INTERNATIONAL FARM EXPERIENCE PROGRAMME YFC Centre, N A C, Stoneleigh Park, Kenilworth, Warwickshire CV8 2LG ✆ (01203) 696584

Provides assistance to young
agriculturalists and **horticulturalists**
by finding places in farms/nurseries
abroad, enabling them to broaden their
knowledge of agricultural and
horticultural methods. Opportunities
for placements in arable, sheep or dairy
farming. Participants usually live and
work with a farming family and the work
is matched as far as possible with
participant's requirements. Entails
physical work and practical involvement.
Basic wage plus board and lodging. 7-12
months, beginning March and July.
✦ Ages 18-28. Applicants must have at
least 2 years practical experience, one of
which may be at agricultural college, and
intend to make a career in agriculture/
horticulture. Valid driving licence
necessary. Participants pay own
fares and insurance. Registration fee
£70 plus programme fee. ✎ *Apply 2-3
months in advance. UK nationals only.*

WILLING WORKERS ON ORGANIC FARMS (WWOOF NZ) c/o Andrew and Jane Strange, PO Box 1172, Nelson, New Zealand ✆ (64 25) 345711

A non-profitmaking organisation which
aims to help organic farmers and
smallholders whose work is often
labour-intensive as it does not rely on
the use of artificial fertilisers/pesticides.
Provides **volunteers** with first-hand
experience by spending some time on
one of 450 farms and smallholdings.
✦ Ages 16+. Placements arranged on a
fix-it-yourself basis. Anti-tetanus
vaccination recommended. No fares or
wages paid. ✎ *Write 2-3 months in
advance enclosing £8 or equivalent for a list
of farms and further information.*

NORTHERN IRELAND

INFO

Tourist office
Northern Ireland Tourist Board, River House, 48 High Street, Belfast BT1 2DS
✆ Belfast (01232) 2315906
London office: 11 Berkeley Street, London W1X 6LN ✆ 0171-493 0601

Youth hostels
YHA Northern Ireland, 56 Bradbury Place, Belfast BT7 1RU
✆ Belfast (01232) 324733

Youth & student information
USIT, Fountain Centre, Belfast BT1 6ET
✆ Belfast (01232) 324073

Entry regulations governing overseas applicants for work in Northern Ireland are as under **Great Britain**.

CHILDREN'S PROJECTS

CHILDREN'S COMMUNITY HOLIDAYS PO Box 463, Belfast BT12 5HB ✆ **Belfast (01232) 245650**
Provides holidays in residential centres and converted schools throughout Northern Ireland for some 800 children aged 8-15 from all kinds of backgrounds, handicapped and able-bodied, Catholic and Protestant. All holidays include games, handicrafts, storytelling, music and exploring the countryside; some feature activities such as canoeing, horse riding, theme games and climbing. **Volunteers** required as monitors, each taking responsibility for a group of 6-8. ♦ Ages 17+. Applicants should have a strong interest in caring for children; fluent English also required. Experience not necessary; training given. Hours as required during holidays; each holiday lasts 7 days, July-August, preceded by a 7-day training course. Pocket money £25 per holiday. Full board accommodation, insurance and travel costs within Northern Ireland provided.

PAX CHRISTI 9 Henry Road, London N4 2LH © 0181-800 4612
An international Catholic movement for peace. **Volunteers** needed on playschemes for Catholic and Protestant children and young people from housing estates, based at schools, community centres and youth clubs in Belfast, Dungannon and Antrim. The schemes aim to ease tension and promote integration by providing happy and creative play opportunities for those for whom there is otherwise very little provision. Each scheme daily attracts up to 500 participants, and has 6-20 volunteers who work in international teams and in close collaboration with the local community. Work involves helping to plan, organise and supervise activities including sports, games, hiking, nature studies, drama, arts and crafts, weekend camping trips and talent shows. ⊕ Ages 18+. Experience with children desirable and volunteers must be self-disciplined, energetic, committed to community living, sensitive to the local situation, prepared to work together as an international team and to take considerable personal responsibility and initiative. Approx 30 hour, 5 day week; some weekend work. 3-5 weeks, July/August. Self-catering accommodation in schools, empty houses, youth clubs, church halls or with families provided, plus food. Help may be given with travel costs if necessary. Volunteers arrange own insurance. Essential that the Northern Ireland history and current situation is studied before arrival.

COMMUNITY WORK

THE CORRYMEELA COMMUNITY Volunteer Coordinator, Corrymeela Centre, 5 Drumaroan Road, Ballycastle, Northern Ireland BT54 6QU © Ballycastle (0126 57) 62626
An interdenominational Christian community working for reconciliation in Northern Ireland, and promoting a concern for peace and justice in the wider world. The Community's summer programme lasts 8 weeks, during which time **volunteers** are needed. Groups using the centre include single-parent or prisoners' families, cross-community exchanges, special needs groups and youth groups. Volunteers join with and become part of the groups, assisting them in any way necessary. Other areas of work include cooking, housekeeping, organising arts, crafts and outdoor activities, and coordinating daily worship. ⊕ Ages 18+. Applicants must be prepared to work long hours and enjoy being with people of all ages. 1-3 weeks; longer-term positions also available. Work is challenging and tiring, but very rewarding. Full board accommodation provided, with one day off per week. No fares or wages paid, although transport can be provide from Belfast. All applicants are requested to attend a preparation weekend. ✎ *Completed application forms to be submitted by late April. Overseas volunteers accepted.*

SHARE HOLIDAY VILLAGE Smith's Strand, Lisnaskea, Co Fermanagh, Northern Ireland © **Lisnaskea (0136 57) 22122**
A registered charity providing a residential activity centre for the integration of able-bodied and disabled people as well as respite care for families. **Volunteers** are employed to act as carer-companions, mainly to senior citizen guests resident at Share during the summer, some quite able-bodied, others confined to wheelchairs. Alternatively, volunteers may be assigned to work with families who have a relative with multiple sclerosis. Work involves accompanying guests on day excursions, serving meals and providing general care and companionship. ⊕ Ages 18-30. Caring experience/qualifications useful but not essential; volunteers must be keen workers with a lively personality and should speak good English. 7 day week, end June-mid September. Full board accommodation, employer's liability insurance and £10

per week pocket money provided. Training weekend held for citizens of Northern Ireland and the Irish Republic; other nationals receive basic training on arrival. ♨ *Apply by 1 April.* **PH W**

CONSERVATION

CONSERVATION VOLUNTEERS (NORTHERN IRELAND) 159 Ravenhill Road, Belfast BT6 0BP, Northern Ireland

The Northern Ireland region of the British Trust for Conservation Volunteers, a charity promoting practical conservation work for **volunteers**. Organises numerous projects on nature reserves, country estates, NT properties and country parks. Recent projects have included restoring the famous Brandy Pad smugglers' route in the Mourne Mountains; planting marram grass and constructing brushwood fencing to protect the sand dune system at Ballyholme; rebuilding a boundary wall surrounding a wildflower meadow at Ardglass; and habitat management in an urban fringe woodland in Belfast. Instruction given in the traditional techniques of drystone walling, fencing, coppicing, woodland and wetland management, and many other conservation skills. Approx 12 volunteers work on each task with an experienced leader; beginners welcome. ⊕ Ages 16+ (17+ for non-UK residents). 7/8 hour day with one day off per week. 1+ weeks or weekends, all year. Accommodation in training centre, tents, youth hostels or cottages, food and insurance provided. Cost from £12, weekend breaks, £36 for 1 week. Tasks qualify under the Duke of Edinburgh's Award Scheme.

When writing to any organisation it is essential to mention Working Holidays 1995 and enclose a stamped, self-addressed A4 envelope, or if in another country, an addressed A4 envelope and at least two IRCs (International Reply Coupons, available from post offices).

NATIONAL TRUST NORTHERN IRELAND REGION Regional Volunteer Organiser, Rowallane House, Saintfield, Ballynahinch, Co Down BT24 7LH, Northern Ireland ✆ Saintfield (01238) 510721

A major conservation charity, organising several workcamps each year at Castle Ward on the shores of Strangford Lough. Typical projects include scrub clearance, fencing, conservation work and helping with the wildfowl collection. ⊕ Ages 16+. July-August. Basecamp accommodation provided in stone houses. Participants should take sleeping bags. **B D PH W** depending on task. *All nationalities welcome.*

MONITORS & INSTRUCTORS

GLEN RIVER YMCA National Centre, Donard Park, Newcastle, Co Down BT33 0GR, Northern Ireland ✆ Newcastle (0139 67) 23172 ☷ (0139 67) 23172

Offers a wide range of outdoor activities aiming to introduce young people to nature and improve their quality of life in a Christian atmosphere. Volunteers are needed to work as **counsellors, instructors, domestic assistants** and **day camp leaders**. Training given in activities such as orienteering, ropes course, archery, adventure and nature walks. Opportunities for canoeing, climbing, abseiling and bouldering as well as to participate in domestic and other duties related to the running of the centre. Applicants should agree with the aims and purposes of the YMCA, be willing to support Christian values and faith, be articulate, enjoy working with children and fit easily into the staff team. ⊕ Ages 18+; preferably 20+. Good knowledge of English required. Applicants are required to produce references as to suitability to work with children. 6 day week, June-August. £18 per week pocket money, accommodation, meals and public liability insurance provided. Participants pay own travel and personal insurance.

WORKCAMPS

INTERNATIONAL VOLUNTARY SERVICE NORTHERN IRELAND
122 Great Victoria Street, Belfast BT2 7BG, Northern Ireland
℗ Belfast (01232) 238147
The Northern Irish branch of Service Civil International, which promotes international reconciliation through volunteer exchange. **Volunteers** are needed on international workcamps Recent projects have included decorating and landscaping at an educational resource centre in Coleraine committed to healing the divisions between the two communities within Northern Ireland; helping Tools for Self Reliance in Derry to refurbish old tools for use in the Third World; working with children and volunteers from an east Belfast community to make banners, masks, giant puppets and hats for an alternative festival parade; and planting trees at a number of sites as a symbolic contribution to international peace.
⚓ Ages 18+. Applicants should be prepared to work hard and contribute to team life. Overseas volunteers should be able to speak basic English. 35-40 hour week. 2-3 weeks especially June-September. Food, shared accommodation and insurance provided. No fares or wages paid. Membership fee £15 (£5 unwaged). Registration fee £35 (£25 unwaged). **B D PH**

🎓 *Applicants in Northern Ireland should apply direct; applicants in the rest of the UK should apply to International Voluntary Service, Old Hall, East Bergholt, Colchester, Essex CO7 6TQ. Applications from outside the UK: please see information on page 30.*

APPLYING FOR A JOB

When writing to **any** organisation it is **essential** to mention **Working Holidays 1995** and enclose a **stamped, self-addressed A4 envelope**, or if in another country, an **addressed A4 envelope** and at least two **IRCs** (International Reply Coupons, available from post offices). Enquiries received without SAEs/IRCs are **unlikely** to be answered. **Before applying**, read carefully all the information given. Pay **particular** attention to:

- skills/qualifications/experience required

- the period of employment expected

- age limits or nationality restrictions

- application deadlines

- any other points, especially details of insurance cover, and other costs such as travel and accommodation.

When applying include the following:

- your name, address, date of birth, marital status, nationality, sex

- details of your education, qualifications, relevant experience, skills, languages spoken

- your period of availability for work

- a passport-size photo, particularly if you will be working with the public

- anything else recommended in the listing (such as a *cv*)

INFO

Royal Norwegian Embassy
25 Belgrave Square, London SWIX
8QD ✆ 0171-235 7151

British Embassy
Thomas Heftyesgate 8, 0244 Oslo
✆ (47) 22 55 24 00

Tourist office
Norwegian National Tourist Office,
Charles House, 5-11 Lower Regent
Street, London SWIY 4LR
✆ 0171-839 6255

Youth hostels
Norske Vandrerhjem, Dronningensgate
26, 0154 Oslo ✆ (47) 22 42 14 10
✉ (47) 22 42 44 76

Youth & student information
Universitetenes Reisebyra (Norwegian
Student Travel Office), Universitets-
sentret, Blindern, Boks 55, Oslo 3

Norwegian Foundation for Youth
Exchange, Rolf Hofmosgate 18, 0655
Oslo 6

Entry regulations Nationals of the
UK/EU/EEA do not need a visa, nor do
they require a work permit in order to
take up employment. They may stay for
up to 3 months to seek employment,
provided they are financially self-
supporting. If their stay exceed 3
months they should apply in person at
the nearest police station for a
residence permit. All other nationals
require a work permit for all types of
employment. This can only be obtained
before arrival, when a job has been
secured with an employer who has been
approved to employ foreign personnel.
An Offer of Employment form must be
completed and signed by the employer
before a work permit can be applied for.
Permits are very difficult to obtain and
only people with special skills are
accepted, if a Norwegian national cannot
fill the job. The application will be sent

to the authorities in Norway, who normally take 3-6 months; in special cases and at peak times this may be longer. A current full passport is required for employment purposes.

Job advertising Frank L Crane (London) Ltd, International Press Representation, 5/15 Cromer Street, Grays Inn Road, London WC1H 8LS ℗ 0171-837 3330 can place job advertisements in *Dagbladet.*

Travel Freedom Pass allows 3, 5 or 10 days unlimited rail travel in 1 month on the railways of Norway. Cost from £68 (under 26) or £89 (26+). Available from British Rail International Rail Centre, Victoria Station, London SW1V 1JY ℗ 0171-834 2345.

ScanRail Pass is a flexible rail pass for Scandinavia, valid for unlimited travel during 5 days within 15 days, 10 days in 1 month and 1 month consecutive. Cost from £94 (under 26) or from £125 (26+) for 5 days. Discounts are offered on certain ferry and bus routes. Details from Norwegian State Railways, 21-24 Cockspur Street, London SW1Y 5DA ℗ 0171-930 6666.

Campus Travel can arrange Eurotrain, Inter-Rail and student/youth fares for travel to destinations in Norway. Offices throughout the UK, including 52 Grosvenor Gardens, London SW1W 0AG ℗ 0171-730 3402 or ℗ 0131-668 3303 for Scottish telephone bookings.

Information centres Use It, Mollergata 3, 0179 Oslo ℗ (47) 22 41 51 32 ⊡ (47) 22 42 63 71 is a youth information centre that can help with budget accommodation and tourist information. Publishes an alternative guide to Oslo called *Streetwise.* Open early June-late August, Mondays-Fridays, 0730-1800 and Saturdays, 0900-1400.

Publications Lonely Planet's *Scandinavian and Baltic Europe on a Shoestring* £10.95 offers practical, down-to-earth information for the low-budget, independent traveller in Norway.

The Rough Guide to Scandinavia £10.99 provides comprehensive background information on Norway plus details on getting there, getting around, places to explore and cheap places to stay.

Michael's Guide to Scandinavia £10.95 is detailed and concise, providing invaluable practical advice for all kinds of travellers. Published by Inbal Travel.

Culture Shock! Norway £6.95 introduces the reader to the people, customs, ceremonies, food and culture, with checklists of dos and don'ts.

Vacation Work's *Live & Work in Scandinavia* £8.95 is a guide for those interested in finding temporary or permanent work, starting a business or buying a home in Norway, Denmark, Finland, Sweden or Iceland.

All the above guides are available from good bookshops.

AU PAIR / CHILDCARE

ATLANTIS YOUTH EXCHANGE Rolf Hofmosgate 18, 0655 Oslo, Norway ℗ (47) 22 67 00 43 Can place English-speaking **au pairs** in families to provide an experience of Norwegian culture. 9+ months. ⊕ Ages 18-30. Board, lodging and NKr2,300 per month provided. Travel and language course fees paid by applicants.

HELPING HANDS AU PAIR & DOMESTIC AGENCY 39 Rutland Avenue, Thorpe Bay, Essex SS1 2XJ ℗ Southend-on-Sea (01702) 602067 Can place **au pairs** and **mothers' helps.** ⊕ Ages 18-27. Pocket money approx £35 per week for au pairs, higher for mothers' helps. Introduction

fee £40 on acceptance of a family.
🐾 UK nationals only.

COMMUNITY WORK

NANSEN INTERNASJONALE CENTER Barnegården Breivold, Nesset, 1400 Ski, Norway

Long-term relief centre for teenagers with deep social and emotional needs, situated on a renovated farm south of Oslo. **Volunteers** needed to help in all aspects of the work, cooking, cleaning and care of animals, all forming part of the daily routine. Many possibilities for sports, hobbies and excursions; leaders are expected to motivate young people's participation and prepare them for the future. Volunteers must be prepared to work very hard; hours long and tiring. ⊕ Ages 22+. Applicants with practical skills and the initiative to tackle and follow through ideas with the minimum of supervision needed. Driving licence and some experience of working with children essential. Most applicants expected to stay 1 year but there is also a 6 week special summer project. Volunteers receive full board and lodging and NKr500 per week. 🐾 Apply to the Director before April for summer projects.

CONSERVATION

BRITISH TRUST FOR CONSERVATION VOLUNTEERS Room IWH, 36 St Mary's Street, Wallingford, Oxfordshire OX10 0EU ✆ Wallingford (01491) 839766

The largest charitable organisation in Britain to involve people in practical conservation work. Following the success of the UK Natural Break Programme, is now developing a series of working holidays with the aim of introducing the volunteering ethic to communities abroad. It is hoped British **volunteers** will adapt to and learn from local lifestyles as well as participate in the community. In conjunction with the

Nansen Society in Budor, work involves footpath construction, restoration of traditional timber houses and erection of bird boxes.
⊕ Ages 18-70. 2 weeks, July-August. Cost from £165 includes transport from a meeting point in Norway, insurance, food and accommodation in log cabins, with everyone sharing in domestic chores. Volunteers should take a sleeping bag. Membership fee £12. No fares or wages paid.

COURIERS/REPS

EUROCAMP Summer Jobs (Ref WH), PO Box 170, Liverpool L70 1ES ✆ Knutsford (01565) 625522

One of Europe's leading tour operators, specialising in providing quality camping and mobile home holidays for families throughout Europe. **Campsite couriers** required. Work involves cleaning tents and equipment prior to the arrival of new customers; checking, replacing and making repairs on equipment; replenishing gas supplies; keeping basic accounts and reporting on a weekly basis to England. Couriers are also expected to meet new arrivals and assist holidaymakers with any problems that arise; organise activities and parties; provide information on local tourist attractions and maintain an information noticeboard. At the beginning and end of the season couriers also help in erecting and dismantling tents. Couriers need to be flexible to meet the needs of customers and be on hand where necessary; able to organise their own free time as the workload allows.
⊕ Ages 18+. Applicants should be independent, adaptable, reliable, physically fit, have plenty of initiative and relish a challenging and responsible position. Good working knowledge of local languages also necessary. Preference given to those able to work the whole season, April-September/October; contracts also available for first half, April-mid July and second half season, mid July-September/October.

Children's couriers also required, with the energy and enthusiasm to organise a wide range of exciting activities for groups aged 4-13. Experience of working with this age range essential, but language ability is not a requirement. ⊕ Ages 18+. Must be available for the whole season, May-September.

For both positions the salary is £95 per week. Training provided together with tent accommodation with cooking facilities, insurance and return travel. *Early application by telephone preferred; interviews start September/October. UK/EEA passport-holders only.*

FARMWORK

ATLANTIS YOUTH EXCHANGE
Working Guest Programme, Rolf Hofmosgate 18, 0655 Oslo, Norway ☎ (47) 22 67 00 43
Opportunities to stay on a farm as a **working guest**. The work involves haymaking, weeding, milking, picking fruit and vegetables, tractor driving, feeding cattle, painting, housework and/or taking care of the children. Most farmers and/or children speak some English/German. ⊕ Ages 18-30. Farming experience desirable but not essential; applicants must be willing to work hard. Up to 35 hour week; 1½ consecutive free days. 4-12 weeks, all year. Board, lodging and NKr500+ per week pocket money provided. Participants pay own travel costs. Registration fee NKr830; NKr700 refundable if applicant not placed. Some farms may accept 2 people who apply together. *UK applicants should apply through Concordia (Youth Service Volunteers) Ltd, Recruitment Secretary, 8 Brunswick Place, Hove, Sussex BN3 1ET ☎ Brighton (01273) 772086.*

INTERNATIONAL FARM EXPERIENCE PROGRAMME
YFC Centre, N A C, Stoneleigh Park, Kenilworth, Warwickshire CV8 2LG ☎ (01203) 696584
Provides assistance to young **agriculturalists** and **horticulturalists**

by finding places in farms/nurseries abroad, enabling them to broaden their knowledge of agricultural and horticultural methods. Participants usually live and work with a farming family and the work is matched as far as possible with participant's requirements. Entails physical work and practical involvement. Basic wage plus board and lodging. 3-12 months, all year. ⊕ Ages 18-28. Applicants must have at least 2 years practical experience, one of which may be at agricultural college, and intend to make a career in agriculture/horticulture. Valid driving licence necessary. Participants pay own fares and insurance. Registration fee £85. *UK applications to IFEP; others to IFEP partner in home country.*

WORKCAMPS

INTERNASJONAL DUGNAD
Langes Gate 6, 0165 Oslo 1, Norway
The Norwegian branch of Service Civil International, which promotes international reconciliation through work projects. **Volunteers** are invited to take part in international workcamps. Recent projects have included haymaking and painting alongside teenagers at an community for youngsters with social problems near Gol; reconstruction work, gardening and helping in the cafe at the Korhaug Peace Centre; and maintenance and improvement of a bio-organic farm near Fåvang. ⊕ Ages 18+. Applicants should be highly motivated, preferably with workcamp or other voluntary experience, and prepared to work hard as part of a team. 35-40 hour week. 2-4 weeks, June-September. Food, shared accommodation and work accident insurance provided. No fares or wages paid. **B D PH W**

Apply through partner organisation in country of residence. In the UK: International Voluntary Service. See page 30 for registration details and addresses.

POLAND

INFO

Polish Embassy
47 Portland Place, London WIN 3AG
✆ 0171-580 4324/9 📠 0171-323 4018
Visa Section: Consulate General, 73 New
Cavendish Street, London WIN 3AG
✆ 0171-580 0476 📠 0171-323 2320

British Embassy
Aleje Roz 1, 00-556 Warsaw
✆ (48 2) 628 1001-5

Tourist office
Polorbis Travel Ltd, 82 Mortimer Street,
London WIN 7DE ✆ 0171-636 2217

Youth hostels
Polskie Towarzystwo Schronisk
Mlodziezowych, ul Chocimska 28,
00-791 Warsaw

Youth & student information
Almatur, Travel Bureau of the Polish
Students' Association, ul Kopernika 15,
00-364 Warsaw

Juventur Youth Travel Bureau, Gdanska
27/31, 01-633 Warsaw

Entry regulations UK nationals
holding valid passports may stay for up
to 6 months without a visa. Nationals of
most other EU countries and the US do
not require a visa for stays of up to 90
days. Visa-free entry does not apply to
persons arriving to take up employment
in Poland, who should check regulations
with the Polish Consulate General.

Job advertising Frank L Crane
(London) Ltd, International Press
Representatives, 5/15 Cromer Street,
Grays Inn Road, London WC1H 8LS
✆ 0171-837 3330 can place job
advertisements in The Warsaw Voice,
English language weekly.

Travel Freedom Pass allows 3, 5 and 10
days unlimited rail travel in 1 month on
the railways of Poland. Cost from £28
(under 26) or £33 (26+). Available from

British Rail International Rail Centre, Victoria Station, London WIV IJY © 0171-832 2345.

Campus Travel can arrange Eurotrain, Inter-Rail and student/youth fares on all types of travel to Poland. Offices throughout the UK, including a student travel centre at 52 Grosvenor Gardens, London SWIW 0AG © 0171-730 3402 or © 0131-668 3303 for Scottish telephone bookings.

Council Travel, 28A Poland Street, London WIV 3DB © 0171-287 3337 offers Eurotrain under 26 fares and youth/student flights to destinations in Poland, plus travel insurance, guidebooks and travel gear.

Fregata Travel Ltd, 100 Dean Street, London WIV 6AQ © 0171-734 5101 offers express rail travel London-Poznan/ Warsaw from £160 return plus couchettes, and a coach service London-Poznan/Warsaw, from £60 return (youth fare). Also flights London-Warsaw/ Gdansk/Krakow from £168; Manchester-Warsaw from £225, plus tax.

The Polrailpass entitles the holder to unlimited travel on local and express trains. Valid for 8/15/21/30 days, cost from £29. Available from Polorbis Travel Ltd, 82 Mortimer Street, London WIN 7DE © 0171-636 2217.

Publications Lonely Planet's *Eastern Europe on a Shoestring* £13.95, provides practical information on budget travel.

Poland - A Travel Survival Kit £10.95 offers practical, down-to-earth information for independent travellers wanting to explore beyond the usual tourist routes.

The Rough Guide to Poland £9.99 provides comprehensive background information plus details on getting around, places to explore and cheap places to stay.

Vacation Work's *Travellers Survival Kit Eastern Europe* £9.95 is a guide for

travellers containing advice on where to go, budget accommodation and dealing with bureaucracy.

All the above available from bookshops.

FARMWORK

INTERNATIONAL FARM EXPERIENCE PROGRAMME YFC Centre, N A C, Stoneleigh Park, Kenilworth, Warwickshire CV8 2LG © Coventry (01203) 696584
Provides assistance to young **agriculturalists** and **horticulturalists** by finding places on farms and nurseries abroad, enabling them to broaden their knowledge of agricultural and horticultural methods. Participants usually live and work with a farming family and the work is matched as far as possible with participant's requirements. Entails physical work and practical involvement. Basic wage plus board and lodging. 3 months, during the summer. ⊕ Ages 18-28. Applicants must have at least 2 years practical experience, one of which may be at an agricultural college and intend to make a career in agriculture or horticulture. Valid driving licence necessary. Participants pay own fares and insurance. Registration fee £85. ✎ *UK applications to IFEP; others to IFEP partner in home country.*

MONITORS & TEACHERS

ANGLO-POLISH ACADEMIC ASSOCIATION Secretariat, 93 Victoria Road, Leeds LS6 IDR © 0113-275 8121
Volunteers are required to teach English to Polish doctors, teachers, students and families.
⊕ Ages 20-60. Applicants must have clear spoken English and legible handwriting. Teacher training or previous teaching experience desirable

but not essential. 15 hours per week for 3 weeks, July-August. Cultural and recreational activities organised by hosts. Full board accommodation provided but volunteers pay own travel and insurance costs. Travel grant of up to 50% available. **B D PH** 🎓 *Apply before mid June. English native speakers only.*

CENTRAL BUREAU FOR EDUCATIONAL VISITS & EXCHANGES Seymour Mews House, Seymour Mews, London W1H 9PE ✆ 0171-725 9411

Teachers and **sixth formers** are required at English language summer camps held at boarding schools in Poland, each accommodating approx 100 pupils from UNESCO Associated Schools which have specialised courses in foreign languages. The main objective is to provide Polish pupils aged 14-18 with the opportunity of practising English learnt in school and to acquire a deeper awareness of the British way of life. Duties include assisting with the teaching of English, running conversation classes and organising sporting, musical and social activities. ⊕ Ages up to 45. Applicants should be native English speakers, sixth formers willing to assist the staff; or teachers qualified in the teaching of any discipline: EFL or ESL qualifications an advantage. Applicants should have a sense of responsibility, organisational skill, adaptability to new surroundings, a sociable nature and an interest in sports and/or drama and music, plus experience of working with or teaching children. Participants must fully commit themselves to the teaching of English and the organisation of various educational, outdoor and social activities. 4 weeks, July-August, including a 4 day trip to places of interest at the end. Board and accommodation provided, plus honorarium in Polish currency towards pocket money. Travel cost approx £250 including insurance and visa, paid by applicants. Organised by the Polish Ministry of Education and UNESCO. 🎓 *Apply by mid April.*

PRIVATE SCHOOL OF ENGLISH PROGRAM ul Fredry 7, Poznan, Poland

Volunteers required to teach English and organise activities for groups of 10-12 children on summer camps. ⊕ Ages 21-35. 24 hour day; four 2-week camps, June-August. Applicants should be enthusiastic and creative, preferably with experience of working with children. Full board accommodation and pocket money provided. 🎓 *Apply by 30 August. Native English speakers only.*

WORKCAMPS

FOUNDATION FOR INTERNATIONAL YOUTH EXCHANGES (FIYE) ul Nowy Swiat 18/20, 00-920 Warsaw, Poland

A voluntary organisation providing social services to disadvantaged groups and organising activities for young people. **Volunteers** are invited to take part in international workcamps. Recent projects have included working with people with learning disabilities at a residential home in Zbyszyce; assisting with the renovation of an 18th century palace and grounds in Kozłówka; and conducting conversational English classes for groups of Polish teenagers in Siennica. Educational, cultural and recreational activities arranged, including visits to national parks and sports. ⊕ Ages 18+. Applicants should have previous workcamp experience and be fit, prepared to work hard and contribute to team life. 30-35 hour week. 2-4 weeks, July-September. Food and shared accommodation in schools, hostels, houses or tents provided. No fares or wages paid. Volunteers should take out full insurance. 🎓 *Apply through partner organisation in country of residence. In the UK: Christian Movement for Peace, Concordia (Youth Service Volunteers) Ltd, International Voluntary Service, Quaker International Social Projects or United Nations Association International Youth Service. See page 30 for details and addresses.*

INFO

Portuguese Embassy
11 Belgrave Square, London SW1X 8PP
✆ 0171-235 5331-4
Consular section: Silver City House,
62 Brompton Road, London SW3 1BJ
✆ 0171-581 8722-4

British Embassy
Rua de S Domingos à Lapa 37, 1200
Lisbon ✆ (351 1) 396 1191

Tourist office
Portuguese National Tourist Office,
22/25a Sackville Street, London
W1X 1DE ✆ 0171-494 1441

Youth hostels
Associaçâo Portuguesa das Pousadas de
Juventude, Rua Andrade Corvo 46,
1000 Lisbon ✆ (351 1) 571054/522002

Youth & student information
Associacâo de Turismo Estudantil e
Juvenil, PO Box 4586, 4009 Porto

Instituto da Juventude, Avenida da
Liberdade 194, 1200 Lisbon

Turicoop, Turismo Social e Juvenil, Rua
Pascoal de Melo, 15-1, Dto, 1100 Lisbon

Entry regulations UK citizens
intending to work should have a full
passport. UK/EEA nationals may stay
for up to 3 months; those wishing to
stay longer must contact the local
Serviço de Estrangeiros e Fronteiras
(SEF) to obtain a residence permit.
A list of SEF offices is available from the
Consulate General. A work permit and
residence visa are required for non-EEA
nationals; the employer applies for the
permit through the local authorities.
Applications for a residence visa should
be made to the Consulate General at
least 6 months in advance. Workcamp
volunteers do not require work permits.

Job advertising Publicitas Ltd, 517/523
Fulham Road, London SW6 1HD

© 0171-385 7723 can place job advertisements in *Diario de Noticias* (Lisbon daily), *Journal de Noticias* (Oporto daily) and *Expresso* (business weekly).

Anglo-Portuguese News, Apartado 113, 2765 Estoril, Lisbon, can accept all kinds of advertisements, especially for work in families as au pairs or domestics.

Travel Freedom Pass allows 3, 5 or 10 days unlimited rail travel in 1 month on the railways of Portugal. Cost from £66 (under 26) or £84 (26+). Available from British Rail International Rail Centre, Victoria Station, London SW1V 1JY © 0171-834 2345.

Campus Travel can arrange Eurotrain, Inter-Rail and student/youth fares for all types of travel to Portugal. Offices throughout the UK including 52 Grosvenor Gardens, London SW1W 0AG © 0171-730 3402 or © 0131-668 3303 for Scottish telephone bookings.

Council Travel, 28A Poland Street, London W1V 3DB © 0171-287 3337 (offices also in Paris, Nice, Lyon, Munich, Düsseldorf, Tokyo, Singapore and throughout the US) offers Eurotrain under 26 fares and youth/student flights to Portugal, plus travel insurance, guidebooks and travel gear.

STA Travel, 86 Old Brompton Road, London SW7 3LQ/117 Euston Road, London NW1 2SX © 0171-937 9921 (offices also in Birmingham, Bristol, Cambridge, Glasgow, Leeds, Manchester and Oxford) operates flexible low-cost flights between London and Portugal.

Publications The Portuguese National Tourist Office, see above, publish a brochure providing descriptions of regions, information on folklore, fairs, festivals, travel and accommodation.

The Rough Guide to Portugal £9.99 provides background information plus places to explore, details on getting around and cheap places to stay. Available from good bookshops.

Portugal: a guide to employment and opportunities for young people offers advice and contacts for those seeking long and short term teaching posts, office employment, summer jobs, and voluntary work. Available from the Hispanic and Luso Brazilian Council, Canning House, 2 Belgrave Square, London SW1X 8PJ © 0171-235 2303. Price £3 (free to members).

Live and Work in Spain and Portugal £8.95 is a guide for those interested in finding temporary or permanent work, starting a business or buying a home in Iberia. Published by Vacation Work, 9 Park End Street, Oxford OX1 1HJ © Oxford (01865) 241978.

Accommodation Residência Universitâria, Estrada da Costa, 1495 Cruz Quebrada, Lisbon has accommodation for students during August only. 170 beds in double/triple rooms; cost Esc2,000 per day. Apply 2 months in advance. Also offers discounts on train, boat and air travel. Further information from Servicos Sociais da Universidade Técnica de Lisboa, Servico de Cultura e Turismo, Rua Goncalves Crespo 20, 1100 Lisbon.

Turicoop, Turismo Social e Juvenil, Rua Pascoal de Melo, 15-1, Dto, 1100 Lisbon can arrange cheap accommodation for young people in youth hostels, pensions and hotels. Also runs holiday centres and provides information on campsites.

ARCHAEOLOGY

ETCHED IN TIME - PORTUGAL
Ludwig Jaffe & Dr Mila Simoes de Abreu, Av D José 1, n 53, 2780 Oeiras, Portugal ©/▱ (351 1) 442 1359
Volunteers are invited to join international, multi-disciplinary expeditions investigating rock art,

archaeology and ethnography in the Trás-os-Montes region to the north east of Portugal and the Alentejo region to the south. As well as mapping and recording finds, participants may also get involved in conversing with village storytellers and recording their narratives. 1+ weeks, June-September, with 1 day each week set aside for rambling.
⊕ Ages 14+. Applicants should be creative, original individuals who enjoy working as part of a team and are keen to contribute to new and existing lines of research. No previous experience required but an interest in rock art, archaeology, people and places is essential, as is a knowledge of English, Portuguese, Italian or Spanish. Cost £300 per 7-day session covers well-equipped dormitory accommodation and all meals; awards worth up to £150 available to those unable to cover full costs. Applicants arrange own travel and insurance and should bring a sleeping bag, work clothes and sturdy footwear. No fares or wages paid. 🖂 *Send IRC for application form, to be returned at least 1 month in advance.* **B D PH**

INSTITUTO DA JUVENTUDE
Avenida da Liberdade 194, 1200 Lisbon, Portugal
Volunteers are invited to work on international workcamps assisting with archaeological digs and aimed at discovering and preserving Portugal's heritage. Recent projects have included excavating and recording finds at prehistoric sites, Roman baths, castles and other historic monuments. Visits to local places of interest and sports activities arranged.
⊕ Ages 18-25. 40 hour, 5 day week. 2 weeks, July-September. Food, shared accommodation in houses, schools or tents and work accident insurance provided. Participants cook on a rota basis and must take a sleeping bag. No fares or wages paid.

🖂 *Apply through partner organisation in country of residence. In the UK: Quaker International Social Projects or United Nations Association International Youth Service. See page 30 for registration details and addresses.*

CONSERVATION

INSTITUTO DA JUVENTUDE
Avenida da Liberdade 194, 1200 Lisbon, Portugal
Volunteers are invited to work on international workcamps assisting with conservation projects. Recent projects have included restoring 16th-18th century ceramic tiles in Beja; renovating an old watermill in Braga; cleaning up the Esmoriz lagoon; biological and geological studies in natural caves in Portalegre; and coastal protection work in Setúbal. Visits to local places of interest and sports activities arranged.
⊕ Ages 18-25. 40 hour, 5 day week. 2 weeks, July-September. Food, shared accommodation in houses, schools or tents and work accident insurance provided; participants cook on a rota basis and must take a sleeping bag. No fares or wages paid.

🖂 *Apply through partner organisation in country of residence. In the UK: Quaker International Social Projects or United Nations Association International Youth Service. See page 30 for registration details and addresses.*

FARMWORK

INTERNATIONAL FARM EXPERIENCE PROGRAMME
YFC Centre, N A C, Stoneleigh Park, Kenilworth, Warwickshire CV8 2LG ✆ Coventry (01203) 696584
Provides assistance to young **agriculturalists** and **horticulturalists** by finding places in farms/nurseries abroad, enabling them to broaden their knowledge of agricultural and horticultural methods. Participants usually live and work with a farming

family and the work is matched as far as possible with participant's requirements. Entails physical work and practical involvement. Basic wage plus board and lodging. 3-12 months, all year. ⊕ Ages 18-28. Applicants must have at least 2 years practical experience, one of which may be at agricultural college, and intend to make a career in agriculture/horticulture. Valid driving licence necessary. Participants pay own fares and insurance. Registration fee £85. 🖾 UK applications to IFEP. Other applications to IFEP partner in home country.

WORKCAMPS

INSTITUTO DA JUVENTUDE
Avenida da Liberdade 194, 1200 Lisbon, Portugal
Volunteers are invited to work on international workcamps. Recent projects have included renovating a youth hostel in Beja; restoring an old castle in Portalegre; constructing kayaks in Porto; preserving an abandoned village in Viano do Castelo; documenting caves in Serra de Montejunio; and building a children's playground and an open-air theatre in Vila Real.
⊕ Ages 18-25. 40 hour, 5 day week. 2 weeks, July-September. Food, shared accommodation in houses, schools or tents and work accident insurance provided. Participants cook on a rota basis and must take a sleeping bag. No fares or wages paid.

🖾 Apply through partner organisation in country of residence. In the UK: Quaker International Social Projects or United Nations Association International Youth Service. See page 30 for registration details and addresses.

MOVIMENTO CRISTAO PARA A PAZ (MCP) Praça de Republica 18-3°, 3000 Coimbra, Portugal
✆ (351 39) 27459
Volunteers are needed to work in international teams on summer projects

aimed at offering a service in an area of need; promoting self-help within the community; promoting international understanding and the discussion of social problems; and offering young people the chance to live as a group and take these experiences into the context of daily life. Recent projects have included helping to construct an MCP head office and welcome centre in Granja do Ulmeiro; building and decorating a children's playground in the small mountain village of Sanhoane; repair jobs at a home for orphaned and vulnerable children near Porto; and clearing footpaths and forestry work in the mountain area of Lousa.
⊕ Ages 18+. Knowledge of Portuguese, French or English useful. 6 hour day, 50 hour week for 2 weeks, July/August. Food, shared accommodation and work accident insurance provided. No fares or wages paid.

🖾 Apply through partner organisation in country of residence. In the UK: Christian Movement for Peace. See page 30 for registration details and addresses.

GENERAL

EUROYOUTH LTD
301 Westborough Road, Westcliff, Southend-on-Sea Essex SS0 9PT
✆ **Southend-on-Sea (01702) 341434**
Arranges stays where **guests** are offered board and lodging in return for an agreed number of hours English conversation with hosts or their children. Time also available for guests to practise Portuguese.
⊕ Mainly ages 18-25, but sometimes opportunities for ages 13-16 and for older applicants. Open to British students interested in visiting Portugal and living with a local family for a short time. Compulsory language course. 2-3 weeks, June-August. Insurance and travel paid by applicants. Registration fee approx £70. 🖾 Apply at least 12 weeks prior to departure. Limited places.

ROMANIA

INFO

Romanian Embassy
4 Palace Green, London W8 4QD
℡ 0171-937 9666/8
Visa Section: ℡ 0171-937 9667

British Embassy
24 Strada Jules Michelet, 70154 Bucharest
℡ (40 0) 3120 303/4/5/6

Tourist office
Romanian National Tourist Office,
17 Nottingham Street, London W1M
3FF ℡ 0171-224 3692

Entry regulations A visa is required
for all types of visits. Applicants must
present a full passport, valid for at least
3 months after date of anticipated
return. Visas are valid for 3 months
from date of issue and allow stays of 30
days maximum. Further details from
the Visa Section of the Romanian
Embassy.

Travel Campus Travel can arrange
Eurotrain, Inter-Rail and student/youth
fares for all types of travel to
destinations in Romania. Offices
throughout the UK including 52
Grosvenor Gardens, London SW1W
0AG ℡ 0171-730 3402 or ℡ 0131-668
3303 for Scottish telephone bookings.

Council Travel, 28A Poland Street,
London W1V 3DB ℡ 0171-287 3337
(offices also in Paris, Nice, Lyon, Munich,
Düsseldorf, Tokyo, Singapore and
throughout the US) offers Eurotrain
under 26 fares and youth/student flights
to Bucharest, plus travel insurance,
guidebooks and travel gear.

Publications Lonely Planet's *Eastern
Europe on a Shoestring* £13.95, provides
practical information on budget travel.
Available from good bookshops.

CONSERVATION

BRITISH TRUST FOR CONSERVATION VOLUNTEERS Room IWH, 36 St Mary's Street, Wallingford, Oxfordshire OX10 0EU ℗ Wallingford (01491) 839766

The largest charitable organisation in Britain to involve people in practical conservation work. Following the success of the Natural Break Programme in the UK, BTCV is now developing international working holidays with the aim of introducing **volunteers** to practical conservation projects abroad. Recent projects have included surveying and habitat management at a salt lake resort in Braila; and improving nesting sites for white-tailed eagles in the Danube Delta. ⊕ Ages 18-70. 1-2 weeks, July-October. Cost from £100 includes transport from a suitable pick-up point in Romania, insurance cover, food and basic accommodation, with everyone sharing in domestic chores. Volunteers should take a sleeping bag. Membership fee £12. No fares or wages paid.

COURIERS/REPS

CRYSTAL HOLIDAYS Crystal House, The Courtyard, Arlington Road, Surbiton, Surrey KT6 6BW ℗ 0181-241 5111

Tour operator arranging skiing holidays in Poiana Brasov and Sinaia.
Representatives required to meet and greet clients and look after their welfare during their holiday. **Ski guides** and **chalet staff** also required.
⊕ Ages 22-35. Previous experience and fluent Romanian desirable. Chalet staff must have catering qualifications and experience. Approx 60 hour, 6½ or 7 day week, December-April. Basic salary plus commission, travel costs, board, lodging, insurance and uniform provided. 1 week training seminar held beginning of each season. ✉ Apply April/May.

WORKCAMPS

INTERNATIONAL VOLUNTARY SERVICE Old Hall, East Bergholt, Colchester, Essex CO7 6TQ

The British branch of Service Civil International, which promotes international reconciliation through work projects. Recruits for SCI projects in Romania involving international teams of **volunteers**. Recent projects have included organising an activity holiday for orphan children with special needs in Gilau; layaing a footpath and building a small church at an isolated monastery in the mountains; and renovation and conservation work at an arboretum in Simeria.
⊕ Ages 18+. Applicants must have workcamp or other voluntary experience, and should be prepared to work hard as part of a team. 2-4 weeks, July-August. Food, shared accommodation and work accident insurance provided. No fares or wages paid. Registration fee £105 (students or low/unwaged £100) plus £25/£15 membership fee. Preparation days held in Edinburgh/London prior to departure. **B D PH W** welcome.

🖾 *Applicants outside the UK must apply through partner organisation in country of residence. See page 30 for registration details and addresses.*

When writing to any organisation it is essential to mention Working Holidays 1995 and to enclose a stamped, self-addressed A4 envelope, or if in another country, an addressed A4 envelope and at least two IRCs (International Reply Coupons, available from post offices). Enquiries received without SAEs/IRCs are unlikely to be answered.

SPAIN

INFO

Spanish Embassy
24 Belgravia Square, London SW1X
8QA © 0171-235 5555/6/7
Consular section: 20 Draycott Place,
London SW3 2RZ and 22 Manchester
Square, London W1H 5AP
© 0171-581 5921

British Embassy
Calle de Fernando el Santo 16, 28010
Madrid © (34 1) 319 0200

Tourist office
Spanish National Tourist Office, 57/58
St James's Street, London SW1A 1LB
© 0171-499 0901

Youth hostels
Red Española de Albergues Juveniles,
José Ortega y Gasset 71, 28006 Madrid

Youth & student information
TIVE, Oficina Nacional de Intercambio y
Turismo de Jovenes y Estudiantes, José
Ortega y Gasset 71, 28006 Madrid

Entry regulations EEA nationals may
take up employment without a visa or
work permit. If they intend to stay for
over 3 months, a residence card must be
applied for, obtainable from the local
Comisaria de Policia or *Oficina Gubernativa
de Extranjeros* upon presentation of a
valid passport or identity card and a
photocopy of the same, three passport-
sized photographs, a medical certificate
and the contract or offer of
employment. Non-EEA nationals
wishing to work in Spain must apply in
person for the appropriate visa at the
Spanish Consulate in their country of
residence. The Consulate will then
notify the applicant of the decision
taken. In the UK, the Consular fee is
£43.20. Full details of the regulations
governing residence and employment in
Spain are given on information sheets
available from the Consular Section of
the Spanish Embassy, see above.

Spain: a guide to employment and opportunities for young people offers advice and contacts for teaching posts, exchanges, office employment, summer jobs, voluntary work, au pairs and travel. Available from Hispanic & Luso Brazilian Council, Canning House, 2 Belgrave Square, London SW1X 8PJ ✆ 0171-235 2303. Price £3 (free to members).

Travel Freedom Pass allows 3, 5, or 10 days unlimited rail travel in 1 month on the railways of Spain. Cost from £78 (under 26) or £97 (26+). Available from British Rail International Rail Centre, Victoria Station, London SW1V 1JY ✆ 0171-834 2345.

Campus Travel can arrange Eurotrain, Inter-Rail and student/youth fares for travel to destinations throughout Spain. Offices throughout the UK including 52 Grosvenor Gardens, London SW1W 0AG (opposite Victoria Station) ✆ 0171-730 3402 or ✆ 0131-668 3303 for Scottish telephone bookings.

Council Travel, 28A Poland Street, London W1V 3DB ✆ 0171-287 3337 offers Eurotrain under 26 fares and low-cost youth airfares to destinations throughout Spain, plus travel insurance, guidebooks and travel gear.

STA Travel, 86 Old Brompton Road, London SW7 3LQ/117 Euston Road, London NW1 2SX ✆ 0171-937 9921 (offices also in Birmingham, Bristol, Cambridge, Glasgow, Leeds, Manchester and Oxford) operates flights between London and destinations across Spain.

Information centres Usit, Gran Via 88, Edificio España, Grupo 4, Planta 11, Oficina 7, Madrid (Campus Travel's sister organisation) arranges student/youth travel and gives information and advice.

Publications *The Rough Guide to Spain* £9.99, *The Rough Guide to Andalucia* £8.99 and *The Rough Guide to Barcelona and Catalunya* £8.99 provide comprehensive background information plus details on

getting there, getting around, places to explore and cheap places to stay.

Culture Shock Spain £6.95 introduces the reader to the people, customs, ceremonies, food and culture of Spain, with checklists of dos and don'ts.

Vacation Work's *Live and Work in Spain and Portugal* £8.95 is a guide for those interested in finding temporary or permanent work, starting a business or buying a home in Iberia.

All the above guidebooks are available from good bookshops.

ARCHAEOLOGY

INSTITUTO DE LA JUVENTUD
Servicio Voluntario Internacional de España, José Ortega y Gasset 71, 28006 Madrid, Spain
Volunteers with a genuine interest in archaeology required to work on sites throughout Spain. Recent projects have included excavating a Roman aqueduct and cleaning artefacts near Tiermes; recovering Roman remains, including mosaics, in Augusta; and excavating prehistoric remains at Puerto Roque, near the Portuguese border. Some projects include topographic studies, finds classification, lectures and discussions as well as excavation work. Cultural and sports activities and excursions arranged.
⊕ Ages usually 18-26; younger and older volunteers accepted on some camps. 40 hour week. 2/3 weeks, July and August. Food and accommodation in schools, youth hostels, centres or tents, and accident insurance provided. Participants pay own travel costs.

🏛 *Apply through partner organisation in country of residence. In the UK: Concordia (Youth Service Volunteers) Ltd, Quaker International Social Projects or United Nations Association International Youth Service. See page 30 for details.*

AU PAIR / CHILDCARE

Au pair posts are open to males and females aged 17-30, who work a maximum 25 hour week with 1 day free in return for board, lodging and at least Pts24,000 per month pocket money; they should also have at least 10 hours language classes per week. If the au pair is not covered by Spanish social security, the host family must take out private medical insurance, paying at least half the premium. The *Gobierno Civil* and the *Comisaria Provincial de Policia* in the area in which the au pair will be resident are responsible for granting an au pair permit.

ACADEMY AU PAIR AGENCY LTD 42 Cedarhurst Drive, Eltham, London SE9 5LP ✆ 0181-294 1191 📠 0181-850 8932
Can place **au pairs**. ⊕ Ages 18-27. Some knowledge of Spanish essential. Pocket money approx £35-£40 per week. Administration charge £40. **Nannies** and **mothers' helps** positions also available for those with qualifications/experience.

ANGLO PAIR AGENCY 40 Wavertree Road, Streatham Hill, London SW2 3SP ✆ 0181-674 3605
Can place **au pairs** and **au pairs plus**. ⊕ Ages 17-27. Pocket money £30-£50 per week. Placements for experienced **nannies** and **mothers' helps**; salary up to £100 per week. Agency fee £40.

AVALON AGENCY Thursley House, 53 Station Road, Shalford, Guildford, Surrey GU4 8HA ✆ Guildford (01483) 63640
Can place **au pairs**. ⊕ Ages 18-30. Basic knowledge of Spanish needed. Pocket money equal to £35-£35 per week, usually paid monthly. Fee £40 for placement and use of agent in Spain. Summer holiday placements June-August only. Long-term, 6 month-2 year, vacancies to start any time.

BUNTERS AU PAIR & DOMESTIC AGENCY 17 Copper Street, Macclesfield, Cheshire SK11 7LH ✆ Macclesfield (01625) 614534
Can place **au pairs**, **demi pairs** and **mothers' helps**. 6-12 months all year or 10 weeks, summer. ⊕ Ages 18-27. Pocket money £35-£50 per week depending on hours. Placement fee £40. ✉ *Apply before May for summer posts.*

CENTROS EUROPEOS C/Principe 12, 6A, 28012 Madrid, Spain
Arranges **au pair** stays in Madrid, Bilbao, Asturias, Andalusia, Alicante, Galicia, Valencia, Zaragoza and Santander for girls. ⊕ Ages 18+. Pocket money Pts6,000 per week.

HELPING HANDS AU PAIR & DOMESTIC AGENCY 39 Rutland Avenue, Thorpe Bay, Essex SS1 2XJ ✆ Southend-on-Sea (01702) 602067
Can place **au pairs** and **mothers' helps**. ⊕ Ages 18-27. Pocket money approx £35 per week for au pairs, higher for mothers' helps. Introduction fee £40. *UK nationals only.*

HOME FROM HOME Walnut Orchard, Chearsley, Aylesbury, Buckinghamshire HP18 0DA ✆/📠 Aylesbury (01844) 208561
Can place **au pairs** in all areas. ⊕ Ages 18+. Basic knowledge of Spanish preferable. Pocket money £35 per week. Placement fee £40. *UK nationals only.*

JOLAINE AGENCY 18 Escot Way, Barnet, Hertfordshire EN5 3AN ✆ 0181-449 1334 📠 0181-449 9183
Can place **au pairs** and **mothers' helps**. ⊕ Ages 18-27. Weekly pocket money £40+ per week (au pairs), £50+ (mothers' helps). Placement fee £40.

JUST THE JOB (NOTTINGHAM) 32 Dovedale Road, West Bridgford, Nottingham NG2 6JA ✆ 0115-945 2482
Can place **au pairs** on 6+ month placements only. ⊕ Ages 18+. Weekly pocket money £32-£40. *UK nationals only.*

LANGTRAIN INTERNATIONAL
Torquay Road, Foxrock, Dublin 18, Ireland ✆ **(353 1) 289 3876**
Can place **au pairs** in Spanish families. ⚘ Ages 18+. Pocket money £25 per week. Placement fee £60.

MONDIAL AGENCY 32 Links Road, West Wickham, Kent BR4 0QW ✆ 0181-777 0510
Can place **au pairs** in the Barcelona area. ⚘ Ages 18-27. Pocket money approx £35 per week. Service charge £40.

PROBLEMS UNLIMITED AGENCY 86 Alexandra Road, Windsor, Berkshire SL4 1HU ✆ Windsor (01753) 830101
Can place **au pairs**. ⚘ Ages 18-27. Pocket money £30-£35 per week.

STUDENTS ABROAD LTD
11 Milton View, Hitchin, Hertfordshire SG4 0QD ✆ **Hitchin (01462) 438909** ▭ **(01462) 438919**
Can place **au pairs** and **mothers' helps** on mainland and islands. 1 year stay preferred for mothers' helps; summer placements also available for au pairs. ⚘ Ages 18-30, au pairs. Basic knowledge of Spanish useful. Pocket money £35+ per week au pairs, higher for mothers' helps. Service charge £40. 🕮 *Apply early for summer positions.*

CONSERVATION

BRITISH TRUST FOR CONSERVATION VOLUNTEERS
Room IWH, 36 St Mary's Street, Wallingford OX10 0EU ✆ **Wallingford (01491) 839766**
The largest charitable organisation in Britain to involve people in practical conservation work. Following the success of the Natural Break programme in the UK, BTCV is now developing international working holidays with the aim of introducing **volunteers** to practical conservation projects abroad. It is hoped that the British volunteers will adapt to and learn from local lifestyles as well as participate in the community. Recent projects have included habitat management in the Monfragüe National Park; and working with the Sunseed Trust, drystone walling, tree planting and organic gardening. ⚘ Ages 18-70. 1-2 weeks. Cost from £75 includes transport from suitable pick-up in Spain, insurance, food and basic accommodation with everyone sharing domestic chores. Membership fee £12. No fares or wages paid.

INSTITUTO DE LA JUVENTUD
Servicio Voluntario Internacional de España, José Ortega y Gasset 71, 28006 Madrid, Spain
Volunteers are invited to work on conservation projects. Recent projects have included installing signposts along a mountain path near Oviedo; maintaining paths and caves in the natural park of Los Alcornocales near Cadiz; restoring traditional lime kilns in the Basque village of Billabona; and drawing up a botanical inventory near Ciudad Real. ⚘ Ages usually 18-26; older and younger volunteers accepted on some camps. 40 hour week. 2/3 weeks, July and August. Food, accommodation in schools, youth hostels, centres or tents and accident insurance provided. Cultural and sports activities and excursions arranged. Participants pay own travel costs.

🕮 *Apply through partner organisation in country of residence. In the UK: Concordia (Youth Service Volunteers) Ltd, Quaker International Social Projects or United Nations Association International Youth Service. See page 30 for registration details and addresses.*

THE SUNSEED TRUST PO Box 2000WH, Cambridge CB3 0JF
A British registered charity conducting research into sustainable solutions to environmental problems, with emphasis on countering desertification and on discovering technologies and ways of living appropriate to the planet's future. **Volunteers** are invited to work at the Trust's research station near Almeria,

Europe's most parched region. The site covers over 20 hectares and the project generates its own electricity using wind, solar and generator power. Volunteers work alongside staff researching into simple and appropriate systems to improve the fertility of arid and marginal lands. Projects include tree research, organic hydroponics, semi-sealed growing, solar stills and ovens, and pedal power. Work also goes into support sections, such as organic gardening, administration, construction and maintenance, and communications. ⊕ Ages 17+. No experience necessary, but applicants should have a strong interest in the work of the Trust. Project language is English; knowledge of Spanish or French useful. Volunteers may either join as working visitors (24 hour week, 1+ weeks) or on placement (full-time, 6+ weeks). Work available all year round. Cost £50-£80 per week (working visitors) or £35-£50 per week (placements) covers basic accommodation and vegetarian food, with everyone taking turns doing domestic chores. No fares or wages paid. **D PH W** although difficult terrain.

🖎 *Write for further information enclosing £1 or equivalent in stamps or IRCs. Applicants in Spain may apply to Sunseed, Apdo 9, Sorbas, 04270 Almeria.*

COURIERS / REPS

CANVAS HOLIDAYS LTD
12 Abbey Park Place, Dunfermline, Fife KY12 7PD
Resident **couriers, children's couriers**, and **watersports couriers** are required to work on campsites for a holiday company providing accommodation for families in ready-erected fully equipped tents and mobile homes. The work involves a daily routine of tent cleaning as customers arrive and depart, providing information and advice on the local attractions and essential services, helping to sort out problems that might arise, and

organising activities for the children and get-togethers for the families. 7 day week with no fixed hours; the workload varies from day to day. At the beginning and end of the season there is a period of physical work when tents are put up and prepared for the customers or taken down and stored for the winter. Other tasks include administration, book keeping and stock control. Working knowledge of Spanish essential. ⊕ Ages 18-25. Applicants are normally those with a year between school and further education, undergraduates or graduates. They need to be reliable, self-motivated, able to turn their hand to new and varied tasks, and with a sense of humour. 6 months, April-October. Salary £85 per week. Return travel, dependent on successful completion of contract, and accommodation in frame tents provided. 🖎 *Applications accepted anytime, interviews commence early November. UK nationals only.*

CLUB CANTABRICA HOLIDAYS LTD Overseas Department, Holiday House, 146-148 London Road, St Albans, Hertfordshire AL1 1PQ ✆ St Albans (01727) 33141
Organises holidays providing fully equipped tents, caravans and mobile homes. Requires **couriers** and **maintenance staff** for the summer season, early May-early October. ⊕ Ages 21+. Experience and good knowledge of Spanish an advantage. 6 day week. Wages from £55 per week, plus bonus at end of season. Self-catering accommodation in tents or caravans, travel costs from Watford and insurance provided. 🖎 *Apply enclosing cv and SAE/IRCs. EEA nationals only.*

EUROCAMP Summer Jobs (Ref WH), PO Box 170, Liverpool L70 1ES ✆ Knutsford (01565) 625522
One of Europe's leading tour operators, specialising in providing quality camping and mobile home holidays for families throughout Europe. **Campsite couriers** are required: work involves cleaning tents and equipment prior to

customers' arrival; checking, replacing and making repairs on equipment; replenishing gas supplies; keeping basic accounts and reporting on a weekly basis to England. Couriers are also expected to meet new arrivals and assist holidaymakers with any problems that arise; organise activities and parties; provide information on local tourist attractions and maintain an information noticeboard. At beginning and end of the season couriers also help in erecting and dismantling tents. They need to be flexible to meet the needs of customers and be on hand where necessary; they will be able to organise their own free time as the workload allows.
⊕ Ages 18+. Applicants should be independent, adaptable, reliable, physically fit, have plenty of initiative and relish a challenging and responsible position. Good working knowledge of Spanish also necessary. Preference given to those able to work the whole season, April-September/October; contracts also available for first half season, April-mid July and second half season, mid July-September/October.
Children's couriers also required, with the energy and enthusiasm to organise a wide range of exciting activities for groups of children aged 4-13. Experience of working with these ages essential, but language ability not a requirement.
⊕ Ages 18+. Must be available for the whole season, May-September.
For both positions salary £95 per week. Training, accommodation in frame tent with cooking facilities, insurance and return travel provided.
🕮 Early application by telephone preferred; interviews start September/October.
UK/EEA passport-holders only.

HAVEN EUROPE Northney Marina, Northney Road, Hayling Island, Hampshire PO11 0NL
Tour operator organising self-drive package holidays, with accommodation in luxury mobile homes and tents.
Seasonal **park managers** required for parks in coastal and inland regions. Work involves preparing accommodation,

welcoming guests and dealing with problems that may arise. **Tiger Club couriers** also required, to work with children and organise entertainment.
⊕ Ages 18+. Experience preferred but not essential, as training is given. Knowledge of Spanish essential. 40+ hour week, although hours vary. May-September. Salary according to workload. Accommodation in self-catering mobile homes or tents, personal insurance and travel expenses provided. UK nationals only.

KEYCAMP HOLIDAYS 92-96 Lind Road, Sutton, Surrey SM1 4PL
✆ 0181-395 8170
One of the UK's largest self-drive camping and mobile home tour operators, offering holidays on over 100 campsites in Europe. **Campsite couriers** are required to work for 3-6 months in an outdoor environment. Main duties include providing clients with information, organising social and sporting activities, cleaning mobile homes and tents, and providing activities for children. Period of employment March-July or July-September.
⊕ Ages 18+. Knowledge of Spanish desirable. Accommodation, uniform, training and competitive salary provided.
🕮 Application requests by postcard.
UK/EEA nationals only.

SOLAIRE INTERNATIONAL HOLIDAYS 1158 Stratford Road, Hall Green, Birmingham B28 8AF
✆ 0121-778 5061
Organises camping and mobile home holidays at Salou on the Costa Dorada. **Seasonal staff** required to prepare tents and mobile homes when season begins in May and close down in October. During the season staff act as couriers, ensuring the smooth running of the camps, and undertake some maintenance work. No fixed hours.
⊕ Ages 18+. No previous experience necessary; foreign languages preferable but not essential. Wages £55-£75 per week, accommodation in tents/mobile homes, insurance and travel provided.

VENUE HOLIDAYS
21 Christchurch Road, Ashford, Kent TN23 1XD
Small family company offering self-drive holidays with fully-equipped mobile homes at a campsite on the Costa Brava. **Representatives** required to clean and maintain accommodation, sort out customers' problems and organise social events for adults and children. At the beginning and end of the season reps assist with the setting up and dismantling of the operation. No fixed hours; workload varies from day to day. Season lasts April-October; minimum requirement to work all July and August. ⊕ Ages 18-30. Experience of working with the public and knowledge of Spanish desirable. Applicants should be fit, able to work hard in hot conditions, mentally alert and practical, with a pleasant, easy-going personality. Salary approx £60 per week; possibility of bonuses. Tented accommodation, insurance and return fare provided. ✍ *Postal applications only.*

DOMESTIC

VIGVATTEN NATUR KLUBB
Apartado Numero 3253, 01002 Vitoria-Gasteiz, Spain
Runs summer camps in the Pyrenees, the Urbion mountains and the Basque country for children and teenagers who want to make friends, explore the countryside and improve knowledge of Spanish or English. Requires **cooks**, and **support staff** for catering, cleaning, maintenance and to set up and dismantle camp. Cooks should have experience of cooking for large numbers; relevant qualifications an advantage. Experience preferred for support staff but not essential; certificate of competence in food hygiene useful. ⊕ Ages 18+. Knowledge of English essential, Spanish useful. 2+ weeks, summer. All positions demand a high level of commitment; staff must enjoy working with children and should be patient, diplomatic, responsible, flexible, enthusiastic, reliable and mature, with a sense of humour and the ability to work in a team. Full board accommodation in tents, and accident and liability insurance provided. Wages approx £240 (cooks), £145 (support staff) per 2 week session. Training programme held prior to camp. Staff arrange and pay for own travel. ✍ *Apply enclosing 2 character references by end June. EEA nationals only.*

FARMWORK

INTERNATIONAL FARM EXPERIENCE PROGRAMME YFC
Centre, N A C, Stoneleigh Park, Kenilworth, Warwickshire CV8 2LG
✆ **Coventry (01203) 696584**
Provides assistance to young **agriculturalists** and **horticulturalists** by finding places in farms/nurseries abroad, enabling them to broaden their knowledge of agricultural and horticultural methods. Participants usually live and work with a farming family and the work is matched as far as possible with participant's requirements. Entails physical work and practical involvement. Basic wage plus board and lodging. 3-12 months, all year. ⊕ Ages 18-28. Applicants must have at least 2 years practical experience, one of which may be at agricultural college, and intend to make a career in agriculture/horticulture. Valid driving licence necessary. Participants pay own fares and insurance. Registration fee £85. ✍ *UK applications to IFEP; others to IFEP partner in home country.*

MONITORS & INSTRUCTORS

ACORN VENTURE LTD Personnel
Department, 137 Worcester Road, Hagley, Stourbridge DY9 0NW
An activity holiday company catering for school groups at a centre in Cala Llevadó on the Costa Brava north of Barcelona. **Instructors** required to

supervise activities such as watersports, target sports, climbing, abseiling, orienteering, caving and gorge walking. ⊕ Ages 18+. Previous experience and qualifications such as BCU/RYA essential. Minimum 50 hour, 6 day week. Applicants are expected to work the full season, May-September. Salary approx £40-£45 per week. All meals and accommodation in tents, insurance and cost of return travel from ferry ports provided. ✎ *Apply in writing with cv by end February. If no reply within 28 days assume application unsuccessful.*

CLUB CANTABRICA HOLIDAYS LTD Overseas Department, Holiday House, 146-148 London Road, St Albans, Hertfordshire AL1 1PQ ✆ St Albans (01727) 833141

Organises camping holidays, providing fully equipped tents, caravans and mobile homes. **Kiddies club staff** required for summer season, early May-early October.
⊕ Ages 21+. Nursing, teaching or NNEB qualifications an advantage. Salary from £55 per week, bonus at season end, self-catering accommodation in tents and caravans, travel from Watford and insurance provided.
✎ *Apply enclosing cv. EEA nationals only.*

ROB HASTINGS ADVENTURE LTD 25 Southcourt Avenue, Leighton Buzzard LU7 7QD ✆ Leighton Buzzard (01525) 379881

Small number of **activity instructors** required to work at a centre in the Pyrenees catering for Spanish children undertaking English and Adventure Activities Programme. Applicants should be experienced and qualified climbers, hillwalkers and/or whitewater canoeists. ⊕ Ages 21+. Ability in other adventure pursuits and individual sports (eg fencing, archery, team-building exercises) and/or environmental awareness useful. 6-8 weeks, July and August. Wages from £75 per week depending on qualifications. Full board hotel accommodation and flight provided. UK nationals only.

VIGVATTEN NATUR KLUBB Apartado Numero 3253, 01002 Vitoria-Gasteiz, Spain

Runs summer camps in the Pyrenees, the Urbion mountains and the Basque country for children and teenagers who want to make friends, explore the countryside and improve knowledge of Spanish or English. Combines balanced programme of leisure activities with an adventure holiday. **Monitors** required to organise and direct daytime and outdoor activities including nature walks, mountaineering, orienteering, campfires, quizzes, environmental and farm studies, forest games, talent shows, treasure hunts and mini olympics. Qualified **nurse** also required for each camp. ⊕ Ages 18+. Knowledge of English essential, Spanish useful. 2+ weeks, during the summer. Applicants must have experience of, and enjoy working with children. They should be responsible, energetic, imaginative, patient, enthusiastic, have initiative, a good sense of humour, strong personality and sympathetic nature. Full board accommodation in tents, and accident and liability insurance provided. Wages approx £145 for 2 week session. Training programme held prior to camp. Staff arrange and pay for own travel.
✎ *Apply enclosing 2 character references by end June. EEA nationals only.*

TEACHERS

CENTRO DE IDIOMAS LIVERPOOL Calle Libreros 11, 1°, 28801 Alcala de Henares, Madrid, Spain ✆ (34 1) 881 3184

Small number of **English teachers** required by language school 30km from Madrid to teach at the school and at companies and schools in nearby towns. ⊕ Ages 22-30. Applicants must have an English degree, elementary Spanish, a recognised TEFL qualification and previous TEFL experience. 25 hour, 5 day week, mid-September-June. 9 month contract; salary Pts 1,400 per hour. Insurance provided. Help given with finding accommodation.

🕮 *Apply by July; interviews held in Britain during August. EEA nationals only.*

CENTROS EUROPEOS C/Principe 12, 6 A, 28012 Madrid, Spain

Teachers with enthusiasm, imagination, and good communication skills are required to teach English, French, and occasionally German or Italian to small groups of mainly adult students. Classes take place within companies or privately. ⊕ Ages 20+. Applicants should have a university background and be reliable, conscientious and vivacious. Some experience preferred. Those without experience, but who have the necessary qualities and who attend an introductory course, may be accepted. Some knowledge of Spanish helpful but not essential. 15-25 hour week, October-June only; no summer positions. Pts2,250 per hour. Accommodation can be arranged with families. Travel and insurance paid by applicants. **PH** *Native speakers only.*

ESCUELAS DE IDIOMAS BERLITZ DE ESPAÑA Ms Susan Taylor, Gran Via 80, 4°, 28013 Madrid, Spain ℂ (34 1) 542 3586

Opportunities for graduates of any discipline to **teach English** as a foreign/second language to adult professionals at beginner through to advanced levels at language centres in Madrid, Barcelona, Bilbao, Sevila, Valencia and Palma de Mallorca. Also possibility of teaching English for Special Purposes in commerce, finance, science and engineering. Work may involve frequent travel within and around the city of allocation. Irregular timetable hours, 0800-2130, and Saturday mornings. ⊕ Ages 21+. Applicants should be mature, responsible, flexible regarding timetable, and have an outgoing personality. TEFL training/experience not necessary; full in-house training provided. 9 month contracts; details of salary on application. 🕮 *Applicants should send cv and recent photograph. Interviews held in Spain in early September.*

THE MANGOLD INSTITUTE Avda Marques de Sotelo 5, Pasaje Rex, 46002 Valencia, Spain ℂ (34 6) 352 7714/351 4556

Offers day and evening courses at all levels in languages, secretarial skills and computing. Languages taught include English, French, German, Italian and Russian. **EFL teachers** and **secretarial staff** needed in Valencia and surrounding areas; native English speakers with knowledge of Spanish preferred. ⊕ Ages 25+. Teachers should have 1+ year's experience. 34 hour week. 9+ months, October onwards, teachers; April-June and October-December, secretarial staff. Wages approx Pts130,000 per month, depending on qualifications. Accommodation approx Pts2,500 per day, full board. Staff should allow Pts3,500 per month, medical insurance.

WORKCAMPS

INSTITUTO DE LA JUVENTUD Servicio Voluntario Internacional de España, José Ortega y Gasset 71, 28006 Madrid, Spain

Volunteers are invited to work in international workcamps on a variety of manual projects. Recent projects have included renovating an old youth hostel in Asturias; reconstructing a bridge and the city walls in Vallodolid; gardening in the grounds of a monastery in Madrid; renovating a Red Cross centre on Tenerife; and reconstructing old houses in a village in Soria. Cultural and sports activities and excursions arranged. ⊕ Ages usually 18-26; older and younger applicants accepted on some camps. 2/3 weeks, July and August. Food, accommodation in schools, youth hostels, centres or tents, and accident insurance provided. Participants pay own travel costs.

🕮 *Apply through partner organisation in country of residence. In the UK: Concordia (Youth Service Volunteers) Ltd, Quaker International Social Projects or United*

Nations Association International Youth Service. See page 30 for registration details and addresses.

SCI-CATALUNYA Carrer del Carme 95, baixos 2a, 08001 Barcelona, Spain
SCI-MADRID Colón, 14 primero, 28004 Madrid, Spain
Volunteers are needed to work in international teams on workcamps organised by SCI-Catalunya, the Catalan branch of Service Civil International, and the local group based in Madrid. Recent projects have included working at a centre for disabled people in Barcelona, sharing their daily life and helping with leisure activities; working with residents at a drug addicts' rehabilitation centre in Terrassa; building a greenhouse and nurseries near Villamalea to conserve Iberian plants in danger of extinction; and construction work and care of animals at a centre for injured wild animals in Majadahonda.
⊕ Ages 18+. Applicants should be highly motivated, preferably with workcamp or other voluntary experience, and prepared to work hard as part of a team. Good knowledge of Spanish or Catalan essential on most camps. 40 hour week. 2-4 weeks, June-September. Shared accommodation, food and work accident insurance provided. No fares or wages paid. **B D PH W**

✎ Apply through partner organisation in country of residence. In the UK: International Voluntary Service. See page 30 for registration details and addresses.

G E N E R A L

ACORN VENTURE LTD Personnel Department, 137 Worcester Road, Hagley, Stourbridge, West Midlands DY9 0NW
Activity holiday company catering for school groups at a centre in Cala Llevadó on the Costa Brava, north of Barcelona. **Site managers** required to coordinate activities, organise evening

entertainments, and make sure groups have all they need. **General maintenance staff** and qualified **nurses** also required.
⊕ Ages 18+. Applicants should have some previous experience and fluency in Spanish. Minimum 50 hour, 6 day week. Applicants are expected to work the full season, May-September. Salary approx £40-£70 per week according to position. All meals and accommodation in tents, insurance and cost of return travel from ferry ports provided. ✎ Apply in writing with cv by end January. If no reply within 28 days assume application unsuccessful.

CLUB PUNTA ARABI
Apartado 73, Es Caná, 07840 Santa Eulalia del Río, Ibiza, Baleares, Spain ✆ **(34 71) 33 06 50/51**
▥ **(34 71) 33 91 67**
Bungalow holiday village organising club style holidays, mainly for German nationals. **Organisers, DJs, sports instructors** and **theatre people** required. 60 hour week for 4-5 months, during the summer. Accommodation, salary and insurance provided.
⊕ Ages 20-30. Fluent German essential; all staff should have relevant experience and enjoy working for and with people.
✎ Apply October-February. EEA nationals only.

EUROYOUTH LTD
301 Westborough Road, Westcliff, Southend-on-Sea Essex SSO 9PT
✆ **Southend-on-Sea (01702) 341434**
Arranges holiday guest stays where **guests** are offered board and lodging in return for an agreed number of hours English conversation with hosts or their children. Time also available for guests to practise Spanish if desired.
⊕ Mainly ages 18-25, but sometimes opportunities for older applicants. 2-3 weeks, occasionally 1-2 months, mainly July and August. Travel and insurance arranged by applicants, but tickets at reduced rates can be obtained on request. Registration fee approx £70.
✎ Apply at least 12 weeks prior to departure date. UK nationals only.

INFO

Swedish Embassy
11 Montagu Place, London W1H 2AL
✆ 0171-724 2101
Consular Section: ✆ 0171-914 6413

British Embassy
Skarpögatan 6-8/Box 27819, 115 93
Stockholm ✆ (46 8) 671 9000

Tourist office
Swedish Travel & Tourism Council,
73 Welbeck Street, London W1M 8AN
✆ 0171-935 9784 (1000-1300)
✆ 0891 200280 (24 hours).

Youth hostels
STF Drottninggatan 31/Box 25, 101 20
Stockholm ✆ (46 8) 790 3100

Youth & student information
SFS Resebyrå, Kungsgatan 4/Box 7144,
103 87 Stockholm

Entry regulations Nationals of the
UK and other EU/EEA countries wishing
to visit Sweden do not need a visa, nor
do they require a work permit in order
to take up employment. They may stay
for up to 3 months to seek employment,
provided they are financially self-
supporting. Should their stay exceed 3
months they should apply for a
residence permit. All other nationals
require a work permit for all types of
employment. Applications should be
made to the Swedish Embassy or
Consulate once an offer of employment
has been secured. Work permits are
issued for a specific job and period and
applicants will be notified of the decision
by the Embassy.

Job advertising Frank L Crane
(London) Ltd, International Press
Representation, 5/15 Cromer Street,
Grays Inn Road, London WC1H 8LS
✆ 0171-837 3330 can place ads in the
Svenska Dagbladet (Stockholm),
Goteborgs-Posten (Gothenburg) and
Sydsvenska Dagbladet (Malmö).

Travel Freedom Pass allows 3, 5 or 10 days unlimited rail travel in 1 month on the railways of Sweden. Cost from £68 (under 26) or £92 (26+). Available from British Rail International Rail Centre, Victoria Station, London SW1V 1JY ✆ 0171-834 2345.

Campus Travel can arrange Eurotrain, Inter-Rail and student/youth fares for travel by plane, train, boat and bus to destinations in Sweden. Offices throughout the UK including a student travel centre at 52 Grosvenor Gardens, London SW1W 0AG (opposite Victoria Station) ✆ 0171-730 3402 or ✆ 0131-668 3303 for Scottish bookings.

Council Travel, 28A Poland Street, London W1V 3DB ✆ 0171-287 3337 (offices also in Paris, Nice, Lyon, Munich, Düsseldorf, Tokyo, Singapore and throughout the US) offers Eurotrain under 26 fares and competitive airfares to destinations in Sweden, plus travel insurance, guidebooks and travel gear.

The ScanRail pass is a flexible rail pass for Scandinavia, valid for unlimited travel during 5 days within 15 days, 10 days within 1 month and 1 month consecutive. Cost from £94 (ages under 25) or from £125 (ages 25+) for 5 days. Discounts are offered on certain ferry and bus routes. Available from Norwegian State Railways, 21-24 Cockspur Street, London SW1Y 5DA ✆ 0171-930 6666.

Publications Lonely Planet's *Scandinavian and Baltic Europe on a Shoestring* £10.95 offers practical, down-to-earth information for the low-budget, independent traveller in Sweden.

The Rough Guide to Scandinavia £10.99 provides comprehensive background information on Sweden, with details on getting there, getting around, places to explore and cheap places to stay.

Michael's Guide to Scandinavia £10.95 is detailed and concise, providing invaluable practical advice for all kinds of travellers. Published by Inbal Travel.

Vacation Work's *Live & Work in Scandinavia* £8.95 is a guide for those interested in finding temporary or permanent work, starting a business or buying a home in Sweden, Denmark, Finland, Norway or Iceland.

All the above guidebooks are available from good bookshops.

Sweden Holiday Guide is a free magazine providing general information on travel to and around the country, places of interest, public services, medical treatment, eating, accommodation and outdoor activities, plus maps and colour photographs. Also *Holiday Guide for the Disabled*. Available from the Swedish Travel & Tourism Council, see above. **PH**

COURIERS/REPS

EUROCAMP Summer Jobs (Ref WH), PO Box 170, Liverpool L70 1ES ✆ **Knutsford (01565) 625522** One of Europe's leading tour operators, specialising in providing quality camping and mobile home holidays for families throughout Europe.

Campsite couriers required. Work involves cleaning tents and equipment prior to the arrival of new customers; checking, replacing and making repairs on equipment; replenishing gas supplies; keeping basic accounts and reporting on a weekly basis to England. Couriers are also expected to meet new arrivals and assist holidaymakers with any problems that arise; organise activities and parties; provide information on local tourist attractions and maintain an information noticeboard. At the beginning and end of the season couriers are also expected to help in erecting and dismantling tents. Couriers need to be flexible to meet the needs of customers and be on hand where necessary; they will be able to organise their own free time as the workload allows.

⊕ Ages 18+. Applicants should be independent, adaptable, reliable, physically fit, have plenty of initiative and relish a challenging and responsible position. Good working knowledge of Swedish also necessary. Preference given to those able to work the whole season, April-September/October; contracts also available for first half season, April-mid July and second half season, mid July-September/October. **Children's couriers** also required, with the energy and enthusiasm to organise a wide range of exciting activities for groups aged 4-13. Experience of working with this age range essential, but language ability is not a requirement. ⊕ Ages 18+. Must be available for the whole season, May-September.

For both positions the salary is £95 per week. Training provided together with accommodation in frame tent with cooking facilities, insurance and return travel. ✆ *Early application by telephone preferred; interviews start September/ October. UK/EEA passport-holders only.*

FARMWORK

INTERNATIONAL FARM EXPERIENCE PROGRAMME
YFC Centre, N A C, Stoneleigh Park, Kenilworth, Warwickshire CV8 2LG ✆ **Coventry (0203) 696584**
Provides assistance to young **agriculturalists** and **horticulturalists** by finding places in farms and nurseries abroad, enabling them to broaden their knowledge of agricultural and horticultural methods. Participants live and work with a farming family and the work is matched as far as possible with the participant's requirements. 3-12 months, all year. Entails physical work and practical involvement. Basic wage plus board and lodging.
⊕ Ages 18-28. Applicants must have at least 2 years practical experience, one of which may be at an agricultural college, and intend to make a career in agriculture or horticulture. Valid driving

licence necessary. Participants pay own fares and insurance. Registration fee £85. ✆ *UK applications to IFEP. Other applications to IFEP partner in host country.*

WORKCAMPS

INTERNATIONELLA ARBETSLAG (IAL) Barnangsgatan 23, 11 641 Stockholm, Sweden
The Swedish branch of Service Civil International, which promotes international reconciliation through work projects. **Volunteers** are invited to take part in international workcamps where the work may vary from manual labour to social activities or study. Recent projects have included making terraces down a slope and working in a biodynamic garden at a community near Delsbo; building a traditional shipyard to renovate a turn-of-the-century sailing boat in Vastervik; and constructing turf houses using traditional Sami methods in a wildlife village in Solberget. Study themes are linked to the camps.
⊕ Ages 18+. Applicants should be highly motivated and prepared to work hard as part of a team. 35-40 hour week.
2 weeks, June-September. Food, shared accommodation and work accident insurance provided. No fares or wages paid. **B D PH W**

✉ *Apply through partner organisation in country of residence.*
In the UK: International Voluntary Service. See page 30 for registration details and addresses.

SWITZERLAND

INFO

Swiss Embassy
16-18 Montagu Place, London W1H
2BQ ✆ 0171-723 0701
Consulate General: Sunley Building,
24th floor, Piccadilly Plaza, Manchester
M1 4BT ✆ 0161-236 2933

British Embassy
Thunstraße 50, 3005 Bern
✆ (41 31) 352 5021/6

Tourist office
Swiss National Tourist Office, Swiss
Centre, Swiss Court, London W1V 8EE
✆ 0171-734 1921

Youth hostels
Schweizer Jugendherbergen,
Engestraße 9, Postfach, 3001 Bern
✆ (41 31) 302 5503

Youth & student information
Swiss Student Travel Office, SSR-Reisen,
Bäckerstraße 4c, Postfach, 8026 Zürich

Entry regulations British passport-
holders and holders of passports from
most west European countries do not
require a visa for purposes other than
employment. An Assurance of a
Residence Permit is required for all
types of employment; this is a
combination of both residence and work
permits, entitling the holder to live in a
particular canton and work for a
specified employer. It should be
obtained by the prospective employer
from the Cantonal Aliens Police before
the applicant's arrival in Switzerland.
This procedure also applies to au pairs
and trainees. The number of permits
granted is extremely limited and only
applicants offering specific skills or
qualifications are likely to succeed. As a
rule, only those who have been offered a
job which cannot be filled by a Swiss
national have a chance of receiving a
permit. The few jobs for which permits
may be granted are mainly in the hotel
and catering trades, in shops and on

farms. Seasonal permits are granted to holders of Assurance of a Residence Permits after arrival in Switzerland for seasonal employment in the building, hotel and holiday industry for a period of 4/5-9 months; entry and exit dates must be adhered to. The Federal Office for Industry, Crafts and Labour in Bern publishes a booklet covering information on entry and residence, living and working conditions, taxes and insurance; available from the Swiss Embassy.

Job advertising Publicitas Ltd, 517/523 Fulham Road, London SW6 1HD ✆ 0171-385 7723 can place adverts in the *Basler Zeitung* (Basle daily), *Der Bund* (Bern daily), *Journal de Genève* (high class daily), *Neue Zürcher Zeitung* (leading high class daily), *24 Heures* (Lausanne daily) and other newspapers.

Travel Freedom Pass allows 3, 5 or 10 days unlimited rail travel in 1 month on the railways of Switzerland, including most Swiss private railways. Cost from £66 (under 26) or £86 (26+). Available from British Rail International Rail Centre, Victoria Station, London SW1V 1JY ✆ 0171-834 2345.

Campus Travel can arrange Eurotrain, Inter-Rail and student/youth fares for travel to destinations in Switzerland. Offices throughout the UK, including 52 Grosvenor Gardens, London SW1W 0AG (opposite Victoria Station) ✆ 0171-730 3402 or ✆ 0131-668 3303 for Scottish telephone bookings.

Council Travel, 28A Poland Street, London W1V 3DB ✆ 0171-287 3337 (offices also in Paris, Nice, Lyon, Munich, Düsseldorf, Tokyo, Singapore and throughout the US) offers Eurotrain under 26 fares and charter flights to destinations in Switzerland.

STA Travel Ltd, 86 Old Brompton Road, London SW7 3LQ/117 Euston Road, London NW1 2SX ✆ 0171-937 9921 (offices throughout the UK) offers flexible, low cost flights to Switzerland.

Swiss National Tourist Office, see above, issues the Swiss Pass which gives unlimited travel on rail, boat and postbus routes, trams and buses in 24 towns, and reductions on mountain railways and cable cars. Valid for 4, 8, 15 or 31 days, cost from £91.

Publications *Michael's Guide to Switzerland* £7.95 is detailed and concise, providing a invaluable practical advice for all kinds of travellers. Lonely Planet's *Switzerland - A Travel Survival Kit* £8.95 offers practical information for budget travellers. Both available from good bookshops.

Travel Tips for Switzerland covers formalities and facilities including accommodation, sports and culture. Available from the Swiss National Tourist Office, see above.

Accommodation *Student Lodgings at University Cities in Switzerland* gives the addresses of student accommodation. Available from the Swiss National Tourist Office, see above.

AU PAIR / CHILDCARE

HELPING HANDS AU PAIR & DOMESTIC AGENCY 39 Rutland Avenue, Thorpe Bay, Essex SS1 2XJ ✆ **Southend-on-Sea (01702) 602067** Can place **au pairs** and **mothers' helps**. ⌖ Ages 18-27. Pocket money approx £35 per week for au pairs, higher for mothers' helps. Introduction fee £40. *UK nationals only.*

HOME FROM HOME Walnut Orchard, Chearsley, Aylesbury, Buckinghamshire HP18 0DA ✆/✉ **Aylesbury (01844) 208561** Can place **au pairs**. ⌖ Ages 18+. Minimum stay 1 year. Pocket money £35 per week. Placement fee £40. *UK nationals only.*

LANGTRAIN INTERNATIONAL
Torquay Road, Foxrock, Dublin 18, Ireland ℭ (353 1) 289 3876
Can place **au pairs** in German-speaking cantons. ⚥ Ages 18+. Pocket money £25-£40 per week. Placement fee £60.

STUDENTS ABROAD LTD
11 Milton View, Hitchin, Hertfordshire SG4 0QD ℭ Hitchin (01462) 438909 ☐ (01462) 438919
Can place **au pairs** and occasionally **nannies** for 1 year stay. ⚥ Ages 18-27 for au pairs. Knowledge of French, German or Italian helpful. Pocket money approx £35-£40 per week. Service charge £40.

COMMUNITY WORK

SERVICE CIVIL INTERNATIONAL
Gerberngasse 21a, 3000 Bern 13, Switzerland
Service Civil International promotes international reconciliation through work projects. **Volunteers** needed to work in international teams on community projects. Recent projects have included working on a holiday camp for handicapped and able bodied children in the Canton of Bern; working with young people at a Rudolf Steiner school in the Canton of Vaud; and constructing a chicken house and making the garden accessible for wheelchairs, at a centre for seriously physically handicapped young people in Geneva. ⚥ Ages 18+. Applicants should be highly motivated, preferably with previous workcamp or other voluntary experience, and prepared to work hard as part of a team. Good knowledge of German needed on some camps. 35-40 hour week. 2-4 weeks, June-September. Food, shared accommodation and work accident insurance provided. No fares or wages paid. **B D PH W**

🐝 *Apply through partner organisation in country of residence. In the UK: International Voluntary Service. See page 30 for registration details and addresses.*

CONSERVATION

AWSR - IUK Post Box 1, 9101 Herisau, Switzerland
ℭ/☐ (41 71) 515103
Volunteers needed for conservation work at international camps in Zermatt, Saas Fee, Sustenpass/Steingletscher and possibly Schwägalp. Small teams go out from the basecamp to work on a variety of projects, which may include building footpaths and small bridges; environmental protection on alpine roads and rivers and lake shores; or repairing damage caused by avalanches. ⚥ Ages 18-26. Knowledge of German required. 5-7 hour day, excluding travel to and from workplace. 5 day week. 8-22 days; mid June-end August. Full board accommodation provided, plus SF6 per day pocket money. Volunteers must take mountain boots, warm clothes, rainwear, sleeping bag, first aid kit, pocket knife, torch, sunglasses and signal whistle; anyone arriving insufficiently equipped will not be accepted. Volunteers pay their own travel costs. Registration fee SF50.
🐝 *Apply at least 4 weeks before intended date of arrival; applications confirmed 2+ weeks before starting date.*

SERVICE CIVIL INTERNATIONAL
Gerberngasse 21a, 3000 Bern 13, Switzerland
Service Civil International promotes international reconciliation through work projects. **Volunteers** needed to work in international teams on projects which have recently included reconstructing a mountain path at Cimalmotto; clearing alpine meadows and constructing a fountain at Scareglia; and building a settlement in Bern using traditional materials.
⚥ Ages 18+. Knowledge of French or German useful. Applicants should be highly motivated, preferably with previous workcamp or voluntary experience, and prepared to work hard as part of a team. 35-40 hour week. 2-4 weeks, June-September. Food,

shared accommodation and work accident insurance provided. No fares or wages paid. **B D PH W**

🕮 *Apply through partner organisation in country of residence. In the UK: International Voluntary Service. See page 30 for registration details and addresses.*

COURIERS / REPS

BLADON LINES Personnel Department, 56-58 Putney High Street, London SW15 1SF
℄ **0181-785 2200**
Opportunities for **representatives** in ski resorts, looking after guests, giving information, organising transfers and ensuring everything is running smoothly.
⊕ Ages 24+. Relevant experience an advantage, and fluent French or German essential. Applicants must be prepared to work hard but will get time to ski. December-May. Salary £50-£100, depending on the size of the resort. Board, lodging, return travel, insurance, ski pass and ski hire provided. Small charge made for uniform. Training course held in London before departure. Also a couple of places in each resort for **ski guides** who act as assistant reps and whose work involves showing guests around the slopes, helping with coach transfers and organising *après ski*.
⊕ Ages 22+; good spoken French or German an advantage. Applicants should have good leadership qualities and be proficient skiers. Salary approx £50 per week. A week's training held in Val d'Isère before the season starts.
EEA nationals only.

**CANVAS HOLIDAYS LTD
12 Abbey Park Place, Dunfermline, Fife KY12 7PD**
Resident **couriers, children's couriers** and **watersports couriers** required to work on campsites for a holiday company providing accommodation for families in ready-erected fully equipped tents and mobile homes. The work involves a daily routine of tent cleaning as customers arrive and depart, providing information and advice on the local attractions and essential services, helping to sort out problems that might arise and organising activities for the children and get-togethers for the families. 7 day week job with no fixed hours; the workload varies from day to day. At the beginning and end of the season there is a period of physical work when tents are put up and prepared for the clients or dismantled and stored for the winter. Other tasks include administration, book keeping and stock control.
⊕ Ages 18-25. Working knowledge of French or German essential. Applicants are normally those in a gap year, undergraduates or graduates. They need to be reliable, self-motivated, able to turn their hand to new and varied tasks, and with a sense of humour. 6 months, April-October. Return travel, dependent on successful completion of contract, and accommodation in frame tents provided. Salary £85 per week.
🕮 *Applications accepted any time; interviews commence early November. UK nationals only.*

CRYSTAL HOLIDAYS Crystal House, The Courtyard, Arlington Road, Surbiton, Surrey KT6 6BW
℄ **0181-241 5111**
Tour operator arranging air and self-drive holidays to the Swiss Lakes, and winter skiing holidays in Château d'Oex, Saas Fee, Verbier, Wengen and Zermatt. **Representatives** required to meet and greet clients and be responsible for their welfare during their holiday. **Ski guides** also needed during winter season.
⊕ Ages 22-35. Previous experience desirable and fluent German/French essential. Approx 60 hour, 7 day week, May-October and December-April. Basic salary plus commission, board, lodging, insurance, travel costs and uniform provided. 1 week training seminar held at beginning of each season. 🕮 *Apply January/February for summer season, April/May for winter.*

ESPRIT HOLIDAYS LTD
Oaklands, Reading Road North,
Fleet, Hampshire GU13 8AA
℘ Fleet (01252) 625177
Organises winter ski holidays in the
Swiss Alps. Requires **resort
representatives** to deal with most
aspects of a guest's holiday: dealing with
ski hire, lift passes, ski schools and any
immediate problems arising from chalet
operations or guests' requirements.
⊕ Ages 23+. Applicants must speak
French, should have a minimum parallel
skiing standard and should be able to
work on their own initiative. Experience
of working in service industry desirable.
Hours will vary; 6 day week, December-
April. Board, accommodation, pocket
money plus lift pass, skis, boots and ski
jacket provided. Full medical insurance
cover; travel costs paid if season
completed. 6 day training programme
provided in France in December.
⌦ Apply June/July. UK nationals only.

EUROCAMP Summer Jobs (Ref
WH), PO Box 170, Liverpool L70
1ES ℘ Knutsford (01565) 625522
One of Europe's leading tour operators,
specialising in providing quality camping
and mobile home holidays for families
throughout Europe. **Campsite
couriers** required: work involves
cleaning tents and equipment prior to
the arrival of new customers; checking,
replacing and making repairs on
equipment; replenishing gas supplies;
keeping basic accounts and reporting on
a weekly basis to England. Couriers are
also expected to meet new arrivals and
assist holidaymakers with any problems
that arise; organise activities and parties;
provide information on local tourist
attractions and maintain an information
noticeboard. At the beginning and end
of the season couriers are also expected
to help in erecting and dismantling tents.
Couriers need to be flexible to meet the
needs of customers and be on hand
where necessary; they will be able to
organise their own free time as the
workload allows.
⊕ Ages 18+. Applicants should be

independent, adaptable, reliable, fit, have
plenty of initiative and relish a
challenging and responsible position.
Good working knowledge of French/
German also necessary. Preference
given to those able to work the whole
season, April-September/October;
contracts also available for first half
season, April-mid July and second half
season, mid July-September/October.
Children's couriers are also required,
with the energy and enthusiasm to
organise a wide range of exciting
activities for groups of children aged
4-13. Experience of working within this
age range is essential, but language ability
is not a requirement.
⊕ Ages 18+. Must be available for the
whole season, May-September.
For both positions the salary is £95 per
week. Accommodation in frame tent
with cooking facilities, insurance, training
and return travel provided.
⌦ Early application by telephone preferred;
interviews start September/October.
UK/EEA passport-holders only.

SKI TOTAL 10 Hill Street,
Richmond, Surrey ℘ 0181-948 3535
Tour operator arranging skiing holidays.
Opportunities for ski **resort managers**
to organise all aspects of clients'
holidays, supervise staff and ensure
standards are maintained with possible
ski guiding up to 3½ days per week.
⊕ Ages 23+. Applicants must be hard
working, resourceful, patient, outgoing,
experienced resort managers, who get
along with and can handle people well at
all levels. Salary £70-£90 per week.
**Ski guides/technicians/handymen/
women** also required. Duties include
clearing snow, fitting gas bottles, repairs,
maintenance, unloading deliveries and ski
guiding approx 4 days per week.
⊕ Ages 21+. Applicants should be hard
working, friendly, good skiers with ski
technician experience and a clean driving
licence. Some French/German useful.
Salary £50-£70 per week. All staff work
a 40-50 hour, 6 day week, December-
April. Accommodation, board, full
medical insurance and travel fares

provided. I week pre-season training programme at resort. ⚞ *Apply from June onwards. UK nationals only.*

VENTURE ABROAD Richmond House, High Street, Cranleigh, Surrey GU6 8RF ℗ Cranleigh (01483) 273027

Representatives required by a tour operator specialising in European holidays for youth groups. Work involves assisting and advising groups staying in Adelboden, Grindelwald, Gstaad, Meiringen and Interlaken, in the Bernese Oberland, helping to them to get the most out of their stay. Representatives meet groups on arrival, provide general local information, hire coaches, escort on excursions and act as guides. ⊕ Ages 19+. University students with knowledge of French or German and evidence of leadership qualities preferred. 50 hour week, end June-end August. Salary £90 per week, self-catering accommodation and insurance provided. Basic training given before departure. ⚞ *Apply enclosing* cv.

DOMESTIC

BLADON LINES Personnel Department, 56-58 Putney High Street, London SW15 1SF ℗ 0181-785 2200

Opportunities for **cooks** and **cleaners** to work in the ski resorts of Verbier, Wengen and Zermatt. Also opportunities for **chalet girls**, whose work involves cleaning chalets, making beds, caring for guests, shopping and preparing meals. ⊕ Ages 21+. Experience and/or qualifications in catering/domestic work essential. Hours very variable; applicants must be prepared to work hard but will get time to ski. December-May. Salary approx £45 per week, ski pass and ski hire, board, lodging, return travel and insurance provided. Small charge made for uniform. One day briefing in London before departure. *EEA nationals only.*

CRYSTAL HOLIDAYS Crystal House, The Courtyard, Arlington Road, Surbiton, Surrey KT6 6BW ℗ 0181-241 5111

Tour operator arranging skiing holidays in Château d'Oex, Saas Fee, Verbier, Wengen and Zermatt. **Chalet staff** required to cook daily breakfast, afternoon tea and 3-course evening meal, and keep chalets clean and tidy. ⊕ Ages 20-35. Catering qualifications or experience essential. Approx 60 hour, 6½ day week, December-April. Basic salary plus commission; board, lodging, insurance, travel costs and uniform provided. I week training seminar held at beginning of the season. ⚞ *Apply April/May.*

ESPRIT HOLIDAYS LTD Oaklands, Reading Road North, Fleet, Hampshire GU13 8AA ℗ Fleet (01252) 625177

Organises winter ski holidays in the Swiss Alps. Requires **chalet staff** to shop, cook, clean and host guests. **Nannies** also required to run in-chalet crèches and Snowclub, caring for children aged 4 months to 8 years. ⊕ Ages 18+. Chalet staff should have City and Guilds 706 or equivalent qualification. Nannies should be NNEB, BTEC or RGN qualified. French language useful but not essential. Hours vary; 6 day week, December-April. Board, accommodation, pocket money, lift pass, skis, boots and ski jacket provided. Full medical insurance cover; travel costs paid if season completed. 4 day training programme in France in December. ⚞ *Apply June/July. UK nationals only.*

JOBS IN THE ALPS AGENCY PO Box 388, London SW1X 8LX

Can provide work for **hall and night porters**, **waiters**, **waitresses**, and occasionally **receptionists** or **barmaids**, in hotels with international clientèle. Some 120 winter and 80 summer jobs available. Good knowledge of French or German required. Limited number of other jobs such as

chambermaids and kitchen helpers, and in mountain cafés, may be available for those with limited languages. Some jobs available in village cafés for girls with good French.
✤ Ages 18+. Applicants must be prepared to work hard and to a high standard, alongside an international workforce. 8½ hour day, with afternoons usually free. 2 days free per week, 1 of which may be paid in lieu during the high season. Jobs are for the whole season, December-April or June-September. Pay from approx £140 per week, board, lodging and insurance provided. Interview fee £1, plus £30 service charge and £15 per week levy depending on length of contract. ✐
Closing dates for interviews: 30 September (winter) or 30 April (summer). EEA nationals only.

SILVER SKI HOLIDAYS
Conifers House, Grove Green Lane, Maidstone, Kent ME14 5JW
Couples required to staff ski chalets. Work involves hosting and running a fully catered chalet programme; providing breakfast, afternoon tea and dinner as well as a ski guiding service.
✤ Ages 23/25-40. Applicants must be able to demonstrate some catering/housekeeping experience and should preferably run their own home in UK. They should be skiers of above average ability with an outgoing personality. French useful but not essential. Hours vary; 6 day week for approx 20 weeks, December-May; must work whole season. Board, accommodation, pocket money plus commission provided. 2 week training programme.
✐ *Apply May-October. UK nationals only.*

SKI TOTAL 10 Hill Street,
Richmond, Surrey ✆ 0181-948 3535
Tour operator arranging skiing holidays. Requires chalet staff to do catering, cleaning, washing up, bedmaking for 8-12 people in self-contained chalets.
✤ Ages 21+. Applicants should be experienced, capable and hard working with plenty of cooking experience. Sense

of humour, patience and ability to get on with groups of people of varied ages and backgrounds essential, as is knowledge of French/German and a clean driving licence. Salary £50 per week.
Cooks also required, to cater for 14-30 people per week, run a kitchen and supervise junior staff.
✤ Ages 21+. Applicants must have experience and a proven record of cooking for large numbers. Driving licence and some French/German useful. Salary £60-£80 per week.
Opportunities for chalet helpers/assistant cooks to do cooking, cleaning, washing up, making beds.
✤ Ages 19+. Applicants must have experience, aptitude for hard work, enthusiasm, sense of humour and an outgoing personality. Salary £40 per week.
All staff work a 40-50 hour, 6 day week, December-April. Accommodation, board, full medical insurance and travel costs provided. 1 week pre-season training programme at resort.
✐ *Apply from June onwards.*
UK nationals only.

VILLAGE CAMPS Chalet Seneca,
1854 Leysin, Switzerland
Organises a range of holidays in American-style camps for children aged 8-16 from the international business and diplomatic communities. Opportunities for chalet girls to work on winter ski camps in Anzere, Leysin and Morgins. Chalet girls are responsible for some kitchen work, dining room service, house cleaning and preparing the chalet for the weekly arrival of guests.
✤ Ages 21+. Applicants should be friendly and capable of dealing with groups of people of different ages and nationalities. English is the first language; priority consideration given to applicants with additional French and German language skills. 45 hour week, December-Easter. Accommodation, ski pass, accident and liability insurance provided. Wages SF200 per week. Applicants pay their own travel costs. Compulsory pre-camp training course.

FARMWORK

INTERNATIONAL FARM EXPERIENCE PROGRAMME YFC Centre, N A C, Stoneleigh Park, Kenilworth, Warwickshire CV8 2LG ℗ Coventry (01203) 696584

Provides assistance to young **agriculturalists** and **horticulturalists** by finding places in farms/nurseries abroad, enabling them to broaden their knowledge of agricultural and horticultural methods. Participants usually live and work with a farming family and the work is matched as far as possible with participant's requirements. Entails physical work and practical involvement. Basic wage plus board and lodging. 3-12 months, all year.
⚜ Ages 18-28. Applicants must have at least 2 years practical experience, 1 year of which may be at agricultural college, and intend to make a career in agriculture/horticulture. Valid driving licence necessary. Participants pay own fares and insurance. Registration fee £85. ⚓ *UK applications to IFEP; others to IFEP partner in home country.*

LANDDIENST-ZENTRALSTELLE Postfach 728, Mühlegasse 13, 8025 Zürich, Switzerland ℗ (41 1) 261 4488   ▭ (41 1) 261 4432

Workers required for **agricultural** and **domestic work** on small farms in French and German-speaking cantons. Work involves cleaning out cowstalls, haymaking, grass cutting, poultry feeding, transporting milk, manure spreading and spraying, vegetable and fruit picking, wood cutting, gardening and housework.
⚜ Ages 17+. Basic knowledge of French or German essential. Maximum 48 hour week, Sundays free. 3-8 weeks, March-October; or in French speaking cantons: mid April-end June and mid August-end September. Full board and lodging, insurance and SF20+ per day pocket money provided. It is not possible to place 2 people with the same farmer. Applications should be made 4 weeks before intended date of arrival, and

successful applicants will be sent details of arrangements before they are due to start work.

⚓ *UK applicants may apply through Concordia (Youth Service Volunteers) Ltd, Recruitment Secretary, 8 Brunswick Place, Hove, Sussex BN3 1ET ℗ Brighton (01273) 772086. Administration fee £25.*

WILLING WORKERS ON ORGANIC FARMS (WWOOF-CH) Thomas Schwager, Postfach 615, 9001 St Gallen, Switzerland ℗/▭ (41 71) 232415

A non-profitmaking organisation which aims to help organic farmers and smallholders whose work is often labour intensive as it does not rely on the use of artificial fertilisers or pesticides. Provides **volunteers** with first-hand experience of organic farming and gardening. Places on some 80 farms.
⚜ Ages 16+. Approx 30 hour week. 1-2+ weeks, all year. Full board and lodging provided in the farmhouse, tent or caravan; volunteers should take a sleeping bag. No wages paid, although long-term volunteers may receive small payment as arranged with host. Helpers pay own travel costs. Insurance and anti-tetanus vaccination recommended. Families welcome on some farms. Membership fee SF15; US$15 from abroad.

MONITORS & INSTRUCTORS

PGL SKI EUROPE Brentham House, 45c High Street, Hampton Wick, Kingston-upon-Thames, Surrey KT1 4DG ℗ 0181-977 7755

A company with its own ski school, operating holidays for groups and school parties. Part-time **ski instructors** are required for winter sports in the Bernese Oberland, Grisons and Valais regions. Work involves 6 hours teaching per day. BASI or full foreign qualifications essential, together with a high level of teaching skill. Knowledge of foreign languages useful; fluent English a prerequisite. 1-4 week periods over Christmas, the New Year, February and April. Instructors receive full board accommodation and ski pass, plus travel expenses London/resort, and have access to the same facilities as the clients. Wages approx £90-£135 per week, depending on qualifications. 𝕏 *Interviews held May-November.*

VILLAGE CAMPS Chalet Seneca, 1854 Leysin, Switzerland

Organises a range of holidays in American-style camps for children aged 8-16 from the international business and diplomatic communities. Opportunities for **counsellors, special activity counsellors, programme leaders, special instructors, ski counsellors** and **nurses.** Staff live, work and play with the children and are responsible for their safety, health and happiness. **Counsellors** plan, organise and direct daytime and evening programmes, accompany campers on excursions and may be called upon to supervise other counsellors and take charge of a camper group. Evening activities include sports, films, competitions, fondues and discos. **Special activity counsellors** having a high degree of proficiency organise, execute and instruct specific programmes such as sports, arts and crafts, nature study and basic computer science. Counsellors with a substantial amount of leadership experience can be appointed **programme leaders**, which includes running a camp programme and direction and supervision of adult counsellors. **Assistant** and **junior counsellors** are responsible for supporting counsellors in all activities and assisting with special activities as required. **Specialist instructors** should have 2 years training and experience and be able to instruct children of all ability levels; responsible for the concentrated teaching of their subject at a speciality camp such as football, golf, tennis, computer science or French and English language. **Ski counsellors** must be good parallel skiers, with a thorough understanding of mountain safety. **Nurses** are responsible for the health and welfare of campers and counsellors, attending to accidents and maintaining an infirmary. ♠ Ages 21+, 26+ for programme leaders. Applicants must have training and/or experience of working with children and have an interest in children from many ethnic and religious backgrounds. English is the first language; priority consideration given to applicants with additional French, Italian or German language skills. For day camps preference is given to applicants living within commuting distance of the camp. 45 hour week. Summer camps 1+ months, June-August; 1½ days plus 3 evenings free per 2 week session. Winter camps 1-4 weeks, December-Easter; 2 evenings free per week. Full board accommodation, accident and liability insurance provided, but not travel costs. Summer wages SF325 per two week session; winter wages SF100 per week plus ski pass for area worked. Wages for day camps are paid per 10 day session: counsellors, special activity counsellors and nurses SF275; assistant counsellors SF225; junior counsellors SF150. Compulsory pre-camp training course arranged for all staff. Summer camps organised in Leysin; winter camps at Saas Fee, Anzere, Leysin, Saas Grund and Morgins.

TEACHERS

SWISS FEDERATION OF PRIVATE SCHOOLS Service Scolaire, rue du Mont-Blanc, PO Box 1488, 1211 Geneva 1, Switzerland

Publishes *Private Schools in Switzerland* (5 IRCs by surface mail, 10 IRCs by airmail), a booklet giving full details of schools to which **teachers** may apply, many international, from elementary to adult formation and including finishing schools. Many of them have English-speaking sections which prepare for

GCSE and A level exams, and include commercial, technical, secretarial, language and domestic branches with sports facilities. 📖 *Does not arrange placements; apply direct to the schools.*

SWISS NATIONAL TOURIST OFFICE Swiss Centre, Swiss Court, London WIV 8EE ✆ 0171-734 1921

Can provide a booklet, *Switzerland - Country for Children*, published by the Association Suisse des Homes d'Enfants. Contains a large selection of schools and homes for children to which **teachers** may apply. Some offer tutoring in English of American/English curricula.

WORKCAMPS

ATD QUART MONDE
1733 Treyvaux, Switzerland
An international voluntary organisation which develops a human rights approach to overcoming poverty. Brings together people from all walks of life in partnership with the most disadvantaged families, to support the efforts of the very poor in overcoming poverty and taking an active role in their community. **Volunteers** are invited to take part in an international workcamp involving manual work at the Treyvaux centre; or to join street workshops organised in Fribourg, Geneva or Basle, sharing skills with parents, young people and children whose sense of creativity has never been challenged. Workshops are organised in very disadvantaged areas where holidays too often mean boredom and violence. ⊕ Ages 18+. No experience necessary but applicants should be interested in better understanding the causes and effects of persistent poverty and willing to work hard with others as a team. 2-3 weeks, July (workcamps) or 1-3 weeks, July/August (workshops). Approx 40 hour week. Accommodation provided; applicants are asked to take a sleeping bag and to contribute towards living expenses. No fares or wages paid. 📖 *Write for further details.*

GRUPPO VOLUNTARI DELLA SVIZZERA ITALIANA CP 12, 6517 Arbedo, Switzerland

Exists to promote communal activity for the good of society and recruits **volunteers** to assist in reconstruction, maintenance and other essential work after natural disasters. Projects have included helping the inhabitants of Fusio which was struck by a flood; building river bridges in the Mogno region; excavating an aqueduct in Borgnone; and restoring a small church in Ces. Sports, social and cultural activities arranged. ⊕ Ages 18+. Applicants should enjoy living and working together and want to help the community in which they are based. No previous experience or special skills required. 30 hour week. 1-3 weeks, July and August. Self-catering accommodation provided. Fee SF100.

SERVICE CIVIL INTERNATIONAL Gerberngasse 21a, 3000 Bern 13, Switzerland

Promotes international reconciliation through work projects. **Volunteers** are needed to work in international teams on manual/social projects which have recently included building a bread oven and woodwork at the abandoned and remote mountain village of Ces; painting, haymaking, building a sand pit and helping in the restaurant at a village in the Jura mountains; and rebuilding an abandoned area in the Canton of Ticino, as a cultural camp for courses, group projects and therapeutic groups. ⊕ Ages 18+. Applicants should be highly motivated, preferably with previous workcamp or other voluntary experience, and prepared to work hard as part of a team. Some camps require knowledge of French or German. 25-40 hour week. 2-4 weeks, June-September. Food, shared accommodation and work accident insurance provided. No fares or wages paid. **B D PH W**

⊕ *Apply through partner organisation in country of residence. In the UK: International Voluntary Service. See page 30 for registration details and addresses.*

INFO

Turkish Embassy
43 Belgrave Square, London SW1X 8PA
✆ 0171-235 5252/3/4
Consulate General: Rutland Lodge,
Rutland Gardens, London SW7 1BW
✆ 0171-589 0360

British Embassy
Sehit Ersan Caddesi 46/A Cankaya,
Ankara ✆ (90 312) 468 6230/42

Tourist office
Turkish Information Office, 1st floor,
170-173 Piccadilly, London W1V 9DD
✆ 0171-734 8681

Youth & student information
Gençtur, Yerebatan Caddesi 15/3,
Sultanahmet, 34410 Istanbul

Entry regulations A work visa is
required for all types of employment.
This may be applied for from the
Consulate General once an offer of
work has been secured. Alternatively,
the prospective employer may make the
necessary application to the Turkish
authorities. In either case the applicant
will be informed of the decision by the
Consulate. British visitors to Turkey
require a visa; this can be obtained at
the point of entry and is valid for 3
months. Most other European and
North American nationals do not
require visas; check requirements with
the Turkish Consulate. Persons who
enter Turkey as a tourist are not
permitted to take up employment.

Travel Freedom Pass allows 3, 5 or 10
days unlimited rail travel in 1 month on
the railways of Turkey. Cost from £17
(under 26) or £22 (26+). Available from
British Rail International Rail Centre,
Victoria Station, London W1V 1JY
✆ 0171-834 2345.

Campus Travel can arrange Eurotrain,
Inter-Rail and student/youth fares for
travel by plane, train, boat or bus to

destinations in Turkey. Offices throughout the UK, including a student travel centre at 52 Grosvenor Gardens, London SW1W 0AG (opposite Victoria Station) ✆ 0171-730 3402 or ✆ 0131-668 3303 for Scottish bookings.

Council Travel, 28A Poland Street, London W1V 3DB ✆ 0171-287 3337 (offices also in Paris, Nice, Lyon, Munich, Düsseldorf, Tokyo, Singapore and throughout the US) offers Eurotrain under 26 fares to destinations in Turkey, and flexible low-cost youth/student charter flights to Turkey, plus travel insurance, guidebooks and travel gear.

North-South Travel Ltd, Moulsham Mill, Parkway, Chelmsford CM2 7PX ✆ Chelmsford (01245) 492882 arranges competitively priced, reliably planned flights to all parts of Turkey. All profits go to projects in the developing world.

STA Travel, 86 Old Brompton Road, London SW7 3LQ/117 Euston Road, London NW1 2SX ✆ 0171-937 9921 (offices also in Birmingham, Bristol, Cambridge, Glasgow, Leeds, Manchester and Oxford) operates flexible low-cost flights between London and destinations throughout Turkey, and also offers accommodation and tours.

Publications Lonely Planet's *Turkey - A Travel Survival Kit* £12.95 offers practical, down-to-earth information for independent travellers wanting to explore beyond the usual tourist routes.

The Rough Guide to Turkey £9.99 provides comprehensive background information plus details on getting there, getting around, places to explore and cheap places to stay.

Michael's Guide to Turkey £10.95 is detailed and concise, providing invaluable practical advice for all kinds of travellers. Published by Inbal Travel.

All the above are available from good bookshops.

Turkey Travel Guide is a booklet containing information, useful tips, addresses and an accommodation list. This plus various brochures and maps available from the Turkish Information Office, see above.

A U P A I R /
C H I L D C A R E

ANGLO PAIR AGENCY
40 Wavertree Road, Streatham Hill, London SW2 3SP
✆ **0181-674 3605**
Can place **au pairs** and **au pairs plus**. Minimum stay 6 months. ⊕ Ages 17-27. Pocket money £30-£50 per week. Also placements for experienced nannies and mothers' helps; salary up to £100 per week. Agency fee £40.

JOLAINE AGENCY **18 Escot Way, Barnet, Hertfordshire EN5 3AN** ✆ **0181-449 1334** ⊐⊐ **0181-449 9183** Can place **au pairs** and **mothers' helps**. ⊕ Ages 18+. Pocket money from £30 per week. Placement fee £40.

M O N I T O R S &
T E A C H E R S

CENTRAL BUREAU FOR EDUCATIONAL VISITS & EXCHANGES **Seymour Mews House, Seymour Mews, London W1H 9PE** ✆ 0171-725 9411 **Teachers** and **sixth formers** are required at two English language summer schools run under the auspices of the Turkish Ministry of Education. The schools are attended by approx 60 Turkish pupils and 7 Turkish staff, and are in the Mediterranean coastal town of Antalya, based at camping sites near the sea front. The main objective is to provide Turkish pupils aged 11-16 with the opportunity of practising English learnt in school, and by spending 3

weeks in the company of a group of British teachers and young people to acquire a deeper awareness of the British way of life. Duties include assisting with the teaching of English as a foreign language, running conversation classes and organising sporting, musical and social activities.
④ Ages up to 45. Applicants should be native English speakers, sixth formers willing to assist the staff; or teachers qualified in the teaching of any discipline. EFL or ESL qualifications an advantage. Applicants should have a sense of responsibility, organisational skill, adaptability to new surroundings, a sociable nature and an interest in sports and/or drama and music, plus experience of working with or teaching children. Participants must fully commit themselves to the teaching of English and the organisation of various educational, outdoor and social activities. 3 weeks, July-August, including excursions to places of interest and the opportunity to spend weekends with Turkish families. Board and accommodation provided, plus honorarium in Turkish currency towards pocket money. Travel cost approx £250 including insurance, paid by applicants.
🕮 Apply by mid April.

WORKCAMPS

GENÇTUR Yerebatan Caddesi 15/3, Sultanahmet, 34410 Istanbul, Turkey ℗ (90 212) 520 5274/5 ☎ (90 212) 519 0864
Volunteers are invited to participate on international workcamps, working in groups of 15-20 volunteers from 4-5 different countries in small villages throughout Turkey. Recent projects have including making paths and working in the park around a castle in Milas; assisting with practical tasks to prepare for a festival in the ruins of the ancient city of Troy; painting and whitewashing village schools in the Aladog area; and organising activities for children at a summer camp in Gallipolli.

④ Ages 18-35. 6-7 hour day, with I free day per week. 2 weeks, June-September. Working language is English. Accommodation provided in schools; volunteers should take a sleeping bag. Food supplied by the villagers or, occasionally, self-catering. Volunteers pay own travel expenses and insurance, and must attend an orientation meeting in Istanbul before each camp. **D**

🕮 Apply through partner organisation in country of residence.
In the UK: Concordia (Youth Service Volunteers) Ltd, International Voluntary Service, Quaker International Social Projects or United Nations Association International Youth Service. See page 30 for registration details and addresses.

GSM GENÇLIK ACTIVITELERI SERVISI Mr Ertugrul Senoglu, Yüksel Caddesi 44/6, 06420 Kizilay- Ankara, Turkey ℗ (90 312) 433 2200
Requires volunteers for workcamps throughout Turkey. Recently, GSM has been working with local councils to develop green areas in town centres, including a natural recreation area along the banks of the river Kizilirmak in the town of Avanos, Central Anatolia; and transforming a derelict area into a public park in the historical town of Silifke on the Mediterranean. Tasks involve fencing, building paths and preparing the ground for planting. 5 hour day, weekends free. 2 weeks, July-September.
④ Ages 18-28. Excursions organised at weekends. Board and lodging provided in small hotels/pensions. Volunteers pay their own travel costs and £70 registration fee.

🕮 Apply through partner organisation in country of residence.
In the UK: Christian Movement for Peace, Concordia (Youth Service Volunteers) Ltd, Quaker International Social Projects or United Nations Association International Youth Service.
See page 30 for registration details and addresses.

GENERAL

EUROYOUTH LTD
301 Westborough Road, Westcliff, Southend-on-Sea, Essex SS0 9PT
✆ Southend-on-Sea (01702) 341434
Holiday guest stays arranged where **guests** are offered board and lodging in return for an agreed number of hours English conversation with hosts or their children. Time also available for guests to practise the host language.
⚘ Mainly ages 17-25, but sometimes opportunities for older applicants.
Open to anyone whose mother tongue is English, interested in visiting Turkey and living with a local family for a short time. 2-3 weeks, and occasionally 1-2 months, mainly July and August, but also during the year. Travel and insurance arranged by applicants, but tickets at reduced rates can be obtained on request. Registration fee approx £70.
🎓 Apply at least 12 weeks prior to scheduled departure date.

SUNSAIL The Port House, Port Solent, Portsmouth PO6 4TH
✆ Portsmouth (01705) 214330
📠 (01705) 219827
Crew members are required to work aboard cruising yachts sailing in flotillas off the Lycian coast. Vacancies for RYA qualified and experienced **skippers**, responsible for the wellbeing of up to 13 yachts and 60 holidaymakers, giving daily briefings on navigation and providing sailing assistance where necessary.
Also qualified **diesel mechanics** needed, responsible for maintaining the marine diesel engines and repairing any other onboard items.
Hostesses also required to look after laundry, accounting, cleaning of boats, advising holidaymakers on shops and restaurants, and organising social events and barbecues.
Also vacancies for qualified and experienced **hotel managers, chefs, cooks, bar staff, receptionists** and **windsurfing instructors** to work at watersports clubs throughout Turkey; also NNEB qualified **nannies/nurses** to look after children during the day.
⚘ Ages 21-35 for all posts. Relevant qualifications and experience essential; sailing experience desirable; conversational French/German an advantage. Staff should be enthusiastic, hardworking, loyal and honest with an outgoing personality. 45-50 hour, 6 day week, plus social hours in the evenings. Staff must work the full season, March/April-October/November. Salary £55-£95 per week, depending on position. Accommodation provided on board yachts in flotillas; in hotels with meals for club staff. Return travel and 50% insurance paid.
🎓 Apply December-March.

When writing to any organisation it is essential to mention Working Holidays 1995 and to enclose a stamped, self-addressed A4 envelope, or if in another country, an addressed A4 envelope and at least two IRCs (International Reply Coupons, available from post offices). Enquiries received without SAEs/IRCs are unlikely to be answered.

UNITED STATES

INFO

US Embassy
24 Grosvenor Square, London
WIA IAE ✆ 0171-499 9000
Visa section: 5 Upper Grosvenor Street,
London WIA 2JB ✆ 0891 200290

British Embassy
3100 Massachusetts Avenue NW,
Washington, DC 20008
✆ (1 202) 462 1340

Tourist office
United States Travel and Tourism
Administration, PO Box 1EN, London
WIA 1EN ✆ 0891 616000

Youth hostels
American Youth Hostels Inc, 1332
1 Street NW, Suite 800, Washington,
DC 20005

Youth & student information
Council on International Educational
Exchange (CIEE), 205 East 42nd Street,
New York, NY 10017

ISSTA, Suite 1204, 211 East 43rd Street,
New York, NY 10017

Student Travel Network, Suite 307,
Geary Street, San Francisco, CA 94108

Student Travel Network, Suite 728, 6151
West Century Boulevard, Los Angeles,
CA 90034

US-UK Educational Commission,
62 Doughty Street, London WC1N 2LS
✆ 0171-404 6994

Entry regulations A visa is required
for all types of temporary employment,
whether paid or unpaid. The applicant
must generally either be the beneficiary
of a petition approved by the US
Immigration and Naturalization Service
or qualify as an exchange visitor.
Exchange visitor programmes are
operated by a number of organisations;

anyone wanting to work in the US should check whether they qualify under one of the programmes and if so should apply as early as possible. Once an application has been accepted, the participant will receive form IAP-66 for a non-immigrant Exchange Visitor Visa, which should be posted, with a completed visa application (form OF-156) to the visa branch of the US Embassy, address above; or for residents of Northern Ireland to the American Consulate General, Queens House, 14 Queen Street, Belfast BT1 6EQ. Holders of non-immigrant Exchange Visitor Visas may work only under the terms of the programme and are not eligible to seek other employment while in the country. They are automatically exempt from paying social security and income tax. Participants should not plan to stay longer than the duration of the programme, though the visa is valid for a period of travel, normally of 2/3 weeks, at the end of the programme. Changing to another visa is a complicated procedure, there is no guarantee that it will be granted; full details available from the visa branch at the US Embassy. **B D PH W** Generally, handicapped people are not ineligible to receive visas.

Travel Campus Travel offers low-cost, flexible student/youth fares to destinations throughout the US, with the facility to enter via one city and leave from another. Also offer wide range of options for internal travel by air, rail or coach and can book adventure tours and treks. Offices throughout the UK including a student travel centre at 52 Grosvenor Gardens, London SW1W 0AG (opposite Victoria Station) ℂ 0171-730 8111 or ℂ 0131-668 3303 for Scottish telephone bookings.

Council Travel, 28A Poland Street, London W1V 3DB ℂ 0171-437 7767 (offices also in Paris, Nice, Lyon, Munich, Düsseldorf, Tokyo, Singapore and across the US) offer low cost student/youth airfares to destinations in the US, plus insurance, guidebooks and travel gear.

Amtrak's National USA Pass offers unlimited travel on trains in the US; cost from $218 (15 days). Regional USA Pass offers unlimited travel on trains on key routes in 4 major regions; cost from $188 (15 days). Bicycle boxes available. Details from Long-Haul Leisurail, PO Box 113, Bretton, Peterborough, PE3 8HY ℂ Peterborough (01733) 335599.

Ameripass offers unlimited bus travel in the US, from £50 (4 days). **B D PH W** Helping Hand service enables a companion to travel free to assist a handicapped person who needs help in travelling on a bus. Doctor's certificate of eligibility required; wheelchairs and other aids carried free. All tickets must be purchased in Britain. Details from Greyhound International, Sussex House, London Road, East Grinstead, West Sussex RH19 1LD ℂ East Grinstead (01342) 317317 ▭ (01342) 328519.

North-South Travel Ltd, Moulsham Mill, Parkway, Chelmsford CM2 7PX ℂ Chelmsford (01245) 492882 arranges competitively priced, reliably planned flights to all parts of America. All profits go to projects in the developing world.

STA Travel, 86 Old Brompton Road, London SW7 3LQ/117 Euston Road, London NW1 2SX ℂ 0171-937 9971 (offices also throughout Britain and the US) operates flexible low-cost flights with open-jaw facility between London and destinations throughout the US. Internal flights, accommodation, tours and air passes also available.

If you're a driver, an economical way to see the US, especially from the east to west coast, is to offer your services to an automobile transporting company, who specialise in delivering cars all over the US. AAACON has branches in most major cities; *Yellow Pages* also list others under *Automobile and Truck Transporting*. You generally need to be over 21, and in possession of an International Driving Licence. Be prepared to be finger printed, photographed, or to submit character references. Deposit of $100-$200 also required, repayable upon safe delivery, and you will probably have to pay your own fuel and toll costs.

Publications Rough Guides provide comprehensive background information plus details on getting there, getting around, places to explore and cheap places to stay. Titles include *USA* £12.99, *California* £9.99, *Florida* £7.99, *New York* £8.99, *Pacific Northwest* £9.99 and *San Francisco* £8.99.

Vacation Work's *Travellers Survival Kit USA & Canada* £9.95, is a down-to-earth, entertaining guide for travellers to North America. Describes how to cope with the inhabitants, officialdom and way of life in the US and Canada. Also *Live & Work in USA & Canada* £8.99, a guide for those interested in finding work, starting a business or buying a home in North America.

Writer's Digest Books *Summer Jobs USA 1995* £10.95, gives details of thousands of summer jobs for students in the US and Canada. Includes a section giving advice on legal requirements and visa procedures. Also *Internships USA 1995* £19.95, which lists career-oriented positions enabling students and graduates to train through a period of work with an established employer.

All the above guidebooks available from good bookshops.

The Moneywise Guide to North America £11.10 including UK postage, provides information for anyone travelling on a budget, with useful details on getting around. Published by BUNAC, 16 Bowling Green Lane, London EC1R OBD ℗ 0171-251 3472.

North America Rail & Bus Guide is an essential handbook for budget travellers including timetables, details of passes and travel bargains, maps, street plans and practical advice. Available from Thomas Cook Publications, PO Box 227,

Peterborough PE3 6SB ℗ Peterborough (01733) 505821/268943, price £7.75 including UK postage.

Accommodation The Council on International Educational Exchange, 205 East 42nd Street, New York, NY 10017 publishes *Where to Stay USA*, a paperback listing over 1,700 places to spend the night from $6, including hostels, motels, campsites and university halls of residence. Special section for foreign visitors. Available in the UK from Council Travel, see above, price £6.95.

Ys Way International, 224 East 47th Street, New York, NY 10017 offers inexpensive accommodation at YMCAs in New York and other major cities in the US and Canada. Average cost per night is $40 including use of sports facilities. Details in the UK from Travel Cuts, 295A Regent Street, London W1R 7YA ℗ 0171-637 3161.

ARCHAEOLOGY

Archaeological Fieldwork Opportunities Bulletin $10.50 plus $3.00 postage, lists sites throughout the US where excavation and research are being carried out. Details given of staff needed at each site. Also lists field schools providing practical training for students. Published annually in January by the Archaeological Institute of America, 675 Commonwealth Avenue, Boston, MA 02215, United States.

EARTHWATCH EUROPE Belsyre Court, 57 Woodstock Road, Oxford ℗ Oxford (01865) 516366 Aims to support field research in a wide range of disciplines including archaeology, ornithology, animal behaviour, nature conservation and ecology. Support is given to researchers as a grant and in the form of volunteer assistance. Recent projects involving **volunteers** have included excavating Apache sites in Texas; searching for evidence of the Homol'ori people,

ancestors to the Hopi, in Arizona; excavating slave cabins in Tennessee to uncover the lives of plantation slaves; and recording prehistoric petroglyphs at the Grand Gulch canyon in Utah.
⊕ Ages 16-80. No special skills required, but each expedition may, because of its nature, demand some talent or quality of fitness. Volunteers should be fit, able to cope with new situations and work with people of different ages and backgrounds, and a sense of humour will help. 2-3 weeks, all year. Members share costs, from £340-£2,000, which includes meals, transport and all necessary field equipment, but does not include the cost of travel to the staging area, although assistance may be given in arranging it. Membership fee £25 entitles members to join an expedition, attend evening and weekend members' events, and receive magazines and newsletters providing the information necessary to choose a project.
B D PH W depending on project.

LUBBOCK LAKE LANDMARK
The Director, Box 43191 TTU, Lubbock, TX 79409, United States
Volunteers are needed for research on Paleo-Indian, Archaic, Ceramic, Protohistoric and Historic remains.
⊕ Ages 18+. Applicants should be willing to work hard. 6+ weeks, June-August. Basic accommodation, food, major equipment, instruction and training provided. Volunteers pay own fares, personal expenses and $40 for small equipment needs. Academic credit available. Sponsored by the Museum of Texas Tech University. D PH W
⚏ Apply by 1 May.

MISSION SAN ANTONIO ARCHAEOLOGICAL SCHOOL
Dr Robert Hoover, Social Sciences Department, California Polytechnic State University, San Luis Obispo, CA 93407, United States
Volunteers required to assist research into Spanish colonial archaeology. Since 1976 the School has been excavating the 18th century site, including the Indian dormitories, the first brick and tile kiln excavated in Spanish California and the nearby barracks, and examining historical and cultural materials from the vine-grower's house to interpret the role of agriculture in educating the converts to the culture of 18th century Spain. Work involves excavating, recording and laboratory processing of the shops wing. Evening lectures and activities arranged; opportunities for weekend sightseeing.
⊕ Ages 18+. Applicants must be in good health. Interest and dedication essential; no experience necessary. Knowledge of English required. 35 hour, 5 day week. 6 weeks, beginning mid June-end July. Cost approx $850 per 6 weeks, includes board and accommodation as guests of the Mission's Franciscan friars. Housekeeping chores are cooperative. No fares, wages or insurance paid.

PASSPORT IN TIME/USDA FOREST SERVICE
Passport in Time Clearinghouse, PO Box 18364, Washington, DC 20036, United States ✆ (1 202) 293 0922
Provides opportunities for individuals and families to work as volunteers under the supervision of professional archaeologists and historians. Work involves excavation, survey, analysis, historic structure restoration and interpretation. Projects take place in forests throughout the US; recent projects have included excavating a 19th century gold prospector's site in Idaho; recording prehistoric cliff-dwellings and pictographs in New Mexico; locating and mapping Custer's trail to Little Bighorn in North Dakota; recording abandoned pioneer homesteads in the Oregon Coast Range; and mapping a ghost town in Wyoming.
⊕ Ages 18+ in most cases, unless accompanied by adult. No special skills or experience required but volunteers must have an interest in history, a willingness to learn and good spoken English. Commitment varies by project from 1 day to 2 weeks. Basic training given in archaeological techniques.

Campsites available near to projects; insurance cover provided. Volunteers are responsible for own travel, food and incidental costs. Newsletter provides project details and application form. **B D PH** at discretion of project leader.

AU PAIR / CHILDCARE

The au pair programme is open equally to males as well as females; the emphasis is as much on community involvement as on childcare. You must be a citizen of a western European country with a fair degree of fluency in English, childcare experience (such as babysitting) and able to drive; most families prefer nonsmokers. References and a medical certificate required. Work involves active duties including feeding and playing with children, and passive supervision. Up to 45 hour week spread over a maximum of 5½ days, with 1 full weekend free each month. ⊕ Ages 18-25. Positions last 12 months; also 10 week summer programme, see Camp America, below. Return flight, approx $100 per week pocket money, board and accommodation, medical insurance, $300 for a study course, 2 weeks holiday, and opportunities to travel provided. Applicants interviewed, and, if accepted, matched according to interests and experience with a host family and issued with a J-1 Exchange Visitor Visa authorised by the US Government. Short orientation programme held on arrival; au pairs have access to a local counsellor during their stay. Agencies require a good faith deposit of up to $500, refunded on completion of the programme. The following agencies can arrange au pair placements on authorised programmes:

ACADEMY AU PAIR AGENCY LTD 42 Cedarhurst Drive, Eltham, London SE9 5LP ✆ 0181-294 1191 ▭ 0181-850 8932
12 month **au pair** programme, as above.

AMERICAN INSTITUTE FOR FOREIGN STUDY Au Pair in America Programme, Department WH, 37 Queens Gate, London SW7 5HR ✆ 0171-581 7322
12 month **au pair** programme, as above. Good faith deposit of $500, refundable upon successful placement completion and return to Europe. **B D PH W** applications considered. ☏ ✆ *0800 413116 for brochure and application form.*

AVALON AGENCY Thursley House, 53 Station Road, Shalford, Guildford, Surrey GU4 8HA ✆ **Guildford (01483) 63640**
Can place **au pairs**. ⊕ Ages 18-27. 1 year programme, as above. Must be drivers, preferably nonsmokers with approx 1 year experience/qualifications. Refundable deposit against airfare.

CAMP AMERICA Dept WH1, 37A Queens Gate, London SW7 5HR
Exchange Visitor Programme offering limited places for females as **family companions** in selected American families. Participants live as a member of the family, responsible for care and supervision of the children aged 0-10, and undertake light household duties. ⊕ Ages 18 (by 1 June)-24. Applicants must have a genuine love of children, enthusiasm to work and play with them imaginatively, and the ability to adapt to different lifestyles. Driving licence preferred. 10 weeks, June-September. 1½ days free per week. Pocket money $400, return flight from London, orientation, sightseeing and lodging in New York, and transfer provided. Applicants must be willing to work hard, fit, with doctor's certificate of good health, and good English. 1-8 weeks at end for travel; cost not included. Deposit £50. Medical insurance fee £105. ☏ *Apply September-May. Interviews throughout Europe and Australia.*

CBR AU PAIR 63 Foregate Street, Worcester WR1 1DE ✆ **Worcester (01905) 26671**
12 month **au pair** programme, as above.

Good faith bond of £350, repaid when programme is successfully completed.

EXPERIMENT IN INTERNATIONAL LIVING
Au Pair Homestay, Otesaga, West Malvern Road, Malvern, Worcestershire WR14 4EN
✆ **Malvern (01684) 562577**
A non-profitmaking organisation aiming to promote international understanding as a means of achieving world peace. Operates a 12 month **au pair** programme, as above. £350 good faith bond, returnable at end of year. *British nationals only; other EEA nationals should apply to the EIL office in their own country.*

JUST THE JOB (NOTTINGHAM)
32 Dovedale Road, West Bridgford, Nottingham NG2 6JA
✆ **0115-945 2482**
12 month **au pair** programme, as above. Area organiser for East Midlands, Edinburgh, Dundee, Aberdeen, Inverness and Stirling. *UK applicants only.*

STUDENTS ABROAD LTD
11 Milton View, Hitchin, Hertfordshire SG4 0QD *✆* **Hitchin (01462) 438909** *▱* **(01462) 438919**
12 month **au pair** programme, as above. Good faith deposit of £300 refunded on successful completion of programme.
✎ Applicants should be resident in the UK and available for interview and to complete formalities. EEA passport-holders only.

COMMUNITY WORK

BENEDICTINE LAY VOLUNTEERS
Summer Program, Mother of God Monastery, Box 254, Watertown, SD 57201, United States
The Program is designed for people interested in experiencing life in a monastic community, and is offered in the expectation that the volunteer might serve and at the same time grow spiritually. **Volunteers** serve primarily in South Dakota, in rural parishes, on summer day camp programmes, with Native American children, as well as in the monastery and the Harmony Hill Centre. Orientation provided to the monastery life and ministries. Sharing in the life of the religious community, such as reflection and days of prayer, is an important aspect of the programme.
✦ Ages 18+. 2-10 weeks, June-August. Board and lodging provided. Volunteers pay own travel and insurance costs.
✎ Apply by 1 April.

HABITAT FOR HUMANITY OF GREATER MIAMI
17300 SW 177 Avenue, Miami, FL 33187, United States *✆* **(1 305) 252 8606**
A not-for-profit organisation working towards eliminating substandard living conditions by providing houses for the economically disadvantaged. **Volunteers** needed to help construct homes in partnership with families in some of the poorest areas of South Florida, to replace housing destroyed by Hurricane Andrew which left 250,000 people homeless. Work involves almost all aspects of woodframe construction, with tasks allocated according to volunteers' skills, local needs, material availability, weather and other factors. Includes general carpentry, framing, roofing, painting and landscaping.
✦ Ages 14+. Experience useful but not essential; enthusiasm and ability to speak English required. 7 hour day, 5 day week; work available all year. Board, accommodation and supplementary accident insurance; cost $10 per day. Long-term volunteers may be eligible to $40 per week wages. No fares paid. **B D PH W** *✎ May also apply through Habitat for Humanity International, 121 Habitat Street, Americus, GA 31709-3498, United States.*

SERVICE CIVIL INTERNATIONAL
Route 2, Box 506, Crozet, VA 22932, United States
Promotes international reconciliation through work projects. **Volunteers** are needed to work on community projects. Recent projects have included gardening and small construction projects at a

centre providing free holistic healthcare to the community in West Virginia; hosting a youth camp at an Indian reservation in New Jersey, preparing food, leading hikes, and assisting with arts, crafts, fishing and other activities; and providing personal care and a recreational programme for a group of mentally handicapped adults in the Blue Ridge Mountains, Virginia.

⊕ Ages 18+. Applicants should be highly motivated, preferably with previous workcamp or voluntary experience, and prepared to work hard as part of a team. 3-8 weeks, June-August. Food, shared accommodation and work accident insurance provided. No fares or wages paid. **B D PH** some camps unsuitable for wheelchairs.

Apply through partner organisation in country of residence. In the UK: International Voluntary Service. See page 30 for registration details and addresses.

THE SIOUX INDIAN YMCA
PO Box 218, Dupree, SD 57623, United States

First founded in 1879 and today serve in 31 communities on 5 reservations in South Dakota, the only YMCAs operated by and serving primarily Indian people. **Volunteers** are required to live and work individually on small, remote reservation communities. Projects may include developing recreational and children's activities; work in elementary and pre-schools; assisting with the nutrition program for the elderly; and developing libraries and tutoring. Time not spent in formally organised activity may be spent in recreation and community development activities. What is done largely depends on the volunteer's own abilities and the needs of the community and local YMCA. The personal relationships formed are at least as important as the specific activities carried out.

⊕ Ages 18+. Volunteers should speak good English, and preferably be skilled in recreation, leadership development, childcare and working with people.

A love of children and people in general, and an ability to adapt to a different socio-economic and cultural setting also necessary. Because of the poverty/alcohol syndrome on the reservation, volunteers are expected not to drink alcohol for the project period. Those from all religious faiths and commitments are accepted, but are expected to respect and participate in the Christian life of the community. Time commitment should be to a 24 hour day, 7 day week, 3-12 months. Full board accommodation provided with families or in small community buildings. Volunteers arrange own insurance and travel. Help given in obtaining a visa. Orientation and evaluation sessions arranged. **PH** depending on ability.

VOLUNTEERS FOR PEACE INC
43 Tiffany Road, Belmont, VT 05730, United States

Independent, non-aligned, non-profit organisation working for peace through youth exchanges and voluntary service. **Volunteers** are invited to work on community projects. Recent projects have included renovation work and preparing and serving meals at a residential self-help centre for homeless people in New York; renovation work at a ranch for formerly abused/neglected children in Maryland; building and renovating housing for low-income families in Connecticut; and painting, woodwork and repair work at an HIV/AIDS supportive community in Harlem.

⊕ Ages 18-35. Applicants should preferably be already involved in the peace movement, as well as highly motivated, fit and prepared to work hard as part of a team. 2/3 weeks, June-August. Food, shared accommodation and work accident insurance provided. No fares or wages paid. **B D PH**

Apply through partner organisation in country of residence.
In the UK: International Voluntary Service or United Nations Association International Youth Service. See page 30 for registration details and addresses.

WINANT-CLAYTON VOLUNTEERS ASSOCIATION

The Coordinator, 38 Newark Street, London E1 2AA
℗ 0171-375 0547

A community service exchange scheme which aims to offer assistance to city projects in the eastern states and provide insights into a different culture. **Volunteers** are assigned to social work agencies; projects include assisting at rehabilitation centres and homes for emotionally disturbed children, working with the elderly and housebound, AIDS projects, and day camps/centres for deprived inner city teenagers/children. ⊕ Ages 19+. Applicants should have experience of work with children, youth and community or other voluntary social work. They should be flexible, with a sense of humour and real interest in people. Hours comparable to full-time staff. 3 months, June-September, including time for own travel. 2 days free per week. Board, accommodation and pocket money provided. Volunteers pay travel and insurance costs; small grants may be available. Participants should take enough money to support themselves during free time at the end of the project. Orientation course organised. Registration fee £10. **B D PH W** depending on ability.
※ Apply by mid January. UK residents only.

CONSERVATION

Helping Out In The Outdoors $10 including postage lists hundreds of parks, forests and other land agencies all over the US requiring **volunteers**. Most positions are for campground hosts, trail crews and wilderness rangers. Published annually in November by the American Hiking Society, see below.

AMERICAN HIKING SOCIETY

Volunteer Vacations, PO Box 20160, Washington, DC 20041-2160, United States
Volunteers required for trail crews of 10-20 people working in national parks, state parks, wilderness areas and forests. Crews build and maintain trails and help with a variety of projects designed to make these areas safe, attractive and accessible. Recent projects have included cleaning and painting cabins on Hasselborg Lake in Alaska; heavy maintenance work on the Bull Frog Trail in Arizona's Mayatyal Wilderness; and water drainage and clearance in the Indian Heaven Wilderness, Washington. ⊕ Ages 18+. Volunteers should be experienced hikers who are in good physical condition, comfortable in remote, primitive settings and willing to work hard. 1 and 2 week projects, all year. Supervision, safety equipment, tools and food provided; volunteers should take their own sleeping bags and tents. Registration fee $50 payable with application form, refundable if not accepted for programme. **D**

APPALACHIAN MOUNTAIN CLUB Volunteer Trail Opportunities, Box 298, Gorham, NH 03581, United States
℗ (1 603) 466 2721

Maintains over 1,400 miles of trail in the northeast. **Volunteers** invited to join the conservation corps and work on trail crews in the Delaware Water Gap, the Berkshires, the Catskills and the White Mountains, constructing and maintaining shelters and trails, relocating sections and building new routes. Also 10 day service trips in Alaska, Montana, Maine, Wyoming and elsewhere. ⊕ Ages 18-65+. Trailwork experience helpful but not essential; enthusiasm and willingness to learn and work to your best ability more important. Good health and backpacking experience also valuable; fluency in English essential. 1 week or 10 days, June-September. Approx 40 hours per week; weekends free. Full board and accommodation in basecamps or tents provided. Volunteers arrange own travel and insurance. Training provided in the use of handtools, safety procedures and maintenance techniques. Project fees $35-$60 (1 week), $95-$195 (10 days).

APPALACHIAN TRAIL CONFERENCE PO Box 10, Newport, VA 24128, United States
✆ (1 703) 544 7388

The Appalachian Trail is the world's first continuously marked footpath, stretching for 2,155 miles from Maine through Georgia. The trail has been maintained by volunteers since its construction in the 1920s/30s as a place where workers in cities could go to take a break and learn about nature. Volunteers are invited to join teams of 6-8 helping with trail design, building and maintenance, shelter and bridge construction, rehabilitation of eroded trail, clearing and open-areas management and various other tasks. Also a few paid positions for experienced trail crew leaders, camp coordinators and roving caretakers. ⊕ Ages 18+. No experience necessary for volunteer positions, as trail skills are taught by professionals. Applicants must be fit, enthusiastic, adaptable, willing to follow instructions and safety rules and happy to share in camp chores. 1-2+ weeks, May-October. Approx 40 hours per week, with 2 days off. Accommodation provided in tents or cabins, with time off spent at base camp. All meals and insurance provided, but not travel costs. B D depending on ability and project. ⊠ Apply by 1 March.

ARCOSANTI HC 74, Box 4136, Mayer, AZ 86333, United States
✆ (1 602) 632 7135   ▥ (1 602) 632 5111

An experimental city in the making, located in the high desert of Arizona, and constructed according to the arcology concept of Paolo Soleri, with architecture and ecology working together to produce an alternative to urban sprawl. When finished, it will be an energy efficient, pedestrian university town for 5,000 on 25 acres, surrounded by natural wilderness or farmland. By taking advantage of solar heat, by limiting the use of the car and by incorporating Soleri's multi-use designs into the city structure it is hoped to demonstrate that cities need not be ugly, unhealthy and wasteful structures. Volunteers are invited to participate in the project by learning about techniques and helping to build and maintain solar buildings. Work involves concrete construction, interior finishing, bronze foundry work, gardening and landscaping. ⊕ Ages 18+. Relevant experience in architecture, carpentry, mechanics, building, ceramics, bronze foundry work or environmental studies welcome but not essential. Participants must attend a 5 week workshop, which includes a 1 week orientation and training seminar followed by 4 weeks' work. Cost $400 for seminar, plus $75 per week to cover board and accommodation. After initial 5 weeks, participants may be considered for residency and volunteer work, paying only for meals and $25 weekly fee. No fares or wages paid. ⊠ Completed applications to be received at least 2 weeks in advance.

BACKCOUNTRY VOLUNTEERS PO Box 86, North Scituate, MA 02060-0086, United States
✆ (1 617) 545 7019

Recruits volunteers for trail crews of 10-12 people working primarily in national parks, forests and state parks throughout the US, building new trails, maintaining old ones and helping with other tasks. Projects have included building bridges in Yellowstone National Park, weeding out non-native plants in Hawaii's Haleakala National Park, and reconstructing trails in Alaska. ⊕ Ages 13-70. Ages 16-18 must have parental consent; under 16s must be accompanied by an adult. Volunteers must be experienced backpackers in good physical condition, able to do hard manual work in rugged conditions. Relevant skills and experience welcome but not essential. Projects run all year, usually 10 days in a 2 week period, with time off for relaxation and hiking. Supervision, tools and safety equipment provided; in most cases food also provided. Volunteers should take a sleeping bag and camping equipment. No fares or wages paid. Registration fee

$40 payable on acceptance. **D** 🖂 *Send large SAE and 2 IRCs.*

BRITISH TRUST FOR CONSERVATION VOLUNTEERS
Room IWH, 36 St Mary's Street, Wallingford, Oxfordshire OX10 0EU ✆ **Wallingford (01491) 839766**
The largest charitable organisation in Britain to involve people in practical conservation work. Following the success of the UK programme, aims to introduce **volunteers** to practical conservation projects abroad. It is hoped that British volunteers will adapt to and learn from local lifestyles as well as participate in the community. Recent projects have included footpath work in the Berkshire Mountains, in the White Mountains in New Hampshire, on the Appalachian Trails, and continuing work on the Bay Circuit Trail in Boston.
⊕ Ages 18-70. 2 weeks. The work is quite arduous. Cost from £175 includes transport from a suitable pick up point in the US, insurance, food and basic accommodation with everyone sharing domestic chores. Membership fee £12. No fares or wages paid.

CASCADIA QUEST
4649 Sunnyside Avenue North, Seattle, WA 98013, United States
Aims to bring together young people from all over the world to work as **volunteers** on environmental projects in Cascadia, a bio-region comprising southern British Columbia (Canada) and Washington, Oregon and Idaho. Projects include stream restoration, tree-planting, erosion control and improving wildlife habitat.
⊕ Ages 18-24. Previous workcamp or other voluntary experience an advantage; volunteers should be motivated to work hard as part of a team. 3 weeks, spring, summer and autumn. Orientation and evaluation programmes held in Seattle at the beginning and end of project. Food and accommodation provided; volunteers cover their own travel, insurance and personal expenses.

🖂 *Apply through partner organisation in country of residence. In the UK: United Nations Association International Youth Service. See page 30 for registration details and addresses.*

EARTHWATCH EUROPE **Belsyre Court, 57 Woodstock Road, Oxford** ✆ **Oxford (01865) 516366**
Aims to support field research in a wide range of disciplines including ornithology, archaeology, animal behaviour, nature conservation and ecology. Support is given to researchers as a grant and in the form of volunteer assistance. Recent projects involving **volunteers** have included tracking timber wolves in Minnesota to find out how traffic and the presence of humans affects their behaviour; documenting the distribution of saltmarsh plants in Chesapeake Bay, Virginia, to see how they may survive a rise in sea level; and studying the feeding patterns of musk-oxen and caribou in Alaska in an attempt to boost numbers.
⊕ Ages 16-80. No special skills are required, but each expedition may, because of its nature, demand some talent or quality of fitness. Volunteers should be generally fit, able to cope with new situations and work with people of different ages and backgrounds, and a sense of humour will help. 2-3 weeks, all year. Members share the costs of the project, from £340-£2,000 which includes meals, transport and all necessary field equipment, but does not include the cost of travel to the staging area, although assistance may be given in arranging it. Membership fee £25 entitles members to join an expedition, attend evening and weekend events, and receive magazines and newsletters providing all the information necessary to choose a project. **B D PH W** depending on project.

STUDENT CONSERVATION ASSOCIATION INC **PO Box 550, Charlestown, NH 03603, United States**
Aims to provide resource management agencies with qualified and motivated

volunteers, who get educational opportunities and professional work experience in conservation and resource management in over 200 national parks, forests, wildlife refuges and similar areas throughout the US, including Hawaii and Alaska. Specific duties vary with location, but may include trail patrol, wildlife management, visitor contact, natural science interpretation, forestry, archaeological surveys or recreation management. Recent opportunities have included organising guided walks, hikes and cave tours around Mount St Helens, Washington; radio-tracking endangered red wolves in the Great Smoky Mountains, Tennessee; studying the effect of recent forest-fires upon elk behaviour in Yellowstone National Park, Wyoming; identifying and sampling marine fish, invertebrates and vegetation in the Everglades, Florida; monitoring Canada geese nesting in the Aleutian islands of the Alaskan Peninsula; and patrolling the wilderness areas of the Grand Canyon. ⊕ Ages 16+. Volunteers should have an interest in conservation or resource management. Some posts may require specific experience in public speaking, hiking or other outdoor activities, or in a particular academic field. Fluency in English essential; knowledge of other languages helpful. 12+ weeks, all year. 40 hour week. Accommodation in apartment, trailer or ranger station, information and assistance with visas, partial travel reimbursement, $45-$90 per week to cover food expenses, and a uniform allowance, if required, training, guidance and supervision provided. B D PH W depending on position and abilities. ✎ *Write 4 months in advance for application material. Competition for places strong. Application fee of $20 must accompany completed application form.*

VOLUNTEERS FOR PEACE INC
43 Tiffany Road, Belmont, VT 05730, United States
Independent, nonaligned, non-profit American organisation working for peace through youth exchanges and voluntary service. Volunteers are invited to work in international teams on summer projects. Recent projects have included restoring historic buildings such as lighthouses at wildlife refuges on the coast of Maine; landscaping and transplanting work on a nature trail and building a maple tree syrup sap house at a rural community in Southern New Hampshire; constructing a straw-bale structure with solar panels at an ecological farming and education centre in New Jersey; trail construction and maintenance alongside members of the Forest Service in Alaska; and working on shoreline restoration, landscaping and carpentry projects at Baxter State Park near the coast of Maine.
⊕ Ages 18+. Applicants should be highly motivated and prepared to work hard as part of a team. 6 hour day, 30-36 hour week. 2-3 weeks July-August. Food, shared accommodation and work accident insurance provided. No fares or wages paid. **B D PH**

✎ *Apply through partner organisation in country of residence. In the UK: International Voluntary Service or United Nations Association International Youth Service. See page 30 for registration details and addresses.*

DOMESTIC

BRITISH UNIVERSITIES NORTH AMERICA CLUB (BUNAC)
16 Bowling Green Lane, London EC1R 0BD ✆ **0171-251 3472**
Operates KAMP (Kitchen and Maintenance Programme), an Exchange Visitor Programme offering opportunities to work on summer camps as domestic or maintenance staff. The camps are permanent sites catering for 40-600 children at one time, and can be organised privately, by the YMCA, Girl Scouts or Salvation Army, or can be institutional camps for the physically, mentally or socially handicapped. Vacancies exist for **kitchen assistants, dining room staff, chambermaids, cleaners, laundry workers,**

dishwashers, assistant cooks and bakers, porters, janitors and nightwatchmen. Ground staff and general maintenance workers also required for mowing, weeding, plumbing, carpentry, electrical work, building, painting, cleaning and repairing. Relevant skills required for some jobs. ⊕ Ages 18+. Also vacancies for drivers, ⊕ ages 21+ with full UK and international drivers licences, to transport children, staff and equipment. Applicants must be full-time students studying at HND, 2 year BTEC or degree level in Britain, or gap year students who will be returning to an unconditional place at university. They should like children and sports, and must be cooperative, energetic, sociable, conscientious, outgoing and cheerful. June-August. Hours vary from camp to camp, but can be long; the work is hard and often tedious and staff have to organise their own free time. Most camps allow staff to use recreational facilities. 8-10 hour day, 5½-6 day week. Contracts are for the full camp period, normally 9 weeks, but occasionally longer. Cost £69 towards flight to New York, transfer to camp, full board and basic accommodation in wooden cabins at camp, and visa charges. Insurance cost approx £86. Participants receive a salary of approx $520, at the end of the camp. Approx 6 weeks are free at the end of the programme for independent travel; advice can be provided on onward travel. Friends can sometimes be placed on the same camp. Applicants will receive a list of jobs available, with details of size, type and location of camps, types of work available and any special facilities. Two references required of all applicants. Compulsory orientation programmes held at Easter throughout Britain. Membership fee £3.50. ⚱ Apply from October-November; directory available January/February.

Irish applications to USIT, Aston Quay, O'Connell Bridge, Dublin 2 © (353 1) 6778117.

CAMP AMERICA Dept WH2, 37A Queens Gate, London SW7 5HR
An Exchange Visitor Programme enabling young people to spend the summer in the US. Openings at summer camps on the Campower programme, working in utility areas. Assignments include working with automatic washing and drying machines in the **laundry**; helping with food preparation, serving, dish and pot washing in the **kitchen**; **dining room service**; **indoor and outdoor work**, grass cutting, painting, moving and clearing rubbish, cleaning and general repair work; **driving** camp vehicles; and general **secretarial work**. Experienced **cooks** and **bakers** also required. On some camps workers are needed before camp opens, preparing the activity and living areas for the children. 10+ hour day. ⊕ Students aged 18+. Pocket money $350. The programmes include return flight from London, orientation, sightseeing and accommodation in New York, transfer to camp, plus full board and lodging. Applicants must have be willing to work hard, fit, with a doctor's certification of good health, and speak good English. 1-6 weeks left free at the end of the camp for travel, the cost of which is not included in the programme. Deposit £50. Medical insurance fee £105. ⚱ Apply September-May.

GOLDEN ACRES FARM & RANCH Box WH, Gilboa, NY 12076, United States © (1 813) 786 2251 (2 December-14 April) or © **(1 607) 588 7329** (15 April-1 December)
A 600 acre farm and ranch resort in the Catskill Mountains of New York State. Requires **waiting staff, cooks, chambermaids** and **dishwashers**. ⊕ Ages 19+. Applicants must be English speaking and have previous experience of working with people. 40-55 hour, 6 day week, May-September; several jobs are available from 1 August. All staff must work until the first Monday in September. Wages $4.25 per hour, plus 2 bonuses of up to $40 per week upon successful completion of contract.

Full board dormitory accommodation provided, cost $9.55 per day. All staff are given training and may use most of the resort facilities. Excursions organised to local places of interest. Staff must pay own travel and insurance costs, and organise own visa/work permit through an approved scheme operator. ✍ Applications accepted 1 November-30 May.

FARMWORK

INTERNATIONAL AGRICULTURAL EXCHANGE ASSOCIATION YFC Centre, N A C, Stoneleigh Park, Kenilworth, Warwickshire CV8 2LG ✆ Coventry (01203) 696578

Operates opportunities for young people involved with **agriculture, horticulture** or **home management** to acquire practical work experience in the rural sector, and to strengthen and improve their knowledge and understanding of the way of life in other countries. Participants are given an opportunity to study practical methods on approved training farms and work as trainees, gaining experience in their chosen field. Types of farm include cropping, dairy, beef, sheep and mixed farms (crops plus dairy/beef) and a limited number of horticultural enterprises. Participants undertake paid work on the farm, approx 40 hours per week, and live as a member of the host family. Full board and lodging, insurance cover and a minimum net weekly wage of £50-£60 provided. All programmes include 3 weeks unpaid holiday. 3 day orientation seminar at the beginning of each programme at agricultural colleges and universities throughout the United States. Stopovers (2-4 days) in South Pacific (for 14 month programme) arranged en route.

⊕ Ages 18-30. Applicants should be single, and have good practical experience in the chosen training category, plus a valid driving licence. 7 months, (departing March); 14 months - 7 in Australia plus 7 in the US (departing September). Cost from £1,800 covers airfare, work permit, administration fee, orientation courses seminar, information meetings, insurance, supervision, placement with host family and travel costs to placement. £200 deposit.

✍ Apply at least 4 months in advance. UK and Irish passport holders only. Applicants in other countries should contact corresponding exchange body. American applicants requiring an exchange should apply to IAEA, 1000 1st Avenue South, Great Falls, MT 59401 ✆ (800) 272 4996.

INTERNATIONAL FARM EXPERIENCE PROGRAMME YFC Centre, N A C, Stoneleigh Park, Kenilworth, Warwickshire CV8 2LG ✆ Coventry (01203) 696584

Provides assistance to young **agriculturalists** and **horticulturalists** by finding places in farms/nurseries abroad to enable them to broaden their knowledge of agricultural and horticultural methods. IFEP is the UK representative for several programmes providing applicants with the opportunity to experience North American farm life. The University of Minnesota MAST/PART Program involves 12 months practical experience or 5-8 months on a farm/nursery followed by 3 months in the University. There are a variety of farms and the training is matched as far as possible with the applicants' requirements. Salary $575 per month including board and lodging. The Ohio State University Program involves 12 months practical experience or 9 months on a farm/nursery followed by 3 months at the University. Salary from $4. 25 per hour. OSU also offers classes for a 3 month period for each participant at reasonable cost. The National FFA Organisation also offers agricultural and horticultural placements for 3, 6 or 12 months. CAEP and Experience International offer further programme options.

⊕ Ages 18-28. Applicants must have at least 2 years' practical experience, or at least 1 year at agricultural college and 1 year's practical experience, and intend to make a career in agriculture or horticulture. Valid driving licence necessary. Applicants pay own travel and insurance. Registration fee £175 plus programme fee. ⚘ *UK applications to IFEP. Other applications to IFEP partner in home country.*

MONITORS & TEACHERS

AMERICAN CAMPING ASSOCIATION 5000 State Road 67 North, Martinsville, IN 46151-7902, United States

Publishes *Guide to Accredited Camps* $18.95 including airmail postage, listing over 2,000 residential and day camps throughout the US. Written primarily for parents choosing a camp for their children, it also includes a section on the camp job market which is estimated to provide more than 330,000 full-time posts. The majority of opportunities are for **counsellors** in over 50 activity areas, including outdoor living, sports, climbing, horse riding, ocean biology projects, drama and music. The guide also gives details of practical job finding services operated by the American Camping Association. **B D PH**

BRITISH UNIVERSITIES NORTH AMERICA CLUB (BUNAC) 16 Bowling Green Lane, London EC1R 0BD ✆ 0171-251 3472

A non-profit, non-political educational student club which aims to encourage interest and understanding between students in Britain and North America. Its camp counsellor programme, BUNACAMP, enables some 4,000 young people to work on summer camps across the US, but mostly in the north east, upper mid west, south east and west coast. Camps are permanent sites

and cater for 40-600 children at a time. They can be organised privately, by the YMCA, Girl Scouts, Salvation Army or they can be institutional camps for the physically, mentally or socially handicapped. Work involves living, working and playing with groups of 3-8 children aged 6-16.

General counsellors are responsible for the full-time supervision of their group and ensure that the children follow the set routine, and should be able to provide counsel and friendship and must therefore have fairly general experience and aptitude in the handling of children. **Specialist counsellors** must have a sporting or craft interest, qualifications or skills plus ability and enthusiasm to organise or teach specific activities. These include sports, watersports, music, arts and crafts, science, pioneering, entertainments and dance. Staff with **secretarial skills** are needed for office work; there are also vacancies for **counsellors** in institutional camps.

⊕ Ages 19½ (by 1 July)-35. Applicants must be resident in UK, single, hard working as hours are long, with a genuine love of children and relevant experience. They should be able to show firm, fair leadership and be flexible, cooperative, energetic, conscientious, cheerful, patient, positive and able to adapt to new situations, and to function enthusiastically in a structured setting. 8/9+ weeks, with 1 day off most weeks, mid June-end August, followed by 1-6 weeks free for travel after the camp. Return flight, overnight hostel accommodation, transfer to camp, orientation and training, guide to North America, plus board and lodging at the camp provided. Counsellors live with the children in log cabins or tents. Registration fee £59. Insurance fee approx £85. Salary approx $390; $450 for ages 21+. Suitable for students, teachers, social workers and others with relevant qualifications. Interviews throughout the UK, mid November-early May. Compulsory orientation programme at

Easter. Membership fee £3.50
♨ *Early application advisable.*
Irish applications to USIT, Aston Quay,
O'Connell Bridge, Dublin 2 ℭ *(353 1) 677*
8117.

CAMP AMERICA Dept WH3, 37A Queens Gate, London SW7 5HR

An Exchange Visitor Programme which recruits young people to work on summer camps in the US, mainly in New England, the middle Atlantic and mid-west states. Camps can be organised privately, by agencies such as the Boy Scouts, Jewish Youth Centres and YMCA, or they can be institutional, organised specially for the handicapped and the learning disabled.

General counsellors are responsible for the care and supervision of a group of 8-10 children aged 6-16. Involves working, playing and living with children 24 hours a day; duties include supervising the camp and personal cleanliness, helping maintain a high level of camp morale, ensuring that campers receive proper medical care, supervising rest hours, conducting activities and being on duty several nights a week. **Specialist counsellors** are responsible for instructing the children in specific activities such as sports, waterfront, sciences, arts and crafts, pioneering and performing arts. Other counsellors may be responsible for both activities and general work. **Nurses** and **student nurses** also required as camp aides. ⊕ Ages 18 (by 1 June)-35. Applicants must be flexible, cooperative and adaptable, like and get on with children, prepared to work with young people intensively in an outdoor educational environment, and be willing to adjust to camp life. They must be fit, with a doctor's certification of good health, and speak good English. Applicants must be available June-September.

Programme includes return flight, orientation in the US, transfer to camp, full board and lodging for 9 weeks at camp plus pocket money of $150-$450, according to age and experience. Up to 8 weeks free at the end of the camp for

travel, the cost of which is not included in the programme. Refundable deposit £50. Medical insurance fee £105. ♨ *Apply September-May.*

CAMP COUNSELORS USA (CCUSA) 154A Heath Road, Twickenham, London TW1 4BN ℭ 0181-744 9060 or 27 Woodside Gardens, Musselburgh EH21 7LJ ℭ 0131-665 5843

Recruits **counsellors** to work with children on summer camps, usually instructing in a specific skill or sport. ⊕ Ages 19-28. Applicants must be fluent in English with previous experience of working with children and a recognised qualification in their particular skill or sport. 9+ weeks, June-September, with 1 day off per week. Full board accommodation provided; return fare paid plus approx $300-$650 pocket money for 9 weeks. Orientation in Britain and the US before work begins. Cost £85 administration and £75 full insurance cover. ♨ *Apply by 1 April.*

THE SIOUX INDIAN YMCA PO Box 218, Dupree, SD 57623, United States

First founded in 1879 and today serve in 31 communities on five reservations in South Dakota, and are the only YMCAs operated by and serving primarily Indian people. **Volunteers** are needed to work at a residential summer camp on the Oahe Reservoir of the Missouri River. Volunteers will provide partial leadership for a workcamp as it prepares the campground, and will assume staff responsibilities for four week-long camp sessions. Staff live in teepees with campers, without electricity and running water; applicants should have skills suitable for primitive camping. Activities may include basketball, volleyball, arts and crafts, storytelling, hiking, swimming, canoeing, baseball and group games. ⊕ Ages 18+. Volunteers should be mature and committed, with definite camp skills, prepared to accept the disciplines of camp routine. They should be creative, responsible and flexible, speak good English, and be skilled in recreation, leadership development, childcare and working with people. A love of children and people in general, the ability to adapt to a different socio-economic setting and to relate meaningfully to other cultures are also necessary. Because of the poverty/alcohol syndrome on the reservation, volunteers are expected not to drink alcohol during the project. Those from all religious faiths and commitments accepted, but are expected to respect and participate in the Christian life of the community. 10 weeks, summer. Commitment should be to a 24-hour day, 7-day week. Volunteers arrange own insurance and travel. Orientation and evaluation sessions arranged. Help given in obtaining a visa. **PH** depending on mobility and abilities.

WORKCAMPS

COUNCIL ON INTERNATIONAL EDUCATIONAL EXCHANGE (CIEE) 205 East 42nd Street, New York, NY 10017, United States

Volunteers are invited to take part in international workcamps in various states including California, Colarado, Hawaii, Idaho, Iowa, Florida, Maine, Montana, Nevada, New York and Utah, run by a non-governmental organisation seeking to promote international understanding and friendship. Recent projects have included leading 5-10 day tours for adults with learning disabilities from New York to locations such as Niagara and the Catskills; restoring pond shorelines and dunes at the Cape Cod National Seashore; building trails and improving wildlife habitats in the Ozark Mountains; and preparing for Independence Day celebrations in the Golden Gate National Park.
⊕ Ages 18/20+. Applicants should be highly motivated and prepared to work hard as part of a team of international volunteers. Approx 35 hours per week for 3 weeks, July-September. Food and self-catering accommodation provided.

Participants should take work clothes and a sleeping bag and must pay their own travel costs. **B D PH W** depending on project.

Apply through partner organisation in country of residence. In the UK: United Nations Association International Youth Service. See page 30 for details.

SERVICE CIVIL INTERNATIONAL Route 2, Box 506, Crozet, VA 22932, United States

Service Civil International promotes international reconciliation through work projects. **Volunteers** are invited to work in international teams on workcamps. Recent projects have included harvesting, marketing and farm improvements, greenhouse and deck work, at an organic farm near Boulder in the foothills of the Rocky mountains; digging to extend wolf enclosures and expand visitor areas at a mountain wolf sanctuary in Colorado; and cleaning the banks of the Clark Fork River and replanting native species in Montana.
⊕ Ages 18+. Applicants should be highly motivated, preferably with previous workcamp or voluntary experience, and prepared to work hard as part of a team. 30-40 hour week. 2-4 weeks, June-September. Food, shared accommodation and work accident insurance provided. No fares or wages paid. **B D PH**

Apply through partner organisation in country of residence. In the UK: International Voluntary Service. See page 30 for registration details and addresses.

VOLUNTEERS FOR PEACE INC 43 Tiffany Road, Belmont, VT 05730, United States

Volunteers are invited to work on international workcamps organised by this independent, nonaligned, non-profit American organisation working for peace through youth exchanges and voluntary service. Recent projects have included the maintenance and repair of a traditional Alaskan fishing camp, painting

the buildings at a rehabilitation centre for birds of prey, helping young native students make their own regalia and painting Native Alaskan art on classroom walls; working in a recycling centre and staffing a display of Third World crafts in Indiana; creating trails and outdoor prayer and meditation spots, building maintenance, grounds upkeep and landscaping at a retreat centre in Virginia; and painting and renovation work in an African American community in Brooklyn. Opportunities for study groups, social and cultural activities, all linked to camp themes.
✪ Ages 18-35. Applicants should preferably be already involved in the peace movement, and be highly motivated, fit and prepared to work hard as part of a team. 2/3 weeks, June-August. Food, shared accommodation and work accident insurance provided. No fares or wages paid. **B D PH** but unsuitable for wheelchairs.

☙ *Apply through partner organisation in country of residence.*
In the UK: International Voluntary Service or United Nations Association International Youth Service. See page 30 for registration details and addresses.

GENERAL

BRITISH UNIVERSITIES NORTH AMERICA CLUB (BUNAC)
16 Bowling Green Lane, London EC1R 0BD ✆ **0171-251 3472**
A non-profit, non-political educational student club which aims to encourage interest and understanding between students in Britain and North America. Operates the **Work America Programme**, a general work and travel Exchange Visitor Program for full-time college and university students and gap year students resident in Britain ✪ aged 18+ who wish to work and travel in the US and who will be returning to unconditional places at university at the end of the summer. The Programme is sponsored in the UK

by the Council on International Educational Exchange (CIEE). Participants can visit the US between 15 June-3 October, working for a maximum of 15 weeks; most work about 8 weeks and travel for 4. Members receive a handbook on how to get to the US and a job directory which lists hundreds of jobs including hotel, restaurant and shop work, making and selling fudge, ice cream, sandwiches, soft drinks and fast food, laundry work, and helping in amusement parks. Alternatively members can go to the US on the basis of personal funds or on sponsorship and find a job once they are there. Compulsory orientation programmes held throughout Britain and upon arrival give advice on finding and choosing a job, obtaining a visa, income tax, accommodation, travel, food and budgeting. Flights arranged and include overnight accommodation in New York, cost £379; information also provided on onward travel, together with a guide to budget travel in North America and Mexico. Assistance provided by the summer office and by CIEE in New York. Cost £81 covers visa and administration costs. Insurance £86. Wages average $200+ per week. Participants can earn enough to cover the cost of the return flight, plus travel and all living expenses. Operates a loan scheme to help with flight costs. To qualify, participants must be able to provide evidence that they can support themselves during their stay, with $300-$600 in traveller's cheques, depending on whether they have a job offer, personal funds or individual sponsorship. Membership fee £3.50.
✪ *Apply for information in November.*

GRAND VIEW LODGE GOLF & TENNIS CLUB **South 134 Nokomis Avenue, Nisswa, MN 56468, United States** ✆ **(1 218) 963 2234**
A luxurious resort situated on the edge of Gull Lake in Minnesota, with guest cabins, golf courses, tennis courts and beach. Requires **waiting staff, cooks, housekeepers, bartenders, clerks,**

beach attendants, shop staff and children's counsellors.
⊕ Ages 18-28. Applicants must be English speaking; previous experience preferred. 35 hour, 5-6 day week, mid August-mid October. Wages $4.25 per hour, plus $0.35 per hour distribution. All staff must purchase uniforms on arrival. Full board accommodation provided in dormitories or cabins, cost $150 per month. Free use of resort facilities in spare time; occasional evening entertainments such as films, water skiing or bowling also organised.
Staff must pay own travel and insurance costs, and organise own visa/work permit through an approved scheme operator. ✍ *Apply between 1 January and 15 April.*

INTERNSHIP USA PROGRAMME
Council on International Educational Exchange (CIEE), 33 Seymour Place, London W1H 6AT ✆ **0171-706 3008** ☎ **0171-724 8468**
Enables students to complete a period of **work experience** of up to 1 year in the US, with optional travel period preceding or following placement.
⊕ Ages 18+. Applicants must be enrolled in full time further or higher education (HND level or above) on a course where practical experience forms an integral part. They must find their own work placement and, either through payment from their employer or through other means, finance their own visit to the US. Administration fees £125 for a stay of up to 6 months or £150 for 6-12 months. Participants must have insurance cover for the length of the stay. Official documentation and assistance with visa application provided, as are orientation materials covering issues such as social security, taxes, housing, American culture and transportation; plus 24 hour emergency assistance with any problems whilst in the US. ✍ *Apply all year round, at least 2 months in advance.*

Applications in France to CIEE, 1 place de l'Odéon, 75006 Paris ✆ (33 1) 46 34 16 10

Applications in Germany to CIEE, Thomas Mann Straße 33, 5300 Bonn ✆ (49 228) 6597 46/7.

INVOLVEMENT CORPS INC
15515 Sunset Boulevard, Suite 108, Pacific Palisades, CA 90272, United States ✆/☎ **(1 310) 459 1022**
Works in association with the Involvement Volunteers Association Inc network to find unpaid volunteer placements. **Volunteers** of all ages can participate in either individual placements or team tasks. Placements relate to conservation in urban or rural areas; farm programmes; sand dune restoration; bird observatory research; national parks; forestry reserves; passive recreation areas; or social service in special schools for disabled children. Volunteers must be able to speak English, arrange their own visitor visas, and organise their own international travel and insurance. Involvement Corps provides advice on placements, itinerary planning, low cost accommodation and banking, as well as a communications base in the area of operations. Cost $300. **B D**

✍ *In Europe, apply to Involvement Volunteers-Deutschland, Postfach 110224, 37047 Göttingen, Germany ✆ (49 551) 33 765 ☎ (49 551) 33 787*

In Australia, New Zealand and the Asia Pacific region, apply to Involvement Volunteers Association Inc, PO Box 218, Port Melbourne, Victoria 3207, Australia ✆/☎ (61 3) 646 5504

When writing to any organisation it is essential to mention Working Holidays 1995 and enclose a stamped, self-addressed A4 envelope, or if in another country, and addressed A4 envelope and at least two IRCs (International Reply Coupons, available from post offices).

WORLDWIDE

INFO

Travel Eurolines, 23 Crawley Road, Luton LU1 1HX ✆ Luton (01582) 404511 or ✆ 0171-730 0202 offers a wide range of coach services to over 270 destinations in Europe, including daily services to Paris, Amsterdam, Brussels, Frankfurt and Cologne.

The British Rail International Rail Centre, Victoria Station, London SW1V 1JY ✆ 0171-834 2345 can issue those under 26 with Euro-Youth low-cost rail tickets to any one of 200 selected destinations in mainland Europe. Also issues Inter-Rail passes providing unlimited travel on the railways of up to 27 countries in Europe and around the Mediterranean; cost from £179 (1 zone, 15 days, under 26) to £269 (19 countries, 1 month, 26+). European timetables and assistance with journey planning also available.

Odyssey International, 21 Cambridge Road, Waterbeach, Cambridge CB5 9NJ ✆ Cambridge (01223) 861079 aims to match like-minded travelling partners. An advice line is run by members who have just returned from abroad giving details of visa problems, vaccination requirements and employment prospects. Publishes a quarterly newsletter detailing travel offers. Annual membership £25. **B D PH W** welcome.

On The Rails Around Europe £11.35 including UK postage, is designed to help rail pass holders make the most of touring by train. Also *Thomas Cook Rail Map of Europe* £5.55 including UK postage, shows passenger lines throughout Europe and in countries bordering the Mediterranean. Both available from Thomas Cook Publications, PO Box 227, Peterborough PE3 6SB ✆ Peterborough (01733) 505821/268943.

Travellers Survival Kit Europe £6.95, is a practical guide covering over 35 countries, including details on the cost of food and accommodation, rules of the road, car hire, health tips, public transport, shopping hours, where to get help and information and many useful addresses. Available from Vacation Work Publications, 9 Park End Street, Oxford OX1 1HJ © Oxford (01865) 241978.

The Traveller's Handbook £14.95 (£9.95 to members), is an 900-page reference and source book for independent travellers, with chapters on travel, health, clothing, luggage and survival kits, where to stay, photography, choosing maps, passports, visas, permits, insurance, currency and Customs. Also includes special chapters for students, single women and disabled people. Published by WEXAS International, 45-49 Brompton Road, London SW3 1DE © 0171-589 0500.

Accommodation Backpackers Resorts International, 3 Newman Street, Nambucca Heads, NSW 2448, Australia © (61 18) 666888 ☎ (61 66) 847100 is a chain of over 250 independently owned and operated hostels catering for backpackers in Australia, Canada, Fiji, Ireland, New Zealand, Papua New Guinea, South Africa, the US and a number of other countries. VIP card entitles the holder to a variety of savings including discount accommodation at hostels; details in the UK from The Imaginative Traveller, 14 Barley Mow Passage, Chiswick, London W4 4PH © 0181-742 3113 ☎ 0181-742 3045.

YMCA World Directory £4 including UK postage, lists over 2,400 YMCAs in 90+ countries offering accommodation for both sexes. Available from National Council of YMCAs, 640 Forest Road, London E17 3DZ © 0181-520 5599.

International Youth Hostel Handbook Vol I gives addresses and brief details of all the permanent hostels in Europe and around the Mediterranean. Large folding map showing locations. Published annually in March. *International Youth Hostel Handbook Vol II* details hostels in Australasia, America and Asia. Price £6.99 each. Available from YHA shops or by post (add 61p per book for UK postage) from YHA Adventure Shops plc, 14 Southampton Street, London WC2E 7HY © 0171-836 8541.

Publications *Work Your Way Around the World* £9.95 includes first-hand accounts and details on preparation, working a free passage, opportunities in tourism, fruit picking, farming, teaching, domestic work, business and industry. Also details seasonal and temporary employment. *Directory of Summer Jobs Abroad 1995* £7.95 details vacancies in over 40 countries, including information on jobs offered, wages given and addresses of employers. *Working in Ski Resorts - Europe and North America* £8.95 has information on finding winter work. All available from Vacation Work Publications, 9 Park End Street, Oxford OX1 1HJ © Oxford (01865) 241978.

World Service Enquiry is a free booklet giving information on organisations who can be contacted for details of workcamp, community and voluntary work opportunities for 1-3 months. Published by Christians Abroad, 1 Stockwell Green, London SW9 9HP © 0171-737 7811.

A R C H A E O L O G Y

Archaeological Fieldwork Opportunities Bulletin US$10.50 + $3.00 postage, lists sites where excavation and research are being carried out. Details are given of staff and volunteers needed at each site. Also lists field schools which provide practical training. Published annually in January by the Archaeological Institute of America, 675 Commonwealth Avenue, Boston, MA 02215, United States.

**ARCHAEOLOGY ABROAD
The Secretary, 31-34 Gordon Square, London WC1H 0PY**
Provides information on opportunities for archaeological fieldwork and

excavations outside Britain. 3 bulletins published annually which provide details of digs and addresses of where to apply.

COMMUNITY WORK

THE ACROSS TRUST
Bridge House, 70/72 Bridge Road, East Molesey, Surrey KT8 9HF
℡ 0181-783 1355 ▭ 0181-783 1622
Set up in 1972 with the aim of taking bed-bound and severely handicapped people to Lourdes, the Trust now operates 15 jumbo ambulances purpose built for the long-distance transportation of sick, handicapped and disabled people on accompanied tours, holidays and pilgrimages across Europe. As well as Lourdes, destinations include towns in Spain, Belgium, Switzerland, Austria, Germany, Israel, Holland, Ireland, Poland and other European countries. Qualified **doctors**, **nurses** and unqualified **helpers** needed on tours, caring for, living, learning and laughing with the handicapped and sick throughout the journey. Willingness to help the unable is the most important requirement; muscle power also helpful for pushing and lifting wheelchairs. Work can be demanding, requiring love, understanding and self-sacrifice. Satisfaction comes in knowing the lives of unable travellers have been made happier and their courage renewed. ⊕ Ages 16+. Most holidays last 10 days, March-November. Volunteers pay their own expenses and travel costs, from £399-£700, which also covers full board hotel accommodation and insurance.

THE DISAWAY TRUST 2 Charles Road, Merton Park, London SW19 3BD ℡ 0181-543 3431
Enables physically disabled people to take holidays, and needs able-bodied **volunteers** to look after disabled holidaymakers aged 16-80 on a 1:1 basis, helping with all personal needs, ensuring they gain the greatest possible enjoyment. 1994 holidays were arranged to Orléans, Cardiff and Rhodes.

⊕ Ages 18+. Experience not necessary; those who have never assisted disabled people before particularly welcome. 8-10 days, May-late September. Volunteers pay 50% of the cost of the holiday, from £190-£400, to cover transport, half board accommodation, excursions and insurance.

PROJECT PHOENIX TRUST
56 Burnaby Road, Southend-on-Sea, Essex SS1 2TL
℡ Southend-on-Sea (01702) 466412
Runs overseas study tours and holidays for adults who would not be able to travel without physical assistance, or who are prepared to give help in order that others may travel. Able-bodied **helpers** are needed to provide care for disabled adults. Holidays last 7-14 days, spring and September, and have included Provence, Egypt, Tunisia, Rome, Pompeii, Venice, Vienna, Florence, Spain, Bruges, Athens, Israel, Sweden and Leningrad. ⊕ Ages 20+. Long hours and hard but rewarding work. Helpers should be strong and fit as tasks include pushing and lifting wheelchairs, and night attendance for turning patients in bed. Experience of caring for disabled people welcome, but not essential, providing there is genuine motivation to help. Accommodation in twin-bedded rooms shared by one handicapped and one able-bodied person. Volunteers are required to contribute 25% of the full costs, and organise their own insurance, pocket money and travel to and from London. ✉ *Apply well in advance; most places are allocated in January/February.*

YOUNG DISABLED ON HOLIDAY 33 Longfield Avenue, Heald Green, Cheadle, Cheshire SK8 3NH
Volunteers needed to help on holidays abroad for young physically disabled people. Activities include sightseeing, theatre visits, discos, shopping and adventure pastimes. ⊕ Ages 18-35. Applicants should have a sense of fun and adventure. Each disabled person has at least 1 helper.

1 week, April-October. Volunteers are expected to contribute 40% of holiday costs.

CONSERVATION

EARTHWATCH EUROPE Belsyre Court, 57 Woodstock Road, Oxford ℂ Oxford (01865) 516366
Aims to support field research in a wide range of disciplines including animal behaviour, nature conservation and ecology. Support is given as a grant and in the form of volunteer assistance. Recent projects involving **volunteers** have included monitoring the feeding habits of baby lemurs in Madagascar; analysing water samples in the fragile wetlands of Mallorca; saving the leatherback turtle in the Virgin Islands; and examining coral communities in Fiji. Also support projects in eastern Europe, including studying the effects of acid rain on the forests of Bohemia; reclaiming industrial wasteland in Bulgaria and monitoring the impact of wolves on Poland's red deer population.
⊕ Ages 16-75. No special skills required although each expedition may, because of its nature, demand some talent or quality of fitness. Volunteers should be generally fit, able to cope with new situations and work with people of different ages and backgrounds, and a sense of humour will help. 2-3 weeks, all year. Members share the costs of the expedition, from £340-£2,000, which includes meals, transport and all necessary field equipment, but does not include the cost of travel to the staging area, although assistance may be given in arranging it. Membership fee £25 entitles members to attend evening and weekend events, and receive magazines/newsletters providing all the information necessary to choose a project.
B D PH W depending on project.

EUROPE CONSERVATION Via Giusti 5, 20154 Milan, Italy ℂ (39 2) 33 10 33 44 ☎ (39 2) 33 10 40 68
A non-profitmaking organisation

founded in Italy in 1989 to gather funds for conservation projects and promote voluntary programmes. **Volunteers** are invited to help researchers on some 20 projects worldwide, assisting with aspects such as observing and recording behaviour, collecting and analysing data, photo-identification or radio-tracking. Recent projects have included studying fin and sperm whales in the Ligurian Sea; recording the behaviour of griffon vultures on the Croatian island of Cres; research into the nesting habits of sea turtles in Turkey, and radio-tracking chamois in Italy's Lake Garda region.
⊕ Ages 18+. Experience not essential for most projects, but volunteers must be highly motivated, fit, enthusiastic and responsible. Italian is official language on most projects, but researchers also speak English and sometimes French or German. 1-4 weeks, usually during the summer. Cost 300,000-1,300,000 Lire depending on project, covers membership fee, accommodation and contribution to costs. Insurance approx 2,000 Lire per day. Volunteers pay own travel expenses and contribute to communal food kitty. ✎ *Apply from May onwards for summer projects.*

Applications in Belgium to E CO Belgium, Parc de Mariemont, 7170 Manage ℂ (32 64) 21 69 55 ☎ (32 64) 26 27 18

Applications in France to E CO France, BP 44, 41260 La Chaussée St Victor ℂ (33) 54 55 16 16 ☎ (33) 54 55 16 19

Applications in Germany to E CO Germany, Am Fronhof 4, 53177 Bonn

Applications in Switzerland to E CO Switzerland, CP 14, 6924 Sorengo (Lugano) ℂ/☎ (41 91) 551 538

EUROPEAN CAMPUSES FOR HERITAGE AND ENVIRONMENT c/o 41 cours Jean Jaurès, 84000 Avignon, France ℂ (33) 90 85 51 15 ☎ (33) 90 86 82 19
Students are invited to participate as **volunteers** in the preservation of

Europe's architectural and environmental heritage, by joining summer campuses sponsored by the European Union and other interested organisations. In 1994 campuses were held in Belgium, Bulgaria, the Czech Republic, Denmark, France, Germany, Great Britain, Greece, Hungary, Ireland, Italy, the Netherlands, Poland, Portugal, the Russian Federation and Spain. Projects included excavating and signposting an ancient Viking encampment on Denmark's Fyn Island; doing field research into 18th century coal pits in the Royal Forest of Dean, Great Britain; developing a tourist circuit linking heritage sites and beauty spots along Ireland's Connemara coast; drawing up proposals for forest fire prevention in northwest Crete; and producing a sustainable development plan incorporating organic market gardening, fish farming and rural tourism, in Hungary's Hortobagy Park. ⊕ Ages 18+. Each campus is led by academic personnel and includes field study as well as practical work. Students should have an academic background consistent with the subject matter of the campus of their choice, such as landscaping, architecture, ecology, geography, economics, tourism, town planning or archaeology. Knowledge of campus language (often English or French) essential. 2-3 weeks, June-September. Board and lodging provided; may be basic depending on local conditions. Participation fee 70 ECUs covers repatriation insurance. Students pay own travel costs. ✒ *Apply direct to campus organiser before end of June; details from address above.*

TRAVELER'S EARTH REPAIR NETWORK (TERN) Friends of the Trees Society, PO Box 1064, Tonasket, WA 98855, United States ℗/☎ (1 509) 485 2705
A networking service for travellers wanting to make a positive contribution to the environment. TERN links travellers with contacts and hosts involved in reforestation, forest preservation, sustainable agriculture, permaculture and other areas of work related to trees and conservation. Travellers fill out a form listing experience, interests and countries they want to work in, and TERN will run a computer search to supply a list of suitable contacts and hosts. Visits range from weekends to seasonal apprenticeships. Most hosts offer food and accommodation in exchange for help, but there may be a nominal charge. Cost US$50 ($35 for students) for 20 references.

COURIERS / REPS

AIFS UK LTD 15-17 Young Street, London W8 5EH ℗ **0171-376 0800** ☎ **0171-376 0789**
American educational travel company for high school students and teachers requires **tour directors** to lead educational tours of Europe. Tours last 9-23 days, Easter-August, and directors work continuously with their group for the duration of the tour. ⊕ Ages 21+. Previous experience desirable but not essential. Applicants must be effective communicators with a desire to share their knowledge and interest of the major cities of Europe. Good grasp of European history and culture essential for preparing and presenting commentary. Fluency in at least one major European language also required. Good organisational and leadership skills needed to run all operational aspects of the tour, although thorough training will be given. Full board hotel accommodation provided, plus salary, travel expenses and insurance whilst on tour. ✒ *Apply October-February to Courier Office.*

CONTIKI SERVICES LTD Wells House, 15 Elmfield Road, Bromley, Kent BR1 1LS
Coach tour operator specialising in European camping and hotel tour holidays for ages 18-35. Requires **site representatives** responsible for cooking, cleaning accommodation and

maintaining good public relations with clients and suppliers. **Mobile cooks** also required for tours through Europe, Scandinavia and Eastern Bloc countries to cook for groups of up to 50 people, maintain mobile kitchen and equipment and work to a high standard of hygiene. ⊕ Ages 23-35. Previous experience, leadership and public relations skills useful. Applicants should be motivated, enthusiastic young people who enjoy hard work and have a keen sense of responsibility. 7 day week with long, irregular hours; approx 30 weeks, March-November. Fixed salary with performance-related incentive, board, accommodation, transport to and from designated place of employment and medical insurance provided. Short training course held in February. £150 refundable bond held as security against non-completion of contract. ✎ *Apply January-September. EEA nationals only.*

EF EDUCATIONAL TOURS
118 Cromwell Road, London SW7 4ET ✆ 0171-244 6900
Tour directors required to lead educational tours of Europe made up of American and Canadian high school students and their teachers. Groups travel principally by coach, and tour directors have full responsibility for the group, supervising hotel check-ins and coach transfers, liaising with teachers, solving problems and providing journey commentaries. Applicants must have self-confidence and a good working knowledge of major European cities. Language skills an advantage. ⊕ Ages 23+. Tours last 9-35 days and run during Easter and June-July. Directors are continuously with the group throughout the tour. Salary under review. Full board hotel accommodation, travel expenses and insurance provided on tour. **PH** ✎ *French applications to EF, 9 rue Duphot, 75001 Paris* ✆ *(33 1) 40 15 09 06*

Italian applications to EF, Viale Pasteur 70, 00144 Rome ✆ *(39 6) 678 2564*

SPECIALISED TRAVEL LTD
12-15 Hanger Green, London W5 3EL ✆ 0181-998 1761
Couriers required to escort groups of musicians (choirs, bands and orchestras) throughout the UK, mainland Europe and the former Soviet Union. Work involves being responsible for all daily events; confirming accommodation, transportation, concert arrangements and leading sightseeing excursions. ⊕ Ages 20+. Applicants should have excellent organisation skills, leadership qualities and initiative; a knowledge of touring would be an advantage. Languages necessary according to specific tour/country. Vacancies March-August. Tours last approx 2 weeks. Hours vary according to schedule. Accommodation provided. Salary £50 per day plus expenses. ✎ *Apply late summer/autumn. All nationalities welcome.*

THOMSON HOLIDAYS Overseas
Personnel Department, Greater London House, Hampstead Road, London NW1 7SD ✆ 0171-387 9321
Britain's largest holiday company, operating throughout the world.
Overseas representatives required to meet guests at airport and transfer them by coach to their hotel, organise social occasions and generally give assistance and advice on hotel and resort facilities. Should be flexible and may be moved to different resorts during the season. ⊕ Ages 21-35. Applicants should be fluent in English and at least one of the following: Spanish, Italian, French, German, Greek or Portuguese. The work involves close contact with guests and experience with the general public is essential. No set working hours as representatives are expected to be on call to deal with any problems. Salary paid monthly in the UK with commission on excursion sales.
Children's representatives also required, which involves organising activities, supervising meals, reading bedtime stories, and ensuring the safety of the children is maintained at all times. Variable hours of work.

⊕ Ages 19-30. Applicants must have childcare or nursing experience, should be friendly, and like children. Salary paid monthly in the UK. Accommodation, meals and uniform provided. For all jobs applicants must have a high degree of patience, tact, sense of responsibility, a friendly, outgoing nature, and the ability to use initiative. Applicants must be available to work April-end October.

TRAVELSPHERE LTD Compass House, Rockingham Road, Market Harborough, Leicestershire LE16 7QD ℰ **Market Harborough (01858) 410456**
Couriers required to escort groups of adult and elderly passengers on coaching holidays throughout Europe, including Austria, Belgium, the Czech and Slovak Republics, France, Germany, Norway, Poland, Portugal, Spain and Switzerland. Work involves checking into accommodation, organising welcome meetings, guiding excursions and generally looking after passengers to ensure they have an enjoyable holiday. ⊕ Ages 20-35. Experience of courier work not essential but applicants must have a friendly, outgoing personality and an ability to deal with the general public. Experience of travelling in Europe useful. Good spoken English and one other European language required. 4 months, May-October. Couriers work long hours, but work is rewarding. Pay is at daily rate plus commission on sale of excursions. Half board accommodation generally provided, plus full insurance, travel costs and training. 🕮 *Apply in writing between 1 November and 31 January enclosing a photograph.*

FARMWORK

WILLING WORKERS ON ORGANIC FARMS (WWOOF) W Tree, Buchan, Victoria 3885, Australia
A non-profitmaking organisation which aims to provide voluntary help to organic farmers and smallholders whose work is often labour-intensive as it does not rely on the use of artificial fertilisers or pesticides. Publishes a list of 400 **volunteer** work opportunities, including farmwork, available in 48 countries not yet served by a WWOOF group. Volunteers apply direct to organisations on the list. Cost £8.

LEADERS & GUIDES

SHERPA EXPEDITIONS 131A Heston Road, Hounslow, Middlesex TW5 0RD ℰ **0181-577 2717**
Tour operator organising mountain walking holidays for groups of 15 people in Europe, South America, Africa, Nepal, India, Eastern Europe, Russia and the former Soviet Union. Requires **trek leaders** and **trainee trek leaders**. Duties involve operating airport transfers, acting as guide and group leader along trekking route, liaising with local operators, hoteliers and support staff, and being responsible for the welfare of the group. Treks last 1-4 weeks and run throughout the year. Salary £130 per week plus normal living expenses; return travel paid plus medical and baggage insurance. ⊕ Ages 23-60. Trekking experience, First Aid certificate and high level of physical fitness essential; mountain leadership qualification desirable. Knowledge of languages useful for some treks. Training programme and manuals provided in London. 🕮 *Apply January-March for summer season; April-July for winter season.*

MONITORS & INSTRUCTORS

CLUB MED 106-110 Brompton Road, London SW3 1JJ ℰ **0171-225 1066**
Qualified tennis, riding, golf, windsurfing, swimming, archery, scuba diving, water

skiing and sailing **instructors,
playgroup leaders, arts and circus
school instructors** and **children's
activities monitors** are required to
work in holiday villages in Europe and
north Africa. Applicants should be
single, possess relevant qualifications and
experience, must have minimum A level
French, and, if possible, one other
language such as German/Italian.
⊕ Ages 20-30. 5 months, May-October.
It should be noted that applications
cannot be made to work in a specific
country; preference to work in a
particular country can be indicated once
applicants have worked for a few
seasons. *Apply with cv, November-
January. EEA nationals only.*

WORKCAMPS

**GLOBAL VOLUNTEERS 375 E
Little Canada Road, St Paul, MN
55117, United States** ℗ **(1 612) 482
1074** ⎚ **(1 612) 482 0925**
A private not-for-profit corporation
founded in 1984 with the aim of
establishing a foundation for peace
through international understanding.
Invites **volunteers** to live and work
with local people in the southern United
States, Costa Rica, Indonesia, Jamaica,
Mexico, Poland, Russia, Spain, Tanzania
and Vietnam. Projects include teaching
English, tutoring in classrooms, home
building, repair and painting, and other
community restoration projects. Work
is under the direction of local project
leaders and a trained team leader.
⊕ Ages 18+ unless accompanied by an
adult. 1-4 weeks, minimum 4 hour day,
all year. No experience necessary but
volunteers must have an open mind,
should be flexible and willing to serve
local people. Cost US$300-US$2,185
includes board, accommodation, land
transportation and administration.
Volunteers arrange and pay for own
international travel and insurance.
B D PH *Apply at least 2 months in
advance.*

**WORLD COUNCIL OF
CHURCHES Ecumenical Youth
Action, 150 route de Ferney, PO
Box 2100, 1211 Geneva 2,
Switzerland** ℗ **(41 22) 791 6111**
Within the Ecumenical Youth Action
programme there are opportunities for
young people to participate as
volunteers in international workcamps,
contributing to local and national
development schemes. Recent
workcamps have been held in Africa, Asia
the Caribbean, Europe and the Middle
East. Volunteers assist local groups in
manual work such as agriculture,
construction and renovation of buildings.
The camps have theological reflections
and discussions on vital issues affecting
the local situation.
⊕ Ages 18-30. 2-4 weeks, July and
August. Volunteers pay travel and
insurance costs and contribute approx
$5 per day towards camp expenses.

GENERAL

**CHRISTIAN SERVICE CENTRE
Holloway Street West, Lower
Gornal, West Midlands DY3 2DZ**
Matches the personnel needs of
missions and Christian organisations in
Britain and abroad with the availability of
those offering themselves for service,
and also provides a counselling and
advisory service for prospective
workers. Both short and long-term
paid and voluntary positions are available
throughout the year in a wide variety of
areas, ranging from **pioneer
missionary work, agriculture,
community development** and
engineering, to jobs in the fields of
**radio, literacy, publicity, translation,
accountancy** and **administration,** and
short-term work in a variety of areas.
Vacancies in Britain also cover
**maintenance staff, cooks,
housekeepers, social workers,
secretaries** and **book-keepers** in
residential, rehabilitation or conference
centres, and **secretarial posts** in
mission offices.

✦ Ages 17+. Experience/qualifications needed vary from post to post, as do hours, wages/pocket money, and provision of board, lodging and insurance cover. Issue a *Job File* listing current longer-term vacancies in the UK, cost £16.50 for 8 issues, and *STS Directory*, a brochure listing short-term service opportunities, cost £2.15 including postage.

CLUB MED 106-110 Brompton Road, London SW3 1JJ
✆ 0171-225 1066
Receptionists, hostesses, cashiers, bar staff, administrative staff, boutique staff, dressmakers, physiotherapists, lifesavers and **nurses** are required to work in holiday villages in Europe and north Africa. Applicants should be single, possess relevant qualifications and experience, must speak fluent French, and, if possible, one other language such as German.
✦ Ages 20-30. 6 months, April-October. It should be noted that applications cannot be made to work in a specific country; preference to work in a particular country can be indicated once applicants have worked for a few seasons. ✎ *Apply with cv, November-January. EEA nationals only.*

CONTIKI TRAVEL Wells House, 15 Elmfield Road, Bromley, Kent BR1 1LS ✆ 0181-290 6777
Coach tour operator specialising in European camping and hotel tour holidays for 18-35s. Requires **tour managers** responsible for the day-to-day running of the tour, ensuring itineraries are adhered to, booking restaurants and excursions, giving historical, geographical and cultural talks to groups of 50+, directing drivers around Europe, negotiating borders, organising money exchange and dealing with local agents. **Tour drivers** with British PSV licence also required to assist the tour manager in the overall organisation of the tour, ensure clients have a safe and comfortable journey and

keep a high standard of coach cleanliness.
✦ Ages 23-35. Basic knowledge of Europe essential; experience of leadership and public relations useful. Applicants must be motivated, enthusiastic young people who enjoy hard work and have a keen sense of responsibility. 6-18 weeks, March-October. Board, accommodation, medical insurance and training provided. Fixed salary with performance-related incentive. ✎ *Apply September-January. EEA nationals only.*

CREWIT Shute Hill Cottage, Malborough, Kingsbridge, Devon TQ7 3SG ✆ Kingsbridge (01548) 561897
Operates a **crew placement service** bringing boat owners and amateur crew members together. Opportunities include crewing for amateur/professional skippers, cruising or delivery to Europe, Mediterranean, North Atlantic, West Indies and the United States.
✦ All ages. Experience not essential but wider opportunities for the most experienced. Period and hours of work vary. None of the positions are paid, but accommodation is provided on board; expenses shared. Annual membership fee £29.90. ✎ *Apply any time. All nationalities welcome.*

THE CRUISING ASSOCIATION Crewing Service, Ivory House, St Katharine Dock, London E1 9AT ✆ 0171-481 0881
Maintains a register of people interested in **crewing yachts**, designed to put potential crews and skippers in contact. Applicants must be proficient sailors. None of the positions offered is paid, and skippers may expect a contribution towards expenses. Cost £18 to join the register.

INVOLVEMENT VOLUNTEERS ASSOCIATION INC PO Box 218, Port Melbourne, Victoria 3207, Australia ✆/☐ (61 3) 646 5504
A not-for-profit organisation set up to

find unpaid individual and team **volunteer** placements for people of all ages with community based organisations involved in practical conservation or social service programmes in Australia, Austria, Fiji, Germany, India, Italy, Latvia, New Zealand, Thailand and the US. Projects include development of national parks and walking trails in Fiji, New Zealand or Latvia; assisting landholder groups with extensive revegetation programmes in Australia and Thailand; bird breeding and research in Austria, Australia, Germany and the US; wetland development in Australia and New Zealand; and caring assistance at an institution for the rehabilitation of children in Germany or a pavement health clinic in India. Volunteers must be able to speak English as well as the local language in some cases, arrange their own visitor visas, and organise their own international travel and insurance. Involvement Volunteers provides advice, placements, itinerary planning, meeting on arrival, initial accommodation, introductions to banking, taxation and a communications base for mail. Cost AU$400 plus AU$35 placement fee. **B D**

🐚 *For placements in Europe, apply to Involvement Volunteers-Deutschland, Postfach 110224, 34047 Göttingen, Germany © (49 551) 33 765 ⌨ (49 551) 33 787.*

For placements in North America, apply to Involvement Corps Inc, 15515 Sunset Boulevard, Suite 108, Pacific Palisades, CA 90272, United States ©/⌨ (1 310) 459 1022.

SHERPA EXPEDITIONS
131A Heston Road, Hounslow, Middlesex TW5 0RD © **0181-577 2717**
Tour operator organising mountain walking holidays for groups of 15 people in Europe, South America, Africa, Nepal, India, Eastern Europe, Russia and the former Soviet Union. Requires **support drivers** to provide transport services

on trek, including driving the vehicle between home country and destination, driving between campsites and transporting baggage. Also maintenance of vehicle and camping equipment, acting as cook, shopping for food and recording expenditure.
⊕ Ages 23-60. Applicants must have a full driving licence, good and imaginative cooking skills, a friendly and outgoing nature, travel experience, physical fitness and adaptability. Knowledge of languages useful for some treks. 1-4 week treks run throughout the year. Salary £90 per week plus normal living expenses; return travel, medical and baggage insurance paid. Training programme and manuals provided in London. 🐚 *Apply January-March for summer season; April-July for winter season.*

WORLD OF EXPERIENCE EQUESTRIAN EMPLOYMENT AGENCY **52 Kingston Deverill, Warminster, Wiltshire BA12 7HF** © **Warminster (01985) 844102**
Agency arranging all types of work with horses throughout Europe and further afield, for **grooms**, **riding instructors**, **stud hands**, **nanny-grooms**, **trainees** and other staff.
⊕ Ages 18+. Relevant previous experience essential; driving licence and equine qualifications useful. Conditions vary depending on job; usually 6 day week, 8-12+ hours per day. Accommodation plus wages from £50-£200 per week. Applicants must be available for at least 3 months, preferably 6-12 months. Applicants pay own travel costs, which are usually reimbursed by the employer. Agency advises on travel and visas. 🐚 *Apply 4-6 weeks in advance of starting date.*

When writing to any organisation it is essential to mention Working Holidays 1995 and enclose a stamped, self-addressed A4 envelope, or if in another country, an addressed A4 envelope and at least two IRCs (International Reply Coupons, available from post offices).

A year out, between school and university or work, is a rare chance to stand back, assess where life has brought you so far, and seize the freedom offered to take on a completely different challenge. All the vital advice and information you need to arrange a successful and enjoyable year out is in the Central Bureau guide **A YEAR BETWEEN**.

From industrial placements in research in the UK to working on a cattle ranch in Australia; from trekking through Bali, Lombok and Java to tracking Arctic foxes in Norway; from teaching in Spain to working with kids on community projects in Scotland, **A YEAR BETWEEN** has hundreds of opportunities and a wealth of information for a great gap year.

A YEAR BETWEEN lists over 100 organisations and employers offering year between placements in Britain and 80 other countries. Whatever the opportunity, in whatever country, **the guide** gives very full details. Any age restrictions are noted, the period of work on offer, salary and terms, including whether accommodation, insurance or travel are included is listed, and application deadlines are given together with details of where the work is overseas, and any address in the home country to which application can be made. But we don't stop there.

A YEAR BETWEEN carries information on a wide range of other useful details: a personal checklist covering the pros, cons and options of taking a year out, offering a programmed series of questions to enable participants to evaluate their potential; authoritative advice on planning & preparation, useful books and other resources; accounts from students and placing organisations alike, providing first hand reports vital to those considering taking a year out; and for potential volunteers, some challenging words on commitment.

A YEAR BETWEEN has opportunities detailed under seven headings: Training/work experience; Discovery/leadership; Conservation/land use; Teaching/instructing; Community & social service; Youth work/childcare; and Christian service. **The guide** also provides advice on further study options, on travel, insurance and health requirements. In fact, just about everything you'll need to know in order not only to get a successful placement but to make the whole experience worthwhile, fulfilling and as trouble-free as possible.

A YEAR BETWEEN has opportunities for those aged 17+; from 4 weeks up to a whole year; from accountancy placements to zoology expeditions; from Australia to Zimbabwe. For further information on the Bureau's publications and programmes contact the Information Desk on ✆ 0171-725 9448.

A YEAR BETWEEN is published biannually.   Second edition   ISBN 0 900087 98 6   £8.99

REPORT FORM

Up-to-date reports enable us to improve the accuracy and standard of information in our guidebooks, and monitor the opportunities available. Your completion and return of this form to the Information, Print & Design Unit, Central Bureau for Educational Visits & Exchanges, Seymour Mews, London W1H 9PE, would therefore be much appreciated. **All reports will be treated in strict confidence.**

Name and address of employing organisation(s)

Where work was undertaken

Period of work

Type of work

Ratio of work : free time

Salary/terms of employment

Food and accommodation provided? Yes ❑   No ❑

Were you offered visits/excursions? Yes ❑   No ❑

Age group of other participants

PLEASE TURN OVER

Nationality of other participants

Any other comments

Knowledge of foreign languages

Have you travelled overseas before?　　　Yes ❑　　　No ❑

If yes, which countries?

Have you been on a working holiday before?　Yes ❑　　　No ❑

Name

Address

Age　　　　　　　　　　Occupation

Signed　　　　　　　　　Date